The Editor

DANIEL HELLER-ROAZEN is the Arthur W. Marks '19 Professor of Comparative Literature and the Council of the Humanities at Princeton University. He is the author of *The Enemy of All: Piracy and the Law of Nations; The Inner Touch: Archaeology of a Sensation*, awarded the Aldo and Jeanne Scaglione Prize for Comparative Literature Studies in 2008; *Echolalias: On the Forgetting of Language*; and *Fortune's Faces: The Roman de la Rose and the Poetics of Contingency*. He has published articles on classical, medieval, and modern literature and philosophy and has edited, translated, and introduced Giorgio Agamben's *Potentialities: Collected Essays in Philosophy*. Heller-Roazen's books have been translated into many languages.

W. W. NORTON & COMPANY, INC.
Also Publishes

ENGLISH RENAISSANCE DRAMA: A NORTON ANTHOLOGY
edited by David Bevington et al.

THE NORTON ANTHOLOGY OF AFRICAN AMERICAN LITERATURE
edited by Henry Louis Gates Jr. and Nellie Y. McKay et al.

THE NORTON ANTHOLOGY OF AMERICAN LITERATURE
edited by Nina Baym et al.

THE NORTON ANTHOLOGY OF CHILDREN'S LITERATURE
edited by Jack Zipes et al.

THE NORTON ANTHOLOGY OF DRAMA
edited by J. Ellen Gainor, Stanton B. Garner Jr., and Martin Puchner

THE NORTON ANTHOLOGY OF ENGLISH LITERATURE
edited by M. H. Abrams and Stephen Greenblatt et al.

THE NORTON ANTHOLOGY OF LITERATURE BY WOMEN
edited by Sandra M. Gilbert and Susan Gubar

THE NORTON ANTHOLOGY OF MODERN AND CONTEMPORARY POETRY
edited by Jahan Ramazani, Richard Ellmann, and Robert O'Clair

THE NORTON ANTHOLOGY OF POETRY
edited by Margaret Ferguson, Mary Jo Salter, and Jon Stallworthy

THE NORTON ANTHOLOGY OF SHORT FICTION
edited by R. V. Cassill and Richard Bausch

THE NORTON ANTHOLOGY OF THEORY AND CRITICISM
edited by Vincent B. Leitch et al.

THE NORTON ANTHOLOGY OF WORLD LITERATURE
edited by Sarah Lawall et al.

THE NORTON FACSIMILE OF THE FIRST FOLIO OF SHAKESPEARE
prepared by Charlton Hinman

THE NORTON INTRODUCTION TO LITERATURE
edited by Alison Booth and Kelly J. Mays

THE NORTON READER
edited by Linda H. Peterson and John C. Brereton

THE NORTON SAMPLER
edited by Thomas Cooley

THE NORTON SHAKESPEARE, BASED ON THE OXFORD EDITION
edited by Stephen Greenblatt et al.

For a complete list of Norton Critical Editions, visit
www.wwnorton.com/college/English/nce_home.htm

A NORTON CRITICAL EDITION

THE ARABIAN NIGHTS

THE HUSAIN HADDAWY TRANSLATION
BASED ON THE TEXT EDITED BY MUHSIN MAHDI

CONTEXTS
CRITICISM

Selected and Edited by

DANIEL HELLER-ROAZEN

PRINCETON UNIVERSITY

W. W. NORTON & COMPANY

New York • London

W. W. Norton & Company has been independent since its founding in 1923, when William Warder Norton and Mary D. Herter Norton first published lectures delivered at the People's Institute, the adult education division of New York City's Cooper Union. The firm soon expanded its program beyond the Institute, publishing books by celebrated academics from America and abroad. By mid-century, the two major pillars of Norton's publishing program—trade books and college texts—were firmly established. In the 1950s, the Norton family transferred control of the company to its employees, and today—with a staff of four hundred and a comparable number of trade, college, and professional titles published each year—W. W. Norton & Company stands as the largest and oldest publishing house owned wholly by its employees.

Library of Congress Cataloging-in-Publication Data

Arabian nights. English.
    The Arabian nights / the Husain Haddawy translation ; based on the text edited by Muhsin Mahdi ; contexts, criticism selected and edited by Daniel Heller-Roazen. — 1st ed.
        p. cm. — (A Norton critical edition)
    Includes bibliographical references.
    ISBN 978-0-393-92808-2 (pbk.)
    1. Arabian nights.   I. Haddawy, Husain.   II. Mahdi, Muhsin.
III. Heller-Roazen, Daniel.   IV. Title.
    PJ7715.M87 2010
    398.22—dc22

                                                                2009039285

W. W. Norton & Company, Inc., 500 Fifth Avenue
New York, N.Y. 10110
www.wwnorton.com

W. W. Norton & Company Ltd., Castle House
75/76 Wells Street, London W1T 3QT

1 2 3 4 5 6 7 8 9 0

Contents

Contexts   351

Criticism   379

Preface

Few works of literature are as familiar and as beloved as *The Arabian Nights*. But few remain also as unknown. Everyone can call to mind an image of Aladdin and his magic lamp, Ali Baba and the Forty Thieves, Sinbad and his travels, and it is difficult to forget Shahrazad. But who can say from where these many figures came? In English, at least, *The Arabian Nights* is a literary work of relatively recent date. The first versions of the tales in our language appeared barely two hundred years ago. They followed the French edition of *The Thousand and One Nights* by Antoine Galland, which was published in twelve volumes between 1704 and 1718. Ushering into European letters a body of marvelous stories from the Middle East, Galland's version of the tales achieved almost instant success, and not only in France. His quickly become the first of many Western translations from the "Arabian," and by the end of the nineteenth century many of the languages of Europe had their *Nights*. The story of the proliferation of editions, re-editions, revisions, and renditions of this classic of translation is complex. Understandably, it has been studied more than once.[1] But the book that is the source of the many versions possesses a mystery all its own. Galland translated his *Nights* above all from a fourteenth-century manuscript, which he arranged to have sent to him from Syria to France. To this day, this medieval manuscript remains the oldest surviving edition of the work in any tongue. Muhsin Mahdi used it as the basis for his groundbreaking critical edition of the *Nights* in Arabic, which he published in 1984. Hussain Haddawy translated this authoritative text for the version of *The Arabian Nights* that Norton brought out in 1990, whose text constitutes the source of all but one of the tales printed in this Critical Edition.

Because of its antiquity, the fourteenth-century manuscript edited by Galland and Mahdi possesses unique authority among the editions of the *Nights*. But in itself, the Syrian manuscript shows few signs of originality. In its day, it may well not have been unique. A document dating from the twelfth century found among the

---

1. For a synthesis of the scholarship, see Muhsin Mahdi, *The Thousand and One Nights* (Leiden: E. J. Brill, 1995), pp. 11–86.

discarded papers of the Cairo Synagogue already refers to a book
called *The Thousand and One Nights*.[2] Two Arabic authors of the
tenth century, Al-Mas'ūdī and Ibn al-Nadīm, also allude in passing
to a collection that seems by all appearances to be the *Nights*.[3]
Al-Mas'ūdī calls this work *A Thousand Nights* (*Alf layla*), reporting
that it is a translation of an older Persian text, titled *A Thousand Stories* (*Hāzar afsāneh*). Starting in the nineteenth century, several
modern scholars availed themselves of the methods of philological
reconstruction, taking it one step further. They argued that the Persian basis for the Arabic might also have been a translation. The first
and framing story in *The Arabian Nights*, after all, is set in India.
Could its first language, the modern scholars naturally wondered,
not have been an older tongue, such as Sanskrit? Critical discussions of the genesis of the tales continue to this day. But this much
is by now beyond all doubt: the origin of *The Thousand and One
Nights* is impenetrably obscure. As far back as one looks, there are
translations and retranslations; no absolutely primal version can be
found. There is, moreover, no one author to whom one might attrib-
ute the whole collection; from edition to edition, the work remains
obstinately unsigned. Finally, one cannot be certain of the language
in which the anthology was first conceived. From its inception, so to
speak, *The Arabian Nights* lacks any stable historical and linguistic
point of inception.

Long before its entry into the languages of Europe, *The Thousand
One Nights*, therefore, seems to have already possessed one fundamental trait that it retains today: that of being a work in movement,
caught in the passage from territory to territory, culture to language,
language to language. One might be tempted to construe this lack of
a certain origin as a limitation to the integrity of this work, which,
unlike some others, cannot reveal to its reader its first and ultimate
literary and linguistic form. But that would be to misunderstand
much of what is proper to *The Arabian Nights*. This work acquired
its characteristically varied shape precisely in the process by which it
was repeatedly compiled and recompiled in ever changing circumstances. Edited without ever being authored, it grew to its present
form through a process closer to sedimentation than creation. It
may be for this reason that the *Nights*, itself a universe of stories,
has confronted its readers with the image of more worlds than one.
For the European and American publics who discovered it thanks to
Galland, the compendium long laid claim to offering the classic representation of the Islamic East. It was for them a collection not of

2. See S. D. Goitein, "The Oldest Documentary Evidence for the Title Alf Laila wa-Laila,"
   Journal of the American Oriental Society 78 (1959), pp. 301–2.
3. See Al-Mas'ūdī (p. 353 herein) and Ibn al-Nadīm (p. 354 herein). Cf., also in Horovitz
   (p. 386 herein).

A *Thousand and One Nights*, as the Arabic has it, but more pointedly of
Arabian Nights' Entertainments, as W. E. Lane's famous retranslation
of the title read. Writers from Coleridge to George Eliot, Robert Louis
Stevenson, Hofmannsthal, Proust, and Borges found in this book the
privileged archive of the culture, mores, beliefs, and literature of "the
Orient."[4] It is hardly surprising that Arabic writers, for their part, have
rarely shared that view. A traditional judgment in the Arabic tradition,
represented also by such a modern scholar as Francesco Gabrieli, main-
tains to the contrary that the *Nights* is neither especially "Arabian" in
content nor particularly literary in form.[5] Several reasons may be cited
for this claim. The *Nights* differs from the bulk of the great works of Arabic letters in lacking an author and, by extension, a single guarantor.[6]
More crucially, awareness of a fact of language dominates the traditional criticism. *The Thousand and One Nights* is written in a simple and
almost colloquial idiom, suggesting translation or folklore, if not both.
In its literary texture, *The Arabian Nights* is essentially foreign to the
eloquent diction and syntax of Arabic belles lettres.

The kernel of the collection can easily be identified. It is the tale of
Shahrazad, the learned young woman who in the prologue to the
work outwits King Shahrayar. When the *Nights* open, the monarch of
"India and Indochina" has been cuckolded. Outraged, he has
promptly executed his wife, determining never again to let himself be
betrayed. He resolves, from now on, each day to wed a woman; he
will spend one night with her and then have her executed at dawn.
He puts his plan immediately into effect. Shahrazad, the daughter of
one of Shahrayar's viziers, has learned of these happenings; resolving
to do what she can to save the people of her land, she begs her father
to offer her in marriage to the king. Her father ultimately does as she
wishes. The wedding concluded, Shahrazad now puts a request to
her new husband: she asks that her sister, Dinarzad, join them both
in their private bedchamber. The king obeys. "When the night wore
on," we learn, Dinarzad "waited until the king had satisfied himself
with her sister Shahrazad and they were by now all fully awake. Then
Dinarzad cleared her throat and said, 'Sister, if you are not sleepy, tell
us one of your lovely little tales to while away the night, before I bid
you good-bye at daybreak, for I don't know what will happen to you
tomorrow.'" Thus the queen begins to recount a tale so captivating
that the king finds himself compelled to hear it through to its end —
even, or especially, if to do so takes more than a single night. At dawn,

4. Jorge Luis Borges, "The Thousand and One Nights," in *Seven Nights*, trans. Eliot Weinberger (New York: New Directions, 1984), p. 42.
5. See Gabrieli (p. 426 herein).
6. On the function of authorship in classical Arabic letters, see Abdelfattah Kilito, *The
Author and His Doubles: Essays on Classical Arabic Culture*, trans. Michael Cooperson,
with a foreword by Roger Allen (Syracuse, N.Y.: Syracuse University Press, 2001).

the story still has not reached its final chapter. Desirous of hearing more, the king thus postpones the execution of his bride, if only by one more day and night. And, each dawn, he will do so again.

Although Shahrazad retreats from *The Arabian Nights* as a character after the prologue, her shadowy presence can be detected throughout the tales that ensue, and not only in the stories of despots outwitted by the young women they would master. By virtue of its form, the collection continues to remind the reader of the dire conditions in which its storytelling comes to pass. Between one night and another, the so-called frame narrative explicitly emerges. As dawn breaks, morning overtakes the queen, and she lapses into silence. The queen's sister, beneath the royal bed, then exclaims: " 'Sister! What an entertaining story!' Shahrazad replied, 'What is this compared to what I shall tell you tomorrow night if the king spares me and lets me live!' " Translators of the *Nights* have often omitted these lines, no doubt because, though minimally varying in diction, they are unmistakably formulaic. But the truth is that they are of capital importance. Recalling the shape of the work as a series of "nights" rather than "tales," these interjections attest to the narrative constraints that define *The Arabian Nights* as a whole. The most obvious among them is that imposed by the murderous and jealous king: in this collection, storytelling works to ward off death. As such, the act of narration here has a double role to play; simultaneously, it defers and anticipates an imminent execution. The figure of such a liberating if transitory speech returns more than once in the queen's wondrous tales. Often it comes to be doubled by its fatal mirror image; then we read not of a story that emancipates the teller but of a tale that, by contrast, puts to death the one who hears it. One might well ponder the relation between the two types of narrative. Who runs the greater risk in the *Nights*, the one who speaks or the one who listens, the writer or the reader, Shahrazad or Shahrayar? This much, in any case, is certain: from the moment the queen begins to speak, the end is always near. Nights must be counted, be it up to a thousand and one, because time, from the beginning, has grown short.

Shahrazad's recurrent appearances in the work bear witness to a fundamental law that defines the structure of the collection as a whole. It can be simply stated: starting with the first night, *The Arabian Nights* sets in motion at least two narratives, which are both simultaneous and noncoincident. At each point in the compendium, there is the tale of Shahrazad, which continues unabated from night to night. But there are also the tales she tells so as to continue living and speaking from day to day. These two levels of storytelling define the order of *The Arabian Nights*. In a sense, they are but one, for the narrative of Shahrazad's avoidance of her death is none other than the narrative of her storytelling and so, too, of the tales she tells. In another sense, however, the two orders must be considered formally distinct. That the work insists on their separation can be gleaned from a simple fact: the narrative of Shahrazad can be divided into nights, which do not coincide with the queen's stories. In no edition of *The Arabian Nights* are these two units in any sense commensurable. *A Thousand and One Nights* does not equal a thousand and one stories. If one considers the fourteenth-century manuscript edited by Mahdi, one finds, for instance, two hundred and seventy-one nights; the count for the stories will vary, depending on one's reading, but the total tales will in any case be fewer than forty. One might cite a formal reason for this fact, which involves the structure of narrative in the collection. In *The Arabian Nights*, one story may be stretched over more than one night; conversely, in a single night one story can end and another can begin. But there is another reason for these facts, and it is to be found within the tale of Shahrazad itself. A moment's reflection allows one to understand why, as a rule, nights and stories in this work cannot—must not—coincide. If they did, Shahrazad, ending her tale at dawn, would leave her satisfied spouse but one course of action: to execute her forthwith.

Whereas the tale of the queen's telling is divided into nights, the stories Shahrazad recounts, therefore, are ordered according to other rules of concatenation. Some tales last many nights; others emerge and vanish almost imperceptibly, like those enigmatic stories some characters in the stories name without ever recounting. But one constant can always be observed: the two levels of storytelling in *The Arabian Nights* run alongside each other without ever perfectly coinciding. Their complex relation of difference constitutes what one might name "the poetry of narrative" in this work. The term *poetry*, in such a setting, ought not to be misleading. For a precise definition of the word, one may turn to Jean-Claude Milner, who has proposed an enlightening account of the distinction between prose and verse. Milner has argued that poetry can be defined as a variety of discourse in which it is possible to contrast and even to oppose two types of limits: a syntactical limit, such as the end of the sentence, and a purely phonological limit, such as the end of the line.[7] Since *enjambment* is the term traditionally given to the occurrence of this opposition, one may also reformulate the thesis in the following manner: "there exists verse from the moment there exists the possibility of enjambment."[8] Where, in other words, a sentence may always momentarily be interrupted before its syntactic end, we are no longer in the terrain of prose. We are in the world of verse.

7. Jean-Claude Milner, "Réflexions sur le fonctionnement du vers français," in *Ordres et raisons de langue* (Paris: Éditions du Seuil, 1982), pp. 283–391, esp. p. 300, proposition 21.
8. Milner, "Réflexions," p. 301.

One need only recall the double order that defines *The Arabian Nights* to grasp the value of such an account of poetry for the structure of Shahrazad's book of tales. The two types of limits at play in verse correspond, in fact, to the two narrative series that define the *Nights*, each of which possesses a characteristic form and duration. There is Shahrazad's tale, which begins with the prologue; divided night by night, it lasts as long as the work itself. Then there are the tales she tells, which possess unequal lengths. Modern editions, such as Norton's, designate the secondary tales by chapter titles. The contemporary reader thus encounters such units as "The Story of The Merchant and the Demon," "The First Old Man's Tale," and "The Story of the Fisherman and the Demon." These are logical segments, introduced for comprehensible reasons by scholars; they reflect what one might term "narrative limits." But within the *Nights*, Shahrazad edits her tales by other means, dividing up her stories according to principles that are not those of action. Although the reader may discern the beginning and the ending of each story by the titles the modern editor chooses to include in the text, the readers inscribed within the book—Shahrayar and Dinarzad—perceive the tales, for this reason, as divided by a type of limit that in no way depends on narrated action. This is what one might call a *nonnarrative* or *metrical limit*. In *The Arabian Nights*, it is stable, no doubt because it is linked to the movements of the sun: it is dawn. Daybreak is the line by which Shahrazad breaks one tale in two, even— or especially—when the action of the tale is not yet complete. In the *Nights*, this is a structural necessity, which implies a preponderance of what one might well term *narrative enjambment*. Just as poetry may be defined as that discourse in which it is possible to oppose a syntactic limit to a nonsyntactic limit (the end of the line), so *The Arabian Nights* may be defined as that collection of tales in which it is possible to oppose a narrative limit to a nonnarrative limit (the end of the night). Where, in other words, a story may always momentarily be interrupted before the conclusion of its action, we are no longer in the terrain of mundane storytelling. We are in the wondrous world of Shahrazad.

This world conceals one final marvel, which has not always been perceived as such. It can be grasped most readily with respect to the characteristic trait of verse. Developing Milner's definition of poetry, Giorgio Agamben has drawn a simple yet astonishing conclusion, whose consequences for *The Arabian Nights* are numerous: "If poetry is defined precisely by the possibility of enjambment, it follows that the last verse of the poem is not a verse."[9] That the last

---

9. Giorgio Agamben, *The End of the Poem: Studies in Poetics*, trans. Daniel Heller-Roazen (Stanford, Calif.: Stanford University Press, 1999), p. 112.

phrase of a poem cannot be interrupted by the metrical break that ties one line to the next line seems clear enough. But if one accepts that there can be poetry only as long as there may be line breaks, can the last line truly be considered a line? Agamben's statement presents the end of the poem as an impossible point of nonverse in verse, to which each poetic composition, in unfolding, grows ever closer. This point, too, has its precise *pendant* in *The Arabian Nights*. It suffices to recall that the collection is structured in such a way that each story, as a rule, is interrupted at daybreak, day after day, before being carried on again for many, many nights. To be precise: for a thousand and one nights. But what happens on the thousand and first night? If one admits that in *The Arabian Nights* it is always possible to oppose a narrative limit to a nonnarrative limit, such that each tale may be interrupted at daybreak before its end, one will be obligated to concede a strange and perplexing fact: the last night of *The Arabian Nights* cannot be one of *The Arabian Nights*! The thousand and first night must be a night that knows no end, a night that will never reach dawn—not so much "another night," one might assert, as something other than any night at all.[1] More than one troubling consequence follows from this simple fact. Doubtless, the first involves an apparently straightforward question of arithmetic: if the thousand and first night cannot be a night, how, one might well ask, could one ever count a thousand and one of them?

Each edition of *The Arabian Nights* has had to confront the bewildering question of how it might be possible for this near endless work properly to conclude. Not all editors have granted that it could. In the "Terminal Essay" to his translation of the work, Richard Burton records one "popular superstition" concerning the *Nights*: "no one can read through them without dying."[2] But that seemingly decisive dictum is hardly unequivocal. Are we to infer that someone (Shahrayar or Shahzarad?) did read the work to its end, paying the price, or that, instead, no one but a genie or a demon could accomplish such a feat? It is perhaps no accident that the fourteenth-century Syrian manuscript falls so dramatically short of *The Thousand and One Nights* announced by its title. Truncated at the two hundred and seventieth daybreak, it delivers little more than a quarter of the promised goods. Later readers and writers, storytellers and retellers, had to advance unaided toward the point that the queen had simultaneously anticipated and deferred. Some would later claim that the king listened to the end, was delighted, and so commanded that all the tales of the

---

1. On the last night, cf. Abdelfattah Kilito, *L'Œil et l'aiguille: Essais sur "les Mille et une nuits"* (Paris, La Découverte, 1992), p. 27; Michael Wood, "The Last Night of All," *PMLA* 122:5 (2007), p. 1396.
2. Richard Burton, "Terminal Essay," *The Thousand Nights and a Night*, vol. VI (New York: The Heritage Press, 1934), p. 3722.

past nights be recorded. This would have been the genesis of our earthly book, the copy of the unwritten original. To be transcribed, our text would then have required but one supplementary event: beginning anew, so that all the stories might regularly be recorded, night after night. Others instead maintained that the king listened to the end and, satisfied at last, uttered his ultimate command: the queen was to be executed, the stories forgotten. Might our book, incomplete and secondary, have emerged from this act of willful oblivion? Poe's "The Thousand-and-Second Tale of Scheherazade" offers its own answers, as do Proust's great novel and Ṭāhā Ḥusayn's *Dreams of Scheherazade*. Borges, for his part, once suggested that the true end lay in the middle—in the tale of the six hundred and second night: "This is the night that the king hears from the queen his own story. He hears the beginning of his story, which comprises all others and also— monstrously—comprises itself."[3] Monstrous or marvelous, perhaps monstrous and marvelous at once, *The Arabian Nights* in any case always conceals one final mystery. It is no less unknown in its end than in its origin and still, like the storytelling queen, no less beguiling.

---

3. Jorge Luis Borges, "Partial Magic in the Quixote," in *Labyrinths: Selected Stories and Other Writings*, ed. Donald A. Yates and James E. Irby, preface by André Maurois (New York: New Directions, 1962), pp. 193–196, p. 195. Cf. "Garden of the Forking Paths," in *Labyrinths*, pp. 44–54, p. 51.

A Note on the Text

All the texts from *The Arabian Nights I* have been translated from the oldest existing edition of *The Thousand and One Nights*, the fourteenth-century Syrian manuscript edited by Muhsin Mahdi.

"The Story of Sindbad the Sailor," from *The Arabian Nights II*, has been translated from the Bulaq edition (1835).

For a discussion of the Arabic texts, the reader may consult the two introductions by Hussain Haddawy (*The Arabian Nights I*, pp. xiii–xxxiv, esp. xiii–xix; *The Arabian Nights II*, pp. ix–xvii).

The Text of
THE ARABIAN NIGHTS

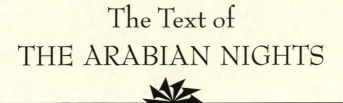

FOREWORD

In the Name of God the Compassionate,
the Merciful. In Him I Trust

PRAISE BE TO GOD, the Beneficent King, the Creator of the world and man, who raised the heavens without pillars and spread out the earth as a place of rest and erected the mountains as props and made the water flow from the hard rock and destroyed the race of Thamud, 'Ad, and Pharaoh of the vast domain.[1] I praise Him the Supreme Lord for His guidance, and I thank Him for His infinite grace.

To proceed, I should like to inform the honorable gentlemen and noble readers that the purpose of writing this agreeable and entertaining book is the instruction of those who peruse it, for it abounds with highly edifying histories and excellent lessons for the people of distinction, and it provides them with the opportunity to learn the art of discourse, as well as what happened to kings from the beginnings of time. This book, which I have called *The Thousand and One Nights*, abounds also with splendid biographies that teach the reader to detect deception and to protect himself from it, as well as delight and divert him whenever he is burdened with the cares of life and the ills of this world. It is the Supreme God who is the True Guide.

---

1. No specific Egyptian pharaoh is referred to here. Thamud and 'Ad were two neighboring tribes of the Arabian peninsula that were destroyed by natural disasters. They are referred to in pre-Islamic poetry and the Quran, and their destruction is cited as an example of God's wrath against blasphemy.

PROLOGUE

[The Story of King Shahrayar and Shahrazad, His Vizier's Daughter]

IT IS RELATED—but God knows and sees best what lies hidden in the old accounts of bygone peoples and times—that long ago, during the time of the Sasanid dynasty,[2] in the peninsulas of India and Indochina, there lived two kings who were brothers. The older brother was named Shahrayar, the younger Shahzaman. The older, Shahrayar, was a towering knight and a daring champion, invincible, energetic, and implacable. His power reached the remotest corners of the land and its people, so that the country was loyal to him, and his subjects obeyed him. Shahrayar himself lived and ruled in India and Indochina, while to his brother he gave the land of Samarkand to rule as king.

Ten years went by, when one day Shahrayar felt a longing for his brother the king, summoned his vizier[3] (who had two daughters, one called Shahrazad, the other Dinarzad) and bade him go to his brother. Having made preparations, the vizier journeyed day and night until he reached Samarkand. When Shahzaman heard of the vizier's arrival, he went out with his retainers to meet him. He dismounted, embraced him, and asked him for news from his older brother, Shahrayar. The vizier replied that he was well, and that he had sent him to request his brother to visit him. Shahzaman complied with his brother's request and proceeded to make preparations for the journey. In the meantime, he had the vizier camp on the outskirts of the city, and took care of his needs. He sent him what he required of food and fodder, slaughtered many sheep in his honor, and provided him with money and supplies, as well as many horses and camels.

For ten full days he prepared himself for the journey; then he appointed a chamberlain in his place, and left the city to spend the night in his tent, near the vizier. At midnight he returned to his palace in the city, to bid his wife good-bye. But when he entered the palace, he found his wife lying in the arms of one of the kitchen boys. When he saw them, the world turned dark before his eyes and, shaking

---

2. A dynasty of Persian kings who ruled from c. 226 to 641 C.E.
3. The highest state official or administrator under a caliph or a king (literally, "one who bears burdens").

his head, he said to himself, "I am still here, and this is what she has done when I was barely outside the city. How will it be and what will happen behind my back when I go to visit my brother in India? No. Women are not to be trusted." He got exceedingly angry, adding, "By God, I am king and sovereign in Samarkand, yet my wife has betrayed me and has inflicted this on me." As his anger boiled, he drew his sword and struck both his wife and the cook. Then he dragged them by the heels and threw them from the top of the palace to the trench below. He then left the city and, going to the vizier, ordered that they depart that very hour. The drum was struck, and they set out on their journey, while Shahzaman's heart was on fire because of what his wife had done to him and how she had betrayed him with some cook, some kitchen boy. They journeyed hurriedly, day and night, through deserts and wilds, until they reached the land of King Shahrayar, who had gone out to receive them.

When Shahrayar met them, he embraced his brother, showed him favors, and treated him generously. He offered him quarters in a palace adjoining his own, for King Shahrayar had built two beautiful towering palaces in his garden, one for the guests, the other for the women and members of his household. He gave the guesthouse to his brother, Shahzaman, after the attendants had gone to scrub it, dry it, furnish it, and open its windows, which overlooked the garden. Thereafter, Shahzaman would spend the whole day at his brother's, return at night to sleep at the palace, then go back to his brother the next morning. But whenever he found himself alone and thought of his ordeal with his wife, he would sigh deeply, then stifle his grief, and say, "Alas, that this great misfortune should have happened to one in my position!" Then he would fret with anxiety, his spirit would sag, and he would say, "None has seen what I have seen." In his depression, he ate less and less, grew pale, and his health deteriorated. He neglected everything, wasted away, and looked ill.

When King Shahrayar looked at his brother and saw how day after day he lost weight and grew thin, pale, ashen, and sickly, he thought that this was because of his expatriation and homesickness for his country and his family, and he said to himself, "My brother is not happy here. I should prepare a goodly gift for him and send him home." For a month he gathered gifts for his brother; then he invited him to see him and said, "Brother, I would like you to know that I intend to go hunting and pursue the roaming deer, for ten days. Then I shall return to prepare you for your journey home. Would you like to go hunting with me?" Shahzaman replied, "Brother, I feel distracted and depressed. Leave me here and go with God's blessing and help." When Shahrayar heard his brother, he thought that his dejection was because of his homesickness for his country. Not wishing to coerce him, he left him behind, and set out with his retainers and men. When they entered the wilderness, he deployed his men in a circle to begin trapping and hunting.

After his brother's departure, Shahzaman stayed in the palace and, from the window overlooking the garden, watched the birds and trees as he thought of his wife and what she had done to him, and sighed in sorrow. While he agonized over his misfortune, gazing at the heavens and turning a distracted eye on the garden, the private gate of his brother's palace opened, and there emerged, strutting like a dark-eyed deer, the lady, his brother's wife, with twenty slave girls, ten white and ten black. While Shahzaman looked at them, without being seen, they continued to walk until they stopped below his window, without looking in his direction, thinking that he had gone to the hunt with his brother. Then they sat down, took off their clothes, and suddenly there were ten slave girls and ten black slaves dressed in the same clothes as the girls. Then the ten black slaves mounted the ten girls, while the lady called, "Mas'ud, Mas'ud!" and a black slave jumped from the tree to the ground, rushed to her, and, raising her legs, went between her thighs and made love to her. Mas'ud topped the lady, while the ten slaves topped the ten girls, and they carried on till noon. When they were done with their business, they got up and washed themselves. Then the ten slaves put on the same clothes again, mingled with the girls, and once more there appeared to be twenty slave girls. Mas'ud himself jumped over the garden wall and disappeared, while the slave girls and the lady sauntered to the private gate, went in and, locking the gate behind them, went their way.

All of this happened under King Shahzaman's eyes. When he saw this spectacle of the wife and the women of his brother the great king—how ten slaves put on women's clothes and slept with his brother's paramours and concubines and what Mas'ud did with his brother's wife, in his very palace—and pondered over this calamity and great misfortune, his care and sorrow left him and he said to himself, "This is our common lot. Even though my brother is king and master of the whole world, he cannot protect what is his, his wife and his concubines, and suffers misfortune in his very home. What happened to me is little by comparison. I used to think that I was the only one who has suffered, but from what I have seen, everyone suffers. By God, my misfortune is lighter than that of my brother." He kept marveling and blaming life, whose trials none can escape, and he began to find consolation in his own affliction and forget his grief. When supper came, he ate and drank with relish and zest and, feeling better, kept eating and drinking, enjoying himself and feeling happy. He thought to himself, "I am no longer alone in my misery; I am well."

For ten days, he continued to enjoy his food and drink, and when his brother, King Shahrayar, came back from the hunt, he met him happily, treated him attentively, and greeted him cheerfully. His brother, King Shahrayar, who had missed him, said, "By God, brother, I missed you on this trip and wished you were with me." Shahzaman thanked him and sat down to carouse with him, and when night fell, and food was brought before them, the two ate and drank, and again Shahzaman ate and drank with zest. As time went by, he continued to eat and drink with appetite, and became light-hearted and carefree. His face regained color and became ruddy, and his body gained weight, as his blood circulated and he regained his energy; he was himself again, or even better. King Shahrayar noticed his brother's condition, how he used to be and how he had improved, but kept it to himself until he took him aside one day and said, "My brother Shahzaman, I would like you to do something for me, to satisfy a wish, to answer a question truthfully." Shahzaman asked, "What is it, brother?" He replied, "When you first came to stay with me, I noticed that you kept losing weight, day after day, until your looks changed, your health deteriorated, and your energy sagged. As you continued like this, I thought that what ailed you was your homesickness for your family and your country, but even though I kept noticing that you were wasting away and looking ill, I refrained from questioning you and hid my feelings from you. Then I went hunting, and when I came back, I found that you had recovered and had regained your health. Now I want you to tell me everything and to explain the cause of your deterioration and the cause of your subsequent recovery, without hiding anything from me." When Shahzaman heard what King Shahrayar said, he bowed his head, then said, "As for the cause of my recovery, that I cannot tell you, and I wish that you would excuse me from telling you." The king was greatly astonished at his brother's reply and, burning with curiosity, said, "You must tell me. For now, at least, explain the first cause."

Then Shahzaman related to his brother what happened to him with his own wife, on the night of his departure, from beginning to end, and concluded, "Thus all the while I was with you, great King, whenever I thought of the event and the misfortune that had befallen me, I felt troubled, careworn, and unhappy, and my health deteriorated. This then is the cause." Then he grew silent. When King Shahrayar heard his brother's explanation, he shook his head, greatly amazed at the deceit of women, and prayed to God to protect him from their wickedness, saying, "Brother, you were fortunate in killing your wife and her lover, who gave you good reason to feel troubled, careworn, and ill. In my opinion, what happened to you has never happened to anyone else. By God, had I been in your place, I would have killed at least a hundred or even a thousand women. I would have been furious; I would have gone mad. Now praise be to God who has delivered you from sorrow and distress. But tell me what has caused you to forget your sorrow and regain your health?" Shahzaman replied, "King, I wish that for God's sake you would excuse me from telling you." Shahrayar said, "You must." Shahzaman replied, "I fear that you will feel even more troubled and careworn than I." Shahrayar asked, "How could that be, brother? I insist on hearing your explanation."

Shahzaman then told him about what he had seen from the palace window and the calamity in his very home—how ten slaves, dressed like women, were sleeping with his women and concubines, day and night. He told him everything from beginning to end (but there is no point in repeating that). Then he concluded, "When I saw your own misfortune, I felt better—and said to myself, 'My brother is king of the world, yet such a misfortune has happened to him, and in his very home.' As a result I forgot my care and sorrow, relaxed, and began to eat and drink. This is the cause of my cheer and good spirits."

When King Shahrayar heard what his brother said and found out what had happened to him, he was furious and his blood boiled. He said, "Brother, I can't believe what you say unless I see it with my own eyes." When Shahzaman saw that his brother was in a rage, he said to him, "If you do not believe me, unless you see your misfortune with your own eyes, announce that you plan to go hunting. Then you and I shall set out with your troops, and when we get outside the city, we shall leave our tents and camp with the men behind, enter the city secretly, and go together to your palace. Then the next morning you can see with your own eyes."

King Shahrayar realized that his brother had a good plan and ordered his army to prepare for the trip. He spent the night with his brother, and when God's morning broke, the two rode out of the city with their army, preceded by the camp attendants, who had gone to drive the poles and pitch the tents where the king and his army were to camp. At nightfall King Shahrayar summoned his chief chamberlain and bade him take his place. He entrusted him with the army and ordered that for three days no one was to enter the city. Then he and his brother disguised themselves and entered the city in the dark. They went directly to the palace where Shahzaman resided and slept there till the morning. When they awoke, they sat at the palace window, watching the garden and chatting, until the light broke, the day dawned, and the sun rose. As they watched, the private gate opened, and there emerged as usual the wife of King Shahrayar, walking among twenty slave girls. They made their way under the trees until they stood below the palace window where the two kings sat. Then they took off their women's clothes, and suddenly there were ten slaves, who mounted the ten girls and made love to them. As for the lady, she called, "Mas'ud, Mas'ud," and a black slave jumped from the tree to the ground, came to her, and said, "What do you want, you slut? Here is Sa'ad al-Din Mas'ud." She laughed and fell on her back, while the slave mounted her and like the others did his business with her. Then the black slaves got up, washed themselves, and, putting on the same clothes, mingled with the girls. Then they walked away, entered the palace, and locked the gate behind them. As for Mas'ud, he jumped over the fence to the road and went on his way.

When King Shahrayar saw the spectacle of his wife and the slave girls, he went out of his mind, and when he and his brother came down from upstairs, he said, "No one is safe in this world. Such doings are going on in my kingdom, and in my very palace. Perish the world and perish life! This is a great calamity, indeed." Then he turned to his brother and asked, "Would you like to follow me in what I shall do?" Shahzaman answered, "Yes. I will." Shahrayar said, "Let us leave our royal state and roam the world for the love of the Supreme Lord. If we should find one whose misfortune is greater than ours, we shall return. Otherwise, we shall continue to journey through the land, without need for the trappings of royalty." Shahzaman replied, "This is an excellent idea. I shall follow you."

Then they left by the private gate, took a side road, and departed, journeying till nightfall. They slept over their sorrows, and in the morning resumed their day journey until they came to a meadow by the seashore. While they sat in the meadow amid the thick plants and trees, discussing their misfortunes and the recent events, they suddenly heard a shout and a great cry coming from the middle of the sea. They trembled with fear, thinking that the sky had fallen on the earth. Then the sea parted, and there emerged a black pillar that, as it swayed forward, got taller and taller, until it touched the clouds. Shahrayar and Shahzaman were petrified; then they ran in terror and, climbing a very tall tree, sat hiding in its foliage. When they looked again, they saw that the black pillar was cleaving the sea, wading in the water toward the green meadow, until it touched the shore. When they looked again, they saw that it was a black demon, carrying on his head a large glass chest with four steel locks. He came out, walked into the meadow, and where should he stop but under the very tree where the two kings were hiding. The demon sat down and placed the glass chest on the ground. He took out four keys and, opening the locks of the chest, pulled out a full-grown woman. She had a beautiful figure, and a face like the full moon, and a lovely smile. He took her out, laid her under the tree, and looked at her, saying, "Mistress of all noble women, you whom I carried away on your wedding night, I would like to sleep a little." Then he placed his head on the young woman's lap, stretched his legs to the sea, sank into sleep, and began to snore.

Meanwhile, the woman looked up at the tree and, turning her head by chance, saw King Shahrayar and King Shahzaman. She lifted the demon's head from her lap and placed it on the ground. Then she came and stood under the tree and motioned to them with her hand, as if to say, "Come down slowly to me." When they realized that she had seen them, they were frightened, and they begged her and implored her, in the name of the Creator of the heavens, to excuse them from climbing down. She replied, "You must come down to me." They motioned to her, saying, "This sleeping demon is the enemy of mankind. For God's sake, leave us alone." She replied, "You must come down, and if you don't, I shall wake the demon and have him kill you." She kept gesturing and pressing, until they climbed down very slowly and stood before her. Then she lay on her back, raised her legs, and said, "Make love to me and satisfy my need, or else I shall wake the demon, and he will kill you." They replied, "For God's sake, mistress, don't do this to us, for at this moment we feel nothing but dismay and fear of this demon. Please, excuse us." She replied, "You must," and insisted, swearing, "By God who created the heavens, if you don't do it, I shall wake my husband the demon and ask him to kill you and throw you into the sea." As she persisted, they could no longer resist and they made love to her, first the older brother, then the younger. When they were done and withdrew from her, she said to them, "Give me your rings," and, pulling out from the folds of her dress a small purse, opened it, and shook out ninety-eight rings of different fashions and colors. Then she asked them, "Do you know what these rings are?" They answered, "No." She said, "All the owners of these rings slept with me, for whenever one of them made love to me, I took a ring from him. Since you two have slept with me, give me your rings, so that I may add them to the rest, and make a full hundred. A hundred men have known me under the very horns of this filthy, monstrous cuckold, who has imprisoned me in this chest, locked it with four locks, and kept me in the middle of this raging, roaring sea. He has guarded me and tried to keep me pure and chaste, not realizing that nothing can prevent or alter what is predestined and that when a woman desires something, no one can stop her." When Shahrayar and Shahzaman heard what the young woman said, they were greatly amazed, danced with joy, and said, "O God, O God! There is no power and no strength, save in God the Almighty, the Magnificent. 'Great is women's cunning.'" Then each of them took off his ring and handed it to her. She took them and put them with the rest in the purse. Then sitting again by the demon, she lifted his head, placed it back on her lap, and motioned to them, "Go on your way, or else I shall wake him."

They turned their backs and took to the road. Then Shahrayar turned to his brother and said, "My brother Shahzaman, look at this

sorry plight. By God, it is worse than ours. This is no less than a
demon who has carried a young woman away on her wedding night,
imprisoned her in a glass chest, locked her up with four locks, and
kept her in the middle of the sea, thinking that he could guard her
from what God had foreordained, and you saw how she has managed to sleep with ninety-eight men, and added the two of us to
make a hundred. Brother, let us go back to our kingdoms and our
cities, never to marry a woman again. As for myself, I shall show you
what I will do."

Then the two brothers headed home and journeyed till nightfall.
On the morning of the third day, they reached their camp and men,
entered their tent, and sat on their thrones. The chamberlains,
deputies, princes, and viziers came to attend King Shahrayar, while
he gave orders and bestowed robes of honor, as well as other gifts.
Then at his command everyone returned to the city, and he went to
his own palace and ordered his chief vizier, the father of the two girls
Shahrazad and Dinarzad, who will be mentioned below, and said to
him, "Take that wife of mine and put her to death." Then Shahrayar
went to her himself, bound her, and handed her over to the vizier,
who took her out and put her to death. Then King Shahrayar
grabbed his sword, brandished it, and, entering the palace chambers, killed every one of his slave girls and replaced them with
others. He then swore to marry for one night only and kill the
woman the next morning, in order to save himself from the wickedness and cunning of women, saying, "There is not a single chaste
woman anywhere on the entire face of the earth." Shortly thereafter
he provided his brother Shahzaman with supplies for his journey
and sent him back to his own country with gifts, rarities, and money.
The brother bade him good-bye and set out for home.

Shahrayar sat on his throne and ordered his vizier, the father of
the two girls, to find him a wife from among the princes' daughters.
The vizier found him one, and he slept with her and was done with
her, and the next morning he ordered the vizier to put her to death.
That very night he took one of his army officers' daughters, slept
with her, and the next morning ordered the vizier to put her to death.
The vizier, who could not disobey him, put her to death. The third
night he took one of the merchants' daughters, slept with her till the
morning, then ordered his vizier to put her to death, and the vizier
did so. It became King Shahrayar's custom to take every night the
daughter of a merchant or a commoner, spend the night with her,
then have her put to death the next morning. He continued to do
this until all the girls perished, their mothers mourned, and there
arose a clamor among the fathers and mothers, who called the
plague upon his head, complained to the Creator of the heavens,
and called for help on Him who hears and answers prayers.

Now, as mentioned earlier, the vizier, who put the girls to death, had an older daughter called Shahrazad and a younger one called Dinarzad. The older daughter, Shahrazad, had read the books of literature, philosophy, and medicine. She knew poetry by heart, had studied historical reports, and was acquainted with the sayings of men and the maxims of sages and kings. She was intelligent, knowledgeable, wise, and refined. She had read and learned. One day she said to her father, "Father, I will tell you what is in my mind." He asked, "What is it?" She answered, "I would like you to marry me to King Shahrayar, so that I may either succeed in saving the people or perish and die like the rest." When the vizier heard what his daughter Shahrazad said, he got angry and said to her, "Foolish one, don't you know that King Shahrayar has sworn to spend but one night with a girl and have her put to death the next morning? If I give you to him, he will sleep with you for one night and will ask me to put you to death the next morning, and I shall have to do it, since I cannot disobey him." She said, "Father, you must give me to him, even if he kills me." He asked, "What has possessed you that you wish to imperil yourself?" She replied, "Father, you must give me to him. This is absolute and final." Her father the vizier became furious and said to her, "Daughter, 'He who misbehaves, ends up in trouble,' and 'He who considers not the end, the world is not his friend.' As the popular saying goes, 'I would be sitting pretty, but for my curiosity.' I am afraid that what happened to the donkey and the ox with the merchant will happen to you." She asked, "Father, what happened to the donkey, the ox, and the merchant?" He said:

[The Tale of the Ox and the Donkey]

THERE WAS A prosperous and wealthy merchant who lived in the countryside and labored on a farm. He owned many camels and herds of cattle and employed many men, and he had a wife and many grown-up as well as little children. This merchant was taught the language of the beasts, on condition that if he revealed his secret to anyone, he would die; therefore, even though he knew the language of every kind of animal, he did not let anyone know, for fear of death. One day, as he sat, with his wife beside him and his children playing before him, he glanced at an ox and a donkey he kept at the farmhouse, tied to adjacent troughs, and heard the ox say to the donkey, "Watchful one, I hope that you are enjoying the comfort and the service you are getting. Your ground is swept and watered, and they serve you, feed you sifted barley, and offer you clear, cool water to drink. I, on the contrary, am taken out to plow in the middle of the night. They clamp on my neck something they call yoke and plow, push me all day under the whip to plow the field, and drive me beyond my endurance until my sides are lacerated, and my neck is flayed. They work me from nighttime to nighttime, take me back in the dark, offer me beans soiled with mud and hay mixed with chaff, and let me spend the night lying in urine and dung. Meanwhile you rest on well-swept, watered, and smoothed ground, with a clean trough full of hay. You stand in comfort, save for the rare occasion when our master the merchant rides you to do a brief errand and returns. You are comfortable, while I am weary; you sleep, while I keep awake."

When the ox finished, the donkey turned to him and said, "Greenhorn, they were right in calling you ox, for you ox harbor no deceit, malice, or meanness. Being sincere, you exert and exhaust yourself to comfort others. Have you not heard the saying 'Out of bad luck, they hastened on the road'? You go into the field from early morning to endure your torture at the plow to the point of exhaustion. When the plowman takes you back and ties you to the trough, you go on butting and beating with your horns, kicking with your hoofs, and bellowing for the beans, until they toss them to you; then you begin to eat. Next time, when they bring them to you, don't eat or even touch them, but smell them, then draw back and lie down on the hay and straw. If you do this, life will be better and kinder to you, and you will find relief."

As the ox listened, he was sure that the donkey had given him good advice. He thanked him, commended him to God, and invoked His blessing on him, and said, "May you stay safe from harm, watchful one." All of this conversation took place, daughter, while the merchant listened and understood. On the following day, the plowman came to the merchant's house and, taking the ox, placed the yoke upon his neck and worked him at the plow, but the ox lagged behind. The plowman hit him, but following the donkey's advice, the ox, dissembling, fell on his belly, and the plowman hit him again. Thus the ox kept getting up and falling until nightfall, when the plowman took him home and tied him to the trough. But this time the ox did not bellow or kick the ground with his hoofs. Instead, he withdrew, away from the trough. Astonished, the plowman brought him his beans and fodder, but the ox only smelled the fodder and pulled back and lay down at a distance with the hay and straw, complaining till the morning. When the plowman arrived, he found the trough as he had left it, full of beans and fodder, and saw the ox lying on his back, hardly breathing, his belly puffed, and his legs raised in the air. The plowman felt sorry for him and said to himself, "By God, he did seem weak and unable to work." Then he went to the merchant and said, "Master, last night, the ox refused to eat or touch his fodder."

The merchant, who knew what was going on, said to the plowman, "Go to the wily donkey, put him to the plow, and work him hard until he finishes the ox's task." The plowman left, took the donkey, and placed the yoke upon his neck. Then he took him out to the field and drove him with blows until he finished the ox's work, all the while driving him with blows and beating him until his sides were lacerated and his neck was flayed. At nightfall he took him home, barely able to drag his legs under his tired body and his drooping ears. Meanwhile the ox spent his day resting. He ate all his food, drank his water, and lay quietly, chewing his cud in comfort. All day long he kept praising the donkey's advice and invoking God's blessing on him. When the donkey came back at night, the ox stood up to greet him, saying, "Good evening, watchful one! You have done me a favor beyond description, for I have been sitting in comfort. God bless you for my sake." Seething with anger, the donkey did not reply, but said to himself, "All this happened to me because of my miscalculation. 'I would be sitting pretty, but for my curiosity.' If I don't find a way to return this ox to his former situation, I will perish." Then he went to his trough and lay down, while the ox continued to chew his cud and invoke God's blessing on him.

"YOU, MY DAUGHTER, will likewise perish because of your miscalculation. Desist, sit quietly, and don't expose yourself to peril. I advise you out of compassion for you." She replied, "Father, I must go to the king, and you must give me to him." He said, "Don't do it." She insisted, "I must." He replied, "If you don't desist, I will do to you what the merchant did to his wife." She asked, "Father, what did the merchant do to his wife?" He said:

[The Tale of the Merchant and His Wife]

AFTER WHAT HAD happened to the donkey and the ox, the merchant and his wife went out in the moonlight to the stable, and he heard the donkey ask the ox in his own language, "Listen, ox, what are you going to do tomorrow morning, and what will you do when the plowman brings you your fodder?" The ox replied, "What shall I do but follow your advice and stick to it? If he brings me my fodder, I will pretend to be ill, lie down, and puff my belly." The donkey shook his head, and said, "Don't do it. Do you know what I heard our master the merchant say to the plowman?" The ox asked, "What?" The donkey replied, "He said that if the ox failed to get up and eat his fodder, he would call the butcher to slaughter him and skin him and would distribute the meat for alms and use the skin for a mat. I am afraid for you, but good advice is a matter of faith; therefore, if he brings you your fodder, eat it and look alert lest they cut your throat and skin you." The ox farted and bellowed.

The merchant got up and laughed loudly at the conversation between the donkey and the ox, and his wife asked him, "What are you laughing at? Are you making fun of me?" He said, "No." She said, "Tell me what made you laugh." He replied, "I cannot tell you. I am afraid to disclose the secret conversation of the animals." She asked, "And what prevents you from telling me?" He answered, "The fear of death." His wife said, "By God, you are lying. This is nothing but an excuse. I swear by God, the Lord of heaven, that if you don't tell me and explain the cause of your laughter, I will leave you. You must tell me." Then she went back to the house crying, and she continued to cry till the morning. The merchant said, "Damn it! Tell me why you are crying. Ask for God's forgiveness, and stop questioning and leave me in peace." She said, "I insist and will not desist." Amazed at her, he replied, "You insist! If I tell you what the donkey said to the ox, which made me laugh, I shall die." She said, "Yes, I insist, even if you have to die." He replied, "Then call your family," and she called their two daughters, her parents and relatives, and some neighbors. The merchant told them that he was about to die, and everyone, young and old, his children, the farmhands, and the servants began to cry until the house became a place of mourning. Then he summoned legal witnesses, wrote a will, leaving his wife and children their due portions, freed his slave girls, and bid his family good-bye, while everybody, even the witnesses, wept. Then the wife's parents approached her and said, "Desist, for if your husband had not known for certain that he would die if he revealed his secret, he wouldn't have gone through all this." She replied, "I will not change my mind," and everybody cried and prepared to mourn his death.

Well, my daughter Shahrazad, it happened that the farmer kept fifty hens and a rooster at home, and while he felt sad to depart this world and leave his children and relatives behind, pondering and about to reveal and utter his secret, he overheard a dog of his say something in dog language to the rooster, who, beating and clapping his wings, had jumped on a hen and, finishing with her, jumped down and jumped on another. The merchant heard and understood what the dog said in his own language to the rooster, "Shameless, no-good rooster. Aren't you ashamed to do such a thing on a day like this?" The rooster asked, "What is special about this day?" The dog replied, "Don't you know that our master and friend is in mourning today? His wife is demanding that he disclose his secret, and when he discloses it, he will surely die. He is in this predicament, about to interpret to her the language of the animals, and all of us are mourning for him, while you clap your wings and get off one hen and jump on another. Aren't you ashamed?" The merchant heard the rooster reply, "You fool, you lunatic! Our master and friend claims to be wise, but he is foolish, for he has only one wife, yet he does not know how to manage her." The dog asked, "What should he do with her?"

The rooster replied, "He should take an oak branch, push her into a room, lock the door, and fall on her with the stick, beating her mercilessly until he breaks her arms and legs and she cries out, 'I no longer want you to tell me or explain anything.' He should go on beating her until he cures her for life, and she will never oppose him in anything. If he does this, he will live, and live in peace, and there will be no more grief, but he does not know how to manage." Well, my daughter Shahrazad, when the merchant heard the conversation between the dog and the rooster, he jumped up and, taking an oak branch, pushed his wife into a room, got in with her, and locked the door. Then he began to beat her mercilessly on her chest and shoulders and kept beating her until she cried for mercy, screaming, "No, no, I don't want to know anything. Leave me alone, leave me alone. I don't want to know anything," until he got tired of hitting her and opened the door. The wife emerged penitent, the husband learned good management, and everybody was happy, and the mourning turned into a celebration.

"IF YOU DON'T relent, I shall do to you what the merchant did to his wife." She said, "Such tales don't deter me from my request. If you wish, I can tell you many such tales. In the end, if you don't take me to King Shahrayar, I shall go to him by myself behind your back and tell him that you have refused to give me to one like him and that you have begrudged your master one like me." The vizier asked, "Must you really do this?" She replied, "Yes, I must."

Tired and exhausted, the vizier went to King Shahrayar and, kissing the ground before him, told him about his daughter, adding that he would give her to him that very night. The king was astonished and said to him, "Vizier, how is it that you have found it possible to give me your daughter, knowing that I will, by God, the Creator of heaven, ask you to put her to death the next morning and that if you refuse, I will have you put to death too?" He replied, "My King and Lord, I have told her everything and explained all this to her, but she refuses and insists on being with you tonight." The king was delighted and said, "Go to her, prepare her, and bring her to me early in the evening."

The vizier went down, repeated the king's message to his daughter, and said, "May God not deprive me of you." She was very happy and, after preparing herself and packing what she needed, went to her younger sister, Dinarzad, and said, "Sister, listen well to what I am telling you. When I go to the king, I will send for you, and when you come and see that the king has finished with me, say, 'Sister, if you are not sleepy, tell us a story.' Then I will begin to tell a story, and it will cause the king to stop his practice, save myself, and deliver the people." Dinarzad replied, "Very well."

At nightfall the vizier took Shahrazad and went with her to the great King Shahrayar. But when Shahrayar took her to bed and began to fondle her, she wept, and when he asked her, "Why are you crying?" she replied, "I have a sister, and I wish to bid her good-bye before day-break." Then the king sent for the sister, who came and went to sleep under the bed. When the night wore on, she woke up and waited until the king had satisfied himself with her sister Shahrazad and they were by now all fully awake. Then Dinarzad cleared her throat and said, "Sister, if you are not sleepy, tell us one of your lovely little tales to while away the night, before I bid you good-bye at daybreak, for I don't know what will happen to you tomorrow." Shahrazad turned to King Shahrayar and said, "May I have your permission to tell a story?" He replied, "Yes," and Shahrazad was very happy and said, "Listen":

THE FIRST NIGHT

[The Story of the Merchant and the Demon]

It is said, O wise and happy King, that once there was a prosper-ous merchant who had abundant wealth and investments and com-mitments in every country. He had many women and children and kept many servants and slaves. One day, having resolved to visit another country, he took provisions, filling his saddlebag with loaves of bread and with dates, mounted his horse, and set out on his jour-ney. For many days and nights, he journeyed under God's care until he reached his destination. When he finished his business, he turned back to his home and family. He journeyed for three days, and on the fourth day, chancing to come to an orchard, went in to avoid the heat and shade himself from the sun of the open country. He came to a spring under a walnut tree and, tying his horse, sat by the spring, pulled out from the saddlebag some loaves of bread and a handful of dates, and began to eat, throwing the date pits right and left until he had had enough. Then he got up, performed his ablu-tions, and performed his prayers.

But hardly had he finished when he saw an old demon, with sword in hand, standing with his feet on the ground and his head in the clouds. The demon approached until he stood before him and screamed, saying, "Get up, so that I may kill you with this sword, just as you have killed my son." When the merchant saw and heard the demon, he was terrified and awestricken. He asked, "Master, for what crime do you wish to kill me?" The demon replied, "I wish to kill you because you have killed my son." The merchant asked, "Who has killed your son?" The demon replied, "You have killed my son." The merchant said, "By God, I did not kill your son. When and how could that have been?" The demon said, "Didn't you sit down, take out some dates from your saddlebag, and eat, throwing the pits right and left?" The merchant replied, "Yes, I did." The demon said, "You killed my son, for as you were throwing the stones right and left, my son happened to be walking by and was struck and killed by one of them, and I must now kill you." The merchant said, "O my lord, please don't kill me." The demon replied, "I must kill you as you killed him—blood for blood." The merchant said, "To God we belong and to God we return. There is no power or strength, save in God the Almighty, the Magnificent. If I killed him, I did it by mistake. Please forgive me." The demon replied, "By God, I must kill you, as you killed my son." Then he seized him and, throwing him to the ground, raised the sword to strike him. The merchant began to weep and mourn his family and his wife and children. Again, the demon raised his sword to strike, while the merchant cried until he was drenched with tears, saying, "There is no power or strength, save in God the Almighty, the Magnificent." Then he began to recite the following verses:

> Life has two days: one peace, one wariness,
> And has two sides: worry and happiness.
> Ask him who taunts us with adversity,
> "Does fate, save those worthy of note, oppress?
> Don't you see that the blowing, raging storms
> Only the tallest of the trees beset,
> And of earth's many green and barren lots,
> Only the ones with fruits with stones are hit,
> And of the countless stars in heaven's vault
> None is eclipsed except the moon and sun?
> You thought well of the days, when they were good,
> Oblivious to the ills destined for one.
> You were deluded by the peaceful nights,
> Yet in the peace of night does sorrow stun."

When the merchant finished and stopped weeping, the demon said, "By God, I must kill you, as you killed my son, even if you weep blood." The merchant asked, "Must you?" The demon replied, "I must," and raised his sword to strike.

But morning overtook Shahrazad, and she lapsed into silence, leaving King Shahrayar burning with curiosity to hear the rest of the story. Then Dinarzad said to her sister Shahrazad, "What a strange and lovely story!" Shahrazad replied, "What is this compared with what I shall tell

*you tomorrow night if the king spares me and lets me live? It will be
even better and more entertaining." The king thought to himself, "I will
spare her until I hear the rest of the story; then I will have her put to
death the next day." When morning broke, the day dawned, and the sun
rose; the king left to attend to the affairs of the kingdom, and the vizier,
Shahrazad's father, was amazed and delighted. King Shahrayar governed all day and returned home at night to his quarters and got into
bed with Shahrazad. Then Dinarzad said to her sister Shahrazad,
"Please, sister, if you are not sleepy, tell us one of your lovely little tales
to while away the night." The king added, "Let it be the conclusion of
the story of the demon and the merchant, for I would like to hear it."
Shahrazad replied, "With the greatest pleasure, dear, happy King":*

THE SECOND NIGHT

It is related, O wise and happy King, that when the demon raised
his sword, the merchant asked the demon again, "Must you kill me?"
and the demon replied, "Yes." Then the merchant said, "Please give
me time to say good-bye to my family and my wife and children,
divide my property among them, and appoint guardians. Then I shall
come back, so that you may kill me." The demon replied, "I am
afraid that if I release you and grant you time, you will go and do
what you wish, but will not come back." The merchant said, "I swear
to keep my pledge to come back, as the God of Heaven and earth is
my witness." The demon asked, "How much time do you need?" The
merchant replied, "One year, so that I may see enough of my children, bid my wife good-bye, discharge my obligations to people, and
come back on New Year's Day." The demon asked, "Do you swear
to God that if I let you go, you will come back on New Year's Day?"
The merchant replied, "Yes, I swear to God."

After the merchant swore, the demon released him, and he mounted
his horse sadly and went on his way. He journeyed until he reached
his home and came to his wife and children. When he saw them, he
wept bitterly, and when his family saw his sorrow and grief, they
began to reproach him for his behavior, and his wife said, "Husband,
what is the matter with you? Why do you mourn, when we are
happy, celebrating your return?" He replied, "Why not mourn when
I have only one year to live?" Then he told her of his encounter with
the demon and informed her that he had sworn to return on New
Year's Day, so that the demon might kill him.

When they heard what he said, everyone began to cry. His wife
struck her face in lamentation and cut her hair, his daughters wailed,

and his little children cried. It was a day of mourning, as all the children gathered around their father to weep and exchange good-byes. The next day he wrote his will, dividing his property, discharged his obligations to people, left bequests and gifts, distributed alms, and engaged reciters to read portions of the Quran in his house. Then he summoned legal witnesses and in their presence freed his slaves and slave girls, divided among his elder children their shares of the property, appointed guardians for his little ones, and gave his wife her share, according to her marriage contract. He spent the rest of the time with his family, and when the year came to an end, save for the time needed for the journey, he performed his ablutions, performed his prayers, and, carrying his burial shroud, began to bid his family good-bye. His sons hung around his neck, his daughters wept, and his wife wailed. Their mourning scared him, and he began to weep, as he embraced and kissed his children good-bye. He said to them, "Children, this is God's will and decree, for man was created to die." Then he turned away and, mounting his horse, journeyed day and night until he reached the orchard on New Year's Day.

He sat at the place where he had eaten the dates, waiting for the demon, with a heavy heart and tearful eyes. As he waited, an old man, leading a deer on a leash, approached and greeted him, and he returned the greeting. The old man inquired, "Friend, why do you sit here in this place of demons and devils? For in this haunted orchard none come to good." The merchant replied by telling him what had happened to him and the demon, from beginning to end. The old man was amazed at the merchant's fidelity and said, "Yours is a magnificent pledge," adding, "By God, I shall not leave until I see what will happen to you with the demon." Then he sat down beside him and chatted with him. As they talked . . .

But morning overtook Shahrazad, and she lapsed into silence. As the day dawned, and it was light, her sister Dinarzad said, "What a strange and wonderful story!" Shahrazad replied, "Tomorrow night I shall tell something even stranger and more wonderful than this."

THE THIRD NIGHT

When it was night and Shahrazad was in bed with the king, Dinarzad said to her sister Shahrazad, "Please, if you are not sleepy, tell us one of your lovely little tales to while away the night." The king added, "Let it be the conclusion of the merchant's story." Shahrazad replied, "As you wish":

I heard, O happy King, that as the merchant and the man with the deer sat talking, another old man approached, with two black hounds, and when he reached them, he greeted them, and they returned his greeting. Then he asked them about themselves, and the man with the deer told him the story of the merchant and the demon, how the merchant had sworn to return on New Year's Day, and how the demon was waiting to kill him. He added that when he himself heard the story, he swore never to leave until he saw what would happen between the merchant and the demon. When the man with the two dogs heard the story, he was amazed, and he too swore never to leave them until he saw what would happen between them. Then he questioned the merchant, and the merchant repeated to him what had happened to him with the demon.

While they were engaged in conversation, a third old man approached and greeted them, and they returned his greeting. He asked, "Why do I see the two of you sitting here, with this merchant between you, looking abject, sad, and dejected?" They told him the merchant's story and explained that they were sitting and waiting to see what would happen to him with the demon. When he heard the story, he sat down with them, saying, "By God, I too like you will not leave, until I see what happens to this man with the demon." As they sat, conversing with one another, they suddenly saw the dust rising from the open country, and when it cleared, they saw the demon approaching, with a drawn steel sword in his hand. He stood before them without greeting them, yanked the merchant with his left hand, and, holding him fast before him, said, "Get ready to die." The merchant and the three old men began to weep and wail.

But dawn broke and morning overtook Shahrazad, and she lapsed into silence. Then Dinarzad said, "Sister, what a lovely story!" Shahrazad replied, "What is this compared with what I shall tell you tomorrow night? It will be even better; it will be more wonderful, delightful, entertaining, and delectable if the king spares me and lets me live." The king was all curiosity to hear the rest of the story and said to himself, "By God, I will not have her put to death until I hear the rest of the story and find out what happened to the merchant with the demon. Then I will have her put to death the next morning, as I did with the others." Then he went out to attend to the affairs of his kingdom, and when he saw Shahrazad's father, he treated him kindly and showed him favors, and the vizier was amazed. When night came, the king went home, and when he was in bed with Shahrazad, Dinarzad said, "Sister, if you are not sleepy, tell us one of your lovely little tales to while away the night." Shahrazad replied, "With the greatest pleasure":

THE FOURTH NIGHT

It is related, O happy King, that the first old man with the deer approached the demon and, kissing his hands and feet, said, "Fiend and King of the demon kings, if I tell you what happened to me and that deer, and you find it strange and amazing, indeed stranger and more amazing than what happened to you and the merchant, will you grant me a third of your claim on him for his crime and guilt?" The demon replied, "I will." The old man said:

[The First Old Man's Tale]

DEMON, THIS DEER is my cousin, my flesh and blood. I married her when I was very young, and she a girl of twelve, who reached womanhood only afterward. For thirty years we lived together, but I was not blessed with children, for she bore neither boy nor girl. Yet I continued to be kind to her, to care for her, and to treat her generously. Then I took a mistress, and she bore me a son, who grew up to look like a slice of the moon. Meanwhile, my wife grew jealous of my mistress and my son. One day, when he was ten, I had to go on a journey. I entrusted my wife, this one here, with my mistress and son, bade her take good care of them, and was gone for a whole year. In my absence my wife, this cousin of mine, learned soothsaying and magic and cast a spell on my son and turned him into a young bull. Then she summoned my shepherd, gave my son to him, and said, "Tend this bull with the rest of the cattle." The shepherd took him and tended him for a while. Then she cast a spell on the mother, turning her into a cow, and gave her also to the shepherd.

When I came back, after all this was done, and inquired about my mistress and my son, she answered, "Your mistress died, and your son ran away two months ago, and I have had no news from him ever since." When I heard her, I grieved for my mistress, and with an anguished heart I mourned for my son for nearly a year. When the Great Feast of the Immolation[4] drew near, I summoned the shepherd and ordered him to bring me a fat cow for the sacrifice. The cow he brought me was in reality my enchanted mistress. When I bound her and pressed against her to cut her throat, she wept and cried, as if saying, "My son, my son," and her tears coursed down her cheeks. Astonished and seized with pity, I turned away and asked the shepherd to bring me a different cow. But my wife shouted, "Go on. Butcher her,

4. A four-day Muslim feast that celebrates the pilgrimage to Mecca and that is marked by the slaughtering of sheep and cattle as sacrificial offerings to God.

for he has none better or fatter. Let us enjoy her meat at feast time." I
approached the cow to cut her throat, and again she cried, as if saying,
"My son, my son." Then I turned away from her and said to the shepherd, "Butcher her for me." The shepherd butchered her, and when he
skinned her, he found neither meat nor fat but only skin and bone. I
regretted having her butchered and said to the shepherd, "Take her all
for yourself, or give her as alms to whomever you wish, and find me a
fat young bull from among the flock." The shepherd took her away and
disappeared, and I never knew what he did with her.

Then he brought me my son, my heartblood, in the guise of a fat
young bull. When my son saw me, he shook his head loose from the
rope, ran toward me, and, throwing himself at my feet, kept rubbing his
head against me. I was astonished and touched with sympathy, pity,
and mercy, for the blood hearkened to the blood and the divine bond,
and my heart throbbed within me when I saw the tears coursing over
the cheeks of my son the young bull, as he dug the earth with his hoofs.
I turned away and said to the shepherd, "Let him go with the rest of the
flock, and be kind to him, for I have decided to spare him. Bring me
another one instead of him." My wife, this very deer, shouted, "You
shall sacrifice none but this bull." I got angry and replied, "I listened to
you and butchered the cow uselessly. I will not listen to you and kill this
bull, for I have decided to spare him." But she pressed me, saying, "You
must butcher this bull," and I bound him and took the knife . . .

*But dawn broke, and morning overtook Shahrazad, and she lapsed
into silence, leaving the king all curiosity for the rest of the story. Then her
sister Dinarzad said, "What an entertaining story!" Shahrazad replied,
"Tomorrow night I shall tell you something even stranger, more wonderful, and more entertaining if the king spares me and lets me live."*

THE FIFTH NIGHT

*The following night, Dinarzad said to her sister Shahrazad, "Please,
sister, if you are not sleepy, tell us one of your little tales." Shahrazad
replied, "With the greatest pleasure":*

I heard, dear King, that the old man with the deer said to the
demon and to his companions:

I took the knife and as I turned to slaughter my son, he wept, bellowed, rolled at my feet, and motioned toward me with his tongue. I
suspected something, began to waver with trepidation and pity, and

finally released him, saying to my wife, "I have decided to spare him, and I commit him to your care." Then I tried to appease and please my wife, this very deer, by slaughtering another bull, promising her to slaughter this one next season. We slept that night, and when God's dawn broke, the shepherd came to me without letting my wife know, and said, "Give me credit for bringing you good news." I replied, "Tell me, and the credit is yours." He said, "Master, I have a daughter who is fond of soothsaying and magic and who is adept at the art of oaths and spells. Yesterday I took home with me the bull you had spared, to let him graze with the cattle, and when my daughter saw him, she laughed and cried at the same time. When I asked her why she laughed and cried, she answered that she laughed because the bull was in reality the son of our master the cattle owner, put under a spell by his stepmother, and that she cried because his father had slaughtered the son's mother. I could hardly wait till daybreak to bring you the good news about your son."

Demon, when I heard that, I uttered a cry and fainted, and when I came to myself, I accompanied the shepherd to his home, went to my son, and threw myself at him, kissing him and crying. He turned his head toward me, his tears coursing over his cheeks, and dangled his tongue, as if to say, "Look at my plight." Then I turned to the shepherd's daughter and asked, "Can you release him from the spell? If you do, I will give you all my cattle and all my possessions." She smiled and replied, "Master, I have no desire for your wealth, cattle, or possessions. I will deliver him, but on two conditions: first, that you let me marry him; second, that you let me cast a spell on her who had cast a spell on him, in order to control her and guard against her evil power." I replied, "Do whatever you wish and more. My possessions are for you and my son. As for my wife, who has done this to my son and made me slaughter his mother, her life is forfeit to you." She said, "No, but I will let her taste what she has inflicted on others." Then the shepherd's daughter filled a bowl with water, uttered an incantation and an oath, and said to my son, "Bull, if you have been created in this image by the All Conquering, Almighty Lord, stay as you are, but if you have been treacherously put under a spell, change back to your human form, by the will of God, Creator of the wide world." Then she sprinkled him with the water, and he shook himself and changed from a bull back to his human form.

As I rushed to him, I fainted, and when I came to myself, he told me what my wife, this very deer, had done to him and to his mother. I said to him, "Son, God has sent us someone who will pay her back for what you and your mother and I have suffered at her hands." Then, O demon, I gave my son in marriage to the shepherd's daughter, who turned my wife into this very deer, saying to me, "To me this is a pretty form, for she will be with us day and night, and it is better to turn her into a pretty deer than to suffer her sinister looks." Thus she stayed with us, while the days and nights followed one another, and the months and years went by. Then one day the shepherd's daughter died, and my son went to the country of this very man with whom you have had your encounter. Some time later I took my wife, this very deer, with me, set out to find out what had happened to my son, and chanced to stop here. This is my story, my strange and amazing story.

The demon assented, saying, "I grant you one-third of this man's life."

Then, O King Shahrayar, the second old man with the two black dogs approached the demon and said, "I too shall tell you what happened to me and to these two dogs, and if I tell it to you and you find it stranger and more amazing than this man's story will you grant me one-third of this man's life?" The demon replied, "I will." Then the old man began to tell his story, saying . . .

But dawn broke, and morning overtook Shahrazad, and she lapsed into silence. Then Dinarzad said, "This is an amazing story," and Shahrazad replied, "What is this compared with what I shall tell you tomorrow night if the king spares me and lets me live!" The king said to himself, "By God, I will not have her put to death until I find out what happened to the man with the two black dogs. Then I will have her put to death, God the Almighty willing."

THE SIXTH NIGHT

When the following night arrived and Shahrazad was in bed with King Shahrayar, her sister Dinarzad said, "Sister, if you are not sleepy, tell us a little tale. Finish the one you started." Shahrazad replied, "With the greatest pleasure":

I heard, O happy King, that the second old man with the two dogs said:

[The Second Old Man's Tale]

DEMON, AS FOR my story, these are the details. These two dogs are my brothers. When our father died, he left behind three sons, and left us three thousand dinars,[5] with which each of us opened a shop

---

5. Gold coins, the basic Muslim money units.

and became a shopkeeper. Soon my older brother, one of these very dogs, went and sold the contents of his shop for a thousand dinars, bought trading goods, and, having prepared himself for his trading trip, left us. A full year went by, when one day, as I sat in my shop, a beggar stopped by to beg. When I refused him, he tearfully asked, "Don't you recognize me?" and when I looked at him closely, I recognized my brother. I embraced him and took him into the shop, and when I asked him about his plight, he replied, "The money is gone, and the situation is bad." Then I took him to the public bath, clothed him in one of my robes, and took him home with me. Then I examined my books and checked my balance, and found out that I had made a thousand dinars and that my net worth was two thousand dinars. I divided the amount between my brother and myself, and said to him, "Think as if you have never been away." He gladly took the money and opened another shop.

Soon afterward my second brother, this other dog, went and sold his merchandise and collected his money, intending to go on a trading trip. We tried to dissuade him, but he did not listen. Instead, he bought merchandise and trading goods, joined a group of travelers, and was gone for a full year. Then he came back, just like his older brother. I said to him, "Brother, didn't I advise you not to go?" He replied tearfully, "Brother, it was foreordained. Now I am poor and penniless, without even a shirt on my back." Demon, I took him to the public bath, clothed him in one of my new robes, and took him back to the shop. After we had something to eat, I said to him, "Brother, I shall do my business accounts, calculate my net worth for the year, and after subtracting the capital, whatever the profit happens to be, I shall divide it equally between you and myself." When I examined my books and subtracted the capital, I found out that my profit was two thousand dinars, and I thanked God and felt very happy. Then I divided the money, giving him a thousand dinars and keeping a thousand for myself. With that money he opened another shop, and the three of us stayed together for a while. Then my two brothers asked me to go on a trading journey with them, but I refused, saying, "What did you gain from your ventures that I can gain?"

They dropped the matter, and for six years we worked in our stores, buying and selling. Yet every year they asked me to go on a trading journey with them, but I refused, until I finally gave in. I said, "Brothers, I am ready to go with you. How much money do you have?" I found out that they had eaten and drunk and squandered everything they had, but I said nothing to them and did not reproach them. Then I took inventory, gathered all I had together, and sold everything. I was pleased to discover that the sale netted six thousand dinars. Then I divided the money into two parts, and said to my brothers, "The sum of three thousand dinars is for you and myself to use on our trading journey. The other three thousand I shall bury in the ground, in case what happened to you happens to me, so that when we return, we will find three thousand dinars to reopen our shops." They replied, "This is an excellent idea." Then, demon, I divided my money and buried three thousand dinars. Of the remaining three I gave each of my brothers a thousand and kept a thousand for myself. After I closed my shop, we bought merchandise and trading goods, rented a large seafaring boat, and after loading it with our goods and provisions, sailed day and night, for a month.

But morning overtook Shahrazad, and she lapsed into silence. Then her sister Dinarzad said, "Sister, what a lovely story!" Shahrazad replied, "Tomorrow night I shall tell you something even lovelier, stranger, and more wonderful if I live, the Almighty God willing."

THE SEVENTH NIGHT

The following night Dinarzad said to her sister Shahrazad, "For God's sake, sister, if you are not sleepy, tell us a little tale." The king added, "Let it be the completion of the story of the merchant and the demon." Shahrazad replied, "With the greatest pleasure":

I heard, O happy King, that the second old man said to the demon:

For a month my brothers, these very dogs, and I sailed the salty sea, until we came to a port city. We entered the city and sold our goods, earning ten dinars for every dinar. Then we bought other goods, and when we got to the seashore to embark, I met a girl who was dressed in tatters. She kissed my hands and said, "O my lord, be charitable and do me a favor, and I believe that I shall be able to reward you for it." I replied, "I am willing to do you a favor regardless of any reward." She said, "O my lord, marry me, clothe me, and take me home with you on this boat, as your wife, for I wish to give myself to you. I, in turn, will reward you for your kindness and charity, the Almighty God willing. Don't be misled by my poverty and present condition." When I heard her words, I felt pity for her, and guided by what God the Most High had intended for me, I consented. I clothed her with an expensive dress and married her. Then I took her to the boat, spread the bed for her, and consummated our marriage. We sailed many days and nights, and I, feeling love for her, stayed with her day and night, neglecting my brothers. In the meantime they, these very dogs, grew jealous of me, envied me for my increasing merchandise and wealth, and coveted all our possessions. At last they decided to betray me and, tempted by the Devil, plotted to kill me. One night they waited until I was asleep beside my wife; then they carried the two of us and threw us into the sea.

When we awoke, my wife turned into a she-demon and carried me out of the sea to an island. When it was morning, she said, "Husband, I have rewarded you by saving you from drowning, for I am one of the demons who believe in God. When I saw you by the seashore, I felt love for you and came to you in the guise in which you saw me, and when I expressed my love for you, you accepted me. Now I must kill your brothers." When I heard what she said, I was amazed and I thanked her and said, "As for destroying my brothers, this I do not wish, for I will not behave like them." Then I related to her what had happened to me and them, from beginning to end. When she heard my story, she got very angry at them, and said, "I shall fly to them now, drown their boat, and let them all perish." I entreated her, saying, "For God's sake, don't. The proverb advises 'Be kind to those who hurt you.' No matter what, they are my brothers after all." In this manner, I entreated her and pacified her. Afterward, she took me and flew away with me until she brought me home and put me down on the roof of my house. I climbed down, threw the doors open, and dug up the money I had buried. Then I went out and, greeting the people in the market, reopened my shop. When I came home in the evening, I found these two dogs tied up, and when they saw me, they came to me, wept, and rubbed themselves against me. I started, when I suddenly heard my wife say, "O my lord, these are your brothers." I asked, "Who has done this to them?" She replied, "I sent to my sister and asked her to do it. They will stay in this condition for ten years, after which they may be delivered." Then she told me where to find her and departed. The ten years have passed, and I was with my brothers on my way to her to have the spell lifted, when I met this man, together with this old man with the deer. When I asked him about himself, he told me about his encounter with you, and I resolved not to leave until I found out what would happen between you and him. This is my story. Isn't it amazing?

The demon replied, "By God, it is strange and amazing. I grant you one-third of my claim on him for his crime."

Then the third old man said, "Demon, don't disappoint me. If I told you a story that is stranger and more amazing than the first two would you grant me one-third of your claim on him for his crime?" The demon replied, "I will." Then the old man said, "Demon, listen":

But morning overtook Shahrazad, and she lapsed into silence. Then her sister said, "What an amazing story!" Shahrazad replied, "The rest is even more amazing." The king said to himself, "I will not have her put to death until I hear what happened to the old man and the demon; then I will have her put to death, as is my custom with the others."

THE EIGHTH NIGHT

The following night Dinarzad said to her sister Shahrazad, "For God's sake, sister, if you are not sleepy, tell us one of your lovely little tales to while away the night." Shahrazad replied, "With the greatest pleasure":

I heard, O happy King, that the third old man told the demon a story that was even stranger and more amazing than the first two. The demon was very much amazed and, swaying with delight, said, "I grant you one-third of my claim on him for his crime." Then the demon released the merchant and departed. The merchant turned to the three old men and thanked them, and they congratulated him on his deliverance and bade him good-bye. Then they separated, and each of them went on his way. The merchant himself went back home to his family, his wife, and his children, and he lived with them until the day he died. But this story is not as strange or as amazing as the story of the fisherman.

Dinarzad asked, "Please, sister, what is the story of the fisherman?" Shahrazad said:

[The Story of the Fisherman and the Demon]

IT IS RELATED that there was a very old fisherman who had a wife and three daughters and who was so poor that they did not have even enough food for the day. It was this fisherman's custom to cast his net four times a day. One day, while the moon was still up, he went out with his net at the call for the early morning prayer. He reached the outskirts of the city and came to the seashore. Then he set down his basket, rolled up his shirt, and waded to his waist in the water. He cast his net and waited for it to sink; then he gathered the rope and started to pull. As he pulled little by little, he felt that the net was getting heavier until he was unable to pull any further. He climbed ashore, drove a stake into the ground, and tied the end of the rope to the stake. Then he took off his clothes, dove into the water, and went around the net, shaking it and tugging at it until he managed to pull it ashore. Feeling extremely happy, he put on his clothes and went back to the net. But when he opened it, he found inside a dead donkey, which had torn it apart. The fisherman felt sad and depressed and said to himself, "There is no power and no strength save in God, the Almighty, the Magnificent," adding, "Indeed, this is a strange catch!" Then he began to recite the following verses:

> O you who brave the danger in the dark,
> Reduce your toil, for gain is not in work.
> Look at the fisherman who labors at his trade,
> As the stars in the night their orbits make,
> And deeply wades into the raging sea,
> Steadily gazing at the swelling net,
> Till he returns, pleased with his nightly catch,
> A fish whose mouth the hook of death has cut,
> And sells it to a man who sleeps the night,
> Safe from the cold and blessed with every wish.
> Praised be the Lord who blesses and withholds:
> This casts the net, but that one eats the fish.

But morning overtook Shahrazad, and she lapsed into silence. Then her sister Dinarzad said, "Sister, what a lovely story!" Shahrazad replied, "Tomorrow night I shall tell you the rest, which is stranger and more wonderful, if the king spares me and lets me live!"

THE NINTH NIGHT

The following night Dinarzad said to her sister Shahrazad, "Sister, if you are not sleepy, finish the fisherman's story." Shahrazad replied, "With the greatest pleasure":

I heard, O happy King, that when the fisherman finished reciting his verses, he pushed the donkey out of the net and sat down to mend it. When he was done, he wrung it out and spread it to dry. Then he waded into the water and, invoking the Almighty God, cast the net and waited for it to sink. Then he pulled the rope little by little, but this time the net was even more firmly snagged. Thinking that it was heavy with fish, he was extremely happy. He took off his clothes and, diving into the water, freed the net and struggled with it until he reached the shore, but inside the net he found a large jar full of nothing but mud and sand. When he saw this, he felt sad and, with tears in his eyes, said to himself, "This is a strange day! God's we are and to God we return," and he began to recite the following verses:

> O my tormenting fate, forbear,
> Or if you can't, at least be fair.
> I went to seek, my daily bread,
> But they said to me it was dead.
> And neither luck nor industry
> Brought back my daily bread to me.
> The Pleiades[6] many fools attain,
> While sages sit in dark disdain.

Then the fisherman threw the jar away, washed his net, and, wringing it out, spread it to dry. Then he begged the Almighty God for forgiveness and went back to the water. For the third time, he cast the net and waited for it to sink. But when he pulled it up, he found nothing inside but broken pots and bottles, stones, bones, refuse, and the like. He wept at this great injustice and ill luck and began to recite the following verses:

> Your livelihood is not in your own hands;
> Neither by writing nor by the pen you thrive.
> Your luck and your wages are by lot;
> Some lands are waste, and some are fertile lands.
> The wheel of fortune lowers the man of worth,
> Raising the base man who deserves to fall.
> Come then, O death, and end this worthless life,
> Where the ducks soar, while the falcons are bound to earth.
> No wonder that you see the good man poor,
> While the vicious exalts in his estate.
> Our wages are alloted; 'tis our fate
> To search like birds for gleanings everywhere.
> One bird searches the earth from east to west,
> Another gets the tidbits while at rest.

Then the fisherman raised his eyes to the heavens and, seeing that the sun had risen and that it was morning and full daylight, said, "O Lord, you know that I cast my net four times only. I have already cast it three times, and there is only one more try left. Lord, let the sea

---

6. The Pleiades, a cluster of stars in the constellation of Taurus.

serve me, even as you let it serve Moses."[7] Having mended the net, he
cast it into the sea, and waited for it to sink. When he pulled, he found
that it was so heavy that he was unable to haul it. He shook it and
found that it was caught at the bottom. Saying "There is no power or
strength save in God, the Almighty, the Magnificent," he took off his
clothes and dove for the net. He worked at it until he managed to free
it, and as he hauled it to the shore, he felt that there was something
heavy inside. He struggled with the net, until he opened it and found a
large long-necked brass jar, with a lead stopper bearing the mark of a
seal ring.[8] When the fisherman saw the jar, he was happy and said to
himself, "I will sell it in the copper market, for it must be worth at least
two measures of wheat." He tried to move the jar, but it was so full and
so heavy that he was unable to budge it. Looking at the lead stopper,
he said to himself, "I will open the jar, shake out the contents, then
roll it before me until I reach the copper market." Then he took out a
knife from his belt and began to scrape and struggle with the lead
stopper until he pried it loose. He held the stopper in his mouth, tilted
the jar to the ground, and shook it, trying to pour out its contents, but
when nothing came out, he was extremely surprised.

After a while, there began to emerge from the jar a great column of
smoke, which rose and spread over the face of the earth, increasing
so much that it covered the sea and rising so high that it reached the
clouds and hid the daylight. For a long time, the smoke kept rising
from the jar; then it gathered and took shape, and suddenly it shook
and there stood a demon, with his feet on the ground and his head in
the clouds. He had a head like a tomb, fangs like pincers, a mouth
like a cave, teeth like stones, nostrils like trumpets, ears like shields,
a throat like an alley, and eyes like lanterns. In short, all one can say
is that he was a hideous monster. When the fisherman saw him, he
shook with terror, his jaws locked together, and his mouth went dry.
The demon cried, "O Solomon,[9] prophet of God, forgive me, forgive
me. Never again will I disobey you or defy your command."

*But morning overtook Shahrazad, and she lapsed into silence. Then
Dinarzad said, "Sister, what a strange and amazing story!" Shahrazad
replied, "Tomorrow night I shall tell you something stranger and more
amazing if I stay alive."*

---

7. When Moses and the Jews fled from Egypt, pursued by Pharaoh and his army, Moses
   struck the water of the Red Sea with his stick, and the sea parted, so that he and his
   people were able to cross safely into Sinai, while his pursuers were drowned. Moses is a
   prophet in Islam, as well.
8. A ring that houses a precious or semiprecious stone (usually agate) engraved with the
   name of a person and used to imprint a signature; it is in other instances engraved with
   talismanic words and used as a charm.
9. The Old Testament king and son of David.

THE TENTH NIGHT

The following night, when Shahrazad was in bed with King Shahrayar, her sister Dinarzad said, "Please, sister, finish the story of the fisherman." Shahrazad replied, "With the greatest pleasure":

I heard, O happy King, that when the fisherman heard what the demon said, he asked, "Demon, what are you saying? It has been more than one thousand and eight hundred years since the prophet Solomon died, and we are now ages later. What is your story, and why were you in this jar?" When the demon heard the fisherman, he said, "Be glad!" The fisherman cried, "O happy day!" The demon added, "Be glad that you will soon be put to death." The fisherman said, "You deserve to be put to shame for such tidings. Why do you wish to kill me, I who have released you and delivered you from the bottom of the sea and brought you back to this world?" The demon replied, "Make a wish!" The fisherman was happy and asked, "What shall I wish of you?" The demon replied, "Tell me how you wish to die, and what manner of death you wish me to choose." The fisherman asked, "What is my crime? Is this my reward from you for having delivered you?" The demon replied, "Fisherman, listen to my story." The fisherman said, "Make it short, for I am at my rope's end."

The demon said, "You should know that I am one of the renegade, rebellious demons. I, together with the giant Sakhr, rebelled against the prophet Solomon, the son of David, who sent against me Asif ibn-Barkhiya, who took me by force and bade me be led in defeat and humiliation before the prophet Solomon. When the prophet Solomon saw me, he invoked God to protect him from me and my looks and asked me to submit to him, but I refused. So he called for this brass jar, confined me inside, and sealed it with a lead seal on which he imprinted God's Almighty name. Then he commanded his demons to carry me and throw me into the middle of the sea. I stayed there for two hundred years, saying to myself, 'Whoever sets me free during these two hundred years, I will make him rich.' But the two hundred years went by and were followed by another two hundred, and no one set me free. Then I vowed to myself, 'Whoever sets me free, I will open for him all the treasures of the earth,' but four hundred years went by, and no one set me free. When I entered the next hundred years, I vowed to myself, 'Whoever delivers me, during these hundred years, I will make him king, make myself his servant, and fulfill every day three of his wishes,' but that hundred years too, plus all the intervening years, went by, and no one set me free. Then I raged and raved and growled and snorted and said to myself, 'Whoever delivers me from now on, I will either put him to the worst of deaths or let him choose for himself the manner of death.' Soon you came by and set me free. Tell me how you wish to die."

When the fisherman heard what the demon said, he replied, "To God we belong and to Him we return. After all these years, with my bad luck, I had to set you free now. Forgive me, and God will grant you forgiveness. Destroy me, and God will inflict on you one who will destroy you." The demon replied, "It must be. Tell me how you wish to die." When the fisherman was certain that he was going to die, he mourned and wept, saying, "O my children, may God not deprive us of each other." Again he turned to the demon and said, "For God's sake, release me as a reward for releasing you and delivering you from this jar." The demon replied, "Your death is your reward for releasing me and letting me escape." The fisherman said, "I did you a good turn, and you are about to repay me with a bad one. How true is the sentiment of the following lines:

> Our kindness they repaid with ugly deeds,
> Upon my life, the deeds of men depraved.
> He who the undeserving aids will meet
> The fate of him who the hyena saved."

The demon said, "Be brief, for as I have said, I must kill you." Then the fisherman thought to himself, "He is only a demon, while I am a human being, whom God has endowed with reason and thereby made superior to him. He may use his demonic wiles on me, but I will use my reason to deal with him." Then he asked the demon, "Must you kill me?" When the demon replied, "I must," the fisherman said, "By the Almighty name that was engraved on the ring of Solomon the son of David, will you answer me truthfully if I ask you about something?" The demon was upset and said with a shudder, "Ask, and be brief!"

But morning overtook Shahrazad, and she lapsed into silence. Then Dinarzad said, "Sister, what an amazing and lovely story!" Shahrazad replied, "What is this compared with what I shall tell you tomorrow night if the king spares me and lets me live! It will be even more amazing."

THE ELEVENTH NIGHT

The following night Dinarzad said to her sister Shahrazad, "Sister, if you are not sleepy, finish the story of the fisherman and the demon." Shahrazad replied, "With the greatest pleasure":

I heard, O King, that the fisherman said, "By the Almighty name, tell me whether you really were inside this jar." The demon replied, "By the Almighty name, I was imprisoned in this jar." The fisherman said, "You are lying, for this jar is not large enough, not even for your hands and feet. How can it be large enough for your whole body?" The demon replied, "By God, I was inside. Don't you believe that I was inside it?" The fisherman said, "No, I don't." Whereupon the demon shook himself and turned into smoke, which rose, stretched over the sea, spread over the land, then gathered, and, little by little, began to enter the jar. When the smoke disappeared completely, the demon shouted from within, "Fisherman, here I am in the jar. Do you believe me now?"

The fisherman at once took out the sealed lead stopper and hurriedly clamped it on the mouth of the jar. Then he cried out, "Demon, now tell me how you wish to die. For I will throw you into this sea, build a house right here, and sit here and stop any fisherman who comes to fish and warn him that there is a demon here, who will kill whoever pulls him out and who will let him choose how he wishes to die." When the demon heard what the fisherman said and found himself imprisoned, he tried to get out but could not, for he was prevented by the seal of Solomon the son of David. Realizing that the fisherman had tricked him, the demon said, "Fisherman, don't do this to me. I was only joking with you." The fisherman replied, "You are lying, you the dirtiest and meanest of demons," and began to roll the jar toward the sea. The demon shouted, "Don't, don't!" But the fisherman replied, "Yes, yes." Then in a soft and submissive voice the demon asked, "Fisherman, what do you intend to do?" The fisherman replied, "I intend to throw you into the sea. The first time you stayed there for eight hundred years. This time I will let you stay until Doomsday. Haven't I said to you, 'Spare me, and God will spare you. Destroy me, and God will destroy you'? But you refused, and persisted in your resolve to do me in and kill me. Now it is my turn to do you in." The demon said, "Fisherman, if you open the jar, I will reward you and make you rich." The fisherman replied, "You are lying, you are lying. Your situation and mine is like that of King Yunan and the sage Duban." The demon asked, "What is their story?" The fisherman said:

[The Tale of King Yunan and the Sage Duban]

DEMON, THERE WAS once a king called Yunan, who reigned in one of the cities of Persia, in the province of Zuman.[1] This king was afflicted with leprosy, which had defied the physicians and the sages, who, for all the medicines they gave him to drink and all the ointments

1. Modern Armenia.

they applied, were unable to cure him. One day there came to the city of King Yunan a sage called Duban. This sage had read all sorts of books, Greek, Persian, Turkish, Arabic, Byzantine, Syriac, and Hebrew, had studied the sciences, and had learned their groundwork, as well as their principles and basic benefits. Thus he was versed in all the sciences, from philosophy to the lore of plants and herbs, the harmful as well as the beneficial. A few days after he arrived in the city of King Yunan, the sage heard about the king and his leprosy and the fact that the physicians and the sages were unable to cure him. On the following day, when God's morning dawned and His sun rose, the sage Duban put on his best clothes, went to King Yunan and, introducing himself, said, "Your Majesty, I have heard of that which has afflicted your body and heard that many physicians have treated you without finding a way to cure you. Your Majesty, I can treat you without giving you any medicine to drink or ointment to apply." When the king heard this, he said, "If you succeed, I will bestow on you riches that would be enough for you and your grandchildren. I will bestow favors on you, and I will make you my companion and friend." The king bestowed robes of honor on the sage, treated him kindly, and then asked him, "Can you really cure me from my leprosy without any medicine to drink or ointment to apply?" The sage replied, "Yes, I will cure you externally." The king was astonished, and he began to feel respect as well as great affection for the sage. He said, "Now, sage, do what you have promised." The sage replied, "I hear and obey. I will do it tomorrow morning, the Almighty God willing." Then the sage went to the city, rented a house, and there he distilled and extracted medicines and drugs. Then with his great knowledge and skill, he fashioned a mallet with a curved end, hollowed the mallet, as well as the handle, and filled the handle with his medicines and drugs. He likewise made a ball. When he had perfected and prepared everything, he went on the following day to King Yunan and kissed the ground before him.

But morning overtook Shahrazad, and she lapsed into silence. Then her sister Dinarzad said, "What a lovely story!" Shahrazad replied, "You have heard nothing yet. Tomorrow night I shall tell you something stranger and more amazing if the king spares me and lets me live!"

THE TWELFTH NIGHT

The following night Dinarzad said to her sister Shahrazad, "Please, sister, finish the rest of the story of the fisherman and the demon." Shahrazad replied, "With the greatest pleasure":

I heard, O King, that the fisherman said to the demon:

The sage Duban came to King Yunan and asked him to ride to the playground to play with the ball and mallet. The king rode out, attended by his chamberlains, princes, viziers, and lords and eminent men of the realm. When the king was seated, the sage Duban entered, offered him the mallet, and said, "O happy King, take this mallet, hold it in your hand, and as you race on the playground, hold the grip tightly in your fist, and hit the ball. Race until you perspire, and the medicine will ooze from the grip into your perspiring hand, spread to your wrist, and circulate through your entire body. After you perspire and the medicine spreads in your body, return to your royal palace, take a bath, and go to sleep. You will wake up cured, and that is all there is to it." King Yunan took the mallet from the sage Duban and mounted his horse. The attendants threw the ball before the king, who, holding the grip tightly in his fist, followed it and struggled excitedly to catch up with it and hit it. He kept galloping after the ball and hitting it until his palm and the rest of his body began to perspire, and the medicine began to ooze from the handle and flow through his entire body. When the sage Duban was certain that the medicine had oozed and spread through the king's body, he advised him to return to his palace and go immediately to the bath. The king went to the bath and washed himself thoroughly. Then he put on his clothes, left the bath, and returned to his palace.

As for the sage Duban, he spent the night at home, and early in the morning, he went to the palace and asked for permission to see the king. When he was allowed in, he entered and kissed the ground before the king; then, pointing toward him with his hand, he began to recite the following verses:

> The virtues you fostered are great;
> For who but you could sire them?
> Yours is the face whose radiant light
> Effaces the night dark and grim.
> Forever beams your radiant face;
> That of the world is still in gloom.
> You rained on us with ample grace,
> As the clouds rain on thirsty hills,
> Expending your munificence,
> Attaining your magnificence.

When the sage Duban finished reciting these verses, the king stood up and embraced him. Then he seated the sage beside him, and with attentiveness and smiles, engaged him in conversation. Then the king bestowed on the sage robes of honor, gave him gifts and endowments, and granted his wishes. For when the king had looked at himself the morning after the bath, he found that his body was clear of leprosy, as clear and pure as silver. He therefore felt exceedingly happy and in a very generous mood. Thus when he went in the morning to the reception hall and sat on his throne, attended by the Mamluks[2] and chamberlains, in the company of the viziers and the lords of the realm, and the sage Duban presented himself, as we have mentioned, the king stood up, embraced him, and seated him beside him. He treated him attentively and drank and ate with him.

But morning overtook Shahrazad, and she lapsed into silence. Then her sister Dinarzad said, "Sister, what a lovely story!" Shahrazad replied, "The rest of the story is stranger and more amazing. If the king spares me and I am alive tomorrow night, I shall tell you something even more entertaining."

THE THIRTEENTH NIGHT

The following night Dinarzad said to her sister Shahrazad, "Sister, if you are not sleepy, tell us one of your lovely little tales to while away the night." Shahrazad replied, "With the greatest pleasure":

I heard, O happy King who is praiseworthy by the Grace of God, that King Yunan bestowed favors on the sage, gave him robes of honor, and granted his wishes. At the end of the day he gave the sage a thousand dinars and sent him home. The king, who was amazed at the skill of the sage Duban, said to himself, "This man has treated me externally, without giving me any draught to drink or ointment to apply. His is indeed a great wisdom for which he deserves to be honored and rewarded. He shall become my companion, confidant, and close friend." Then the king spent the night, happy at his recovery from his illness, at his good health, and at the soundness of his body. When morning came and it was light, the king went to the royal reception hall and sat on the throne, attended by his chief officers, while the princes, viziers, and lords of the realm sat to his right and left. Then the king called for the sage, and when the sage entered and kissed the ground before him, the king stood up to salute him, seated him beside him, and invited him to eat with him. The king treated him intimately, showed him favors, and bestowed on him robes of

2. Literally "slaves," members of a military force, originally of Caucasian slaves, who made themselves masters of Egypt in 1254 C.E. until their massacre in 1811.

honor and many other gifts. Then he spent the whole day conversing
with him, and at the end of the day he ordered that he be given a
thousand dinars. The sage went home and spent the night with his
wife, feeling happy and thankful to God the Arbiter.

In the morning, the king went to the royal reception hall, and the
princes and viziers came to stand in attendance. It happened that
King Yunan had a vizier who was sinister, greedy, envious, and fretful,
and when he saw that the sage had found favor with the king, who
bestowed on him much money and many robes of honor, he feared
that the king would dismiss him and appoint the sage in his place;
therefore, he envied the sage and harbored ill will against him, for
"nobody is free from envy." The envious vizier approached the king
and, kissing the ground before him, said, "O excellent King and glorious Lord, it was by your kindness and with your blessing that I rose to
prominence; therefore, if I fail to advise you on a grave matter, I am
not my father's son. If the great King and noble Lord commands,
I shall disclose the matter to him." The king was upset and asked,
"Damn you, what advice have you got?" The vizier replied, "Your
Majesty, 'He who considers not the end, fortune is not his friend.'
I have seen your Majesty make a mistake, for you have bestowed
favors on your enemy who has come to destroy your power and steal
your wealth. Indeed, you have pampered him and shown him many
favors, but I fear that he will do you harm." The king asked, "Whom
do you accuse, whom do you have in mind, and at whom do you point
the finger?" The vizier replied, "If you are asleep, wake up, for I point
the finger at the sage Duban, who has come from Byzantium." The
king replied, "Damn you, is he my enemy? To me he is the most faithful, the dearest, and the most favored of people, for this sage has
treated me simply by making me hold something in my hand and has
cured me from the disease that had defied the physicians and the
sages and rendered them helpless. In all the world, east and west,
near and far, there is no one like him, yet you accuse him of such a
thing. From this day onward, I will give him every month a thousand
dinars, in addition to his rations and regular salary. Even if I were to
share my wealth and my kingdom with him, it would be less than he
deserves. I think that you have said what you said because you envy
him. This is very much like the situation in the story told by the vizier
of King Sindbad[3] when the king wanted to kill his own son."

*But morning overtook Shahrazad, and she lapsed into silence. Then
her sister Dinarzad said, "Sister, what a lovely story!" Shahrazad replied,
"What is this compared with what I shall tell you tomorrow night! It
will be stranger and more amazing."*

---

3. Not to be confused with Sindbad the Sailor.

THE FOURTEENTH NIGHT

The following night, when the king got into bed and Shahrazad got in with him, her sister Dinarzad said, "Please, sister, if you are not sleepy, tell us one of your lovely little tales to while away the night." Shahrazad replied, "Very well":

I heard, O happy King, that King Yunan's vizier asked, "King of the age, I beg your pardon, but what did King Sindbad's vizier tell the king when he wished to kill his own son?" King Yunan said to the vizier, "When King Sindbad, provoked by an envious man, wanted to kill his own son, his vizier said to him, 'Don't do what you will regret afterward.'"

[The Tale of the Husband and the Parrot]

I HAVE HEARD it told that there was once a very jealous man who had a wife so splendidly beautiful that she was perfection itself. The wife always refused to let her husband travel and leave her behind, until one day when he found it absolutely necessary to go on a journey. He went to the bird market, bought a parrot, and brought it home. The parrot was intelligent, knowledgeable, smart, and retentive. Then he went away on his journey, and when he finished his business and came back, he brought the parrot and inquired about his wife during his absence. The parrot gave him a day-by-day account of what his wife had done with her lover and how the two carried on in his absence. When the husband heard the account, he felt very angry, went to his wife, and gave her a sound beating. Thinking that one of her maids had informed her husband about what she did with her lover in her husband's absence, the wife interrogated her maids one by one, and they all swore that they had heard the parrot inform the husband.

When the wife heard that it was the parrot who had informed the husband, she ordered one of her maids to take the grinding stone and grind under the cage, ordered a second maid to sprinkle water over the cage, and ordered a third to carry a steel mirror and walk back and forth all night long. That night her husband stayed out, and when he came home in the morning, he brought the parrot, spoke with it, and asked about what had transpired in his absence that night. The parrot replied, "Master, forgive me, for last night, all night long, I was unable to hear or see very well because of the intense darkness, the rain, and the thunder and lightning." Seeing that it was summertime, during the month of July, the husband replied, "Damn you, this is no season for rain." The parrot said, "Yes, by God, all night long, I saw what I told you." The husband, concluding that the parrot had lied about his wife and had accused her falsely, got angry, and he grabbed the parrot and, taking it out of the cage, smote it on the ground and killed it. But after the parrot's death, the husband heard from his neighbors that the parrot had told the truth about his wife, and he was full of regret that he had been tricked by his wife to kill the parrot.

King Yunan concluded, "Vizier, the same will happen to me."

But morning overtook Shahrazad, and she lapsed into silence. Then her sister Dinarzad said, "What a strange and lovely story!" Shahrazad replied, "What is this compared with what I shall tell you tomorrow night! If the king spares me and lets me live, I shall tell you something more amazing." The king thought to himself, "By God, this is indeed an amazing story."

THE FIFTEENTH NIGHT

The following night Dinarzad said to her sister Shahrazad, "Please, sister, if you are not sleepy, tell us one of your lovely little tales, for they entertain and help everyone to forget his cares and banish sorrow from the heart." Shahrazad replied, "With the greatest pleasure." King Shahrayar added, "Let it be the remainder of the story of King Yunan, his vizier, and the sage Duban, and of the fisherman, the demon, and the jar." Shahrazad replied, "With the greatest pleasure":

I heard, O happy King, that King Yunan said to his envious vizier, "After the husband killed the parrot and heard from his neighbors that the parrot had told him the truth, he was filled with remorse. You too, my vizier, being envious of this wise man, would like me to kill him and regret it afterward, as did the husband after he killed the parrot." When the vizier heard what King Yunan said, he replied, "O great king, what harm has this sage done to me? Why, he has not harmed me in any way. I am telling you all this out of love and fear for you. If you don't discover my veracity, let me perish like the vizier who deceived the son of the king." King Yunan asked his vizier, "How so?" The vizier replied:

[The Tale of the King's Son and the She-Ghoul]

IT IS SAID, O happy King, that there was once a king who had a son who was fond of hunting and trapping. The prince had with him a vizier appointed by his father the king to follow him wherever he went. One day the prince went with his men into the wilderness, and when he chanced to see a wild beast, the vizier urged him to go after it. The prince pursued the beast and continued to press in pursuit until he lost its track and found himself alone in the wilderness, not knowing which way to turn or where to go, when he came upon a girl, standing on the road, in tears. When the young prince asked her, "Where do you come from?" she replied, "I am the daughter of an Indian king. I was riding in the wilderness when I dozed off and in my sleep fell off my horse and found myself alone and helpless." When the young prince heard what she said, he felt sorry for her, and he placed her behind him on his horse and rode on. As they passed by some ruins, she said, "O my lord, I wish to relieve myself here." He let her down and she went into the ruins. Then he went in after her, ignorant of what she was, and discovered that she was a she-ghoul, who was saying to her children, "I brought you a good, fat boy." They replied, "Mother, bring him to us, so that we may feed on his innards." When the young prince heard what they said, he shook with terror, and fearing for his life, ran outside. The she-ghoul followed him and asked, "Why are you afraid?" and he told her about his situation and his predicament, concluding, "I have been unfairly treated." She replied, "If you have been unfairly treated, ask the Almighty God for help, and he will protect you from harm." The young prince raised his eyes to Heaven . . .

But morning overtook Shahrazad, and she lapsed into silence. Then her sister Dinarzad said, "What a strange and lovely story!" Shahrazad replied, "What is this compared with what I shall tell you tomorrow night! It will be even stranger and more amazing."

THE SIXTEENTH NIGHT

The following night Dinarzad said, "Please, sister, if you are not sleepy, tell us one of your lovely little tales." Shahrazad replied, "I shall with pleasure":

I heard, O King, that the vizier said to King Yunan:

When the young prince said to the she-ghoul, "I have been unfairly treated," she replied, "Ask God for help, and He will protect you from harm." The young prince raised his eyes to Heaven and said, "O Lord, help me to prevail upon my enemy, for 'everything is within your power.'" When the she-ghoul heard his invocation, she gave up and departed, and he returned safely to his father and told him about the vizier and how it was he who had urged him to pursue the beast and drove him to his encounter with the she-ghoul. The king summoned the vizier and had him put to death.

The vizier added, "You too, your Majesty, if you trust, befriend, and bestow favors on this sage, he will plot to destroy you and cause your death. Your Majesty should realize that I know for certain that he is a foreign agent who has come to destroy you. Haven't you seen that he cured you externally, simply with something you held in your hand?" King Yunan, who was beginning to feel angry, replied, "You are right, vizier. The sage may well be what you say and may have come to destroy me. He who has cured me with something to hold can kill me with something to smell." Then the king asked the vizier, "My vizier and good counselor, how should I deal with him?" The vizier replied, "Send for him now and have him brought before you, and when he arrives, strike off his head. In this way, you will attain your aim and fulfill your wish." The king said, "This is good and sound advice." Then he sent for the sage Duban, who came immediately, still feeling happy at the favors, the money, and the robes the king had bestowed on him. When he entered, he pointed with his hand toward the king and began to recite the following verses:

> If I have been remiss in thanking you,
> For whom then have I made my verse and prose?
> You granted me your gifts before I asked,
> Without deferment and without excuse.
> How can I fail to praise your noble deeds,
> Inspired in private and in public by my muse?
> I thank you for your deeds and for your gifts,
> Which, though they bend my back, my care reduce.

The king asked, "Sage, do you know why I have had you brought before me?" The sage replied, "No, your Majesty." The king said, "I brought you here to have you killed and to destroy the breath of life within you." In astonishment Duban asked, "Why does your Majesty wish to have me put to death, and for what crime?" The king replied, "I have been told that you are a spy and that you have come to kill me. Today I will have you killed before you kill me. 'I will have you for lunch before you have me for dinner.'" Then the king called for the executioner and ordered him, saying, "Strike off the head of this sage and rid me of him! Strike!"

When the sage heard what the king said, he knew that because he had been favored by the king, someone had envied him, plotted against him, and lied to the king, in order to have him killed and get rid of him. The sage realized then that the king had little wisdom, judgment, or good sense, and he was filled with regret, when it was useless to regret. He said to himself, "There is no power and no strength, save in God the Almighty, the Magnificent. I did a good deed but was rewarded with an evil one." In the meantime, the king was shouting at the executioner, "Strike off his head." The sage implored, "Spare me, your Majesty, and God will spare you; destroy me, and God will destroy you." He repeated the statement, just as I did, O demon, but you too refused, insisting on killing me. King Yunan said to the sage, "Sage, you must die, for you have cured me with a mere handle, and I fear that you can kill me with anything." The sage replied, "This is my reward from your Majesty. You reward good with evil." The king said, "Don't stall; you must die today without delay." When the sage Duban became convinced that he was going to die, he was filled with grief and sorrow, and his eyes overflowed with tears. He blamed himself for doing a favor for one who does not deserve it and for sowing seeds in a barren soil and recited the following verses:

> Maimuna was a foolish girl,
> Though from a sage descended,
> And many with pretense to skill
> Are many on dry land upended.

The executioner approached the sage, bandaged his eyes, bound his hands, and raised the sword, while the sage cried, expressed regret, and implored, "For God's sake, your Majesty, spare me, and God will spare you; destroy me, and God will destroy you." Then he tearfully began to recite the following verses:

> They who deceive enjoy success,
> While I with my true counsel fail
> And am rewarded with disgrace.
> If I live, I'll nothing unveil;
> If I die, then curse all the men,
> The men who counsel and prevail.

Then the sage added, "Is this my reward from your Majesty? It is like the reward of the crocodile." The king asked, "What is the story of the crocodile?" The sage replied, "I am in no condition to tell you a story. For God's sake, spare me, and God will spare you. Destroy me, and God will destroy you," and he wept bitterly.

Then several noblemen approached the king and said, "We beg your Majesty to forgive him for our sake, for in our view, he has done nothing to deserve this." The king replied, "You do not know the reason why I wish to have him killed. I tell you that if I spare him, I will surely perish, for I fear that he who has cured me externally from my affliction, which had defied the Greek sages, simply by having me hold a handle, can kill me with anything I touch. I must kill him, in order to protect myself from him." The sage Duban implored again, "For God's sake, your Majesty, spare me, and God will spare you. Destroy me, and God will destroy you." The king insisted, "I must kill you."

Demon, when the sage realized that he was surely going to die, he said, "I beg your Majesty to postpone my execution until I return home, leave instructions for my burial, discharge my obligations, distribute alms, and donate my scientific and medical books to one who deserves them. I have in particular a book entitled *The Secret of Secrets*, which I should like to give you for safekeeping in your library." The king asked, "What is the secret of this book?" The sage replied, "It contains countless secrets, but the chief one is that if your Majesty has my head struck off, opens the book on the sixth leaf, reads three lines from the left page, and speaks to me, my head will speak and answer whatever you ask."

The king was greatly amazed and said, "Is it possible that if I cut off your head and, as you say, open the book, read the third line, and speak to your head, it will speak to me? This is the wonder of wonders." Then the king allowed the sage to go and sent him home under guard. The sage settled his affairs and on the following day returned to the royal palace and found assembled there the princes, viziers, chamberlains, lords of the realm, and military officers, as well as the king's retinue, servants, and many of his citizens. The sage Duban entered, carrying an old book and a kohl[4] jar containing powder. He sat down, ordered a platter, and poured out the powder and smoothed it on the platter. Then he said to the king, "Take this book, your Majesty, and don't open it until after my execution. When my head is cut off, let it be placed on the platter and order that it be pressed on the powder. Then open the book and begin to ask my head a question, for it will then answer you. There is no power and no strength save in God, the Almighty, the Magnificent. For God's sake, spare me, and God will spare you; destroy me, and God will destroy you." The king replied, "I must kill you, especially to see how your head will speak to me." Then the king took the book and ordered the executioner to strike off the sage's head. The executioner drew his sword and, with one stroke, dropped the head in the middle of the platter, and when he pressed the head on the powder, the bleeding stopped. Then the sage Duban opened his eyes and said, "Now, your Majesty, open the book." When the king opened the book, he found the pages stuck. So he put his finger in his mouth,

---

4. Cosmetic, used by Eastern, especially Muslim, women to darken the eyelids.

wetted it with his saliva, and opened the first page, and he kept opening the pages with difficulty until he turned seven leaves. But when he looked in the book, he found nothing written inside, and he exclaimed, "Sage, I see nothing written in this book." The sage replied, "Open more pages." The king opened some more pages but still found nothing, and while he was doing this, the drug spread through his body—for the book had been poisoned—and he began to heave, sway, and twitch.

But morning overtook Shahrazad, and she lapsed into silence. Then her sister Dinarzad said, "Sister, what an amazing and entertaining story!" Shahrazad replied, "What is this compared with what I shall tell you tomorrow night if the king spares me and lets me live!"

THE SEVENTEENTH NIGHT

The following night Dinarzad said to her sister Shahrazad, "Please, sister, if you are not sleepy, tell us one of your lovely little tales to while away the night." The king added, "Let it be the rest of the story of the sage and the king and of the fisherman and the demon." Shahrazad replied, "Very well, with the greatest pleasure":

I heard, O King, that when the sage Duban saw that the drug had spread through the king's body and that the king was heaving and swaying, he began to recite the following verses:

> For long they ruled us arbitrarily,
> But suddenly vanished their powerful rule.
> Had they been just, they would have happily
> Lived, but they oppressed, and punishing fate
> Afflicted them with ruin deservedly,
> And on the morrow the world taunted them,
> "'Tis tit for tat; blame not just destiny."

As the sage's head finished reciting the verses, the king fell dead, and at that very moment the head too succumbed to death. Demon, consider this story.

But morning overtook Shahrazad, and she lapsed into silence. Then her sister Dinarzad said, "Sister, what an entertaining story!" Shahrazad replied, "What is this compared with what I shall tell you tomorrow night if I live!"

THE EIGHTEENTH NIGHT

The following night, Dinarzad said to her sister Shahrazad, "Please, sister, if you are not sleepy, tell us one of your lovely little tales to while away the night." The king added, "Let it be the rest of the story of the fisherman and the demon." Shahrazad replied, "With the greatest pleasure":

I heard, O King, that the fisherman said to the demon, "Had the king spared the sage, God would have spared him and he would have lived, but he refused and insisted on destroying the sage, and the Almighty God destroyed him. You too, demon, had you from the beginning agreed to spare me, I would have spared you, but you refused and insisted on killing me; therefore, I shall punish you by keeping you in this jar and throwing you into the bottom of the sea." The demon cried out, "Fisherman, don't do it. Spare me and save me and don't blame me for my action and my offense against you. If I did ill, you should do good. As the saying goes, 'Be kind to him who wrongs you.' Don't do what Imama did to 'Atika." The fisherman asked, "What did Imama do to 'Atika?" The demon replied, "This is no time and this narrow prison is no place to tell a story, but I shall tell it to you after you release me." The fisherman said, "I must throw you into the sea. There is no way I would let you out and set you free, for I kept imploring you and calling on you, but you refused and insisted on killing me, without any offense or injury that merits punishment, except that I had set you free. When you treated me in this way, I realized that you were unclean from birth, that you were ill-natured, and that you were one who rewards good with ill. After I throw you into the sea, I shall build me a hut here and live in it for your sake, so that if anyone pulls you out, I shall acquaint him with what I suffered at your hands and shall advise him to throw you back into the sea and let you perish or languish there to the end of time, you the dirtiest of demons." The demon replied, "Set me free this time, and I pledge never to bother you or harm you, but to make you rich." When he heard this, the fisherman made the demon pledge and covenant that if the fisherman released him and let him out, he would not harm him but would serve him and be good to him.

After the fisherman secured the demon's pledge, by making him swear by the Almighty Name, he opened the seal of the jar, and the smoke began to rise. When the smoke was completely out of the jar, it gathered and turned again into a full-fledged demon, who kicked the jar away and sent it flying to the middle of the sea. When the fisherman saw what the demon had done, sure that he was going to meet with disaster and death, he wet himself and said, "This is a bad omen." Then he summoned his courage and cried out, "Demon, you have sworn and given me your pledge. Don't betray me. Come back, lest the Almighty God punish you for your betrayal. Demon, I repeat to you what the sage Duban said to King Yunan, 'Spare me, and God will spare you; destroy me, and God will destroy you.'" When the demon heard what the fisherman said, he laughed, and when the fisherman cried out again, "Demon, spare me," he replied, "Fisherman, follow me," and the fisherman followed him, hardly believing in his escape, until they came to a mountain outside the city. They climbed over to the other side and came to a vast wilderness, in the middle of which stood a lake surrounded by four hills.

The demon halted by the lake and ordered the fisherman to cast his net and fish. The fisherman looked at the lake and marveled as he saw fish in many colors, white, red, blue, and yellow. He cast his net, and when he pulled, he found four fish inside, one red, one white, one blue, and one yellow. When he saw them, he was full of admiration and delight. The demon said to him, "Take them to the king of your city and offer them to him, and he will give you enough to make you rich. Please excuse me, for I know no other way to make you rich. But don't fish here more than once a day." Then, saying, "I shall miss you," the demon kicked the ground with his foot, and it opened and swallowed him. The fisherman, O King, returned to the city, still marveling at his encounter with the demon and at the colored fish. He entered the royal palace, and when he offered the fish to the king, the king looked at them . . .

But morning overtook Shahrazad, and she lapsed into silence. Then Dinarzad said, "Sister, what an amazing and entertaining story!" Shahrazad replied, "What is this compared with what I shall tell you tomorrow night if the king spares me and lets me live!"

THE NINETEENTH NIGHT

The following night Dinarzad said to her sister Shahrazad, "Sister, tell us the rest of the story and what happened to the fisherman." Shahrazad replied, "With the greatest pleasure":

I heard, O King, that when the fisherman presented the fish to the king, and the king looked at them and saw that they were colored, he took one of them in his hand and looked at it with great amazement. Then he said to his vizier, "Take them to the cook whom the emperor of Byzantium has given us as a present." The vizier took the fish and brought them to the girl and said to her, "Girl, as the saying goes, 'I save my tears for the time of trial.' The king has been presented these four fish, and he bids you fry them well." Then the vizier went back to report to the king, and the king ordered him to give the fisherman four hundred dirhams.[5] The vizier gave the money to the fisherman, who, receiving it, gathered it in the folds of his robe and went away, running, and as he ran, he stumbled and kept falling and getting up, thinking that he was in a dream. Then he stopped and bought some provisions for his family.

So far for the fisherman, O King. In the meantime the girl scaled the fish, cleaned them, and cut them into pieces. Then she placed the frying pan on the fire and poured in the sesame oil, and when it began to boil, she placed the fish in the frying pan. When the pieces were done on one side, she turned them over, but no sooner had she done this than the kitchen wall split open and there emerged a maiden with a beautiful figure, smooth cheeks, perfect features, and dark eyes. She wore a short-sleeved silk shirt in the Egyptian style, embroidered all around with lace and gold spangles. In her ears she wore dangling earrings; on her wrists she wore bracelets; and in her hand she held a bamboo wand. She thrust the wand into the frying pan and said in clear Arabic, "O fish, O fish, have you kept the pledge?" When the cook saw what had happened, she fainted. Then the maiden repeated what she had said, and the fish raised their heads from the frying pan and replied in clear Arabic, "Yes, yes. If you return, we shall return; if you keep your vow, we shall keep ours; and if you forsake us, we shall be even." At that moment the maiden overturned the frying pan and disappeared as she had come, and the kitchen wall closed behind her.

When the cook came to herself, she found the four fish charred, and she felt sorry for herself and afraid of the king, saying to herself, "'He broke his lance on his very first raid.'" While she remonstrated with herself, the vizier suddenly stood before her, saying, "Give me the fish, for we have set the table before the king, and he is waiting for them." The girl wept and told the vizier what she had seen and witnessed and what had happened to the fish. The vizier was astonished and said, "This is very strange." Then he sent an officer after the fisherman, and he returned a while later with the fisherman. The vizier shouted at him, saying, "Bring us at once four more fish like the ones you brought us before, for we have had an accident with them." When he followed with threats, the fisherman went home and, taking his fishing gear, went outside the city, climbed the

---

5. Small silver coins; in Iraq the dirham is one twentieth of a dinar.

mountain, and descended to the wilderness on the other side. When
he came to the lake, he cast his net, and when he pulled up, he found
inside four fish, as he had done the first time. Then he brought them
back to the vizier, who took them to the girl and said, "Fry them in
front of me, so that I can see for myself." The girl prepared the fish
at once, placed the frying pan over the fire, and threw them in.
When the fish were done, the wall split open, and the maiden
appeared in her elegant clothes, wearing necklaces and other jewelry and holding in her hand the bamboo wand. Again she thrust the
wand into the frying pan and said in dear Arabic, "O fish, have you
kept the pledge?" and again the fish raised their heads and replied,
"Yes, yes. If you return, we shall return; if you keep your vow, we
shall keep ours; and if you forsake us, we shall be even."

*But morning overtook Shahrazad, and she lapsed into silence. Then
Dinarzad said, "What an entertaining story!" Shahrazad replied,
"What is this compared with what I shall tell you tomorrow night if
I live, the Almighty God willing!"*

THE TWENTIETH NIGHT

*The following night Dinarzad said to her sister Shahrazad, "Please,
sister, if you are not sleepy, tell us one of your lovely little tales to while
away the night." Shahrazad replied, "With the greatest pleasure":*

I heard, O happy King, that after the fish spoke, the maiden overturned the frying pan with the wand and disappeared into the opening from which she had emerged, and the wall closed behind her.
The vizier said to himself, "I can no longer hide this affair from the
king," and he went to him and told him what had happened to the
fish before his very eyes.

The king was exceedingly amazed and said, "I wish to see this with
my own eyes." Then he sent for the fisherman, who came after a
little while, and the king said to him, "I want you to bring me at once
four more fish like the ones you brought before. Hurry!" Then he
assigned three officers to guard the fisherman and sent him away.
The fisherman disappeared for a while and returned with four fish,
one red, one white, one blue, and one yellow. The king commanded,
"Give him four hundred dirhams," and the fisherman, receiving the
money, gathered it in the folds of his robe and went away. Then the
king said to the vizier, "Fry the fish here in my presence." The vizier
replied, "I hear and obey," and he called for a stove and a frying pan

and sat to clean the fish. Then he lit the fire and, pouring the sesame oil, placed the fish in the frying pan.

When they were almost done, the palace wall split open, and the king and vizier began to tremble, and when they looked up, they saw a black slave who stood like a towering mountain or a giant descendant of the tribe of 'Ad.[6] He was as tall as a reed, as wide as a stone bench, and he held a green palm leaf in his hand. Then in clear but unpleasant language, he said, "O fish, O fish, have you kept the pledge?" and the fish raised their heads from the frying pan and said, "Yes, yes. If you return, we shall return; if you keep your vow, we shall keep ours; and if you forsake us, we shall be even." At that moment, the black slave overturned the frying pan, in the middle of the hall, and the fish turned into charcoal. Then the black slave departed as he had come, and the wall closed behind him. When the black slave disappeared, the king said, "I cannot sleep over this affair, for there is no doubt a mystery behind these fish." Then he bade the fisherman be brought before him again.

When the fisherman arrived, the king said to him, "Damn you, where do you catch these fish?" The fisherman replied, "My lord, I catch them in a lake that lies among four hills, on the other side of the mountain." The king turned to the vizier and asked, "Do you know this lake?" The vizier replied, "No, by God, your Majesty. For sixty years, I have hunted, traveled, and roamed far and wide, sometimes for a day or two, sometimes for a month or two, but I have never seen or known that such a lake existed on the other side of the mountain." Then the king turned to the fisherman and asked him, "How far is this lake from here?" The fisherman replied, "King of the age, it is one hour from here." The king was astonished, and he ordered his soldiers to be ready. Then he rode out with his troops, behind the fisherman, who led the way under guard, muttering curses on the demon as he went.

They rode until they were outside the city. Then they climbed the mountain, and when they descended to the other side, they saw a vast wilderness that they had never seen in all their lives, as well as the four hills and the lake in whose clear water they saw the fish in four colors, red, white, blue, and yellow. The king stood marveling; then he turned to the vizier, princes, chamberlains, and deputies and asked, "Have any of you ever seen this lake before?" They replied, "Never." He asked, "And none of you knew where it was?" They kissed the ground before him and replied, "By God, your Majesty, till now we have never in our lives seen this lake or known

6. Tribe supposedly destroyed by God's wrath; see n. 1, p. 3.

about it, even though it is close to our city." The king said, "There is a mystery behind this. By God, I shall not return to the city until I find the answer to the mystery behind this lake and these fish in four colors." Then he ordered his men to halt and pitch the tents, and he dismounted and waited.

When it was dark, he summoned the vizier, who was an experienced and wise man of the world. The vizier came to the king, without being seen by the soldiers, and when he arrived, the king said, "I wish to reveal to you what I intend to do. At this very hour, I shall go all by myself to look for an answer to the mystery of this lake and these fish. Early tomorrow morning you shall sit at the entrance of my tent and tell the princes that the king is indisposed and that he has given you orders not to let anyone be admitted to his presence. You must not let anyone know about my departure and absence, and you must wait for me for three days." The vizier, unable to disobey him, abided by the order, saying, "I hear and obey."

Then the king packed, prepared himself, and girded himself with the royal sword. Then he climbed one of the four hills, and when he reached the top, he journeyed on for the rest of the night. In the morning, when the sun rose and steeped the mountaintop with light, the king looked and sighted a dark mass in the distance. When he saw it, he was glad, and he headed in its direction, saying to himself, "There may be someone there to give me information." He journeyed on, and when he arrived, he found a palace, built under a lucky star, with black stones and completely overlaid with iron plates. It had double doors, one open, one shut. Pleased, the king knocked gently at the door and waited patiently for a while without hearing any reply. He knocked again, this time more loudly than before, but again waited without hearing any reply or seeing anyone. He knocked for the third time and kept knocking repeatedly but once more waited without hearing any reply or seeing anyone. Then he said to himself, "There is no doubt that there is no one inside, or perhaps the palace is deserted." Summoning his courage, he entered and shouted from the hallway, "O inhabitants of the palace, I am a stranger and a hungry traveler. Have you any food? Our Lord will requite you and reward you for it." He shouted a second and a third time but heard no reply. Feeling bold and determined, he advanced from the hallway into the center of the palace and looked around, but saw no one.

But morning overtook Shahrazad, and she lapsed into silence. Then Dinarzad said, "Sister, what an amazing and entertaining story!" Shahrazad replied, "What is this compared with what I shall tell you tomorrow night if I live, the Almighty God willing!"

THE TWENTY-FIRST NIGHT

*The following night Dinarzad said to her sister Shahrazad, "For God's
sake, sister, if you are not sleepy, tell us one of your lovely little tales to
while away the night." Shahrazad replied, "With the greatest pleasure":*

I heard, O King, that the king walked to the center of the palace
and looked around, but saw no one. The palace was furnished with
silk carpets and leather mats and hung with drapes. There were also
settees, benches, and seats with cushions, as well as cupboards. In
the middle there stood a spacious courtyard, surrounded by four
adjoining recessed courts facing each other. In the center stood a
fountain, on top of which crouched four lions in red gold, spouting
water from their mouths in droplets that looked like gems and
pearls, and about the fountain singing birds fluttered under a high
net to prevent them from flying away. When the king saw all this,
without seeing anyone, he was astonished and regretted that he
found none to give him any information. He sat pensively by one of
the recessed courts, when he heard sad moans and lamentations and
the following plaintive verses:

> My soul is torn between peril and toil;
> O life, dispatch me with one mighty blow.
> Lover, neither a bankrupt nor a noble man
> Humbled, by love's law do you pity show.
> Ev'n from the breeze I jealously used to guard you,
> But at the blow of fate the eyes blind go.
> When, as he pulls to shoot, the bowstring breaks
> What can the bowman facing his foes do?
> And when the foes begin to congregate
> How can he then escape his cruel fate?

When the king heard the lamentation and the verses, he rose and
moved toward the source of the voice until he came to a doorway
behind a curtain, and when he lifted the curtain, he saw at the upper
end of the room a young man sitting on a chair that rose about
twenty inches above the floor. He was a handsome young man, with
a full figure, clear voice, radiant brow, bright face, downy beard, and
ruddy cheeks, graced with a mole like a speck of amber, just as the
poet describes it:

> Here is a slender youth whose hair and face
> All mortals envelope with light or gloom.
> Mark on his cheek the mark of charm and grace,
> A dark spot on a red anemone.

The king greeted the seated young man, pleased to see him. The young man wore a long-sleeved robe of Egyptian silk with gold embroidery, and on his head he wore an Egyptian conical head covering, but his face showed signs of grief and sorrow. When the king greeted him, the young man greeted him back courteously and said, "Pardon me, sir, for not rising, for you deserve even a greater honor." The king replied, "Young man, you are pardoned. I myself am your guest, having come to you on a serious mission. Pray tell me the story behind the lake and the colored fish, as well as this palace and the fact that you sit alone and mourn with no one to console you." When the young man heard this, his tears began to flow over his cheeks until they drenched his breast. Then he sang the following *Mawwaliya* verses:[7]

> Say to the man whom life with arrows shot,
> "How many men have felt the blows of fate!"
> If you did sleep, the eyes of God have not;
> Who can say time is fair and life in constant state?

Then he wept bitterly. The king was astonished and asked, "Young man, why do you cry?" The young man replied, "Sir, how can I refrain from crying in my present condition?" Then he lifted the skirt of his robe, and the king saw that while one half of the young man, from the navel to the head, was human flesh, the other half, from the navel to the feet, was black stone.

But morning overcame Shahrazad, and she lapsed into silence. Then King Shahrayar thought to himself, "This is an amazing story. I am willing to postpone her execution even for a month, before having her put to death." While the king was thinking to himself, Dinarzad said to her sister Shahrazad, "Sister, what an entertaining story!" Shahrazad replied, "What is this compared with what I shall tell you tomorrow night if I live, the Almighty God willing!"

THE TWENTY-SECOND NIGHT

The following night Shahrazad said:

I heard, O King, that when the king saw the young man in this condition, he felt very sad and sorry for him, and said with a sigh, "Young man, you have added one more worry to my worries. I came

---

7. Poems in colloquial language, often sung to the accompaniment of a reed pipe.

to look for an answer to the mystery of the fish, in order to save them, but ended up looking for an answer to your case, as well as the fish. There is no power and no strength save in God, the Almighty, the Magnificent. Hurry up, young man, and tell me your story." The young man replied, "Lend me your ears, your eyes, and your mind." The king replied, "My ears, my eyes, and my mind are ready." The young man said:

[The Tale of the Enchanted King]

MY STORY, AND the story of the fish, is a strange and amazing one, which, if it could be engraved with needles at the corner of the eye,[8] would be a lesson to those who would consider. My lord, my father was the king of this city, and his name was King Mahmud of the Black Islands. For these four hills were islands. He ruled for seventy years, and when he died, I succeeded him and married my cousin. She loved me very much, so much so that if I was away from her even for a single day, she would refuse to eat and drink until I returned to her. In this way, we lived together for five years until one day she went to the bath and I ordered the cook to grill meat and prepare a sumptuous supper for her. Then I entered this palace, lay down in this very spot where you are sitting now, and ordered two maids to sit down, one at my head and one at my feet, to fan me. But I felt uneasy and could not go to sleep. While I lay with my eyes closed, breathing heavily, I heard the girl at my head say to the one at my feet, "O Mas'uda, what a pity for our poor master with our damned mistress, and him so young!" The other one replied, "What can one say? May God damn all treacherous, adulterous women. Alas, it is not right that such a young man like our master lives with this bitch who spends every night out." Mas'uda added, "Is our master stupid? When he wakes up at night, doesn't he find that she is not by his side?" The other replied, "Alas, may God trip the bitch our mistress. Does she leave our master with his wits about him? No. She places a sleeping potion in the last drink he takes, offers him the cup, and when he drinks it, he sleeps like a dead man. Then she leaves him and stays out till dawn. When she returns, she burns incense under his nose, and when he inhales it, he wakes up. What a pity!"

My lord, when I heard the conversation between the two maids, I was extremely angry and I could hardly wait for the night to come. When my wife returned from the bath, we had the meal served but

---

8. I.e., if a master calligrapher could by a miracle of his art write the entire story at the corner of an eye, it would then be read as a double miracle, one for the extraordinary events, one for the extraordinary art.

ate very little. Then we retired to my bed and I pretended to drink the contents of the cup, which I poured out, and went to sleep. No sooner had I fallen on my side than my wife said, "Go to sleep, and may you never rise again. By God, your sight disgusts me and your company bores me." Then she put on her clothes, perfumed herself with burning incense and, taking my sword, girded herself with it. Then she opened the door and walked out. My lord, I got up . . .

But morning overtook Shahrazad, and she lapsed into silence. Then Dinarzad said, "O my lady, what an amazing and entertaining story!" Shahrazad replied, "What is this compared with what I shall tell you tomorrow night!"

THE TWENTY-THIRD NIGHT

The following night Dinarzad said to her sister Shahrazad, "Please, sister, if you are not sleepy, tell us one of your lovely little tales." Shahrazad replied, "With the greatest pleasure":

It is related, O King, that the enchanted young man said to the king:

Then I followed her, as she left the palace and traversed my city until she stood at the city gate. There she uttered words I could not understand, and the locks fell off and the gate opened by itself. She went out, and I followed her until she slipped through the trash mounds and came to a hut built with palm leaves, leading to a domed structure built with sun-dried bricks. After she entered, I climbed to the top of the dome, and when I looked inside, I saw my wife standing before a decrepit black man sitting on reed shavings and dressed in tatters. She kissed the ground before him and he raised his head and said, "Damn you, why are you late? My black cousins were here. They played with the bat and ball, sang, and drank brewed liquor. They had a good time, each with his own girlfriend, except for myself, for I refused even to drink with them because you were absent."

My wife replied, "O my lord and lover, don't you know that I am married to my cousin, who finds me most loathsome and detests me more than anyone else? Were it not for your sake, I would not have let the sun rise before reducing his city to rubble, a dwelling place for the bears and the foxes, where the owl hoots and the crow crows, and would have hurled its stones beyond Mount Qaf."⁹ He replied,

9. Legendary mountain cited for its remoteness.

"Damn you, you are lying. I swear in the name of black chivalry that as of tonight, if my cousins visit me and you fail to be present, I will never befriend you, lie down with you, or let my body touch yours. You cursed woman, you have been playing with me like a piece of marble, and I am subject to your whims, you cursed, rotten woman." My lord, when I heard their conversation, the world started to turn black before my eyes, and I lost my senses. Then I heard my wife crying and imploring, "O my lover and my heart's desire, if you remain angry at me, whom else have I got, and if you turn me out, who will take me in, O my lord, my lover, and light of my eye?" She kept crying and begging until he was appeased. Then, feeling happy, she took off her outer garments, and asked, "My lord, have you anything for your little girl to eat?" The black man replied, "Open the copper basin," and when she lifted the lid, she found some leftover fried rat bones. After she ate them, he said to her, "There is some brewed liquor left in that jug. You may drink it." She drank the liquor and washed her hands and lay beside the black man on the reed shavings. Then she undressed and slipped under his tatters. I climbed down from the top of the dome and, entering through the door, grabbed the sword that my wife had brought with her, and drew it, intending to kill both of them. I first struck the black man on the neck and thought that I had killed him.

But morning overtook Shahrazad, and she lapsed into silence. Then Dinarzad said, "Sister, what an entertaining story!" Shahrazad replied, "Tomorrow night I shall tell you something more entertaining if I live!"

THE TWENTY-FOURTH NIGHT

The following night Dinarzad said to her sister Shahrazad, "For God's sake, sister, if you are not sleepy, tell us one of your lovely little tales." Shahrazad replied, "With the greatest pleasure":

I heard, O King, that the enchanted young man said to the king:

My lord, I struck the black man on the neck, but failed to cut the two arteries. Instead I only cut into the skin and flesh of the throat and thought that I had killed him. He began to snort violently, and my wife pulled away from him. I retreated, put the sword back in its place, and went back to the city. I entered the palace and went to sleep in my bed till morning. When my wife arrived and I looked at her, I saw that she had cut her hair and put on a mourning dress.

She said, "Husband, don't reproach me for what I am doing, for I have received news that my mother has died, that my father was killed in the holy war, and that my two brothers have also lost their lives, one in battle, the other bitten by a snake. I have every reason to weep and mourn." When I heard what she said, I did not reply, except to say, "I don't reproach you. Do as you wish."

She mourned for an entire year, weeping and wailing. When the year ended, she said to me, "I want you to let me build inside the palace a mausoleum for me to use as a special place of mourning and to call it the house of sorrows." I replied, "Go ahead." Then she gave the order, and a house of mourning was erected for her, with a domed mausoleum and a tomb inside. Then, my lord, she moved the wounded black man to the mausoleum and placed him in the tomb. But, although he was still alive, from the day I cut his throat, he never spoke a word or was able to do her any good, except to drink liquids. She visited him in the mausoleum every day, morning and evening, bringing with her beverages and broth, and she kept at it for an entire year, while I held my patience and left her to her own devices. One day, while she was unaware, I entered the mausoleum and found her crying and lamenting:

> When I see your distress,
> It pains me, as you see.
> And when I see you not,
> It pains me, as you see.
> O speak to me, my life,
> My master, talk to me.

Then she sang:

> The day I have you is the day I crave;
> The day you leave me is the day I die.
> Were I to live in fear of promised death,
> I'd rather be with you than my life save.

Then she recited the following verses:

> If I had every blessing in the world
> And all the kingdom of the Persian king,
> If I see not your person with my eyes,
> All this will not be worth an insect's wing.

When she stopped crying, I said to her, "Wife, you have mourned and wept enough and further tears are useless." She replied,

"Husband, do not interfere with my mourning. If you interfere again, I will kill myself." I kept quiet and left her alone, while she mourned, wept, and lamented for another year. One day, after the third year, feeling the strain of this drawn-out, heavy burden, something happened to trigger my anger, and when I returned, I found my wife in the mausoleum, beside the tomb, saying, "My lord, I have not had any word from you. For three years I have had no reply." Then she recited the following verses:

> O tomb, O tomb, has he his beauties lost,
> Or have you lost yourself that radiant look?
> O tomb, neither a garden nor a star,
> The sun and moon at once how can you host?

These verses added anger to my anger, and I said to myself, "Oh, how much longer shall I endure?" Then I burst out with the following verses:

> O tomb, O tomb, has he his blackness lost,
> Or have you lost yourself that filthy look?
> O tomb, neither a toilet nor a heap of dirt,
> Charcoal and mud at once how can you host?

When my wife heard me, she sprang up and said, "Damn you, dirty dog. It was you who did this to me, wounded my beloved, and tormented me by depriving me of his youth, while he has been lying here for three years, neither alive nor dead." I said to her, "You, dirtiest of whores and filthiest of all venal women who ever desired and copulated with black slaves, yes it was I who did this to him." Then I grabbed my sword and drew it to strike her. But when she heard me and realized that I was determind to kill her, she laughed and said, "Get away, you dog. Alas, alas, what is done cannot be undone; nor will the dead come back to life, but God has delivered into my hand the one who did this to me and set my heart ablaze with the fire of revenge." Then she stood up, uttered words I could not understand, and cried, "With my magic and cunning, be half man, half stone." Sir, from that instant, I have been as you now see me, dejected and sad, helpless and sleepless, neither living with the living nor dead among the dead.

But morning overtook Shahrazad, and she lapsed into silence. Then Dinarzad said, "Sister, what an amazing and entertaining story!" Shahrazad replied, "Tomorrow night I shall tell you something more entertaining if the king spares me and lets me live!"

THE TWENTY-FIFTH NIGHT

The following night Dinarzad said to her sister Shahrazad, "Sister, if you are not sleepy, tell us one of your lovely little tales to while away the night." Shahrazad replied, "With the greatest pleasure":

It is related, O King, that the enchanted young man said to the king:

"After my wife turned me into this condition, she cast a spell on the city, with all its gardens, fields, and markets, the very place where your troops are camping now. My wife turned the inhabitants of my city, who belonged to four sects, Muslims, Magians,[1] Christians, and Jews, into fish, the Muslims white, the Magians red, the Christians blue, and the Jews yellow. Likewise, she turned the islands into four hills surrounding the lake. As if what she has done to me and the city is not enough, she strips me naked every day and gives me a hundred lashes with the whip until my back is lacerated and begins to bleed. Then she clothes my upper half with a hairshirt like a coarse rug and covers it with these luxurious garments." Then the young man burst into tears and recited the following verses:

> O Lord, I bear with patience your decree,
> And so that I may please you, I endure,
> That for their tyranny and unfair use
> Our recompense your Paradise may be.
> You never let the tyrant go, my Lord;
> Pluck me out of the fire, Almighty God.

The king said to the young man, "Young man, you have lifted one anxiety but added another worry to my worries. But where is your wife, and where is the mausoleum with the wounded black man?" The young man replied, "O King, the black slave is lying in the tomb inside the mausoleum, which is in the adjoining room. My wife comes to visit him at dawn every day, and when she comes, she strips me naked and gives me a hundred lashes with the whip, while I cry and scream without being able to stand up and defend myself, since I am half stone, half flesh and blood. After she punishes me, she goes to the black slave to give him beverages and broth to drink. Tomorrow at dawn she will come as usual." The king replied, "By God, young man, I shall do something for you that will go down in

---

1. Zoroastrian priests. Zoroastrianism is the religion of ancient Persia, based on the recognition of the dual principle of good and evil or light and darkness.

history and commemorate my name." Then the king sat to converse with the young man until night fell and they went to sleep.

The king got up before dawn, took off his clothes, and, drawing his sword, entered the room with the domed mausoleum and found it lit with candles and lamps and scented with incense, perfume, saffron, and ointments. He went straight to the black man and killed him. Then he carried him out and threw him in a well inside the palace. When he came back, he put on the clothes of the black man, covered himself, and lay hiding at the bottom of the tomb, with the drawn sword hidden under his clothes.

A while later, the cursed witch arrived, and the first thing she did was to strip her husband naked, take a whip, and whip him again and again, while he cried, "Ah wife, have pity on me; help me; I have had enough punishment and pain; have pity on me." She replied, "You should have had pity on me and spared my lover."

But morning overtook Shahrazad, and she lapsed into silence. Then Dinarzad said, "Sister, what an amazing and entertaining story!" Shahrazad replied, "What is this compared with what I shall tell you tomorrow night if I live!" King Shahrayar, with a mixture of amazement, pain, and sorrow for the enchanted youth, said to himself, "By God, I shall postpone her execution for tonight and many more nights, even for two months, until I hear the rest of the story and find out what happened to the enchanted young man. Then I shall have her put to death, as I did the others." So he said to himself.

THE TWENTY-SIXTH NIGHT

The following night Dinarzad said to Shahrazad, "Sister, if you are not sleepy, tell us one of your lovely little tales to while away the night." Shahrazad replied, "With the greatest pleasure":

I heard, O King, that after the witch punished her husband by whipping him until his sides and shoulders were bleeding and she satisfied her thirst for revenge, she dressed him with the coarse hairshirt and covered it with the outer garments. Then she headed to the black man, with the usual cup of drink and the broth. She entered the mausoleum, reached the tomb, and began to cry, wail, and lament, saying, "Lover, denying me yourself is not your custom. Do not be stingy, for my foes gloat over our separation. Be generous with your love, for forsaking is not your custom. Visit me, for my life

is in your visit. O my lord, speak to me; O my lord, entertain me."
Then she sang the following verses of the *Mufrad*[2] variety:

> For how long is this cruel disdain,
> Have I not paid with enough tears?
> O lover, talk to me,
> O lover, speak to me,
> O lover, answer me.

The king lowered his voice, stammered, and, simulating the accent
of black people, said, "Ah, ah, ah! There is no power and no strength
save in God the Almighty, the Magnificent." When she heard him
speak, she screamed with joy and fainted, and when she came to herself, she cried, "Is it true that you spoke to me?" The king replied,
"Damn you, you don't deserve that anyone should speak to you or
answer you." She asked, "What is the cause?" He replied, "All day
long you punish your husband, while he screams for help. From sunset till dawn he cries, implores, and invokes God against you and me,
with his deafening and enervating cries that deprive me of sleep. If it
had not been for this, I would have recovered a long time ago, and
this is why I have not spoken to you or answered you." She said, "My
lord, if you allow me, I shall deliver him from his present condition."
He replied, "Deliver him and rid us of his noise."
    She went out of the mausoleum, took a bowl, and, filling it with
water, uttered a spell over it, and the water began to boil and bubble
as in a caldron over fire. Then she sprinkled the young man with the
water and said, "By the power of my spell, if the Creator has created
you in this form, or if he has turned you into this form out of anger
at you, stay as you are, but if you have been transformed by my
magic and cunning, turn back to your normal form, by the will of
God, Creator of the world." The young man shook himself at once
and stood up, erect and sound, and he rejoiced and thanked God for
his deliverance. Then his wife said to him, "Get out of my sight and
don't ever come back, for if you do and I see you here, I shall kill
you." She yelled at him, and he went away.
    Then she returned to the mausoleum and, descending to the
tomb, called out, "My sweet lord, come out and let me see your
handsome face." The king replied in a muffled voice, "You have rid
me of the limb, but failed to rid me of the body." She asked, "My
sweet lord, what do you mean by the body?" He replied, "Damn you,
cursed woman, it is the inhabitants of this city and its four islands,

---

2. Literally "single," a verse form.

for every night at midnight, the fish raise their heads from the lake to implore and invoke God against me, and this is why I do not recover. Go to them and deliver them at once; then come back to hold my hand and help me rise, for I am beginning to feel better already." When she heard him, she rejoiced and replied joyfully, "Yes, my lord, yes, with God's help, my sweetheart." Then she rose, went to the lake, and took a little of its water.

But morning overtook Shahrazad, and she lapsed into silence. Then Dinarzad said, "What an amazing and entertaining story!" Shahrazad replied, "What is this compared with what I shall tell you tomorrow night if the king spares me and I live!"

THE TWENTY-SEVENTH NIGHT

The following night Dinarzad said to her sister Shahrazad, "If you are not sleepy, tell us one of your lovely little tales to while away the night." Shahrazad replied, "With the greatest pleasure":

It is related, O King, that the wife uttered some words over the lake, and the fish began to dance, and at that instant the spell was lifted, and the townspeople resumed their usual activities and returned to their buying and selling. Then she went back to the palace, entered the mausoleum, and said, "My lord, give me your gracious hand and rise." The king replied in a muffled voice, "Come closer to me." She moved closer, while he urged her "Come closer still," and she moved until her body touched his. Then he pushed her back and with one stroke of the sword sliced her in half, and she fell in two to the ground.

Then the king went out and, finding the enchanted young man waiting for him, congratulated him on his deliverance, and the young man kissed his hand, thanked him, and invoked God's blessing on him. Then the king asked him, "Do you wish stay here or come with me to my city?" The young man replied, "King of the age, and Lord of the world, do you know the distance between your city and mine?" The king replied, "It is a half-day journey." The young man said, "O King, you are dreaming, for between your city and mine it is a full year's journey. You reached us in half a day because the city was enchanted." The king asked, "Still, do you wish to stay here in your city or come with me?" The young man replied, "O King, I shall not part from you, even for one moment." The king was happy and said, "Thank God who has given you to me. You shall be a son to me, for I have never had one." They embraced, holding each other closely, and felt happy. Then they walked together back to the palace, and when they entered the palace, the enchanted young king announced to the eminent men of his kingdom and to his retinue that he was going on a journey.

He spent ten days in preparation, packing what he needed, together with the gifts that the princes and merchants of the city had given him for his journey. Then he set out with the king, with his heart on fire to be leaving his city for a whole year. He left, with fifty Mamluks and many guides and servants, bearing one hundred loads of gifts, rarities, and treasures, as well as money. They journeyed on, evening and morning, night and day, for a whole year until God granted them safe passage and they reached their destination. Then the king sent someone to inform the vizier of his safe return, and the vizier came out with all the troops and most of the townspeople to meet him. Having given him up for lost, they were exceedingly happy, and the city was decorated and its streets were spread with silk carpets. The vizier and the soldiers dismounted and, kissing the ground before the king, congratulated him on his safety and invoked God's blessing on him.

Then they entered the city, and the king sat on his throne and, meeting with the vizier, explained to him why he had been absent for an entire year. He told him the story of the young man and how he, the king, had dealt with the young man's wife and saved him and the city, and the vizier turned to the young man and congratulated him on his deliverance. Then the princes, viziers, chamberlains, and deputies took their places, and the king bestowed on them robes of honor, gifts, and other favors. Then he sent for the fisherman, who was the cause of saving the young man and the city, and when the fisherman stood before the king, the king bestowed on him robes of honor, and then asked him, "Do you have any children?" The fisherman replied that he had one boy and two girls. The king had them brought before him, and he himself married one of the girls, while he married the other to the enchanted young man. Moreover, the king took the fisherman's son into his service and made him one of his attendants. Then he conferred authority on the vizier, appointing him king of the city of the Black Islands, supplied him with provisions and fodder for the journey, and ordered the fifty Mamluks, who had come with them, as well as a host of other people, to go with him. He also sent with him many robes of honor and many fine gifts for all the princes and prominent men there. The vizier took his leave, kissed the king's hand, and departed. The king, the enchanted young man, and the fisherman lived peacefully thereafter, and the fisherman became one of the richest men of his time, with daughters married to kings.

But morning overtook Shahrazad, and she lapsed into silence. Then Dinarzad said, "What an amazing and entertaining story!" Shahrazad replied, "What is this compared with what I shall tell you tomorrow night if the king spares me and lets me live!"

THE TWENTY-EIGHTH NIGHT

The following night Dinarzad said to her sister Shahrazad, "Sister, if you are not sleepy, tell us one of your lovely little tales." Shahrazad replied, "With the greatest pleasure":

[The Story of the Porter and the Three Ladies]

I HEARD, O happy King, that once there lived in the city of Baghdad[3] a bachelor who worked as a porter. One day he was standing in the market, leaning on his basket, when a woman approached him. She wore a Mosul[4] cloak, a silk veil, a fine kerchief embroidered with gold, and a pair of leggings tied with fluttering laces. When she lifted her veil, she revealed a pair of beautiful dark eyes graced with long lashes and a tender expression, like those celebrated by the poets. Then with a soft voice and a sweet tone, she said to him, "Porter, take your basket and follow me." Hardly believing his ears, the porter took his basket and hurried behind her, saying, "O lucky day, O happy day." She walked before him until she stopped at the door of a house, and when she knocked, an old Christian came down, received a dinar from her and handed her an olive green jug of wine. She placed the jug in the basket and said, "Porter, take your basket and follow me." Saying, "Very well, O auspicious day, O lucky day, O happy day," the porter lifted the basket and followed her until she stopped at the fruit vendor's, where she bought yellow and red apples, Hebron peaches and Turkish quinces, and seacoast lemons and royal oranges, as well as baby cucumbers. She also bought Aleppo jasmine and Damascus lilies, myrtle berries and mignonettes, daisies and gillyflowers, lilies of the valley and irises, narcissus and daffodils, violets and anemones, as well as pomegranate

---

3. Then and now capital of Iraq, at that time capital of the Abbasid caliphate and its empire, situated on the Tigris River. It is the scene of several of the stories of the *Nights*.
4. Then and now an important city in northern Iraq.

blossoms. She placed everything in the porter's basket and asked him to follow her.

Then she stopped at the butcher's and said, "Cut me off ten pounds of fresh mutton." She paid him, and he cut off the pieces she desired, wrapped them, and handed them to her. She placed them in the basket, together with some charcoal, and said, "Porter, take your basket and follow me." The porter, wondering at all these purchases, placed his basket on his head and followed her until she came to the grocer's, where she bought whatever she needed of condiments, such as olives of all kinds, pitted, salted, and pickled, tarragon, cream cheese, Syrian cheese, and sweet as well as sour pickles. She placed the container in the basket and said, "Porter, take your basket and follow me." The porter carried his basket and followed her until she came to the dry grocer's, where she bought all sorts of dry fruits and nuts: Aleppo raisins, Iraqi sugar canes, pressed Ba'albak figs, roasted chick-peas, as well as shelled pistachios, almonds, and hazelnuts. She placed everything in the porter's basket, turned to him, and said, "Porter take your basket and follow me."

The porter carried the basket and followed her until she came to the confectioner's, where she bought a whole tray full of every kind of pastry and sweet in the shop, such as sour barley rolls, sweet rolls, date rolls, Cairo rolls, Turkish rolls, and open-worked Balkan rolls, as well as cookies, stuffed and musk-scented kataifs, amber combs, ladyfingers, widows' bread, Kadi's tidbits, eat-and-thanks, and almond pudding. When she placed the tray in the basket, the porter said, to her, "Mistress, if you had let me know, I would have brought with me a nag or a camel to carry all these purchases." She smiled and walked ahead until she came to the druggist's, where she bought ten bottles of scented waters, lilywater, rosewater scented with musk, and the like, as well as ambergris, musk, aloewood, and rosemary. She also bought two loaves of sugar and candles and torches. Then she put everything in the basket, turned to the porter, and said, "Porter, take your basket and follow me." The porter carried the basket and walked behind her until she came to a spacious courtyard facing a tall, stately mansion with massive pillars and a double door inlaid with ivory and shining gold. The girl stopped at the door and knocked gently.

But morning overtook Shahrazad, and she lapsed into silence. Then her sister said, "Sister, what a lovely and entertaining story!" Shahrazad replied, "What is this compared with what I shall tell you tomorrow night if the king spares me and lets me live! May God grant him long life."

THE TWENTY-NINTH NIGHT

The following night Dinarzad said to her sister Shahrazad, "Sister, if you are not sleepy, tell us one of your little tales to while away the night." Shahrazad replied, "I hear and obey":

I heard, O wise and happy King, that as the porter stood with the basket, at the door, behind the girl, marveling at her beauty, her charm, and her elegant, eloquent, and liberal ways, the door was unlocked, and the two leaves swung open. The porter, looking to see who opened the door, saw a full-bosomed girl, about five feet tall. She was all charm, beauty, and perfect grace, with a forehead like the new moon, eyes like those of a deer or wild heifer, eyebrows like the crescent in the month of Sha'ban,[5] cheeks like red anemones, mouth like the seal of Solomon, lips like red carnelian, teeth like a row of pearls set in coral, neck like a cake for a king, bosom like a fountain, breasts like a pair of big pomegranates resembling a rabbit with uplifted ears, and belly with a navel like a cup that holds a pound of benzoin ointment. She was like her of whom the poet aptly said:

> On stately sun and full moon cast your sight;
> Savor the flowers and lavender's delight.
> Your eyes have never seen such white in black,
> Such radiant face with hair so deeply dark.
> With rosy cheeks, Beauty proclaimed her name,
> To those who had not yet received her fame.
> Her swaying heavy hips I joyed to see,
> But her sweet, slender waist brought tears to me.

When the porter saw her, he lost his senses and his wits, and the basket nearly fell from his head, as he exclaimed, "Never in my life have I seen a more blessed day than this!" Then the girl who had opened the door said to the girl who had done the shopping, "Sister, what are you waiting for? Come in and relieve this poor man of his heavy burden." The shopper and the porter went in, and the door-keeper locked the door and followed them until they came to a spacious, well-appointed, and splendid hall. It had arched compartments and niches with carved woodwork; it had a booth hung with drapes; and it had closets and cupboards covered with curtains. In the middle stood a large pool full of water, with a fountain in the center, and at the far end stood a couch of black juniper wood, covered with white silk and set with gems and pearls, with a canopylike mosquito

---

5. The eighth month of the lunar Muslim year.

net of red silk, fastened with pearls as big as hazelnuts or bigger. The curtain was unfastened, and a dazzling girl emerged, with genial charm, wise mien, and features as radiant as the moon, She had an elegant figure, the scent of ambergris, sugared lips, Babylonian eyes, with eyebrows as arched as a pair of bent bows, and a face whose radiance put the shining sun to shame, for she was like a great star soaring in the heavens, or a dome of gold, or an unveiled bride, or a splendid fish swimming in a fountain, or a morsel of luscious fat in a bowl of milk soup. She was like her of whom the poet said:

> Her smile reveals twin rows of pearls
> Or white daisies or pearly hail.
> Her forelock like the night unfurls;
> Before her light the sun is pale.

The third girl rose from the couch and strutted slowly until she joined her sisters in the middle of the hall, saying, "Why are you standing? Lift the load off this poor man." The doorkeeper stood in front of the porter, and the shopper stood behind him, and with the help of the third girl, they lifted the basket down and emptied its contents, stacking up the fruits and pickles on one side and the flowers and fresh herbs on the other. When everything was arranged, they gave the porter one dinar and said . . .

But morning overtook Shahrazad, and she lapsed into silence. Then Dinarzad said to her sister Shahrazad, "What an amazing and entertaining story!" Shahrazad replied, "If I am alive tomorrow night, I shall tell you something stranger and more amazing than this."

THE THIRTIETH NIGHT

The following night Dinarzad said to her sister Shahrazad, "Sister, tell us the rest of the story of the three girls." Shahrazad replied, "With the greatest pleasure":

I heard, O King, that when the porter saw how charming and beautiful the girls were and saw how much they had stacked of wine, meat, fruits, nuts, sweets, fresh herbs, candles, charcoal, and the like for drinking and carousing, without seeing any man around, he was very astonished and stood there, hesitant to leave. One of the girls asked him, "Why don't you go? Do you find your pay too little?" and, turning to her sister, said, "Give him another dinar." The porter replied, "By God, ladies, my pay is not little, for I deserve not even two dirhams, but I have been wondering about your situation and the absence of anyone to entertain you. For as a table needs four legs to stand on, you being three, likewise need a fourth, for the pleasure of men is not complete without women, and the pleasure of women is not complete without men. The poet says:

> For our delight four things we need, the lute,
> The harp, the zither, and the double flute,
> Blending with the scent of four lovely flowers,
> Roses, myrtles, anemones, and gillyflowers.
> Only in four such things join together,
> Money, and wine, and youth, and a lover.

You are three and you need a fourth, a man." His words pleased the girls, who laughed and said, "How can we manage that, being girls who keep our business to ourselves, for we fear to entrust our secrets where they may not be kept. We have read in some book what ibn al-Tammam[6] has said:

> Your own secret to none reveal;
> It will be lost when it is told.
> If your own breast cannot conceal,
> How can another better hold?"

When the porter heard their words, he replied, "Trust me; I am a sensible and wise man. I have studied the sciences and attained knowledge; I have read and learned, and presented my knowledge and cited my authorities. I reveal the good and conceal the bad, and I am well-behaved. I am like the man of whom the poet said:

> Only the faithful does a secret keep;
> None but the best can hold it unrevealed.
> I keep a secret in a well-shut house
> Of which the key is lost and the lock sealed."

When the girls heard what he said, they replied, "You know very well that this table has cost us a lot and that we have spent a great deal of money to get all these provisions. Do you have anything to pay in return for the entertainment? For we shall not let you stay unless we see your share; otherwise you will drink and enjoy yourself with us

---

6. Actually Abu-Tamman, an Arab poet of the ninth century, and author of the *Hamasa*.

at our expense." The mistress of the house said, "'Without gain, love is not worth a grain.'" The doorkeeper added, "Have you got anything, my dear? If you are emptyhanded, go emptyhanded." But the shopper said, "Sisters, stop teasing him, for by God, he served me well today; no one else would have been as patient with me. Whatever his share will come to, I shall pay for him myself." The porter, overjoyed, kissed the ground before her and thanked her, saying, "By God, it was you who brought me my first business today and I still have the dinar you gave me; take it back and take me, not as a companion but as a servant." The girls replied, "You are very welcome to join us."

Then the shopper, girding herself, began to arrange this and that. She first tidied up, strained the wine, stacked up the flasks, and arranged the bowls, goblets, cups, decanters, plates, and serving spoons, as well as various utensils in silver and gold. Having prepared all the requisites, she set the table by the pool and laid it with all kinds of food and drink. Then she invited them to the banquet and sat down to serve. Her sisters joined her, as did the porter, who thought that he was in a dream. She filled the first cup and drank it, filled the second and offered it to one of her sisters, who drank it, filled a third and gave it to the other sister to drink, and filled a fourth and gave it to the porter, who held it in his hand and, saluting with a bow, thanked her and recited the following verses:

> Drink not the cup, save with a friend you trust,
> One whose blood to noble forefathers owes.
> Wine, like the wind, is sweet if o'er the sweet,
> And foul if o'er the foul it haply blows.

Then he emptied his cup, and the doorkeeper returned his salute and recited the following verses:

> Cheers, and drink it in good health;
> This wine is good for your health.

The porter thanked her and kissed her hand. After the girls had drunk again and had given the porter more to drink, he turned to his companion, the shopper, saying, "My lady, your servant is calling on you," and recited the following verses:

> One of your slaves is waiting at your door,
> With ample thanks for your ample favor.

She replied "By God, you are welcome. Drink the wine and enjoy it in good health, for it relieves pain, hastens the cure, and restores health."

The porter emptied his cup and, pouring out another, kissed her hand, offered it to her, and proceeded to recite the following verses:

> I gave her pure old wine, red as her cheeks,
> Which with red fire did like a furnace glow.
> She kissed the brim and with a smile she asked,
> "How can you cheeks with cheeks pay what you owe?"
> I said, "Drink! This wine is my blood and tears,
> And my soul is the fragrance in the cup."
> She said, "If for me you have shed your blood,
> Most gladly will I on this red wine sup."

The girl took the cup, drank it off, then sat by her sister.

Thus receiving the full and returning the empty, they went on drinking cup after cup until the porter began to feel tipsy, lost his inhibitions, and was aroused. He danced and sang lyrics and ballads and carried on with the girls, toying, kissing, biting, groping, rubbing, fingering, and playing jokes on them, while one girl thrust a morsel in his mouth, another flirted with him, another served him with some fresh herbs, and another fed him sweets until he was in utter bliss. They carried on until they got drunk and the wine turned their heads. When the wine got the better of them, the doorkeeper went to the pool, took off her clothes, and stood stark naked, save for what was covered of her body by her loosened hair. Then she said, "Whee," went into the pool, and immersed herself in the water.

But morning overtook Shahrazad, and she lapsed into silence. Then Dinarzad said, "What an amazing and entertaining story!" Shahrazad replied, "What is this compared with what I shall tell you tomorrow night!"

THE THIRTY-FIRST NIGHT

The following night Dinarzad said, "Sister, if you are not sleepy, tell us one of your lovely little tales to while away the night." Shahrazad replied, "With the greatest pleasure":

I heard that the doorkeeper went into the pool, threw water on herself, and, after immersing herself completely, began to sport, taking water in her mouth and squirting it all over her sisters and the porter. Then she washed herself under her breasts, between her thighs, and inside her navel. Then she rushed out of the pool, sat naked in the porter's lap and, pointing to her slit, asked, "My lord and my love, what is this?" "Your womb," said he, and she replied, "Pooh, pooh, you have no shame," and slapped him on the neck. "Your vulva," said he, and the other sister pinched him, shouting, "Bah, this is an ugly word." "Your cunt," said he, and the third sister boxed him on the chest and knocked him over, saying, "Fie, have some shame." "Your clitoris," said he, and again the naked girl slapped him, saying, "No." "Your pudenda, your pussy, your sex tool," said he, and she kept replying, "No, no." He kept giving various other names, but every time he uttered a name, one of the girls hit him and asked, "What do you call this?" And they went on, this one boxing him, that one slapping him, another hitting him. At last, he turned to them and asked, "All right, what is its name?" The naked girl replied, "The basil of the bridges." The porter cried, "The basil of the bridges! You should have told me this from the beginning, oh, oh!" Then they passed the cup around and went on drinking for a while.

Then the shopper, like her sister, took off all her clothes, saying, "Whee," went into the pool, and immersed herself completely in the water. Then she washed herself under the belly, around the breasts, and between the thighs. Then she rushed out, threw herself in the porter's lap, and asked, "My little lord, what is this?" "Your vulva," said he, and she gave him a blow with which the hall resounded, saying, "Fie, you have no shame." "Your womb," said he, and her sister hit him, saying, "Fie, what an ugly word!" "Your clitoris," said he, and the other sister boxed him, saying, "Fie, fie, you are shameless." They kept at it, this one boxing him, that one slapping him, another hitting him, another jabbing him, repeating, "No, no," while he kept shouting, "Your womb, your cunt, your pussy." Finally he cried, "The basil of the bridges," and all three burst out laughing till they fell on their backs. But again all three slapped him on the neck and said, "No, this is not its name." He cried, "All right, what is its name?" One of them replied, "Why don't you say 'the husked sesame'?" He cried out, "The husked sesame! Thank God, we are finally there." Then the girl put on her clothes and they sat, passing the cup around, while the porter moaned with sore neck and shoulders.

They drank for a while, and then the eldest and fairest of the three stood up and began to undress. The porter touched his neck and began to rub it with his hand, saying, "For God's sake, spare my neck and shoulders," while the girl stripped naked, threw herself into the pool, and immersed herself. The porter looked at her naked body, which looked like a slice of the moon, and at her face, which shone like the full moon or the rising sun, and admired her figure, her breasts, and her swaying heavy hips, for she was naked as God had created her. Moaning "Oh, oh," he addressed her with the following verses:

> If I compare your figure to the bough,
> When green, I err and a sore burden bear.
> The bough is fairest when covered with leaves,
> And you are fairest when completely bare.

When the girl heard his verses, she came quickly out of the pool, sat in his lap and, pointing to her slit, asked, "O light of my eyes, O sweetheart, what is the name of this?" "The basil of the bridges," said he, but she replied, "Bah!" "The husked sesame," said he, and she replied, "Pooh!" "Your womb," said he, and she replied, "Fie, you have no shame," and slapped him on the neck. To make a long story short, O King, the porter kept declaring, "Its name is so," and she kept saying "No, no, no, no." When he had had his fill of blows, pinches, and bites until his neck swelled and he choked and felt miserable, he cried out, "All right, what is its name?" She replied, "Why don't you say the Inn of Abu Masrur?" "Ha, ha, the Inn of Abu Masrur," said the porter. Then she got up, and after she put on her clothes, they resumed their drinking and passed the cup around for a while.

Then the porter stood up, took off his clothes, and, revealing something dangling between his legs, he leapt and plunged into the middle of the pool.

But morning overtook Shahrazad, and she lapsed into silence. Then Dinarzad said to her sister Shahrazad, "Sister, what a lovely and entertaining story!" Shahrazad replied, "What is this compared with what I shall tell you tomorrow night if the king spares me and lets me live!" The king said to himself, "By God, I will not have her put to death until I hear the rest of the story. Then I shall do to her what I did to the others."

THE THIRTY-SECOND NIGHT

The following night Dinarzad said to her sister Shahrazad, "Sister, if you are not sleepy, tell us one of your lovely little tales." Shahrazad replied, "With the greatest pleasure":

I heard, O King, that when the porter went down into the pool, he bathed and washed himself under the beard and under the arms; then he rushed out of the pool, planted himself in the lap of the fairest girl, put his arms on the lap of the doorkeeper, rested his legs in the lap of the shopper and, pointing to his penis, asked, "Ladies, what is this?" They were pleased with his antics and laughed, for his disposition agreed with theirs, and they found him entertaining. One of them said, "Your cock," and he replied, "You have no shame; this is an ugly word." The other said, "Your penis," and he replied, "You should be ashamed; may God put you to shame." The third said,

"Your dick," and he replied, "No." Another said, "Your stick," and he replied "No." Another said, "Your thing, your testicles, your prick," and he kept saying, "No, no, no." They asked, "What is the name of this?" He hugged this and kissed that, pinched the one, bit the other, and nibbled on the third, as he took satisfaction, while they laughed until they fell on their backs. At last they asked, "Friend, what is its name?" The porter replied, "Don't you know its name? It is the smashing mule." They asked, "What is the meaning of the name the smashing mule?" He replied, "It is the one who grazes in the basil of the bridges, eats the husked sesame, and gallops in the Inn of Abu Masrur." Again they laughed until they fell on their backs and almost fainted with laughter. Then they resumed their carousing and drinking and carried on until nightfall.

When it was dark, they said to the porter, "Sir, it is time that you get up, put on your slippers, and show us your back." The porter replied, "Where do I go from here? The departure of my soul from my body is easier for me than my departure from your company. Let us join the night with the day and let each of us go his way early tomorrow morning." The shopper said, "By God, sisters, he is right. For God's sake and for my sake, let him stay tonight, so that we may laugh at him and amuse ourselves with him, for who will live to meet with one like him again? He is a clever and witty rogue." They said, "You cannot spend the night with us unless you agree to abide by our condition, that whatever we do and whatever happens to us, you shall refrain from asking for any explanation, for 'speak not of what concerns you not, lest you hear what pleases you not.' This is our condition; don't be too curious about any action of ours." He replied, "Yes, yes, yes, I am dumb and blind." They said, "Rise, then, go to the entrance, and read what is inscribed on the door and the entrance." He got up, went to the door, and found on the door and the entrance the following inscription written in letters of gold, "Whoever speaks of what concerns him not hears what pleases him not." The porter came back and said, "I pledge to you that I will not speak of what concerns me not."

Then the shopper went and prepared supper, and after they had something to eat, they lighted the lamps, and, sticking the aloewood and ambergris into the wax, they lighted the candles, and the incense burned, rose, and filled the hall. Then they changed the plates, laid the table with wine and fresh fruits, and sat to drink. They sat for a long time, eating, drinking, engaging in refined conversation, bantering, and laughing, and joking, when suddenly they heard a knocking at the door. Without showing much concern, one of the girls rose, went to the door, and returned after a while, saying, "Sisters, if you listen to me, you will spend a delightful night, a night to remember." They asked, "How so?" She replied, "At this very moment, three one-eyed dervishes[7] are standing at the door, each with a shaven head, shaven beard, and shaven eyebrows, and each blind in the right eye. It is a most amazing coincidence. They have just arrived in Baghdad from their travel, as one can see from their condition, and this is their first time in our city. Night overtook them and, being strangers with no one to go to and unable to find a place to sleep, they knocked at our door, hoping that someone would give them the key to the stable or offer them a room for the night. Sisters, each one of them is a sight, with a face that would make a mourner laugh. Would you agree to let them in for this one time, so that we may amuse ourselves with them tonight and let them go early tomorrow morning?" She continued to persuade her sisters until they consented, saying, "Let them in, but make it a condition that they 'speak not of what concerns them not, lest they hear what pleases them not.'"

Pleased, she disappeared for a while and returned, followed by three one-eyed dervishes, who greeted them, bowed, and stood back. The three girls rose to greet them, extended welcomes, expressed delight at their visit, and congratulated them on their safe arrival. The three dervishes thanked them and again saluted with bows, and when they saw the beautiful hall, the well-set table laden with wine, nuts, and dried fruits, the burning candles, the smoking incense, and the three girls, who had thrown off all restraint, they exclaimed with one voice, "By God, this is fine." When they turned and looked at the porter, who, sore from the beating and slapping and intoxicated with the wine, lay almost unconscious, they said, "Whether an Arab or a foreigner, he is a brother dervish." The porter sat up and, fixing his eyes on them, said, "Sit here without meddling. Haven't you read the inscription on the door, which is quite clearly written, 'Speak not of what concerns you not, lest you hear what pleases you not'? Yet as soon as you come in you wag your tongues at us." They replied, "O mendicant, we ask for God's forgiveness. Our heads are in your hands." The girls laughed and made peace between the dervishes and the porter; then the shopper offered the dervishes something to eat, and after they ate, they all sat down to carouse and drink, with the doorkeeper replenishing the cups as they passed them around. Then the porter asked, "Friends, can you entertain us with something?"

But morning overtook Shahrazad, and she lapsed into silence. Then her sister Dinarzad said, "Sister, what a lovely and entertaining story!" Shahrazad replied, "What is this compared with what I shall tell you tomorrow night if I live!"

7. Members of a Muslim order of mendicant monks, vowed to a life of poverty.

THE THIRTY-THIRD NIGHT

The following night Dinarzad said to her sister Shahrazad, "Sister, if you are not sleepy, tell us one of your lovely little tales to while away the night." Shahrazad replied, "With the greatest pleasure":

I heard, O King, that the dervishes, heated with the wine, called for musical instruments, and the doorkeeper brought them a tambourine, a flute, and a Persian harp. The dervishes rose, and one took the tambourine, another the flute, another the Persian harp, tuned their instruments, and began to play and sing, and the girls began to sing with them until it got very loud. While they were thus playing and singing, they heard a knocking at the door and the doorkeeper went to see what was the matter.

Now the cause of that knocking, O King, was that it happened on that very night that the Caliph Harun al-Rashid and Ja'far[8] came into the city, as they used to do every now and then, and as they walked through, they passed by the door and heard the music of the flute, the harp, and the tambourine, the singing of the girls, and the sounds of people partying and laughing. The caliph said, "Ja'far, I would like to enter this house and visit the people inside." Ja'far replied, "O Prince of the Faithful, these are people who are intoxicated and who do not know who we are, and I fear that they may insult us and abuse us." The caliph said, "Don't argue; I must go in and I want you to find a pretext to get us in." Ja'far replied, "I hear and obey." Then Ja'far knocked at the door, and when the doorkeeper came and opened the door, he stepped forward, kissed the ground before her, and said, "O my lady, we are merchants from the city of Mosul, and we have been in Baghdad for ten days. We have brought with us our merchandise and have taken lodgings at an inn. Tonight a merchant of your city invited us to his home and offered us food and drink. We drank and enjoyed ourselves and sent for a troop of musicians and singing women and invited the rest of our companions to join us. They all came and we had a good time, listening to the girls blow on the flutes, beat the tambourines, and sing, but while we were enjoying ourselves, the prefect of the police raided the place, and we tried to escape by jumping from walls. Some of us broke our limbs and were arrested, while some escaped safely. We have come now to seek refuge in your house, for, being strangers in your city, we are afraid that if we continue to walk

---

8. Harun al-Rashid was the fifth Abbasid caliph, who ruled from 786 to 809 C.E.; his rule is considered to be the golden age of the Arab empire, and his court in Baghdad is idealized in the *Nights*. Ja'far al-Barmaki was Harun al-Rashid's vizier and frequent companion, to whose family Harun delegated the administrative duties of the empire until, grown suspicious of their rising power, he had Ja'far and virtually the entire clan exterminated.

the streets, the prefect of the police will stop us, discover that we are intoxicated, and arrest us. If we go to the inn, we shall find the door locked for, as is the rule, it is not to be opened till sunrise. As we passed by your house, we heard the sounds of music and the noise of a lovely party and hoped that you would be kind enough to let us join you to enjoy the rest of the night, giving us the chance to pay you for our share. If you refuse our company, let us sleep in the hallway till the morning, and God will reward you. The matter is in your magnanimous hands and the decision is yours, but we will not depart from your door."

After the doorkeeper had listened to Ja'far's speech, looked at their dress, and seen that they were respectable, she went back to her sisters and repeated Ja'far's story. The girls felt sorry for them and said, "Let them in," and she invited them to come in. When the caliph, together with Ja'far and Masrur,[9] entered the hall, the entire group, the girls, the dervishes, and the porter, rose to greet them, and then everyone sat down.

But morning overtook Shahrazad, and she lapsed into silence. Then Dinarzad said, "What a lovely and entertaining story!" Shahrazad replied, "What is this compared with what I shall tell you tomorrow night if I stay alive!"

THE THIRTY-FOURTH NIGHT

The following night Dinarzad said to her sister Shahrazad, "Please, if you are not sleepy, tell us the rest of the story of the three girls." Shahrazad replied, "Very well":

It is related, O King, that when the caliph, together with Ja'far and Masrur, entered and sat down, the girls turned to them and said, "You are welcome, and we are delighted to have you as our guests, but on one condition?" They asked, "What is your condition?" The girls replied, "That you will be eyes without tongues and will not inquire about whatever you see. You will 'speak not of what concerns you not, lest you hear what pleases you not.'" They replied, "Yes, as you wish, for we have no need to meddle." Pleased with them, the girls sat to entertain them, drinking and conversing with them. The caliph was astonished to see three dervishes, all blind in the right eye, and he was especially astonished to see girls with such beauty, charm, eloquence, and generosity, in such a lovely place, with a music band consisting of

9. A black eunuch who was Harun al-Rashid's executioner and bodyguard.

three one-eyed dervishes. But he felt that at that moment he could not ask any questions. They continued to converse and drink, and then the dervishes rose, bowed, and played another round of music; then they sat down and passed the cup around.

When the wine had taken hold, the mistress of the house rose, bowed, and, taking the shopper by the hand, said, "Sister, let us do our duty." Both sisters replied, "Very well." The doorkeeper got up, cleared the table, got rid of the peels and shells, replenished the incense, and cleared the middle of the hall. Then she made the dervishes sit on a sofa at one side of the hall and seated the caliph, Ja'far, and Masrur on another sofa at the other side of the hall. Then she shouted at the porter, saying, "You are very lazy. Get up and lend us a hand, for you are a member of the household." The porter got up and, girding himself, asked, "What is up?" She replied, "Stand where you are." Then the shopper placed a chair in the middle of the hall, opened a cupboard, and said to the porter, "Come and help me." When the porter approached, he saw two black female hounds with chains around their necks. He took them and led them to the middle of the hall. Saying, "It is time to perform our duty," the mistress of the house came forward, rolled up her sleeves, took a braided whip, and called to the porter, "Bring me one of the bitches." The porter dragged one of the bitches by the chain and brought her forward, while she wept and shook her head at the girl. As the porter stood holding the chain, the girl came down on the bitch with hard blows on the sides, while the bitch howled and wept. The girl kept beating the bitch until her arm got weary. Then she stopped, threw the whip away, and, taking the chain from the porter, embraced the bitch and began to cry. The bitch too began to cry, and the two cried together for a long time. Then the girl wiped the bitch's tears with her handkerchief, kissed her on the head, and said to the porter, "Take her back to her place, and bring me the other." The porter took the bitch to the cupboard and brought the other bitch to the girl, who did to her as she had done to the first, beating her until she fainted. Then she took the bitch, cried with her, kissed her on the head, and asked the porter to take her back to her sister, and he took her back. When those who were present saw what happened, how the girl beat the bitch until the bitch fainted, and how she cried with the bitch and kissed her on the head, they were completely amazed and began to speak under their breath. The caliph himself felt troubled and lost all patience as he burned with curiosity to know the story of these two bitches. He winked to Ja'far, but Ja'far, turning to him, said with a sign, "This is not the time to inquire."

O happy King, when the girl finished punishing the two bitches, the doorkeeper said to her, "My lady, go and sit on your couch, so that I in turn may fulfill my desire." Saying, "Very well," the girl went to the far end of the hall and seated herself on the couch, with the caliph, Ja'far, and Masrur seated in a row to her right and the dervishes and the porter, to her left, and although the lamps glowed, the candles burned, and the incense filled the place, these men were depressed and felt that their evening was spoiled. Then the door-keeper sat on the chair.

But morning overtook Shahrazad, and she lapsed into silence. Then Dinarzad said to her sister, "Sister, what an amazing and entertaining story!" Shahrazad replied, "What is this compared with what I shall tell you tomorrow night if I live!"

The Thirty-Fifth Night

The following night, Dinarzad said to her sister Shahrazad, "Sister, if you are not sleepy, tell us one of your lovely little tales to while away the night." Shahrazad replied, "Very well":

I heard, O happy King, that the doorkeeper sat on the chair and said to her sister the shopper, "Get up and pay me my due." The shopper rose, entered a chamber, and soon brought back a bag of yellow satin with two green silk tassels ornamented with red gold and two beads of pure ambergris. She sat in front of the doorkeeper, drew a lute out of the bag, and with its side resting on her knee, held it in her lap. Then she tuned the lute and, plucking the strings with her fingertips, began to play and sing the following verses of the *Kan wa Kan* variety:[1]

> My love, you are my aim,
> And you are my desire.
> Your company is constant joy,
> Your absence, hellish fire.
> You are the madness of my life,
> My one infatuation,
> A love in which there is no shame,
> A blameless adoration.
> The shirt of agony I wore
> Revealed my secret passion,

---

1. A verse form in quatrains, which originated in Baghdad. At first the subject matter consisted of narratives that began with the word *kan*, meaning "once upon a time"; later the form included love lyrics and maxims.

Betrayed my agitated heart
And left me in confusion.
My tears to all declared my love,
As o'er my cheeks they flowed,
My treacherous tears betrayed me
And all my secrets showed.
O, cure me from my dire disease;
You are the sickness and the cure,
But he whose remedy you are
Will suffer evermore.
Your brilliant eyes have wasted me,
Your jet-black hair has me in thrall,
Your rosy cheeks have vanquished me
And told my tale to all.
My hardship is my martyrdom,
The sword of love, my death.
How often have the best of men
This way ended their breath?
I will not cease from loving you,
Nor unlock what is sealed.
Love is my law and remedy,
Whether hid or revealed.
Blessed my eyes that gazed on you,
O treasured revelation;
Which has left me confused, alone,
In helpless adoration.

When the girl finished the poem, her sister let out a loud cry and moaned, "Oh, oh, oh!" Then she grabbed her dress by the collar and tore it down to the hem, baring her entire body, and fell down in a swoon. When the caliph looked at her, he saw that her whole body, from her head to her toe, bore the marks of the whip, which left it black and blue. Seeing the girl's condition and not knowing the cause, he and his companions were troubled, and he said to Ja'far, "By God, I will not wait a moment until I get to the bottom of this and ask for an explanation for what has happened, the flogging of the girl, the whipping of the two bitches, then the crying and the kissing." Ja'far replied, "My lord, this is not the time to ask for an explanation, especially since they have imposed on us the condition that we speak not of what concerns us not, for 'he who speaks of what concerns him not hears what pleases him not.'"

Then the shopper rose and, entering the chamber, came out with a fine dress that she put on her sister, replacing the one her sister had torn, and sat down. The sister said to the shopper, "For God's sake, give me some more to drink," and the shopper took the cup, filled it, and handed it to her. Then the shopper held the lute in her lap, improvised a number of measures, and sang the following verses:

> If I bemoan your absence, what will you say?
> If I pine with longing, what is the way?
> If I dispatch someone to tell my tale,
> The lover's complaint no one can convey.
> If I with patience try to bear my pain,
> After the loss of love, I can't endure the blow.
> Nothing remains but longing and regret
> And tears that over the cheeks profusely flow.
> You, who have long been absent from my eyes,
> Will in my loving heart forever stay.
> Was it you who have taught me how to love,
> And from the pledge of love never to stray?

When the sister finished her song, the girl cried out, "Oh, oh, oh!" and, overcome by passion, again grabbed her dress by the collar and tore it to the hem. Then she shrieked and fell down in a swoon. Again the shopper entered the chamber and came out with a dress even better than the first. Then she sprinkled her sister's face with rosewater, and when her sister came to herself, she put the dress on her. Then the sister said, "For God's sake, sister, pay me and finish off, for there remains only this one song." "With the greatest pleasure," replied the shopper, and she took the lute and began to play and sing the following verses:

> How long shall I endure this cruel disdain?
> Have I not paid enough with tears of woe?
> For how long suffer your willful neglect,
> As if it were a vengeful, envious foe?
> Be kind! Your cruel ways inflict a cruel pain,
> Master, 'tis time to me you pity show.
> O gentlemen, avenge this thrall of love,
> Who neither sleep nor patience does now know.
> Is it the law of love that one my love enjoys,
> While I alone do empty-handed go?
> My lord, let him my unjust tyrant be;
> Many the toils and trials I undergo.

When she finished her song . . .

But morning overtook Shahrazad, and she lapsed into silence. Then Dinarzad said, "Sister, what an amazing and entertaining story!" Shahrazad replied, "Tomorrow night I shall tell you something stranger, more amazing, and more entertaining if the king spares me and lets me live!"

THE THIRTY-SIXTH NIGHT

The following night Dinarzad said to her sister Shahrazad, "Sister, tell us the rest of the girls' story." Shahrazad said:

It is related, O King, that when the girl heard the third song, she cried out, "By God, this is good." Then she grabbed her dress and tore it, and, as she fell down in a swoon, she revealed on her chest marks like welts from a whip. The dervishes muttered. "We wish that we had never entered this house, but had rather spent the night on the rubbish mounds outside the city, for our visit has been spoiled by such heartrending sights." The caliph turned to them and asked, "How so?" and they replied, "O distinguished gentleman, our minds are troubled by this matter." The caliph asked, "But you are members of the household; perhaps you can explain to me the story of these two black bitches and this girl." They replied, "By God, we know nothing and we have never laid eyes on this place until tonight." Surprised, the caliph said, "Then this man who sits beside you should know the explanation." They winked at the porter, questioning him, but he replied, "By the Almighty God, 'In love all are alike,' for even though I have been raised in Baghdad, never in my life have I entered this house until today. I did spend an amazing day with them. Still, I kept wondering that they were all women without men." They said to him, "By God, we took you to be one of them, but now we find that you are in the same predicament as we are."

Then the caliph said, "Adding Ja'far and Masrur, we are seven men, and they are only three women, without even a single man. Let us ask them for an explanation; if they don't answer by choice, they will answer by force." They agreed to proceed with this plan, but Ja'far said, "This is not right; let them be, for we are their guests and, as you know, they made a condition that we promised to keep. It is better to keep silent about this matter, for little remains of the night, and soon each of us will go his own way." Then he winked at the caliph and whispered to him, "O Commander of the Faithful, be patient for this one last hour of the night, and tomorrow morning I will come back and bring them before you to tell us their story." But the caliph yelled at him, saying, "Damn it, I can no longer wait for an explanation. Let the dervishes question them." Ja'far replied, "This is not a good idea." Then they talked at length and disputed as to who should first put the question, and at last all agreed on the porter.

When the girls heard their clamor, one of them asked, "Men, what is the matter?" The porter approached her and said, "My lady, these men express the wish that you acquaint them with the story of the two black bitches and why you punish them and then weep over them, and they wish to know the story of your sister and how it was that she got flogged with the whip, like a man. That is all; that is what they want to know." Turning to them, the girl asked, "Is it true what he says about you?" They all replied, "Yes," except Ja'far, who remained silent. When the girl heard their reply, she said, "O guests, you have wronged us. Have we not told you of our condition, that 'he who speaks of what concerns him not will hear what pleases him not'? We took you into our home and fed you with our food, but after all this you meddled and did us wrong. Yet the fault is not so much yours as hers who let you in and brought you to us." Then she rolled up her sleeves and struck the floor three times, crying out, "Come at once," and a door opened and out came seven black men, with drawn swords in their hands. Then with the palm of the sword, each man dealt one of the men a blow that threw him on his face to the ground, and in no time they had the seven guests tied by the hands and bound each to each. Then they led them in a single file to the center of the hall, and each black man stood with his sword drawn above the head of his man. Then they said to the girl, "O most honorable and most virtuous lady, permit us to strike off their heads." She replied, "Wait a while until I question them, before you strike off their heads." The porter cried, "God protect me. O lady, slay me not for another's sin. All these men have sinned and offended, except me. By God, we had a delightful day. If only we could have escaped these one-eyed dervishes, whose entrance into any city blights it, destroys it, and lays it waste!" Then he began to weep and recite the following verses:

> Fair is the forgiveness of mighty men,
> And fairest when to weakest men 'tis shown.
> Break off not the first friendship for the last,
> By the bond of the love that has between us grown.

The girl, despite her anger, laughed, and, coming up to the group, said, "Tell me who you are, for you have only one hour to live. Were you not men of rank or eminent among your people or powerful rulers, you would not have dared to offend us." The caliph said to Ja'far, "Damn it, tell her who we are, lest we be slain by mistake." Ja'far replied, "This is part of what we deserve." The caliph yelled at him, saying, "This is no time for your witticisms." Then the lady approached the dervishes and asked, "Are you brothers?" They replied, "No, by God, mistress, we are not, nor are we mendicants." Then she asked one of them, "Were you born blind in one eye?" and he replied, "No, by God my lady. It was an amazing event and a strange mischance that caused me to lose my eye, shave off my beard, and become a dervish. Mine is a tale that, if it were engraved with needles at the corner of the eye, would be a warning to those who wish to consider." Then she questioned the second dervish, and he said the same, and questioned the third, and again he replied like the other two. Then they added, "By God, lady, each one of us comes from a different city, and each one of us is the son of a king, a prince sovereign over land and people." The girl turned to the black men and said, "Whoever tells us his tale and explains what has happened to him and what has brought him to our place, let him stroke his head and go,[2] but whoever refuses, strike off his head."

But morning overtook Shahrazad, and she lapsed into silence. Then Dinarzad said to her sister, "What an amazing and entertaining story!" Shahrazad replied, "What is this compared with what I shall tell you tomorrow night if I stay alive!"

THE THIRTY-SEVENTH NIGHT

The following night Dinarzad said to her sister Shahrazad, "Sister, if you are not sleepy, tell us one of your lovely little tales to while away the night." Shahrazad replied, "With the greatest pleasure":

I heard, O King, that after the girl spoke, the first to come forth was the porter, who said, "Mistress, you know that the reason I came to this place was that I was hired as a porter by this shopper, who led me from the vintner to the butcher, and from the butcher to the greengrocer, and from the greengrocer to the fruit vendor, and from the fruit vendor to the dry grocer, then to the confectioner, to the druggist, and finally to this house. This is my tale." The girl replied, "Stroke your head and go." But he replied, "By God, I will not go until I hear the tales of the others."

Then the first dervish came forward and said:

[The First Dervish's Tale]

MY LADY, THE CAUSE of my eye being torn out and my beard being shaved off was as follows. My father was a king, and he had a brother who was also a king and who had a son and a daughter. As the years went by and we grew up, I used to visit my uncle every now and then, staying with him for a month or two and returning to my

---

2. I.e., stroke your head in satisfaction, or in appreciation that you still have it, and go.

father. For between my uncle's son and myself there grew a firm friendship and a great affection. One day I visited my cousin, and he treated me with unusual kindness. He slaughtered for me many sheep, offered me clear wine, and sat with me to drink. When the wine got the better of us, my cousin said, "Cousin, I would like to acquaint you with something that I have been preparing a whole year for, provided that you do not try to hinder me." I replied, "With the greatest pleasure." After he made me take a binding oath, he got up and quickly disappeared, but a while later came back with a woman wearing a cloak, a kerchief, and a headdress, and smelling of a perfume so sweet as to make us even more intoxicated. Then he said, "Cousin, take this lady and go before me to a sepulcher in such and such a graveyard," describing it so that I knew the place. Then he added, "Enter with her into the sepulcher and wait for me there." Unable to question or protest because of the oath I had taken, I took the lady and walked with her until we entered the graveyard and seated ourselves in the sepulcher. Soon my cousin arrived, carrying a bowl of water, a bag of mortar, and an iron adze. He went straight to a tomb, broke it open with the adze, and set the stones to one side. Then he went on digging into the earth of the tomb until he came upon an iron plate, the size of a small door, that covered the length and width of the tomb. He raised the plate, and there appeared below it a vaulting, winding staircase. Then turning to the lady, he said with a sign, "Make your choice," and she went down the staircase and disappeared. Then he turned to me and said, "Cousin, there is one last favor to ask." I asked, "What is it?" He said, "After I descend into this place, place the iron plate and the earth back over us."

But morning overtook Shahrazad, and she lapsed into silence. Then her sister said, "Sister, what an entertaining story!" Shahrazad replied, "What is this compared with what I shall tell you tomorrow night!"

THE THIRTY-EIGHTH NIGHT

The following night Dinarzad said to her sister Shahrazad, "For God's sake, sister, if you are not sleepy, tell us one of your lovely little tales." King Shahrayar added, "Tell us the rest of the story of the king's son." Shahrazad replied, "With the greatest pleasure":

I heard, O happy King, that the first dervish said to the girl:

After I followed his instructions, I returned, suffering from a hangover, and spent the night in one of my uncle's houses, which he had given me to use before he went on a hunting trip. When I woke up in the morning and recalled the events of the previous night, I thought that it was all a dream. Being in doubt, I inquired about my cousin, but no one could tell me anything about him. Then I went to the graveyard and searched for the sepulcher, but I could not find it or remember anything about it. I kept wandering from sepulcher to sepulcher and from tomb to tomb, without stopping to eat or drink, until night set in. I was getting worried about my cousin, and as I wondered where the vaulted staircase led to, I began to recall the events little by little, as one recalls what happens in a dream. Finally I went back to the house, ate a little, and spent a restless night. Having recollected everything he and I did that night, I returned the following morning to the graveyard and wandered about, searching till nightfall, without finding the sepulcher or figuring out a way that might lead me to it. I went back to the graveyard for a third day and a fourth and searched for the sepulcher from early morning till nightfall without success, until I almost lost my sanity with frustration and worry. At last, realizing that I had no other recourse, I resolved to go back to my father's city.

When I arrived there and entered the city gate, I was immediately set upon, beaten, and bound. When I inquired, asking, "What is the cause?" I was told, "The vizier has plotted against your father and betrayed him. Being in league with the entire army, he has killed your father and usurped his power and ordered us to lie in wait for you." Then they carried me off in a swoon and brought me before him. O great lady, it so happened that the vizier and I were bitter enemies, for I was the cause of tearing out one of his eyes. Being fond of shooting with the crossbow, I stood one day on my palace roof, when a bird alighted at the palace of the vizier, who by coincidence also stood on his palace roof. When I shot at the bird, the missile missed him and instead hit the vizier and pierced the corner of his eye, and that was the cause of his grudge against me; therefore, when they brought me before him, he thrust his finger into my eye, gouged it out, and made it ooze over my cheek. Then he bound me, placed me in a chest, and handed me over to my father's swordsman, saying, "Ride your horse, draw your sword, and take this one with you into the wilderness. Then kill him and let the beasts and vultures devour his flesh." The executioner followed the vizier's order and led me into the wilderness. Then he dismounted, taking me out of the chest, and looked at me and was about to kill me. I wept bitterly over what had happened to me until I made him weep with me. Then looking at him, I began to recite the following verses:

My shield I deemed you from the foeman's dart,
But you did prove to be that very dart.
I counted on your aid in all mishaps,
Just as the left hand comes to aid the right.
Stand then as one absolved, away from me,
And let the foes at me their arrows aim,
For if our friendship you cannot maintain,
Between yourself and me there is no claim.

When the executioner heard my verses, he felt pity for me, and he spared me and set me free, saying, "Run with your life and never return to this land, for they will kill you and kill me with you." The poet says:

If you suffer injustice, save yourself,
And leave the house behind to mourn its builder.
Your country you'll replace by another,
But for yourself, you'll find no other self.
Nor with a mission trust another man,
For none is as loyal as you yourself.
And did the lion not struggle by himself,
He would not prowl with such a mighty mane.

Hardly believing in my escape, I kissed his hand and thought that losing my eye was certainly better than dying.

Then I journeyed slowly until I reached my uncle's city. When I went to him and told him about my father's death and the loss of my eye, he said to me, "I too have enough woes, for my son is missing, and I do not know what has happened to him, nor do I have any news about him." Then he wept bitterly, reviving my old grief and arousing my pity. Unable to remain silent, I acquainted him with what his son had done, and he was exceedingly happy and said, "Come and show me the sepulcher." I replied, "By God, uncle, I have lost the way to it, and I no longer know which one it is." He said, "Let us go together." Then he and I went secretly to the graveyard, and when I came to the center, I suddenly recognized the sepulcher and was exceedingly happy at the prospect of finding out what lay below the staircase and what had happened to my cousin. We entered the sepulcher, opened the tomb, and, removing the earth, found the iron plate. My uncle led the way, and we descended about fifty steps, and as we reached the bottom of the staircase, we met a great cloud of smoke that almost blinded our eyes. My uncle cried, "There is no power and no strength, save in God, the Almighty, the Magnificent." Then we saw a hallway, and as we advanced a little, we came to a hall resting on pillars and lighted by very high skylights. We wandered about and saw a cistern in the center, saw large jars and sacks full of flour, grains, and the like, and at the end of the hall saw a bed covered with a canopy. My uncle went up to the bed, and when he lifted the curtain, he found his son and the lady who had gone down with him, lying in each other's arms, but saw that the two had turned to black charcoal. It was as if they had been cast into a raging fire, which burned them thoroughly until they were reduced to charcoal. When my uncle saw this spectacle, he expressed satisfaction and spat in his son's face, saying, "This is your punishment in this world, but there remains your punishment in the world to come." Then he took off his shoe and struck his son, hard on the face.

But morning overtook Shahrazad, and she lapsed into silence. Then her sister Dinarzad said to her, "Sister, what an entertaining story!" Shahrazad replied, "What is this compared with what I shall tell you tomorrow night if I stay alive!"

THE THIRTY-NINTH NIGHT

The following night Dinarzad said to her sister Shahrazad, "Sister, if you are not sleepy, tell us one of your lovely little tales to while away the night." The king added, "Let it be the completion of the first dervish's tale." Shahrazad replied, "With the greatest pleasure":

I heard, O happy King, that the first dervish said to the girl:

My lady, when my uncle struck his son's face with the shoe, as he and the lady lay there in a charred heap, I said to him, "For God's sake, uncle, don't make me feel worse; I feel worried and sorry for what happened to your son; yet as if he has not suffered enough, you strike him on the face with your shoe." He replied, "Nephew, you should know that this son of mine was madly in love with his sister, and I often forbade him from seeing her but went on saying to myself, 'They are only children.' But when they grew up, they did the ugly deed and I heard about it, hardly believing my ears. I seized him and beat him mercilessly, saying, 'Beware, beware of that deed, lest our story spread far and wide even to every remote province and town and you be dishonored and disgraced among the kings, to the end of time. Beware, beware, for this girl is your sister, and God has forbidden her to you.' Then, nephew, I secluded her from him, but the cursed girl was in love with him, for the devil had possessed her

and made the affair attractive in her eyes. When they saw that I had
separated them from each other, he built and prepared this subterranean place, dug up the well, and brought whatever they needed of
provisions and the like, as you see. Then, taking advantage of my
going to the hunt, he took his sister and did what you saw him do.
He believed that he would be enjoying her for a long time and that
the Almighty God would not be mindful of their deed." Then he
wept, and I wept with him. Then he looked at me and said, "You are
my son in his place," and when he thought of what had happened to
his two children, his brother's murder, and the loss of my eye, he
wept again and I wept with him over the trials of life and the misfortunes of this world. Then we climbed out of the tomb and I replaced
the iron plate cover over my cousin and his sister, and without being
detected by anyone, we returned home.

But hardly had we sat down when we heard the sounds of kettle-
drums, little drums, and trumpets, the din of men, the clanking of
bits, the neighing of horses, and the orders to line up for battle,
while the world became clouded with dust raised by the galloping of
horses and the tramping of men. We were bewildered and startled,
and when we asked, we were told that the vizier who had usurped
my father's kingdom had levied his soldiers and prepared his armies,
and taking a host of bedouins[3] into service, had invaded us with
armies like the desert sand, whom no one could count and no one
could withstand. They took the city by surprise, and the citizens,
being unable to oppose them, surrendered the place to the vizier. My
uncle was slain and I escaped to the outskirts of the city, thinking to
myself, "If I fall into the vizier's hands, he will kill me and kill Sayir,
my father's swordsman." My sorrows were renewed and my anxiety
grew, as I pondered over what had happened to my uncle and my
cousins and over the loss of my eye, and I wept bitterly. I asked
myself, "What is to be done? If I show myself in public, the people of
my city and all my father's soldiers will recognize me as they recognize the sun and will try to win favor with the vizier by killing me."
I could think of no way to escape and save my life except to shave my
beard and eyebrows. I did so, changed my clothes for those of a
mendicant, and assumed the life of a dervish. Then I left the city,
undetected by anyone, and journeyed to this country, with the intention of reaching Baghdad, hoping that I might be fortunate to find
someone who would assist me to the presence of the Commander of
the Faithful, the Vice Regent of the Supreme Lord, so that I might
tell him my tale and lay my case before him. I arrived this very night,
and as I stood in doubt at the city gate, not knowing where I should

3. Arab nomads of the desert.

go, this dervish by my side approached me, showing the signs of travel, and greeted me. I asked him, "Are you a stranger?" and when he replied, "Yes," I said, "I too am a stranger." As we were talking, this other dervish by our side joined us at the gate, greeted us, and said, "I am a stranger." We replied, "We are strangers too." Then the three of us walked as night overtook us, three strangers who did not know where to go. But God drove us to your house, and you were kind and generous enough to let us in and help me forget the loss of my eye and the shaving off of my beard.

The girl said to him, "Stroke your head and go." He replied, "By God, I will not go until I hear the tales of the others."

But morning overtook Shahrazad, and she lapsed into silence. Then Dinarzad said, "Sister, what an entertaining story!" Shahrazad replied, "What is this compared with what I shall tell you tomorrow night if the king spares me and lets me live!" The king said to himself, "By God, I shall postpone her execution until I hear the tales of the dervishes and the girls, then have her put to death like the rest."

THE FORTIETH NIGHT

The following night Dinarzad said to her sister Shahrazad, "Sister, if you are not sleepy, tell us one of your lovely little tales." Shahrazad replied, "With the greatest pleasure":

It is related, O happy King, that those who were present marveled at the tale of the first dervish. The caliph said to Ja'far, "In all my life I have never heard a stranger tale." Then the second dervish came forward and said:

[The Second Dervish's Tale]

BY GOD, MY LADY, I was not born one-eyed. My father was a king, and he taught me how to write and read until I was able to read the Magnificent Quran in all the seven readings.[4] Then I studied jurisprudence in a book by al-Shatibi[5] and commented on it in the presence

---

4. A "reading" is a distinct manner of reciting, punctuating, and vocalizing a text of the Quran.
5. Well-known writer on Muslim jurisprudence.

of other scholars. Then I turned to the study of classical Arabic and
its grammar until I reached the height of eloquence, and I perfected
the art of calligraphy until I surpassed all my contemporaries and all
the leading calligraphers of the day, so that the fame of my eloquence
and calligraphic art spread to every province and town and reached
all the kings of the age.

One day the king of India sent my father gifts and rarities worthy
of a king and asked him to send me to him. My father fitted me with
six riding horses and sent me along with the posted couriers. I bade
him good-bye and set out on my journey. We rode for a full month
until one day we came upon a great cloud of dust, and when a little
later the wind blew the dust away and cleared the air, we saw fifty
horsemen who, looking like glowering lions in steel armor . . .

*But morning overtook Shahrazad, and she lapsed into silence. Then
her sister said, "Sister, what an amazing and entertaining story!"
Shahrazad replied, "What is this compared with what I shall tell you
tomorrow night if I stay alive!"*

THE FORTY-FIRST NIGHT

*The following night Dinarzad said, "Sister, if you are not sleepy, tell
us one of your lovely little tales to while away the night." Shahrazad
replied, "Very well":*

I heard, O happy King, that the second dervish, the young son of
the king, said to the girl:

When we looked at them closely, we discovered that they were
highwaymen, and when they saw that we were a small company with
ten loads of goods—these were gifts—they thought that we were
carrying loads of money, drew their swords, and pointed their spears
at us. We signaled to them, saying, "We are messengers to the great
king of India; you cannot harm us." They replied, "We are neither
within his dominions nor under his rule." Then they killed all my
men and wounded me. But while the highwaymen were scrambling
for the gifts that were with us, I escaped and wandered away without
knowing where I was heading or in which direction to go. I was
mighty and became lowly; I was rich and became poor.

*But morning overtook Shahrazad, and she lapsed into silence. Then
her sister said, "What a strange and entertaining story!" Shahrazad*

replied, "What is this compared with what I shall tell you tomorrow
night if the king spares me and lets me live!"

THE FORTY-SECOND NIGHT

The following night Shahrazad said:

I heard, O happy King, that the second dervish said to the girl:

After I was robbed, I fared on, and when night approached, I
climbed the side of a mountain and took shelter for the night in
a cave till daybreak. Then I journeyed till nightfall, feeding on the
plants of the earth and the fruits of the trees, and slept till daybreak.
For a month I traveled in this fashion until I came to a fair, peaceful,
and prosperous city, teeming with people and full of life. It was the
time when winter had departed with its frost and spring had arrived
with its roses. The streams were flowing, the flowers blooming, and
the birds singing. It was like the city of which the poet said:

> Behold a peaceful city, free from fear,
> Whose wonders make it a gorgeous heaven appear.

I felt both glad and sad at the same time, glad to reach the city, sad
to arrive in such a wretched condition, for I was so tired from walking
that I was pale with exhaustion. My face and my hands and feet were
chapped, and I felt overwhelmed with worry and grief. I entered the
city, not knowing where to go, and chanced to pass by a tailor sitting
in his shop. I greeted him, and he returned my greeting, and detecting in me traces of better days, he welcomed me and, inviting me to
sit with him, talked freely to me. He asked me who I was, and I told
him about myself and what had happened to me. He felt sad for me
and said, "Young man, do not reveal your secret to anyone, for the king
of this city is your father's greatest enemy, and there is a blood feud
between them." Then he brought some food, and we ate together.
When it was dark, he gave me a recess next to his in the shop, and
brought me a blanket and other necessities.
    It stayed with him for three days; then he asked me, "Don't you
have any skill with which you can earn your living?" I replied, "I am a
jurist, a man of letters, a poet, a grammarian, and a calligrapher." He
said, "Such skills are not much in demand in our city." I replied, "By
God, I have no other skills, save what I have mentioned to you." He
said, "Gird yourself, take an axe and a rope, and go and hew wood in

the wilderness for your livelihood. But lest you perish, keep your secret to yourself and don't let anyone know who you are, until God sends you relief." Then he bought me an axe and a rope and put me under the charge of certain woodcutters. I went out with them, cut wood all day long, and came back, carrying my bundle on my head. I sold the wood for half a dinar and brought the money to the tailor. In such work I spent an entire year.

One day I went out into the wilderness, and having penetrated deep, I came to a thick patch of trees in a meadow irrigated by running streams. When I entered the patch, I found the stump of a tree, and when I dug around it with my axe and shoveled the earth away, I came upon a ring that was attached to a wooden plank. I raised the plank and beneath it I found a staircase. I descended the steps, and as I reached the bottom, I came to a subterranean palace, solidly built and beautifully designed, a palace so splendid that a better one I have never seen. I walked inside and saw a beautiful girl who looked as radiant as a brilliant pearl or the shining sun and whose speech banished all sorrow and captivated even the sensible and the wise. She was about five feet tall, with a beautiful figure, firm breasts, soft cheeks, and a fair complexion. Through the night of her tresses, her face beamed, and above her smooth bosom, her mouth gleamed, as the poet said of one like her:

> Four things that never meet do here unite
> To shed my blood and to ravage my heart,
> A radiant brow and tresses that beguile
> And rosy cheeks and a glittering smile.

But morning overtook Shahrazad, and she lapsed into silence. Then Dinarzad said, "Sister, what a strange and entertaining story!" Shahrazad replied, "What is this compared with what I shall tell you tomorrow night if the king spares me and lets me live!"

THE FORTY-THIRD NIGHT

The following night, Dinarzad said to her sister Shahrazad, "Sister, if you are not sleepy, tell us one of your lovely little tales to while away the night." Shahrazad replied, "Very well":

I heard, O happy King, that the second young dervish said to the girl:

When the girl looked at me, she asked, "What are you, a man or a demon?" I replied, "I am a human being." She asked, "What brought you here? I have lived in this place for twenty-five years without ever seeing any human being." I said—for I found her words sweet and touching and she captivated my heart—"My good fortune brought me here to dispel my care, or perhaps your good fortune, to banish your sorrow." Then I related to her my mishaps, and she felt sad for me and said, "I too shall tell you my tale. I am the daughter of Afti-marus, king of the Ebony Island. He married me to one of my cousins, but on my wedding night a demon snatched me up, flew away with me, and a while later set me down in this place. Then he brought me all I needed of food and drink and sweets and the like. Once every ten days he comes to spend a night with me—for he took me after he had already a family. If ever I need him for anything by night or by day, I have only to touch the two lines engraved on the doorstep, and he will be with me before I lift my fingers. He has been away for four days, so there remain only six days before he comes again. Would you like to spend five days with me and leave on the day before he arrives?" I replied, "Yes, indeed, 'if only dreams were true!'"

She was pleased and she rose and took me by the hand through an arched doorway that led to a bath. She took off my clothes and took off hers and, entering the bath, she bathed me and washed me. When we came out, she dressed me with a new gown, seated me on a couch, and, giving me a large cup of juice to drink, sat conversing with me for a while. Then she set some food before me, and I ate my fill. Then she offered me a pillow, saying, "Lie down and rest, for you are tired." I lay down and slept, forgetting every care in the world and regaining my energy. When I awoke, some time later, I found her massaging me. I sat up, thanked her, and commended her to God, feeling very much refreshed. Then she asked, "Young man, are you ready to drink?" I replied, "Yes, let us drink," and she went to a cupboard and took out a sealed flask of old wine and, setting a sumptuous table, began to sing the following lines:

> Had we known of your coming, our dark eyes
> Or throbbing heart for you we would have spread,
> Or with our cheeks would have covered the earth,
> So that over the eyelids you might tread.

My love for her began to possess my whole being and my sorrow departed. We sat drinking till nightfall, and I spent with her a delight-ful night the like of which I never spent in all my life. When we awoke, delight followed delight till midday, and I was so drunk that I almost lost consciousness and began to stagger right and left. I said, "My beautiful one, let me carry you up and deliver you from this prison." She laughed and replied, "O my lord, sit still, hold your peace, and be content, for of every ten days only one is for the demon and nine for you." I said—as drink had got the better of me—"This very instant I shall smash the doorstep with the engraved inscription and let the demon come, so that I may kill him, for I am used to killing demons by the tens." When she heard my words, she grew pale and said, "No, for God's sake, don't do it." Then she recited the following lines:

> You, who seek separation, hold your reins,
> For its horses are much too swift and free.
> Hold, for betrayal is the rule of life
> And severance the end of amity.

But in my drunkenness, I kicked the step with my foot.

But morning overtook Shahrazad, and she lapsed into silence. Then Dinarzad said, "What a strange and entertaining story!" Shahrazad replied, "What is this compared with what I shall tell you tomorrow night if the king spares me and lets me live!"

THE FORTY-FOURTH NIGHT

The following night Dinarzad said, "Sister, if you are not sleepy, tell us one of your lovely little tales to while away the night." Shahrazad replied, "Very well":

It is related, O happy King, that the second dervish said to the girl:

As soon as I kicked the step, there was thunder and lightning, and the earth began to tremble and everything turned dark. I became sober at once and cried out to her, "What is happening?" She replied, "The demon is coming. O my lord, get up and run for your life." I fled up the staircase, but in my great terror I left my sandals and my iron axe behind. I had not reached the top when I saw the palace floor split asunder and the demon appear, saying, "What disaster has led you to trouble me like this?" She replied, "My lord, today I felt depressed and took a little wine to lighten my heart. Then I got up to go and relieve myself, but I felt tipsy and fell against the step." The demon cried, "You are lying, you whore," and, looking about, saw my sandals and my axe, and asked, "Whose are these?" She replied, "I have never set eyes on them till this moment. They must have stuck to your clothes and you brought them with you." The demon said, "I will not be deceived by this ruse, you slut." Then he seized her, stripped her naked and, binding her hands and feet to four stakes, proceeded to torture her and make her confess."

O lady, it was not easy for me to hear her cries, but trembling with fear, I climbed the staircase slowly until I was outside. Then I placed the trapdoor as it was before and covered it with earth. I felt very sad and extremely sorry, as I thought of the girl, her beauty, her kindness, and her generous treatment, how she had lived quietly for twenty-five years and how in one night I had brought her this calamity. And when I remembered my father and my country, how life turned against me and I became a woodcutter, and how for a brief moment it befriended me and punished me again, I wept bitterly, blamed myself, and repeated the following verses:

> My fate does fight me like an enemy
> And pursues helpless me relentlessly.
> If once it chooses to treat me kindly,
> At once it turns, eager to punish me.

Then I walked on until I came to my friend the tailor, whom I found most anxiously waiting for me. He was glad to see me and asked, "Brother, where did you stay last night? I was worried about you; praise be to God for your safety." I thanked him for his friendly concern and, retiring to my recess, sat thinking about what had happened to me, blaming myself for my rashness, for had I not kicked the step, nothing would have happened. As I sat, absorbed in such thoughts, my friend the tailor came to me and said, "There is outside an old Persian gentleman, who has your iron axe and your sandals. He had taken them to the woodcutters, saying, 'I went out this morning to answer the call to prayer and stumbled on this axe and these sandals. Take a look at them and tell me to whom they belong and where I may find him.' The woodcutters recognized your axe and told him where to find you, saying, 'This axe belongs to a young man, a foreigner who lives with the tailor.' At this very moment he is sitting at the entrance of the shop. Go to him and take your axe from him." When I heard what he said, I felt faint and turned pale and, while we stood there talking, the floor of my recess split asunder and there emerged the old Persian gentleman, who was that very demon. He had tortured the girl almost to her death, but she did not confess. So he took the axe and the sandals, saying, "If I am truly the son of Satan's daughter, I shall bring you back the owner of the axe." Then he assumed the guise of a Persian gentleman and came to find me. When the ground split asunder and he emerged . . .

But morning overtook Shahrazad, and she lapsed into silence. Then Dinarzad said, "Sister, what a strange and entertaining story!" Shahrazad replied, "What is this compared with what I shall tell you tomorrow night if the king spares me and lets me live!"

THE FORTY-FIFTH NIGHT

The following night Dinarzad said to her sister Shahrazad, "Sister, if you are not sleepy, tell us one of your little tales." Shahrazad replied, "Very well":

It is related, O King, that the second dervish said to the girl:

As soon as the demon emerged, he snatched me up from my recess, soared high in the sky, and flew away with me. When he landed a while later, he kicked the ground with his foot, split it asunder, and, carrying me in a swoon, plunged under the earth and emerged with me in the middle of the palace where I had spent the night. There I saw the girl stripped naked, her limbs tied, and her sides bleeding, and my eyes filled with tears. The demon untied her and, covering her, said, "You slut, isn't it true that this man is your lover?" Looking at me, she replied, "I don't know this man at all and I have never laid eyes on him till this very moment." He said, "Damn you, all this torture, and you refuse to confess!" She said, "I don't know this man, and I cannot tell lies about him and let you kill him." He replied, "If you don't know him, take this sword then and strike off his head." She took the sword and, coming up to me, stood facing me. I signaled her with my eyes, and she understood and winked back, meaning, "Aren't you the one who has brought all this upon us?" I signaled again, "This is the time for forgiveness," and she replied with words written with tears on her cheeks:

> My eyes spoke for my tongue to let him know,
> And love betrayed what I tried to conceal.
> When we last met and shed our thoughts in tears,
> Tongue-tied, I let my eyes my heart reveal.
> He signed with his eyes, and I understood;
> I winked, and he knew what my eyes did say.
> Our eyebrows carried out our task so well,
> As mute we stood and let love have its sway.

Then the girl threw the sword away and stepped back, saying, "How can I strike the neck of one I do not know and be guilty of his blood?" The demon said, "You cannot bear to kill him because he has slept with you. You have suffered all this torture, yet you have not confessed. It is clear that only like feels for and pities like." Then he turned to me and said, "You human being, do you too not know this woman?" I replied, "Who may she be, for I have never laid eyes on her till this very moment?" He said, "Then take this sword and strike her head off, and I will believe that you do not know her and let you go free." I replied, "I will do it," and I took the sword and sprang toward her.

But morning overtook Shahrazad, and she lapsed into silence. Then Dinarzad said, "Sister, what an entertaining story!" Shahrazad replied, "What is this compared with what I shall tell you tomorrow night if I stay alive!"

THE FORTY-SIXTH NIGHT

The following night Dinarzad said to her sister Shahrazad, "Tell us the rest of the story." Shahrazad replied, "Very well":

I heard, O happy King, that the second dervish said to the girl:

When I took the sword and went up to her, she winked at me, meaning, "Bravo! This is how you repay me!" I understood her look and pledged with my eyes, "I will give my life for you." Then we stood for a while, exchanging looks, as if to say:

> Many a lover his beloved tells
> With his eyes' language what is in his heart.
> "I know what has befallen," seems to say,
> And with a glance he does his thoughts impart.
> How lovely are the glances of the eyes,
> How graceful are the eyes with passion fraught.
> One with his looks a lover's message writes,
> Another with his eyes reads what his lover wrote.

I threw the sword away, stepped back, and said, "Mighty demon, if a woman, who is befuddled, thoughtless, and inarticulate, refuses to strike off the head of a man she does not know, how can I, a man, strike off the head of a woman I do not know? I can never do such a deed, even if I have to die for it." The demon replied, "You two are conniving against me, but I am going to show you the result of your misdeeds." Then he took the sword and struck the girl, severing her arm from her shoulder and sending it flying. Then he struck again and severed the other arm and sent it flying. She looked at me, as she lay in the throes of death, and with a glance bade me good-bye. O my lady, at that moment I longed for death, and for a moment

I fell into a swoon. "This is the punishment of those who deceive," said the demon and, turning to me, added, "O human being, it is in our law that if a wife deceives her husband, she is no longer lawful to him, and he must kill her and get rid of her. I snatched this woman away on her wedding night, when she was merely a girl of twelve who knew no man but myself. I used to come to her every ten days in the semblance of a Persian gentleman, to spend a night with her. When I became certain that she had deceived me, I killed her, for she was no longer lawful to me. As for you, even though I am not certain whether you are the culprit, I cannot let you go unharmed. Tell me into what animal you wish me to turn you with my magic, a dog, an ass, or a lion. Do you prefer to be a bird or a beast?" I replied, hoping that he might spare me, "O demon, it is more befitting to you to pardon me, even as the envied pardoned the envier." The demon asked, "And how was that?" and I began to tell him:

[The Tale of the Envious and the Envied]

It is related, O demon, that there lived in a certain city two men who dwelt in adjoining houses separated by a common wall. One of them envied the other, gave him the evil eye, and did his utmost to hurt him. He was so obsessed that his envy grew until he could hardly eat or enjoy the pleasure of sleep. But the envied did nothing but prosper, and the more the envious strove to injure him, the more he throve and flourished. At last the envy and malice of his neighbor came to his attention, and he left the neighborhood and moved to another city, saying, "By God, because of him, I will even depart from this world." There he bought himself a piece of land that had an old irrigation well, built a hermitage that he furnished with straw mats and other necessities, and devoted himself to the worship of the Almighty God. The mendicants began to flock to him from every quarter, and his fame spread throughout the city.

Soon the news reached his envious neighbor, how he had prospered and how even the eminent men of the city called on him. So the neighbor journeyed to that city, and when he entered the hermitage, the envied received him with cheerful greetings, warm welcome, and great respect. Then the envious said; "I would like to acquaint you with something that has caused me to come to you. Let us walk aside in the hermitage, so that I may tell you what it is." The envied got up, and as the envious held him by the hand, they walked to the far end of the hermitage. Then the envious said, "Friend, bid your mendicants enter their cells, for I will not tell you, except in private, so that none may hear us." Accordingly, the envied said to the mendicants, "Retire to your cells," and they did so. Then the envious

said, "Now, as I was telling you, my tale . . ." and he walked with
him slowly until they reached the edge of the old well. Suddenly the
envious pushed the envied and, without being seen by anyone, sent
him tumbling into the well. Then he left the hermitage and went
away, believing that he had killed him.

*But morning overtook Shahrazad, and she lapsed into silence. Then
Dinarzad said, "Sister, what a strange and entertaining story!" Shahrazad
replied, "What is this compared with what I shall tell you tomorrow night
if I stay alive!"*

THE FORTY-SEVENTH NIGHT

*The following night Dinarzad said to her sister Shahrazad, "Sister, if
you are not sleepy, tell us what happened to the envious after he
pushed the envied into the well." Shahrazad replied, "Very well":*

It is related, O King, that the second dervish said to the girl that
he told the demon:

Demon, I heard that the envious threw the envied into the ancient
well. That well happened to be haunted by a group of demons who
caught him and, letting him down little by little, seated him on a
rock. Then they asked each other, "Do you know who this man is?"
and the answer was "No." But one of them said, "This man is the
envied who, flying from the envious, came to live in our city, built
this hermitage, and has ever since delighted us with his litanies and
his recitals of the Quran. But the envious journeyed until he rejoined
him, tricked him, and threw him into this well where you now are. It
so happens that this very night the fame of this man has come to the
attention of the king of this city, and he is planning to visit him tomorrow morning, on account of his daughter." Someone asked him, "What
is the matter with her?" He replied, "She is possessed, for the demon
Maimun ibn-Damdam is madly in love with her, but if this man knew
the remedy, her cure would be as easy as can be." One of them asked,
"What is the remedy?" He replied, "This man has in the hermitage a
black cat with a white spot the size of a dirham at the end of his tail.
If he plucks seven white hairs from the white spot, burns them, and
fumigates her with the smoke, the demon will depart from her head,
never to return, and she will be cured that very instant." O demon,
all of this conversation took place while the envied listened. When
the day dawned, the mendicants came out in the morning and found

the holy man climbing out of the well, and he grew even greater in
their esteem. Then the envied endeavored to look for the black cat
and, when he found it, he plucked seven hairs from the white spot
on its tail and kept them with him.

In the meantime hardly had the sun risen when the king arrived
with his troops. He dismounted with the lords of the realm, bidding
the rest of his troops stand outside. When he entered the hermitage,
the envied welcomed him and, seating him by his side, asked, "Shall
I tell you the cause of your visit?" The king replied, "Yes." The envied
continued: "You have come to visit me with the intention of consulting
me about your daughter." The king said, "O man of God, you're right."
The envied said, "Send someone to fetch her, and God the Almighty
willing, she will recover presently." The king gladly sent for his daughter, and they brought her in, bound and fettered. The envied made her
sit behind a curtain and, taking out the hairs, burned them and fumi-
gated her with the smoke. At that moment he who was in her head
cried out and departed from her, and she instantly recovered her sanity and, veiling her face, asked, "What has happened to me and who
brought me here?" The king felt unequaled joy, and he kissed his
daughter's eyes and kissed the holy man's hand. Then turning to the
great lords of the realm, he asked, "What do you say to this, and what
does he who has cured my daughter deserve?" They answered, "He
deserves to have her for a wife." The king said, "You are right." Then
he married her to him, and the envied became son-in-law to the king.
A short time later the vizier died, and the king asked, "Whom shall
I make vizier?" They answered, "Your son-in-law," and the envied
became vizier. And a short time later, the king also died, and his men
asked each other, "Whom shall we make king?" The answer was, "The
vizier," and the envied became a monarch, a sovereign king.

One day, as he was riding with his equipage . . .

*But morning overtook Shahrazad, and she lapsed into silence. Then
Dinarzad said, "What a strange and entertaining story!" Shahrazad
replied, "What is this compared with what I shall tell you tomorrow
night if the king spares me and lets me live!"*

THE FORTY-EIGHTH NIGHT

*The following night Dinarzad said, "Sister, if you are not sleepy, tell
us what happened to the envious and the envied." Shahrazad replied,
"Very well":*

I heard, O King, that the second dervish said to the girl that he told the demon:

One day, as the envied rode with his royal equipage at the head of his princes, viziers, and lords of the realm, his eyes fell on the envious. He turned to one of his viziers and commanded, "Bring me that man, but do not alarm him or frighten him." The vizier left and came back with the envious neighbor. The king said, "Give him one thousand weights of gold from my treasury, provide him with twenty loads of goods he trades in, and send him with an escort to his own town." Then the envied bade him farewell and went away without reproaching him for what he had done to him.

I said to the demon, "O demon, consider the mercy of the envied on the envious, who had envied him from the beginning, borne him great malice, pursued him, followed him, and thrown him into the well to kill him. Yet the envied did not respond in kind, but instead of punishing the envious, he forgave him and treated him magnanimously." Then, O my lady, I wept until I could weep no more and recited the following verses:

> Pardon my crime, for every mighty judge
> Is used to mercy some offenders show.
> I stand before you guilty of all sins,
> But you the ways of grace and mercy know.
> For he who seeks forgiveness from above,
> Should pardon the offenders here below.

The demon replied, "I will not kill you, but in no way will I pardon you and let you go unharmed. I have spared you from death, but I will put you under a spell." Then he snatched me up and flew with me upward until the earth appeared like a white cloud. Soon he set me down on a mountain and, taking a little dust, mumbled some incantation and sprinkled me with the dust, saying, "Leave your present form and take the form of an ape." At that very instant, I became an ape, and he flew away and left me behind.

When I saw that I was an ape, I wept for myself and blamed life, which is fair to none. Then I descended the mountain and found a vast desert, over which I journeyed for a month until I reached the seashore. As I stood on the shore, looking at the sea, I saw in the offing a ship sailing under a fair wind and cleaving the waves. I went to a tree and, breaking off a branch, began to signal the ship with it, running back and forth and waving the branch to and fro, but being unable to speak or cry out for help, I began to despair. Suddenly the ship turned and began to sail toward the shore, and when it drew near, I found that it was a large ship, full of merchants and laden with spices and other goods. When the merchants saw me, they said to the captain, "You have risked our lives and property for an ape, who brings bad luck with him wherever he goes." One of them said, "Let me kill him." Another said, "Let me shoot him with an arrow." And a third said, "Let us drown him." When I heard what they said, I sprang up and held the hem of the captain's gown like a suppliant, as my tears began to flow over my face. The captain and all the merchants were amazed, and some of them began to feel pity for me. Then the captain said, "Merchants, this ape has appealed to me for protection, and I have taken him under my care. Let none of you hurt him in any way, lest he become my enemy." Then he treated me kindly, and I understood whatever he said and did his bidding, although I could not respond to him with my tongue.

For fifty days the ship sailed on before a fair wind until we came to a great city, vast and teeming with countless people. No sooner had we entered the port and cast anchor than we were visited by messengers from the king of that city. They boarded the ship and said, "Merchants, our king congratulates you on your safe arrival, sends you this roll of paper, and bids each of you write one line on it. For the king's vizier, a man learned in state affairs and a skilled calligrapher, has died, and the king has sworn a solemn oath that he will appoint none in his place, save one who can write as well as he could." Then they handed the merchants a roll of paper, ten cubits long and one cubit wide, and each of the merchants who knew how to write wrote a line. When they came to the end, I snatched the scroll out of their hands, and they screamed and scolded me, fearing that I would throw it into the sea or tear it to pieces, but I signed to them that I wanted to write on it, and they were exceedingly amazed, saying, "We have never yet seen an ape write." The captain said to them, "Let him write what he likes, and if he merely scribbles, I will beat him and chase him away, but if he writes well, I will adopt him as my son, for I have never seen a more intelligent or a better-behaved ape. I wish that my son had this ape's understanding and good manners," Then I held the pen, dipped it in the inkpot, and in Ruqa' script[6] wrote the following lines:

> Time's record of the favors of the great
> Has been effaced by your greater favor.
> Of you your children God will not deprive,
> You, being to grace both mother and father.

6. The scripts named are all calligraphic varieties of the cursive, curvilinear Arabic script.

Then under these, in Muhaqqiq script I wrote the following lines:

> His pen has showered bounty everywhere
> And without favor favored every land.
> Yet even the Nile, which destroys the earth,
> Cannot its ink use with such mighty hand.

And in Raihani script I wrote the following lines:

> I swore, whoever uses me to write,
> By the One, Peerless, Everlasting God,
> That he would never any man deny
> With one of the pen's strokes his livelihood.

Then in Naskhi script I wrote the following lines:

> There is no writer who from death will flee,
> But what his hand has written time will keep.
> Commit to paper nothing then, except
> What you would like on Judgment Day to see.

Then in Thuluth script I wrote the following lines:

> When the events of life our love condemned
> And painful separation was our end,
> We turned to the inkwell's mouth to complain,
> And voiced with the pen's tongue our parting's pain

Then in Tumar script I wrote the following lines:

> When you open the inkwell of your boon
> And fame, let the ink be munificence and grace.
> Write good and generous deeds while write you can;
> Both pen and sword such noble deeds will praise.

Then I handed them the scroll, and they took it back in amazement.

But morning overtook Shahrazad, and she lapsed into silence. Then Dinarzad said, "Sister, what an amazing and entertaining story!" Shahrazad replied, "What is this compared with what I shall tell you tomorrow night if I stay alive!"

THE FORTY-NINTH NIGHT

The following night Dinarzad said, "Sister, tell us the rest of the story." Shahrazad replied, "Very well":

It is related, O happy King, that the second dervish said to the girl:

The messengers took the scroll and returned with it to the king, and when he looked at it, my writing pleased him and he said, "Take this robe of honor and this she-mule to the master of these seven scripts." The men smiled, and seeing that their smiling had made the king angry, they said, "O King of the age and sovereign of the world, the writer of these lines is an ape." The king asked, "Is it true what you say?" They replied, "Yes, by your bounty, the writer is an ape." The king was greatly amazed and said, "I wish to see this ape." Then he dispatched his messengers with the she-mule and the robe, "Dress him with this robe, place him on the she-mule, and bring him to me, together with his master."

As we sat on board, we saw the king's messengers suddenly appear again. They took me from the captain, dressed me with the robe, and, placing me on the she-mule, walked behind me in a procession, which caused a great commotion in the city. Everyone came out, crowding to gaze at me and enjoy the spectacle. By the time I reached the king, the whole city was astir, and the people were saying to each other, "The king has taken an ape for vizier."

When I entered into the presence of the king, I prostrated myself and then stood up and bowed three times. Then I kissed the ground once, before the chamberlains and statesmen and knelt on my knees. Those who were present marveled at my fine manners, most of all the king himself, who said, "This is a wonder." Then he gave permission to his retinue to leave, and everyone left, save for the king, one servant, one little Mamluk,[7] and myself. Then, he ordered a table of food set before him, and motioned to me to eat with him. I rose, kissed the ground before him, and, after I washed my hands seven times, I sat back on my knees and, as good manners require, took only a little to eat. Then I took a pen and an inkwell and over a board wrote the following lines:

> Wail for the crane well-stewed in tangy sauce;
> Mourn for the meat, either well baked or fried;
> Cry for the hens and daughters of the grouse
> And the fried birds, even as I have cried.
> Two different kinds of fish are my desire,

---

7. See n. 2, p. 39.

Served on two loaves of bread, zestful though plain,
While in the pan that sizzles o'er the fire
The eggs like rolling eyes fry in their pain.
The meat when grilled, O what a lovely dish,
Served with some pickled greens; that is my wish.
'Tis in my porridge I indulge at night,
When hunger gnaws, under the bracelets' light.
O soul, be patient, for our fickle fate
Oppresses one day, only to elate.

The king read the verses and pondered. Then they removed the
food, and the butler set before us a choice wine in a glass flagon.
The king drank first and offered me some. I kissed the ground before
him, took a sip, and wrote the following lines over the flagon:

For my confession they burned me with fire
And found that I was for endurance made.
Hence I was borne high on the hands of men
And given to kiss the lips of pretty maid.

When the king read the verses, he marveled and said, "If a man had
such cultivation, he would excel all the men of his time." Then he
set before me a chessboard and with a sign asked, "Do you play?"
I kissed the ground before him and nodded "Yes." Then the two of us
arranged the pieces on the board and played a game, and it was a
draw. We played a second game, and I won. Then we played for the
third time, and I attacked and won again, and the king marveled at
my skill. Once more I took the inkwell and the pen and over the
chessboard wrote the following lines:

Two armies all day long with arms contend,
Bringing the battle always to a head.
But when night's cover on them does descend
The two go sleeping in a single bed.

As the king read these lines, he was overwhelmed with admiration
and delight, and said to the servant, "O Muqbil, go to your lady, Sitt
al-Husn, and tell her that her father the king summons her to come
and look at this strange ape and enjoy this wonderful spectacle."
The eunuch disappeared and came back a while later with the
king's daughter. When she entered and saw me, she veiled her face
and said, "O father, have you lost your sense of honor to such a
degree that you expose me to men?" Astonished, the king asked,
"Daughter, there is no one here, save this little Mamluk, this your
mentor who brought you up, and I your father. From whom do you
veil your face?" She replied, "From this young man who has been

cast under a spell by a demon who is the son of Satan's daughter. He turned him into an ape after he killed his own wife, the daughter of Aftimarus, king of the Ebony Island. This whom you think an ape is a wise, learned, and well-mannered man, a man of culture and refinement." The king was amazed and, looking at me, asked, "Is it true what my daughter said?" I replied with a nod, "Yes." Then he turned to his daughter and asked, "For God's sake, daughter, how did you know that he is enchanted?" She replied, "O father, there was with me from childhood a wily and treacherous old woman who was a witch. She taught me witchcraft, and I copied and memorized seventy domains of magic, by the least of which I could within the hour transport the stones of your city beyond Mount Qaf and beyond the ocean that surrounds the world." The king was amazed and said to his daughter, "O daughter, may God protect you. You have had such a complete power all this time, yet I never knew it. By my life, deliver him from the spell, so that I may make him vizier and marry you to him." She replied, "With the greatest pleasure." Then she took a knife . . .

But morning overtook Shahrazad, and she lapsed into silence. Then Dinarzad said, "Sister, what a strange and entertaining story!" Shahrazad replied, "What is this compared with what I shall tell you tomorrow night, if the king spares me and lets me live!"

THE FIFTIETH NIGHT

The following night Dinarzad said to her sister Shahrazad, "Sister, if you are not sleepy, tell us one of your lovely little tales." Shahrazad replied, "Very well":

I heard, O King, that the second dervish said to the girl:

The king's daughter took a knife engraved with names in Hebrew characters and, drawing a perfect circle in the middle of the palace hall, inscribed on it names in Kufic letters,[8] as well as other talismanic words. Then she muttered charms and uttered spells, and in a short time the world turned dark until we could no longer see anything and thought that the sky was falling on our heads. Suddenly we were

---

8. The rectilinear Arabic script characteristic of the early Qurans.

startled to see the demon descending in the semblance of a lion as big as a bull, and we were terrified. The girl cried, "Get away, you dog!" The demon replied, "You traitor, you have betrayed me and broken the oath. Have we two not taken an oath that neither would cross the other?" She said, "Cursed one, how could I keep a pledge with one like you?" The demon cried, "Then take what you have brought on yourself," and with an open mouth he rushed toward the girl, who quickly plucked a hair from her head and as she waved the hair in the air and muttered over it the hair turned into a keen sword blade with which she struck the lion, cutting him in half. But while the two halves went flying, the head remained and turned into a scorpion. The girl quickly turned into a huge serpent, and the two fought a bitter battle for a long time. Then the scorpion turned into a vulture and flew outside the palace, and the girl changed into an eagle and flew after the vulture. The two were gone for a long time, but suddenly the ground split asunder, and there emerged a piebald tomcat, which meowed, snorted, and snored. He was followed by a black wolf, and the two battled in the palace for a long time, and when the cat saw that he was losing to the wolf, he screamed, turned into a worm, and crept into a pomegranate that was lying beside the fountain. The pomegranate swelled until it was as big as a striped watermelon, and the wolf turned immediately into a snow white rooster. The pomegranate flew in the air and fell on the marble floor of the raised hall, breaking to pieces, and as the seeds scattered everywhere, the rooster fell to picking them. He picked them all, save for one that lay hidden at the edge of the fountain. Then the rooster began to cry and crow, flap his wings, and motion with his beak, as if to ask us, "Are there any seeds left?" But we did not understand, and he let out such a loud shriek that we thought that the palace was falling on our heads. Then the rooster chanced to turn and saw the seed at the edge of the fountain. He rushed to pick it . . .

But morning overtook Shahrazad, and she lapsed into silence. Then Dinarzad said, "Sister, what an amazing and entertaining story!" Shahrazad replied, "What is this compared with what I shall tell you tomorrow night if the king spares me and lets me live!"

THE FIFTY-FIRST NIGHT

The following night Dinarzad said to her sister Shahrazad, "Sister, if you are not sleepy, tell us the rest of the story." Shahrazad replied, "With the greatest pleasure":

I heard, O King, that the second dervish said to the girl:

O lady, the rooster, glad to see the seed, rushed to pick it, when it rolled into the fountain, became a fish, and dove into the water. The rooster turned immediately into a bigger fish and plunged after it, and the two disappeared into the bottom of the fountain for a very long time. Then we heard loud shouts, shrieks, and howls, which made us tremble, and a while later the demon came out as a burning flame, followed by the girl, who was also a burning flame. The demon blew fire and sparks from his mouth, nostrils, and eyes and battled the girl for a long time until their flames engulfed them, and the smoke filled the palace until we were resigned to suffocate, as we stood stricken by fear for our lives, certain of disaster and perdition, and, as the fire raged and became more intense, we cried, "There is no power and no strength save in God, the Almighty, the Magnificent." Suddenly, before we could notice, the demon darted as a flame out of the fire, and with one leap stood in the hall before us, blowing fire in our faces, and the girl pursued him, with a loud cry. As the demon blew fire at us, the sparks flew, and, as I stood there in the semblance of an ape, one of them hit my right eye and destroyed it. A second spark hit the king, burning half of his face, including his beard and chin, and knocking out a row of his teeth. A third spark hit the servant in the chest and killed him instantly. At that moment, as we felt certain of destruction and gave ourselves up for lost, we heard a cry, "God is great, God is great! He has conquered and triumphed; He has defeated the infidel." It was the cry of the king's daughter, who had at that very moment defeated the demon. We looked and saw a heap of ashes.

Then the girl came up to us and said, "Bring me a bowl of water," and crying, "In the name of the Almighty God and His covenant, be yourself again," she sprinkled me with the water, and I shook and stood "a full-fledged man." Then she cried out, "The fire! The fire! O father, I am going to miss you, for I have been wounded by one of the demon's arrows, and I shall not live much longer. Although I am not used to fighting demons, I had no trouble until the pomegranate broke to pieces and I became a rooster. I picked all the seeds but overlooked the one that contained the very soul of the demon. Had I picked it up, he would have died instantly, but I overlooked it. I fought him under the earth and I fought him in the sky, and every time he initiated a domain of magic, I countered with a greater domain and foiled him until I opened the domain of fire. Few open it and survive, but I exceeded him in cunning, and with God's help I killed him. God will protect you in my place." Then she implored again, "The fire! The fire!"

But morning overtook Shahrazad, and she lapsed into silence. Then Dinarzad said, "Sister, what an entertaining story!" Shahrazad replied, "What is this compared with what I shall tell you tomorrow night if I stay alive!"

THE FIFTY-SECOND NIGHT

The following night Dinarzad said to her sister Shahrazad, "Sister, if you are not sleepy, tell us one of your little tales." Shahrazad replied, "Very well":

I heard, O King, that the second dervish said to the girl:

When the king's daughter implored, "The fire! The fire!" her father said, "Daughter, it would be a wonder if I too do not perish, for this your servant died instantly, and this young man has lost an eye." Then he wept and made me weep with him. Soon the girl implored again, "The fire! The fire!" as a spark shot at her legs and burned them, then flew to her thighs, then to her bosom, while she kept crying out, "The fire! The fire!" until all of her body burned to a heap of ashes. By God, mistress, I grieved sorely for her, wishing to have been a dog, an ape, or even a dead man, instead of seeing that girl fight, suffer, and burn to ashes. When the father saw that his daughter was dead, he beat his face, and as I did likewise and cried, the statesmen and the servants came in and were amazed to see two heaps of ashes and the king in a bad way. Then they attended him, and when he regained consciousness and told them about his daughter's calamity, their grief grew greater and they mourned for her for seven days. Then the king bade a vaulted tomb be built over his daughter's ashes, but the demon's ashes he bade be scattered to the wind.

Then the king lay ill for a full month, but when God granted him recovery and he regained his health and his beard grew again, he summoned me before him and said, "Young man, listen to what I have to say to you, and don't disobey me, lest you perish." I replied, "My lord, tell me, for I shall never disobey an order of yours." He said, "We have enjoyed the happiest of lives, safe from misfortunes of the world, until you came with your black face and brought disaster with you. My daughter died for your sake, my servant perished, and I myself barely escaped destruction. You were the cause of all this, for ever since we laid eyes on you, we have been unfortunate. Would that we never saw you, for we have paid for your deliverance with our destruction. Now I want you to leave our city and depart in peace, but if I ever see you again, I will kill you." Then he yelled at me, and I went forth from his presence, dumbfounded and deaf and blind to everything.

Before leaving the city, I went to the bath and shaved off my beard and eyebrows, and when I came out, I put on a black woolen robe and departed. I left the king's capital in dismay and tears, not knowing where I should go, and when I recalled everything that had happened to me, how I had entered the city and in what condition I was leaving it, my grief grew worse. O mistress, every day I ponder my misfortune, the loss of my eye and the death of the two girls. I weep bitterly and repeat these verses:

> The Lord of Mercy sees me stand perplexed,
> Beset by ills, whence came I cannot see.
> I will endure until I patience tire
> And God fulfills my wish by His decree.
> I will endure until God sees that I
> Bitterness worse than aloes have endured.
> Nor would I have tasted such bitterness,
> Had my weak patience such a teste endured.
> Nor would I have endured such bitterness,
> Had my weak patience endured such decree.
> He who says that life is made of sweetness
> A day more bitter than aloes will see.

Then I journeyed through many regions and visited many countries, with the intention of reaching Baghdad and the hope of finding someone there who would help me to the presence of the Commander of the Faithful, so that I might tell him my tale and acquaint him with my misfortune. I arrived here this very night and found this man my brother standing about. I greeted him and asked, "Are you a stranger?" and he replied, "Yes, I am a stranger." Soon this other man joined us and said, "I am a stranger," and we replied, "We too are strangers like you." Then the three of us walked on, as night descended on us, until God brought us to your house. Such then is the cause of losing my eye and shaving off my beard.

The girl said to him, "Stroke your head and go," but he replied, "By God, I will not leave until I hear the tales of the others." Then the black men untied him, and he stood by the side of the first dervish.

But morning overtook Shahrazad, and she lapsed into silence. Then her sister said, "Sister, what a strange and entertaining story!" Shahrazad replied, "What is this compared with what I shall tell you tomorrow night if I stay alive!"

THE FIFTY-THIRD NIGHT

The following night Dinarzad said, "Please, sister, if you are not sleepy, tell us a tale to while away the night." The king added, "Finish the dervishes' tale." Shahrazad replied, "Very well":

It is related, O King, that the third dervish said:

[The Third Dervish's Tale]

O GREAT LADY, the story behind the shaving off of my beard and the loss of my eye is stranger and more amazing than theirs, yet it is unlike theirs, for their misfortune took them by surprise, whereas I knowingly brought misfortune and sorrow upon myself. My father was a great and powerful king, and when he died, I inherited the kingdom. My name is 'Ajib ibn-Khasib, and my city stood on the shore of a vast sea that contained many islands. My fleet numbered fifty merchantmen, fifty small pleasure boats, and one hundred and fifty ships fitted for battle and holy war. One day I decided to go on an excursion to the islands, and I carried with me a month's supply and went there, enjoyed myself, and came back. A while later, driven by a desire to give myself to the sea, I fitted ten ships, carried two months' supply, and set out on my voyage. We sailed for forty days, but on the night of the forty-first, the wind blew from all directions, the sea raged with fury, buffeting our ships with huge waves, and a dense darkness descended upon us. We gave ourselves up for lost and said, "'Even if he escapes, the foolhardy deserves no praise.'" We prayed to the Almighty God and implored and supplicated, but the blasts continued to blow and the sea continued to rage till dawn. Then the wind died down, the waves subsided, and the sea became calm and peaceful, and when the sun shone on us, the sea lay before us like a smooth sheet.

Soon we came to an island, where we landed and cooked and ate some food. We rested for two days and we set out again and sailed for ten days, but as we sailed, the sea kept expanding before us and the land kept receding behind us. The captain was puzzled and said to the lookout man, "Climb to the masthead and look." The lookout man climbed, and after he looked for a while, came down and said, "I looked to my right and saw nothing but sky and water, and I looked to my left and saw something black looming before me. That is all I saw." When the captain heard what the lookout man said, he threw his turban to the deck, plucked out his beard, beat his face, and said, "O King, I tell you that we are all going to perish. There is no power and no strength save in God, the Almighty, the

Magnificent," and he began to weep and made us weep with him. Then we said to him, "Captain, explain the matter." He replied, "My lord, we lost our course on the night of the storm, and we can no longer go back. By midday tomorrow, forced by the currents, we will reach a black mountain of a metal called the magnetic stone. As soon as we sail below the mountain, the ship's sides will come apart and every nail will fly out and stick to the mountain, for the Almighty God has endowed the magnetic stone with a mysterious virtue that makes the iron love it. For this reason and because of the many ships that have been passing by for a long time, the mountain has attracted so much iron that most of it is already covered with it. On the summit facing the sea, there is a dome of Andalusian brass,[9] supported by ten brass pillars, and on top of the dome there is a brass horse with a brass horseman, bearing on his breast a lead tablet inscribed with talismans. O King, it is none but this rider who destroys the people, and they will not be safe from him until he falls from his horse." Then, O my lady, the captain wept bitterly, and certain that we would perish, we too wept for ourselves with him. We bade each other good-bye, and each of us charged his friend with his instructions, in case he was saved.

We never slept a wink that night, and in the morning we began to approach the magnetic mountain, so that by midday, forced by the currents, we stood below the mountain. As soon as we arrived there, the planks of the ship came apart, and the nails and every iron part flew out toward the mountain and stuck together there. Some of us drowned and some escaped, but those who did escape knew nothing about the fate of the others. As for me, O my lady, God spared me that I might suffer what He had willed for me of hardship and misery. I climbed on one of the planks of the ship, and it was thrown immediately by the wind at the foot of the mountain. There I found a path leading to the summit, with steps carved out of the rock.

But morning overtook Shahrazad, and she lapsed into silence. Then Dinarzad said, "Sister, what a strange and entertaining story!" Shahrazad replied, "What is this compared with what I shall tell you tomorrow night if I stay alive!"

---

9. In this context a reference not to the southern region of contemporary Spain, Andalusia, but rather to the geographical territory know to the classical Islamic world as "Al-Andalus," i.e., the entire Iberian Peninsula, including both Spain and Portugal.

THE FIFTY-FOURTH NIGHT

The following night Dinarzad said to her sister Shahrazad, "Please, sister, if you are not sleepy, tell us the rest of the story of the third dervish." Shahrazad replied, "Very well":

O my lord, I heard that the third dervish said to the girl:

When I saw the path on the side of the mountain, I invoked the name of the Almighty God, hung against the rock, and began to climb little by little. And the Almighty God bade the wind be still and helped me with the ascent, so that I reached the summit safely and went directly to the dome. Glad at my safe escape, I entered the dome, performed my ablutions, and prayed, kneeling down several times in thanksgiving to the Almighty God for my safety. Then I fell asleep under the dome overlooking the sea and heard in a dream a voice saying, "O 'Ajib, when you wake from your sleep, dig under your feet, and you will find a brass bow and three lead arrows inscribed with talismans. Take the bow and arrows and shoot at the horseman to throw him off the horse and rid mankind of this great calamity. When you shoot at him, he will fall into the sea, and the horse will drop at your feet. Take the horse and bury it in the place of the bow. When you do this, the sea will swell and rise until it reaches the level of the dome, and there will come to you a skiff carrying a man of brass (a man other than the man you will have thrown), holding in his hands a pair of paddles. Ride with him, but do not invoke the name of God. He will row you for ten days until he brings you to the Sea of Safety. Once there, you will find those who will convey you to your native land. All this will be fulfilled, providing that you do not invoke the name of God."

Then I awoke and eagerly sprang up to do the voice's bidding. I shot at the horseman, and he fell from the horse into the sea, while the horse dropped at my feet, and when I buried the horse in the place of the bow, the sea swelled and rose until it came up to me. Soon I saw a skiff in the offing, coming toward me, and I praised and thanked the Almighty God. When the skiff came up to me, I saw there a man of brass, bearing on his breast a lead tablet inscribed with names and talismans. I climbed into the skiff without uttering a word, and the boatman rowed with me through the first day and the second and on to the ninth, when I happily caught sight of islands, hills, and other signs of safety. But in my excess of joy, I praised and glorified the Almighty God, crying, "There is no god but God." No sooner had I done that than the skiff turned upside down and sank, throwing me into the sea. I swam all day until my shoulders were

numb with fatigue and my arms began to fail me, and when night
fell and I was in the middle of nowhere, I became resigned to drown.
Suddenly there was a violent gust of wind, which made the sea
surge, and a great wave as tall as a mountain swept me and with one
surge cast me on dry land; for God had willed to preserve my life. I
walked ashore, wrung out my clothes, and spread them to dry. Then
I slept the whole night.

In the morning I put on my clothes and went to scout and see
where I was. I came to a cluster of trees, circled around them, and as
I walked further, I found out that I was on a small island in the
middle of the sea. I said, "There is no power and no strength save in
God, the Almighty, the Magnificent," and while I was thinking about
my situation, wishing that I was dead, I suddenly saw in the distance
a ship with human beings on board, making for the island. I climbed
a tree and hid among the branches. Soon the ship touched land, and
there came ashore ten black men, carrying shovels and baskets.
They walked on until they reached the middle of the island. Then
they began to dig into the ground and to shovel the earth away until
they uncovered a slab. Then they returned to the ship and began to
haul out sacks of bread and flour, vessels of cooking butter and
honey, preserved meat, utensils, carpets, straw mats, couches, and
other pieces of furniture—in short, all one needs for setting up
house. The black men kept going back and forth and descending
through the trapdoor with the articles until they had transported
everything that was in the ship. When they came out of the ship
again, there was a very old man in their middle. Of this man nothing
much was left, for time had ravaged him, reducing him to a bone
wrapped in a blue rag through which the winds whistled east and
west. He was like one of whom the poet said:

> Time made me tremble; ah! how sore that was
> For with his might does time all mortals stalk.
> I used to walk without becoming tired;
> Today I tire although I never walk.

The old man held by the hand a young man who was so splendidly
handsome that he seemed to be cast in beauty's mold. He was like
the green bough or the tender young of the roe, ravishing every heart
with his loveliness and captivating every mind with his perfection.
Faultless in body and face, he surpassed everyone in looks and inner
grace, as if it was of him that the poet said:

> With him to make compare Beauty they brought,
> But Beauty hung his head in abject shame.
> They said, "O Beauty, have you seen his like?"
> Beauty replied, "I have ne'er seen the same."

My lady, they walked until they reached the trapdoor, went down, and were gone for a long time. Then the old man and the black men came out without the young man and shoveled the earth back as it was before. Then they boarded the ship, set sail, and disappeared.

I came down from the tree and, going to the spot they had covered, began to dig and shovel away. Having patiently cleared the earth away, I uncovered a single millstone, and when I lifted it up, I was surprised to find a winding stone staircase. I descended the steps, and when I came to the end, I found myself in a clean, white-washed hall, spread with various kinds of carpets, beddings, and silk stuffs. There I saw the young man sitting on a high couch, leaning back on a round cushion, with a fan in his hand. A banquet was set before him, with fruits, flowers, and scented herbs, as he sat there all alone. When he saw me, he started and turned pale, but I greeted him and said, "My lord, set your mind at ease, for there is nothing to fear. I am a human being like you, my dear friend, and like you, the son of a king. God has brought me to you to keep you company in your loneliness. But tell me, what is your story, and what causes you to dwell under the ground?"

But morning overtook Shahrazad, and she lapsed into silence. Then Dinarzad said, "Sister, what a strange and entertaining story!" Shahrazad replied, "What is this compared with what I shall tell you tomorrow night if I stay alive!"

THE FIFTY-FIFTH NIGHT

The following night Dinarzad said to her sister Shahrazad, "Please, sister, if you are not sleepy, tell us the rest of the story of the king's son and the young man under the ground." Shahrazad replied, "With the greatest pleasure":

I heard, O King, that the third dervish said to the girl:

My lady, when I asked the young man to tell me his story, and he was assured that I was of his kind, he rejoiced and regained his composure. Then he made me draw near to him and said, "O my brother, my case is strange and my tale is amazing. My father is a very wealthy jeweler, who deals even with kings and who has many black and white slaves as well as traders who travel on ships to trade for him. But he was not blessed with a child. One night he dreamt that he was going to have a son who would be short-lived, and he woke up in the morning, feeling depressed. My mother happened to conceive on the following night, and my father noted the date of her conception. When the months passed and her time came, she gave birth to me, and my father was exceedingly happy. Then the astrologers and wise men, noting my birth date, read my horoscope and said, 'Your son will live fifteen years, after which there will be a conjunction of the stars, and if he can escape it, he will live. For there stands in the salty sea a mountain called the magnetic mountain, on top of which stands a brass horseman riding on a brass horse and holding in his mouth a lead tablet. Fifty days after this horseman falls from the horse, your son will die, and his killer will be the man who will have thrown the horseman off the horse, a man named 'Ajib, son of King Khasib.' My father was stricken with grief. But he raised me and educated me as the years went by until I was fifteen. Ten days ago, the news reached my father that the brass horseman has been thrown into the sea by a man called King 'Ajib, son of King Khasib. When my father heard the news, he wept bitterly at our impending separation and became like a madman. Then for fear that 'Ajib, son of King Khasib, would kill me, my father built me this house under the ground and brought me in the ship with everything I need for the duration of fifty days. Ten days have already passed, and there remain only forty days until the conjunction of the stars is over and my father comes back to take me home. This is my story and the cause of my loneliness and isolation."

My lady, when I heard his narrative and strange tale, I said to myself, "I am the one who overthrew the brass horseman, and I am 'Ajib, son of King Khasib, but by God, I will never kill him." Then I said to him, "O my lord, may you be spared from death and safe from harm. God willing, there is nothing to worry about or fear. I will stay with you to serve you and entertain you these forty days. I will help you and go home with you, and you in turn will help me to return to my native land, and God will reward you." My words pleased him, and I sat to chat with him and entertain him.

When night came, I got up and, lighting a candle, I filled and lit three oil lamps. Then I offered him a box of sweets, and after we both ate and savored some, we sat and chatted most of the night. When he fell asleep, I covered him, and then I too lay down and slept. When I woke up in the morning, I heated some water for him and gently woke him up, and when he awoke, I brought him the hot water, and he washed his face and thanked me saying, "God bless you, young man. By God, when I escape the man who is called 'Ajib, son of Khasib, and God saves me from him, I will make my father reward you and grant you every favor." I replied, "May all your days be free from harm, and may God set my appointed day before yours!" Then I offered him something to eat, and after the two of us ate I rose and cut pieces of wood for checkers and set the pieces on the checkerboard. We diverted and amused ourselves, playing and eating and drinking till nightfall. Then I rose, lit the lamps, and offered him some sweets, and after we ate and savored some, we sat and chatted, then went to sleep.

My lady, in this way we passed many days and nights, and I became an intimate friend of his, felt a great affection for him, and forgot my cares and sorrows. I said to myself, "The astrologers lied when they told his father, 'Your son will be killed by one called 'Ajib, son of Khasib,' for by God, this is I and in no way will I kill him," and for thirty-nine days I kept serving him, entertaining him, and carousing with him through the night. On the night of the fortieth day, feeling glad at his safe escape, he said, "Brother, I have now completed forty days. Praise be to God who has saved me from death by your blessed coming. By God, I shall make my father reward you and send you to your native land. But, brother, kindly heat some water for me, so that I may wash my body and change my clothes." I replied, "With the greatest pleasure." Then I rose, heated some water, and took the young man into a little room where I gave him a good bath and put on him fresh clothes. Then I spread for him a high bed, covered with a leather mat, and there he lay down to rest, tired from his bath. He said to me, "Brother, cut me up a water-melon and sweeten the juice with sugar." I rose and, bringing back a fine watermelon, set it on a platter, saying, "My lord, do you know where the knife is?" He replied, "Here it is, on the high shelf over my head." I sprang up and, reaching over him in haste, drew the knife from the sheath, and as I stepped back, I slipped on the leather mat, as had been foreordained, and fell prostrate on the young man, and the knife, which was in my hand, pierced his heart and killed him instantly. When I saw that he was dead and realized that it was I who had killed him, I let out a loud scream, beat my face, tore my clothes, and cried, "O people, O God's creatures, there remained for this young man only one day out of the forty, yet he still met his death at my hand. O God, I ask for your forgiveness, wishing that I had died before him. These my afflictions I suffer, draught by bitter draught, 'so that God's will may be fulfilled.'"

But morning overtook Shahrazad, and she lapsed into silence. Then Dinarzad said, "What a strange and entertaining story!" Shahrazad replied, "What is this compared with what I shall tell you tomorrow night if I stay alive!"

THE FIFTY-SIXTH NIGHT

The following night Dinarzad said to her sister Shahrazad, "Sister, if you are not sleepy, tell us the rest of the story of the third dervish." Shahrazad replied, "With the greatest pleasure":

I heard, O King, that the third dervish said to the girl:

My lady, when I was sure that I had killed him, as the God above had foreordained, I rose and, ascending the stairs, replaced the trap- door and covered it with earth. Then I looked toward the sea and saw the ship that had brought him, cleaving the waters toward the island to fetch him. I said to myself, "The moment they come and see their boy slain and find that I am his slayer, they will surely kill me." I headed toward a nearby tree and, climbing it, hid among the branches, and hardly had I done so when the ship reached the island and touched the shore, and the black servants came out with the old father of the young man I had killed. They came to the spot, and when they removed the earth, they were surprised to find it soft. They went down and found the young man lying down, with his face still glowing after the bath, dressed in clean clothes and the knife deep in his heart. When they examined him and found that he was dead, they shrieked, beat their faces, wept, wailed, and invoked awful curses on the murderer. His father fell into such a deep swoon that the black servants thought that he was dead. At last he came to himself, and they wrapped the young man in his clothes and carried him up, together with the old man. Then one of the slaves went and came back with a seat covered with silk, and they carried the old man, laid him there, and sat by his head. All this took place under the tree in which I hid, watching everything they did and listening to everything they said. My heart felt hoary before my head turned gray because of the afflictions, misfortunes, calamities, and sorrows I had suffered. O my lady, the old man remained in a swoon till close to sunset. When he came to himself, looked at his son, and recalled what had happened—that what he feared had come to pass—he wept, beat his face, and recited the following verses:

> By my life, hurry; they have gone away,
> And my tears from my eyes profusely flow.
> Their resting place is far, O far away;
> What shall I say of them, what shall I do?
> I wish that I had never seen their sight.
> Helpless I stand and no solution know.
> Comfort and consolation can I find
> When burning sorrow sets my heart aglow?

O luck, off with me to their dwelling place;
Cry out to them about my tears that flow
They died and left my heart with burning pain,
The fire that in the loving breast did glow.
I wish that death would take me to their place;
Forever lasts the bond between us two.
For God's sake, luck, be careful with our fate,
Our pending union, careful be and slow.
How blessed we lived together in one home
A life of bliss that did no hindrance know
Until with parting's arrow we were shot,
And who can of such arrows bear the blow?
By death was felled the noblest of the tribe,
The age's pearl, with beauty on his brow.
I mourned or silently I seemed to say,
"I wish that death had not hastened the blow.
On me and mine did envy fix his eye,
O son, I'd have given my life for you.
How can I meet you soon, my only one,
My son, for whom I would my soul bestow?
Your gifts you lavished like the bounteous moon,
And like the moon your fame did rise and grow.
If moon I call you, no, the moon goes down,
And if I call you sun, the sun sinks low.
O you, whose beauties were on every tongue,
You whom the virtues did with grace endow,
For you I will forever grieve and mourn;
No other love but you I'll ever know.
Longing for you your father has consumed,
But helpless now he stands since death felled you.
Some evil eyes on you have had their feast,
Would they were pierced or black and blind did grow."

Then the old man took a breath, and with a deep sigh his soul left his body. The black servants shrieked and, throwing dust on their heads and faces, wailed and cried bitterly. Then they carried the old man and his son to the ship and laid them down side by side. Soon they set sail and vanished from my sight. Then I descended from the tree and went back to the underground dwelling. When I entered, I saw some of the young man's belongings, which reminded me of him, and I repeated the following verses:

I see their traces and with longing pine
In their empty dwelling, and my tears flow.
And Him who has their loss decreed I beg,
That He may on me their return bestow.

But morning overtook Shahrazad, and she lapsed into silence. Then her sister said, "Sister, what a strange and entertaining story!" Shahrazad replied, "What is this compared with what I shall tell you tomorrow night if I stay alive!"

THE FIFTY-SEVENTH NIGHT

The following night Dinarzad said to her sister Shahrazad, "If you are not sleepy, tell us the rest of the dervish's story." Shahrazad said:

I heard, O King, that the third dervish said to the girl:

My lady, for a month I lived on the island, spending my day in the open and my night in the underground hall, until one day I noticed that the water on the west side of the island was receding little by little. By the end of the month dry land appeared on the east side, and I felt happy and certain of my safety. I waded through the shallow water, and when I reached permanent dry land, I saw nothing but sand as far as the eye can see. Then I noticed a great fire raging in the distance, and I gathered my energy and braved the sand toward the fire, saying to myself, "Someone must surely have kindled such a fire, and there perhaps is where I can find help," and I repeated the following verses:

> Perhaps my fate will his own bridle turn
> And bring good fortune, O my fickle fate,
> Replacing past ills with present good deeds,
> My needs to answer and my hopes elate.

When I drew near, I found out that the fire was in reality a palace overlaid with copper plates that, as the sun shone on them, glowed and from a distance appeared like a fire. I was glad to see the palace and sat down to rest, but hardly had I done so when I was approached by ten neatly dressed young men accompanied by an old man, and I was astonished to see that each young man was blind in the right eye, and marveled at this coincidence. When they saw me, they greeted me, delighted to see me, and when they asked me about myself, I told them about my misfortunes. Marveling at my tale, they took me into the palace, where I saw ranged around the hall ten couches, each with blue bedding and blue coverlet, with a smaller couch in the middle, covered likewise in blue. We entered and each young man took his seat on a couch, and the old man seated himself on the smaller couch in the middle, saying to me, "Young man, sit down on the floor and do not inquire about our situation or the loss of our eyes." Then he rose and one by one set before each of them his own food and did the same for me. After we ate, he offered us wine, each in his own cup, and they sat to carouse and ask me about my extraordinary case and strange adventures, and I told them my tale until most of the night was gone. Then the young men said to the old man, "Old man, will you give us our due, for it is time to go to bed?" The old man rose, entered a chamber, and came back, carrying on his head ten trays, each covered with a blue cover. He set a tray before each young man and, lighting ten candles, stuck one on each tray. Then he drew off the covers, and there appeared on each tray nothing but ashes, powdered charcoal, and kettle soot. Then, rolling up their sleeves, every young man blackened his face and smeared his clothes with soot and ashes, beat his breast and face, and wept and wailed, crying out again and again, "'We would be sitting pretty but for our curiosity.'" They carried on like this until it was close to sunrise. Then the old man rose and heated some water for them, and the young men ran, washed themselves, and put on clean clothes.

My lady, when I saw what the young men had done and how they had blackened their faces, I was filled with bewilderment and curiosity and forgot my own misfortunes. Unable to remain silent, I asked them, "What brought this on, after we frolicked and enjoyed ourselves? You seem, God be praised, perfectly sane, and such actions befit only madmen. I ask you by all that is dearest to you to tell me your tale and the cause of losing your eyes and smearing your faces with soot and ashes." They turned to me and said, "Young man, don't let our youth and our behavior deceive you. It is better for you not to ask." Then they laid out some food, and we began to eat, but my heart was still on fire and I burned with curiosity to find out the cause of their action, especially after having eaten and drunk with them. Then we sat to converse until late afternoon, and when it got dark, the old man offered us wine, and we sat drinking till past midnight. Then the young men said, "Give us our due, old man, for it is time to go to bed." The old man rose, disappeared, then came back a while later with the same trays, and the young men repeated what they had done the previous night.

My lady, to make a long story short, I stayed with them for a full month, and every night they did the same thing and washed themselves early in the morning, while I watched, marveling at their action, until my curiosity and my anxiety increased to the point that I was no longer able to eat or drink. At last I said to them, "Young men, if you don't relieve me and tell me why you blacken your faces and repeat, 'We would be sitting pretty but for our curiosity,' let me relieve myself of such sights by leaving you and going home, for as the saying goes, 'Better for me and meet to see you not, for if the eye sees nought, the heart grieves not.'" When they heard my words, they came up to me and said, "Young man, we have kept our secret from you only out of pity for you, so that you would not suffer what we have suffered." I replied, "You must tell me." They said, "Young man, listen to our advice and don't ask, lest you become one-eyed like us." I repeated, "I must know the secret." They replied, "Young man, when you find out the secret, remember that we will no longer harbor you nor let you stay with us again."

Then they fetched a ram, slaughtered it, skinned it, and made the skin into a sack. Then they said, "Take this knife and get into the sack, and we shall sew you up in it. Then we shall go away and leave you alone. Soon a bird called Rukh[1] will pick you up with his talons, fly with you high in the air for a while; then you will feel that he has set you down on a mountain and moved away from you. When you feel that the bird has done so, rip the skin open with this knife and come out, and when the bird sees you, he will fly away. Proceed immediately and walk for half a day, and you will see before you a towering palace, built with sandal- and aloewood and covered with plates of red gold, studded with emeralds and all kinds of precious stones. Enter the palace, and you will have your wish, for we have all entered that palace, and that was the cause of losing our eyes and blackening our faces. It would be too tedious to tell you the whole story, for each of us has his own tale for losing his right eye."

But morning overtook Shahrazad, and she lapsed into silence. Then Dinarzad said, "Sister, what a strange and entertaining story!" Shahrazad replied, "What is this compared with what I shall tell you tomorrow night if I stay alive!"

THE FIFTY-EIGHTH NIGHT

The following night Dinarzad said to her sister Shahrazad, "Please, sister, if you are not sleepy, tell us the rest of the story of the third dervish." Shahrazad replied, "With the greatest pleasure":

It is related, O King, that King 'Ajib, the third dervish, said:

When the young men finished their explanation, they let me into the skin sack, sewed me up, and returned to the palace. Soon I felt

---

1. The phoenix, a mythological bird.

the white bird approach, and snatching me up with his talons, he flew away with me for a while and set me down on the mountain. I ripped the skin open and came out, and when the bird saw me, he flew away. I proceeded immediately to walk until I reached the palace and found it to be exactly as they had described it. The door stood open, and when I entered, I found myself in a spacious and lovely hall as vast as a playground. It was surrounded by forty chambers with doors of sandal- and aloewood, covered with plates of red gold and graced with silver handles. At the far end of the hall, I saw forty girls, sumptuously dressed and lavishly adorned. They looked like moons, so lovely that none could tire of gazing on them. When they saw me, they said in one voice, "O lord, welcome, O master, welcome! and good cheer to you, lord! We have been expecting one like you for months. Praised be God who has sent us one who is as worthy of us as we are of him." Then they raced toward me and made me sit on a high couch, saying, "This day, you are our lord and master, and we are your maids and servants, at your beck and call." Then while I sat marveling at their behavior, they rose, and some of them set food before me; others warmed water and washed my hands and feet and changed my clothes; others mixed juice and gave me to drink; and they all gathered around me, joyful at my coming. Then they sat down to converse with me and question me till nightfall.

But morning overtook Shahrazad, and she lapsed into silence. Then Dinarzad said, "Sister, what a strange and entertaining story!" Shahrazad replied, "What is this compared with what I shall tell you tomorrow night if the king spares me and lets me live!"

THE FIFTY-NINTH NIGHT

The following night Dinarzad said to her sister Shahrazad, "Sister, if you are not sleepy, tell us the rest of the story." Shahrazad replied, "Very well":

It is related, O King, that the third dervish said to the girl:

My lady, the girls sat around me, and when night came, five of them rose and set up a banquet with plenty of nuts and fragrant herbs. Then they brought the wine vessels and we sat to drink, with the girls sitting all around me, some singing, some playing the flute, the psalter, the lute, and all other musical instruments, while the bowls and cups went round. I was so happy that I forgot every sorrow in the world, saying to myself, "'This is the life; alas, that it is fleeting.'" I enjoyed myself with them until most of the night was gone and we were drunk. Then they said to me, "O our lord, choose from among us whomever you wish to spend this night with you and not return to be your bedfellow again until forty days will have passed." I chose a girl who had a lovely face and dark eyes, with black hair, joining brows, and a mouth with slightly parted teeth. Perfect in every way, like a willow bough or a stalk of sweet basil, her beauty struck the eye and bewildered the mind. She was like the one of whom the poet said,

> She bent and swayed like a ripe willow bough,
> O more lovely, sweet, and delicious sight!
> She smiled and her glittering mouth revealed
> The flashing stars that answered light with light.
> She loosened her black tresses, and the morn
> Became a dusky, black, and darkling night,
> And when her radiant face shone in the dark,
> From east to west the gloomy world turned bright.
> 'Tis foolish to compare her to a roe;
> How can such fledgling thing such beauties show,
> Such lovely body, such honeydew lips,
> Such sweet nectar to drink, such joy to know,
> Such wide eyes that with the arrows of love
> The tortured victim pierce; how can the roe?
> I loved her madly like a pagan boy,
> No wonder when with love one is laid low.

That night I slept with her and spent the best of nights.

But morning overtook Shahrazad, and she lapsed into silence. Then her sister said, "Sister, what a strange and entertaining story!" Shahrazad replied, "What is this compared with what I shall tell you tomorrow night if I stay alive!"

THE SIXTIETH NIGHT

The following night Dinarzad said to her sister Shahrazad, "Please, sister, tell us the rest of the story of the third dervish." Shahrazad replied, "Very well":

I heard, O King, that the third dervish said to the girl:

When it was morning, the girls took me to a bath in the palace, and after they bathed me, they dressed me in fine clothes. Then they served food, and after we ate they served wine, and as the cup was passed around, we drank into the night. Then they said, "Choose from among us whomever you wish to spend the night with; we are your maids, awaiting your command." I chose a girl with a lovely face and a soft body, like her of whom the poet said:

> I saw two caskets on her bosom fair,
> Shielded with musk seals from lovers' embrace.
> Against assault she guarded them with darts
> And arrowy glances from her lovely face.

I spent with her a lovely night, and when morning came, I bathed and put on new clothes.

My lady, to make a long story short, for a full year I lived with them a carefree life, eating and drinking, carousing, and spending every night with one of them. But one day, at the beginning of the new year, they began to wail and cry, bidding me farewell, clinging to me, and weeping. Amazed at their behavior, I asked, "What is the matter, for you are breaking my heart?" They replied, "We wish that we had never known you, for we had lived with many men but never met one more pleasant than you. May God never deprive us of you," and they wept. I asked, "Why do you weep, for to me your tears are gall?" They replied with one voice, "The reason is our separation from you, of which none other than you yourself is the cause. If you listen to us, we will not be separated, but if you disobey us, we will. Our hearts tell us that you will not obey and that it will happen, and this is the cause of our weeping." I said, "Explain the matter." They replied, "Our lord and master, we are the daughters of kings, and we have lived together here for many years. It has been our custom to go away once a year for forty days and return to live here for the rest of the year, eating and drinking and taking our pleasure and enjoying ourselves here. Now this is how you will disobey us. We are about to leave for forty days. We commit to you now all the keys to this palace, which contains one hundred chambers. Eat and drink and enjoy looking around in every chamber, for each one you open will occupy you a full day, but there is one chamber you must never open or even approach, for it is its opening that will cause our separation. You have ninety-nine chambers to open and to enjoy looking at what is in them as you please, but if you open the one with the door of red gold, that will cause our separation."

But morning overtook Shahrazad, and she lapsed into silence. Then Dinarzad said, "Sister, what a strange and entertaining story!" Shahrazad replied, "What is this compared with what I shall tell you tomorrow night if I stay alive!"

THE SIXTY-FIRST NIGHT

The following night Shahrazad said:

I heard, O happy King, that the third dervish said to the girl:

My lady, the forty girls said, "O our lord, the cause of our separation is in your hand. For God's sake and for our sake, enjoy looking
into all ninety-nine chambers, but don't open the hundredth, lest we
be separated. Be patient for forty days, and we shall come back to
you." Then one of them came up to me, embraced me, wept, and
repeated the following verses:

> When she drew near to bid adieu, her heart
> Burning with love and longing in her breast,
> Her tears and mine, wet pearls and carnelians,
> A necklace made for her and came to rest.

I bid her farewell, saying, "By God, I will never open that door."
Then the girls left, shaking at me admonishing fingers.
When they departed and I was left alone in the palace, I said to
myself, "By God, I will never open that door and never cause our separation." Then I went and opened the first chamber, and when I
entered, I found myself in a garden with streams, trees, and abundant
fruits. It was a garden like Paradise, with tall trees, intertwining
branches, ripe fruits, singing birds, and running waters. Pleased with
the sight, I walked through the trees, enjoying the perfume of the
flowers and the song of the birds, which hymned together the glory of
the Almighty One. I saw apples like those of which the poet said:

> Two colors, in one apple joining, seemed
> Two cheeks in the embrace of love's desire,
> Two cheeks that, as from sleep they startled stood,
> One yellow turned with fright, one burned with fire.

And I saw pears sweeter than sugar and rosewater and more aromatic than musk and ambergris and saw quinces like those of which
the poet said:

> The quince has gathered every pleasing taste,
> Thereby the queen of fruits she has been crowned.
> Her taste is wine, a waft of musk her scent.
> Her hue is gold, her shape, like the moon, round.

And I saw plums so lovely that they dazzled the eyes like polished
rubies. At last I went out of the garden and closed the door.

The following day I opened another door, and when I entered, I found myself in a large field full of palm trees and encircled by a running stream whose banks were covered with roses, jasmine, mignonettes, irises, daffodils, narcissus, violets, daisies, gillyflowers, and lilies of the valley; and as the breeze blew over these aromatic plants, the whole field was filled with the sweet aroma. After I enjoyed and diverted myself there for a while, I went out and closed the door. Then I opened a third door and found myself in a large hall covered with all kinds of colored marble, rare metals, and precious stones and hung with cages of aloe- and sandalwood, full of all kinds of singing birds, such as nightingales, thrushes, pigeons, ringdoves, turtledoves, silver doves, and Nubian doves. There I enjoyed myself, felt happy, and forgot my cares.

Then I went to sleep, and in the morning I opened a fourth door and found myself in a large hall, surrounded by forty chambers whose doors stood open. I entered every chamber and found them full of jewels, such as pearls, emeralds, rubies, corals, and carbuncles, as well as gold and silver. I was amazed at such abundance and said to myself, "Such wealth could belong only to the greatest of kings, for no ordinary monarch could assemble such a fortune, not even if all the monarchs of the world joined together." I felt happy and carefree, saying to myself, "I am the king of the age, for these jewels and this wealth are mine, and these girls belong to me and to me alone." O my lady, I enjoyed myself in chamber after chamber until thirty-nine days had passed and there remained only one day and one night. During that time, I had opened all ninety-nine chambers, and there remained only the hundredth, the one the girls had cautioned me not to open.

But morning overtook Shahrazad, and she lapsed into silence. Then Dinarzad said to her sister, "Sister, what an amazing and entertaining story!" Shahrazad replied, "What is this compared with what I shall tell you tomorrow night if the king spares me and lets me live!"

THE SIXTY-SECOND NIGHT

The following night Shahrazad said:

I heard, O happy King, that the dervish said:

There remained only that one chamber to complete the hundred, and I began to feel obsessed and tempted with it, as Satan urged me to open it and cause my undoing. Even though there remained but one night for the appointed time for the girls to return and spend a

whole year with me, I was no longer able to restrain myself and, suc-
cumbing to the devil, at last opened the door plated with gold. As
soon as I entered, I was met by a perfume that, as I smelled it, sent
me reeling to the floor and made me swoon for a long time. When I
came to myself, I summoned my courage and entered the chamber. I
found the floor strewn with saffron and saw lamps of gold and silver,
fed with costly oils, and saw fragrant candles burning with aloes and
ambergris. I also saw two incense burners, each as large as a knead-
ing bowl, full of glowing embers in which burned the incense of
aloewood, ambergris, musk, and frankincense, and as the incense
burned, the smoke rose to blend with the odors of the candles and
the saffron, filling the chamber with perfume.

O my lady, I then saw a deep-black horse as black as the darkest
night, bridled and ready with a saddle of red gold, as it stood before
two mangers of clear crystal, one filled with husked sesame, the other
with rosewater scented with musk. When I saw the horse, I was
exceedingly amazed, and said to myself, "There is something of great
importance about this horse." Then the devil took hold of me again,
and I took the horse from his place and led him outside the palace. I
got on his back and tried to ride him, but he refused to move. I kicked
him, but he did not stir. Then I took the whip and hit him angrily, and
as soon as he felt the blow, he neighed with a sound like roaring
thunder and, spreading a pair of wings, flew up with me and disappeared in the sky. A while later he landed on the roof of another
palace and, throwing me off his back, lashed my face with his tail
with a blow so hard that it gouged out my eye and made it roll on my
cheek, leaving me one-eyed. I cried, "There is no power and no
strength save in God, the Almighty, the Magnificent. I have taunted
the one-eyed young men until I became one-eyed like them."

I looked down from the terrace of the palace and saw again the
ten couches with the blue bedding and realized that the palace was
the same one that belonged to the ten one-eyed young men who had
admonished me and whose admonition I had refused to follow. I
went down from the roof and sat down amid the couches, and hardly
had I done so when I saw the young men and their old companion
approaching. When they saw me, they cried, "You are not welcome
or wanted here. By God, we will not let you stay. May you perish." I
replied, "All I wanted to know was why you smeared your faces with
blue and black soot." They said, "Each of us suffered the same misfortune as you did. We all lived the best of lives in bliss, feeding on
chicken, sipping wine from crystal cups, resting on silk brocade, and
sleeping on the breasts of fair women. We had to wait one more day to
gain a year of pleasures, such food and drink and such entertainment,
but because of our curious eyes, we lost our eyes, and now, as you

see, we are left to mourn our misfortune." I said, "Do not blame me
for what I did, for I have become like you. Indeed, I want you to
bring me all ten black trays to blacken my face," and I burst into
bitter tears. They replied, "By God, by God, we will never harbor you
or let you stay with us. Get out of here, go to Baghdad, and find
someone to help you there."

When I saw that there was no avail against their harsh treatment
and when I recalled the miseries written on my forehead, how I killed
the young man and how 'I would be sitting pretty but for my curiosity,'
I could no longer stand it. I shaved off my beard and eyebrows,
renounced everything, and roamed the world, a one-eyed dervish.
Then God granted me safe passage and I reached Baghdad on the
evening of this very night. Here I met these two men standing at a
loss, and I greeted them and said, "I am a stranger," and they replied,
"We are strangers like you." We formed an extraordinary group, for by
coincidence, all three of us happened to be blind in the right eye. This,
my lady, was the cause of losing my eye and shaving off my beard.

It is related, O happy King, that after the girl heard the dervishes'
tales, she said to them, "Stroke your heads and go your way," but
they replied, "By God, we will not go until we hear our companions'
tales." Then, turning to the caliph, Ja'far, and Masrur, the girl said,
"Tell us your tales." Ja'far stood forth and said, "O my lady, we are
citizens of Mosul who have come to your city for trade. When we
arrived here, we took lodgings in the merchants' inn and we traded
and sold our goods. Tonight a merchant of your city held a party and
invited all the merchants in the inn, including our group, to his
house, where we had a good time, with choice wine, entertainment,
and singing girls. Then there was argument and yelling among some
of the guests, and the prefect of police raided the place. Some of us
were arrested and some escaped. We were among those who escaped,
and when we went to the inn, late at night, we found the door locked,
not to be opened again till sunrise. We wandered helplessly, not
knowing where to go, for fear that the police would catch up with us,
arrest us, and humiliate us. God drove us to your house, and when we
heard the beautiful singing and the sound of carousing, we knew that
there was a company having a party inside and said to ourselves that
we would enter at your service and spend the rest of our night with
you to entertain you and to make our pleasure complete. It pleased
you to offer us your hospitality and to be generous and kind. This was
the cause of our coming to you."

The dervishes said, "O our lady and mistress, we wish you to grant
us as a favor the lives of these three men and to let us depart with
gratitude." Looking at the entire group, the girl replied, "I grant you

your lives, as a favor to all." When they were outside the house, the caliph asked the dervishes, "Men, where are you going, for it is still dark?" They replied, "By God, sir, we do not know where to go." He said, "Come and sleep at our place." Then, turning to Ja'far, the caliph said, "Take these men home with you for the night and bring them before me early tomorrow morning, so that we may chronicle for each his adventure that we have heard tonight." Ja'far did as the caliph bade him, while the caliph returned to his palace. But the caliph was agitated and stayed awake, pondering the mishaps of the dervishes and how they had changed from being sons of kings to what they were now, and burning with curiosity to hear the stories of the flogged girl and the other with the two black bitches. He could not sleep a wink and waited impatiently for the morning.

No sooner had the day dawned than he sat on his throne, and when Ja'far entered and kissed the ground before him, he said, "This is no time for dawdling. Go and bring me the two ladies, so that I may hear the story of the two bitches, and bring the dervishes with you," yelling at him, "Hurry!" Ja'far withdrew and came back soon with the three girls and the three dervishes. Then placing the dervishes next to him and the girls behind a curtain, he said, "Women, we forgive you because of your generosity and kindness to us. If you do not know who is the one sitting before you, I shall introduce him. You are in the presence of the seventh of the sons of 'Abbas, al-Rashid, son of al-Mahdi son of al-Hadi and brother of al-Saffah son of Mansur. Take courage, be frank, and tell the truth and nothing but the truth, and do not lie, for 'you should be truthful even if the truth sends you to burning Hell.' Explain to the caliph why you beat the two black bitches, why you weep after you beat them, and why they weep with you."

But morning overtook Shahrazad, and she lapsed into silence. Then Dinarzad said, "Sister, what a strange and amazing story!" Shahrazad replied, "What is this compared with what I shall tell you tomorrow night if the king spares me and lets me live!"

THE SIXTY-THIRD NIGHT

The following night Shahrazad said:

I heard, O happy King, that when the girl who was the mistress of the house heard what Ja'far said to her on behalf of the Commander of the Faithful, she said:

[The Tale of the First Lady,
the Mistress of the House]

MY CASE IS so strange and my tale is so amazing that were it engraved with needles at the corner of the eye, it would be a lesson for those who wish to consider. The two black bitches are my sisters by the same mother and father. These two girls, the one whose body bears the marks of the rod and the other who is the shopper are sisters by another mother. When our father died and the inheritance was divided, the three of us lived with our mother, while the other two sisters lived with their own mother. After a while, our mother also died, leaving us three thousand dinars, which we divided equally among ourselves. Since I was the youngest of the three, my two sisters prepared their dowries and got married before me.

The husband of the eldest sister bought merchandise with his money and hers, and the two of them set out on their travels. They were absent for five years, during which time he threw away and wasted all her money. Then he deserted her, leaving her to wander alone in foreign lands, trying to find her way back home. After five years she returned to me, dressed like a beggar in tattered clothes and a dirty old cloak. She was in a most miserable plight. When I saw her, I was stunned, and I asked her, "Why are you in this condition?" She replied, "Words are useless, for 'the pen has brought to pass that which had been decreed.'" O Commander of the Faithful, I took her at once to the bath, dressed her with new clothes, prepared for her some broth, and gave her some wine to drink. I took care of her for a month, and then I said to her, "Sister, you are the eldest, and you have now taken the place of our mother. You and I will share my wealth equally, for God has blessed my share of the inheritance, and I have made much money by spinning and producing silk." I treated her with the utmost kindness, and she lived with me for a whole year, during which time our minds were on our other sister. Shortly she too came home in a worse plight than the first. I treated her just as I had treated the other, clothing her and taking care of her.

A little later, they said to me, "Sister, we would like to get married, for it is not fitting that we live without husbands." I replied, "Sister, there is little good in marriage, for it is hard to find a good man. You got married, but nothing good came of it. Let us stay together and live by ourselves." But, O Commander of the Faithful, they did not listen to my advice and married again without my consent. This time I was obliged to provide them with dowries from my own pocket. Soon their husbands betrayed them; they took what they could, cleared out, and left their wives behind. My two sisters came to me with apologies, saying, "Sister, although you are younger than the two of us in years, you are older in wisdom. We will never mention marriage again. Take us back, and we shall be your servants to earn our upkeep." I replied, "Sisters, none is dearer to me than you." I took them in and treated them even more generously than before. We spent the third year together, and all that time my wealth kept increasing, and my circumstances kept getting better and better.

One day, O Commander of the Faithful, I resolved to take my merchandise to Basra.[2] I fitted a large ship and loaded it with merchandise, provisions, and other necessities. Then we set out, and for many days we sailed under a fair wind. Soon we discovered that we had strayed from our course, and for twenty days we were lost on the high seas. At the end of the twentieth day, the lookout man, climbing the masthead, cried out, "Good news!" Then he joyfully came down, saying, "I have seen what seems to be a city that looks like a fat pigeon." We were happy, and in less than an hour our ship entered the harbor, and I disembarked to visit the city. When I came to the gate, I saw people standing there with staves in their hands, but as I drew nearer, I saw that they had been turned by a curse into stone. I went into the city and saw that all the people in their shops had been turned into stone. Not one of them breathed or gave a sign of life. I walked through the streets and found out that the entire city had been turned into hard stone. When I came to the upper end of the city, I saw a door plated with red gold, draped with a silk curtain, and hung with a lamp. Saying to myself, "By God, this is strange! Can it be that there are human beings here!" I entered through the door and found myself in a hall that led to another and then another, and as I kept going from hall to hall all alone, without meeting anyone, I became apprehensive. Then I entered the harem quarters and found myself in an apartment bearing the royal insignia and hung throughout with drapes of gold brocade. There I saw the queen, the king's wife, wearing a dress decorated with opulent pearls, each as big as a hazelnut, and a crown studded with precious stones.

But morning overtook Shahrazad, and she lapsed into silence. Then Dinarzad said to her sister, "Sister, what an entertaining story!" Shahrazad replied, "What is this compared with what I shall tell you tomorrow night if the king spares me and lets me live!"

2. Then and now a port city in southern Iraq, situated on the Shat al-Arab, a waterway formed by the confluence of the Tigris and the Euphrates and going into the Arabian, or Persian, Gulf.

THE SIXTY-FOURTH NIGHT

The following night Shahrazad said:

I heard, O King, that the girl who was the mistress of the house said to the caliph:

O Commander of the Faithful, the queen wore a crown studded with all kinds of gems, and the apartment was spread with silk tapestries embroidered with gold. In the middle of the hall I saw an ivory bed plated with burnished gold, set with two bosses of green emeralds, and draped with a canopylike net strung with pearls. I saw something glitter, sending rays through the net, and when I approached and put my head in, I saw there, O Commander of the Faithful, set on a pedestal, a gem as big as an ostrich egg, with an incandescent glow and a brilliant light that dazzled the eyes. I also saw silk bedding and a silk coverlet, and beside the pillow, I saw two lighted candles. But there was nobody in the bed. I marveled at the sight, and astonished to find the gem and the two lighted candles, I said to myself, "Someone must have lighted these candles." Then I proceeded to other rooms and came to the kitchen, then the wine cellar, then the king's treasure chambers. I continued to explore the palace, going from room to room, absorbed in the wonderful sights and the amazing state of the city's inhabitants, until I forgot myself and was surprised by the night. I searched for the gate of the castle, but I lost my way and could not find it, and for a long time I wandered in the dark without finding a place of refuge save the canopied bed with the candles. I lay down there, covered myself with the coverlet, and tried to go to sleep, but I could not.

At midnight I heard a sweet voice chanting the Quran. I rose, glad to hear someone, and followed the voice until I came to a chamber, whose door stood ajar. I peered through and saw what looked like a place of worship and recitation, with a prayer niche lighted with hanging lamps and two candles. On a prayer carpet stood a section of the Quran set on a stand, and on the carpet sat a handsome young man reciting the Holy Book. I was amazed to find that this young man was the only one among the people of the city to have escaped the curse and thought that there was a mystery behind this. I opened the door and, entering the chamber, greeted him and said, "Blessed be God who has granted you to me, to be the cause of our deliverance and help our ship return to our native land. O holy man, by the Holy Book you are reciting, answer my question." He looked at me with a smile and said, "O good woman, tell me first what caused you to come here, and I shall relate to you what happened to me and to the people of this city and why they were cursed while I was not." I told him our story and how our ship had strayed for twenty days. Then I questioned him again about the city and its people, and he replied, "O sister, be patient, and I shall tell you." Then he closed the Quran, put it aside, and seated me, O Commander of the Faithful . . .

But morning overtook Shahrazad, and Dinarzad said, "O sister, what a strange and entertaining story!" Shahrazad replied, "Sister, what is this compared with what I shall tell you tomorrow night if the king spares me and lets me live!"

THE SIXTY-FIFTH NIGHT

The following night Shahrazad said:

It is related, O happy King, that the girl who was the mistress of the house said to the caliph:

O Commander of the Faithful, the young man placed the Quran in the prayer niche and seated me by his side. When I looked at him, I saw a face as beautiful as the full moon, like the one of whom the poet said:

> The stargazer one night charted the stars
> And saw his fair form shining like a moon
> Who vied in brilliance with the hiding sun
> And left in darkness the bewildered moon.

It was a face on which the supreme God has bestowed the robe of beauty, which was embroidered with the grace of his perfect cheeks. He was like the one of whom the poet said:

> By his enchanting eyelids and his slender waist,
> By his beguiling eyes so keen, so fair,
> By his sharp glances and his tender sides,
> By his white forehead and his jet black hair,
> By eyebrows that have robbed my eyes of sleep
> And made me subject to their mighty will,
> By lovely sidelocks that curl, coil, and charm
> And all rejected lovers with their beauty kill,
> By the soft myrtle of his rosy cheeks,
> By his carnelian lips and mouth of pearls,
> Which sends the fragrance of the honey breath,

And the sweet wine which in its sweetness purls,
By his graceful neck and his boughlike frame,
Which bears two pomegranates on the breast,
By his charming, tender, and slender waist,
And hips that quiver while they move or rest,
By his soft silky skin and charming touch
And all the beauty that his own does seem,
By his open hand and his truthful tongue,
And noble pedigree and high esteem,
By these I swear that his life-giving breath
Gives the musk being and perfumes the air,
That the sun pales before him and the moon
Is nothing but a paring of his nail; I swear.

O Commander of the Faithful, I looked at him and sighed, for he had captivated my heart. I said to him, "O my dear lord, tell me the story of your city." He said, "O woman of God, this city is the capital of my father the king whom you must have seen turned into black stone inside this cursed palace, together with my mother the queen whom you found inside the net. They and all the people of the city were Magians[3] who, instead of the Omnipotent Lord, worshiped the fire, to which they prayed and by which they swore. My father, who had been blessed with me late in life, reared me in affluence, and I grew and throve. It happened that there lived with us a very old woman who used to teach me the Quran, saying, " 'You should worship none but the Almighty God,' " and I learned the Quran without telling my father or the rest of my family. One day we heard a mighty voice proclaiming, 'O people of this city, leave your fire worship and worship the Merciful God.' But they refused to obey. A year later the voice cried out again and did the same the following year. Suddenly one morning the city turned into stone, and none was saved except myself. Here I sit now, as you see, to worship God, but I have grown weary of loneliness, for there is none to keep me company."

I said to him (for he had captured my heart and mastered my life and soul), "Come with me to the city of Baghdad, for this girl standing before you is the head of her family, mistress over servants and slaves, and a businesswoman of considerable wealth, part of which is on the very ship that, after straying, now anchors outside your city, by the will of God who drove us here that I might meet you." I continued to press him, O Commander of the Faithful, until he consented. I spent that night, hardly believing my fortune, asleep at his feet. When morning dawned, we rose and, taking from his father's treasure chambers whatever was light in weight and great in worth, the two of us went

---

3. Zoroastrian priests; see n. 1, p. 61.

from the castle to the city and found the captain, my sisters, and my servants looking for me. When they saw me, they were happy, and when I related to them the story of the young man and the city, they were amazed. But when my two sisters, these very bitches, saw the young man with me, they envied me, O Commander of the Faithful, and harbored ill feelings toward me. Then we went aboard, all of us feeling happy at our gain, most of all I, because of the young man, and sat waiting for the wind to blow before setting sail.

But morning overtook Shahrazad, and she lapsed into silence. Then Dinarzad said, "O sister, what a strange and entertaining story!" Shahrazad replied, "What is this compared with what I shall tell you tomorrow if the king spares me and lets me live!"

THE SIXTY-SIXTH NIGHT

The following night Shahrazad said:

It is related, O happy King, that the girl who was the mistress of the house said to the caliph:

O Commander of the Faithful, when the wind began to blow, we set sail, and, as we sat chatting, my sisters asked me, "Sister, what will you do with this young man?" I replied, "I will make him my husband." Then I turned to him and said, "O my lord, I want you to follow my wish that when we reach Baghdad, our native city, I offer you myself in marriage as your maidservant, and we will be husband and wife." The young man replied, "Yes, indeed, for you are my lady and my mistress, and I will obey you in everything." Then I turned to my sisters and said, "Whatever goods we have brought are yours; my only reward is this young man; he is mine and I am his." But my sisters turned green with envy over him and harbored ill feelings toward me. We sailed on under a fair wind until we entered the Sea of Safety and began to approach Basra. When night came, and the young man and I fell asleep, my two sisters, who had been waiting patiently, carried me with my bed and threw me into the sea. They did the same thing to the young man. He drowned, but I was saved; I wish that I had drowned with him. I was cast on a raised island, and when I came to myself and saw myself surrounded by water, I realized that my sisters had betrayed me, and I thanked God for my safety. Meantime, the ship sailed on like a flash of lightning, while I stood alone through the night.

When morning dawned, I saw a dry strip of land connecting the island to the shore. I crossed it; then I wrung out my clothes and spread them to dry in the sun. When they were dry, I ate some dates and drank some fresh water I had found there; then I proceeded to walk until there remained only two hours between me and the city. As I sat to rest, I suddenly saw a long serpent, as thick as the trunk of a palm tree, gliding sideways and sweeping the sand in her way, as she speeded toward me. When she drew near, I saw that she was being pursued by a long and slender serpent, as slender as a spear and as long as two. He had seized her by the tail, while she, with a tongue about ten inches long, rolling in the dust, and eyes streaming with tears, wriggled right and left, trying to escape. Feeling pity for her, O Commander of the Faithful, I ran toward a big stone, picked it up, and calling on God for help, hit him with it and killed him. As soon as he rolled dead, the serpent opened a pair of wings, flew up, and disappeared from my sight.

Then I sat down to rest and dozed off, and when I awoke, I saw a black girl, together with two bitches, sitting at my feet, massaging them. Sitting up, I asked, "O friend, who are you?" She replied, "How soon you have forgotten me. I am she for whom you have done the good deed and sowed the seed of gratitude. I am the serpent who was in distress until it pleased you, with the help of the Almighty God, to kill my foe. In order to reward you, I hurried after the ship and carried to your house everything that belonged to you. Then I ordered my attendants to sink the ship, for I knew how you had been kind to your sisters all your life and how they had treated you, how out of envy over the young man, they threw you both into the sea and caused him to drown. Here they are, these two black bitches, and I swear by the Creator of the heavens that if you disobey my command, I will take you and imprison you under the earth." Then the girl shook and, turning into a bird, picked up me and my two sisters and flew up with us until she set us down in my house, where I found all my property, which she had brought from the ship. Then she said to me, "I swear by 'Him who made the two seas flow'—this is my second oath—that if you disobey my command, I will turn you into a bitch like them. I charge you to give them every night three hundred blows with the rod, as a punishment for what they did." I replied, "I shall obey," and she departed and left me. Since that time, I have been forced to punish them every night until they bleed. I feel very sorry for them, and, knowing that I am not to blame for their punishment, they forgive me. This is the cause of my beating them and crying with them, and this is my story and the end of my history.

When she finished, the caliph was greatly amazed. Then the Commander of the Faithful ordered Ja'far to ask the second girl to explain to them the cause of the rod marks on her sides and chest. She said:

O Commander of the Faithful, when my father died . . .

But morning overtook Shahrazad, and she lapsed into silence. Then her sister said, "O sister, what an entertaining story!" Shahrazad replied, "What is this compared with what I shall tell you tomorrow night if the king spares me and lets me live!"

THE SIXTY-SEVENTH NIGHT

The following night Shahrazad said:

I heard, O happy King, that the flogged girl said to the Commander of the Faithful:

[The Tale of the Second Lady, the Flogged One]

When my father died, he left me a great deal of money. Shortly thereafter, I married the wealthiest man in Baghdad, and for a year I lived with him the happiest of lives. Then he too died and left me my legal share of the inheritance, which was ninety thousand dinars. I lived a prosperous life, buying so much gold jewelry, clothes, and embroideries that I had ten complete changes of clothes, each costing one thousand dinars, and my reputation spread in the city. One day, as I was sitting at home, an old woman came to me, and what an old woman she was, with a pallid, scabby skin; a bent body; matted gray hair; a gray, freckled face; broken teeth; plucked-out eyebrows; hollow, bleary eyes; and a runny nose. She was like the one of whom the poet said:

> Seven defects are planted in her face,
> The least of which is but the curse of fate
> A bleary frown that covers all the face,
> A mouth full of stones, or a mowed-down pate.

She greeted me and, kissing the ground before me, said, "My lady, I have an orphan daughter, and tonight is her unveiling and wedding night, but we are brokenhearted, for we are strangers in this city, and we do not know anyone. If you come to her wedding, you will earn a reward in Heaven, for when the ladies of this city will hear that you are coming, they too will come, and you shall honor us with your presence and make her happy." Then the old woman repeated the following verses:

> We own that your visit is an honor
> That cannot be performed by another.

She wept and implored me until I felt pity for her and agreed to her request. I said, "Yes, I shall do it for the sake of the Almighty God, and she will not be unveiled to her bridegroom, save in my clothes, ornaments, and jewelry." Overjoyed, the old woman bent and kissed my feet, saying, "May God reward you and comfort you, as you have comforted me, but my lady, do not trouble yourself yet. Be ready at suppertime, and I shall come and fetch you." When she left, I proceeded to string the pearls, assemble the embroideries, and pack the ornaments and jewelry, not knowing what God had in store for me. At nightfall the old woman arrived with a happy smile and, kissing my hand, said, "Most of the ladies of the city are already assembled in our house, and they are waiting for you and looking forward to your coming." I rose, put on my outer garment, and, wrapping myself in my cloak, followed the old lady with my maids behind me. We walked on until we came to a well-swept and -watered alley and stood before a door draped with a black curtain hung with a lamp covered with gold filigree, bearing the following inscription in letters of gold:

> I am the house of mirth
> And eternal laughter.
> Inside a fountain flows
> With a healing water,
> With myrtle, daisy, rose,
> And clove pink for border.

The old woman knocked at the door, and when it was opened we entered and saw silk carpets covering the floor and saw two rows of lighted candles that formed an avenue leading from the door to the upper end of the hall. There stood a couch of juniper wood, encrusted with gems and hung with a canopylike red-speckled silk curtain. Suddenly, O Commander of the Faithful, a girl came out from behind the curtain, shining like the half moon. Indeed, her face was as radiant as the full moon or the rising sun, just like her of whom the poet said:

> To her inferior Caesar she was sent,
> A gift nobler than all her Persian kings.
> The roses blossomed on her rosy cheeks,
> Staining with crimson dye such lovely things.

Slender and sleepy-eyed and languorous,
She won from Beauty all of Beauty's ploys,
As if her forelock sat upon her brow
A night of gloom before a dawn of joys.

The girl came down from the couch and said to me, "Welcome and greetings to my dear and illustrious sister." Then she recited the following verses:

If the house could know who has visited,
It would rejoice and kiss the very dust,
As if to say, "Only the generous
Has by his gifts such welcome merited."

Then she came up to me, O Commander of the Faithful, and said, "O my lady, I have a brother who is more handsome by far than I. He has noticed you at some wedding feasts and other festive occasions, and, seeing your great beauty and charm and hearing that, like him, you are the head of your clan, he has decided that he would like to tie his knot with you, so that you may become husband and wife." I replied, "Yes, I hear and obey." O Commander of the Faithful, no sooner had I uttered these words than she clapped her hands and a door opened and out came a finely dressed young man in the bloom of youth, all beauty and perfect grace. He was sweetly coquettish, with a fine figure, eyebrows arching like a bow, and eyes that bewitched the heart with their holy magic. He was like him of whom the poet said:

He has a face as bright as the young moon,
And joys as pearls he scatters as a boon.

As soon as I looked at him, I was attracted to him. He sat beside me and chatted with me for a while; then the girl clapped her hands a second time, and a door opened and out came a judge and four witnesses, who sat and wrote the marriage contract. Then the young man made me pledge that I would not look at any other man, and he was not satisfied until I took a solemn oath. I was feeling very happy and impatient for the night to come. When it finally came, we retired to our room, and I spent with him the best of nights. In the morning he slaughtered many sheep in thanksgiving, showed me favors, and treated me lovingly. For a full month thereafter, I lived with him a most happy life.

One day, wishing to buy certain fabric, I asked him for permission to go to the market. He consented, and I went with the old woman and two maids. When we entered the silk-mercers' market, the old woman said, "O my lady, here is a very young merchant who has a large stock of goods and every kind of fabric you may desire, and no one in the market has better goods. Let us go into his shop, and there you can buy whatever you wish." We entered his shop, and I saw that he was slender, handsome, and very young, like him of whom the poet said:

> Here is a slender youth whose hair and face
> All mortals envelope with light or gloom.
> Mark on his cheek the mark of charm and grace,
> A dark spot on a red anemone.

I said to the old lady, "Let him show us some nice fabric." She replied, "Ask him yourself." I said, "Don't you know that I have sworn not to speak to any man except my husband?" So she said to him, "Show us some fabric," and he showed us several pieces, some of which I liked. I said to the old woman, "Ask him for the price." When she asked him, he replied, "I will sell them for neither silver nor gold but for a kiss on her cheek." I said, "God save me from such a thing." But the old woman said, "O my lady, you needn't talk to him or he to you; just turn your face to him and let him kiss it; that is all there is to it." Tempted by her, I turned my face to him. He put his mouth on my cheek and bit off with his teeth a piece of my flesh. I fainted, and when I came to myself, a long time later, I saw that he had locked the shop and departed, while the old woman, in a display of grief, sorrowed over my bleeding face.

But morning overtook Shahrazad, and she lapsed into silence.

THE SIXTY-EIGHTH NIGHT

The following night Shahrazad said:

I have heard, O happy King, that the flogged girl said to the Commander of the Faithful:

The old woman, expressing anguish, grief, and sorrow, said, "O my lady, God has saved you from something worse. Take heart and let us go, before the matter becomes public. When you get home, pretend to be sick, and cover yourself up, and I will bring you powders and plasters that will heal your cheek within three days." I rose, and we walked slowly until we reached the house, where I collapsed on the floor with pain. Then I lay in bed, covered myself up, and drank some wine.

In the evening my husband came in and asked, "O my darling, what is the matter with you?" I replied, "I have a headache." He lighted a candle and, coming close to me, looked at my face and, seeing the wound on my cheek, asked, "What caused this?" I replied, "When I went today to the market to buy some fabric, a camel driver with a load of firewood jostled me in a narrow passage, and one of the pieces tore my veil and cut my cheek, as you see." He said, "Tomorrow I shall ask the governor of the city to hang every camel driver in this city." I replied, "O my lord, this does not warrant hanging innocent men and bearing the guilt of their death." He asked, "Then who did it?" I replied, "I was riding a rented donkey, and when the donkey driver drove it hard, it stumbled and threw me to the ground, and I fell on a piece of glass that happened to be there and cut my cheek." He said, "By God, I shall not let the sun rise before I go to Ja'far the Barmakid[4] and ask him to hang every donkey driver and every sweeper in this city." I said, "By God, my lord, this is not what really happened to me. Don't hang people because of me." He asked, "What then is the real cause of your wound?" I replied, "I suffered what God had foreordained for me." He kept pressing me relentlessly, and I kept mumbling and resisting him until he drove me to speak rudely to him. At that moment, O Commander of the Faithful, he cried out and a door opened and out came three black slaves who, at his bidding, dragged me out of my bed and threw me down on my back in the middle of the room. Then he ordered one slave to sit on my knees, the other to hold my head, and the third to draw his sword, saying to him, "You, Sa'd, strike her and with one blow cut her in half and let each of you carry one half and throw it into the Tigris river for the fish to feed upon. This is the punishment of those who violate the vow." Then he grew angrier and recited the following verses:

> If there be one who shares the one I love,
> I'll kill my love even though my soul dies,
> Saying, "Better nobly to die, O soul,
> Than share a love for which another vies."

Then he ordered the slave to strike me with the sword. When the slave was sure of the command, he bent down to me and said, "O my lady, have you any wish, for this is the last moment of your life?" I replied, "Get off me, so that I may tell him something." I raised my head and, thinking of my condition and how I had fallen from high esteem into disgrace and from life into death, I wept bitterly and choked with sobs. But my husband looked at me angrily and recited the following verses:

---

4. Harun al-Rashid's vizier; see n. 3, p. 77.

Tell her who for another lover left,
Bored with me, and repaid me with disdain,
That even though I suffered first, I found
Contentment in what was between us twain.

When I heard his words, O Commander of the Faithful, I wept
and, looking at him, replied with the following verses:

You set my poor heart burning with your love
And left my eyes to smart and went to sleep,
While all alone I thought of you and wept
And in my sorrow did a vigil keep.
You promised to be faithful to the end,
But when you had my heart, you broke the vow.
I loved you in all childish innocence;
Kill not that love, for I am learning now.

But when he heard my verses, O Commander of the Faithful, he
grew even angrier and, giving me a furious look, recited the following verses:

'Twas not boredom that bid me leave my love,
But a sin that imposed such fate on me.
She wished to let another share our love,
But faith forbade me such a blasphemy.

I wept and implored and, looking at him, recited the following
verses:

You left me burdened with the weight of love,
Being too weak even a shirt to wear.
I marvel not that my soul wastes away
But that my body can your absence bear.

When he heard my words, he cursed me and scolded me. Then
looking at me, he recited the following verses:

You left me to enjoy another love
And showed disdain, a deed I could not do.
If you dislike my presence, I will leave
And rue the end of love, as you did rue,
And take another lover for myself,
For love was killed not by me but by you.

Then he yelled at the slave, saying, "Cut her in half and rid me of
her, for her life is worthless." O Commander of the Faithful, as we

argued in verse, I grew certain of death and gave up myself for lost, but suddenly the old woman rushed in and, throwing herself at my husband's feet, said tearfully, "O son, by the rights of rearing you up, by the breasts that nursed you, and by my service to you, pardon her for my sake. You are still young, and you should not bear the guilt of her death, for as it is said, 'Whoever slays shall be slain.' Why bother with such a worthless woman? Drive her out of your hearth and heart." She kept weeping and imploring until he relented and said, "But I must brand her and leave a permanent mark on her." Then he ordered the slaves to strip me of all my clothes and stretch me on the floor, and when they sat on me to pin me down, he rose and, fetching a quince rod, fell with blows on my sides until I despaired of life and lost consciousness. Then he bade the slaves take me to my own home as soon as it was dark and let the old woman show them the way.

Following their master's command, they took me away, threw me into my house, and departed. I remained unconscious till the morning. Then I treated myself with ointments and drugs, but my body remained disfigured from the beating and my sides bore the marks of the rod. I lay sick in bed for four months, and when I recovered and was able to get up, I went to look for my husband's house but found it in ruin. The entire alley, from beginning to end, was torn down, and on the site of the house stood piles of rubbish. Unable to find out how this had come about, I went to this woman, my sister on my father's side, and found her with these two black bitches. I greeted her and told her my story, and she said, "O my sister, who is safe from the accident of life and the misfortunes of the world?" Then she repeated the following verses:

> Such is the world; with patience it is best
> The loss of wealth or loss of love to breast.

Then, O Commander of the Faithful, she told me her story, what her sisters had done to her, and what had become of them.

We lived together without thinking of any man, and everyday, this girl, the shopper, would come by and go to the market to buy for us what we needed for the day and the night. We lived like this for a long time until yesterday, when our sister went to shop as usual and returned with the porter, whom we allowed to stay to divert us. Less than a quarter of the night had passed when these three dervishes joined us, and we sat to converse, and when a third of the night had gone by, three respectable merchants from Mosul joined us and told us about their adventures. We had pledged the guests to accept a condition, and when they broke the pledge, we treated them accordingly. Then we questioned them about themselves, and when they told us their tales, we pardoned them and they departed. This morning we were unexpectedly summoned to your presence. This is our story.

The caliph, O happy King, marveled at their tales and their adventures.

But morning overtook Shahrazad, and she lapsed into silence. Then Dinarzad said, "O sister, what a strange, amazing, and entertaining story!" Shahrazad replied, "What is this compared with what I shall tell you tomorrow night if the king spares me and lets me live!"

THE SIXTY-NINTH NIGHT

The following night Shahrazad said:

It is related, O glorious King, that the caliph, marveling at these adventures, turned to the first girl and said, "Tell me what happened to the demon serpent who had cast a spell on your sisters and turned them into bitches. Do you know her whereabouts, and did she set with you the date of her return to you?" The girl replied, "O Commander of the Faithful, she gave me a tuft of hair, saying 'Whenever you need me, burn two of the hairs, and I will be with you at once, even if I am beyond Mount Qaf.'" The caliph asked, "Where is the tuft of hair?" She brought it, and he took it and burned the entire tuft. Suddenly the whole palace began to tremble, and the serpent arrived and said, "Peace be with you, O Commander of the Faithful! This woman has sown with me the seed of gratitude, and I cannot reward her amply enough, for she killed my enemy and saved me from death. Knowing what her sisters had done to her, I felt bound to reward her by avenging her. At first, I was about to destroy them once and for all, but I feared that their deaths would be hard on her; therefore, I cast a spell on them and turned them into bitches. Now, if you wish me to release them, O Commander of the Faithful, I will do it gladly, for your wish is my command, O Commander of the Faithful!" The caliph replied, "O spirit, release them and let us deliver them from their misery. After you release them, I will look into the case of this flogged girl, and may the Almighty God help me and make it easy for me to solve her case and discover who wronged her and usurped her rights, for I am sure that she is telling the truth." The she-demon replied, "O Commander of the Faithful, not only will I release these two bitches, but I will also reveal to you who

abused and beat this girl. In fact, he is the nearest of all men to you."
Then she took, O King, a bowl of water, and muttering a spell over it
in words no one could understand, sprinkled the two sisters with the
water and turned them back into their original form.

Then the she-demon said, "O Commander of the Faithful, the man
who beat this girl is your son al-Amin brother of al-Ma'mun. He had
heard of her beauty and charm, and he tricked her into a legal marriage. But he is not to blame for beating her, for he pledged her and
bound her by a solemn oath not to do a certain thing, but she broke the
pledge. He was about to kill her but, reflecting on the sin of murder
and fearing the Almighty God, contented himself with flogging her and
sending her back to her home. Such is the story of the second girl,
and God knows all." When the caliph heard what the she-demon
said and found out who had flogged the girl, he was exceedingly
amazed and said, "Praise be to the Almighty God who has blessed me
and helped me to release these two women and deliver them from sorcery and torture and who has blessed me a second time and revealed to
me the cause of that woman's misfortune. By God, I am now going to
do a deed by which I will be remembered." Then the caliph, O King,
summoned his son al-Amin and questioned him to confirm the truth of
the story. Then he assembled together the judge and witnesses, the
three dervishes, the first girl and her two sisters who had been cast
under a spell, and the flogged girl and the shopper. When they were all
assembled, he married the first girl and her sisters who had been cast
under a spell to the three dervishes, who were the sons of kings. He
made the three dervishes chamberlains and members of his inner
circle, giving them money, clothes, horses, a palace in Baghdad, and
everything they needed. He married the flogged girl to his son al-Amin,
under a new marriage contract, showered her with wealth and ordered
the house to be rebuilt and made even better than before. Then the
commander of the Faithful himself married the third girl, the shopper.
The people marveled at the caliph's wisdom, tolerance, and generosity
and, when all the facts were revealed, recorded these stories.

[The Story of the Three Apples]

A FEW DAYS later the caliph said to Ja'far, "I wish to go into the city
to find out what is happening and to question the people about the
conduct of my administrators, so that I may dismiss those of whom
they complain and promote those they praise." Ja'far replied, "As you
wish." When it was night, the caliph went into the city with Ja'far and
Masrur and walked about the streets and markets, and as they made
their way through an alley, they met a very old man carrying a basket

and a fishnet on his head and holding a staff in his hand. The caliph said to Ja'far, "This is a poor man in need." Then he asked the old man, "Old man, what is your trade?" and the old man replied, "My lord, I am a fisherman with a family, and I have been out fishing since midday without luck or anything with which to buy supper for my family; I feel helpless and disgusted with life, and I wish that I was dead." The caliph said to him, "Fisherman, would you go back with us to the Tigris,[5] stand at the riverbank, and cast the net for me, and whatever you happen to catch, I shall buy from you for one hundred dinars?"

Delighted, the old fisherman replied, "Yes, my lord," and went back with them to the Tigris. He cast his net, and when he gathered his rope and pulled it up, he found inside the net a locked, heavy chest. The caliph gave the fisherman one hundred dinars and bade Masrur carry the chest back to the palace. When they broke it open, they found inside a basket of palm leaves sewn with a red woolen thread. Cutting the basket open, they saw inside a piece of carpet and, lifting it out, saw a woman's cloak folded in four. When they removed the cloak, they found at the bottom of the chest a girl in the bloom of youth, as fair as pure silver. She had been slain and cut to pieces.

But morning overtook Shahrazad, and she lapsed into silence. Then Dinarzad said, "O sister, what an entertaining story!" Shahrazad replied, "What is this compared with what I shall tell you tomorrow night if I stay alive!"

THE SEVENTIETH NIGHT

The following night Shahrazad said:

I heard, O happy King, that the girl had been cut into nineteen pieces. When the caliph looked at her, he felt sad and sorry for her, and with tears in his eyes turned to Ja'far and said angrily, "You dog of a vizier, people are being killed and thrown into the river in my city, while I bear the responsibility till Doomsday. By God, I will avenge this girl and put her murderer to the worst of deaths. If you do not find me her killer, I will hang you and hang forty of your kinsmen with you." He was exceedingly angry and cried a disquieting cry at Ja'far, who said, "O Commander of the Faithful, grant me three days'

---

5. One of the two great rivers that cross Iraq from north to south, the other being the Euphrates.

delay." The caliph replied, "Granted." Then Ja'far withdrew and went into the city, vexed and sad, not knowing what to do. He said to himself, "Where shall I find the murderer of this girl, so that I may bring him before the caliph? If I bring him one of the men from jail, I will be guilty of his blood. I don't know what to do, but there is no power and no strength, save in God, the Almighty, the Magnificent." He stayed at home the first day, and the second, and by noon of the third day the caliph sent some of his chamberlains to fetch him. When he came into the presence of the caliph, the caliph asked him, "Where is the murderer of the girl?" Ja'far replied, "O Commander of the Faithful, am I an expert in detecting a murder?" The caliph was furious at his answer. He yelled at him and commanded that he be hanged before the palace, bidding a crier to cry throughout Baghdad, "Whoever wishes to see the hanging of the vizier Ja'far with forty of his Barmaki kinsmen let him come before the palace and look at the spectacle." Then the governor of the city and the chamberlains brought Ja'far and his kinsmen and made them stand under the gallows.

But while they waited to see the handkerchief at the window (this was the usual signal), and while the crowd wept for Ja'far and his kinsmen, a neatly dressed young man pushed his way through the crowd toward Ja'far. He had a bright face, with dark eyes, fair brow, and rosy cheeks covered with a downy beard, and graced with a mole like a disk of ambergris. When he finally made his way and stood before Ja'far, he kissed his hand and said, "May I spare you from such a horrible fate, O Grand Vizier, most eminent prince, and refuge of the poor? Hang me for the murder of the girl, for I am the one who murdered her." When Ja'far heard the young man's confession, he rejoiced at his own deliverance but grieved for the young man. But while Ja'far was talking to him, an old man, well-advanced in years, pushed his way through the crowd until he reached Ja'far and said, "O Vizier and mighty lord, do not believe what this young man is saying, for none has murdered the girl but I. Punish me for her death, for if you do not, I will call you to account before the Almighty God." But the young man cried out, "O Vizier, none murdered her but I." The old man said, "Son, you are still very young, while I am an old man who has had enough of life; I will give my life for you." And turning to Ja'far, he continued, "None murdered the girl but I. Hurry up and hang me, for my life is over, now that she is dead."

When Ja'far heard the conversation, he was amazed, and he took both the young man and the old man with him and went to the caliph. After kissing the ground before him seven times, he said, "O Commander of the Faithful, I have brought you the murderer of the girl. Each of these two men, the young man and the old man, claims that he is the murderer. Here they stand before you." The caliph, looking at the young man and the old man, asked, "Which of you killed the girl and threw her into the river?" The young man replied, "I murdered her," and the old man said, "None killed her but I." Then the caliph said to Ja'far, "Hang them both." But Ja'far said, "O Commander of the Faithful, since only one of them is guilty, it will be unjust to hang the other too." The young man said, "By Him who raised the firmament, I am the one who four days ago killed the girl, placed her in a basket of palm leaves, covered her with a woman's cloak, placed a piece of carpet over it, sewed the basket with a red woolen thread, and threw her into the river. In the name of God and His Judgment Day, I ask you to punish me for her death; do not let me live after her." The caliph, marveling at what the young man said, asked him, "What caused you to kill her wrongfully, and what caused you to come forward on your own?" The young man replied, "O Commander of the Faithful, our story is such that were it engraved with needles at the corner of the eye, it would be a lesson to those who would consider." The caliph said, "Relate to us what happened to you and her." The young man replied, "I hear and obey the command of God and the Commander of the Faithful." Then the young man . . .

But morning overtook Shahrazad, and she lapsed into silence.

THE SEVENTY-FIRST NIGHT

The following night Shahrazad said:

I heard, O happy King, that the young man said:

O Commander of the Faithful, the murdered girl was my wife and the mother of my children. She was my cousin, the daughter of this old man, my uncle, who gave her to me in marriage when she was still a young virgin. We lived together for eleven years, during which time God blessed her and she bore me three sons. She was well-behaved toward me and served me exceedingly well, and I in turn loved her very much. On the first day of this month she fell gravely ill and kept getting worse, but I took great care of her until by the end of the month she slowly began to recover.

One day, before going to the bath, she said to me, "Husband, I want you to satisfy a desire of mine." I replied, "I hear and obey, even if it were a thousand desires." She said, "I have a craving for an apple. If I could only smell it and take a bite, I wouldn't care if I die afterward." I replied, "It shall be done." Then I went and looked for apples but could not find any anywhere in your whole city. Had I found any, I would have paid a dinar for one. Vexed at my failure to satisfy her craving, I went home and said, "Wife, I was unable to find any apples." She was upset and, being still ill, suffered a relapse that night. As soon as it was morning, I went out and made the rounds of the orchards, one by one, but found no apples anywhere. At last a very old gardener answered my inquiry, saying, "Son, no apples can be found, except in the orchards of the Commander of the Faithful in Basra, where they are stored by the gardener. I went home and, driven by my love and solicitude for her, I prepared myself for the journey. For two full weeks, O Commander of the Faithful, I journeyed day and night, returning finally with three apples I had bought from the gardener for three dinars. But when I handed them to her, she showed no pleasure in them but laid them aside. Then she suffered another relapse, lay ill, and made me worried about her for ten days.

One day, as I sat in my shop, buying and selling fabrics, I suddenly saw an ugly black slave, as tall as a reed and as broad as a bench, passing by. He was holding in his hand one of the three apples for which I had journeyed for half a month. I called after him, saying, "My good slave, where did you get this apple?" He replied, "I got it from my mistress, for I went to see her today and found her lying ill with three apples by her side. She told me that her pimp of a husband had journeyed for half a month to bring them. After I ate and drank with her, I took one of the apples with me." When I heard what he said, O Commander of the Faithful, the world turned black before my eyes. I locked up my shop and went home, mad with resentment and fury. When I got home and looked for the apples, I found only two, and when I asked her, "Wife, where is the other apple?" she raised her head and replied, "By God, husband, I don't know." This convinced me that the slave had told the truth, and I took a sharp knife and, stealing behind her silently, knelt on her breast, worked the knife into her throat, and cut off her head. Then I quickly placed her in a basket, covered her with a woman's cloak, placed a piece of carpet on top of it, and sewed the basket. Then I placed the basket inside a chest, carried it on my head, and threw it into the Tigris. For God's sake, O Commander of the Faithful, avenge her on me and hang me quickly, or I will call you to account on her behalf before the Almighty God. For when I threw her into the river and went home, I found my eldest son crying, and when I asked him, "What is the matter with you?" he replied, "O father, this morning I stole one of the three apples you had brought back for my mother. I took it and went to the market, and as I was standing with my brothers, a tall black slave came by and snatched it from my hand. I protested, saying, 'For God's sake, good slave, this is one of the apples for which my father journeyed for half a month to Basra to bring back to my mother who was ill. Don't get me into trouble.' But he paid no attention to me, and when I begged him for a second and a third time, he slapped me and went off with it. Scared of my mother, I went with my brothers outside the city and we stayed there in fear until it started to get dark. For God's sake, father, say nothing to her of this, or her illness will get worse." When I heard my son's words and saw him trembling and weeping, O Commander of the Faithful, I realized that I had killed my wife wrongfully and that she had died unjustly; the accursed slave, hearing about the apples from my son, had slandered her and lied about her. When I realized that, I wept and made my sons weep with me, and when this old man, my uncle and her father, came in, I related to him what had happened, and he wept and made us weep with him till midnight, and for three days afterward we mourned for her and grieved over her unjust death, and all because of that black slave. This is the story of the murdered girl. So by your fathers and forefathers, I beg you to avenge her unjust death on me and kill me for my mistake, for I have no life left after her.

When the caliph heard his words . . .

But morning overtook Shahrazad, and she lapsed into silence.

THE SEVENTY-SECOND NIGHT

The following night, Shahrazad said:

I heard, O happy King, that when the caliph heard the young man's story, he was very much amazed and said, "By God, I will hang none but the accursed slave and I will do a deed that will quench the thirst for vengeance and please the Glorious King." Then he said to Ja'far, "Go into the city and bring me the slave, or I will strike your neck." Ja'far left in tears, saying to himself, "There is no escape from death this time, for 'the jar cannot be saved every time,' but the All-powerful and Omnipotent God who saved me the first time may save me yet a second time. By God, I will stay home for three days until God's will is accomplished." He stayed home the first day and the second, and by noon of the third day, giving himself up for lost, Ja'far summoned the judges and witnesses and made his will. Then he called his children to him, bade them farewell, and wept. Soon a messenger from the caliph arrived, saying, "The caliph is in a great rage and he swears that this day shall not pass before you are hanged." Ja'far wept and made all his slaves and members of his household weep for him. After he bade his children and all the members of his household farewell, his little daughter, who was very pretty and whom he loved more than all the others, came up to him, and he embraced her and kissed her, as he wept at parting from his family and his children. But as he embraced her to comfort her, pressing her hard to his aching heart, he felt something round in her pocket. He asked her, "My little girl, what is in your pocket?" and the little one replied, "It is an apple with the name of our Lord the caliph written on it. Rayhan our slave brought it, but he would not let me have it until I gave him two dinars for it." When Ja'far heard her mention the apple and the slave, he shrieked and, putting his hand in her pocket, took out the apple and, recognizing it, cried out, "O Speedy Deliverer!"

Then he bade the slave be brought before him, and when the slave came, Ja'far said, "Damn you, Rayhan, where did you get this apple?" The slave replied, "Although 'a lie may save a man, the truth is better and safer.' By God, my lord, I did not steal this apple from your palace or from the palace of the Commander of the Faithful or from his gardens. Four days ago, as I was walking through one of the alleys of the city, I saw some children at play, and when one of them dropped this apple, I beat him and snatched it from him. He cried and said to me, 'Kind gentleman, this apple belongs to my mother who is ill. She had told my father that she had a craving for apples, and he journeyed for half a month to Basra and brought her back three apples, of which I stole this one; give it back to me.' But I refused to give it back to him; instead, I brought it here and sold it to my little lady for two dinars. This is the story of the apple." When Ja'far heard his words, he marveled at the story and at the discovery that the cause of all the trouble turned out to be none other than one of his own slaves. He rejoiced and, taking the slave by the hand, led him before the caliph and related to him the whole story from beginning to end. The Commander of the Faithful was greatly astonished and laughed until he fell on his back. Then he asked Ja'far, "Do you mean to tell me that this slave of yours is the cause of all the trouble?" Ja'far replied, "Yes, Commander of the Faithful." Seeing that the caliph was greatly struck by the coincidences of the story, Ja'far said to the Commander of the Faithful, "Do not marvel at this story, for it is not as amazing as the story of the two viziers, Nur al-Din Ali al-Misri and Badr al-Din Hasan al-Basri." The caliph asked, "O my vizier, is the story of these two viziers truly more amazing than this one?" Ja'far replied, "Yes, it is indeed more amazing and more extraordinary, but I will not relate it to you, save on one condition." Eager to hear the story, the caliph said, "Come on, my vizier, and let me hear it. If it is indeed more amazing than the events we have just witnessed, I will pardon your slave, but if it is not, I will kill him. Come on: tell me what you know." Ja'far said:

[The Story of the Two Viziers, Nur al-Din Ali al-Misri and Badr al-Din Hasan al-Basri]⁶

I HEARD, O Commander of the Faithful, that a long time ago there lived in the province of Egypt a just, trusted, kind, generous, courageous, and powerful king, who associated with the learned and loved the poor. He had a wise, experienced, and influential vizier who was careful, cautious, and skilled in the affairs of state. This vizier, who was a very old man, had two sons who were like two moons or two lovely deer in their perfect elegance, beauty, and grace. The elder was called Shams al-Din Muhammad, the younger, Nur al-Din Ali. The younger surpassed his brother in beauty; indeed in his day God had created none more beautiful. One day as it had been foreordained, their father the vizier died, and the king mourned him and summoned the two sons, bestowed on them robes of honor and other favors and said, "You shall take your father's place and be joint viziers of Egypt." They kissed the ground before him and withdrew and for a full month they performed the ceremonial mourning for their father. Then they assumed their position, taking turns, each performing his duty for a week at a time, and each accompanying the king on one journey at a time. The two lived in the same house and their word was one.

It happened that one night, before the elder brother was to set out on a journey with the king the next morning, the two brothers sat chatting. The elder brother said, "Brother, I wish that you and I would marry two sisters, draw our marriage contracts on the same day, and go in to our wives on the same night." Nur al-Din replied, "Brother, do as you wish, for this is an excellent idea, but let us wait until you come back from your journey, and with God's blessing we shall seek two girls in marriage." The elder brother said to Nur al-Din, "Tell me, brother, if you and I perform our wedding on the same day and consummate our marriage on the same night and if your wife and mine conceive on our wedding night and at the end of their pregnancy give birth on the same day and if your wife gives birth to a boy and my wife to a girl, tell me, will you marry your son to my daughter?" Nur al-Din replied, "Yes, brother Shams al-Din," adding, "But what dowry will you require from my son for your daughter?" The elder brother replied, "I will take at least three thousand dinars, three orchards, and three farms in addition to an amount specified in the contract." Nur al-Din replied, "Brother Shams al-Din, why

6. Fictitious names, like most of the names in the *Nights*. Al-Misri means "of Egypt," and al-Basri means "of Basra."

such an excessive dowry? Are we not brothers, and is not each of us a vizier who knows his obligations? It behooves you to offer your daughter to my son without a dowry, for the male is worthier than the female. But you treat me like the man who said to another who came to ask for help 'Very well, I will help you, but wait till tomorrow,' prompting the other to repeat the following verses:

> When one postpones the favor for a day,
> The wise man knows that he has answered, 'Nay.'"

Shams al-Din said, "Enough of your comments. Damn you for comparing your son to my daughter and thinking that he is worthier than she; by God, you lack understanding and wisdom. You say that we are partners in the vizierate, without realizing that I let you share it with me, only in order to spare your feelings by letting you assist me. By God, I will never marry my daughter to your son, not even for her weight in gold. I will never marry her to your son and have him for a son-in-law, not even if I have to suffer death." When Nur al-Din heard his brother's words, he became very angry and asked, "Will you indeed not marry your daughter to my son?" Shams al-Din replied, "No, I will never consent to that, for he is not worth even a paring of her nail. Were I not on the eve of a journey, I would make an example of you, but when I come back, I will show you how I will vindicate my honor." Nur al-Din's anger grew so great that he was beside himself with rage, but he hid what he felt, while the brother sulked, and the two spent the night far apart, each full of wrath against the other.

As soon as it was morning, the king went to the pyramids, accompanied by the Vizier Shams al-Din, whose turn it was to go with him. When Shams al-Din departed, Nur al-Din got up, still full of anger, opened his treasure chamber and, taking gold only, filled a small saddlebag. He recalled how his brother had scolded him and insulted him, and he recited the following verses:

> Travel, and new friends will succeed the friends you lost,
> And toil, for life's sweets do through toil come.
> To stay wins you no honor nor from exile saves;
> Set out to roam the world and leave your home.
> When water stands, it stagnant turns and stinks
> But tastes so sweet when it does flow and run.
> And if the sun stood in its orbit still,
> Both Arabs and barbarians would tire of the sun,
> And if the full moon did not wane and set,
> No watchful eyes would the moon's rising mark.
> If in the lair the lion stayed, in the bow the dart,
> Neither would catch the prey, or hit the mark.

Deep in the mine, gold dust is merely dust,
And in its native ground, fuel aloewood.
Gold, when extracted, grows much in demand.
And when exported, aloe fetches gold.

When he finished reciting these verses, he ordered one of his pages to saddle his Arabian she-mule, with her sturdy saddle and saddle-cloth. She was a particularly fine riding animal, with dappled gray skin, ears like sharp reed pens, and legs like pillars. He ordered the page to saddle her with all her trappings, to place the saddlebags on her back, and to cover them with a soft seat of silk carpeting. Then he said to his pages and slaves, "I am leaving the city on an excursion in the vicinity of Qalyubiya to divert myself for a night or two, for I have been very depressed lately. Let none of you follow me." Then he took some provisions, mounted the she-mule, and leaving Cairo,[7] entered the desert. At midday, he reached a town called Bilbis, where he dismounted to rest and have something to eat. Then he took some food for himself and forage for his she-mule and left the town and, spurring his she-mule, fared forth in the desert. By nightfall, he reached the town of al-Sa'idiya, where he dismounted to spend the night at the post station. He walked the she-mule seven or eight times, then gave her some fodder to eat, and after he himself ate some food, he spread the carpet he had used for a seat and, placing the saddlebags under his head, lay down, still seething with anger, saying to himself, "By God, I will ride on even if I wander as far as Baghdad." In the morning, he resumed his journey and, chancing to meet a courier, O Commander of the Faithful, he accompanied him on his she-mule, stopping whenever the courier stopped and riding whenever he rode, until God granted him safe passage and he reached the city of Basra.

It happened that as he approached the outskirts of the city, the vizier of Basra was also traveling on the same road, and when the vizier overtook him and saw that he was a handsome and well-mannered young man, he drew near him, greeted him, and inquired about his situation. Nur al-Din Ali told the vizier about himself and said, "I quarreled with my family and pledged myself not to go back until I visit all the countries of the world, even if I perish and meet my end before I achieve my aim." When the vizier of Basra heard his words, he said to him, "O my son, do not go any further, for most of the regions are waste, and I fear for your safety. " Then he took Nur al-Din Ali home with him and treated him with kindness and generosity, for he was beginning to feel a great affection for him. Then the vizier said to him, "O my son, I am a very old man whom God has never blessed with a son, but I have a daughter who is your equal in beauty.

7. Then and now the capital of Egypt, situated on the Nile River near the pyramids.

Many wealthy and eminent men have asked for her hand, but I have rejected them all, but since I have affection for you, will you accept my daughter as your wife and maid and be a husband to her? If you marry her, I will go to the king and tell him that you are like a son to me and I will advance your cause and make you vizier in my place, so that I may be able to stay at home and rest. For by God, son, I am advanced in years and I am weary and worn out. You shall be a son to me and shall have control over my possessions and over the vizierate in the province of Basra." When Nur al-Din heard the vizier's words, he bowed his head a while, then finally looked up and said, "I hear and obey." The vizier was overjoyed, and he bade his servants prepare food and sweets and decorate the large hall used for wedding feasts, and they at once did as he bade. Then he gathered his friends and invited the prominent and the wealthy men of Basra, and when they were all assembled, he said, "I have a brother who is the vizier of Egypt. He has been blessed with a son and I, as you know, have been blessed with a daughter. When his son and my daughter reached the age of marriage, he sent his son to me, and now I would like to draw their marriage contract, so that he may consummate his marriage here. After the wedding, I shall prepare him for the journey and send him back with his wife." They replied, "This is an excellent idea and a happy and praiseworthy plan. May God crown your good fortune with happiness and may He keep your course blameless."

But morning overtook Shahrazad, and she lapsed into silence.

THE SEVENTY-THIRD NIGHT

The following night Shahrazad said:

I heard, O happy King, that Ja'far said to the caliph:

The prominent men of Basra said, "May God keep your course blameless." Then the witnesses arrived, and the servants brought the tables and laid out the banquet, and the guests ate until they were satisfied, and when the sweets were offered, they enjoyed their fill. Then the servants cleared the tables, and the witnesses came forward and signed the marriage contract, and when the incense rose, the guests departed.

Then the vizier ordered his servants to take Nur al-Din Ali al-Misri to the bath and sent him a full attire worthy of a king, as well as towels, incense, and whatever he needed. A little later, Nur al-Din

came back from the bath, looking like the full moon or the rising
sun, like him of whom the poet said:

> The scent is musk, the cheek a rose,
> The teeth are pearls, the mouth is wine,
> The frame a bough, the hip a barge,
> The hair is night, the face a moon divine.

He went in to his father-in-law and kissed his hand, and the vizier
stood up to greet him, treated him with respect, and seated him
beside him. Then turning to him, he asked, "Son, I would like you to
tell me why you left your family, and how it is that they allowed you
to depart. Hide nothing from me and tell me the truth, for it is said:

> Be truthful, even though the truth
> May torment you with hellish fire,
> And please the Lord and not his slaves,
> In order to avoid His ire.

I wish to take you to the king and let you have my position." When Nur
al-Din heard what his father-in-law said, he replied, "O great Vizier and
mighty lord, I am not of humble origin, nor did I leave my family with
their consent. My father was a vizier." And he told him about what
happened after his father died and about the dispute between himself
and his brother (but there is no point in repeating the story), adding
"Finally, you were kind and gracious to me and you married me to your
daughter. This is my story." When the vizier heard Nur al-Din's story, he
was amazed and said with a smile, "My son, you quarreled even before
getting married and having children! Now, son, go in to your wife, and
tomorrow I shall take you to the king and acquaint him with our case,
and I hope that God will grant you every blessing."

It so chanced, as God had willed and ordained, that on the very
same night on which Nur al-Din consummated his marriage in
Basra, his brother Shams al-Din Muhammad consummated his own
marriage to a girl in Egypt. This is how it came about.

It is related that Ja'far said to the caliph:

I heard that at the time Nur al-Din set out from Egypt, his elder
brother Shams al-Din journeyed with the king of Egypt, and they were
absent for a month. When they returned, the king went to his palace,
while Shams al-Din went home, and when he looked for his brother
and could not find him, he asked his servants and was told, "O our
lord, no sooner had the sun risen on the very morning you set out on
your journey than he was already far away. He said that he would stay

away for a night or two, but we have not heard from him ever since."
When he heard what they said, he felt very sorry to lose his brother and
said to himself, "He must have run away, and I must pursue him even
to the remotest corners of the land." Then he sent couriers after Nur
al-Din, who had already reached Basra. When the couriers reached
Aleppo but heard no news about Nur al-Din, and returned emptyhanded, Shams al-Din despaired of finding him and said to himself,
"There is no power and no strength, save in God, the Almighty, the
Magnificent. I went too far in quarreling with him over the marriage."

Some time later, the Almighty God willed that Shams al-Din should
seek in marriage the daughter of one of the merchants of Cairo, that he
should draw up the marriage contract on the very same day that his
brother drew up his in Basra and that he should consummate his marriage on the very same night that his brother consummated his own
with the vizier's daughter in Basra. So the Almighty and Glorious God,
in order that his decree over his creatures be fulfilled, for a purpose
of his own, let it come to pass, O Commander of the Faithful, that
these two brothers drew up their marriage contracts on the very same
day and consummated their marriages on the very same night, one in
Cairo and the other in Basra. Subsequently, the wife of Shams al-Din
Muhammed, the vizier of Egypt, gave birth to a girl, and the wife of
Nur al-Din Ali al-Misri, the vizier of Basra, gave birth to a boy, a boy
who put to shame both the moon and sun. He had a neck as white as
marble, a radiant brow, and rosy cheeks, and on the right cheek, he had
a mole like a disc of ambergris. He was like one of whom the poet said:

> Here is a slender youth whose hair and face
> All mortals envelope with light and gloom.
> Mark on his cheek the mark of charm and grace,
> A dark spot on a red anemone.

That child, who had a figure as slender as a bough, was endowed by
God with beauty, charm, and perfect grace, so that he captured the
heart with his loveliness and captivated the mind with his perfection. He was so faultless in character and looks that the deer stole
from him their necks and eyes and every other grace. He was like
him of whom the poet said:

> With him to make compare Beauty they brought,
> But Beauty hung his head in abject shame.
> They said, "O Beauty, have you seen his like?"
> Beauty replied, "I have ne'er seen the same."

Nur al-Din Ali named him Badr al-Din Hasan, and his grandfather
the vizier of Basra rejoiced in him and gave banquets in his honor
and distributed presents worthy of kings.

One day, the vizier took Nur al-Din Ali, the vizier of Egypt, with him and went up to the king. When Nur al-Din entered before the king, he kissed the ground before him and repeated the following verses, for he was a cultivated, intelligent, generous, and gentle man:

> May you long live in glory, night and day,
> And may eternal bliss attend your way.

The king thanked Nur al-Din for the compliment and asked his vizier, "Who is this young man with you?" and the vizier repeated Nur al-Din's story from beginning to end, adding, "O King, I would like my lord Nur al-Din to take my place as vizier, for he is an eloquent man, and I your slave have become a very old man, weak in body and mind. As a favor, in consideration of my service to your Majesty, I beg you to appoint him vizier in my place, for he is more qualified than I," and he kissed the ground before the king. When the king looked at Nur al-Din, the vizier of Egypt, and scrutinized him, he was pleased with him and took a liking to him. So he granted the vizier's request, bestowed on Nur al-Din a full robe of honor, presented him with one of his best she-mules, and allotted him stipends and allowances. Then Nur al-Din and his father-in-law went home, feeling happy and saying to each other, "The newborn Hasan has brought us good fortune."

The next day Nur al-Din went up to the king and, sitting in the vizier's seat, carried out all the usual duties of viziers, signing, instructing, judging, and granting, for nothing was beyond him. And the king took him into favor. Then Nur al-Din Ali al-Misri went home, happy and pleased with his position as vizier and with the powers and favors the king had bestowed on him.

The days and nights went by, and he continued to raise and rejoice in his son Badr al-Din Hasan, who grew and thrived, becoming ever more beautiful and charming. When the boy was four years old, his grandfather the old vizier, his mother's father, fell ill and willed all his wealth to him, and when the grandfather died, they mourned him and gave banquets for a whole month. Nur al-Din continued to be the vizier of Basra, as his son Badr al-Din continued to grow and thrive. When he was seven years old, Nur al-Din entered him in a school and charged the tutor to take care of him, saying, "Take care of this boy and give him a good education and teach him good manners." At school everybody was as pleased with Badr al-Din as could be, for he was intelligent, perceptive, sensible, well-mannered, and articulate, and for two full years, under his tutor's guidance, he continued to read and learn.

But morning overtook Shahrazad, and she lapsed into silence.

THE SEVENTY-FOURTH NIGHT

The following night Shahrazad said:

I heard, O King, that Ja'far said to the caliph:

By the time Badr al-Din was twelve years old, he had learned to read and write the Arabic language, as well as calligraphy, mathematics, and jurisprudence; furthermore, the Almighty God had bestowed on his fine figure the robe of beauty, charm, and perfect grace, so that he was like the one of whom the poet eloquently said:

> In perfect beauty he vies with the moon,
> In his fine figure, with the slender bough.
> The sun sets in his cheeks' anemones;
> The rising moon shines in his radiant brow.
> All grace is his, as if he does the earth
> With beauty from his boundless grace endow.

Yet while he was growing up, he never ventured into the city until one day his father Nur al-Din Ali had him fully attired, placed him on a she-mule, and went with him through the city, on his way to the king. When the people looked at him and saw his face, they invoked God to save his beauty from harm, raising their voices in prayer for him and his father, as they crowded around him to look at his beauty, charm, and perfect grace. From that time on he rode with his father every day, and everyone who saw him marveled at his loveliness, for he was like the one of whom the poet said:

> When he appeared, they said, "May he be blessed,
> And glory to the God who fashioned such a one."
> Above all lovely men he was the king,
> And they his subjects all, excepting none.
> The nectar of his mouth tasted so sweet,
> And like a row of pearls his white teeth shone.
> He garnered all the beauty of the world,
> Leaving all mortals helpless and undone.
> And on his cheeks beauty for all to see,
> Proclaimed, "No one is beautiful but he."

He bent coquettishly like a willow bough, and his cheeks resembled roses and anemones. With sweet speech, and a smile so radiant as to put the full moon to shame, he was the lovers' trial and delight.

When he reached the age of twenty, his father, Nur al-Din Ali, having grown feeble, summoned him and said, "Son, you should know that this world is temporary while the next is eternal. I wish to instruct you in what I have learned and understood. I have five admonitions for you." Then he recalled his home and country and, thinking of his brother Shams al-Din, began to weep over his separation from those he loved and from his distant home, and as passion raged within him, he sighed deeply and repeated the following verses:

> I blame you and proclaim my ardent love.
> My body is here, my heart with you still.
> I did not wish to leave you, but our fate
> And God's decree defeat the human will.

When he finished reciting the verses and stopped weeping, he said to his son, "Son, before I give you advice, you should know that you have an uncle who is a vizier in Egypt and whom I left without his consent, as it had been foreordained." Then he took a roll of paper and wrote down what had happened between him and his brother before his departure. Then he wrote down what had happened to him in Basra and how he had become a vizier, recording the date of the day on which he got married and the night on which he consummated the marriage, noting that he was less than forty years old on the day of the quarrel. He concluded by stating that this was his letter to his brother whom he commended to God's care. Then he folded and sealed the scroll, saying, "O Hasan, my son, keep this scroll, and don't ever part with it." Hasan took it and hid it by sewing it into the skullcap of his turban, while his eyes filled with tears for parting from his father, who was entering the throes of death.

But a while later his father opened his eyes and said, "O Hasan, my son, my first advice is that you should not mix or associate with anyone. If you do not, you will avoid trouble, for safety is in keeping aloof. I have heard the poet say:

> There is no man whose friendship you can trust,
> Nor is there true friend in adversity.
> Then live alone and lean for help on none.
> Let this advice of mine your lesson be.

Second, O my son, oppress no one, lest fortune oppress you, for fortune is for you one day but against you another, and its gifts are a loan to be repaid. I have heard the poet say:

> Be careful and restrain your hasty wish;
> Be merciful to all, and they will mercy show.
> The hand of God is above every hand,
> And every tyrant shall another know.

Third, hold your tongue and let your faults distract you from the faults of others. Preserve silence, for it is said, 'In silence safety.' I have heard the poet say:

> Silence is fair, safe taciturnity,
> So, if you speak, do not a babbler be.
> For if your silence may once bother you,
> Your uttered words you will forever rue.

Fourth, O my son, beware of drinking wine, for wine is the root of all evil, because it robs man of reason. Beware, beware of drinking wine. I have heard the poet say:

> I have all wine forsworn
> And joined its many detractors,
> For wine leads man astray
> And opens all the evil doors.

Last, O my son, protect your wealth, so that it may protect you, and watch over it, so that it may watch over you. Do not squander your substance, lest you become dependent on the meanest of men, and guard your money, for money is a salve. I have heard the poet say:

> When my wealth dwindles, all friends disappear;
> When it increases, all are friends to me.
> How many men for money were my friends,
> And when it went, how many left my company!

Follow my advice." He continued to exhort his son until his soul left his body. Then they burned incense around him and buried him.

But morning overtook Shahrazad, and she lapsed into silence. Then Dinarzad said, "Sister, what an entertaining story!" Shahrazad replied, "What is this compared with what I shall tell you tomorrow night if I stay alive!"

THE SEVENTY-FIFTH NIGHT

The following night Dinarzad said, "O sister, tell us the rest of the story." Shahrazad replied, "With the greatest pleasure":

It is related, O King, that Ja'far said to the caliph:

After the vizier died, his son Badr al-Din sat in mourning for two full months, without riding out or attending on the king until the king finally grew angry at him, summoned one of his chamberlains, and made him vizier. Then he bade him take chamberlains and envoys, seize the assets of the deceased Vizier Nur al-Din Ali, confiscate all his money, and seal up all his houses, goods, and possessions, without leaving a penny. The new vizier took with him chamberlains, envoys, guards, clerks, and treasury inspectors, and proceeded to the house of the Vizier Nur al-Din Ali. It happened that there was among the troops a man who had been one of the Mamluks of the Vizier Nur al-Din Ali, and when he heard this order, he spurred his horse and hurried to Badr al-Din Hasan. He found him sitting at the gate of his house, with downcast head and broken heart. He dismounted and, kissing his hand, said, "O my lord and son of my lord, hurry up, hurry up before death catches up with you." Badr al-Din Hasan trembled and asked, "What is the matter?" The Mamluk replied, "The king is angry with you. He has ordered your arrest, and calamity is behind me on its way to you. Run for your life, and don't fall into their hands, for they will not spare you." Badr al-Din Hasan was terribly alarmed, and he paled and asked, "Brother, is there time for me to go into the house?" The Mamluk replied, "No, my lord. Rise this instant and flee your house." Badr al-Din rose, repeating the following verses:

> If you suffer injustice, save yourself,
> And leave the house behind to mourn its builder.
> Your country you'll replace by another,
> But for yourself you'll find no other self.
> Nor with a mission trust another man,
> For none is as loyal as you yourself.
> And did the lion not struggle by himself,
> He would not prowl with such a mighty mane.

He put on his shoes, and, covering his head with the hem of his outer robe, left in confusion, full of anxiety and fear, not knowing where he was proceeding or in which direction he was heading. At last he decided to go to his father's sepulcher, and as he made his way among the tombs, he let fall from his head the hem of his outer robe, which was adorned with bands of brocaded taffeta embroidered with the following lines in gold:

> You who with the dew and stars
> Do with face so radiant vie,
> May your fortune stay the same
> And your glory ever high.

As he was walking, he met a Jew on his way to the city. He was a moneychanger carrying a basket, and when he saw Badr al-Din, he greeted him.

But morning overtook Shahrazad, and she lapsed into silence. Then Dinarzad said, "What an entertaining story!" Shahrazad replied, "What is this compared with what I shall tell you if I live!"

THE SEVENTY-SIXTH NIGHT

The following night, Dinarzad said to her sister, "Tell us the rest of the story." Shahrazad said:

It is related, O King, that Ja'far said to the caliph:

When the Jew saw Badr al-Din, he kissed his hand and said, "My lord, where are you going, for it is near the end of the day; and you are lightly dressed and you look unhappy?" Badr al-Din replied, "I was asleep a while ago and saw my father in a dream. I woke up and came to visit him before nightfall." The Jew replied, "My lord and master, before he died, your father had a seafaring trade, and many of his ships have just arrived with his goods. I would like to ask you as a favor not to sell the cargo to anyone but me." Badr al-Din Hasan replied, "Very well." The Jew said, "I will this instant buy from you the cargo of the first ship to arrive, for a thousand dinars." Then he took out of the basket a sealed purse, opened it, and, setting up the scales, weighed twice until he had a thousand dinars. Badr al-Din Hasan said, "It is sold to you." Then the Jew said, "My lord, write me an acknowledgment on a piece of paper." Badr al-Din Hasan took a piece of paper and wrote on it, "Badr al-Din Hasan al-Basri has sold to Isaac the Jew the cargo of the first ship to arrive, for a thousand dinars, and has received the money." The Jew said, "Put the paper into the purse," and Badr al-Din placed the paper into the purse, tied it, sealed it, and attached it to his belt. Then he left the Jew and continued to make his way among the tombs until he reached his father's sepulcher. There he sat and wept for a while and recited the following verses:

> Since you left me, home is no longer home,
> Nor is the neighbor neighbor, since you went away,
> Nor is the friend who kept me company
> The friend I knew, nor is the day bright day,
> Nor are the sun and moon that shone with light,

The same, for they will never shine again.
In desolation you have left the world,
In gloomy darkness, every field and plain.
O, may the crow that at our parting crowed
His feathers lose and without shelter stand.
My patience fails; my body wastes away;
How many veils are torn by death's cruel hand!
I wonder, will our nights come back again,
And will the old home once more hold us twain?

Badr al-Din Hasan wept at his father's tomb for a full hour, thinking of his plight and feeling at a loss what to do or where to go. As he wept, he laid his head on his father's tomb until he fell asleep— Glory be to Him who sleeps not. He slept on till it was dark, when his head rolled off the tomb and he fell on his back and, with arms and legs outstretched, lay sprawling against the tomb.

It happened that the cemetery was haunted by a demon who sought shelter there in the daytime and flew to another cemetery at night. When night came, the demon came out and was about to fly away, when he saw a man, fully dressed, lying on his back. When he drew near him and looked at his face, he was startled by and amazed at his beauty.

But morning overtook Shahrazad, and she lapsed into silence. Then Dinarzad said, "Sister, what an entertaining story!" Shahrazad replied, "What is this compared with what I shall tell you tomorrow night if I stay alive!"

THE SEVENTY-SEVENTH NIGHT

The following night Shahrazad said:

It is related, O King, that Ja'far said to the caliph:

When the demon looked at Hasan al-Basri, who lay asleep on his back, he marveled at his beauty, saying to himself, "This can be none other than one of the children of Paradise, whom God has created to tempt all mortals." He looked upon him for a long time; then he flew up in the air, rising until he was between the heaven and the earth, where he ran into a flying she-demon. He asked her, "Who are you?" and she replied, "I am a she-demon." Then he greeted her and asked her, "She-demon, will you come with me to my cemetery to see what the Almighty God has created among men?" She replied, "Very well." Then they both flew down to the cemetery, and as they stood there, the demon asked, "In all your life, have you ever seen a young man more beautiful than this one?" When the she-demon looked at Badr al-Din and examined his face, she said, "Glory be to Him who has no rival. By God, brother, by your leave, I will tell you about an extraordinary thing I witnessed this very night in the land of Egypt." The demon said, "Tell me." The she-demon said, "Demon, you should know that there is in the city of Cairo a king who has a vizier named Shams al-Din Muhammad. That vizier has a daughter who is about twenty years old and who bears the most striking resemblance to this young man, for with an elegant and fine figure, she is endowed with beauty, charm, and perfect grace. When she approached the age of twenty, the king of Egypt heard of her and, summoning the vizier her father, said to him, 'Vizier, it has come to my knowledge that you have a daughter, and I wish to demand her of you in marriage.' The vizier replied, 'O King, accept my apology and do not reproach me but grant me your indulgence. As you know, I had a brother called Nur al-Din, who shared the vizierate with me in your service. It happened that one night we sat discussing marriage and children, but the next morning he disappeared, and for twenty years I have never heard of him. Recently, however, I heard, O King of the age, that he had died in Basra, where he was a vizier, leaving behind a son. Having recorded the date of the day I got married, the night I went in to my wife, and the day she gave birth, I have reserved my daughter for her cousin; besides, there are plenty of other women and girls for our lord the king.' When the king heard the vizier's answer, he was angry."

But morning overtook Shahrazad, and she lapsed into silence. Then Dinarzad said, "Sister, what an entertaining story!" Shahrazad replied, "What is this compared with what I shall tell you tomorrow night if I stay alive!"

THE SEVENTY-EIGHTH NIGHT

The following night Shahrazad said:

It is related, O King, that Ja'far said to the caliph:

The she-demon said to the demon, "The king, angry at the answer of his vizier Shams al-Din, said to him, 'Damn you, Someone like me asks the likes of you for his daughter in marriage, yet you put me off with a lame excuse,' and he swore to marry her to none but the meanest of his servants. It happened that the king had a hunchbacked groom with two humps, one behind and one in front, and he sent for the hunchback and, summoning witnesses, ordered the vizier to draw the marriage contract between his daughter and the hunchback that very day, swearing that he would have the hunchback led in procession and that he would have him go in to his bride that very night. I have just now left the princes and their Mamluks waiting for the hunchback at the door of the bath, with lighted candles in their hands, in order to lead him in procession when he comes out. As for the vizier's daughter, she has been dressed and decked out with jewelry by her attendants, while her father is placed under guard until the hunchback goes in to her. O demon, I have never seen anyone as beautiful or delightful as that girl." The demon replied, "You are lying; this young man is more beautiful than she." The she-demon said, "By the Lord of this world, none is worthy of her but this young man. It would be a pity to waste her on that hunchback." The demon replied, "Let us take him up, carry him in his sleep to the girl, and leave them alone together." She said, "Very well," and the demon carried Badr al-Din Hasan al-Basri and flew with him up in the air, while the she-demon flew by his side. Then he came down at the gate of Cairo and, setting Badr al-Din on a bench, awakened him.

When Badr al-Din woke up and found himself in an unknown city, he started to make inquiries, but the demon jabbed him and, handing him a thick candle, said to him, "Go to the bath, mix with the Mamluks and the crowd of people, and walk with them until you come to the wedding hall. Then press ahead and enter the hall as if you are one of the candle bearers. Stand at the right side of the hunchbacked bridegroom, and whenever the bride's attendants, the singing women, or the bride herself approaches you, take a handful of gold from your pocket and give it to the women. Don't hesitate, and whenever you put your hand in your pocket and take it out, it will be full of gold. Take it and give it to those who approach you. Do not wonder, for this is not by your power or strength but by the power, the strength, and the will of God, so that His wise decree may be fulfilled upon His creatures." Then Badr al-Din Hasan rose, lighted the candle, and walked until he came to the bath, where he found the hunchbacked bridegroom already on horseback. So he mixed with the people in the guise and manner already mentioned, wearing a double turban.

But morning overtook Shahrazad, and she lapsed into silence. Then Dinarzad said, "Sister, what an entertaining story!" Shahrazad replied, "What is this compared with what I shall tell you tomorrow night if the king spares me and lets me live!"

THE SEVENTY-NINTH NIGHT

Shahrazad said:

It is related, O King, that Ja'far said to the caliph:

Badr al-Din Hasan walked in the procession, and whenever the singing women stopped to sing and collect money from the people, he put his hand in his pocket and, finding it full of gold, took a handful and cast it in the singing women's tambourines until they were full of dinars. The singing women and all the people were amazed at his beauty and grace, and he continued in this fashion until they reached the palace of the vizier (who was his uncle), where the doormen drove back the people, and forbade them to enter. But the singing women said, "By God, we will not enter unless this wonderful young man enters with us, for in all our life we have never seen anyone more beautiful or more generous, and we will not unveil the bride except in his presence, for he has given out a golden treasure in her honor." So they brought him into the wedding hall and seated him on the dais to the right of the hunchback. The wives of the princes, viziers, chamberlains, and deputies, as well as every other woman present, each veiled to the eyes and holding a large lighted candle in her hand, lined up in two opposite rows, extending from the dais to the bride's throne, which stood in front of the door from which she was to emerge. When the women saw Hasan al-Basri's beauty and grace and looked on his face, which was as bright as the new moon and as dazzling as the full moon, and looked on his body, which swayed like a willow bough, they loved his charm and flirtatious looks, and when he showered them with money, they loved him even more. They crowded around him with their lighted candles and gazed on his beauty and envied him his charm, winking at each other, for every one of them desired him and wished that she was lying in his lap. Everyone said, "None deserves our bride but this young man. What a pity to waste her on the worthless hunchback! May God curse him who brought this about!" and they cursed the king. The hunchback, who was wearing a brocaded robe of honor and a double turban, with his neck buried between his shoulders, sat rolled up like a ball, looking more like a toy than a man. He was like him of whom the poet said:

> O for a hunchback who can hide his hump
> Like a pearl hidden in an oyster shell,
> Or one who looks like a castor oil branch
> From which dangles a rotten citric lump.

Then the women began to curse the hunchback and to jeer at him, while they prayed for Badr al-Din Hasan and ingratiated themselves with him.

Then the singing women beat their tambourines and played their flutes, as the attendants emerged with the bride.

But morning overtook Shahrazad, and she lapsed into silence. Then Dinarzad said to her sister, "Sister, what an amazing and entertaining story!" Shahrazad replied, "What is this compared with what I shall tell you tomorrow night if the king spares me and lets me live!"

THE EIGHTIETH NIGHT

The following night Shahrazad said:

It is related, O King, that Ja'far said to the caliph:

As Badr al-Din Hasan sat on the bench next to the hunchback, the attendants emerged with his cousin. They had combed her hair and, inserting sacks of musk, braided her tresses, and after they had perfumed her with the incense of cardamom and ambergris, they decked her with robes and jewelry worthy of the Persian kings. She paraded in a robe embroidered in gold with dazzling figures of all kinds of birds and beasts, with eyes and bills of precious stones and feet of rubies and green beryl. She wore a very rare and precious necklace, set with large, round gems that dazzled the eye and staggered the mind. As the attendants led the way with lighted camphor candles, her face shone under the candlelight, looking more brilliant than the full moon when it shines on the fourteenth night. With eyes sharper than a bare sword, lashes that captivate the heart, rosy cheeks, and a swinging gait, she advanced, dazzling the eyes with beauty beyond description. The singing women received her by playing on the tambourines and all sorts of musical instruments. Meanwhile, Badr al-Din Hasan al-Basri sat while the women gazed on him, like the moon among the stars, with a radiant brow, a neck as white as marble, a face as bright as the moon, and a rosy cheek graced with a mole like a disk of ambergris.

As the bride approached, swaying gracefully, and unveiled her face, the hunchback rose and bent to kiss her, but she turned her head from him, slipped away, and stood before Badr al-Din Hasan, her cousin, causing the singing women to cry out aloud and the people to clamor.

Badr al-Din Hasan put his hand in his pocket and, again finding it full of dinars, took out a handful and cast it in the singing women's tambourines, and he kept taking out handfuls and throwing them to them, while they commended him to God and signaled to him with their fingers, meaning to say, "We wish that this bride was yours." And as every woman at the wedding gazed on him, he smiled, while the hunchback sat alone like a monkey. Then Badr al-Din Hasan began to move excitedly, surrounded by servants and slave girls, who were carrying on their heads large trays full of gold pieces and dinars, part as a gift for the bride, part for distribution to the public. When the bride made her way to him and stood before him, he kept staring at her, contemplating the beauty that God had bestowed on her alone, while the servants scattered the gold pieces over the heads of the young and the old. And he was happy and rejoiced at what he saw.

But morning overtook Shahrazad, and she lapsed into silence. Then Dinarzad said, "Sister, what a strange and entertaining story!" Shahrazad replied, "What is this compared with what I shall tell you tomorrow night if I stay alive!"

THE EIGHTY-FIRST NIGHT

The following night Shahrazad said:

It is related, O King, that Ja'far said to the caliph:

The attendants presented the bride, in her first dress,[8] as she swayed coquettishly, to the delight and amazement of Badr al-Din Hasan and everyone present. When he looked at his cousin in her red satin dress and saw her blooming radiant face, he was happy and rejoiced at what he saw, for she was like the one of whom the excellent poet said:

> Like the sun above a reed in the dunes, she flamed,
> Clad in a pomegranate red attire,
> And offered me the bounty of her cheeks
> And her lips' wine to quench my burning fire.

Then they changed her dress and put on a blue one, and she reappeared like the shining moon, with jet black hair, soft cheeks, smiling mouth, swelling bosom, firm wrists, and opulent limbs. She was like her of whom the noble poet said:

---

8. The custom still prevails in some parts of the Middle East to present the bride in different dresses to the bridegroom.

> She came in lapis blue, O heavenly sight,
> A moon of summer on a winter's night.

Then they clad her with another dress and, letting down her long tresses, which were as black as the deep night, veiled her face with her abundant hair, save for her eyes, which pierced the hearts with their keen arrows. She was like her of whom the poet said:

> Veiling her cheeks with hair, she came to charm,
> And like a dove appeared to lovers' harm.
> I said, "You veil the morning with the night."
> Said she, "No, 'tis the moon that I veil from the light."

Then they clad her with the fourth dress, and she reappeared like the rising sun, swaying coquettishly, turning gracefully like a deer, and piercing the hearts with the arrows of her eyes. She was like her of whom the poet said:

> The sun of beauty she to all appears,
> With coy reserve and with coquettish grace.
> And when the sun beholds her radiant smile,
> He in the clouds hastens to hide his face.

Then they presented her in the fifth dress, which revealed her wonders, as she swayed her hips and shook her ringlets and curving side tresses, like a willow bough or a deer bending to drink. She was like her of whom the poet said:

> She comes like a full moon on a fair night,
> With dainty limbs and with a slender waist,
> With eyes that subdue all men with their charm,
> With cheeks that vie with rubies at their best.
> She trails her jet black hair over her hips;
> Beware the serpents of her curls, beware!
> Her sides are soft, but alas, alas!
> A heart harder than stones lies hidden there.
> From arching brows she sends her darting looks,
> Which, although distant, never miss the mark.
> When I embrace her waist to press her to my heart,
> Her swelling breasts repel and push me back.
> Ah, how her beauty all outshines, and how
> Her fair shape puts to shame the tender bough.

Then they presented her in the sixth dress, which was green. In this she attained the height of beauty, shaming a bronze spear with her slender form and the bending bough with her softness and supple grace and outshining the rising moon with her radiant face. She surpassed every fair woman in the world and broke every heart, as the poet said of one like her:

> There was a maid with such polish and grace
> That e'en the sun seemed borrowed from her face.
> Bedecked in green she came, fair to behold,
> As a pomegranate bud the green leaves enfold.
> And when we asked, "What do you call this dress?"
> She answered in sweet words meant to impress,
> "Since I have tortured many with my arts,
> In this dress, I call it Breaker of Hearts."

But morning overtook Shahrazad, and she lapsed into silence. Then her sister Dinarzad said, "Sister, what an amazing and entertaining story!" Shahrazad replied, "What is this compared with what I shall tell you tomorrow night if I stay alive!"

THE EIGHTY-SECOND NIGHT

The following night Shahrazad said:

It is related, O King, that Ja'far said to the caliph:

Whenever the attendants presented the bride in a new dress and brought her before the hunchback, she turned her head from him and, moving away, stood before Badr al-Din Hasan, who took out a handful of gold from his pocket and gave it to the singing women. This went on until she was unveiled in all seven dresses, and the attendants signaled to the guests to depart. Everyone departed, except Badr al-Din and the hunchback, while the attendants took the bride inside to undress her and prepare her for the bridegroom. The hunchback turned to Badr al-Din and said, "You have favored us and cheered us with your presence. Would you please rise and leave us now?" Saying "Very well," Badr al-Din rose and made his way to the hallway where he was met by the demon and she-demon, who asked, "Where are you going? Wait here, and when the hunchback comes out to go to the privy to relieve himself, go back to the bedroom and lie in the canopied bed, and when the bride comes and speaks to you, say, 'It is I who am your husband, for the king has planned all this only to laugh at the hunchback, whom we hired for ten dirhams and a bowl of food and then got rid of.' Then proceed to take her virginity and consummate your marriage. We have no sympathy for the hunchback in this matter, for none but you deserves this young woman."

While they were talking, the hunchback came out and went into the privy. While he sat, defecating so much that the shit kept coming from his ass, the demon suddenly emerged from the water bowl in the privy, in the shape of a black tomcat, and said "Meow, meow." The hunchback cried, "Away with you, unlucky cat!" But the cat grew and swelled until he became as big as an ass-colt, braying, "Hee-haw, hee-haw!" The hunchback was startled, and in his fear, he smeared his legs with shit, screaming, "O people of the house, help me!" Then the ass grew even bigger and became a buffalo, and in a human voice said, "Damn you, hunchback!" The hunchback quaked and was so terrified that he slipped on the toilet with his clothes on, saying, "Yes, indeed, O king of the buffaloes!" The demon cried out, "Damn you, you mean hunchback! Is the world so small that you had to marry none but my mistress?" The hunchback replied, "My lord, I am not to blame, for they forced me to marry her, and I did not know that she had a buffalo for a lover. What would you like me to do?" The demon said, "I swear to you that if you leave this place or say anything before sunrise, I will wring your neck. As soon as the sun rises, depart and never return to this house or let us hear from you again." Then the demon seized the hunchback and turned him upside down, with his head stuck in the toilet and his feet up in the air, saying to him, "I will stand here to watch you, and if you try to leave before sunrise, I will seize you by the legs and dash your head against the wall. Be careful with your life."

So much for the hunchback. As for Badr al-Din Hasan, when the hunchback entered the privy, Badr al-Din went straightaway into the net covering the bed and sat there waiting. Soon the bride came in, accompanied by an old woman who stood at the opening of the net and said, "You misshapen man, take God's gift, you trash!" and departed, while the bride, whose name was Sit al-Husn, entered the bed, and when she saw Badr al-Din Hasan sitting there, she exclaimed, "O my dear, are you still here? By God, I wish that you and the hunchback were partners in me." When Badr al-Din heard her words, he said, "Sit al-Husn, why should the filthy hunchback share you with me?" Sit al-Husn replied, "Why shouldn't he? Is he not my husband?" Badr al-Din replied, "Lady, God forbid. The wedding was nothing but a masquerade. Haven't you noticed that the attendants, the singing women, and all your relatives presented you to me, while they laughed at him? Your father knows very well that we hired the hunchback for ten dirhams and a bowl of food and then got rid of him."

When Sit al-Husn heard his words, she laughed and said, "By God, my little lord, you have made me happy and put my heart at ease. Take me and hold me in your lap." She had no trousers on, so Badr al-Din also took off his trousers and, taking from his belt the purse containing the thousand dinars he had received from the Jew, he wrapped it in his trousers and laid them under the mattress. Then taking off his turban, which he laid over the wrapping cloth on the seat, he remained only in his shirt and skullcap and stood hesitating. But Sit al-Husn drew him to her, saying, "O my love, you are keeping me waiting. Quench my desire with your love and let me enjoy your loveliness!" Then she recited these verses:

> For God's sake, rest your legs between my thighs,
> For that is all I now want in the world,
> And let me hear your voice again, O love!
> For I long for you and await your word,
> While my right arm, like your own binding lace,
> My arm alone, enjoys the tight embrace.

But morning overtook Shahrazad, and she lapsed into silence. Then Dinarzad said, "Sister, what an amazing and entertaining story!" Shahrazad replied, "What is this compared with what I shall tell you tomorrow night if I stay alive!"

THE EIGHTY-THIRD NIGHT

The following night Shahrazad said:

It is related, O King, that Ja'far said to the caliph:

Badr al-Din Hasan and Sit al-Husn embraced, and he took her virginity and consummated the marriage. Then she placed one arm under his neck and the other under his shoulder, and with neck on neck and cheek on cheek they went to sleep. as if they seemed to say:

> Cleave to the one you love and ignore calumny,
> For those who envy never favor love.
> Two lovers in one bed, no fairer sight
> Has mercy's Lord created from above.
> Bosom to bosom in each other's arm,
> They lie in bliss, clad in their own delight.
> For when two hearts unite in love's embrace,

The world and all its chatter seem so trite.
Therefore, if ever you your true love find,
O rare occasion, you should never part,
And you who chide the lovers for their love,
Why not instead reform the wicked heart?

When they were fast asleep, the demon said to the she-demon, "Take up the young man, and let us return him to the place where he was asleep, before morning overtakes us." The she-demon took up Badr al-Din Hasan, as he lay asleep without trousers clad only in his thin sequin shirt with its Moroccan gold embroidery and in his striped blue skullcap, and flew away with him, while the demon flew by her side. But no sooner had the Glorious and Almighty God bidden the day dawn and the announcers of prayer climbed to the minaret tops to proclaim the Almighty One, than the angels shot the two demons with shooting stars. The demon was consumed by fire while the she-demon was saved by the Almighty God and was able to come down safely with Badr al-Din Hasan, at the very moment when, as fate would have it, she had reached the city of Damascus,[9] and there she left him by one of the city gates and departed.

When the day dawned and it was light, the city gate was opened and the people came out and, seeing a handsome young man clad in nothing but a light shirt and a skullcap and snoring as he lay in a deep sleep from the exhaustion of the previous night, the candle procession, the presentation of the bride, and his other activities, said, "Lucky is he with whom he spent the night! He should have waited until the boy put on his clothes." Another said, "What a pity for such young people! Look at this young man! Perhaps he came out of the tavern, seeking something and, being drunk, fell asleep without clothes, or perhaps he could not find the door of his house and wandered until he came to the city gate and, finding it shut, fell asleep here." As everyone offered an opinion, the breeze blew and raised his shirt, revealing legs and thighs and belly and navel as clear as crystal and softer than cream. The bystanders cried out, "O lovely, lovely!" and their cries awakened Badr al-Din Hasan al-Basri, who, finding himself lying at the city gate, surrounded by a huge crowd of people, asked in astonishment, "Good people, where am I, and why do you crowd around me?" They replied, "We found you lying here, at the time of the morning call to prayer, and this is all we know about you. Where did you sleep last night?" He replied, "By God, good people, I slept in Cairo last night." One of them said, "Listen to him!" Another said, "Give him a hard kick!" Another said, "Son, you are mad; how can you sleep in Cairo and wake up in Damascus?"

9. Then and now the capital of Syria.

Badr al-Din replied, "By God, good people, last night I slept in the city of Cairo; yesterday I was in the city of Basra; and this morning I am in Damascus." One of them said, "By God, this is a good one; by God, this is a good one!" Another said, "Well, well!" Another said, "He is mad," and everybody began to shout, "He is mad," thus making him a madman in spite of himself and affirming to each other, "There is no doubt of his madness; what a pity for this young man!" Then they said to him, "Son, return to your senses. Who in the world could be in Basra yesterday, in Cairo last night, and in Damascus this morning?" Badr al-Din Hasan replied, "I was truly a bridegroom in Cairo last night." They said, "No doubt, you must have dreamt and seen all this in your sleep." Badr al-Din was no longer sure of himself and began to wonder, but finally said to them, "By God, brothers, it was not in a dream that I went to Cairo and they unveiled the bride before me and before the hunchback. If it was a dream, then where are my gold purse, my dagger, my turban, and my robe?" He was utterly confused.

But morning overtook Shahrazad, and she lapsed into silence. Then Dinarzad said to her sister, "What an amazing and entertaining story!" Shahrazad replied, "What is this compared with what I shall tell you tomorrow night if the king spares me and lets me live!"

THE EIGHTY-FOURTH NIGHT

The following night Shahrazad said:

It is related, O King, that Ja'far said to the caliph:

When the people cried out, "He is mad," Badr al-Din began to run, and they followed him, shouting, "Madman! Madman!" He entered the city and ran through the markets, with the crowd pressing on him, until he took refuge in a cook's shop. This cook had been a scoundrel and a robber until he repented, became reformed, and opened a cookshop. Yet all the people of Damascus were still frightened by him and afraid of his mischief. When they saw Badr al-Din enter his shop, they retreated, dispersed, and went their ways. The cook looked at Badr al-Din and asked, "Young man, where do you come from?" Badr al-Din told him his story from beginning to end (but there is no point in repeating it here). The cook said, "This is a strange story. Keep it to yourself until God sends you relief, and stay with me in this shop, for I am childless and I will adopt you as my son." Badr al-Din replied, "Very well," Then the cook went to the market, bought him some clothes, and had him put them on. Then he took him before witnesses and adopted him formally, and from that day Badr al-Din became known in Damascus as the cook's son, living with him and sitting by the scales in the shop.

So much for Badr al-Din Hasan; as for his cousin Sit al-Husn, when she woke up at dawn and did not find Badr al-Din by her side, she thought that he had gone to the privy. While she was waiting, her father, the Egyptian vizier Shams al-Din Muhammad the brother of Nur Al-Din Ali who was the father of Badr al-Din Hasan, came out, feeling unhappy because of the wrong he had suffered at the hands of the king, who had forced him to marry his daughter to the meanest of servants, a lump of a hunchback. He walked about until he came to his daughter's bed and, standing by the net, called out to his daughter, "Sit al-Husn!" She replied, "Here I am, here I am," and she came out, with a face that had turned more radiant and beautiful from the embraces of that deerlike Badr al-Din, and kissed her father's hand. He said to her, "You cursed girl, you seem mighty pleased with that abominable hunchback!"

But morning overtook Shahrazad, and she lapsed into silence. Then Dinarzad said, "Sister, what a strange and entertaining story!" Shahrazad replied, "What is this compared with what I shall tell you tomorrow night if I live!"

THE EIGHTY-FIFTH NIGHT

The following night Shahrazad said:

It is related, O King, that Ja'far said to the caliph:

When Sit al-Husn heard her father say to her, "You seem mighty pleased with that abominable hunchback!" she smiled and said, "Stop, father! It was enough what I had suffered yesterday at the hands of the women who taunted me and mocked me with that mean hunchback, who is not worthy even to bring my husband his mule or his shoes. By God, in all my life I have never had a better night than last night. Stop mocking me with the hunchback, whom you had hired to ward off the evil eye from my young bridegroom!" When her father heard what she said, he glared at her and said, "Damn you, what is this talk! Hasn't the hunchback slept with you?" The girl replied, "Stop mentioning the hunchback, that worthless creature! May God curse him. I slept in the lap of none but my true husband, the one with the dark eyes and the arched black eyebrows." Her father yelled at her, "Damn you, shameless woman! Have you lost your senses?" She replied, "Ah, for God's sake, father, stop torturing me and being hard on me. I swear by God that my husband, who took my virginity and made me pregnant, is a handsome young man, who is in the privy at this very moment."

Her father went to the privy and there he found the hunchback standing upside down, with his head stuck in the toilet and his feet in the air. The vizier was taken aback and called out, "You hunchback!" The hunchback replied, "Yeah, yeah." The vizier asked, "Why are you in this position, and who did this to you?" The hunchback replied, "Couldn't you people have found anyone for me to marry except a girl who consorts with buffaloes and takes demons for lovers?"

But morning overtook Shahrazad, and she lapsed into silence. Then Dinarzad said, "Sister, what a strange and entertaining story!" Shahrazad replied, "What is this compared with what I shall tell you tomorrow night if the king spares me and lets me live!"

THE EIGHTY-SIXTH NIGHT

The following night Shahrazad said:

It is related, O King, that Ja'far said to the caliph:

When the hunchback said to the father of the bride, "Couldn't you people have found anyone for me to marry except a girl who consorts with buffaloes and takes demons for lovers? May God curse the Devil and my wretched lot," the vizier said to him, "Get up and go!" But the hunchback said, "I am not crazy, for the sun has not risen yet, and I will not go from here until the sun rises. Yesterday I came here to relieve myself when a black tomcat suddenly emerged and screamed at me. Then he kept getting bigger until he was as big as a buffalo and spoke to me in a way that made me obey him. Leave me and go your way, and may God reward you and curse the bride!" But the vizier took him out of the toilet, and the hunchback, in that same condition, went at once to the king and told him what had happened to him at the hands of the demon.

Meanwhile, the father of the bride went back inside the house, amazed and bewildered, not knowing what to make of his daughter. He went to her and said, "Damn it, tell me your secret!" She replied, "Ah, father, what secret? By God, last night I was presented to a young man who spent the night with me, took my virginity, and made me pregnant. Here on this chair is his turban, and here are his robe and his dagger, and here under the mattress are his trousers, wrapped around something. The vizier took his nephew's turban and, turning it in his hand, examined it and said, "By God, this is a vizier's turban, tied in the style of Mosul." When he examined it further, he felt inside it a scroll, folded, sealed, and sewn into the lining. Then he unfolded the trousers and found the purse with the thousand dinars and the piece of paper. When he unfolded the paper, he read, "Badr al-Din Hasan al-Basri has sold to Isaac the Jew the cargo of the first ship to arrive for a thousand dinars and has received the money," and as soon as he read it, he screamed and fell into a swoon.

But morning overtook Shahrazad, and she lapsed into silence. Then Dinarzad said, "Sister, what a strange and entertaining story!" Shahrazad replied, "What is this compared with what I shall tell you tomorrow night if the king spares me and lets me live!"

THE EIGHTY-SEVENTH NIGHT

The following night Shahrazad said:

It is related, O King, that Ja'far said to the caliph:

O Commander of the Faithful, when the vizier Shams al-Din came to himself and recalled what he had discovered, he was amazed, and when he opened the sealed paper and saw that it was in his brother's handwriting, he was even more amazed and said, "Daughter, do you know who the man who took your virginity really was? By God, he is none other than your cousin, and these thousand dinars are your dowry. Glory be to the Omnipotent God who controls everything, for He has turned the cause of my quarrel with my brother Nur al-Din into a just resolution. I wonder how all this came about?" Then he looked at the letter again, and when he saw the date in his brother's handwriting, he kissed it many times, and as he kept looking at the handwriting, he wept, lamented, and repeated these verses:

> I see their traces and with longing pine
> In their empty dwelling, and my tears flow.
> And Him who had decreed their loss I beg
> That He may on me their return bestow.

Then he read the letter and saw the dates of his brother's arrival in Basra, the marriage contract, the consummation of the marriage, the birth of his son Badr al-Din-Hasan, and the year of his death. When the vizier realized what these dates meant, he shook with amazement and delight, for when he compared the events of his life with those of his brother's, he found them parallel, and when he compared the dates of his brother's marriage in Basra, the consummation of that marriage, and the birth of his son, he found them to be identical with his own in Cairo, and when he pondered how shortly thereafter his nephew had arrived and consummated the marriage with his daughter, he concluded that all of this was planned by Providence. Then he took the letter and the piece of paper that he had found inside the purse, went at once to the king, and told him the whole story. The king was very much amazed and ordered that these events be dated and recorded.

Then the vizier went home and waited for his nephew all day long, but he did not show up, and when he waited a second and a third day and kept waiting until the seventh day, without any news or any trace of his nephew, he said, "By God, I will do what has never been done before." He took an inkwell and a sheet of paper and wrote down a description of the entire wedding chamber and its contents. Then he ordered everything put aside, including the turban, the trousers, and the purse.

But morning overtook Shahrazad and she lapsed into silence. Then Dinarzad said, "Sister, what a strange and entertaining story!" Shahrazad replied, "What is this compared with what I shall tell you tomorrow night if the king spares me and lets me live!"

THE EIGHTY-EIGHTH NIGHT

The following night Shahrazad said:

I heard, O happy King, that Ja'far said to the caliph:

Days and months went by, and when her time came, the daughter of the vizier of Egypt gave birth to a boy, who had a face as round as the full moon or the rising sun, a radiant brow, and rosy cheeks. They cut his navel cord and applied kohl to his eyelids, and his grandfather named him 'Ajib and committed him to the care of the nurses, stewardesses, and servants.

'Ajib grew, and when he was seven, his grandfather sent him to school, bidding the tutor educate him and teach him good manners. 'Ajib remained at the school about four years. Then he began to bully, beat, and abuse the other children. At last they got together and

complained to the monitor about their maltreatment at the hands of
'Ajib. The monitor said, "I will tell you what you should do tomorrow,
so that he will stop coming to school and you will never see him again.
When he comes tomorrow, gather around him to play a game and say
to each other, 'No one can join us in this game, unless he tells us the
names of his mother and father, for he who does not know the names
of his parents is a bastard and shall not play with us.'" The children
were pleased, and the next day they came to school, and when 'Ajib
arrived, they gathered around him and one of them said, "We will play
a game, but no one can join in unless he tells us the names of his
mother and father." Everyone said, "Very well." Then one said, "My
name is Majid, my mother's name is Sittita, and my father's name is 'Iz
al-Din," and others said the like, until it was 'Ajib's turn. He said, "My
name is 'Ajib, my mother's name is Sit al-Husn, and my father's name
is Shams al-Din, the vizier." They said, "How can that be? By God, he
is not your father!" He said to them, "Damn you, the Vizier Shams al-
Din is indeed my father." But they laughed at him and clapped their
hands and said, "May God help him! He does not know his father! By
God, he cannot play or sit with us." Then they laughed, and dispersed,
leaving him choking with tears. Then the monitor came to him and said,
"'Ajib, don't you know that the Vizier Shams al-Din is your mother's
father, your grandfather, and not your father? As for your father, neither
you nor we know who he is. For the king married your mother to a
hunchback, but the demons came and slept with her, and your father
is unknown. Unless you find out who he is, you will not be able to face
the schoolchildren, for they will treat you as a bastard. Don't you see
that even though your grandfather is the vizier of Egypt, the merchant's son knows his own father and the grocer's son knows his, but
you don't know your father? 'Ajib, this is a strange business!"

*But morning overtook Shahrazad, and she lapsed into silence. Then
Dinarzad said, "Sister, what a strange and entertaining story!" Shahrazad replied, "What is this compared with what I shall tell you tomorrow night if I stay alive!"*

THE EIGHTY-NINTH NIGHT

The following night Shahrazad said:

I heard, O happy King, that Ja'far said to the caliph:

When 'Ajib heard the insulting remarks of the children and the
monitor, he left at once and came crying to his mother Sit al-Husn.

When she saw him, her heart was on fire for him, and she asked him, "Son, why do you cry? May God never let you cry again!" Sobbing, he told her what had happened; then he asked her, "Who, then, is my father?" She replied, "Your father is the vizier of Egypt." He said, "You are lying. The vizier is your own father; he is my grandfather. Who, then, is my father?" When Sit al-Husn heard him speak of his father, her cousin and husband Badr al-Din Hasan, and recalled her wedding night, she wept bitterly and recited these verses:

> Love in my breast he lit and went away
> And left behind an empty hearth and heart.
> His shrine is too distant to visit now,
> A distance that has kept us worlds apart!
> And when he left, my patience also left,
> So did endurance, so did self-control.
> And when he went away, he took with him
> My joy, my peace, my rest, all; he took all
> And left me my tears of unhappy love,
> Which from my burning eyes profusely flow.
> And when I long to see him once again,
> And with vain longing wait for him to show,
> I trace his image in my empty heart,
> Which wells with thoughts, longing, and deep passion.
> You, whose remembrance wraps me in its warmth,
> Whose love I show, a sign of devotion,
> Is there no ransom for the captive heart,
> And for the afflicted no remedy,
> And for the sick with love no medicine,
> And for the defeated no victory?
> O my dear love, how long this coy disdain?
> When will you come back and be mine again?

While she wept and made her son weep with her, the vizier came in, and when he saw them, he asked, "Why do you weep?" His daughter told him what had happened to her son, and when he remembered his brother and nephew and his daughter's puzzling story, he wept with them. Then he went at once to the king of Egypt and, kissing the ground before him, begged him leave to go eastward to the city of Basra to inquire about his nephew; he also begged him for royal edicts to all the provinces and cities, authorizing him to take custody of Badr al-Din wherever he found him. And he wept before the king, who took pity on him and wrote him letters and edicts to all the provinces and cities. The vizier rejoiced, thanked the king, and invoked God's blessing on him. Then he returned at once to his house, and after he made preparations for the journey, he took his daughter and her son 'Ajib with him and departed.

But morning overtook Shahrazad, and she lapsed into silence. Then Dinarzad said, "Sister, what a strange and entertaining story!" Shahrazad replied, "What is this compared with what I shall tell you tomorrow night if the king spares me and lets me live!"

THE NINETIETH NIGHT

The following night Shahrazad said:

I heard, O happy King, that Ja'far said to the caliph:

The vizier of Egypt, the uncle of Badr al-Din Hasan, journeyed with his daughter and her son for twenty days until he came to the city of Damascus and saw its rivers and birds, just as the poet described them:

> Once in Damascus I spent such a night
> That time swore 't would never the like allow.
> We slept carefree under the wing of night
> Till morning smiled and beamed with dappled brow,
> And dewdrops on the branches hung like pearls,
> Then fell and scattered when the zephyr blew,
> And birds chanted the words traced on the lake,
> As the wind wrote and the clouds the points drew.

The vizier dismounted and pitched his tents at a place called the Plain of Pebbles, saying to his followers, "Let us rest here for two or three days." Then the pages and servants went on their errands into the city, this to sell, that to buy, another to go to the bath. 'Ajib too went into the city to see the sights, followed by a eunuch carrying a red club of knotted almondwood, "with which if one hit a camel, it would go galloping as far as Yemen."[1] When the people of Damascus saw 'Ajib, who in spite of his very young age was all beauty, charm, and perfect grace, just like him of whom the poet said:

> The scent is musk, the cheek a rose,
> The teeth are pearls, the mouth is wine,
> The frame a bough, the hip a barge,
> The hair is night, the face a moon divine,

they followed him, while others ran ahead and waited for him to pass by, so that they might gaze on him, until, as if it had been foreordained,

---

1. A country situated on the southwestern corner of the Arabian peninsula.

the eunuch stopped in front of the shop of 'Ajib's father, Badr al-Din Hasan al-Basri.

Badr al-Din had been living in Damascus for twelve years, during which time the reformed cook died, leaving his shop and all his property to his adopted son, Badr al-Din. In the course of the years Badr al-Din's beard had grown and his understanding had matured. When his son and the servants stood before him . . .

But morning overtook Shahrazad, and she lapsed into silence. Then the king said to himself, "By God, I will not have her put to death until I find out what happened to the vizier Badr al-Din Hasan, his son, his uncle, and his cousin. Then I will have her put to death as I did the others."

THE NINETY-FIRST NIGHT

The following night Shahrazad said:

I heard, O happy King, that Ja'far said to the caliph:

When 'Ajib and the servant stood before Badr al-Din's shop, and he gazed on his son's extraordinary beauty and grace, his heart began to throb, his stomach began to flutter, and he felt happy, as the blood hearkened to the blood, driven by instinctive sympathy and the divine mystery—Glory be to Him who controls everything. Looking at his son's outlandish attire and at his wonderful face, Badr al-Din said to him, "O my lord and master of my life and heart, you for whom I would shed my blood, would you enter my shop to taste my food and make me happy?" (That day he had prepared a pomegranate-seed dish cooked in sugar.) At that moment, he remembered his happy days as a vizier's son, and his eyes filled with tears and he recited the following verses:

> O my beloved, as I shed my tears,
> I should acquaint you with my sorry plight:
> When I avoid you, I yearn for you so
> And feel a passion that does burn and blight.
> 'Tis not that I hate or wish to forget,
> But that such love can such wisdom beget!

'Ajib felt tenderness for him, and his heart throbbed. He turned to the eunuch and said, "Tutor, I feel sympathy and pity for this cook, who seems to have lost a son or a brother. Let us enter his shop and by accepting his hospitality console him; perhaps God will reward this act by reuniting me with my father." When the eunuch heard his words, he was angry and said, "What a fine thing for a vizier's son to eat at a cookshop! While I stand here to protect you with this club even from people's looks, how can I let you enter their shops?" When Badr al-Din heard what the eunuch said, he turned to his son and recited the following verses:

> I marvel that they guard you with one slave,
> While many are enslaved by your own grace,
> The basil of the beard and jewels of the mouth,
> The mole of ambergris and rubies of the face.

Then Badr al-Din turned to the eunuch and said, "Noble lord, will you make me happy by entering my shop, you who are like a chestnut, black without but white within, just like him of whom the poet said?" The eunuch laughed and asked, "For God's sake, what did the poet say?" Badr al-Din recited the following verses:

> Were he not such a fine and trusty man,
> He would not in the court hold such a sway,
> Or guard the harem with such zeal and care
> That even the angels do him homage pay.
> In blackness he excels, but 'tis his deeds,
> His noble deeds that outshine the bright day.

This pleased the eunuch, who laughed and, taking 'Ajib by the hand, entered Badr al-Din's shop. Badr al-Din placed before them a sizzling bowl of pomegranate seeds conserved with almonds and sugar, and they ate and found it extremely delicious. 'Ajib turned to his father and said, "Sit down and eat with us, and may the Almighty God reunite me with the one for whom I long!" Badr al-Din said, "Son, have you too at your tender age suffered the loss of one you love?" 'Ajib replied, "Yes uncle, my heart bleeds for the loss of one I love, and my grandfather and I have been roaming the land in search of him. Alas, how I long to be reunited with him!" Then he wept and Badr al-Din wept at the sight of his son's tears and at the thought of his own separation from his home and mother, in a distant land, and he recited the following verses:

> If ever we meet each other again,
> I will have much about which to complain,
> For no letter can cure the ailing heart,
> Nor can another voice a lover's pain.
> The critics censure my abundant tears,
> But tears are little for lovers to pay.
> When will the Good Lord bring me back my love
> And let my care and sorrow go away?
> If we meet then, I will to you complain,
> For none but I myself can voice such pain.

The eunuch felt pity for Badr al-Din, and after they ate together, he took 'Ajib and departed. But when they left the shop, Badr al-Din felt as if his soul had left his body and had gone with them. He could not bear to be without them even for a single moment; so he closed his shop and followed them.

But morning overtook Shahrazad, and she lapsed into silence. Then Dinarzad said, "Sister, what a strange and entertaining story!" Shahrazad replied, "What is this compared with what I shall tell you tomorrow night if I stay alive!"

THE NINETY-SECOND NIGHT

The following night Shahrazad said:

I heard, O happy King, that Ja'far said to the caliph:

Badr al-Din closed his shop and followed his son, without knowing that he was his son. He walked until he caught up with them before they reached the city gate and kept following them. When the eunuch looked behind and saw him, he said, "Damn it, what do you want?" Badr al-Din replied, "Noble lord, when you departed, I felt that my soul had left me and gone with you; besides, as I have some business outside the Victory Gate, I thought that I would come out to finish it and return." The eunuch was angry and said to 'Ajib, "This is what I feared, and this is what you have done to me. When one is blind, one does not see ahead. Because we entered this fellow's shop and ate an unfortunate mouthful, he takes liberties with us and follows us from place to place." 'Ajib turned around and, seeing the cook following him, reddened with anger and said to the eunuch, "Let him walk like any Muslim, but if he turns in the same direction when we come outside the city and turns toward our tents, we will know that he is following us." Then he bowed his head and walked on, with the eunuch behind him.

Badr al-Din followed them until they came to the Plain of Pebbles and drew near their tents, and when 'Ajib turned around and saw Badr al-Din still following him, he flushed and turned pale, angry and afraid that his grandfather might find out that he had gone into a cookshop and that he had been followed by one of the cooks; and when 'Ajib saw Badr al-Din's eyes fixed on him, for he was like a body without a soul, he thought that they were the eyes of a treacherous or a lewd fellow, and his rage mounted. He bent to the ground, picked up a granite stone weighing a pound, and threw it at his father. It struck him on the forehead, cutting it open from eyebrow to eyebrow, and he fell down in a swoon, with his blood streaming down over his face, while 'Ajib and the eunuch headed to their tents. When Badr al-Din came to himself, he wiped away the blood and, taking off his turban, bandaged his wound with it, blaming himself and saying, "I wronged the boy in closing my shop and following him, making him think that I was some treacherous or lewd fellow." Then he returned to his shop, where every now and then he would feel a bit of nostalgia for his mother in Basra, weep for her, and recite the following verses:

> If you ask fair play of fate, you wrong it,
> For blameless fate is not meant to be fair.
> Take what may please you and be not concerned,
> For in this life, one day is troubled, one day fair.

But morning overtook Shahrazad, and she lapsed into silence. Then Dinarzad said, "Sister, what a strange and entertaining story!" Shahrazad replied, "What is this compared with what I shall tell you tomorrow night if the king spares me and I stay alive!"

THE NINETY-THIRD NIGHT

The following night Shahrazad said:

I heard, O happy King, that Ja'far said to the caliph:

Badr al-Din returned to his shop and resumed selling his food. Meanwhile the vizier, his uncle, stayed in Damascus for three days and departed for Homs, and after he arrived there and finished his search, he departed for Hama, where he spent the night. Again, after he finished his search, he departed, pressing on until he reached Aleppo,[2] where he stayed for two days. Then going through Dyarbakir, Mardin, Sinjar, and Mosul,[3] he fared on until he reached Basra. When he arrived, he went up to meet the king, who received him with honor and esteem and asked the reason for his coming. Shams al-Din related to him his story and told him that his vizier, Nur al-Din Ali of

---

2. Homs, Hama, and Aleppo: then and now cities in Syria.
3. Sinjar and Mosul: then and now cities in northern Iraq. Dyarbakir and Mardin: then and now cities in eastern Turkey.

Egypt, was his brother. The king commended Nur al-Din's soul to the mercy of God and said, "My lord, he lived here for fifteen years; then he died, leaving a son, who stayed here only one month after his father's death and disappeared without any trace or news. But his mother, who was the daughter of my old vizier, is still with us." Shams al-Din asked the king for permission to visit her and meet with her, and the king gave him permission.

He went to his brother Nur al-Din's house and looked around and kissed the threshold. And he thought of his brother Nur al-Din and how he had died in a foreign land, and he recited the following verses:

> I wander through the halls where Leyla lived,
> And in my sorrow kiss the stony walls.
> 'Tis not for the stones that I burn with love
> But for the dear one who dwelt in the halls.

Then he entered the main gate and found himself in a spacious courtyard, at the end of which stood an arched door vaulted over with granite inlaid with multicolored marble. He walked around the house and, casting his eyes on the walls, saw his brother Nur al-Din's name inscribed in letters of gold and Iraqi lapis lazuli.[4] He went up to the inscription and kissed it, and, thinking of his brother and his loss, he wept and repeated the following verses:

> I ask for news of you the rising sun
> And of the lightning's flash of you inquire
> And in the throes of passion pass my night,
> Without complaining of love's hellish fire.
> O my love, if our parting longer lasts
> My pining heart with pain will waste away,
> But if you bless my sad eyes with your sight,
> The day we meet will be a blessed day.
> Think not that I have found another love;
> There is no room for others in my heart.
> Pity a tortured lover, sick with love,
> Whose heart by parting has been torn apart.
> If fate should bless my sad eyes with your sight,
> I would that day offer my thanks to fate.
> May God defeat all those who wish us ill
> And thwart those who slander to separate.

Then he walked in and stopped at the door of the hall.

In the intervening years, his brother's widow, the mother of Badr al-Din Hasan of Basra, had, from the day of her son's disappearance,

---

4. Semiprecious stone of a bright blue color.

given herself up to weeping and lamentation, day and night, and after a long time went by, she made a tomb for her son in the middle of the hall and continued to weep there, day and night. When her brother-in-law reached the hall and stood at the door, he saw her draping the tomb with her flowing hair and heard her invoking her son Badr al-Din Hasan, weeping, and repeating these verses:

> O tomb, O tomb, has he his beauties lost,
> Or have you lost yourself that radiant look?
> O tomb, neither a garden nor a star,
> The sun and moon at once how can you host?

Shams al-Din entered and, after greeting her, informed her that he was her brother-in-law and told her what had happened.

But morning overtook Shahrazad, and she lapsed into silence. Then Dinarzad said, "What a strange and entertaining story!" Shahrazad said, "What is this compared with what I shall tell you tomorrow night if I am alive!"

THE NINETY-FOURTH NIGHT

The following night, Shahrazad said:

I heard, O happy King, that Ja'far said to the caliph:

Shams al-Din told her what had happened and how Badr al-Din had spent a night at his house, ten years ago, but had disappeared in the morning, how on that night the young man had gone in to his daughter, taken her virginity, and made her pregnant, and how when her time came, she gave birth to a boy, concluding, "This boy with me here is the son of your son." When Badr al-Din's mother heard this news of her son, that he was still alive, she looked at her brother-in-law and threw herself at his feet, wept bitterly, and recited the following verses:

> How good is he who tells me they have come,
> For he brings me the best of news to know!
> Were he content with worn-out robes, a heart,
> At parting torn, I would on him bestow.

Then she rose, embraced 'Ajib, pressing him to her heart, kissed him and was kissed by him, and wept. But the vizier said to her, "This is no time for weeping. Get yourself ready and come with us to the land of Egypt, and we will perhaps be reunited with your son, my nephew. This story should be written down!" She rose at once and prepared herself for the journey, while the vizier went to take his leave of the king, who provided him for the journey, sending with him gifts to the king of Egypt, and bade him good-bye.

Shams al-Din set out of Basra on his journey homeward, and he fared on until he reached Aleppo, where he stayed for three days. Then he resumed his journey until he came to Damascus and halted, pitching his tents in the same place and saying to his men, "We shall stay here for two or three days to buy some fabrics, as well as other presents for the king." Then he went on his business. Meanwhile 'Ajib came out and said to the eunuch, "Tutor, let us go into the city to enjoy the sights and see what has become of the cook whose food we ate and whose head I cut, for he was kind to us, but we treated him badly." The eunuch replied, "Very well, let us." Then they left the tents, as the blood tie drew 'Ajib to his father, and walked until they entered the city through the Heavenly Gate. They spent the time at the Umayyad Mosque till close to the time of the afternoon prayer; then they walked through the Grand Market[5] and continued walking until they came to the shop of Badr al-Din Hasan and found him standing there. He had prepared a pomegranate-seed dish, preserved in almonds and sweet julep and flavored with cardamom and rose-water, and the food was ready to serve. When 'Ajib looked at him and saw him marked from eyebrow to eyebrow with the dark scar he had given him with the blow, he felt tenderness for him and was overcome with pity. He said to his father, "Peace be with you! You have been on my mind." When Badr al-Din looked at him, his stomach began to flutter and his heart began to throb, as the blood hearkened to the blood. He bowed his head and tried to reply, but his tongue could not find the words. Then still overwhelmed, he raised his head, looked at his son sadly and imploringly, and recited the following verses:

> I longed to see the one I love, and when
> I did, I stood before him dumb and blind.
> I bowed my head in reverence and awe
> But failed to hide the love that seethed behind.
> My heart was full of troubles and concerns,
> But not a single word bespoke my mind.

Then he said to 'Ajib, "Perhaps you and the noble gentleman will enter my shop and eat my food to heal my broken heart, for by God, I cannot look at you without a throbbing in my heart. When I followed you, the other time, I was beside myself." 'Ajib replied . . .

---

5. The famous market of Damascus whose main street leads to the Umayyad Mosque. The Umayyad Mosque: then and now one of the great mosques of the Muslim world, built between 705 and 714 C.E.

But morning overtook Shahrazad, and she lapsed into silence. Then Dinarzad said, "Sister, what a strange and entertaining story!" Shahrazad replied, "What is this compared with what I shall tell you tomorrow night if the king spares me and lets me live!"

THE NINETY-FIFTH NIGHT

The following night Shahrazad said:

I heard, O happy King, that Ja'far said to the caliph:

Badr al-Din said to his son, "When I followed you, I was beside myself." 'Ajib replied, "You must be very fond of us. You gave us a mouthful of food and, assuming that we owed you something, you tried to dishonor us. This time we will not eat anything unless you swear that you will not hold us under any obligation, follow us, or make any claim on us. Else we will not visit you again. We are staying here for about a week, so that my grandfather may buy presents for the king of Egypt." Badr al-Din said, "Very well, you may do as you please." 'Ajib and the eunuch entered the shop; and Badr al-Din ladled from the top of the pot a bowlful of food and placed it before them. 'Ajib said to him, "Sit down and eat with us," and Badr al-Din was glad and sat down and ate with his son, with his eyes fixed on him, for his whole being yearned for him. 'Ajib said, "Ha, ha, haven't I told you that you are an overbearing lover? Stop staring at my face!" Badr al-Din sighed and recited the following verses:

> Passion for you lies deeply in the heart,
> A secret sealed in darkness, seen by none.
> O you whose beauty shames the shining moon,
> Whose ample grace rivals the rising sun,
> Your radiant face frustrates the burning heart
> And with hopelessness afflicts love's desire.
> Your mouth is nectar, but I die of thirst;
> Your face is Heaven, but I burn in fire.

They ate together, and Badr al-Din kept putting morsels, now in 'Ajib's mouth, now in the eunuch's, until they were satisfied. They rose up, and Badr al-Din poured water on their hands and, loosening a towel from his waist, gave it to them to wipe their hands with, and sprinkled them with rosewater from a casting bottle. Then he ran out of the shop and rushed back with an earthenware pitcher containing a sweet drink, flavored with rosewater and cooled with snow.

He set it before them, saying, "Complete your kindness to me." 'Ajib took the pitcher and drank and passed it to the eunuch, and they kept passing it around until they had had enough and their stomachs felt too full, for they had eaten much more than usual. Then they thanked him and, bidding him good-bye, hurried through the city until they came out through the East Gate and hastened to their tents. 'Ajib went to see his grandmother, Badr al-Din's mother, and she kissed him and, thinking of her son Badr al-Din and his days with her, sighed and wept, until her veil was wet, and recited the following verses:

> Had I not thought that we would meet again,
> I would have after you of life despaired.
> I swear my heart holds nothing but your love,
> By God who knows and has my secret shared.

Then she asked 'Ajib, "Son, where have you been?" and set food before him, and as it had been foreordained, they too had cooked a pomegranate-seed dish, except that this one had less sugar. She gave him a bowlful, together with some bread, and said to the eunuch, "Eat with him." Saying to himself, "By God, I can't even smell the bread," he sat down to eat.

But morning overtook Shahrazad, and she lapsed into silence. Then Dinarzad said, "Sister, what a strange and entertaining story!" Shahrazad replied, "What is this compared with what I shall tell you tomorrow night if the king spares me and I stay alive!"

THE NINETY-SIXTH NIGHT

The following night Shahrazad said:

It is related, O King, that Ja'far said to the caliph:

The eunuch sat down; though his belly was full with what he had already eaten and drunk. 'Ajib dipped a piece of bread in the pomegranate dish and took a bite but found the food insipid, for he too was full. He said, "Bah; what is this awful stuff?" His grandmother was astonished and said, "Son, do you find fault with my food? I cooked it myself, and no cook can compare with me, except my son Badr al-Din Hasan." 'Ajib replied, "Grandmother, we have just now found in the city a cook who had prepared a pomegranate-seed dish whose aroma delights the heart and whose flavor stimulates the appetite. Your food is nothing by comparison." When his grandmother heard his words, she was angry and, turning to the eunuch, said, "Damn you, you are corrupting my son by taking him into the city and letting him eat in cookshops." When the eunuch heard her words, he was frightened and said, "No, by God, my lady, we did not eat anything; we only saw the cookshop in passing." But 'Ajib said, "By God, grandmother, we did enter the shop, and both this time and the other time we ate a pomegranate-seed dish that was better than yours." In her anger, she went and informed her brother-in-law, provoking him against the eunuch, at whom the grandfather yelled, saying, "Damn you, where did you take my grandson?" Afraid of being put to death, the eunuch denied everything, but 'Ajib told on him, saying, "Yes, by God, grandfather, we went into the cookshop and ate until the food came out of our nostrils, and the cook gave us an iced sweet drink." The vizier became angrier and said, "You ill-fated slave, did you take my grandson into a cookshop?" The eunuch continued to deny it until the vizier said to him, "My grandson says that the two of you ate until you were full. If you are telling the truth, then eat this bowlful of pomegranate seeds, which is before you." The eunuch said, "Very well," and took a morsel from the bowl and ate it, but unable to swallow a second, he spat it out and threw it away and, drawing away from the food, said, "By God, my lord, I am full ever since yesterday."

By this the vizier realized the truth and ordered his servants to throw the eunuch down and beat him. Smarting under the blows, the eunuch cried for mercy and said, "My lord, we did enter a cookshop and we did eat a pomegranate-seed dish that was indeed better than this one." His words angered Badr al-Din's mother, who said, "For God's sake, son, and may God reunite me with my own son, you must go and bring me back a bowl of pomegranate dish from that cook, so that your master may judge which is the better and tastier of the two, his or mine." The eunuch replied, "Indeed I will." Then she gave him a bowl and half a dinar, and he went out running until he came to the cookshop and said to Badr al-Din, "Excellent cook, I have made a wager about your cooking in my master's household. Give me half a dinar's worth of your pomegranate dish and it better be good, for I have had a bellyful of beating for entering your shop. Don't let me taste more beating with your food." Badr al-Din laughed and said, "By God, noble lord, no one can cook this dish as well but myself and my mother, and she is far away." Then he ladled out the food, choosing the best parts, covered the bowl, and gave it to the eunuch, who hastened back with it. Badr al-Din's mother took it, and when she tasted the food and noticed its excellent flavor, she knew who had cooked it, shrieked, and fell down in a swoon. The vizier was astonished and sprinkled water on her, and when she carne to herself, she said, "If my son Badr al-Din is still in this world, none has cooked this dish but he."

But morning overtook Shahrazad, and she lapsed into silence. Then Dinarzad said, "Sister, what a strange and entertaining story!" Shahrazad replied, "What is this compared with what I shall tell you tomorrow night if the king spares me and lets me live!"

THE NINETY-SEVENTH NIGHT

The following night Shahrazad said:

It is related, O King, that Ja'far said to the caliph:

Badr al-Din's mother said, "None has cooked this dish but my son Badr al-Din, for none knows how to cook it as well as he." When the vizier heard her words, he rejoiced and felt happy and said, "Alas for you, my nephew! I wonder whether God will ever reunite us with you!" Then he rose at once and called out to his followers, atten-dants, slaves, camel drivers, and porters, about fifty in all, saying, "Take sticks, clubs, and the like and go to the cook's shop and demolish it by breaking everything inside, even the pots and dishes. Then tie him with his turban and, saying 'Are you the one who has cooked this awful pomegranate-seed dish,' bring him here. But let none of you beat him or do him any harm; just bind him and bring him here by force. In the meantime I will go to the vizier's palace and come back." They replied, "Very well."

Then the vizier mounted his horse, rode to the palace, and met with the viceroy of Damascus, showing him the king's edicts. The viceroy kissed them and, after reading them, asked, "Who is your adversary?" The vizier replied, "He is a cook." The viceroy ordered a chamberlain to go to the cookshop, and the chamberlain went with four captains, four palace guards, and six soldiers, leading the way. When they came to the cookshop, they found it in ruins and saw everything in it broken.

For while the vizier was at the palace, his servants rose and, taking sticks, tent poles, clubs, and swords, flew in a hurry until they reached the cookshop and, without speaking to Badr al-Din, fell with their weapons on his pots and utensils, broke his shelves, bowls, dishes, and trays, and destroyed his stoves. When Badr al-Din asked them, "O good people, what is the matter?" they replied by asking him, "Are you the one who cooked the pomegranate dish that the eunuch bought?" He replied, "Yes, I am the one who cooked it, and no one can cook anything like it." They yelled at him, abused him, and continued to demolish the shop until a crowd of people assembled and, seeing about fifty or sixty men demolishing the shop, said, "There must be a grave cause behind this!" Badr al-Din cried out, saying, "O fellow Muslims, what is my crime in cooking this food that you should treat me like this, breaking my dishes and ruining my shop?" They said, "Aren't you the one who cooked the pomegranate dish?" He replied, "Yes, indeed! What is wrong with it that you should do this to me?" But they kept yelling at him, scolding him, and cursing him. Then they surrounded him, took off his turban and, tying him with it, dragged him by force out of the shop, while he screamed, cried, and called for help.

But morning overtook Shahrazad, and she lapsed into silence. Then Dinarzad said, "Sister, what a strange and entertaining story!" Shahrazad replied, "What is this compared with what I shall tell you tomorrow night if the king spares me and lets me live!"

THE NINETY-EIGHTH NIGHT

The following night Shahrazad said:

It is related, O King, that Ja'far said to the caliph:

Badr al-Din kept crying, calling for help, and asking, "What fault did you find with the pomegranate dish?" and they kept asking, "Aren't you the one who cooked the pomegranate dish?" while he kept answering, "Yes, indeed! But what is wrong with it that I should suffer like this?" As they drew close to the tents, the chamberlain, with his captains and other men, caught up with them. He pushed the vizier's servants aside to look at Badr al-Din and, hitting him on the shoulders with his stick, asked him, "You, are you the one who cooked the pomegranate seeds?" Badr al-Din cried with pain from the blow and replied, "Yes, my lord, but I ask you, in the name of God, what is supposed to be wrong with it?" But the chamberlain scolded him and cursed him, saying to his men, "Drag away this dog who has cooked the pomegranate dish." Badr al-Din felt miserable, wept, and said to himself, "What did they find wrong with the pomegranate dish that they should abuse me to this extent?" and he felt frustrated for not knowing what his fault was. The men kept dragging him until they reached the tents, where they waited until the vizier, having gotten the viceroy's permission to depart and having bidden him good-bye, returned to the tents.

As soon as he dismounted, he asked, "Where is the cook?" and they brought Badr al-Din before him. When Badr al-Din saw his uncle the vizier Shams al-Din, he wept and said, "My lord, what is my offense against you?" Shams al-Din replied, "Damn you, aren't you the one who cooked the pomegranate dish?" With a cry of exasperation, Badr al-Din replied, "Yes my lord, and what a misfortune! Does my crime warrant cutting off my head?" Shams al-Din replied, "That misfortune would be the least punishment." Badr al-Din said, "My lord, will you not tell me my crime and what is wrong with the pomegranate dish?" Shams al-Din replied, "Yes, presently," and he called out to his servants, shouting, "Pack up, and let us go." The servants undid the tents at once and made the camels kneel for loading. Then they put Badr al-Din in a chest, which they locked and placed on a camel. Then they departed and journeyed until nightfall, when they stopped to eat. Then they took Badr al-Din out of the chest, fed him, and locked him up again.

They kept traveling in this way until they reached Cairo and dismounted outside the city. Then the vizier ordered the servants to take Badr al-Din out of the chest, and they did so and brought him before the vizier, who sent for wood and a carpenter and said to him, "Make a wooden, crosslike figure." Badr al-Din asked, "What will you do with it?" The vizier replied, "I will crucify you by nailing you on it, and then I will parade you throughout the city, because the pomegranate dish you cooked lacked pepper and tasted awful." Badr al-Din said, "Haven't you done enough, and all because the pomegranate dish lacked pepper?"

But morning overtook Shahrazad, and she lapsed into silence. Then Dinarzad said to her sister, "What a strange and entertaining story!" Shahrazad replied, "What is this compared with what I shall tell you tomorrow night if the king spares me and lets me live!"

THE NINETY-NINTH NIGHT

The following night Shahrazad said:

It is related, O King, that Ja'far said to the caliph:

Badr al-Din said, "Because the pomegranate dish lacked pepper, you have beaten me, smashed my dishes, and ruined my shop, all because the pomegranate dish lacked pepper! Isn't it enough, O Muslims, that you have tied me and locked me up in this chest, day and night, fed me only one meal a day, and inflicted on me all kinds of torture, because the pomegranate dish lacked pepper? Isn't it enough, O Muslims, to have shackled my feet that you should now make a crosslike figure to nail me on, because I have cooked a pomegranate dish that lacked pepper?" Then Badr al-Din pondered in bewilderment and asked, "All right, suppose I did cook the dish without pepper, what should my punishment be?" The vizier replied, "To be crucified." Badr al-Din said, "Alas, are you going to crucify me because the pomegranate dish lacked pepper?" and he appealed for help, wept, and said, "None has been crushed as I have been, and none has suffered what I have suffered. I have been beaten and tortured, my shop has been ruined and plundered, and I am going to be crucified, all because I cooked a pomegranate dish that lacked pepper! May God curse the pomegranate dish and its very existence!" and as his tears flowed, he concluded, "I wish that I had died before this calamity."

When they brought the nails, he cried, lamented, and mourned over his crucifixion. But as night was falling and it was getting dark, the vizier took Badr al-Din, pushed him into the chest, and locked it, saying, "Wait till tomorrow morning, for tonight we have no time left to nail you." Badr al-Din sat inside the chest, crying and saying to himself, "There is no power and no strength, save in God, the Almighty, the Magnificent. Why do I have to be crucified and die? I have not killed anyone or committed any crime; nor have I cursed or blasphemed. My only offense is that I am supposed to have cooked a pomegranate dish that lacked pepper; that is all."

In the meantime the vizier placed the chest on a camel and followed it into the city, after the markets closed, until he came to his house. Later at night the servants arrived with the loaded camels and, making them kneel, carried the equipment and baggage inside. The first thing the vizier did was to say to his daughter Sit al-Husn, "Daughter, praised be God who has reunited you with your cousin and husband. Rise this instant and let the servants prepare the house and arrange the furniture as it was on your wedding night, twelve years ago." The servants replied, "Very well." Then the vizier called for candles, and when they lighted the candles and lanterns and brought him the sheet of paper on which he had written the exact description of the room on the wedding night, he began to read it out to them until everything was arranged as it had been on that night. They put everything in its place, lighting the candles as they had been lighted, and placing the turban on the chair and the trousers and the purse with the thousand dinars under the mattress, as Badr al-Din had placed them on that night. Then the vizier came to the hallway and said to his daughter, "Undress and go to bed, as you did the night he came in to you, and when he comes in, this time, say to him, 'My lord, you have stayed too long in the privy.' Then let him lie beside you and engage him in conversation till the morning, when we will tell him the whole extraordinary story."

But morning overtook Shahrazad, and she lapsed into silence. Then Dinarzad said, "Sister, what a strange and entertaining story!" Shahrazad replied, "What is this compared with what I shall tell you tomorrow night if the king spares me and lets me live!"

THE ONE HUNDREDTH NIGHT

The following night Shahrazad said:

It is related, O King, that Ja'far said to the caliph:

I heard, O Commander of the Faithful, that the vizier went to Badr al-Din, untied him, and, taking off all his clothes, save for a shirt, led him slowly until he came to the door of the room from which the bride had come out to be unveiled before him and in which he had slept with her and taken her virginity. When he looked at the room, he recognized it, and when he saw the bed, the net, and the chair, he was amazed and bewildered. Advancing one foot and drawing the other back, he rubbed his eyes and said to himself in his confusion, "Glory be to the Almighty God! Am I awake or asleep?" Sit al-Husn lifted the net and said to him "Ah, my lord, will you not come in? You have stayed too long in the privy; come back to bed!" When Badr al-Din heard her words and saw her face, he smiled in amazement and said, "By God, you are right; I did stay too long in the privy!" But as he entered the room, he recalled the events of the last ten years, and as he kept looking at the room and recalling those events, he was confounded and felt lost, not knowing what to make of this. He looked at the turban, the robe, and the dagger on the chair, went to the bed and felt the trousers and the purse under the mattress, and finally burst out laughing, and said, "By God, this is a good one; by God, this is a good one!" Sit al-Husn asked, "My lord, why do you stare at the room and laugh for no reason?" When he heard her words, he laughed again and asked, "How long have I been absent from you?" She replied, "Ah, may the Compassionate and Merciful God preserve you! Ah, haven't you gone out but a while ago to relieve yourself and come back? Have you lost your wits?"

Badr al-Din laughed and said, "By God, lady, you are right. I left you and, forgetting myself, fell asleep in the privy. I recall as if I dreamt that I lived in Damascus for ten years, working as a cook, and that one day a young boy and his servant visited my shop." Then, touching his forehead and feeling the scar from the blow, he cried out, "No, by God, it must have been true, for the boy hit me with a stone and cut my forehead open. By God, my friend, it would seem that it really happened." Then he reflected for a while and said, "By God, my lady, it seems to me that when I embraced you and we fell asleep, a little while ago, I dreamt that I went to Damascus without turban or trousers and worked there as a cook." Then he reflected again and said, "Yes, by God, my lady, it seems as if I dreamt that I cooked a pomegranate dish that lacked pepper. Yes, by God, my lady, I must have slept in the privy and seen all this in a dream, except that, by God, my lady, it was a long dream." Sit al-Husn said, "For God's sake, my lord, tell me what else you dreamed?" Badr al-Din replied, "My lady, had I not awakened, they would have crucified me." She asked, "For what reason?" He replied, "Because I cooked a pomegranate dish that lacked pepper. It seemed as if they smashed my dishes, ruined my shop, tied me and shackled me, and put me in a chest. Then they brought a carpenter to make a wooden crosslike figure to nail me on. It all happened because the pomegranate dish lacked pepper. Thank God that all of this happened to me in a dream and not in reality." Sit al-Husn laughed and pressed him to her bosom, and he returned her embrace. But he reflected again and said, "My lady, what happened to me must indeed have been real, but there is no power and no strength, save in God, the Almighty, the Magnificent. By God, what a strange story!"

But morning overtook Shahrazad, and she lapsed into silence. Then Dinarzad said, "Sister, what a strange and entertaining story!" Shahrazad replied, "What is this compared with what I shall tell you tomorrow night if the king spares me and lets me live!"

THE ONE HUNDRED AND FIRST NIGHT

The following night Shahrazad said:

It is related, O King, that Ja'far said to the caliph:

That night Badr al-Din lay down in a state of confusion, now saying, "I was dreaming," now, "I was awake." He kept looking in astonishment at the room, the objects, and the bride, saying to himself, "By God, till now I have not even completed one night with her." Then he would reflect again and say, "It must have been real," until it was morning and his uncle came in, bidding him good morning. When Badr al-Din saw him, he recognized him and was utterly confused. He said, "In fact, aren't you the one who gave the orders to beat, tie, shackle, and crucify me because of the pomegranate dish?" The vizier replied, "Son, the truth is out, for what was hidden has been revealed. You are my true nephew, and I did all this only to be sure that you were indeed the one who had consummated the marriage with my daughter that night. You recognized your turban, your clothes, and your gold purse, as well as the scroll written by my brother and hidden in the lining of your turban. Had the man we brought here been other than you, he would not have recognized these objects." Then he recited the following verses:

> Our fate is fickle, for such is our state
> That one day may depress, one day elate.

Then the vizier called for Badr al-Din's mother, and when she saw her son, she threw herself at him, wept bitterly, and recited the following verses:

> When we meet, we will complain
> Of our afflictions, that day,
> For the feelings of the heart
> No messenger can convey,
> Nor is the voicing of grief
> Keeping the feelings at bay.
> No messenger ever knows
> How to say what I can say.

Then she told him how she had endured after his departure, and he too told her how he had suffered, and they thanked God for their reunion. The following day the vizier went to the king and acquainted him with the situation, and the king was exceedingly amazed and ordered that the story be recorded. Thereafter, the vizier and his nephew and daughter lived the best of lives in prosperity and ease, eating and drinking and enjoying themselves to the end of their days.

Ja'far concluded: "This, O Commander of the Faithful, is what happened to the vizier of Basra and the vizier of Egypt." The caliph said, "By God, Ja'far, this is the wonder of wonders," and ordered that the story be recorded. Then he freed the slave and gave the young man one of his choice concubines, settled on him a sufficient income, and made him one of his companions to the end of his days.

The following night Shahrazad said:

[The Story of the Hunchback]

IT IS RELATED, O King, that there lived once in China a tailor who had a pretty, compatible, and loyal wife. It happened one day that they went out for a stroll to enjoy the sights at a place of entertainment, where they spent the whole day in diversions and fun, and when they returned home at the end of the day, they met on the way a jolly hunchback. He was smartly dressed in a folded inner robe and an open outer robe, with gathered sleeves and an embroidered collarband, in the Egyptian style, and sporting a scarf and a tall green hat, with knots of yellow silk stuffed with ambergris.[6] The hunchback was short, like him of whom the poet 'Antar[7] said:

> Lovely the hunchback who can hide his hump,
> Like a pearl hidden in an oyster shell,
> A man who looks like a castor oil branch,
> From which dangles a rotten citric lump.

He was busy playing on the tambourine, singing, and improvising all kinds of funny gestures. When they drew near and looked at him, they saw that he was drunk, reeking of wine. Then he placed the tambourine under his arm and began to beat time by clapping his hands, as he sang the following verses:

> Go early to the darling in yon jug;
> Bring her to me,
> And fete her as you fete a pretty girl,
> With joy and glee,
> And make her as pure as a virgin bride,
> Unveiled to please,
> That I may honor my friend with a cup
> Of wine from Greece.
> If you, my friend, care for the best in life,
> Life can repay,
> Then at this moment fill my empty cup,
> Without delay.
> Don't you, my tantalizer, on the plain
> The gardens see?

6. Waxy substance secreted by the intestinal tract of the sperm whale, often found floating in the sea, and used in the manufacture of perfume.
7. Pre-Islamic hero, and author of one of the Arabic Golden Odes.

But morning overtook Shahrazad, and she lapsed into silence. Then Dinarzad said to her sister, "What a strange and entertaining story!" Shahrazad replied, "What is this compared with what I shall tell you tomorrow night if the king spares me and lets me live!"

THE ONE HUNDRED AND THIRD NIGHT

The following night Shahrazad said:

It is related, O King, that when the tailor and his wife saw the hunchback in this condition, drunk and reeking of wine, now singing, now beating the tambourine, they were delighted with him and invited him home to sup and drink with them that night. He accepted gladly and walked with them to their home.

Then the tailor went to the market—it was already dark—and bought bread, fried fish, radishes, lemons, and a bowl of honey, as well as a candle to give them light during their carousing. When he returned, he set the bread and fish before the hunchback, and the wife joined them for supper. The tailor and his wife were pleased to have the hunchback with them, saying to each other, "We will spend the night carousing, bantering, and amusing ourselves with this hunchback." They ate until they were satisfied. Then the tailor took a piece of fish and, cramming it in the hunchback's mouth, held it shut and said laughing, "By God, you must swallow the whole piece." The hunchback, unable to breathe, could not wait to chew, and he hastened to swallow the piece, which happened to have a large bone, which stuck in his throat and choked him. When the tailor saw the hunchback's eyes rolled up, he raised his hand and boxed him on the chest, and the hunchback's soul left his body and he slumped lifeless. The tailor and his wife were stunned and, trembling, said, "There is no power and no strength, save in God, the Almighty, the Magnificent. How soon was his appointed hour!" The wife said to her husband the tailor, "Why do you sit still and do nothing? Haven't you heard the poet say:

> How can you sit and let the fire rage on?
> Such idleness brings ruin and destruction."

The tailor asked, "What shall I do?" and she replied, "Rise, carry him in your arms, cover him with a silk shawl, and follow me. If anybody sees us in the dark, we shall say, 'This is our sick boy who took ill a short while ago, and since the doctor could not come to see him, we are taking him there.' If we do that . . ."

But morning overtook Shahrazad, and she lapsed into silence. Then Dinarzad said to her sister, "What a strange and amusing story!" Shahrazad replied, "What is this compared with what I shall tell you tomorrow night if I stay alive!"

THE ONE HUNDRED AND FOURTH NIGHT

The following night Shahrazad said:

It is related, O King, that the tailor carried the hunchback in his arms, covered him with a silk shawl, and followed his wife, who led the way, wailing and saying, "O my boy, may you recover from your illness. Where has this smallpox been lying in wait for us?" so that whoever saw them said, "These two have a child stricken with the smallpox," until someone directed them to the house of a Jewish physician. When the wife knocked at the door, a maid came down, and when she opened the door, she saw a man carrying a sick child. The wife handed her a quarter-dinar and said, "Miss, give this to your master, and let him come down to see my child, who is gravely ill." As soon as the maid went upstairs, the wife went in, saying to her husband, "Let us leave the hunchback here and run." The tailor propped up the hunchback, leaving him standing in the middle of the Jew's staircase, and went away with his wife.

Meanwhile the maid went to the Jew and said to him, "Master, there are people downstairs, carrying a sick child, and they have sent you this quarter-dinar to go down to see him and prescribe for him." When the Jew saw the quarter-dinar as a fee for merely going downstairs, he was pleased and in his joy rose hastily in the dark, saying to the maid, "Bring me light," and descended hurriedly in the dark. But hardly had he taken a step when he stumbled on the hunchback, who fell and rolled to the bottom of the stairs. The Jew was startled and shouted to the maid, "Hurry with the light." When she brought it, he went down and, finding the hunchback dead, said, "O Esdras, O Moses, O Aaron, O Joshua son of Nun! It seems that I have stumbled against this sick fellow, and he has fallen downstairs and died. By the hoof of Esdras's ass, how shall I get this dead body out of my house?" Then he carried the body upstairs, and when he told his wife about it, she said to him, "Why do you sit still? If the day breaks and he is still here, we will both lose our lives. You are naive and careless." Then she recited the following verses:

> You thought well of the days, when they were good,
> Oblivious to the ills life brings to one.
> You were deluded by the peaceful nights,
> Yet in the peace of night does sorrow stun.

But morning overtook Shahrazad, and she lapsed into silence. Then Dinarzad said, "Sister, what a strange and entertaining story!" Shahrazad replied, "What is this compared with what I shall tell you tomorrow night if the king spares me and lets me live!"

THE ONE HUNDRED AND FIFTH NIGHT

The following night Shahrazad said:

I heard, O King, that the Jew's wife said to him, "Why do you sit still? Rise at once and let us carry the body to the roof and throw it into the house of our neighbor, the Muslim bachelor." It happened that the Jew's neighbor was the steward of the king's kitchen, who used to bring home a great deal of cooking butter, which, together with everything else he brought, was eaten by the cats and mice, which caused considerable loss. The Jew and his wife took the hunchback up to the roof, carried him little by little to the steward's house and, holding him by the hands and feet, lowered him until he reached the ground. Then they propped him up against the wall and went away.

No sooner had they descended from the roof than the steward, who had been at a recitation of the Quran, came home in the middle of the night, carrying a lighted candle. He opened the door, and when he entered his house, he found a man standing in the corner, under the ventilator, and said, "By God, this is a fine thing! My food has been stolen by none other than a man. You kept taking the meat and the fat sheep tails and scooping out the cooking butter, and I kept blaming the cats and dogs and mice. I have killed many cats and dogs and have sinned against them, while you have been coming down the windshaft to steal my provisions, but now, by God, I will avenge myself on you with my own hands." Then he took a heavy club and with one leap stood before the hunchback and gave him a heavy blow on the rib cage, and as the hunchback fell, he gave him another blow on the back. Then looking at his face and seeing that he was dead, he cried out, saying, "Alas! I have killed him. There is no power and no strength, save in God, the Almighty, the Magnificent." Then he turned pale with fear for himself, saying, "May God curse the cooking butter and curse this night! To God we belong and to Him we return."

But morning overtook Shahrazad, and she lapsed into silence. Then Dinarzad said to her sister, "What a strange and entertaining story!" Shahrazad replied, "What is this compared with what I shall tell you tomorrow night if the king spares me and lets me live!"

THE ONE HUNDRED AND SIXTH NIGHT

The following night Shahrazad said:

It is related, O happy King, that when the steward saw that the man was a hunchback, he said, "O hunchback, O cursed man! Wasn't it enough for you to be a hunchback, but you had to turn thief too? What shall I do? O Protector, protect me!" Then as it was getting toward the end of the night, he carried the hunchback on his back and went out with him until he reached the entrance of the market, where he set him on his feet against a shop, at the corner of a dark alley, and went away.

Soon there came a prominent Christian tradesman, who had a workshop and was the king's broker. He was drunk, and in his drunkenness he had left home, heading for the bath, thinking that morning prayers were near. He came staggering along until he drew near the hunchback and squatted in front of him to urinate and, happening to look around, suddenly saw a man standing before him. It so happened that early that night, someone had snatched off the Christian's turban, so that when he saw the hunchback standing before him, he thought that he too was going to snatch off his turban. He clenched his fist and boxed the hunchback on the neck, knocking him down. Then crying out for the watchman, he fell in his drunkenness on the hunchback, pummeling him and choking him. When the watchman came up to the lamppost and saw a Christian kneeling on a Muslim and beating him, he asked, "What is the matter?" The Christian replied, "This man tried to snatch off my turban." The watchman said, "Get up from him," and when the Christian got up, the watchman drew close to the hunchback and, finding that he was dead, said, "By God, this is a fine thing, a Christian killing a Muslim!" Then he seized the Christian broker, bound him, and brought him in the night to the house of the chief of the police. The Christian was bewildered, wondering how he could have killed the fellow so quickly with one blow of the fist, as "drunkenness left him and reflection returned." Then he and the hunchback passed the night in the chief's house.

In the morning, the chief went up to the king and informed him that his Christian broker had killed a Muslim. The king ordered that the broker be hanged, and the chief went down and bade the executioner proclaim the sentence. Then the hangman set up a gallows, under which he made the Christian stand, put the rope around his neck and was about to hang him, when the steward of the king's kitchen made his way through the crowd and said to the executioner, "Stop! This man did not kill the fellow; I am the one who killed him." The chief asked, "What did you say?" The steward replied, "I am the one who killed him." Then he related to him his story, how he hit the hunchback with the club and how he carried him and propped him up in the market, adding, "Is it not enough for me to have killed a Muslim, without burdening my conscience with the death of a Christian too? On my own confession, hang no one but me."

But morning overtook Shahrazad, and she lapsed into silence. Then Dinarzad said to her sister, "What a strange and entertaining story!" Shahrazad replied, "What is this compared with what I shall tell you tomorrow night if the king spares me and lets me live!"

THE ONE HUNDRED AND SEVENTH NIGHT

The following night Shahrazad said:

I heard, O happy King, that when the chief heard the steward's words, he said to the hangman, "Release the Christian, and hang this man, on the strength of his confession." The hangman, after releasing the Christian, made the steward stand under the gallows, put the rope around his neck, and was about to hang him, when the Jewish physician made his way through the crowd and cried out to the hangman, "Stop! This man did not kill the fellow; I am the one who killed him. Last night I was sitting at home after the markets closed, when a man and a woman knocked at the door. When the maid went down and opened the door, she found that they had a sick person with them. They gave the maid a quarter-dinar, and she brought it up to me and told me about them, but no sooner had she come up than they rushed in and placed the sick person at the top of the stairs. When I went down, I stumbled on him, and the two of us rolled to the bottom of the stairs, and he died instantly. No one was the cause of his death but I. Then my wife and I carried the dead hunchback to the roof and let him down, through the windshaft, into the house of this steward, which adjoins ours, and left him standing in the corner. When the steward came home, he found a man standing there and, thinking that he was a thief, hit him with a club, knocking him down flat on his face, and concluded that he had killed him, whereas in truth none killed him but I. Is it not enough for me to have involuntarily and unwillingly killed one Muslim, without burdening my conscience with the death of another Muslim? Don't hang him, for no one killed the hunchback but I."

But morning overtook Shahrazad, and she lapsed into silence. Then Dinarzad said to her sister, "What a strange and entertaining story!" Shahrazad replied, "What is this compared with what I shall tell you tomorrow night if the king spares me and lets me live!"

THE ONE HUNDRED AND EIGHTH NIGHT

The following night Shahrazad said:

I heard, O happy King, that when the chief heard the Jew's words, he said to the hangman, "Release the steward and hang the Jew." The hangman seized the Jew and put the rope around his neck, when the tailor made his way through the crowd and said to the hangman, "Stop! This man did not kill him, and none killed him but I." Then turning to the chief, he said, "My lord, none killed the hunchback but I. Yesterday I went out to see the sights, and when I returned in the evening, I met the hunchback, who was drunk and singing and playing on the tambourine. I invited him home with me and then went out, bought fried fish for him, and brought it back. Then we sat to eat, and I took a piece of fish and crammed it down his throat, and he choked on a bone and died instantly. My wife and I were frightened, and we carried him to the Jew's house. We knocked at the door, and when the maid came down and opened the door, I said to her, 'Go up and tell your master that there are a man and a woman downstairs, with a sick person for him to see,' handing her a quarter-dinar to give to her master. As soon as she went up, I carried the hunchback to the top of the stairs, propped him up, and went down and ran with my wife. When the Jew came down, he stumbled against the hunchback and thought that he had killed him." Then the tailor turned to the Jew and asked, "Isn't this the truth?" The Jew replied, "Yes, this is the truth." Then turning back to the chief, the tailor said, "Release the Jew and hang me, since I am the one who killed the hunchback." When the chief heard the tailor's words, he marveled at the adventure of the hunchback and said, "There is a mystery behind this story, and it should be recorded in the books, even in letters of gold." Then he said to the hangman, "Release the Jew and hang the tailor on his own confession." The hangman released the Jew and placed the tailor under the gallows, saying to the chief, "I am tired of stringing up this man and releasing that, without any result." Then he put the rope around the tailor's neck and threw the other end over the pulley.

It happened that the hunchback was the favorite clown of the king of China, who could not bear to be without him even for the batting of an eye, so that when the hunchback got drunk and failed to make his appearance that night . . .

But morning overtook Shahrazad, and she lapsed into silence. Then Dinarzad said, "Sister, what a strange and entertaining story!" Shahrazad replied, "What is this compared with what I shall tell you tomorrow night if the king spares me and lets me live!"

THE ONE HUNDRED AND NINTH NIGHT

The following night Shahrazad said:

I heard, O happy King, that when the hunchback got drunk and failed to make his appearance before the king that night, and when the king waited for him in vain the next day until it was close to noon, he at last inquired about him from one of those present, who replied, "I heard, O King, that the chief of the police found a dead hunchback and caught his murderer. But when he was about to hang him, a second and a third man came forward, and each claimed to be the murderer. They are still there, each telling the chief how the hunchback died." When the king of China heard these words, he called out to one of his chamberlains, saying, "Go down and bring me everyone, the chief, the murdered man, and the murderers." The chamberlain went down at once and arrived just when the hangman had put the rope around the tailor's neck and was about to hoist him up. He cried out to the hangman, "Stop!" and, turning to the chief, relayed to him the king's order. The chief took the tailor, the Jew, the steward, and the Christian, together with the hunchback, carried on a litter, and brought them all before the king. He kissed the ground before him and related to him their adventures with the hunchback, from beginning to end. When the king of China heard the story, he was very much amazed and moved to mirth, and he ordered that the story be recorded, saying to those around him, "Have you ever heard anything more amazing than the adventure of the hunchback?" The Christian broker came forward and, kissing the ground before the king, said, "O King of the age, with your leave, I will tell you a more amazing story that happened to myself, a story that will make even the stone weep." The king replied, "Tell us your story." The Christian said:

[The Christian Broker's Tale:
The Young Man with the Severed Hand
and the Girl]

O KING, I CAME as a stranger to your country, bringing merchandise with me, and was fated to stay here these many years. I was born a Copt,[8] a native of Cairo. My father was a prominent broker, and when he died, I became a broker in his place and worked there for many years. One day, as I was sitting in the market of the fodder merchants in Cairo, a handsome and finely dressed young man, riding a tall ass, came up to me. He saluted me, and I rose in salute. Then he took out a handkerchief containing sesame and asked me, "How much is the measure worth?"

But morning overtook Shahrazad, and she lapsed into silence. Then Dinarzad said, "Sister, what a strange and entertaining story!" Shahrazad replied, "What is this compared with what I shall tell you tomorrow night if the king spares me and lets me live!"

THE ONE HUNDRED AND TENTH NIGHT

The following night Shahrazad said:

I heard, O happy King, that the Christian broker said to the king of China:

O King of the age, I replied to the young man, "It is worth a hundred dirhams." He said, "Take a measurer and some porters and come to the al-Jawli Caravansary,[9] by the Gate of Victory, where you

8. Egyptian Christian.
9. Inn with a large courtyard, where caravans could rest during the night.

will find me." I rose and went to find a buyer, making the rounds of the sesame merchants, confectioners, and fodder dealers, and got one hundred dirhams per measure. Then I took with me four teams of porters and went with them to the al-Jawli Caravansary, where I found the young man waiting for me. As soon as he saw me, he rose and led me to the storeroom, saying, "Let the measurer enter to measure, while the porters load the donkeys." The porters kept loading, one team coming and one team going, until they emptied the storeroom, carrying fifty measures in all, costing five thousand dirhams. Then the young man said to me, "Take ten dirhams per measure for your brokerage, and keep my share of four thousand and five hundred dirhams with you. When I finish selling the rest of my crop, I will come to you and take the money." I replied, "Very well," kissed his hand, and departed, surprised at his liberality.

For a month I sat waiting for him until he finally came and asked, "Where is the money?" I welcomed him and invited him to sit with me and have something to eat, but he refused and said, "Go and get the money, and in a little while I will come back to take it from you." Then he departed on assback, while I went and brought the money and sat waiting for him. But again he did not show up for a month, and I said to myself, "This is indeed a liberal young man. He has left four thousand and five hundred dirhams of his money with me, for two full months, without coming to take it." At last he came back, riding an ass, dressed in fine clothes, and looking as if he had just come from the bath.

But morning overtook Shahrazad, and she lapsed into silence. Then Dinarzad said, "What a strange and entertaining story!" Shahrazad replied, "What is this compared with what I shall tell you tomorrow night if the king spares me and lets me live!"

THE ONE HUNDRED AND ELEVENTH NIGHT

The following night Shahrazad said:

I heard, O happy King, that the Christian broker said to the king of China:

The young man looked as if he had just come from the bath. When I saw him, I left the shop and went up to him, saying, "Sir, will you take your money back?" He replied, "What is the hurry? Wait

until I sell the rest of my crop. Then I'll take it from you, next week."
When he left, I said to myself, "When he comes back next time, I
will invite him to eat with me."

He was absent for the rest of the year, during which I used his
money, trading with it and making a great deal of profit. At the end of
the year, he came back again, dressed in fine clothes. When I saw
him, I went up to him and swore by the New Testament that he must
eat with me as my guest. He agreed, saying, "On condition that what
you spend on me will be from my own money." I replied, "Very well."
Then I went in, prepared the place for him and seated him. Then I
went to the market and, getting enough of beverages, stuffed chickens, and sweets, set them before him, saying, "Please help yourself."
He came to the table and began to eat with his left hand.[1] I said to
myself, "Only God is perfect. Here is a young man who is handsome
and respectable yet so conceited that he does not bother to use his
right hand in eating with me." But I ate with him.

*But morning overtook Shahrazad, and she lapsed into silence. Then
Dinarzad said, "What a strange and entertaining story!" Shahrazad
replied, "What is this compared with what I shall tell you tomorrow
night if the king spares me and lets me live!"*

THE ONE HUNDRED AND TWELFTH NIGHT

The following night Shahrazad said:

I heard, O happy King, that the Christian broker said to the king
of China:

When we finished eating, I poured water on his hand and gave
him something to wipe it with, and after I offered him some sweets,
we sat to chat. I asked him, "Sir, relieve my mind by telling me why
you ate with me with your left hand? Does something ail your right
hand?" When the young man heard my question, he wept and
recited the following verses:

> If Leyla[2] I have for Selma exchanged,
> 'Twas not at will but by necessity.

---

1. Considered a lapse in manners, since the left hand is used for toilet hygiene.
2. The beloved cousin of the Arab poet Kais, known as "Majnun," who went mad because of
   his unrequited love for her; she is a legendary figure in Arabic and Persian poetry and art.

Then he drew his right arm from his bosom and showed it to me. It was a stump, with the hand cut off at the wrist. I was astonished at this, and he said to me, "Don't wonder and say to yourself that I am conceited and have eaten with my left hand out of conceit. There is a strange story behind the cutting off of my hand." I asked, "How came it to be cut off?" Sighing and weeping, he said:

I was a native of Baghdad and the son of one of its most prominent men. When I reached manhood, I heard travelers and other people tell of the land of Egypt, and it stayed in my mind. When my father died and I inherited his business, I prepared a load of merchandise, taking with me all kinds of fabrics of Baghdad and Mosul, including a thousand silk cloaks. Then I left Baghdad and journeyed until I reached Egypt. When I entered Cairo, I unloaded at the Masrur Caravansary, where I unpacked the goods and stored them in the storerooms. Then I gave one of my servants money to prepare some food, and after I and my servants ate and I took a rest, I went out for a walk along Bain al-Qasrain Street and then came back and slept. When I arose, I opened the bales of fabric and said to myself, "I will go to some good market and find out the prices." I took samples and, giving them to one of my servants to carry, put on my finest clothes and walked out until I came to the Jerjes Market. When I entered, I was met by the brokers, who had already heard of my arrival. They took my fabrics and auctioned them, but the pieces failed to fetch even their cost. I was vexed and said to the brokers, "My pieces did not fetch even their cost." But they replied, "Sir, we can tell you how you can make a profit without risk."

But morning overtook Shahrazad, and she lapsed into silence. Then Dinarzad said, "Sister, what a strange and entertaining story!" Shahrazad replied, "What is this compared with what I shall tell you tomorrow night if the king spares me and lets me live!"

THE ONE HUNDRED AND THIRTEENTH NIGHT

The following night Shahrazad said:

I heard, O happy King, that the Christian broker told the king of China that the young man said:

The brokers said, "We can tell you how you can make a profit without risk. You should do what the other merchants do and sell

your goods on credit for a fixed period, on a contract drawn by a
scribe and duly witnessed, employ a money changer, and collect
your money, every Monday and Thursday. In this way you will make
a profit, while you spend your own time enjoying the sights of Cairo
and the Nile." I said, "This is a good idea," and took the brokers and
the porters with me to the caravansary, where I took out the bales of
fabric, and they carried them and went with me to the market, where
I sold them on credit, on a written and duly witnessed contract which
I left with the banker. Then I left the market and returned to the
caravansary.

I lived there, breakfasting every morning on a cup of wine, mutton, pigeons, and sweets, until a month went by, and the time came
when my receipts began to fall due. Then I began to go to the market
every Monday and Thursday and sit in the shop of one or other of
the merchants, while the scribe and money changer went around to
collect the money till past the afternoon prayer, when they would
bring it, and I would count it and give them a receipt for it and take
it and return to the caravansary.

I did this for six days, until one day, which happened to be a Monday, I went early to the bath. When I came out, I put on nice clothes
and returned to my place in the caravansary, where I breakfasted on
a cup of wine and then went to sleep. Then I arose, ate a boiled
chicken and, perfuming myself, went to the market and sat at the
shop of a merchant called Badr al-Din al-Bustani. We sat chatting for
a while, when a lady, wearing a cloak and a magnificent headcloth
and exhaling perfume, came up to the shop, and her beauty at once
captured my heart. She saluted Badr al-Din, raising her upper veil
and revealing a pair of large black eyes. He welcomed her and stood
talking with her, and when I heard her speech, the love of her got
hold of my heart, and I felt a sense of foreboding. Then she asked
him, "Do you have a piece of silk fabric with hunting scenes?" He
showed her one of the pieces he had gotten from me, and she bought
it for one thousand and two hundred dirhams. Then she said to him,
"With your permission, I will take it with me and send you the money
next market day." He replied, "This is not possible, my lady, for this
gentleman is the owner of the piece, and I have to pay him for it
today." She said, "Shame on you, haven't I been buying much from
you at whatever profit you wished, taking the fabric from you and
sending you the money afterwards?" Badr al-Din replied, "Yes,
indeed, but this time, I need the money today." She threw the piece
of fabric back into the shop and said angrily, "You merchants don't
respect anyone. May God blight you all." Then she turned to go.

*But morning overtook Shahrazad, and she lapsed into silence.
Then Dinarzad said, "O sister, what a strange and entertaining story!"*

Shahrazad replied, "What is this compared with what I shall tell you tomorrow night if the king spares me and lets me live!"

THE ONE HUNDRED AND FOURTEENTH NIGHT

The following night Shahrazad said:

I heard, O happy King, that the Christian broker told the king of China that the young man said:

When she threw the piece of fabric back into the shop and turned to go, I felt as if my soul was going with her and cried out to her, "For God's sake, lady, do me a favor and come back." She turned back, saying with a smile, "I am coming back for your sake," and sat in the shop facing me. I asked Badr al-Din, "Sir, what was the price we set for this piece of fabric?" He replied, "One thousand and two hundred dirhams." I said, "I will give you one hundred dirhams as a profit for it. Give me a piece of paper, and I will write you a discharge." I wrote him a discharge, took the piece of fabric, and gave it to the lady, saying to her, "Take it, my lady, and if you wish, bring me the money next market day, or better yet, accept it as a present from me to you." She replied, "May God reward you and grant you a larger share of riches and a longer life than mine." (And the gates of Heaven opened and received Cairo's prayers.) I said to her, "My lady, this piece of fabric is yours, and God willing, many like it, only let me see your face." She turned her head and lifted her veil, and when I took one look, I sighed and lost my senses. Then she let down the veil and, taking the piece of fabric, said, "I will miss you," and departed, while I remained in the shop till past the afternoon prayer, lost in another world. When I asked Badr al-Din about the girl, he said, "She is a lady of wealth, the daughter of a prince who died and left her a great fortune." Then I took my leave of him and went to the caravansary, still thinking of her, and when they set supper before me, I could not eat, and when I lay down, I could not sleep but lay awake till dawn. Then I rose, changed my clothes and, swallowing something for breakfast, hurried to Badr al-Din's shop.

But morning overtook Shahrazad, and she lapsed into silence. Then Dinarzad said, "Sister, what a strange and entertaining story!" Shahrazad replied, 'What is this compared with what I shall tell you tomorrow night if the king spares me and lets me live!"

THE ONE HUNDRED AND FIFTEENTH NIGHT

The following night Shahrazad said:

I heard, O happy King, that the Christian broker told the king of China that the young man said:

Hardly had I been in Badr al-Din's shop, when the lady came up, followed by a maid, and more richly dressed than before. She greeted me, instead of Badr al-Din, and said to me, "Sir, let someone receive the money." I said, "What is the hurry for the money?" She replied, "My dear, may I never lose you," and handed me the money. Then we sat talking, and I dropped some hints, by which she understood that I desired to have an affair with her. She rose hastily and went away, taking my heart with her. I left the shop and walked in the market, when suddenly a black maid came up to me and said, "My lord, my lady wishes to speak with you." I was surprised and said, "No one knows me here." She said, "My lord, how soon you seem to have forgotten her! My lady is the one who was in the merchant's shop today."

I walked with her until we came to the lane of the money changers, and when the lady saw me, she drew me aside and said to me, "My dear, you have found a place in my heart, and from the day I first laid eyes on you, I have been unable to eat and drink." I replied, "I feel the same, and my condition speaks for my plight." She asked, "My dear, your place or mine?" I replied, "I am a stranger here and have no lodging but the caravansary."

But morning overtook Shahrazad, and she lapsed into silence. Then Dinarzad said, "Sister, what a strange and entertaining story!" Shahrazad replied, "What is this compared with what I shall tell you tomorrow night if the king spares me and lets me live!"

THE ONE HUNDRED AND SIXTEENTH NIGHT

The following night Shahrazad said:

It is related, O happy King, that the Christian broker told the king of China that the young man said:

"I have no lodging but the caravansary. Do me a favor and let me come to your place." She replied, "Very well, my lord. Tonight is Friday night, and nothing can be done, but tomorrow, after you perform the morning prayer, ride an ass and ask for the house of the syndic[3] Barqut abu-Shamah, in the Habbaniya quarter, and do not delay, for I will be waiting for you." I said, "Very well," and I bade her good-bye.

I waited impatiently for morning, and as soon as it was daylight, I arose, put on my clothes, and perfumed myself. Then I took fifty dinars in a handkerchief and walked from the Masrur Caravansary to the Zuwayla Gate, where I hired an ass, bidding the driver take me to the Habbaniya quarter. He set off with me and in no time brought me to a side street called al-Taqwa Lane. I bade him go in and inquire about the house of the syndic Barqut, known as abu-Shamah, and he disappeared and soon returned and said, "Very well, dismount." I dismounted and said to him, "Guide me to the house, so that you can find it when you return tomorrow to take me back to the Masrur Caravansary." He took me to the house, and I gave him a quarter-dinar and bade him go.

I knocked at the gate, and there came out two little white maids who said, "Please come in, for our mistress, being overjoyed with you, was unable to sleep last night." I walked through the hallway and came to a hall, raised seven steps above the ground and surrounded by windows, overlooking a garden that delighted the eye with running streams and all kinds of fruits and birds. In the middle of the hall there was a square fountain at whose corners stood four snakes made of red gold, spouting water, as if it were jewels and pearls.

But morning overtook Shahrazad, and she lapsed into silence. Then Dinarzad said, "What a strange and entertaining story!" Shahrazad replied, "What is this compared with what I shall tell you tomorrow night if I stay alive!"

THE ONE HUNDRED AND SEVENTEENTH NIGHT

The following night Shahrazad said:

I heard, O happy King, that the Christian broker told the king of China that the young man said:

I entered the hall, and hardly had I sat down, when the lady came up to me, bedecked in fine clothes and ornaments, with a diadem on her head. Her face was made up, and her eyes were penciled. When

3. Representative of a guild or corporation.

she saw me, she smiled at me, pressed me hard to her bosom and, setting her mouth to mine, sucked my tongue, and I did likewise. Then she said, "Can it be true, my little lord, that you have indeed come to me?" I replied, "Yes, I am with you and I am your slave." She said, "By God, since I first saw you, I have enjoyed neither food nor sleep." I said, "I have felt the same." Then we sat down to converse, while I kept my head bowed. Soon she set before me a tray with the most sumptuous dishes, such as ragout, fricassee, fritters soaked in honey, and chickens stuffed with sugar and pistachio nuts, and we ate until we were satisfied. Then the servants removed the tray, and after we washed our hands and they sprinkled them with rosewater scented with musk, we sat down again to converse, and my love for her took such hold of me that all my wealth seemed little to me in comparison with her. We passed the time in dalliance till nightfall, when the servants set before us a banquet of food and wine, and we sat drinking till midnight. Then we went to bed, and I lay with her till the morning, having never spent a better night. When it was day, I arose and, slipping under the mattress the handkerchief containing the fifty dinars, took my leave of her. She wept and asked, "My lord, when shall I see you again?" I replied, "I will be with you this evening." She saw me to the door and said, "My lord, bring our supper with you."

When I stepped out, I found the driver with whom I had ridden the previous day waiting for me, and I mounted, and he drove the ass to the caravansary. I dismounted but did not pay him, saying, "Come back for me at sunset," and he replied, "Very well," and went away. After I had a little breakfast, I went out to collect the money from the sale of my merchandise. In the meantime I ordered a roasted lamb on a bed of rice, as well as some sweets and, giving a porter directions to the lady's house, sent the food to her. Thus I occupied myself with my business till the end of the day, and when at sunset the driver came for me, I took fifty dinars in a handkerchief, adding two quarter-dinars, and rode the ass, spurring it until in no time I reached the lady's house. I dismounted and gave the driver half a dinar. Then I entered and found that the house was better prepared than ever. When she saw me, she kissed me and said, "I have missed you all day long." Then the servants set the table, and we ate until we were satisfied. Then they brought us wine, and we drank till midnight; then we went to the bedroom and lay together till daylight. When I arose, I left with her the fifty dinars in the handkerchief and went out, finding the driver waiting. I rode to the caravansary, where I slept a while. Then I went out and bought from a delicatessen a pair of homegrown geese on two platters of peppered rice. I also bought colocasia roots, fried and soaked in honey, fruits and nuts, as well as aromatic herbs and candles, and sent them all with a porter to her house. Then I waited impatiently till nightfall, when I again took fifty dinars in a handkerchief and rode with the driver to the house. Again she and I conversed, ate, and lay together, and when I arose in the morning, I again left the handkerchief with her and rode back with the driver to the Masrur Caravansary.

But morning overtook Shahrazad, and she lapsed into silence. Then Dinarzad said to her sister Shahrazad, "What a strange and entertaining story!" Shahrazad replied, "What is this compared with what I shall tell you tomorrow night, if the king spares me and lets me live!"

THE ONE HUNDRED AND EIGHTEENTH NIGHT

The following night Shahrazad said:

I heard, O happy King, that the Christian broker told the king of China that the young man said:

I continued like this, eating and drinking and giving her fifty dinars every night until one day I found myself penniless. Not knowing where to find money and saying to myself, "There is no power and no strength save in God, the Almighty, the Magnificent. This is Satan's doing," I left my lodging at the caravansary and walked along Bain al-Qasran Street until I came to the Zuwayla Gate, where it was so crowded that the gate was blocked up with people. As it had been foreordained, I found myself pressed against a soldier, so that my hand came upon his breast pocket and I felt a purse inside. I looked and, seeing a green tassel hanging from the pocket, realized that it was attached to the purse. The crush grew greater every moment, and just then, a camel, bearing a load of wood, jostled the soldier on the other side, and he turned to ward it off from him, lest it should tear his clothes. And Satan tempted me, and I pulled the tassel and drew out a little blue silk purse, with something clinking inside. Hardly had I held the purse in my hand, when the soldier felt something and, touching his pocket with his hand, found it empty. He turned to me and, raising his mace, struck me with it on the head. I fell to the ground, while the people gathered around us and, holding the soldier back, asked him, "Is it because he pushed you that you struck him with such a blow?" But he shouted at them with curses and said, "This fellow is a thief!" At that moment, I came to myself and got up, and the people looked at me and said, "This nice young man would not steal anything." Some believed him while others did not, and after much debate, some of them were about to rescue me from him, when the chief of the police and the captain and the watchmen entered through the gate and saw the crowd gathered around me and the soldier. The chief asked, "What is the matter?" and they told him what had happened [and the soldier said, "He stole from my pocket a blue silk purse containing twenty dinars"]. The chief asked him, "Was there anyone else with him?" and the soldier replied, "No." Then the chief cried out to the captain, bidding him seize me. Then he said, "Strip him naked," and when they did so and found the purse hidden in my clothes, I fell into a swoon. When the chief saw the purse . . .

But morning overtook Shahrazad, and she lapsed into silence. Then Dinarzad said, "Sister, what a strange and entertaining story!" Shahrazad replied, "What is this compared with what I shall tell you tomorrow night if the king spares me and lets me live!"

THE ONE HUNDRED AND NINETEENTH NIGHT

The following night Shahrazad said:

I heard, O happy King, that the Christian broker told the king of China that the young man said:

When the chief saw the purse, he seized it and took out the gold coins, and when he counted, he found twenty dinars. He was angry and, yelling at the officers to bring me before him, said to me, "Young man, there is no need to force it out of you if you tell me the truth. Did you steal this purse?" I bowed my head and said to myself, "I cannot deny it, for they found the purse in my clothes, but if I confess, I will be in trouble." At last I raised my head and said, "Yes, I took it." When the chief heard my words, he called for witnesses, and they attested my confession. (All of this took place at the Zuwayla Gate.) Then he summoned the executioner, who cut off my right hand, and he would have bidden him cut off my foot too, but as the people said to him, "This is a pitiful young man," and as I implored the soldier, who finally took pity on me and interceded for me with him, the chief left me and went away, while the people remained around me and gave me a cup of wine to drink. As for the soldier, he gave me the purse, saying, "You are a nice young man, and it does not become you to be a thief." Then he left me and went away.

I wrapped my hand in a rag, thrust it into my bosom, and walked until I reached my mistress's house and threw myself on the bed. When she saw that I was pale from the bleeding, she asked, "My darling, what ails you?" I replied, "I have a headache." Worried about me, she said, "Sit up and tell me what has happened to you today, for it is written on your face." When I wept without reply, she said, "It seems as if you are tired of me. For God's sake, tell me what is the matter with you." But even though I kept silent and did not reply, she continued to talk to me till nightfall. Then she brought me food, but I refused it, for fear that she would see me eat with my left hand, and I said to her, "I don't care to eat anything." Again she asked, "Tell me what happened to you today and what is troubling you." I said, "Must I tell you?" Then she gave me wine to drink, saying, "Drink it, for it will make you feel better and help you tell me what happened." I replied, "If I must, then give me the wine." She drank, gave me the cup, and I took it with my left hand.

But morning overtook Shahrazad, and she lapsed into silence. Then Dinarzad said, "Sister, what a strange and entertaining story!" Shahrazad replied, "What is this compared with what I shall tell you tomorrow night if the king spares me and lets me live!"

THE ONE HUNDRED AND TWENTIETH NIGHT

I heard, O happy King, that the Christian broker told the king of China that the young man said:

When she gave me the cup, I took it with my left hand with tears in my eyes. She let out a loud cry and said, "My lord, why do you weep, and why do you hold the cup with your left hand?" I replied, "I have a boil on my right hand." She said, "Put it out, and I will lance it for you." I replied, "It is not ready yet." She kept forcing me to drink until I got drunk and fell asleep. Then she examined my right arm and found it a wrist without a hand, and when she searched me and found the purse and my severed hand wrapped in a handkerchief, she grieved for me and lamented till the morning.

When I awoke, I found that she had made me a dish of broth of five boiled chickens, and after I ate some and drank a cup of wine, I laid down the purse and was about to go out, when she said to me, "Where are you going? Sit down." Then she added, "Has your love for me been so great that you have spent all your substance on me until you finally lost even your hand? I pledge to you that I will die nowhere but at your feet, and you shall soon see the truth of my words." Then she sent for witnesses and drew up a marriage contract, saying, "Write down that everything I own belongs to this young man." After she paid the witnesses their fee, she took me by the hand and, leading me to a chest, said to me, "Look at all these handkerchiefs inside; they contain all the money you brought me. Take your money back, for I can never reward you enough for your precious and dear self," repeating, "Take your money." I locked the money in the chest, forgetting my sorrow and feeling happy, and thanked her. She said to me, "By God, even if I gave my life for you, it would be less than you deserve."

We lived together, but in less than a month, she fell ill and continued to get worse because of her grief for me, and in less than fifty days, she was dead. After I buried her, I found that she had left me countless bequests, including the storeroom and the crop of sesame that you, Christian, sold for me.

But morning overtook Shahrazad, and she lapsed into silence. Then Dinarzad said, "Sister, what a strange and entertaining story!" Shahrazad replied, "What is this compared with what I shall tell you tomorrow night if the king spares me and lets me live!"

THE ONE HUNDRED AND TWENTY-FIRST NIGHT

The following night Shahrazad said:

I heard, O happy King, that the Christian broker told the king of China that the young man said:

"It was because I was busy selling the rest of the goods that I did not have the time to pay attention to you and receive my money from you, but now I have at last sold everything she left me. This then is the reason why I ate with my left hand. Now, by God, Christian, you must not object to what I am about to do, for I have entered your home and eaten your food. I make you a present of all the money you are holding for me from the sale of the sesame, for it is only a portion of what the Supreme God has bestowed on me."

The young man added, "Christian, I have prepared a load of merchandise for trading; will you go aboard with me?" I replied, "Yes, indeed," and agreed to go with him at the beginning of the month. Then after I too bought merchandise, I set out with the young man until we came to your city, O King, where he bought merchandise and went back to Egypt. But it was my lot to stay here. This then is my adventure and strange story. Isn't it, O King, more amazing than the hunchback's story?

The king of China replied, "No, it is not more amazing than the hunchback's story, and I must hang all four of you for the hunchback's death."

Then the steward of the king's kitchen came forward and said to the king of China, "O happy King, if I tell you a story that happened to me last night, before I found the hunchback in my house, and you find it to be more amazing than the hunchback's story, will you grant us our lives and let us go?" The king of China replied, "Yes, if I find it to be more amazing than the story of the hunchback, I will grant all four of you your lives." The steward said:

[The Steward's Tale:
The Young Man from Baghdad and
Lady Zubaida's Maid]

O KING OF THE AGE, last night I was invited to hear a recitation of the Quran, where the doctors of the law, as well as a great many citizens of your city, were assembled. After the reciters finished their recitation, the table was spread, and among the dishes set before us there was a ragout spiced with cumin. But when one of the guests saw the ragout, he held back and abstained from eating. We entreated him to eat of the ragout, but he swore that he would not, and we pressed him until he said, "Don't force me to eat, for I have suffered enough from eating this dish." Then he repeated the following verses:

> Shoulder your drum, my man, and
>   leave your home
> And use the kohl if 'tis the
>   kohl you like.

We said to him, "Tell us the reason of your refusal to eat of the ragout," and as the host insisted, saying, "I swear that you must eat of it," the guest replied, "There is no power and no strength, save in God. If I must eat, then I will first have to wash my hands forty times with soap, forty times with potash, and forty times with galingale,[4] all in all one hundred and twenty times."

---

4. Aromatic root of certain East Indian herbs of the ginger family. "Potash": a crude potassium carbonate obtained from wood or other vegetable ashes.

But morning overtook Shahrazad, and she lapsed into silence. Then Dinarzad said, "What a strange and entertainining story!" Shahrazad replied, "What is this compared with what I shall tell you tomorrow night if the king spares me and lets me live!"

THE ONE HUNDRED AND TWENTY-SECOND NIGHT

The following night Shahrazad said:

It is related, O happy King, that the steward said to the king:

O King of the age, the host ordered his servants to bring the guest water and all that he required to wash his hands, and he washed his hands as he had said. Then he came reluctantly and sat down with us, as if in fear, and dipping his hand into the ragout, began to eat, but with repugnance, while we looked at him with surprise, for his hand and indeed his whole body were shaking, and we noticed that his thumb was cut off and that he ate with four fingers only, so that the food kept slipping awkwardly from his hand. We asked him in amazement, "What happened to your thumb? Did God create you like this, or did you have an accident?" He replied, "By God, it is not only this thumb that is missing, but also that of the other hand, and the great toe of each of my feet, as you will see." Then he bared his left hand and his two feet, and we saw that the left hand was like the right and that each of his feet lacked the great toe. When we saw this, our amazement increased, and we said to him, "We are impatient to hear your story and the reason for cutting off your thumbs and toes and for washing your hands one hundred and twenty times." He said:

My father was one of the most prominent merchants of Baghdad, in the days of the caliph Harun al-Raschid, but he was fond of wine and the lute, so that when he died, he left me nothing. I held a mourning ceremony for him, arranged for recitations of the Quran, and continued to mourn for him for a long time. Then I opened the shop and found that he had left little substance and many debts. So I arranged with his creditors to pay them in installments, and I began to buy and sell and to pay the creditors week by week, until at last I paid off all his debts and began to increase my capital. One day, as I was sitting in the shop early in the morning, there came to the market a beautiful young lady, the like of which I had never seen before, richly dressed and bedecked with jewelry. She was riding a

she-mule, with one black slave walking before and another behind
her. She dismounted and, leaving the she-mule by the entrance,
entered the market. No sooner had she done so, when a well-
groomed eunuch followed her and said, "My lady, go in, but don't let
anyone recognize you, or we will be in trouble." Then he stood guard
before her, while she looked at the shops and, finding none open but
mine, came up to my shop, followed by the eunuch, greeted me, and
sat down.

*But morning overtook Shahrazad, and she lapsed into silence. Then
Dinarzad said, "Sister, what an entertaining story!" Shahrazad replied,
"What is this compared with what I shall tell you tomorrow night if the
king spares me and lets me live!"*

THE ONE HUNDRED AND TWENTY-THIRD NIGHT

The following night Shahrazad said:

I heard, O happy King, that the steward told the king of China
that the young merchant said:

She sat in my shop and unveiled her face, and when I saw it, I
sighed. Then she asked me, "Do you have any fabrics?" I replied,
"My lady, your servant is poor, but wait until the other merchants
open their shops, and I will get you whatever you wish." We sat talking for a while and I was beginning to feel an overwhelming passion
for her. When the merchants opened their shops, I rose and got her
everything she wished, to the value of five thousand dirhams. She
gave the fabrics to the eunuch and went back to the slaves, who
brought her the she-mule, and she mounted and rode away, without
telling me where she lived. Being too embarrassed to mention
money before such a beautiful woman, I vouched to the merchants
for the value of the goods, incurring a debt of five thousand dirhams.
Then I went home, drunk with love, and for a week was unable to
eat or drink or sleep.

*But morning overtook Shahrazad, and she lapsed into silence. Then
Dinarzad said, "Sister, what an entertaining story!" Shahrazad replied,
"What is this compared with what I shall tell you tomorrow night if the
king spares me and lets me live!"*

THE ONE HUNDRED AND TWENTY-FOURTH NIGHT

The following night Shahrazad said:

It is related, O King, that the steward told the king of China that the young merchant said:

A week later the merchants came to me, asking for their money, but I persuaded them to wait, and as soon as another week passed, the lady came up, riding the she-mule and followed, as usual, by the eunuch and the two slaves. She greeted me and, sitting down in the shop, said, "I am late in bringing you the money for the fabrics. Fetch a money changer and receive the amount." I sent for the money changer, and the eunuch counted out the money and gave it to him. Then she and I sat talking until the shops opened, at which time I paid every merchant what I owed him. Then she said to me, "Sir, get me such and such," and I got her what she wanted from the merchants, and she took it and went away, without saying a word about payment. I began to regret what I had done, for the price of what I had bought for her was a thousand dinars, and I said to myself, "What a predicament! She has given me five thousand dirhams but has taken a thousand dinars' worth of goods, and the merchants know only me. There is no power and no strength, save in God, the Almighty, the Magnificent. This woman who tricked me must be a swindler, and I did not even ask her for her address."

She was gone for more than a month, and the merchants began to press me for their money and, finally despairing of ever seeing her again, I put up my property for sale. But one day, while I sat dejected and perplexed, she came in and, sitting in the shop, said, "Fetch the scales and take your money." Then she gave me the money and sat, conversing freely with me, until I was beside myself with joy. Then she asked me, "Do you have a wife?" I replied, "No, I have never been married," and began to weep. She asked, "Why do you weep?" I replied, "It is nothing." Then, giving the eunuch some money, I asked him to act as my go-between with her. But he laughed and said, "By God, she is more in love with you than you are with her. She had no need for the fabrics she bought from you, but she only did it out of love for you. Tell her yourself what you want." She had seen me giving the eunuch the money, so I said to her, "Be charitable and permit your servant to tell you what is on his mind." Then I told her what was on my mind, and she assented and said to the eunuch, "You shall carry my message to him," and saying to me, "Do whatever he asks you," went away. I paid the merchants what I owed them and spent a sleepless night.

A few days later the eunuch came to me . . .

But morning overtook Shahrazad, and she lapsed into silence. Then her sister Dinarzad said, "Sister, what a strange and entertaining story!" Shahrazad replied, "What is this compared with what I shall tell you tomorrow night if the king spares me and lets me live!"

THE ONE HUNDRED AND TWENTY-FIFTH NIGHT

The following night Shahrazad said:

It is related, O King, that the steward told the king of China that the young man said:

When the eunuch came, I treated him generously, and when I asked him about his mistress, he replied, "She is pining with love for you." Then I asked him, "Who is she?" and he said, "She is one of the waiting women who is charged with errands for the Lady Zubaida, the wife of the caliph, who brought her up. By God, she told her lady about you and begged her to marry her to you, but the Lady Zubaida said, 'I will not marry you to him until I see whether he is handsome and whether he is a match for you.' I will take you to the palace at once, and if you succeed in entering without being seen, you may win her in marriage, but if you are found out, you will lose your head. What do you say?" I replied, "I am ready to go with you." Then he said, "As soon as it is night, go to the mosque built by the Lady Zubaida on the Tigris River." I replied, "Very well." Then I went to the mosque, where I performed my evening prayer and passed the night.

Just before daybreak, there came up some servants in a boat, with some empty chests, which they deposited in the mosque and departed. But one of them stayed behind, and when I looked at him closely, I found that he was the eunuch who had come to me earlier. Soon, my lady herself came in, and when she drew near, I rose to greet her, and she sat to converse with me, with tears in her eyes. Then she made me get into one of the chests and locked me in. Then the eunuchs came back with all sorts of things that she kept stowing in the chests until she had filled them all and locked them. Then they placed the chests in the boat and headed downstream to the palace of the Lady Zubaida. I soon began to regret what I had done, saying to myself, "By God, I am undone," and kept weeping and praying to God to deliver me until the boat reached the gate of

the caliph's palace. Then the eunuchs lifted out the chests, including mine, and carried them past the eunuchs in charge of guarding
the harem until they came to a eunuch who seemed to be their
chief. He started up from sleep.

*But morning overtook Shahrazad, and she lapsed into silence. Then
her sister Dinarzad said, "Sister, what an entertaining story!" Shahrazad
replied, "What is this compared with what I shall tell you tomorrow
night if the king spares me and lets me live!"*

THE ONE HUNDRED AND TWENTY-SIXTH NIGHT

The following night Shahrazad said:

I heard, O happy King, that the steward told the king of China
that the young man said:

The chief of the eunuchs started up from sleep and cried out to
the young lady, "Don't delay. You must open these chests." It so happened that the chest he was about to start with was the one in which
I was, and when they brought it to him, I lost my senses and in my
panic wet myself until my urine began to run out of the chest. Then
the young lady said, "Chief, you have ruined me and ruined many
merchants by spoiling the belongings of the Lady Zubaida, for the
chest contains colored dresses and a jar of Zam-zam water.[5] The jar
has just tipped over and the water will make the colors run." The
chief of the eunuchs said, "Take the chest and go." But hardly had
the eunuchs carried me and hurried away with all the other chests,
when I heard a voice crying, "O my, O my, the caliph, the caliph!"
When I heard this, my heart died within me. Then I heard the caliph
ask the young lady, "Hey you, what is in these chests of yours?" She
replied, "Clothes for the Lady Zubaida." He said, "Open them and
let me see," and when I heard this, I knew that I was undone. Then I
heard the young lady say, "O Commander of the Faithful, these
chests contain the clothes and belongings of the Lady Zubaida, and
she does not wish their contents to be seen by anyone." But the
caliph said, "You must open these chests, so that I may see what is in
them. Bring them to me." When I heard the caliph say, "Bring them
to me," I was sure of death. Then the eunuchs brought the chests
up, opening them, one after another, and he kept looking at the

5. From a sacred well in Mecca.

clothes and belongings until there remained only the chest in which I was hiding. They carried me and let me down before him, and I bade life good-bye, being certain that I was going to lose my head and die. The caliph said, "Open the chest, so that I may see what is in it," and the eunuch rushed to open the chest.

But morning overtook Shahrazad, and she lapsed into silence. Then Dinarzad said to her sister Shahrazad, "What a strange and entertaining story!" Shahrazad replied, "What is this compared with what I shall tell you tomorrow night if the king spares me and lets me live!"

The One Hundred and Twenty-Seventh Night

The following night Shahrazad said:

I heard, O King, that the steward told the king of China that the young man said:

The caliph said to the eunuchs, "Open this chest, so that I may see what is in it." But the young lady said, "O my lord, open it in the presence of the Lady Zubaida, for that which is in it is her secret, and she is more particular about this one than all the other chests." When the caliph heard her explanation, he ordered the eunuchs to carry the chests inside, and two of them came and carried the chest in which I was hiding, while I could hardly believe that I was still alive. As soon as the chest was inside the harem, where my friend lived, she rushed in and, opening it, said, "Get out quickly and take this stairway upstairs." I stood up and climbed out of the chest, and hardly had she closed the lid and I climbed the stairs, when the eunuchs came in with the other chests, followed by the caliph. Then they opened everything again before him, while he sat on the chest where I had been hiding. Then he got up and went into the harem.

All this time I sat with my mouth dry from fear until the young lady came upstairs and said to me, "There is no longer anything to fear. Be cheerful and wait until the Lady Zubaida comes to see you, and you may be fortunate and win me." I went downstairs, and as soon as I sat down in the small hall, there came in ten maids, like moons, and stood in two rows, and they were followed by twenty high-bosomed virgins, with the Lady Zubaida, who could hardly walk under the weight of her dresses and ornaments. When she drew near, the maids dispersed and brought her a chair, on which she sat. Then she cried out to the girls, who in turn cried out to me, and I advanced and kissed the ground before her. She motioned me to sit down, and I sat down before her, as she conversed with me and I answered her questions about my condition. She was pleased with me and finally said, "By God, I have not raised this girl in vain. She is like my own child, a trust committed to you by God." Then she bade me stay for ten days in the palace.

But morning overtook Shahrazad, and she lapsed into silence. Then Dinarzad said, "What a strange and entertaining story!" Shahrazad replied, "What is this compared with what I shall tell you tomorrow night if the king spares me and lets me live!"

THE ONE HUNDRED AND TWENTY-EIGHTH NIGHT

The following night Shahrazad said:

I heard that the steward told the king of China that the young man said:

I stayed in the palace ten days and nights, without seeing the young lady. Then the Lady Zubaida consulted the caliph about the marriage of her waiting woman, and he gave permission and assigned ten thousand dirhams for that purpose. Then the Lady Zubaida sent for the judge and witnesses, and they drew up the marriage contract, performed the ceremony, and for ten days thereafter celebrated our wedding with sumptuous meals and sweets. At the end of the ten days, the young lady entered the bath. In the meantime they set before me the supper tray, and as there was among the dishes a great platter of ragout cooked with pistachio nuts, white sugar, rosewater, and cumin, I did not hesitate but, by God, fell upon the ragout and ate until I was satisfied. Then I wiped my hands, for God had willed that I should forget to wash them.

I sat until it grew dark, when they lit the candles and all the musicians and singing women of the palace came in a procession, beating the tambourines and singing all kinds of melodies and songs. They kept parading from room to room, displaying the bride and receiving gifts of money and pieces of silk, until they made the round of the whole palace and brought her to my room. They disrobed her and left her with me, but no sooner did I enter the bed with her and embrace her, hardly believing that she was mine, than, smelling the ragout spiced with cumin on my hand, she let out such a loud scream that the maids rushed in from all sides and stood around her, while I sat alarmed and trembled from fear, not knowing why she had screamed. The maids asked her, "Sister, what is the matter with you?" She replied, "Take this madman away from me." I got up, afraid and bewildered, and asked her, "My lady, what makes you think me mad?" She replied, "Madman, didn't you eat the ragout spiced with cumin without washing your hands? By God, I will punish you for it. Shall the like of you consummate marriage with one like me, with a hand smelling of ragout spiced with cumin?" Then she yelled at the girls, saying, "Throw him to the ground," and they threw me to the ground, and she took a braided whip and fell with it on my back and buttocks until her arm was tired. Then she said to the girls, "Take him and send him to the chief of the police; so that he may cut off the hand with which he ate the ragout without washing it and sparing me the stench." When I heard this, still smarting from the blows, I said to myself. "There is no power and no strength, save in God, the Almighty, the Magnificent." What a calamity! What a great calamity! Did I suffer such a painful beating and will my hand be cut off, just because I ate the ragout spiced with cumin and forgot to wash my hands? May god curse this ragout and its very existence."

But morning overtook Shahrazad, and she lapsed into silence. Then Dinarzad said, "Sister, what a strange and entertaining story!" Shahrazad replied, "What is this compared with what I shall tell you tomorrow night if the king spares me and lets me live!"

THE ONE HUNDRED AND TWENTY-NINTH NIGHT

The following night Shahrazad said:

It is related that the steward told the king of China that the young man said:

The girls interceded with her, saying, "Our lady, this man does not know your worth. Forgive him for our sake." But she said, "He is a madman, and I must punish his hand, so that he may never again eat the ragout without washing it." When the girls interceded again and kissed her hands, saying, "Our lady, for God's sake, don't blame him for what he forgot to do," she yelled at me, cursed me, and went away, and they followed her.

She was gone for ten days, during which a maid brought me food and drink everyday and informed me that the lady was not feeling well because I had eaten the ragout without washing my hands. I was very much amazed and burst out with anger, saying to myself, "What a cursed temper!" adding, "There is no power and no strength, save in God, the Almighty, the Magnificent." When the ten days passed, the maid brought me the food and informed me that the lady was going to the bath, adding, "Bear her anger patiently, for tomorrow she will come to you." When the lady finally came in, she looked at me and said, "May God shame you; couldn't you be patient even for one moment? I will not make peace with you until I punish you for eating the ragout without washing your hands." Then crying out to the girls, who surrounded me and bound me, she took out a sharp blade and, coming up to me, cut off my two thumbs, as you people can see for yourselves, and I fell into a swoon. Meanwhile, she sprinkled the wounds with powder and a store of drugs to stop the flow of blood, and when the blood stopped, the maids gave me wine to drink. As soon as I opened my eyes, I said to her, "I pledge to you that I will never again eat ragout spiced with cumin without washing my hands one hundred and twenty times." The lady replied, "Bravo," and made me take an oath to that effect. So when the food was brought in here, and I saw the ragout spiced with cumin, I turned pale and said to myself, "It was this dish that was the cause of cutting off my thumbs"; so when you forced me to eat of it, I had to fulfill the oath.

But morning overtook Shahrazad, and she lapsed into silence. Then Dinarzad said to her sister Shahrazad, "What a strange and entertaining story!" Shahrazad replied, "What is this compared with what I shall tell you tomorrow night if the king spares me and lets me live!"

THE ONE HUNDRED AND THIRTIETH NIGHT

The following night Shahrazad said:

It is related that the steward told the king of China that the guests asked the young man, "What happened to you after that?" and he said:

When my wounds healed and I recovered, she came to me, and I slept with her. Then I spent the rest of the month with her in the palace until I began to feel depressed, and she finally said to me, "Listen! The caliph's palace is no place for us to live. The Lady Zubaida has given me fifty thousand dinars. Take some money with you and go and buy us a good house." Then she gave me ten thousand dinars, and I took them and went out and bought a beautiful house. Then she moved in with me, and for many years we lived like kings until she died. This then is the cause of the cutting off of my thumbs and the washing of my hands.

After we ate, the party ended and we departed, and afterward I had my adventure with the hunchback.

The king of China said, "By God, this is not more amazing than the story of the roguish hunchback." Then the Jewish physician rose and, kissing the ground before the king, said, "O my lord, I have a story to tell, which is more amazing than this one." The king said, "Let us hear it."

But morning overtook Shahrazad, and she lapsed into silence. Then Dinarzad said, "Sister, what a strange and entertaining story!" Shahrazad replied, "What is this compared with what I shall tell you tomorrow night if the king spares me and lets me live!"

* * *

[The Tailor's Tale: The Lame Young Man from Baghdad and the Barber]

O KING OF THE AGE, the most amazing thing that ever happened to me occurred yesterday, before I met the roguish hunchback. I was invited to an early morning banquet, together with about twenty companions from the city. As soon as the sun rose and they set food before us, the host entered with a handsome stranger, a perfectly beautiful young man, except that he was lame. We stood in salute, in deference to the host, and the young man was about to sit down when, seeing among us a man who was a barber by profession, he refused to sit and started to leave. But the host stopped him and adjured him, asking, "Why do you enter my house and leave at once?" The young man replied, "For God's sake, my lord, don't hinder me. The cause is that ill-omened, ill-behaved, bungling, shameful, and pernicious old barber." When we and the host heard this description of the barber, we took a look at him and began to feel an aversion for him.

But morning overtook Shahrazad, and she lapsed into silence. Then Dinarzad said to her sister, "What a strange and entertaining story!" Shahrazad replied, "What is this compared with what I shall tell you tomorrow night if I stay alive!"

THE ONE HUNDRED AND FORTIETH NIGHT

The following night Shahrazad said:

I heard, O happy King, that the tailor said to the king of China:

When we heard this description of the barber, we said, "None of us will be able to eat and enjoy himself, unless the young man tells us about the barber." The young man said, "O fellows, I had an adventure with this barber in my native city of Baghdad, and he was in fact the cause of my breaking my leg and becoming lame. I have sworn never to sit in the same place or live in the same city with him, and because of him I left Baghdad and settled in this city. Now suddenly, I find him here with you. Not another night shall pass before I depart from here." We begged him to sit down and tell us what had happened between him and the barber, in Baghdad, while the barber turned pale and bowed his head. The young man said:

My father was one of the richest men of Baghdad, and God had blessed him with no other child but myself. When I grew up and reached manhood, he died, and the Almighty God took him under His mercy. He left me great wealth, and I began to dress handsomely and to live the best of lives. It happened that God had made me a hater of women, and one day, as I was walking along one of the streets of Baghdad, a group of women blocked my way and I fled from them into a blind alley. I had not sat long, when a window opened and there appeared, tending some flowers in the window, a young lady, as radiant as the moon and so beautiful that I have never seen one more beautiful. When she saw me, she smiled, setting my heart on fire, and my hatred of women was changed to love. I continued sitting there, lost to the world till close to sundown, when the judge of the city, riding a she-mule, came by, dismounted, and entered the young lady's house, leading me to guess that he was her father. I went home in sorrow and fell on my bed, consumed with passion. My relatives came in and wondered what was the matter with me, but I did not reply. I remained like this for several days until they began to lament over me.

One day an old woman came in to see me and, looking at me, guessed at once what was the matter with me. She sat down at my head, spoke gently to me, and said, "Son, be cheerful; tell me what ails you, and I will help you get what you desire." Her words soothed my heart and we sat talking.

But morning overtook Shahrazad, and she lapsed into silence. Then Dinarzad said, "Sister, what a strange and entertaining story!" Shahrazad replied, "What is this compared with what I shall tell you tomorrow night if the king spares me and lets me live!"

THE ONE HUNDRED AND FORTY-FIRST NIGHT

The following night Shahrazad said:

I heard, O King, that the tailor told the king of China that the young man said to the guests:

The old woman gazed on me and recited the following verses:

> No, by her radiant brow and rosy cheeks,
> My eyes I turned not when she left the place,
> But like an eyeless man, I rolled along,
> In my confusion, stumbling in her trace.
> She was a nimble deer, well-used to run,
> A cruel mistress, with a heart of stone.
> She set my heart and soul on hellish fire
> And I became a misfit, alien and alone,
> Cheeks in the dust and eyes flowing with tears,
> Mourning the old days and love I did crave.
> Helpless I grieve, but what avail the sighs?
> I am dead without her, though not in my grave,
> Haunted by everlasting memories
> Of her face that showed neither joy nor rage.
> Heart, break with grief and let my soul expire,
> O heart of silver in a marble cage!
> Consumed with love, impatient with my fate,
> I watch my rivals pressing in their turn,
> Unable to reproach them for their love.
> O will the good old days ever return?
> How can my soul forbear or how forget
> Her slender body and her lovely face,
> Which like the shining sun dazzled the world
> As I held her in an ardent embrace
> And in the dark tasted the night's delight,
> Lying on green grass that felt like the down
> That graces tender, plump, and rosy cheeks,
> Fondling her cheeks like silk of high renown,
> Clutching them as a miser clutches gold,
> Feeling their softness like silk stuffed with flowers
> Or with a tender heart throbbing unseen!
> O let the watchman come; she had redeemed my hours!
> My love is constant; I have never changed,
> Unlike the others, never turned away,
> But always loved and will forever love;
> Keeping the pledge with honor is my way.
> I swore that if I died from grief, I would not plead;

A stoic lover does not need to sigh,
And I am not a heedless lover, quick to blame
Or to betray, for none knows love as I.
We lived in bliss and boundless happiness
Until I thought our Eden safe from blight,
Thought we would stay secure and never part.
Now all has died and vanished from my sight.
Alas for the days with that black-eyed deer!
If they return and bring her back to me,
I pledge eternal fasting all my days.
For without her I will an outcast be,
Living love's victim to eternity.

But morning overtook Shahrazad, and she lapsed into silence. Then Dinarzad said, "Sister, what an entertaining story!" Shahrazad replied, "What is that compared with what I shall tell you tomorrow night if I live!"

The One Hundred and Forty-Second Night

The following night Shahrazad said:

I heard, O happy King, that the tailor told the king of China that the young man said to the guests:

Then the old woman said to me, "Son, tell me your story." When I told her, she said, "Son, that young lady is the daughter of the judge of Baghdad, and she is kept in strict seclusion. The place where you saw her is her private room, which she occupies by herself alone, while her parents live in the great hall below. I often visit her, and I will undertake to help you, for you will not get to her but through me. Gird your loins." When I heard her words, I was encouraged and began to eat and drink, to the satisfaction of my family.

The old woman left and came back the following morning, crest-fallen, and said, "Son, don't ask how I fared with the young lady when I mentioned you to her. The last thing she said about you was, 'Wretched woman, if you don't stop this talk, I will punish you as you deserve, and if you ever mention him again, I will tell my father.' But by God, son, I must try her again, even if I suffer for it." When I heard what she said, I felt even worse than before and kept repeating, "Alas, how cruel is love!" The old woman visited me every day, while my illness dragged on, until all the physicians and sages and my entire family began to despair of my recovery.

One day the old woman came in and, sitting at my head, whispered to me, out of the hearing of my family, "You must give me a reward for good news." When I heard her words, I sat up and said, "The reward is yours." She said, "My lord, I went yesterday to the young lady, who welcomed me and, seeing that I was brokenhearted and tearful, asked, 'O aunt, what is the matter with you, and why are you unhappy?' I replied tearfully, 'My lady, I have just come from a sick young man, who has been lying, now conscious, now unconscious. His family has given up on him, and he will surely perish because of you.' She asked, as she began to feel pity, 'What is he to you?' I replied, 'He is my son. He saw you some time ago, at your window, watering your flowers, and when he looked at your face and lovely hand, his heart was captivated, and he fell madly in love with you. These were the verses he recited:

> By the rare treasure of your lovely face,
> Don't kill your lover with your cruel disdain.
> His heart is intoxicated with love,
> His wasting body racked and torn with pain.
> By your supple, curving, and graceful frame,
> Your mouth that puts the perfect pearls to shame,
> The piercing arrow from your arching brows
> That found my heart without missing the aim,
> Your slender, melting waist, which is as frail
> As the sad lover who pines for you,
> By the enchanting star of ambergris,
> Gracing your cheek, your victim mercy show.
> And by your curling sidelocks, have pity,
> Be tender, and give him your love divine,
> For by the pearls between your coral lips,
> By your sweet mouth and its delicious wine,
> Your belly, folded in poetic lines
> That lacerate my heart; O painful dream!
> And by your legs, which brought me death and doom,
> Only your love can your lover redeem.

But, my lady, when he sent me to you last time, I fared badly at your hands.'"

But morning overtook Shahrazad, and she lapsed into silence. Then Dinarzad said to her sister, "What a strange and entertaining story!" Shahrazad replied, "What is this compared with what I shall tell you tomorrow night if the king spares me and lets me live!" The king said to himself, "By God, I will not kill her until I hear the rest of the hunchback's story."

THE ONE HUNDRED AND FORTY-THIRD NIGHT

The following night Shahrazad said:

I heard, O happy King, that the tailor told the king of China that the young man said to the guests:

The old woman said, "'O my lady, I fared badly at your hands, and when I went back to him and acquainted him with your reply, he got worse and remained bedridden until I thought that he would surely die and gave him up for lost.' The young lady turned pale and asked, 'Is all this because of me?' I replied, 'Yes, by God, my lady; what is your command?' She replied, 'Let him come here on Friday, before the noon prayer, and when he arrives, I will come down, open the door, and take him upstairs to my room, where he can visit with me for a while and then leave, before my father comes back.'" O fellows, when I heard the old woman's words, my anguish ceased. Then she sat at my head and said, "God willing, be ready on Friday." Then she received the reward I owed her and departed, leaving me completely recovered, to the delight of my family.

I kept waiting, and on Friday the old woman came in and inquired after my health, and I replied that I was hale and hearty. Then I rose, put on my clothes, and scented myself with perfumes and incense. The old woman asked me, "Why don't you go to the bath and wash off the traces of your illness?" I replied, "I have no desire to go to the bath, and I have already washed myself with water, but I do want a barber to shave my head." Then I turned to the servant and said to him, "Get me a sensible and discreet barber who will not give me a headache with his chatter." The servant went out and returned with this wretched old barber. When he entered, he greeted me and I returned his greeting. Then he said to me, "My lord, I see that you are emaciated." I replied, "I have been ill." He said, "May God be kind to you and make you well." I said, "May God hear your prayer." He said, "My lord, be cheerful, for your recovery is at hand," adding, "O my lord, do you want me to shave your head or to let blood?"[6] I said, "Shave my head at once and spare me from your raving, for I am still weak from my illness."

But morning overtook Shahrazad, and she lapsed into silence. Then Dinarzad said to her sister, "What a strange and entertaining story!" Shahrazad replied, "What is this compared with what I shall tell you tomorrow night if the king spares me and lets me live!"

---

6. To this day, in certain parts of the Middle East, barbers function as surgeons and dentists.

THE ONE HUNDRED AND FORTY-FOURTH NIGHT

The following night Shahrazad said:

I heard, O happy King, that the tailor told the king of China that the young man said to the guests:

I said to the barber, "I am still weak from my illness." Then he put his hand in his leather bag and took out an astrolabe[7] with seven plates inlaid with silver and, going into the courtyard, held the instrument up to the sun's rays and looked for some time. Then he said to me, "O my lord, eight degrees and six minutes have elapsed of this day, which is Friday, the eighteenth of Safar, in the six hundred and fifty-third year of Hijra and the seven thousand three hundred and twentieth year of the Alexander era, and the planet now in the ascendant, according to the mathematical calculations on the astrolabe, is Mars, which is in conjunction with Mercury, a conjunction that is favorable for cutting hair. I can also see that you intend to meet another person, and for that the time is inauspicious and ill-advised." I said to him, "By God, fellow, you are pestering me and wearying me with your wretched auguries. I have not brought you here to read the stars, but to shave my head. Proceed at once to perform what I have brought you for, or get out and let me call for another barber to shave my head." He said, "By God, my lord, 'even if you had cooked it in milk, it wouldn't have turned out better.' You have asked for a barber, and God has sent you a barber who is also an astrologer and a physician, versed in the arts of alchemy, astrology, grammar, lexicography, logic, scholastic disputation, rhetoric, arithmetic, algebra, and history, as well as the traditions of the Prophet, according to Muslim and al-Bukhari.[8] I have read many books and digested them, I have had experience of affairs and understood them, and I have studied all sciences and crafts and mastered them. In short, I have tried and mastered everything. It behooves you to give thanks to the Almighty God for what He has sent you and to praise Him for what He has bestowed on you. Follow my advice today, and obey the stars. I offer it to you free of charge, for it is nothing, considering my affection and esteem for you. Your father loved me because of my discretion; therefore, my service is obligatory to you."

When I heard his speech, I said to him, "You will surely be the death of me today."

---

7. Instrument used formerly by astrologers for ascertaining the positions of the heavenly bodies.
8. Two of the compilers of the sayings of the prophet Muhammad.

But morning overtook Shahrazad, and she lapsed into silence. Then Dinarzad said to her sister, "What a strange and entertaining story!" Shahrazad replied, "What is this compared with what I shall tell you tomorrow night if the king spares me and lets me live!"

THE ONE HUNDRED AND FORTY-FIFTH NIGHT

The following night Shahrazad said:

I heard, O happy King, that the tailor told the king of China that the young man said to the guests:

The barber added, "Am I not the one whom, because of my taciturnity, people call the Silent One? My eldest brother is called al-Baqbuq [the Prater], the second al-Haddar [the Babbler], the third al-Buqaybiq [the Gabbler], the fourth al-Kuz al-Aswani [the Stone Mug], the fifth al-Nashshar [the Braggart], the sixth Shaqayiq [the Noisy], while I, because of my taciturnity, al-Samit [the Silent One]." The barber kept talking until I got exasperated and angrily said to my servant, "For the sake of the Almighty God, give him four dinars and let him go. I do not wish to have my head shaved today." When the barber heard my words, he said to me, "O my lord, what kind of talk is this? I swear that I am under an obligation not to accept any money from you until I have served you, and indeed I must serve you, for it is my duty to help you and fulfill your need; and I don't care whether I get paid or not. If you, my lord, don't know my worth, I know yours and know what you deserve because of the esteem I hold for your father." Then he recited the following verses:

> I came one day to my lord to let blood,
> But found out that the season was not good
> And sat and talked of many prodigies
> And my store of knowledge before him strewed.
> Pleased with my talk, he turned and said to me,
> "You are beyond compare, O mine of lore!"
> I said, "O lord of men, you are the source,
> Bestowing wisdom from your boundless store,
> O lord of grace and all munificence,
> O treasure house of knowledge, wit, and sense!"

[He added, "When I recited these same verses to your father], he was pleased and cried out to the servant, saying, 'Give him a hundred and three dinars and a robe of honor,' and the servant did as he bade.

Then I read the signs and, finding the moment auspicious, let blood. When that was done, I could not help asking him, 'By God, my lord, what made you bid the servant give me a hundred and three dinars?' He replied, 'One dinar was for your astrological observation, another for your entertaining conversation, the third for the bloodletting, and the remaining hundred and the robe of honor for your praise of me.'" The barber went on and on until I got so angry that I burst out, crying "May God show no mercy to my father for knowing the likes of you."

But morning overtook Shahrazad, and she lapsed into silence. Then Dinarzad said to her sister, "What a strange and entertaining story!" Shahrazad replied, "What is this compared with what I shall tell you tomorrow night if I am alive!"

THE ONE HUNDRED AND FORTY-SIXTH NIGHT

The following night Shahrazad said:

I heard, O happy King, that the tailor told the king of China that the young man told the guests:

I said to the barber, "For God's sake, spare me your chatter, for I am going to be late." But he laughed and said, "There is no god but God. Glory be to Him who changes not. My lord, I must conclude that your illness has changed you from what you used to be, for I see that you have become foolish, while people usually become wiser, as they grow older. I have heard the poet say:

> Comfort the poor with money, if you can,
> And God's recompense will be yours by right.
> Want is a dire affliction, hard to cure,
> But money can improve a sorry sight.
> And if you meet your fellows, wish them peace,
> And show your parents their due reverence.
> How oft have they, sleepless, waited for you,
> Praying to God to keep his vigilance!

In any case, you are excused, but I worry about you. You should know that your father and grandfather did nothing without consulting me, for it is said, 'He who takes counsel shall not be disappointed,' and 'He who has no mentor will never be a mentor.' And the poet says:

> Before you proceed to do anything,
> Consult a mature man ere venturing.

Indeed, you will find none more experienced than I, and I am here, standing on my feet, ready to serve you. I am not annoyed with you; why should you be annoyed with me?" I said to him, "By God, fellow, you have talked too much; all I want from you is to shave my head and be done with it." He said, "I know that my lord is displeased with me, but I do not hold it against you." I said to him, "My appointment is drawing near; for the sake of the Almighty God, fellow, shave my head and go." And I tore my clothes. When he saw me do this, he took the razor and, sharpening it, came up to me, shaved a few hairs, then held his hand back and said, "My lord, haste is of the devil, for the poet says:

> Be careful and restrain your hasty wish;
> Be merciful to all, and they will mercy show.
> The hand of God is above every hand,
> And every tyrant shall another know.

My lord, I don't think that you know my worth, for you are unaware of my knowledge, wisdom, and high merit." I replied, "Stop meddling, for you have pestered me enough." He said, "My lord, it seems to me that you are in a hurry." I replied, "Yes, yes, yes!" He said, "Don't be in a hurry, for haste is of the devil and leads to regret. I am worried about you, and I would like you to let me know what it is you intend to do, for I fear that it might prove harmful to you. There are still three hours left to the end of prayer," adding, "However, I don't wish to be in doubt about this but I must know for certain the exact time, for speech, when it is conjectural, is flawed, especially in one like me, whose merit is plain and known among men; and it does not befit me to base my statements on conjecture, as do the common sort of astrologers." Then he threw down the razor, went out . . .

But morning overtook Shahrazad, and she lapsed into silence. Then Dinarzad said to her sister, "What a strange and entertaining story!" Shahrazad replied, "What is this compared with what I shall tell you tomorrow night if the king spares me and lets me live!"

THE ONE HUNDRED AND FORTY-SEVENTH NIGHT

The following night Shahrazad said:

I heard, O happy King, that the tailor told the king of China that the young man said to the guests:

The barber threw down the razor, went out with the astrolabe, and came back, counting on his fingers, and said, "According to the learned and wise mathematicians and astrologers, there are exactly three hours left to the end of prayer, neither more nor less." I said to him, "For God's sake, fellow, hold your tongue, for you have tormented me enough." So this cursed fellow took the razor, shaved a few hairs, and said, "By God, I don't know the cause of your haste, and I am concerned about it. You would do better to tell me, for your father and grandfather—may God have mercy on them—did nothing without consulting me."

When I realized that I was not going to get rid of him, I said to myself, "Noon is approaching, and I wish to go to the young lady before the people return from the mosque. If I am delayed much longer, I will not be able to get to her." Then I said to him, "Be quick and stop jabbering, for I have to go to a party at the house of one of my friends." When he heard me speak of a party, he said, "This day of yours is a blessed one for me; you have reminded me that yesterday I invited a group of friends, and I have forgotten to provide something for them to eat till now. What a disgrace in their eyes!" I replied, "Don't worry about it. I have told you that I am going to a party today. All the food and drink in my house shall be yours, if you hurry and shave my head." He said, "God bless you, but tell me what you are giving me, so that I may know and inform my guests." I replied, "I have five different dishes, ten fried chickens, and a roasted lamb." He said, "Bring them out, so that I may see them." I bade one of my servants buy all that and bring it back quickly. The servant did as I bade him, and when the barber saw the food, he said, "My lord, the food is here, but there is no wine." I said to him, "I have two flagons of wine." He said, "Have them brought out." I said to the servant, "Bring them," and when he did, the barber said, "O what an excellent fellow, what a generous soul, and what a noble pedigree! We have the food and wine, but there remain [the perfume and the incense]."

I brought him a box containing five dinars' worth of aloewood, ambergris, and musk, and as time was running out, I said to him, "For God's sake, take the whole box and finish shaving my head." But he replied, "By God, I will not take it until I see the contents, one by one." I bade the servant open the box, and the barber threw down the astrolabe, sat down, and began to turn over the contents, before accepting them. Meanwhile, I waited, with most of my head still unshaven, until I choked with exasperation. Then taking the razor, he came up to me and shaved a little hair, reciting the following verses:

> The growing boy follows his father's suit,
> Just as the tree grows firmly from its root.

Then he added, "By God, my lord, I don't know whether to thank you or thank your father, for my party owes itself entirely to your generosity.

May God preserve it and preserve you. None of my friends is worthy of it; yet they are all decent men, such as Zentut the bathkeeper and Sali' the corn dealer and Sallut the beanseller and Akrasha the grocer and Sa'id the cameldriver and Suwaid the porter and Hamid the garbageman and Abu-Makarish the bath attendant and Qusaim the watchman and Karim the groom. There is not one among them who is disagreeable, contentious, meddlesome, or troublesome. Each has his own dance, which he dances, and his verses, which he sings. But their best quality is that they are like your servant and slave; they neither meddle nor talk too much. The bathkeeper sings enchantingly to the little drum and dances and says, 'I am going out, mother, to fill my jar.' As for the corn dealer . . ."

But morning overtook Shahrazad, and she lapsed into silence. Then Dinarzad said to her sister, "What a strange and entertaining story!" Shahrazad replied, "What is this compared with what I shall tell you tomorrow night if the king spares me and lets me live!"

THE ONE HUNDRED AND FORTY-EIGHTH NIGHT

The following night, Shahrazad said:

I heard, O happy King, that the tailor told the king of China that the young man said to the guests:

The barber said, "The corn dealer sings better than the nightingale and dances and says, 'O wailing mistress, you have not done badly,' which makes the men laugh until their hearts burst from laughter. As for the garbageman, he dances to the tambourine and charms even the birds, as he sings, 'News from my neighbor is locked in a chest.' He is a clever, deft, spirited, quick-witted, and refined fellow, of whose virtues I like to say:

> O my life for a handsome garbageman,
> Whose boughlike gait has set my heart on fire!
> Fate blessed me with him one night, and I said,
> Feeling the ebb and flow of my desire,
> 'You have inflamed my heart,' and he replied,
> 'No wonder that a scavenger can light the pyre!'

Indeed, every one of these men is accomplished in knowing how to divert the mind with mirth and fun. Perhaps my lord would like to join us today and postpone going to his friends, as he had intended, for you still show traces of illness and you may meet there some meddlesome and very talkative people or may encounter a busybody who will give you a headache, while you are still weak from illness."

I said to him, "You have not failed in giving me your good advice," and, in spite of my anger, I laughed, adding, "Perhaps some other time, the Almighty God willing. Finish my business and go in God's peace and enjoy yourself with your friends and companions, for they are waiting for you." He said, "My lord, I only wish to introduce you to the company of these nice fellows, among whom there is not one meddlesome or garrulous man, for since I reached manhood, I have never been able to tolerate the company of a man who meddles ill what concerns him not or who is not, like myself, a man of few words. If you were once to spend some time with them, you would forsake all your friends." I said, "May God grant you joy with them. I must visit you and enjoy their company one of these days." He said, "I wish it were today, but if you are determined not to come with me but to go to your friends today, then let me take to my guests what you have kindly given me for them and leave them to eat and drink without me, while I return to you and go with you to your friends, for there is no formality between me and my friends to prevent me from leaving them and returning to you." I replied, "There is no power and no strength, save in God, the Almighty, the Magnificent. Go to your friends and enjoy yourself with them, and let me go to mine and be with them this day, for they are waiting for me." The barber said, "My lord, God forbid that I leave you and let you go alone." I said, "The party I am going to is private, and you will not be able to get in." He said, "My lord, I believe that you are going to meet a woman and that if you were really going to a party, you would take me with you, for it is the like of me that brings color to places of entertainment, parties, celebrations, and festivals. And if you are planning to be alone with some woman, I am the fittest . . ."

But morning overtook Shahrazad, and she lapsed into silence. Then Dinarzad said to her sister, "What a strange and entertaining story!" Shahrazad said, "What is this compared with what I shall tell you if I stay alive!"

THE ONE HUNDRED AND FORTY-NINTH NIGHT

The following night Shahrazad said:

I heard, O happy King, that the tailor told the king of China that the young man said to the guests:

The barber said, "I am the fittest of all men to help you in your plan and to see that no one sees you entering the place and puts you in jeopardy, for in Baghdad one cannot do anything of the kind, especially on a day like this and in a city whose chief of the police is very powerful, severe, and sharp-tempered." I said to him, "Damn you, wretched old man! Aren't you ashamed to speak to me like this?" He replied, "You silly man, you ask me whether I am not ashamed, yet you hide from me your plan, which I know for certain, while all I wanted was to help you today." Fearful lest my family and neighbors should hear the barber's talk and I be exposed, I remained silent, while he finished shaving my head. By then it was almost noon, and the first and second exhortations to prayer were over and the hour of prayer had come. I said to him, "Take the food and drink to your friends, while I wait for your return and take you with me." I kept trying to cajole and outsmart the cursed fellow, hoping that he would leave me, but he replied, "I think that you are trying to trick me and go alone and cast yourself in some peril from which there is no escape. For God's sake, for God's sake, don't leave until I come back and go with you, so that I may watch for you and see that you don't fall into a trap." I replied, "Very well, but don't be late." Then he took all that I had given him of food, drink, roast lamb, and perfume and went out. But the cursed fellow sent everything to his house with a porter and hid himself in an alley.

As for me, I rose at once, for the announcers of prayer had already chanted the salutations, dressed myself, and went out in a hurry until I came to the house where I had seen the young lady—I did not realize that the cursed barber had followed me. I found the door open, and when I went in, I found the old woman on her feet, waiting for me. I went upstairs to the young lady's room, but hardly had I gone in, when the master of the house returned from the mosque and, entering the house, closed the door behind him. I looked out from the window and saw this cursed barber sitting by the door and said to myself, "How did that devil find me out?" At that moment, as God had decreed my undoing, it happened that a maid had committed some offense for which the master of the house beat her. So she screamed, and when a male slave came to rescue her, the judge beat him also, and the slave too began to scream. The cursed barber concluded that it was I whom the judge was beating and began to tear his clothes, throw dust on his head, and cry out for help. The people began to gather around him, while he kept crying out, "My master is being murdered in the judge's house." Then he ran, shrieking, toward my house, followed by the crowd, and told my family and servants. Before I knew it, they arrived, with torn clothes and disheveled hair, crying out, "Alas for our master!" with the barber at their head, in a sorry state, tearing his clothes and screaming.

But morning overtook Shahrazad, and she lapsed into silence. Then Dinarzad said to her sister, "Sister, what a strange and entertaining story!" Shahrazad replied, "What is this compared with what I shall tell you if the king spares me and lets me live!"

THE ONE HUNDRED AND FIFTIETH NIGHT

The following night Shahrazad said:

It is related, O happy King, that the tailor told the king of China that the young man said to the guests:

My relatives kept crying out, "Alas for our murdered one, alas for our murdered one," while a crowd gathered around them, until the judge, hearing the uproar and the screaming at his door, said to one of his servants, "Go and see what is the matter." The servant went out and came back, saying, "O my lord, there are more than ten thousand men and women at the door, crying out, 'Alas for our murdered one,' and pointing to our house." When the judge heard this, he became apprehensive and worried and, opening the door, went out and saw a great crowd of people. He was amazed and said, "O people, what is the matter?" They replied, "O cursed man, O pig, you have killed our master." He said, "What has your master done to me that I should kill him? My house is open to you." The barber said, "You beat him with a rod and I heard him just now screaming inside the house." The judge repeated, "What has your master done to me that I should beat him, and what brings him into my house?" The barber replied, "Don't be perverse, vile old man. I know everything. Your daughter is in love with him and he with her, and when you found them out, you bade your servants beat him. By God, none shall judge between us and you but the caliph, unless you bring out our master to his relatives, before I go in and bring him out myself and put you to shame." The judge stood blushing and tongue-tied before the crowd and could only mumble, "If you are speaking the truth, come in and fetch him." The barber pushed forward and entered the house.

When I saw the barber enter the house, I looked for an exit or a means of escape or a place to hide but saw none, save a large chest that stood in the room. I got into the chest, pulled the lid down on me, and held my breath. When the barber came into the room, he searched, looking right and left and, seeing nothing but the chest in which I was hiding, placed it on his head and left with it in a hurry. At this I lost my mind and, feeling certain that he would not let me alone, took courage and, opening the chest, threw myself to the ground and broke my leg. I opened the door and saw a great crowd of people. Now I happened to have a good sum of money hidden in my sleeve for such a day; so I took the money out and began to scatter it among the crowd, and while they were busy scrambling for it, I fled, running right and left through the alleys of Baghdad, while the cursed barber, whom nothing could divert, kept running after me from place to place.

But morning overtook Shahrazad, and she lapsed into silence. Then Dinarzad said to her sister, "What a strange and entertaining story!" Shahrazad replied, "What is this compared with what I shall tell you tomorrow night if I stay alive!"

THE ONE HUNDRED AND FIFTY-FIRST NIGHT

The following night Shahrazad said:

I heard, O happy King, that the tailor told the king of China that the young man said to the guests:

I kept running, while the barber ran and shouted after me, "They would have killed you and bereft me of my benefactor and the benefactor of my family, my children, and my friends, but praise be to God who made me triumph over them and helped me deliver my lord from their hands." Then he asked me, "My lord, where do you want to go now? If God had not sent me to you, you would not have escaped destruction at their hands, for no one else could have saved you. How long can I live to protect you? By God, you have nearly undone me by your desire and foolish decision to go alone. But I will not reproach you for your foolishness, for you are a rash and ignorant bumbler."

The young man continued:

As if the barber was not satisfied with what he had inflicted on me, he kept pursuing me and shouting after me through the streets of Baghdad until I lost all patience and in my rage and fury against him took refuge in a caravansary inside the market and sought the protection of the owner, who finally drove the barber away. Then I sat in one of the shops and thought to myself, "If I return home, I will never be able to get rid of this cursed fellow, and he will be with me day and night, while I can't stand even the look of him." So I sent

out at once for witnesses and made a will, dividing the greater part
of my money among my family, and appointed a guardian over them,
bidding him sell the house and be in charge of the old and the
young. Then, in order to get rid of this pander, I took some money
with me and set out on that very day from the caravansary until I
reached this country and settled in your city, where I have been living for some time. When you favored me with your invitation and I
came here, whom should I see but this cursed barber, seated in the
place of honor? How can I then enjoy myself in the company of this
fellow who brought all this upon me, causing me to break my leg,
leave my family and my home and country, and go into exile? Now I
have run into him again, here at your place.

The young man refused to sit down and join us. When we heard
what happened to the young man at the hands of the barber, we
were very much amazed and entertained by the story, and we asked
the barber, "Is what the young man says about you true? And why
did you do it?" He raised his head and replied, "Fellows, I did it out
of my wisdom, good sense, and humanity. Were it not for me, he
would have perished, for none but I was responsible for his escape.
It was good that he suffered in his leg and not in his life. I endured
so much just to do a favor to one who does not deserve it. By God, of
all my six brothers—I am the seventh—there is none less talkative,
less meddlesome, or wiser than I. I will tell you now about an incident that happened to me, in order to prove to you that, unlike all
my brothers, I am neither meddlesome nor talkative."

* * *

[The Tale of the Second Brother,
Baqbaqa the Paraplegic]

MY SECOND BROTHER'S name was Baqbaqa, and he was the para-
plegic. One day, as he was going on some business, he was met by an
old woman, who said, "Fellow, stop for a moment, so that I may propose something to you, and if my proposition pleases you, you may
proceed with the help of the Almighty God." My brother stopped,
and she said, "What I have to say is that I shall take you to a pleasant
place, providing that you don't ask too many questions," adding
"What do you say to a handsome house and a garden with running
waters and fruits and clear wine and a face as lovely as the moon for
you to embrace?" When my brother heard her words, he asked, "Is
all of this in this world?" She replied, "Yes, it is all yours, if you
behave sensibly and refrain from meddling and talking too much."
He replied, "Very well." Then she walked, and he walked behind her,

intent on following her instructions. Then she said, "The young lady to whom you are going likes to have her way and hates to be contradicted. If you follow her wishes, she will be yours." My brother said, "I will never contradict her in anything." Then he followed the old woman until she brought him to a mansion full of servants. When they saw him, they asked, "What are you doing here?" But the old lady replied, "Leave him alone; he is a workman, and we need him."

Then she brought him into a spacious yard, in the middle of which stood the loveliest of gardens, and seated him on a fine couch. Soon he heard a great commotion, and in came a troop of young ladies surrounding a lady as lovely as the full moon. When my brother saw her, he rose and bowed before her, and she welcomed him and bade him be seated. When he sat down, she turned to him and said, "God has chosen you and sent you as a blessing to us." My brother replied, "My lady, the blessing is all mine." Then she called for food, and they brought fine dishes. But as they ate, the lady could not stop laughing, and whenever my brother looked at her, she looked away from her maids, as if she was laughing at them, all the while showing my brother affection and jesting with him until he concluded that she was in love with him and that she would grant him his wish. When they finished eating, the wine was set before them, and there came ten young ladies as lovely as the moon, carrying lutes, who began to sing plaintive songs, which delighted my brother. Then the lady drank the cup, and my brother rose . . .

But morning overtook Shahrazad, and she lapsed into silence. Then Dinarzad said to her sister, "What a strange and entertaining story!" Shahrazad replied, "What is this compared with what I shall tell you tomorrow night if the king spares me and lets me live!"

THE ONE HUNDRED AND FIFTY-SEVENTH NIGHT

The following night Shahrazad said:

I heard, O happy King, that the tailor told the king of China that the barber told the guests that he said to the caliph:

My brother rose, but as he was drinking the cup in greeting, the lady gave him a slap on the neck. He drew back in anger, but as the old woman kept winking at him, he returned and the lady bade him sit. But she hit him again, and as if that was not enough, she ordered her maids to hit him too, all the while saying to the old woman, "I have never seen anything better than this," and the old woman replying, "Yes, by God, my lady." Then the lady ordered her maids to perfume my brother with incense and sprinkle rosewater on him; then she said to him, "May God reward you. You have entered my house and submitted to my condition, for whoever crosses me, I turn him away, but whoever is patient with me I grant him his wish." My brother replied, "My lady, I am your slave." Then she bade all her maids sing with loud voices, and they did as she bade.

Then she cried out to one of the maids, saying "Take my darling with you, take care of him, and bring him back to me soon." My brother rose to go with the maid, not knowing what was intended for him, and as the old woman rose to go with them, he said to her, "Tell me what she wishes this maid to do to me." The old woman replied, "Nothing but good. She wishes to dye your eyebrows and remove your mustaches." My brother said, "The dyeing of the eyebrows will come off with washing, but the plucking out of my mustaches will be hard on me." The old lady said, "Beware of crossing her, for her heart is set on you." So my brother submitted while the maid dyed his eyebrows and plucked out his mustaches. Then she went back to her lady, who said, "There is one more thing; shave his chin, so that he may be beardless." The maid returned to my brother and began to shave his beard, and the old woman said to him, "Be glad, for she would not have done this to you if she had not been passionately in love with you. Be patient, for you are about to have your wish." My brother submitted and sat patiently, while the maid shaved his beard.

Then she brought him to her mistress, who, delighted at the sight, laughed until she fell on her back and said to him, "My lord, you have won my heart with your good nature." Then she conjured him by her life to rise and dance, and he began to dance, while she and the maids grabbed everything around and threw it at him until he fell senseless from the pelting and hitting. When he came to himself, the old woman said to him, "You will have your wish."

But morning overtook Shahrazad, and she lapsed into silence. Then Dinarzad said to her sister, "What a strange and entertaining story!" Shahrazad replied, "What is this compared with what I shall tell you tomorrow night if the king spares me and lets me live!"

THE ONE HUNDRED AND FIFTY-EIGHTH NIGHT

The following night Shahrazad said:

I heard, O happy King, that the tailor told the king of China that the barber told the guests that he said to the caliph:

When my brother came to himself, the old woman said to him, "One more thing and you will have your wish; it is her habit, when she gets intoxicated, to let no one have her until he takes off his shirt and trousers and stands naked. Then she runs away, as if she is trying to escape, while he follows her from place to place until his penis hardens and becomes firmly erect. Then she stops and lets him have her," adding "Rise and take off your clothes." My brother took off all his clothes and stood stark naked. Then the lady herself took off her clothes, except for her trousers, and said to him, "If you want me, follow me until you catch me," adding "Start running," and she began to run from place to place, while, overwhelmed with desire, with his cock sticking straight up in the air, he ran after her like a madman. She entered a dark place and he followed her, stepping on a soft spot, which caved in under him, and before he knew it, he found himself in the middle of the leather market, where the traders were shouting their wares, buying and selling.

When they saw him in that condition, naked, without a beard, and with red eyebrows, they yelled and clapped their hands at him and beat him with hides on his naked body until he fell senseless. Then they set him on an ass and took him to the city gate. When the chief of the police arrived, he asked, "What is this?" They replied, "Lord, this fellow fell from the vizier's house, in this condition." The prefect gave him a hundred lashes and banished him from Baghdad. I went after him, O Commander of the Faithful, brought him back secretly into the city and arranged for his upkeep, and I wouldn't have done it were it not for my generous nature.

But morning overtook Shahrazad, and she lapsed into silence. Then Dinarzad said to her sister, "What a strange and entertaining story!" Shahrazad replied, "What is this compared with what I shall tell you tomorrow night if the king spares me and lets me live!"

* * *

[The Tale of the Fifth Brother, the Cropped of Ears]

MY FIFTH BROTHER, the cropped of ears, was a poor man who used to beg by night and live by day on what he got. When our father, who was an old man, far advanced in years, fell sick and died, he left us seven hundred dirhams, which we divided equally among ourselves, each receiving one hundred dirhams. When my fifth brother received his share, he did not know what to do with it until he thought of buying glass of all kinds and selling it at a profit. He bought a hundred dirhams' worth of glass and, putting it in a large basket, sat to sell it next to a tailor's shop, which had a balustrade at the entrance. My brother leaned against the balustrade and sat, thinking to himself, "I know that I have a capital of a hundred dirhams' worth of glass, which I will sell for two hundred dirhams, with which I will buy more glass which I will sell for four hundred dirhams. I will continue to buy and sell until I have four thousand dirhams, then ten thousand, with which I will buy all kinds of jewels and perfumes and make a great profit. Then I will buy a fine house, together with slaves and horses, and I will eat and drink and carouse and bring every singing man and woman in the city to sing to me, for the Almighty God willing, my capital will be a hundred thousand dirhams."

All this went through his head, while the hundred dirhams' worth of glass sat in the basket before him. He continued, saying to himself, "As soon as I have amassed a hundred thousand dirhams, I will send out marriage brokers to demand for me in marriage the daughters of kings and viziers. In fact, I will ask for the hand of the vizier's daughter, for I have heard that she is singularly beautiful, that she is all perfection and grace. I will give her a dowry of a thousand dinars. If her father consents, well; if not, I will take her by force, in spite of him. When I return home, I will buy ten little slaves as well as clothes fit for kings, and I will get me a saddle of gold and have it set with expensive jewels. Then I will ride and parade in the city, with slaves before me and behind me, while the people salute me and invoke blessings on me. When I go to see the vizier, with slaves on my right and left, he will rise in greeting and, seating me in his place, will sit below me because I am his son-in-law. I will have with me two slaves carrying purses, each with a thouand dinars, one for the dowry, the other as a present, so that the vizier may know my generosity, my magnanimity, and my disdain for the world. Then I will return to my house, and if someone comes to me from the bride, I will give him money and bestow on him a robe of honor, but if he brings me a present, I will not accept it, but will return it, for I will maintain my dignity. Then I will prepare my house and ask them to make the bride ready, and when she is ready, I will bid them lead her to me in a procession. When it is time to unveil the bride, I will put on my best clothes and sit on a seat of silk brocade and lean on a cushion, turning neither right nor left, because of my sense of propriety, and my reticence, gravity, and wisdom. My bride will stand before me like the full moon, in her robes and ornaments, and I, out of a sense of self-respect, dignity, and pride, will not look at her until all those who are present will say to me, 'O our lord and master, your wife and slave stands before you. Be kind to her and grant her a glance, for standing hurts her.' After they kiss the ground before me many times, I will raise my head, give her one look, and bend my head again. They they will take her away, and I will rise and change my clothes for a finer suit. When they bring the bride for the second time, in her second dress, I will not look at her until they stand before me and implore me many times. Then I will give her a quick look; then look down again. I will continue to do this until they finish displaying her."

But morning overtook Shahrazad, and she lapsed into silence. Then Dinarzad said to her sister, "What a strange and entertaining story!" Shahrazad replied, "What is this compared with what I shall tell you tomorrow night if the king spares me and lets me live!"

THE ONE HUNDRED AND SIXTY-THIRD NIGHT

The following night Shahrazad replied, "Very well," and said:

I heard, O happy King, that the tailor told the king of China that the barber told the guests that he said to the caliph:

All this went through my brother's mind. Then he went on, "I will continue to enjoy looking at the bride until they finish presenting her to me. Then I will order one of my servants to fetch a purse of five hundred dinars and, giving it to the attendants of the bride, command them to lead me to the bride chamber. When they lead her in and leave her alone with me, I will look at her and lie by her side, but I will ignore her and will not speak to her, so that she may say that I am a proud man. Then her mother will come in and kiss my hand and say, 'My lord, look at your servant and comfort her, for she craves your favor.' But I will not answer. When she sees this, she will kiss my feet many times and say, 'My lord, my daughter is a young lady who has never seen a man before, and if you disdain her, you will break her heart. Turn to her, speak to her, and comfort her.' Then her mother will give her a cup of wine and say to her, 'Entreat your lord to drink.' When the bride comes to me, I will let her stand, while I recline on a cushion embroidered with gold and silver, and will proudly disdain to look at her, so that she may say that I am an honorable and self-respecting man. I will let her stand until she feels humiliated and learns that I am her master. Then she will say to me, 'My lord, for God's sake, don't refuse the cup from my hand, for I am your servant.' But I will not speak to her, and she will press me, saying, 'You must drink,' and put the cup to my lips. Then I will shake my fist in her face and kick her with my foot like that." So saying, he kicked with his foot and knocked over the basket of glass, which, resting high, fell to the ground, and everything in it was broken.

The tailor [who had overheard some of my brother's conversation with himself] cried out, "All this comes of your pride, you dirty pimp. By God, if it was within my power, I would have you beaten a hundred times and paraded throughout the city." At that moment, O Commander of the Faithful, my brother began to beat on his face, tear his clothes, and weep. The people who were going to the Friday prayers saw him, and some of them pitied him, while others paid no attention to him, as he stood bereft both of capital and profit.

While he wept, a beautiful lady, riding on a she-mule with a saddle of gold and attended by servants, passed by, filling the air with the odor of musk. When she saw my brother weeping in his plight, she felt pity for him and, inquiring about him, was told that he had had a basket of glass, by which he was trying to make a living, but that it had got broken, and that this was the cause of his grief. The lady called one of her servants and said to him, "Give him whatever you have with you," and the servant gave my brother a purse in which he found five hundred dinars. When he saw the money, he almost died of joy and, invoking blessings upon the lady, returned to his house a rich man.

As he sat thinking, he heard a knocking at the door, and when he asked, "Who is it?" a woman answered, "My brother, I would like to have a word with you." He rushed and, opening the door, saw an old woman he did not know. She said to him, "Son, the time of prayer is near, and I have not yet performed my ablutions. I would like you to let me do so in your house." My brother replied, "I hear and obey." Then he asked her to come in, and when she was inside, he gave her a ewer for her ablutions and sat down, still beside himself with joy at the money, which he began to stuff inside his clothes. As he finished doing this, the old woman, finishing her prayers, came near where he sat and prayed a two-bow prayer. Then she invoked blessings on him.

But morning overtook Shahrazad, and she lapsed into silence. Then Dinarzad said to her sister, "What a strange and entertaining story!" Shahrazad replied, "What is this compared with what I shall tell you tomorrow night if I stay alive!"

THE ONE HUNDRED AND SIXTY-FOURTH NIGHT

The following night Shahrazad said:

I heard, O happy King, that the tailor told the king of China that the barber told the guests that he said to the caliph:

When the old woman finished her prayer and invoked blessings on him, he thanked her and, pulling out two dinars, gave them to her, saying to himself, "This is an offering from me." At this, she exclaimed, "How strange! Why do you look at me as if I was a beggar? Take your money and keep it for yourself, for I don't need it; however, I do have for you in this city a woman who has wealth, beauty, and charm." My brother asked, "How could I get such a woman?" The old woman replied, "Take all your money and follow me, and when you are with her, spare neither fair words nor amiability, and you will enjoy her beauty and her wealth to your heart's content." My brother took all his money and went with the old woman, so happy that he could hardly believe himself.

He followed her until she came to the door of a mansion, and when she knocked, the door was opened by a Greek slave girl. The old woman entered and bade my brother follow her, and he entered a spacious hall, spread with carpets and hung with curtains. He sat down, placed the money before him, and, taking off his turban, put it on his knee. Soon in came a young lady, so beautiful and so richly dressed that none better was ever seen. He rose to his feet, and when she looked at him, she smiled in his face and was glad to see him. Then she bade the door be shut and, taking him by the hand, led him to a private room, where she seated him and, sitting beside him, dallied with him for a while. Then she rose and, saying, "Wait until I come back," went away.

He sat by himself, when suddenly a great black slave came in, with a sword in his hand, and said to him, "Damn you, what are you doing here?" My brother was tongue-tied and could not answer. The black slave seized him and, stripping him of his clothes, struck him with the flat of the sword and left him half paralyzed. Then he kept striking him, so severely that my brother fell unconscious. The hideous slave concluded that he was dead, and my brother heard him say, "Where is the salt-woman?" and in came a maid with a large dish full of salt. Then the black slave began to stuff my brother's wounds with salt until he fainted again.

When he came to himself, he lay motionless, for fear that the black slave would discover that he was alive and finish him off. Then the maid went away, and the black slave cried out, "Where is the cellar-woman?" and in came the old woman, who took my brother by the feet and dragged him away and, opening a cellar door, threw him down on a heap of dead bodies. There he remained unconscious, without stirring, for two whole days, but the Almighty and Glorious God made the salt the cause of saving his life, for it stopped the flow of blood. As soon as he found himself able to move, he crept fearfully out of the cellar and made his way to the hallway, where he hid till early morning. When the old woman went out in quest of another

prey, he went out behind her, without her knowledge, and headed
home. There he treated himself for a month until he recovered.
Meanwhile he kept a constant watch on the old woman, while she
took one man after another and led them to that house. But my
brother said nothing. When he regained his health and recovered his
strength, he took a piece of cloth and made it into a bag, which he
filled with glass.

*But morning overtook Shahrazad, and she lapsed into silence. Then
Dinarzad said, "Sister, what a strange and entertaining story!" Shahrazad replied, "What is this compared with what I shall tell you tomorrow night if the king spares me and lets me live!"*

THE ONE HUNDRED AND SIXTY-FIFTH NIGHT

The following night Shahrazad said:

I heard, O happy King, that the tailor told the king of China that
the barber told the guests that he said to the caliph:

He put the glass in the bag and tied it to his waist. Then he disguised himself as a Persian, so that nobody would recognize him,
and hid a sword under his clothes. When he saw the old woman, he
said to her, with a Persian accent, "Old lady, I am a stranger here. Do
you have a pair of scales large enough to weigh five hundred dinars?
I will give you some of it for your trouble." The old woman replied,
"O Persian, my son is a money changer, and he has all kinds of
scales. Come with me before he goes out to his shop, and he will
weigh your gold." My brother said to her, "Lead the way." She led
him until she came to the house, and when she knocked at the door,
the young lady herself came out and opened it. The old woman
smiled in her face and said, "I have brought you a fat piece of meat
today." The young lady, taking my brother by the hand, led him into
the house and sat with him for a while. Then she rose and, saying to
him, "Wait until I come back," went away.
   As soon as she left, the cursed black slave came in, with a bare
sword in his hand, and said to my brother, "Get up, cursed man!" He
sprang behind the slave and, drawing the sword that was hidden
under his clothes, struck him and made his head fly away from his
body. Then he dragged him by the heels to the cellar and cried out,
"Where is the salt-woman?" The maid came with the dish of salt
and, seeing my brother with the sword in his hand, turned to run

away, but he caught up with her and struck off her head. Then he called out, "Where is the cellar-woman?" and when the old woman came in, my brother looked at her and said, "Do you recognize me, you wicked old woman?" She replied, "No, my lord." He said, "I am the one in whose house you prayed and whom you lured here." She said, "Spare me." But he paid no attention to her and struck her with the sword, cutting her in four.

Then he went in search of the young lady, and when she saw him, she lost her mind and asked for mercy. He promised to spare her and asked, "And you, how did you come to be with this black slave?" She replied, "I was a slave to a merchant, and the old woman used to visit me until we became intimate friends. One day she said to me, 'We have at our house today a wedding, the like of which was never seen, and I would like you to be there.' I replied, 'I hear and obey.' Then I rose and, putting on my clothes and jewelry and taking with me a purse with a hundred dinars, followed her until she brought me to this house and bade me enter. As soon as I went in, this black slave seized me, and I have been in this situation for three years, due to the treachery of the old woman. May God curse her!" My brother asked, "Does the black slave keep any money or possessions in this house?" She replied, "Yes, he has plenty, and if you can carry it away, do so with God's help." Then she took my brother and opened for him several chests full of purses, and while he stood there, not knowing what to do, she said to him, "Leave me here and go and bring men to carry the money." He went out at once and hired ten men, but when he returned, he found the door open, and when he went in, he was surprised to find that the young lady had disappeared with the purses, leaving very little money behind, and realized that she had tricked him. He took whatever money was left and, opening the closets, carried away all the clothes, leaving nothing in the house, and spent a happy night.

When he got up in the morning, he found at his door twenty policemen, who seized him, saying "The chief of the police wants you." He implored them to give him time to go into the house, but they would not let him, and although he offered them money and kept imploring and throwing himself at their feet until he was weary, they would not listen. They tied his hands fast behind his back and carried him off. On the way, they were met by one of my brother's old friends, and my brother clung to him and implored him to assist him and help deliver him from the hands of these policemen and their officers. The friend, glad to intercede on his behalf, inquired what was the matter, and the officers replied, "The chief of the police has ordered us to bring this man before him and, having found him and seized him, we are on our way to our superior the chief, according to his orders." My brother's friend said to them, "Good fellows, I will get from him whatever you wish and desire for your trouble. Release him and tell your superior the chief that you could not find him." But they refused and dragged my brother on his face to the chief of the police.

But morning overtook Shahrazad, and she lapsed into silence. Then Dinarzad said, "Sister, what a strange and entertaining story!" Shahrazad replied, "What is this compared with what I shall tell you tomorrow night if I stay alive!"

* * *

THE TWO HUNDRED AND THIRTIETH NIGHT

The following night Shahrazad said:

[The Story of Jullanar of the Sea]

I HEARD, O happy King, that there was once in Persia a great and mighty king whose capital was Khurasan. He ruled over so many provinces and cities and so many people that all the kings of Persia and all their armies paid him homage. He was a sensible, discerning, and pious man who judged fairly between the strong and the weak and treated the offenders with mercy, so that everyone near and far loved him and wished him long life, victory, and success. He had one hundred concubines of all races, each housed in her own apartment, but in all his life he had never been blessed with a son. He used to offer sacrifices, give alms, and do all kinds of favors and good deeds, praying to God to bless him with a son to bring him joy and inherit the kingdom after him. He used to say to himself, "I am afraid that I will die without a son and the kingdom will pass into the hands of strangers."

The slave-merchants knew that he enjoyed having many women and concubines, so that whenever they came by any slave girl, they brought her to him, and if he liked her, he would buy her at the highest price, making the merchant rich. Then he would bestow on him a robe of honor as well as other favors, give him written orders that none should levy any duty or tax on him, and hold him in high esteem. Consequently, the slave-merchants came to him from various provinces and countries to present him with fine mistresses and concubines. But in spite of all these efforts, he remained depressed and anxious for a long time.

But morning overtook Shahrazad, and she lapsed into silence.

THE TWO HUNDRED AND THIRTY-FIRST NIGHT

The following night Shahrazad said:

I heard, O happy King, that in spite of all these efforts, the king remained depressed and anxious for a long time because he was getting old, without having been blessed with a son to inherit the kingdom after him.

One day, as he sat on the throne, with his vizier by his side, with the princes, lords of the realm, and notables sitting before him, and with the Mamluks and servants standing in attendance, a servant came in and said, "O King of the age, there is a merchant at the door, with a girl worthy of our lord the king. He wishes to present her to you, and if she pleases you, he will offer her to you. He says that there is none like her in beauty or charm." The king replied, "Bring him to me." The servant rose and returned with the merchant led by a chamberlain who presented him to the king. The merchant kissed the ground and bowed before the king, who engaged him in conversation and spoke amiably with him until he put him at ease, allaying the awe he felt in the presence of the king. Indeed, it is the mark of kings, sovereigns, and other leaders that when a messenger or a merchant stands before them on some business, they converse with him amiably to allay the awe he feels in their presence.

At last the king turned to the merchant and asked . . .

But morning overtook Shahrazad, and she lapsed into silence.

THE TWO HUNDRED AND THIRTY-SECOND NIGHT

It is related, O happy King, that the king at last turned to the merchant and asked, "Where is the girl whom you consider to be worthy of me?" The merchant replied, "She is beautiful and elegant beyond description, and she is standing at the door with the servants, awaiting your pleasure. With your leave, I will bring her at once." The king gave him leave, and when she came in, the king looked and saw a tall girl, as slender as a spear, wrapped in a silk cloak embroidered with gold. The king rose from his throne and, entering a private chamber, bade the merchant bring in the girl. The merchant brought her before the king, and when he unveiled her, the king looked on her and saw that she was brighter than a banner and more slender than a reed, for she put even the rising moon to shame, with hair hanging down to her anklets in seven tresses like horses' tails or the veil of the night, and with dark eyes, smooth cheeks, heavy hips, and slender waist. When the king saw her, he was dazzled by her beauty and grace, for she was like her of whom the poet said:

> When they unveiled her, I doted at once,
> As she stood there with calm and dignity,
> Neither too little nor too much, faultlessly formed,
> Wrapped tightly in her cloak, in total parity,
> Slender her figure and perfect her height,
> Her lovely body to perfection bred.
> Her hair trailed to the anklets and revealed
> The glory and the envy of her head.

But morning overtook Shahrazad, and she lapsed into silence. Then Dinarzad said to her sister, "What a strange and entertaining story!" Shahrazad replied, "What is this compared with what I shall tell you tomorrow night if I stay alive!"

THE TWO HUNDRED AND THIRTY-THIRD NIGHT

The following night Shahrazad said:

It is related, O happy King, that when the king looked at the girl, he was dazzled by her beauty, captivated by her charm, and overwhelmed by love for her. He turned to the merchant and asked, "Shaikh, what is the price of this girl?" The merchant replied, "O King, I bought her from another merchant for two thousand dinars, and to this date I have traveled for three years and spent one thousand dinars on her to bring her to you, but your slave does not want any money for her; she is a gift to our lord the king." When the king heard this, he bestowed on him a robe of honor and ordered him ten thousand dinars and one of his choice horses. The merchant kissed the ground before him and departed.

Then the king committed the girl to the care of the nurses and attendants, saying to them, "Prepare her and leave her alone in one of my choice private apartments." They replied, "We hear and obey." Then they took care of her and brought her whatever she needed of servants, clothes, and food and drink. Then they took her to the bath and washed her, and when she came out, looking even more charming and beautiful, they dressed her in fine clothes and adorned her with jewelry worthy of her beauty and brought her to an apartment overlooking the sea. For at that time the king resided on the seashore, on an island called the White Island. When in the evening the king went in to her, he saw her standing at the window, looking at the sea, but although she noticed his presence, she neither paid attention to him nor showed him veneration, but continued to look at the sea, without even turning her head toward him. When the king saw this, he surmised that she came from ignorant people who had not taught her manners. But when he looked at her and saw her in her fine clothes and jewelry, which lent her greater beauty and charm and made her look like the twinkling stars or the shining sun, he said to himself, "Glory be to God who created you 'from a humble drop . . . in a safe haven.'" Then he went up to her, as she stood at the window, and embraced her. Then he sat down on the couch and, seating her on his knees, kissed her and marveled at her beauty and grace. Then he bade the maids bring food, and they set the food before him, in plates of gold and silver, worthy of a king and placed in the middle of the table almond pastry in a platter of white crystal. Then the king ate and fed her with his hand, but, while she ate, she kept her head bowed down, without paying any attention to him or looking at him.

But morning overtook Shahrazad, and she lapsed into silence.

The Two Hundred and Thirty-Fourth Night

The following night Shahrazad said:

It is related, O happy King, that the king kept feeding her with his hand, while she kept her head bowed down, without paying any attention to him, looking at him, or speaking to him. He began to talk to her and asked her name, but she kept her head bowed down, without replying, speaking, or uttering a word or a single syllable until the maids removed the table and the king and the girl washed their hands. When the king saw that she did not speak or answer his questions, he said to himself, "Glory be to the Almighty God! How beautiful is this girl but how ignorant! Or else she is dumb, but none save the Exalted and Glorious God is perfect. Were she able to speak, she would be perfect." He felt very sorry for her, and when he inquired of the attendants about her silence, they replied, "O King, by God, she has never said a word to us or uttered a single syllable, but has remained silent, as you see."

Then he summoned his concubines, favorites, and other women and bade them entertain her with all kinds of music and songs. But when they played and sang, the king enjoyed it very much, while she, neither speaking nor smiling, kept her head bowed, looked at them silently, and sulked until she made the king depressed. He dismissed the women and remained alone with her. Then he took off his clothes, lay down in bed, and made her lie beside him. When he looked at her body and saw that it was as fair as pure silver, he was enthralled and felt a great love for her, and when he took her virginity, he discovered that she had been a virgin and he rejoiced and said to himself, "By God, it is amazing that a girl of such beauty and grace, who has been bought and sold as a slave, has remained a virgin. This is a mystery."

Thereafter, he devoted himself totally to her, as she began to assume and occupy a great place in his heart, and he forsook and neglected his favorites, concubines, and all other women and considered her his blessing and his lot in life. He lived with her an entire year as if it were one day, yet she never spoke to him or uttered a single word, and this was very hard on him.

One day he turned to her . . .

But morning overtook Shahrazad, and she lapsed into silence. Then Dinarzad said to her sister Shahrazad, "O sister, what a strange and entertaining story!" Shahrazad replied, "What is this compared with what I shall tell you tomorrow night if the king spares me and lets me live! It will be even stranger."

THE TWO HUNDRED AND THIRTY-FIFTH NIGHT

The following night Shahrazad said:

I heard, O happy King, that at the end of the year, during which the king had grown infatuated and madly in love with the girl, he turned to her one day and said, "O my heart's desire, by God, my whole kingdom is not worth a grain of sand to me when I see you unable to reply or speak to me, for you are dearer to me than my eyes. I have forsaken my concubines, my favorites, and all my other women and made you my lot in life, and I have been patient with you and have been praying to the Almighty God to soften your heart with pity and make you speak one word to me, if you are able to speak. If you are dumb, let me know, in order that I may give up hope. I pray God to bless me with a son from you to bring me joy and inherit the kingdom after me, for I am lonely and forlorn, without relatives or anyone else to help me with the affairs of the kingdom, especially now that I am old and too weak to manage by myself and take care of my people. My lady, if you are able to speak, for God's sake, answer me, for my only wish is to hear one word from you before I die." When the girl heard the king's words, she bowed her head in thought, and, looking up, smiled in his face and said, "O gallant King and valiant lion, may God exalt you and humble your enemies, and may He give you long life and grant you every wish. The Almighty God has accepted your pleadings and entreaties and has answered your prayers. O King, I am bearing your child and the time of my delivery is near, although I do not know whether the child is a boy or a girl. Had it not been for the child, I would not have answered you or spoken to you." When the king heard her words, he was extremely happy and he embraced her and kissed her face, saying, "O my lady, O my darling, God has granted me two blessings and relieved me of two sorrows, blessings which are dearer to me than my entire kingdom, the first, your words after your silence, the second, to hear you say that you are bearing my child."

Then he left her and sat on his throne and in a fit of happiness bade his vizier distribute a hundred thousand dinars in alms to the widows, the orphans, and the homeless, and to all the poor and needy, and the vizier did as he bade. Then the king returned to the girl and said, "O my lady and my heart's delight, how was it that you spent a whole year, lying with me in the same bed day and night, without speaking to me until today? How could you bear it and what was the cause?" She replied, "O King, I am an exile and a captive in a foreign land, with a broken heart aching for my people, a woman all alone without father or brother."

But morning overtook Shahrazad, and she lapsed into silence. Then Dinarzad said to her sister, "O sister, what a strange and entertaining story!" Shahrazad replied, "What is this compared with what I shall tell you tomorrow night if I stay alive!"

THE TWO HUNDRED AND THIRTY-SIXTH NIGHT

The following night Shahrazad said:

I heard, O happy King, that when the king heard her words, he replied, "As for your saying that you are a brokenhearted woman in a foreign land, where is the reason for it, since my entire kingdom is in your hands and I am your slave? But, as for your saying that you have a mother and a father and a brother, where are they and what is your name?"

She replied, "I will tell you my name. I am called Jullanar of the Sea. My father was a sea-king, who then died and left his kingdom to my mother, my brother, and myself, but another sea-king defeated us and took the kingdom from us. My mother is descended from the daughters of the sea, not the daughters of the land and clay. My brother is called Sayih. One day I quarreled with him and left, swearing by the Almighty God that I would throw myself into the hands of a man of the land. I came out of the sea and sat down on the shore of the Island of the Moon, where an old man came up to me and, taking me to his house, tried to make love to me. But I refused and hit him on the head, so hard that I almost killed him! Then he took me out and sold me to that pious, fair, and honorable merchant who bought me for two thousand dinars, and brought me here and sold me to you. Had you not, O King, offered me your kindness and love and preferred me over your favorites, concubines, and all other women, I would never have stayed with you even one single hour but would have thrown myself from this window into the sea and returned to my people. I was also too ashamed to return with child, for fear that my people would distrust me, think ill of me, and refuse to believe, even if I swore to them, that it was a king who had bought me with his money and made me his lot in life."

When the king heard her explanation, he thanked her and kissed her between the eyes and said, "By God, O my lady and my darling, if you leave me even for a single hour, I will die. But for God's sake, tell me how do the people of the sea walk there without sinking and dying?" She replied, "O King, we walk in water just as you people walk on land, without being wetted or hurt by the water," adding, "We do this by virtue of the words inscribed on the seal ring of God's prophet Solomon, son of David—Peace be on him—and stay dry without being touched by the water. You should know, O King, that the time of my delivery is near, and I therefore wish my mother, my uncle's daughters, and my brother to come so that they may see me with you and find out that I am bearing the child of one of the kings of the land, who has bought me with his money and treated me kindly, and so that I may make peace with them; besides, your women are daughters of the land who do not know how to assist in birth the daughters of the sea or how to help them or take care of them properly. Moreover, I wish them to come, so that you may satisfy yourself that I am truly a daughter of the sea and that my father was a king."

When the king heard her explanation, he replied . . .

But morning overtook Shahrazad, and she lapsed into silence.

THE TWO HUNDRED AND THIRTY-SEVENTH NIGHT

The following night Shahrazad said:

I heard, O happy King, that when the king heard Jullanar's explanation, he replied, "Do as you wish, and I will agree with whatever you do." She said, "You should also know, O King, that we walk in the sea and see the daylight and the sun and the sky and see the night and the moon and the stars, without being harmed at all. In the sea there are people of all types and creatures of all kinds, just as there are on land, and more." The king marveled at what she said. Then she took out from her bosom a case of Javanese aloewood and took out from it a bead of the same wood. Then she threw the bead into the fire, whistled, and spoke words that the king did not understand, and there arose a great cloud of smoke. She said to the king, "Rise and hide in a closet, so that you may see my brother, mother, and cousins without being seen by them, for I intend to bring them here and show you the Almighty God's marvelous handiwork and the forms He created in the sea." The king ran and, hiding in a closet, watched what she did.

No sooner had she finished her incantation than the sea began to foam and surge, and suddenly the water split asunder and a young man emerged. He had sprouting mustaches, rosy cheeks, and teeth as glittering as gems. He was more handsome than the moon and as lovely as his sister Jullanar. He was followed by a gray-haired old woman and five young ladies who looked like moons and resembled Jullanar in beauty. The king saw the old woman and the young man and young ladies . . .

But morning overtook Shahrazad, and she lapsed into silence.

THE TWO HUNDRED AND THIRTY-EIGHTH NIGHT

The following night Shahrazad said:

I heard, O happy King, that the king saw the old woman and the young man and young ladies walk on the surface of the water until they reached the palace, while Jullanar went to the window to receive them. When they saw her, they were happy and they leapt and flew like birds and in an instant stood beside her, embracing her tearfully and telling her how much they had missed her. Then they said to her, "O Jullanar, you have been away for three years, and we have been desolate without you, unable to enjoy food or drink."

Jullanar kissed her brother's head and his hands and feet and did the same to her mother and her cousins. Then they sat for a while, expressing to each other how they had suffered during their separation. Then they questioned her about her present situation, with whom she was living, to whom the palace belonged, and who had brought her there. She said to them, "When I left you, I came out from the sea and sat on the shore of the Island of the Moon, where a man found me and sold me to a merchant who sold me to the king of this city for ten thousand dinars. I have had a happy life with him, for he has forsaken all his concubines and slave girls on my account, has turned away even from the affairs of the kingdom, and has devoted himself to me." When her brother heard this, he said, "O sister, rise and let us return to our home and family." When the king heard what the brother said, he lost his senses from shock and fright, saying to himself, "I am afraid that she will listen to her brother, leave me, and cause my death by her departure, for I am madly in love with her, especially since she is bearing my child, and I will die of longing for her and for my son." But when Jullanar heard her brother's words, she laughed and said, "O brother, you should know that the man I am living with is a pious, generous, and honorable man who has never said one bad word to me, who has treated me kindly, and who has given me the best of lives."

But morning overtook Shahrazad, and she lapsed into silence.

THE TWO HUNDRED AND THIRTY-NINTH NIGHT

The following night Shahrazad said:

I heard, O happy King, that Jullanar added, "I am bearing his child, and just as I am the daughter of a king, he too is a king and the son of a king. He has no son, but the Almighty God has been generous to me, and I pray to Him to bless us with a son to inherit his father's kingdom." When her brother and her mother and cousins heard this, they rejoiced and said to her, "You know your place in our heart; if you wish to stay here, we will gladly abide by your wish." She replied, "Yes, by God, I do." When the king heard this, he realized that she truly loved him and that she wished to stay with him and he was grateful to her and loved her even more.

Then Jullanar called for food, and the waiting women set the tables and laid on them all kinds of food, sweets, and fruits. They began to eat but soon said to her, "Your lord is a stranger whom you have praised to us because of your gratitude for his kindness to you and your love for him. We have entered his house without his leave and we have eaten his food, yet he has neither shown us himself nor eaten with us." They were so angry at the king that the fire flamed from their mouths as if from torches. When the king saw this, he was mad with terror, while Jullanar rose and, going into the closet, said to him, "O King, you have seen and heard how I praised you and how they wanted to carry me with them down to the sea and take me home." The king replied, "By God, I was not sure of your love until this moment. May God reward you." She replied, "O King, 'Is the reward of kindness anything but kindness'? You have treated me kindly and generously and you have made me your lot in life; how can I bear to part from you?"

But morning overtook Shahrazad, and she lapsed into silence.

THE TWO HUNDRED AND FORTIETH NIGHT

The following night Shahrazad said:

I heard, O happy King, that Jullanar said to the king, "How can I bear to part from you? You should know that when I praised you to my brother and mother and cousins, they felt a great affection for you and desired to see you, saying, 'We will not leave until we meet him and eat with him, so that his bread and salt may bind us together.'" The king replied, "I hear and obey, but I am afraid of them because of the fire I saw flaming from their mouths, for although I was not near them, I almost died of fright." Jullanar laughed and said, "Do not worry, for they do this only when they are angry, and they got angry this time because I had invited them to eat without you." Then she took the king by the hand and led him to them, as they sat before the food, waiting for him. When he came up to them, he greeted and welcomed them and they greeted him back with utmost respect, sprang up to their feet, and kissed the ground before him. Then they said to him, "O King of the age, we have only one request for you; take care of this unique pearl, Jullanar of the Sea, who is worthy of you just as you are worthy of her. By God, all the kings of the sea sought her hand in marriage, but we rejected them because we could not bear to part from her even for a single moment. Had you not been a pious, upright, honorable, and noble-hearted man, God would not have blessed you with this queen. Glory be to Him who made you cherish her and made her favor you and serve you, for you are like those of whom the poet said:

> She is worthy of none but him,
> And he of none but her,
> That should another seek her hand,
> The earth would be astir."

The king thanked them and thanked Jullanar and sat to converse and eat with them until they had had enough and washed their hands. Then he lodged them in a private apartment where they lived for a full month, during which he never left their company for a single hour.

When the month had passed, Jullanar said, "The time of my delivery is at hand," and the king provided for her all the medicines and potions she needed for herself and her child. Then she went into labor and the women gathered around her, and the labor increased until the Almighty God granted her safe delivery, and she gave birth to a boy as lovely as the moon. When his mother looked at him, she was extremely happy to see him. Then her mother went to the king and announced the birth of his son.

But morning overtook Shahrazad, and she lapsed into silence.

THE TWO HUNDRED AND FORTY-FIRST NIGHT

The following night Shahrazad said:

I heard, O happy King, that Jullanar's mother went to the king, and when she announced the birth of his son, he rejoiced and knelt in gratitude before the Almighty God. Then he bestowed robes of honor, distributed money, and gave gifts. When he was later asked, "What do you wish to name him?" he replied, "I name him Badr," and the boy was called Badr. Then the king bade the princes and chamberlains bid the people decorate the city, and he opened the jails and clothed the widows and orphans and gave alms to the poor and freed many Mamluks, as well as male and female slaves, and held celebrations and gave a magnificent banquet, to which he invited the select few as well as the general public. The celebrations lasted for ten full days.

On the eleventh day, as the king sat with Jullanar and her brother and mother and cousins, Jullanar's brother rose and, taking the newborn Badr, played with him, made him dance, then carried him in his arms, while the king and Jullanar looked at the boy and rejoiced. Suddenly her brother, taking them by surprise, flew with the boy out of the window, far from the shore, and dove with him into the sea. When the king saw the uncle take his son, plunge with him into the sea, and disappear, he let out a great cry, and his soul almost left his body. He tore his clothes and began to weep and wail. When Jullanar saw him in this condition, she said to him, "O King of the age, do not fear or weep for your son. I love him even more than you do, and he is with my brother, who does not mind the sea or fear drowning. If he thought that the boy would be in any danger, he would not have taken him there. Soon he will come back with your son safely, God the Almighty willing."

Soon the sea began to storm and surge and suddenly Sayih, the boy's uncle, emerged safely with the boy and flew into the room with the boy nestling in his arms as quietly as the moon. Then Sayih turned to the king and said, "I hope that you were not frightened when I dove with him into the sea." The king replied. "Yes, by God. Sayih, I thought that he would never return safely." Sayih said, "I took him there to pencil his eyes with a special kohl blessed by the words inscribed on the seal ring of Solomon son of David. When a child is born to us . . ."

But morning overtook Shahrazad, and she lapsed into silence.

THE TWO HUNDRED AND FORTY-SECOND NIGHT

The following night Shahrazad said:

I heard, O happy King, that Jullanar's brother Sayih said to the king, "When a child is born to us, we pencil his eyes, as I have told you. Now you need not fear for him to drown, suffocate, or be harmed in any way by water, for just as you walk on land, we walk in the sea." Then he pulled out from his pocket a sealed bag and, breaking the seal, emptied it, scattering strings of rubies and all kinds of jewels, in addition to three hundred emerald cabochons[9] and three hundred gemstones, as big as pigeon eggs, glittering like the sun. He said, "O King, these big gemstones are a gift for your little son Badr, and these rubies, emeralds, and other jewels are a gift from us to you, since we had not brought you any, being unaware of Jullanar's whereabouts or her situation. But now that we have met you and become one family, I have brought you this gift, and every little while I will bring you another like it, for these rubies and jewels

---

9. Gemstones cut with round unfaceted tops.

are plentiful with us and I can easily get them, since I know their sources and whereabouts better than anyone else on land or in the sea." When the king saw these jewels, he was dazzled and wonderstruck, and he said, "One of these jewels is worth my whole kingdom." Then he thanked the young man Sayih and, turning to Queen Jullanar, said, "I am embarrassed before your brother, for he has generously given me this priceless gift that is beyond the reach of anyone on earth." Queen Jullanar praised her husband and thanked her brother, who said, "O King of the age, it is you who have the prior claim on us, and it behooves us to thank you, for you have treated my sister kindly, and we have entered your dwelling and eaten your food. The poet says:

> Had I for Su'da's love before her wept,
> I would have solace found and never had to rue,
> But she wept first and made me weep and say,
> 'The credit to him who is first to act is due.'

And if we stand at your service, O King of the age, a thousand years, we would not repay you enough." The king thanked him profusely. They stayed with him forty days. Then Jullanar's brother Sayih rose and, kissing the ground before the king, said, "O King of the age, you have done us many favors, but we have imposed on your generosity and now we request one last favor. Grant us leave to depart, for we long for our home, family, and relatives. But we will never cease to serve you and serve my sister Jullanar. By the Omnipotent God, we are not happy to leave you, but what shall we do, since we have been reared in the sea and find uncongenial the life of the land?" When the king heard this, he rose to his feet and bade farewell to the young man and his mother and cousins, as did Jullanar, and they all wept because of the sorrow of separation and said, "We will visit you often." Then they rose and with one leap flew off, dove into the sea, and disappeared from sight, leaving the king in amazement.

The king continued to cherish Jullanar and treat her with the utmost generosity, while the boy grew and flourished and was catered to by many attendants. The king loved him exceedingly because he was very beautiful and because the older he grew, the more beautiful he became. His uncle and grandmother and cousins often came to visit the king, staying with him for a month or two, then going back home, while the boy continued to thrive, so that by the time he was fifteen, he was unequaled in charm, beauty, and perfect grace. By then he had learned grammar, lexicography, penmanship, history, and the Quran, as well as archery and spearplay.

But morning overtook Shahrazad, and she lapsed into silence.

THE TWO HUNDRED AND FORTY-THIRD NIGHT

The following night Shahrazad said:

I heard, O happy King, that the boy had learned the skills of chivalry, such as archery, spearplay, playing with the ball and mallet,[1] and every other skill befitting the son of a king. so that all the people of the city, men and women, spoke of none but him, for he was like him of whom the poet said:

> His downy whiskers grew upon his cheeks
> Like a fine drawing that dazzled my sight.
> He was a lamp suspended from a chain
> Of ambergris, in the dark of the night.

When the boy had learned everything that befits a king, his father, who loved him exceedingly, summoned the princes, the lords of the realm, and the chief officers of state and made them take an oath that they would make his son Badr king over them. They were very happy to take the oath because they loved the old king very much, for he was kind to everyone, spoke courteously, acted benevolently, and never said anything that did not benefit the people. The next day the king rode into the city with the princes, officers of state, and troops until he entered the city square. Then he returned, and when they drew near the royal palace, he and all the princes dismounted to wait on his son, while the new king continued to ride, surrounded by attendants and preceded by officers, who announced his progress, until they came to the entrance of the palace, where he stopped and was assisted by his father and the princess to dismount. Then he sat on the throne, while his father stood before him in the rank of a prince, and he issued edicts, adjudicated between the princes, deposed the unjust and appointed the just, and ruled till close to midday. Then he descended from the throne and went in to his mother Jullanar of the Sea, with the crown on his head, looking like the moon. When his mother saw him, with the king his father standing in attendance before him, she rose and, kissing him, congratulated him on having assumed the kingship and wished him and his father long life and victory over their enemies. He sat with his mother and rested till the hour of the afternoon prayer. Then he rode with his father and the officers of state to the city square, where he played with the ball and mallet till nightfall, then returned to the palace, attended by all the people. He did this every day.

But morning overtook Shahrazad, and she lapsed into silence.

---

1. A form of polo.

THE TWO HUNDRED AND FORTY-FOURTH NIGHT

The following night Shahrazad said:

I heard, O happy King, that during the first year King Badr used to go to the city square every day to play with the ball and mallet and return to sit on the throne to judge the people, doing justice to prince and beggar alike. In the second year he began to go hunting, to tour the cities and provinces under his rule, proclaiming peace and security, and to do what kings usually do. He was unique in his day in chivalry, valor, and fairness to his subjects.

One day the old king went to the bath and caught a chill and, becoming feverish, sensed that he was going to die and go to the next world. Then he got worse, and when he was on the verge of death, he called his son and charged him to take care of his kingdom and of his mother, as well as all his chief officers. Then he summoned all the princes, lords, and prominent men and made them once more swear a binding oath of allegiance to his son. He lingered a few days and died and was admitted to the mercy of the Almighty God. His son King Badr and Jullanar and all the princes and viziers and officers of state mourned over him, and they built him a tomb and buried him.

But morning overtook Shahrazad, and she lapsed into silence.

THE TWO HUNDRED AND FORTY-FIFTH NIGHT

The following night Shahrazad said:

I heard, O happy King, that they buried him and mourned over him for a full month. Jullanar's brother and mother and cousins arrived and offered their condolences, saying, "O Jullanar, although your husband is dead, he has left this noble young man, this fierce lion and radiant moon." Then the lords and chief officers of state went in to Badr and said to him, "O King, mourning is unseemly, except for women. Stop distracting yourself over your father's death and distracting us with you, for he has passed away and 'everyone must die'; indeed, he who died and left a son like you is not dead." Then they entreated him and took him to the bath, and when he came out, he put on a fine robe embroidered with gold and adorned with rubies and other jewels and, placing the royal crown on his head, sat on the throne and took care of the affairs of the people, judging fairly between the strong and the weak and exacting from the prince the right of the beggar, so that all the people loved him and invoked blessings upon him. He lived in this fashion for a full year, while every now and then his relatives of the sea visited him and his mother, and he led a pleasant and a happy life.

One night his uncle came to see his sister Jullanar, and he greeted her and she rose, embraced him, and, seating him beside her, asked, "O my brother, how are you and how are my mother and cousins?" He replied, "They are fine and lack nothing save the sight of your face." Then she called for some food, and after they had eaten and the table had been removed, they began to chat. They spoke of King Badr, his beauty and elegance, his cultivation and wisdom, and his skill in horsemanship, while Badr himself lay reclining nearby. When he heard what his mother and uncle said, he continued to listen to them, pretending to be asleep.

Sayih said to his sister Jullanar, "Sister, your son is now sixteen years old and he is still unmarried, and I am afraid that something may happen to him before he has a son; therefore, it is my wish to marry him to one of the princesses of the sea, one who is his equal in beauty and grace." His sister Jullanar replied, "By God, brother, you are reminding me of something in which I have been negligent. Brother, I wonder who is worthy of him from among the daughters of the kings of the sea? Name them to me, for I know them all." Sayih proceeded to name them to her, while she kept saying, "I do not like her for my son; I will marry him only to a girl who is his equal in beauty and grace and piety and wisdom and cultivation and nobility and dominion and rank and pedigree." Her brother said, "By God, by God, I know none other of the daughters of the kings of the sea, for I have named more than one hundred and none of them pleases you. But, sister, find out whether your son is asleep or not." She replied, "He is asleep; why do you ask?" He said, "Sister, I have just thought of the daughter of one of the kings of the sea, one who is worthy of your son, but I am afraid to name her, lest he be awake and his heart be taken by her, for if we fail to win her easily, all of us, he and we and all the chief officers of state will have to work very hard and devote all our energies to that end, for the poet says:

> Love is at first nothing but harmless play,
> But, once entrenched, it takes your peace away."

When his sister heard this, she replied, "Brother, you are right, but tell me who she is and who is her father, for I know all the kings of the sea and their daughters, and if I judge her worthy of him, I will demand her for him in marriage from her father, even if I have to give all our possessions for her. Tell me who she is, for my son is asleep." He said, "I fear that he may be awake, for the poet says:

> [I loved her when I heard them her descry],
> For sometimes the ear loves before the eye."

Then he added, "Sister, no girl is worthy of your son save Jauhara, the daughter of King al-Shamandal, for she is his equal in beauty, charm, and grace, and there is none on land or in the sea who is sweeter or more delightful than she, with her rosy cheeks, radiant brow, and jewel-like teeth."

But morning overtook Shahrazad, and she lapsed into silence.

THE TWO HUNDRED AND FORTY-SIXTH NIGHT

The following night Shahrazad said:

I heard, O happy King, that Sayih said to his sister, "She has jewel-like teeth, sweet lips, black eyes, a soft body, heavy hips, and a slender waist. When she turns, she shames the deer, and when she sways, she makes jealous the willow bough." When Jullanar heard what her brother said, she replied, "Brother, you are right, for I have seen her many times when she was my companion, when we were children, but it has been eighteen years since I last saw her. Indeed, by God, none but she is worthy of my son, and none but he is worthy of her." King Badr, who was awake, heard what his mother and uncle said, and when he heard their description of Princess Jauhara, the daughter of King al-Shamandal, he fell in love with her at once, but he continued to pretend that he was asleep, even though his heart was on fire with love for her. Then Sayih turned to his sister Jullanar and said, "There is none among the kings of the land or sea who is more powerful, more proud, and more ill-tempered than al-Shamandal. So say nothing to your son about her until we demand her in marriage from her father. If he favors us with his assent, we will praise the Almighty God for His help, and if he refuses to give his daughter in marriage to your son, we will keep quiet and seek another girl in marriage." When Jullanar heard this, she replied, "This is an excellent idea," and they said no more on the subject, while the king spent the night with his heart on fire with love for Princess Jauhara. But even though he was on the burning coals of passion, he concealed his feelings and said nothing of her to his mother and uncle.

Next morning the king and his uncle went to the bath and washed, and when they came out, the servants gave them wine to drink and set food before them, and the king and his uncle and mother ate, until they were satisfied and washed their hands. Then Sayih rose and said to the king and to his sister, "I will miss you, but I beg your leave to return to my mother, for I have been with you many days, and she is waiting and worrying about me." King Badr bade his uncle Sayih farewell and, with his heart still on fire, rode until he came to a meadow with a thicket of trees by the banks of a running stream. When he saw the shade, he dismounted by himself—for he had no retinue or servants with him—intending to sleep, but he recalled his uncle's description of the princess and her beauty and grace, and he wept bitterly.

It so happened, as it was foreordained, that when he had bidden his uncle Sayih farewell and mounted his horse, his uncle looked at him and, seeing that he did not look well, feared that the young king had overheard their conversation, and he said to himself, "I will follow Badr and see what he will do." So he followed him, and when the king dismounted at the bank of the stream, his uncle hid himself. So now, from his safe hiding place, he heard him recite the following verses:

> Who will help me with a hard, full-hipped girl,
> Whose face is bright like the sun, nay brighter.
> My heart is her captive and willing slave,
> Lost in love for al-Shamandal's daughter.
> I will never forget her all my life;
> I will never love anyone but her.

When his uncle Sayih heard these verses, he wrung his hands and said, "There is no power and no strength, save in God, the Almighty, the Magnificent." Then he came out of his hiding and said, "I have heard what you said. O my son, did you hear my conversation with your mother about Jauhara, last night?" King Badr replied, "Yes, uncle, and as soon as I heard what you said about her, I fell in love with her, and now my heart cleaves to her and I cannot give her up." His uncle said, "O King, let us return to your mother and inform her about the situation and tell her that I will take you with me and demand the Princess Jauhara in marriage. Then we will take our leave of her and depart, having informed her, for I fear that if I take you with me without her leave and consent, she will reproach me, and indeed she will be right, for I will be the cause of her separation from you; moreover, the city will be left without a king, and your subjects will be left with none to govern them and look after them, and this will undermine your authority and cause you and your mother to lose the kingdom." When King Badr heard what his uncle said, he replied, "Uncle, I will not return to my mother and consult her in this matter because I know that if I return to consult her, she will not let me go with you. No, I will not return to her." And he wept before his uncle, adding, "I will go with you now without telling her, and I will return to her later." When Sayih heard what his nephew said, he was at a loss and said, "In any case, I can only pray to the Almighty God for help."

When he saw . . .

But morning overtook Shahrazad, and she lapsed into silence.

THE TWO HUNDRED AND FORTY-SEVENTH NIGHT

The following night Shahrazad said:

I heard, O happy King, that when King Badr said to his uncle, "I must go with you," his uncle took off of his finger a seal ring engraved with one of the names of the Almighty God and said to him, "Put this ring on your finger, and it will protect you from the whales and other beasts of the sea." King Badr put the ring on his finger, and they plunged into the sea and fared on until they reached his uncle's palace. When he entered, he saw his grandmother seated with her relatives, and he greeted her and kissed her hand, while she rose and, embracing him, kissed him between the eyes, saying, "O my son, blessed is your coming. How is your mother Jullanar?" He replied, "O grandmother, she is well, and she sends greetings to you and to her cousins."

Then Sayih informed his mother that King Badr had fallen in love with Jauhara, al-Shamandal's daughter, as soon as he had heard of her, and told her the story from beginning to end, adding, "He has come with me, so that I may demand her for him in marriage from her father." When King Badr's grandmother heard what Sayih said, she was angry and upset, and she said to him, "Son, you have made a mistake in mentioning Princess Jauhara, al-Shamandal's daughter, before your nephew, for you know that al-Shamandal is an ill-tempered tyrant who is very proud and very foolish and that all the kings have demanded his daughter in marriage but he has rejected them all and dismissed them, saying, 'You are no match for my daughter in beauty or dominion.' I fear that if you demand her of her father, he will respond to you as he has responded to all the others, and we, given our self-respect, will return disappointed and embarrassed." When Sayih heard what his mother said, he asked her, "Mother, what is to be done? For King Badr fell in love with this girl when I mentioned her to my sister Jullanar, and he says, 'I must demand her of her father in marriage, even if I have to give my whole kingdom for her,' adding that if her father refuses to marry her to him, he will die of love and longing for her."

But morning overtook Shahrazad, and she lapsed into silence.

THE TWO HUNDRED AND FORTY-EIGHTH NIGHT

The following night Shahrazad said:

I heard, O happy King, that Sayih said to his mother, "My nephew is superior to her, for his father was king of all the Persians and he is now their present king. Indeed, none but Jauhara is worthy of him, and none but he is worthy of her. I intend to take to her father necklaces of rubies and other jewels, a present worthy of him, and demand her in marriage. If he objects that he is a king, Badr is also a king, and a handsome king at that, with a greater kingdom, vaster dominion, and many more troops and followers. I must endeavor to fulfill his wish, even if it costs me my life, because I was the cause of his infatuation, and just as I plunged him in the ocean of love, so will I endeavor to marry him to the girl, and the Almighty God will help me in my endeavor." His mother replied, "Do as you wish, but when you speak with al-Shamandal, beware of offending him, for you know his pride and violent temper, and I fear that he will lay hands on you, for he has no respect for anyone." Sayih replied, "I hear and obey."

Then he took two bags full of precious necklaces, emerald cabochons, and rubies and diamonds, and, giving them to his servants to carry, set out for the palace of al-Shamandal. When he arrived, he asked for leave to see the king, and when leave was granted, he entered, kissed the ground before him, and greeted him in the best of manners. When the king saw him, he rose to return the greeting and bade him be seated. When he was seated, the king said to him, "Blessed is your coming. I have missed you in your absence. Tell me your wish, and I will grant it." Sayih rose and, kissing the ground once more before the king, said to him, "O King of the age, my errand is to the Almighty God and to the gallant king and valiant lion, whose fame has spread far and wide and whose praise has been sung in all the provinces and cities, for his justice, his forbearance, his mercy, his generosity, his kindness, and his graciousness." Then he opened the two bags and, emptying out the precious necklaces, the emerald cabochons, and the rubies and diamonds before the king, said to him, "O King, I hope that you will do me a favor and make me happy by accepting my present." King al-Shamandal replied, "There is neither reason nor explanation for such a present. What prompted you to give me this great treasure, and what do you expect in return? Explain your case and tell me your need. If it is in my power, I will grant it at once without further ado; and if I am unable to grant it, I will be excused, for 'God asks nothing of a soul beyond its means.'" Sayih rose and, kissing the ground before the king, said, "O King, my need is within your means; it is in your possession and within your power, for I am not mad enough to ask the king for a favor he is unable to grant."

But morning overtook Shahrazad, and she lapsed into silence.

THE TWO HUNDRED AND FORTY-NINTH NIGHT

The following night Shahrazad said:

I heard, O happy King, that Sayih said to King al-Shamandal, "The sage says, 'If you wish to be denied, ask for what can't be supplied,' but my wish is one that the king is able to grant, for it is at his disposal and his to give." The king said, "Explain your case, tell me your need, and ask your wish." Sayih said, "O King of the age, I come to you as a suitor, seeking the unique pearl, the priceless jewel, and the glorious Princess Jauhara, daughter of our lord the king. O King, do not disappoint your suitor, but desire him who desires you." When the king heard this, he laughed in derision until he fell on his back. Then he said, "O Sayih, I thought you an excellent and wise young man who said nothing but what was reasonable and uttered nothing but what was sensible. What has possessed you and urged you to embark on such a grave venture and dangerous adventure, to seek in marriage the daughters of kings who rule over cities and provinces and who command armies and retinues? Is your self-esteem so high and your sense so little that you dare affront me with such a demand?"

Sayih replied, "O King, may God guide you; I do not seek your daughter for myself, and even if I did, I am her match and more, for you know that my father was one of the kings of the sea, like you, and that our kingdom has been taken from us. I seek her for none other than King Badr, the king of Persia, whose might and fame you know. If you object that you are a great king, King Badr is a great king too, indeed greater, and if you object that your daughter possesses beauty, charm, and grace, King Badr is more beautiful, more charming, and more amiable. Indeed he has no equal in discernment, fairness, courtesy, and generosity. If you grant my request and give him your daughter in marriage, you will have done the right thing and settled the matter, as any wise and sensible man would do, but if you reject us and treat us arrogantly, you will not have treated us properly or fairly. O King, you know that Princess Jauhara, the daughter of our lord the king, must have a husband, for the sage says, 'A girl needs a husband or a grave,' and if you intend to marry her at all, my nephew is worthier of her than any other man, but if you dislike us and refuse to have anything to do with us, you will not find a better man." When King al-Shamandal heard Sayih's words, he was so furious that he almost lost his senses and his soul left his body. He said, "O dog, shall the like of you dare speak to me like this and freely mention my daughter's name in public gatherings, saying that your nephew is a match for her? Who are you, who is your father, who is your sister, who is your nephew, and who is his dog of a father that you should speak such words to me and address me in this manner? Guards, seize this good-for-nothing and strike off his head." The guards drew their swords and attacked Sayih, who fled to the palace gate, where he found his cousins, relatives, followers, and servants.

But morning overtook Shahrazad, and she lapsed into silence.

THE TWO HUNDRED AND FIFTIETH NIGHT

The following night Shahrazad said:

I heard, O happy King, that the young man fled to the palace gate, where he found more than a thousand of his cousins, relatives, members of his entourage, followers, and servants, whom his mother had sent to his aid, armed to the teeth, with coats of mail and spears. When they saw him running, they asked him, "What is the matter?" and he told them what had happened. When they heard what he said, they realized that al-Shamandal was an ill-tempered, arrogant man. They dismounted and, drawing their swords, went in with him to al-Shamandal, whom they found seated on his throne, still raging against Sayih, unaware of their coming and surrounded by his guards, attendants, and servants, who were unprepared for battle. When he saw Sayih's men enter with drawn swords, he cried out to his men, "Damn you, away with the heads of these dogs!" but before long his men were routed and he was seized and bound. When his daughter Jauhara heard that her father had been taken captive and his men and followers had been killed, she fled from the palace to one of the islands and, climbing a tree, hid herself there.

Earlier, when the two clans were still fighting, it happened that some of Sayih's servants came to his mother and told her of the battle, and when King Badr heard about it, he ran away in fear, saying to himself, "All this turmoil is on my account, and none is to answer for it but I." So he ran away, not knowing where to go, until, as it had been foreordained, he came to the same island where Jauhara had taken refuge and, being tired, stopped to rest at the very tree in which she was hiding. He threw himself down, like a dead man, and as he lay on his back to rest, he chanced to look up and saw Princess Jauhara, who looked like the shining moon. He said to himself, "Glory be to God who created this wonderful form! Unless I am wrong, she must be Princess Jauhara. I think that when she heard of the battle between her father and my uncle, she fled to this island and hid in this tree. If she is not Princess Jauhara herself, then she is one who is even more beautiful." He pondered for a while, then said to himself, "I will seize her and question her, and if she is indeed Jauhara, I will ask her to marry me and I will attain my wish." Then he spoke to her, saying, "O end of all desire, who are you and who brought you here?" She looked at him and, seeing that he was a young man as beautiful as the full moon, with a slender figure and a sweet smile, said to him, "O fair young man, I am Princess Jauhara, the daughter of King al-Shamandal. I took refuge in this place because Sayih and his men fought my father, killed most of his men, and bound him and took him prisoner. I fled, fearing for my life."

But morning overtook Shahrazad, and she lapsed into silence.

THE TWO HUNDRED AND FIFTY-FIRST NIGHT

The following night Shahrazad said:

I heard, O happy King, that Princess Jauhara said to King Badr, "Young man, I feared for my life and fled to this island." When Badr heard this, he marveled at this strange coincidence and said to himself, "There is no doubt now that my uncle Sayih has defeated King al-Shamandal," and he felt very happy, adding, "and there is no doubt that I have attained my aim and fulfilled my wish by the capture of her father." Then he looked at her and said to her, "O my lady, come down to me, for I am captured by your eyes and slain by your love. It was on your account and mine that these turmoils and broils took place, for I am Badr, king of Persia, and Sayih is my uncle, who came to your father to demand you in marriage for me. I have left my kingdom and my mother and relatives; I have parted from my friends and companions, and I have come far away from my country for your sake. Our meeting here is a rare coincidence. Come down to me and I will take you to your father's palace, ask my uncle Sayih to release him, and make you my lawful wife."

When Jauhara heard this, she said to herself, "Then it was on the account of this vile good-for-nothing and depraved coward that my father's army has been routed, his men have been killed, and he has been taken prisoner, and on his account that I have been driven far away from home to seek refuge on this island. If I do not find a way to foil him, this worthless fellow will overpower me and have his will of me, for he is in love, and the lover is not blamed for anything he does." So she deceived him with sweet words, acted coquettishly, and made eyes at him, saying, "O my lord, O my darling, are you indeed King Badr, the son of Jullanar of the Sea?" He replied, "Yes, my lady, I am." She said, "May God cut off my father's hand and take his kingdom from him and may He never grant him consolation or return from exile! How could he desire anyone more handsome, more elegant, or more suitable than you? By God, he has little sense or judgment," adding, "O King, if you love me a span, I love you two cubits, for I have fallen in the snares of your love and I am one of your victims. Your love for me has transferred itself to me, and what I feel for you now is manyfold greater than what you feel for me." Then she came down from the tree and, coming up to him, embraced him and kissed him, and his love and desire for her grew even greater. He did not doubt that she loved him and he trusted her and embraced her and kissed her, saying to himself, "By God, my uncle has not done justice to a fortieth part of her charm or a carat of her beauty."

But morning overtook Shahrazad, and she lapsed into silence.

THE TWO HUNDRED AND FIFTY-SECOND NIGHT

The following night Shahrazad said:

I heard, O happy King, that King Badr said to himself, "Or a carat of her beauty." Suddenly Jauhara pressed him to her bosom and, uttering words he could not understand, spat in his face and said, "Leave your human form, you vile good-for-nothing, and turn into a bird, the prettiest of birds, with white feathers and red bill and feet." Hardly had she spoken, when King Badr was suddenly transformed into the prettiest of birds, which shook itself and stood looking at Princess Jauhara.

It happened that Princess Jauhara had with her one of her maids, who was also hiding in the tree, and she said to her, "By God, if I did not fear for my father, who is his uncle's prisoner, I would kill him. May God never bless him or grant him good health! How unlucky was his coming to us, for all this trouble is due to him. Listen, girl, take him and carry him to the Island of Thirst; then leave him there and come back to me quickly." The girl took him in the form of a bird, carried him to the Island of Thirst, and was about to leave him there and return, when she said to herself, "By God, a young man of such beauty and grace does not deserve to die of thirst." So she took him to a large, green island, abounding in trees and fruits and streams and, leaving him there, returned to her mistress and told her that she had left him behind.

Meanwhile, when Sayih, King Badr's uncle, killed King al-Shamandal's guards and followers and took him prisoner, he searched for his daughter Jauhara but could not find her. Then he returned to his palace, or rather his mother's palace, and asked her, "Mother, where is my nephew King Badr?" She replied, "By God, son, I know nothing of him or his whereabouts, for when he heard that you had fought a battle with al-Shamandal, he feared for himself and ran away." When Sayih heard what his mother said, he grieved sorely for his nephew and said, "Mother, by God, this was all for nothing. You were negligent with King Badr, and I fear that he may perish or that one of King al-Shamandal's guards or his daughter Jauhara may catch him and kill him, and we may then have an unfortunate situation with his mother, for I took him with me without her permission." Then he dispatched officers and soldiers to search for King Badr throughout the sea, but they found no trace and heard no news of him, and they returned and told Sayih, compounding his worry and grief. So Sayih sat on al-Shamandal's throne and kept al-Shamandal prisoner but continued to grieve for King Badr.

But morning overtook Shahrazad, and she lapsed into silence.

THE TWO HUNDRED AND FIFTY-THIRD NIGHT

The following night Shahrazad said:

I heard, O happy King, that meanwhile Queen Jullanar waited for her son, after he had departed with his uncle, but when she waited for many days, without seeing him or hearing any news of him, she rose one day and, going down into the sea, headed to her mother's palace. When her mother saw her, she rose to greet her, embraced her, and kissed her, as did her cousins. Then she asked them whether her son King Badr had come down with his uncle Sayih. Her mother replied, "He came with his uncle, who took rubies and other jewels and, presenting them to al-Shamandal, demanded his daughter in marriage for your son, but al-Shamandal refused and attacked your brother with abusive words, and there ensued a battle between al-Shamandal and your brother, to whom I had sent a thousand horsemen, fully armed. Your brother defeated al-Shamandal, killing his officers and soldiers and taking him prisoner. When your son heard of the battle, before finding out that his uncle had won, he feared for himself, as it would seem, and ran away from here without my leave, and since then we have had no news of him." Then Jullanar asked about her brother Sayih, and her mother replied, "He is sitting on al-Shamandal's throne, and he has sent men in every direction to search for your son and Princess Jauhara.

When Jullanar heard her mother's reply, she grieved sorely for her son and wept, and she was furious against her brother Sayih for having taken her son down to the sea without her leave. Then she said to her mother, "O mother, I am worried about our kingdom, for I came to you without letting anyone know, and I fear that if I tarry, someone may maneuver against us and take the kingdom from us. I have no choice but to go back soon and manage the affairs there until the Almighty God resolves the matter. But do not forget my son Badr, or neglect his case, because if he dies, I will certainly die too, for I cannot live or enjoy life without him." Her mother replied, "With all my heart! O my daughter, do not ask how much I have suffered because of his absence and loss." Then she too sent men to look for King Badr.

But morning overtook Shahrazad, and she lapsed into silence.

THE TWO HUNDRED AND FIFTY-FOURTH NIGHT

The following night Shahrazad said:

I heard, O happy King, that Jullanar's mother sent men to search for King Badr, while his mother returned to her kingdom in tears, feeling sad and depressed.

As for Badr, when the maid took him to the island and left him there, as I have mentioned, he stayed there several days in the form of a bird, eating of its fruits and drinking of its waters, not knowing how to fly or where to go. One day, as he perched on a tree branch, there came a bird catcher to the island, looking for game. When he drew close to King Badr and saw him in the form of a bird with white feathers and red bill and feet, which dazzled the eyes and bewildered the mind, he marveled at him and said to himself, "This is a lovely bird, the like of which in color and beauty I have never seen." Then he cast his net, caught it, and took it to the city, saying to himself, "I will sell it." Then he took it down to the market, where a man came by and asked him, "O catcher, how much is this bird?" The catcher asked him, "If you buy it, what will you do with it?" The man replied, "I will kill it and eat it." The catcher said, "Who could have the heart to kill this bird and eat it?" The man said, "You fool, what else is it good for?" The catcher said, "I intend to present it to the king, who will give me much more for it than its value and price and will divert himself by gazing on its beauty, while the most you would give me for it is a dirham; by God, I will not sell it to you even for a dinar."

Then the catcher went to the king's palace and waited there with the bird until the king saw him and, noticing the bird's white feathers and red bill and feet, was taken by its beauty and said to one of his servants, "If that bird is for sale, buy it." The servant came to the catcher and asked, "Will you sell this bird?" The catcher replied, "It is a gift from me to the king." The servant took the bird and brought it to the king, telling him what the catcher had said. The king said, "Go to him and give him ten dinars," and the catcher took the money, kissed the ground, and went away. Then the servant carried the bird to the king's palace and, placing it in a handsome cage, left with it food and water and hung it up.

When the king rode back and dismounted, he asked the servant, "Where is the bird? Bring it and let me look at it, for, by God, it is beautiful." The servant brought the bird and set it before the king.

But morning overtook Shahrazad, and she lapsed into silence.

THE TWO HUNDRED AND FIFTY-FIFTH NIGHT

The following night Shahrazad said:

I heard, O happy King, that the servant brought the cage and set it before the king and, seeing the food untouched, said, "O my lord, I left it this food, but it did not touch it, and I don't know what it will eat, so that I may feed it." But the king continued to gaze on the bird and marvel at its beauty. Then he called for food, and they laid the table before him, and he began to eat. When the bird saw the food and meat, it flew down from the cage and, perching on the table, ate of all that was before the king of bread, meat, sweets, and fruits. When the king saw what the bird ate, he and everyone present were surprised and taken aback, and he said to his attending officers and servants, "Never in all my life have I seen a bird eat like this one." Then he called for his wife to come and see the bird, and a servant went to her and said, "O my lady, the king wishes you to come and divert yourself with the sight of a bird he has bought, for when we brought the food, it flew down from its cage and, perching on the table, ate of all the dishes. O my lady, come and look at it, for it is a beauty and a wonder."

When the queen heard what the servant said, she came in a hurry, but when she saw the bird, she veiled her face and turned to go away. When the king saw his wife veil her face and turn to go away, he rose and said to her, "Why do you veil your face and turn away, when there is none here but the servants and your maids?" She replied, "O King, this is not a bird but a man." When the king heard what his wife said, he replied, "You are lying; how can a bird be a man? O how much my wife likes to joke!" She replied, "By God, I am not joking but telling you the truth. This bird is King Badr, the king of Persia and the son of Jullanar of the Sea."

But morning overtook Shahrazad, and she lapsed into silence. Then Dinarzad said to her sister, "Sister, what a strange and entertaining story!" Shahrazad replied, "What is this compared with what I shall tell you tomorrow night if the king spares me and lets me live!"

THE TWO HUNDRED AND FIFTY-SIXTH NIGHT

The following night Shahrazad said:

I heard, O happy King, that the queen told the king that that bird was King Badr, the king of Persia, that his mother was Jullanar of the Sea, his uncle Sayih, and his grandmother Farasha, and that he had been cast under a spell by Princess Jauhara, the daughter of King al-Shamandal. Then she told him the story from beginning to end, how he had demanded Jauhara in marriage from her father, how her father had refused, and how his uncle Sayih had fought al-Shamandal, defeated him, and taken him prisoner. When the king heard the story, he was amazed and said to his wife, who was the greatest sorceress of her day, "For my sake, deliver him from the spell and do not leave him to suffer in this condition. May God cut off the hand of that harlot Jauhara! How little is her mercy and how great is her perfidy!" His wife said, "O King, say to him, 'King Badr, enter that room,'" and when the bird heard the king's words, it entered the room. Then the queen covered herself with a cloak, veiled her face, and taking in her hand a bowl of water, entered the room. Then she pronounced over the water certain words that none understood and sprinkled the bird with it, saying, "By the power of these mighty names and solemn and holy oaths and by the Almighty God, Creator of heaven and earth, who allocates livelihood, allots the days of life, and resurrects the dead, leave your form as a bird and return to that in which

God created you." Hardly had she finished, when the bird shook violently and became a man, and the king saw before him a handsome young man, than whom there was none lovelier on the face of the earth.

When Badr looked at himself, he said, "Glory be to God, the Creator of all creatures and the Master of their destiny!" Then he kissed the king's hands and feet and said to him, "May God reward you for this!" and the king kissed his head and said to him, "King Badr, tell me your story from beginning to end." Then King Badr told him his entire story, concealing nothing, and the king was very much amazed. Then he said to King Badr, "King Badr, what do you intend to do now?" He replied, "O King of the age, I ask of your bounty a ship with a company of servants and other necessities to convey me to my home and kingdom, for I have been long absent from my mother and relatives and subjects, and I fear that if I tarry much longer, I will lose my kingdom; besides, I fear that my mother is either already dead because of my absence or in all likelihood dying of grief for me, not knowing where I am or whether I am alive or dead. My lord the king has kindly . . ."

But morning overtook Shahrazad, and she lapsed into silence.

THE TWO HUNDRED AND FIFTY-SEVENTH NIGHT

The following night Shahrazad said:

I heard, O happy King, that King Badr begged the king and queen to grant him one more favor and equip him for the journey. The king was moved by his beauty and eloquence and, feeling affection for him, said, "I hear and obey." Then he fitted out a ship for him, furnished it with all the necessities, and manned it with a company of his own servants.

King Badr bade him farewell, embarked, and set sail. He sailed before a fair wind for ten continuous days, but on the eleventh the wind began to blow harder, the sea raged, and the ship rose and fell so helplessly that the sailors were unable to control her. They drifted at the mercy of the waves until the ship hit a rock and broke up. Some men drowned and some escaped, while King Badr rode on one of the planks of the ship, after having almost drowned. For three days and nights he continued to rise and fall with the waves and to drift helplessly with the wind, not knowing in which direction he was going or where he was heading, until on the fourth day the waves cast him on the shore.

When he looked around, he saw a city as white as a fat dove, with high towers and beautiful buildings, built on the water, which was beating against its walls. When he saw the city, he rejoiced, for he was near death with hunger and thirst. He dismounted from the plank and tried to climb ashore to the city, but he was attacked by mules, asses, and horses, as countless as the grains of sand, which kicked him and prevented him from climbing. So he swam around to the other side of the city, but when he came out, he was surprised to find no one there and said to himself, "I wonder to whom this city belongs and why there is no king or inhabitants and whose are these mules, asses, horses, and cattle, which prevented me from climbing."

Then he walked aimlessly, musing on the situation, when suddenly he saw an old man.

But morning overtook Shahrazad, and she lapsed into silence.

THE TWO HUNDRED AND FIFTY-EIGHTH NIGHT

The following night Shahrazad said:

I heard, O happy King, that King Badr suddenly saw an old man, a fava-bean seller, sitting in his shop. He greeted him and the old man returned the greeting and, seeing his handsome face, asked him, "Young man, where do you come from and who brought you to this city?" King Badr told him the whole story, and the old man was very much amazed and asked him, "My son, did you see anyone on the way?" King Badr replied, "Father, no, by God, I did not. Indeed, I was amazed to see the city without inhabitants." The old man said, "Son, come up into the shop, lest you perish." King Badr went up into the shop and sat at the upper end, and the old man rose and brought him some food, saying, "Son, stay inside the shop and eat. Glory be to Him who has saved you from that she-devil." King Badr was frightened, but he ate his fill and washed his hands. Then he turned to the old man and asked, "My lord, what is the meaning of your words? You have made me afraid of this city and its people." The old man replied, "Son, you should know that this city is called the City of the Magicians, and its queen is an enchantress who is as enchanting as the moon. All the beasts you saw were once men like you and me but are now enchanted, for whenever a young man like you enters the city, that blasphemous witch seizes him and enjoys him for forty days and . . ."

But morning overtook Shahrazad, and she lapsed into silence.

THE TWO HUNDRED AND FIFTY-NINTH NIGHT

The following night Shahrazad said:

I heard, O happy King, that the old man said, "Then she casts a spell on him and turns him into a mule or an ass or one of the other beasts you saw. When any of the inhabitants of the city, who are sorcerers like her, wishes to go on an errand, he rides one of those beasts, who kicked you out of pity for you, to prevent you from climbing to the shore, lest she should cast a spell on you as she has done to them, for there is none who equals this cursed queen in the power of her magic. Her name is Lab, which means 'the Sun.'" When King Badr heard what the old man said, he was terrified and shook like a thunderbolt, saying to himself, "Hardly did I believe that I had been delivered from sorcery, when God cast me into the den of worse sorcerers." Then he pondered what to do. When the old man saw him trembling with fear, he said to him, "Son, go and sit at the door of the shop and see how many inhabitants there are in this city. Do not be afraid, for the queen and all the inhabitants respect me and like me and will not cause me any trouble." When King Badr heard what the old man said, he went and sat at the door of the shop to look at the people.

But morning overtook Shahrazad, and she lapsed into silence.

THE TWO HUNDRED AND SIXTIETH NIGHT

The following night Shahrazad said:

I heard, O happy King, that when King Badr sat at the door of the shop to look at the people, he saw numberless people pass by. When they saw him, they marveled at his beauty and, coming up to the old man, asked "Shaikh, is this your most recent captive and prey?" He replied, "No, by God, he is my brother's son who lives far from here, and when I heard that his father was dead, I sent for him, so that I might see him and allay my grief." They said to him, "He is a handsome young man, but we fear for him from Queen Lab, lest she should turn against you and take him from you, for she loves handsome young men." The old man replied, "The queen will not cross me in anything, for she respects me and likes me, and when she hears that he is my nephew, she will not bother him, trouble him, or molest him." Then King Badr lived with the old man for a full month, eating and drinking, and the old man loved him exceedingly.

One day, as King Badr sat at the door of the shop as usual, there appeared a thousand officers riding Arabian horses with gilded saddles, dressed in all kinds of uniforms, girded with jeweled girdles, and holding drawn swords. When they passed by the shop, they saluted the old man and he returned their salute. Then they were followed by a thousand Mamluks dressed in the uniforms of attendants and holding drawn gilded swords, and when they passed by the old man, they saluted him and he returned their salute. Then they were followed by a thousand girls like moons, dressed in silk and satin robes embroidered with gold, and armed with shields and spears. In their midst rode the queen on an Arabian horse with a saddle of gold set with rubies and all kinds of jewels. The girls halted before the old man and saluted him, and he returned their salute. Then the queen came up to him and saluted him, and he rose and kissed the ground before her. Then she looked at him and said, "O Abu 'Abd-Allah, is this handsome, charming, and graceful young man your captive, and when did you catch him?" The old man replied, "No by God, O Queen, he is my brother's son, who had been long absent. When I could no longer live without seeing him, I brought him here to satisfy my longing and dispel my loneliness, for I love him very much; besides, I am an old man and his father is dead, and if he stays with me, he will help me during my lifetime and inherit my estate after my death." The queen replied . . .

But morning overtook Shahrazad, and she lapsed into silence.

THE TWO HUNDRED AND SIXTY-FIRST NIGHT

The following night Shahrazad said:

I heard, O happy King, that the queen said to the old man, "Father, will you give him to me as a gift, for I love him? By the fire and the light, by the hot wind and the cool shade, I will make him my lot in life. Do not fear for him, for I may harm everyone on the face of the earth, but I will not harm him, for you know the mutual esteem you and I hold for each other." The old man replied, "O my Queen, I can neither give him to you as a gift nor surrender him to you." She said, "By the fire and the light, by the hot wind and the cool shade, and by my faith, I will not leave without him. I will not betray him or enchant him, and I will do only what will please him." The old man, who did not dare cross her, fearing for himself and for King Badr, secured an oath from her that she would not harm the young man and that she would return him as she received him. Then he said to her, "When you return from the square tomorrow, I will give him to you." She thanked him and returned to her palace.

Then the old man turned to King Badr and said, "This is the woman I had feared and worried about, but she swore by her Magian[2] faith that she would not harm you or enchant you, and were it not that she respected me and liked me, she would have taken you by force, for it is the custom of this blasphemous witch and queen to do with strangers what I have already told you. May God shame her and curse her and her great malice, wickedness, and depravity." When King Badr heard what the old man said, he replied, "My lord, by God, I am terrified of her, for I tasted enchantment for an entire month, when Princess Jauhara, the daughter of King al-Shamandal, cast a spell over me and made me a lesson to others, until the wife of one of the kings delivered me from the spell. I have tasted the most bitter torments and I know how the enchanted suffers," and he wept. The old man felt sorry for him and said to him, "Do not be afraid, for she may hurt even her relatives, but she will not dare hurt me."

But morning overtook Shahrazad, and she lapsed into silence.

THE TWO HUNDRED AND SIXTY-SECOND NIGHT

The following night Shahrazad said:

I heard, O happy King, that the old man said to King Badr, "She may hurt even her relatives, but she will not dare hurt me. Have you not seen how her troops and retinue stood at my shop and saluted me? By God, son, this infidel refuses to salute even kings, yet whenever she passes by my shop, she stops to salute me and speak with me, as you have seen and heard."

They slept that night, and when it was morning, Queen Lab came with her girls, Mamluks, and attendants, who were armed with swords and spears, stopped at the door of the shop, and saluted the old man. He rose and kissed the ground before her, returning the salute. Then she said to him, "Father, fulfill your pledge and do at once what you have promised me." The old man replied, "Swear to me again that you will never harm him, enchant him, or do to him anything he abhors." She swore again by her faith and unveiled a face like the moon, saying, "Father, how you procrastinate in giving me your handsome nephew! Am I not more beautiful than he?" When King Badr saw her beauty, he was bewitched and said to himself, "By God, she is more beautiful

2. See n. 1, p. 61.

than Jauhara. If she marries me, I will leave my kingdom and stay with her, without returning to my mother; if not, I will at least enjoy her in bed for forty days and nights, and I do not care if she enchants me or kills me afterward. By God, a single night with her is worth a lifetime." Then the old man took King Badr by the hand, saying to her, "Receive from me my nephew Badr and return him to me as you receive him. Do not harm him or take him away from me." She swore for the third time that she would not harm him or enchant him; then she ordered for Badr a handsome, saddled horse, bedecked with gold trappings, and gave the old man a thousand dinars.

But morning overtook Shahrazad, and she lapsed into silence.

THE TWO HUNDRED AND SIXTY-THIRD NIGHT

The following night Shahrazad said:

I heard, O happy King, that the queen gave the old fava-bean seller a thousand dinars and, saying "May God give you more," took King Badr and departed. He rode beside her, looking like the moon, and whenever the people looked at him and at his beauty, they felt sorry for him, saying "By God, such a handsome young man does not deserve to be enchanted by that cursed witch," while he rode silently, having committed himself to the Almighty God. They rode on to the palace, and when they reached the gate, the princes and nobles and servants dismounted and stood in attendance, while she and King Badr dismounted and sat on the throne. Then she dismissed all the princes and chamberlains and notables, and they kissed the ground before her and departed.

Then she took King Badr by the hand and with her maids and male servants went into the palace. It was like a palace in Paradise, with walls adorned with gold, with storerooms full of clothes and vessels, and with a beautiful garden in the middle, with a large pond and birds singing in all kinds of voices and tongues. When King Badr saw this opulent palace, he said to himself, "Glory be to God who in His generosity and clemency blesses those who worship other than Himself." Then Queen Lab sat at a window overlooking the garden, on a couch of ivory with high cushions, and, seating King Badr beside her, embraced him and kissed him. Then she called for food, and the maids brought a table of red gold set with jewels and pearls and spread with all kinds of food and sweets, and the queen and King Badr ate, until they were satisfied, and washed their hands.

Then the maids brought the wine service, vessels of gold and silver and crystal, as well as dishes full of dried fruits and nuts, and flowers and perfumes. Then, at her order, they ushered in ten girls like moons, with all kinds of musical instruments in their hands.

Then the queen filled a cup and drank it off and filled another.

But morning overtook Shahrazad, and she lapsed into silence.

THE TWO HUNDRED AND SIXTY-FOURTH NIGHT

The following night Shahrazad said:

I heard, O happy King, that the queen gave the cup to King Badr, who took it and drank it off, and they continued to drink until they began to get drunk. Then she ordered the girls to sing, and they sang all kinds of songs until King Badr imagined that the palace danced with him in delight, and he became light-headed and happy and forgot his separation from home, saying to himself, "By God, this queen is young and beautiful, and I will never leave her, for her kingdom is vaster than mine and she is fairer than Princess Jauhara." He continued to drink till nightfall, when they lighted the candles and burned the incense until the banquet was as joyous as the one of which the poet said:

> O what a day we spent under the trees,
> Enjoying every pleasure and delight,
> The shining rivulet, the myrtle blue,
> The starry narcissus and roses bright,
> The glittering wine and the brimming cup
> And crackling incense rising in the light!

Queen Lab and King Badr continued to drink, while the singers sang, until most of the night was gone and the queen was completely drunk. Then she dismissed the singing women and, lying in bed, ordered King Badr to lie beside her. Then the maids took off all the clothes they had made him wear, except for a gold-embroidered shirt, like the one Queen Lab was left with, and the two spent the happiest of nights till the morning. Then Queen Lab rose and took King Badr to the bath inside the palace, and they washed themselves, and when they came out, the maids dressed them and brought them cups of wine, which they drank. Then she took King Badr by the hand and with her maids . . .

But morning overtook Shahrazad, and she lapsed into silence.

THE TWO HUNDRED AND SIXTY-FIFTH NIGHT

The following night Shahrazad said:

I heard, O happy King, that the queen took King Badr by the hand and with her maids came out of the bath and went to the banquet room, where they sat and rested for a while. Then the maids set food before them, and they ate and washed their hands. Then the maids removed the table and set the wine service and fruits and nuts and flowers before them, and they drank, while the singing women sang all kinds of melodies and songs till nightfall.

They continued to live like this, eating and drinking and kissing and playing, for forty days. Then Queen Lab asked King Badr, "Which is more enjoyable, this place or the shop of your uncle the fava-bean seller?" He replied, "O Queen, by God, this place is more enjoyable, for my uncle is a poor man." She laughed at his reply, and the two spent the happiest of nights in bed. But when he awoke in the morning, he did not find her beside him and asked himself, "Where could she have gone?" He felt lonely without her, and when he waited for her and she did not return, he arose from bed and, putting on his clothes, searched for her, and when he did not find her, he said to himself, "She may be in the garden." He went into the garden and came to a running stream, beside which he saw a black bird next to a white she-bird, under a large tree full of birds of various colors. He stood and watched the birds, without being seen by them, and saw the black bird leap and mount the white she-bird three times. Soon the she-bird turned into a woman, and when he looked at her closely, he saw that she was none other than Queen Lab, and he realized that the black bird was an enchanted man whom she loved and that she had turned into a she-bird so that the man could make love to her. King Badr was seized with jealousy, and he was resentful and angry with Queen Lab because of the black bird. He returned and lay down on the bed, and a little later she came to him and kissed him and joked with him, but when his anger mounted and he did not speak a single word to her, she guessed what was troubling him and was certain that he had seen the bird mount her. But she kept it to herself and said nothing.

When it was broad daylight, he said to her, "O Queen, I wish you to give me leave to go to my uncle's shop, for I have not laid eyes on him for forty days and I long to see him." She replied, "O Badr, go, but do not stay long, for I cannot bear to be without you or wait a single hour." He replied, "I hear and obey," and, mounting his horse, rode to the old man's shop.

But morning overtook Shahrazad, and she lapsed into silence.

THE TWO HUNDRED AND SIXTY-SIXTH NIGHT

The following night Shahrazad said:

I heard, O happy King, that King Badr rode to the shop of the old fava-bean seller, who ran to greet him, welcomed him, and embraced him. Then he asked, "How have you fared with that infidel?" King Badr replied, "I was well, healthy, and happy till last night, when I awoke and did not see her by my side. When I arose and did not find her, I put on my clothes and searched for her until I went into the garden." Then he told him the story and how he had seen the black bird mount her. When the old man heard this, he said, "The cursed woman has started to play games. You should beware of her and should know that the birds on the tree were all young strangers whom she loved, enjoyed, then turned into birds. The black bird was one of her Mamluks, with whom she was madly in love, but when he cast his eye on one of her women, she cast a spell over him and turned him into a bird. Whenever she lusts for him, she turns herself into a she-bird and lets him mount her, for she still loves him. Now that she knows that you have found out, she will no longer be good to you, but fear nothing, since I will protect you, for there is none better skilled in magic than I, although I do not use it except when I have to. I have delivered many men from her hands, for she has no power over me and she fears me, as do the inhabitants of this city, who are fire worshipers like her. Come back to me tomorrow, and tell me what she does to you, for tonight she will prepare to destroy you. Dissemble with her till tomorrow; then come back, and I will tell you what to do." King Badr bade the old man farewell and returned to the queen.

He found her sitting and waiting for him, and when she saw him, she rose to greet him and welcome him. Then the maids set food before them, and they ate and washed their hands. Then they brought them wine, and she drank and plied him with wine until by midnight he was drunk and unconscious. When she saw him in this condition, she said to him, "I conjure you by God and by the god you worship, if I ask you a question, will you answer me truthfully?" He, being unconscious and not knowing what he was saying, replied, "Yes." She said, "O my lord and my darling, when you looked and did not find me, did you not search for me until you found me in the garden in the form of a white she-bird and saw a black bird mount me, then saw me turn back into my human form?" He replied, "Yes." She said, "That black bird was one of my officers, whom I loved, but one day he cast his eye on one of my women, and I became jealous and turned him into a bird and killed the woman. But I cannot bear to be without him, and whenever I desire him, I turn myself into a she-bird and let him possess me, as you have seen. It is because of this that you are jealous and angry at me, yet, by the fire and the night, you love me and I love you more than ever."

But morning overtook Shahrazad, and she lapsed into silence.

THE TWO HUNDRED AND SIXTY-SEVENTH NIGHT

The following night Shahrazad said:

I heard, O happy King, that the queen said to King Badr, "You love me and I love you, for you are my lot in life." When he heard this, he, being drunk, replied, "Yes, this is how I felt." Then she embraced him and kissed him and, pretending to love him, lay down to sleep, and he lay beside her. In the middle of the night, she rose from bed, while Badr lay awake, pretending to be asleep, and watched with one eye to see what she was doing. She took red sand from a bag and spread it on the floor of the room, and it became a running stream. Then she took out a handful of barley and strewed it in the soil on the bank of the stream and watered it with the water from the stream, and it turned into ears of barley. Then she reaped the barley and ground it into meal. Then she laid the meal aside and, returning to bed, slept beside King Badr till the morning.

When it was morning, King Badr rose and, as soon as he washed his face, asked her leave to visit the old man. She gave him leave and he went to the old man and told him what he had seen. When the old man heard what he said, he laughed and said, "By God, this infidel is plotting mischief against you, but do not mind her." Then he gave him a half-pound of barley meal and said, "Take this with you, and when you arrive and she sees it, she will ask you, 'What will you do with this?' Say to her, 'An extra blessing is a blessing,' and eat some of it. Then she will bring you her own meal and say to you, 'Eat some of this.' But pretend to be eating of hers and eat of this instead. Beware, for if you eat as much as a dirham's weight or even a grain of hers, her spell will have power over you, and, knowing that you have eaten of her meal, she will cast her spell over you, bid you leave your human form, and turn you into any other form she pleases. But if you do not eat of it, you need not worry about her, for her magic will have no power over you and will fail to work on you. She will be abashed and tell you that she was teasing you and will make a show of affection and love, but all this will be nothing but abomination. Then make a show of love and say to her, 'O my lady and my darling, taste of my barley meal.' If she tastes even one grain of it, take water in your hand, throw it in her face, and bid her leave her form and turn into any form you please. Then leave her and come to me, and I will take care of you."

Then King Badr bade the old man farewell and, returning to the palace, went in to the queen. When she saw him, she said, "Welcome!" and she rose and kissed him, saying, "O my lord, you have tarried too long from me." He replied, "I have been with my uncle, who gave me some of this barley meal to eat." She replied, "We have better than this." Then she put his meal in one dish and hers in another and said to him, "Eat of this, for it is better than yours." He pretended to eat of it, and when she thought that he had done so, she took water in her hand and sprinkled him with it, saying, "Leave this form, you vile good-for-nothing, and turn into a mean, barren, ugly, lame mule." But he did not change, and when she saw that he did not change, she went up to him and kissed him, saying, "O my beloved, I was teasing you to see what you would say." He replied, "My lady, as long as you love me, nothing will change me toward you."

But morning overtook Shahrazad, and she lapsed into silence.

THE TWO HUNDRED AND SIXTY-EIGHTH NIGHT

The following night Shahrazad said:

I heard, O happy King, that King Badr said to the queen, "As long as you love me, nothing will change me toward you, for I love you even more than you love me. Eat of my barley meal." She took a mouthful and ate it, and no sooner had it settled in her stomach than she began to convulse. Then King Badr took water in his hand and threw it in her face, saying, "Leave this form and turn into a dappled she-mule," and she became at once a dappled she-mule. When she saw herself in this condition, the tears rolled down her face, and she began to rub her cheeks against his feet. He tried to bridle her, but she would not let him; so he left her and went to the old man and told him what had happened, and the old man took out a bridle, saying, "Bridle her with this, for, when she sees it, she will submit and let you bridle her." King Badr took the bridle and returned to the queen, and when she saw him, she came up to him, and he set the bit in her mouth, and, mounting her, he rode from the palace to the old man's shop. When the old man saw her, he said to her, "May God shame you, O cursed woman! Do you see what He has done to you?" Then he said to King Badr, "My son, it is time for you to leave this city. Ride her and go wherever you like, but beware of relinquishing the bridle to anyone." King Badr thanked him and bade him farewell.

Then he rode on for three days until he came near a city, where he met an attractive gray-headed old man, who asked him, "Son, where are you coming from?" King Badr replied, "From the City of the Magicians." The old man replied, "You are my guest," but while they were conversing, up came an old woman, who, when she looked at the she-mule, began to cry, saying, "This she-mule resembles my son's she-mule, which is dead, and my heart aches for her. O young man, for God's sake, sell her to me." King Badr replied, "Mother, by God, I cannot sell her." She said, "For God's sake, do not refuse me, for my son will surely die if I do not buy him this she-mule," and she pressed him until he said to her, "I will not sell her for less than a thousand dinars." She said to him, "Say to me, 'She is sold to you for a thousand dinars.'" King Badr, saying to himself, "Where could this old woman get a thousand dinars? I will say that the she-mule is sold to her and see where she will get the money," replied, "She is sold to you." When she heard his words, she took out from her pocket a thousand dinars, and when he saw the money, he said to her, "Mother, I was joking with you, for I cannot sell her." But the old man looked at him and said, "Son, you should know that none lies in this city, for whoever lies is put to death." King Badr dismounted from the she-mule . . .

But morning overtook Shahrazad, and she lapsed into silence. Then Dinarzad said to her sister, "O sister, what a strange and entertaining story!" Shahrazad replied, "What is this compared with what I shall tell you tomorrow night if I stay alive!"

THE TWO HUNDRED AND SIXTY-NINTH NIGHT

The following night Shahrazad said:

I heard, O happy King, that King Badr dismounted from the she-mule and delivered her to the old woman, who, as soon as she received her, removed the bit from her mouth, took water in her hand, and sprinkled her with it, saying, "O my daughter, leave this form and return to your human form." The queen was at once restored to her original form, and the two women embraced and kissed each other. Then King Badr realized that the old woman was Queen Lab's mother and that he had been tricked, and he wanted to flee, but there was nowhere to go.

Then the old woman gave a loud whistle, and there appeared before her a demon, as huge as a mountain. She mounted on his back and placed her daughter behind her, and the demon, putting King Badr on his shoulder, flew off with them and soon brought

them to the palace of Queen Lab. When the queen sat down on the
throne, she looked at King Badr and said, "You worthless fellow, here
I am; I have attained my wish and I will show you what I will do to
you and to that wretched old fava-bean seller. O how many favors
have I done him and how ill he has served me, for you succeeded
with me only with his help!" Then she took water and sprinkled him
with it, saying, "Leave this form and turn into the ugliest of birds,
and he at once turned into an ugly bird. Then she put him in a cage
and withheld from him all food and water.

But one of her women took pity on him and gave him food and
water without the queen's knowledge. Then she went to the old man
and told him what had happened and informed him that the queen
intended to destroy his nephew. He thought it over, pondering what
to do with the queen, and finally said, "I must take this city from
her." Then he gave a loud whistle, and there appeared before him a
demon with four wings, to whom he said, "O Barq, take this girl,
who has pitied King Badr and given him food and water, and carry
her to the city of Jullanar of the Sea and her mother Farasha, who
are the most powerful magicians on the face of the earth, and tell
them that King Badr is Queen Lab's captive."

The demon took her, and flying off with her, soon set her down on
the roof of Queen Jullanar's palace. The girl descended from the roof
and, going in to the queen, kissed the ground before her and told her
what had happened to her son from beginning to end. Jullanar rose
and kissed her face and thanked her. Then she ordered the drums to
beat in the city in celebration and informed her family that King Badr
had been found. Then Jullanar and her mother Farasha and her
brother Sayih summoned all the tribes of demons and the troops of
the sea, for the kings of the demons obeyed them ever since the capture of King al-Shamandal. Then they all flew up into the air and,
descending on the City of the Magicians, attacked the city and the
palace and killed all the inhabitants in the twinkling of an eye.

Then Jullanar asked the girl, "Where is my son?" The girl brought
the cage and set it before her, and Jullanar took the bird out of the
cage and, taking water in her hand, sprinkled the bird with it, saying,
"Leave this form and return to your human form, by the power of the
God of the world," and no sooner had she finished than King Badr
changed into "a full-fledged man." Then she embraced him and wept,
as did his uncle Sayih and his grandmother Farasha and his cousins,
who fell on him, kissing his hands and feet. Then Jullanar sent for
'Abd-Allah, the old fava-bean seller, and when he presented himself
to her, she thanked him for his kindness to her son and married him
to the girl whom he had dispatched to her with King Badr's news.

But morning overtook Shahrazad, and she lapsed into silence.

THE TWO HUNDRED AND SEVENTIETH NIGHT

The following night Shahrazad said:

I heard, O happy King, that the old man married the girl, as Jullanar had wished.

Then King Badr said to his mother, "O mother, nothing remains, except that I should get married and unite us all." His mother replied, "My son, this is an excellent idea, but wait until we inquire who is suitable from among the daughters of the kings." His grandmother Farasha and his uncle Sayih and his cousins said, "O King Badr, we will endeavor at once to get you what you desire." Then each of them went out to search throughout the country, while Jullanar sent out her waiting-women on the backs of demons, saying to them, "Leave not a province or a city or a king's palace without noting every beautiful girl there." When King Badr saw what his mother Jullanar had done, he said to her, "Mother, stop this, for none will satisfy me."

But morning overtook Shahrazad, and she lapsed into silence.

THE TWO HUNDRED AND SEVENTY-FIRST NIGHT

The following night Shahrazad said:

I heard, O happy King, that King Badr said to his mother Jullanar, "None will satisfy me, save Princess Jauhara, the daughter of King al-Shamandal, for she is, like her name, truly a jewel." His mother replied, "Son, she is yours." Then she sent at once for King al-Shamandal, who was immediately brought and kissed the ground before her. Then she sent for her son King Badr, informing him that al-Shamandal was in her presence. King Badr came and bade him welcome, and when he demanded his daughter Jauhara in marriage, King al-Shamandal replied, "She is your servant and at your disposal." Then he dispatched some of his officers, bidding them go to his city, inform his daughter Jauhara that he was with King Badr, and bring her back with him. The officers flew up into the air and a while later returned with Princess Jauhara.

When she saw her father, she went up to him, embraced him, and wept. Then he turned to her and said, "O my daughter, I have given you in marriage to this gallant king and valiant lion, King Badr, for he is the best, the most handsome, and the most exalted man in this age, and none is worthy of him but you and none is worthy of you but him." She replied, "O my father, I cannot disobey you; do as you wish." So they summoned the legal witnesses and drew up the marriage contract. Then they beat the drums in celebration and opened the prisons and clothed the widows and orphans and bestowed robes of honor on the princes and lords of the realm. Then they held a wedding feast, giving banquets and celebrating, day and night, for ten days, at the end of which they unveiled the bride in seven different robes. Then King Badr went in to Princess Jauhara and took her virginity, and when he found that she had been a virgin, he rejoiced, and they loved one another exceedingly. Then he bestowed a robe of honor on her father King al-Shamandal, gave him riches, and sent him happy to his home and country. Then King Badr and his wife and mother and relatives continued to enjoy life until they were overtaken by the breaker of ties and destroyer of delights. And this is the completion and the end of their story.

The Story of Sindbad the Sailor

THERE LIVED IN Baghdad, in the time of the Commander of the
Faithful, the Caliph Harun al-Rashid, a man called Sindbad the
Porter, who was poor and who carried loads on his head for hire. One
day, he was carrying a heavy load, and as it was very hot, he became
weary and began to perspire under the burden and the intense heat.
Soon he came to the door of a merchant's house, before which the
ground was swept and watered, and the air was cool, and as there was
a wide bench beside the door, he set his load on the bench to rest and
take a breath. As he did so, there came out of the door a pleasant
breeze and a lovely fragrance; so he remained sitting on the edge of
the bench to enjoy this and heard from within the melodious sounds
of lutes and other string instruments accompanying delightful voices
singing all kinds of eloquent verses. He also heard the sounds of birds
warbling and glorifying the Almighty God, in various voices and
tongues, turtledoves, nightingales, thrushes, doves, and curlews.
At that he marveled to himself and felt a great delight. He went to the
door and saw inside the house a great garden and saw pages, servants, slaves, and attendants, the likes of whom are found only with
kings and sultans. And through the door came the aromas of all kinds
of fine delicious foods and delicious wine.

He raised his eyes to heaven and said, "Glory be to You, O God,
Creator and Provider! You bestow riches on whomever You wish,
without reckoning. O Lord, I ask Your forgiveness of all sins and
repent to You of all faults. O Lord, there is no argument with Your
judgment or Your power. You are not to be questioned on what You do,
for You are omnipotent in every thing. Glory be to You! You enrich
whomever You wish and impoverish whomever You wish. You exalt
whomever You wish and humble whomever You wish. There is no god
but You. How great is Your majesty, how mighty Your dominion, and
how excellent Your government! You have bestowed favors on one you
have chosen of your servants, for the owner of this place is in the
height of comfort, enjoying all kinds of pleasant perfumes, delicious
foods, and fine beverages. You have foreordained and apportioned to
Your creatures what You wish, so that among them some are weary,
some comfortable, and some enjoy life, while some, like me, suffer
extreme toil and misery." Then he recited the following verses:

How many wretched men toil without rest,
And how many enjoy life in the shade!
My weariness increases every day;
'Tis strange, how heavy is the burden on me laid!
Others are prosperous and live in ease,
Having never my heavy burden known,
Living in luxury throughout their life,
Enjoying food and drink and pleasure and renown.
Yet all God's creatures are of the same species;
My soul is like this one's and his like mine,
And yet we are so different, one from one,
As different as is vinegar from wine.
And yet, O Lord, I impugn not Thy ways,
For Thou art wise and just, and all judgment is Thine.

When the porter finished reciting his verses and was about to carry
his load and continue on his way, a young page with a handsome face,
fine build, and rich clothes came out of the door, took his hand, and
said, "Come in and speak with my master, for he is asking for you." The
porter wanted to refuse but could not. He left his load with the doorkeeper in the hallway and went into the house with the page. He found
it to be a handsome mansion, stately but cheerful. Then he came to a
great hall in which he saw noblemen and great lords and saw all kinds
of flowers and fresh and dried fruits and a great variety of exquisite
foods and wines of the finest vintage. And he saw musical instruments
and all kinds of beautiful slave girls, all arranged in the proper order.
At the upper end of that hall sat a venerable and majestic man whose
beard was turning gray on the sides. He had a handsome appearance
and a comely face, and he had an aspect of dignity, reverence, nobility,
and majesty. When Sindbad the Porter saw all this, he was confounded and said to himself, "By God, this place is one of the spots of
Paradise, or else it is the palace of a king or a sultan." Then he assumed
a respectful posture, saluted the assembly, invoked a blessing on them,
kissed the ground before them, and stood with his head bowed in
humility. The master of the house asked him to sit near him, welcomed
him, and spoke kindly to him. Then he set before Sindbad the Porter
various kinds of fine, exquisite, and delicious foods. Sindbad the Porter
invoked God, then ate until he was satisfied and said, "Praise be to
God." Then he washed his hands and thanked the company.

The master of the house then said, "You are welcome, and your day
is blessed. What is your name, and what do you do for a living?" The
porter answered him, "Sir, my name is Sindbad the Porter, and I carry
on my head people's goods for hire." The master of the house smiled
and said to him, "Porter, your name is like mine, for I am called Sindbad the Sailor. I would like you to let me hear the verses you were
reciting when you were at the door." The porter was ashamed and

said, "For God's sake, don't reproach me, for fatigue, hardship, and poverty teach a man ill manners and impudence." The host said to him, "Do not be ashamed, for you have become a brother to me. Recite the verses, for they pleased me when you recited them at the door." The porter recited to him those verses, and when he heard them, he was pleased and delighted. Then he said, "Porter, my story is astonishing, and I will relate to you all that happened to me before I attained this prosperity and came to sit in this place, where you now see me, for I did not attain this good fortune and this place save after severe toil, great hardships, and many perils. How much toil and trouble I have endured at the beginning! I embarked on seven voyages, and each voyage is a wonderful tale that confounds the mind, and everything happened by fate and divine decree, and there is no escape nor refuge from that which is foreordained."

The First Voyage of Sindbad

GENTLEMEN, MY FATHER was one of the most prominent men and richest merchants, who possessed abundant wealth and property. When I was a little boy, he died and left me many buildings and fields. When I grew up, I seized everything and began to eat and drink freely, associated with young friends, wore nice clothes, and passed my life with my friends and companions, believing that this way of life would last forever and that it would benefit me. I lived in this way for a length of time but finally returned to my senses and awoke from my heedlessness and found that my wealth had gone and my condition had changed. When I came to myself and found that I had lost everything, I was stricken with fear and dismay, and I remembered a saying I had heard before, a saying of our Lord Solomon, the son of David, that three things are better than three: the day of death is better than the day of birth; a living dog is better than a dead lion; and the grave is better than the palace. Then I gathered all I had of effects and clothes and sold them, together with what was left of my buildings and property and netted three thousand dirhams, thinking that I might travel abroad and recalling what some poet said:

> A man must labor hard to scale the heights,
> And to seek greatness must spend sleepless nights,
> And to find pearls must plunge into the sea
> And so attains good fortune and eminent be.
> For he who seeks success without labor
> Wastes all his life in a futile endeavor.

I made my resolve and, having been inclined to take a sea voyage, I bought goods and merchandise, as well as provisions and whatever is needed for travel, and embarked with a group of merchants on a boat bound downstream for Basra. From there, we sailed for many days and nights from sea to sea and from island to island, and sold, bought, and bartered until we came to an island that seemed like one of the gardens of Paradise. There the captain docked, cast anchor, and put forth the landing plank. Then all those who were on the ship landed on that island. They set up woodstoves, lighted fires in them, and busied themselves with various tasks, some cooking, some washing, some sightseeing. I myself was among those who went to explore the place, while the passengers assembled to eat and drink and play games and amuse themselves.

While we were thus engaged, the captain, standing on the side of the ship, cried out at the top of his voice, "O passengers, may God preserve you! Run for your lives, leave your gear, and hurry back to the ship to save yourselves from destruction. For this island where you are is not really an island but a great fish that has settled in the middle of the sea, and the sand has accumulated on it, making it look like an island, and the trees have grown on it a long time. When you lighted the fire on it, it felt the heat and began to move, and it will soon descend with you into the sea, and you will all drown. Save yourselves before you perish."

When the passengers heard the captain's warning, they hurried to get into the ship, leaving behind their woodstoves, copper cooking pots, and their other gear, together with their goods. Some made it to the ship, but some did not. The island had moved and sunk to the bottom of the sea with everything that was on it, and the roaring sea with its clashing waves closed over it. I, being one of those left behind on the island, sank in the sea with those who sank, but God the Almighty saved me from drowning and provided me with a large wooden tub that the passengers had been using for washing. I held on to it for dear life, got on it, and began to paddle with my feet, while the waves tossed me to the right and left. Meanwhile, the captain spread the sails and pursued his voyage with those who had made it to the ship, without regard for those who were drowning. I kept looking at the ship until it disappeared from my sight, and as night descended, I became sure of perdition. I remained in this condition for a day and a night, but with the help of the wind and the waves, the tub landed me under a high island, with trees overhanging the water. I seized a branch of a tall tree, clung to it, after I had been on the verge of death, and climbed it to the land. I found my feet numb and my soles bore the marks of the nibbling of fish, something of which I had been unaware because of my extreme exhaustion and distress.

I threw myself on the ground like a dead man and, overcome by stupefaction, lost consciousness till the next day, when the sun rose and I woke up on the island. I found that my feet were swollen and that I was reduced to a helpless condition. So I began to move, sometimes dragging myself in a sitting position, sometimes crawling on my knees, and found that the island had abundant fruits and springs of sweet water. I ate those fruits, and after several days I recovered my strength, felt refreshed, and was able to move about. I reflected and, having made myself a crutch from a tree branch, walked along the shores of the island, enjoying the trees and what the Almighty God had created.

I lived in this manner until one day, as I walked along the shore, I saw an indistinct figure in the distance and thought it a wild beast or one of the creatures of the sea. I walked toward it, without ceasing to look at it, and found that it was a magnificent mare tethered by the seashore. I approached her, but she cried at me with a loud cry, and I was terrified, and as I was about to retreat, a man emerged suddenly from the ground, called to me and pursued me, saying, "Who are you, where do you come from, and what brings you here?" I said to him, "Sir, I am a stranger, and I was on a ship and sank in the sea with some other passengers, but God provided me with a wooden tub, and I got on it and floated until the waves cast me on this island." When he heard my words, he took me by the hand and said, "Come with me." I went with him, and he descended with me to a subterranean vault. We entered a large chamber, and he seated me at the upper end of the chamber and brought me food. I was hungry, and I ate until I was satisfied and felt good. Then he inquired about my situation and what had happened to me. I told him my story from beginning to end, and he marveled at it.

When I finished my story, I said to him, "Sir, I have told you all the particulars of my situation and all that has happened to me. For God's sake, pardon me, for I would like you to tell me who you are, why you live in this subterranean chamber, and why is the mare tethered by the seashore?" He said to me, "I am one of a group of men scattered on this island. We are the grooms of King Mihrajan, in charge of all the horses. Every month, at the new moon, we bring the best mares that have not been bred before and hide in the subterranean chamber, so that no one may see us. Then one of the sea horses comes out to the shore after the scent of the mares and, looking and seeing no one around, mounts one of them. When he finishes with her and dismounts her, he wishes to take her with him, but she cannot follow him, because she is tethered. Then he begins to cry out at her and batter her with his head and hoofs. When we hear his cries, we know that he has dismounted, and we run out, shouting at him, and frighten him back into the sea. Then the mare conceives and bears a mare or a filly worth a fortune, one whose like is not to be found on the face of the earth. This is the time of the coming of the sea horse and, God the Almighty willing, I will take you to King Mihrajan and show you our country. Had you not met us, you would not have found anyone else on this island, and you would have died miserably, and no one would have known of you, but I will save your life and return you to your country." I invoked a blessing on him and thanked him for his help and kindness.

While we were in conversation, a sea horse suddenly came out of the sea and, letting out a great cry, leapt on the mare. When he finished with her, he dismounted and tried to take her with him but could not, as she resisted, neighing at him. The groom took a sword and buckler and ran out, shouting to his companions, "Run to the sea horse," as he hit the buckler with the sword. Then a group of them came out, shouting and brandishing spears. The sea horse, frightened by them, ran away, plunged into the water like a buffalo, and disappeared. As the groom sat down to rest for a while, his companions came, each leading a mare. When they saw me with him, they inquired about my situation, and I repeated to them what I had told him. Then they drew near me and, spreading the table, ate and invited me to eat; so I ate with them. Then they rode the mares and gave me one to ride, and we traveled until we reached the city of King Mihrajan.

Then they went in to see him and acquainted him with my story, and he sent for me, and they led me in and made me stand before him. I saluted him, and he returned my salutation, welcomed me, greeted me in a courteous manner, and inquired about my situation. I related to him what had happened to me and what I had seen from beginning to end, and he marveled at my story, saying, "By God, my son, you have had an extraordinary escape, and had you not been destined to a long life, you would not have escaped from these difficulties, but God be praised for your safety." Then he treated me kindly and honored me and, seating me near him, engaged me in friendly conversation. Then he made me his agent to the port and registrar of all the ships that landed. I stood in his presence to transact his affairs, and he treated me generously, bestowed a fine, rich suit on me, and rewarded me in every way. I became a person of high esteem with him, interceding for the people and facilitating their business.

I remained with him for a long time, but whenever I went to the port, I used to ask the merchants and the sailors about the direction of the city of Baghdad, hoping that someone might inform me and I might go with him and return to my country, but no one knew it, nor knew anyone who went there. I was perplexed, and I had grown weary of my long absence from home, and I continued to feel this way for some time.

One day I went in to see King Mihrajan and found with him a group of Indians. I saluted them and they returned my salutation, welcomed me, and asked me about my country. Then I asked them about theirs, and they told me that they consisted of various races. One is called the Kshatriyas, who are the noblest of their races and who oppress no one, nor inflict violence on anyone. Another is called the Brahmans, who abstain from wine but live in joy, sport, merriment, and prosperity, possessing horses, camels, and cattle. They told me, moreover, that the Indians consist of seventy-two castes, and I marveled at that.

Among other things, I saw in the dominion of King Mihrajan an island called Kabil, on which the beating of drums and tambourines is heard all night long and whose inhabitants are reported by travelers and neighboring islanders to be people of judgment and serious pursuits. I saw in the sea a fish four hundred feet long and saw fish with faces that resembled the faces of owls. During that voyage, I saw many strange and wonderful things, which would take too long to relate to you.

I continued to divert myself with the sights of those islands until one day, as I stood in the port, with a staff in my hand, as was my custom, a large ship approached, carrying many merchants. When it entered the harbor and reached the pier, the captain furled the sails, cast anchor, and put forth the landing plank. Then the crew brought out to shore everything that was in the ship and took a long time in doing so, while I stood writing their account. I said to the captain, "Is there anything left in the ship?" He replied, "Yes, sir, I have some goods in the hold of the ship, but their owner drowned at one of the islands during our voyage here; so his goods remained in our charge, and our intention is to sell them and keep a record, so that we may give the money to his family in the city of Baghdad, the Abode of Peace." I asked the captain, "What was the name of the merchant, the owner of the goods?" He said, "His name was Sindbad the Sailor." When I heard these words, I looked carefully at him and, recognizing him, cried out loudly, saying, "Captain, I am the owner of the goods; I am that Sindbad who landed from the ship on the island, with the other merchants, and when the fish moved, and you called out to us, some of us got into the ship, and the rest sank. I was among those who sank, but God the Almighty preserved me and saved me from drowning by means of a wooden tub that the passengers had used for washing. I got on the tub and paddled with my feet, and the wind and the waves brought me to this island, where I landed and where, with the help of the Almighty God, I met the grooms of King Mihrajan, who brought me with them to this city and took me to the king, to whom I related my story, and he treated me generously and made me clerk of the harbor of this city, and he appreciated my services and rewarded me accordingly. These goods in your charge are my goods and possessions."

The captain said, "There is no power and no strength, save in God, the Almighty, the Magnificent. There is neither conscience nor trust left among men." I said to him, "Captain, why those words, after you heard me telling you my story?" The captain replied, "Because you heard me say that I have with me goods whose owner has drowned, you are trying to take them without any rightful claim, and this is unlawful. We saw the owner drown with many other passengers, none of whom escaped. How can you claim that you are the owner of the goods?" I said to him, "Captain, listen to my story and try to understand, and you will discover my veracity, for lying is the mark of a hypocrite." Then I enumerated to him everything I had with me, from the time I left Baghdad with him until we reached that island, where we sank in the sea, and I mentioned to him some incidents that had occurred between him and me. The captain and the other merchants then became convinced of my veracity, and they recognized me and congratulated me on my safety. All of them said, "We never believed that you had escaped from drowning, but God has granted you a new life." Then they gave me my goods, and we found my name written on them, and nothing was missing. Then I opened them and took out something precious and costly, and the crew of the ship carried it with me to the king as a gift. I told him that this ship is the one in which I had been a passenger and that all my goods were intact and in perfect order and that this present was a part of them. The king was amazed and was even more convinced of my truthfulness in everything I had told him. He felt a deep affection for me, treated me with great generosity, and gave me many presents in return for mine.

Then I sold my goods and all my other property and made a great profit. Then I bought goods, gear, and provisions from that city, and when the merchants were about to depart, I loaded everything I had on the ship and went in to see the king. I thanked him for his kindness and generosity and asked his permission to return to my country and family. He bade me farewell and gave me a great many of the products of that country for my voyage. I bade him farewell and embarked. Then we set sail with the permission of the Almighty God, and fortune served us and fate favored us, as we journeyed day and night until we reached Basra safely.

After staying in Basra for a short time rejoicing in my return to my country, I headed for Baghdad, the Abode of Peace, carrying with me an abundance of merchandise, provisions, and gear of great value. I went to my quarter and entered my house, and all my relatives and friends came to see me. Then I acquired a great number of servants and attendants and concubines and bought slaves, both black and white. Then I bought houses and other properties that exceeded what I had had before. And I associated with friends and companions, exceeding my former habits, and forgot all I had suffered of toil, exile, hardship, and perils, indulging for a long time in amusements and pleasures and delicious food and fine drink. This was my first voyage. Tomorrow, the Almighty God willing, I will tell you the story of the second of my seven voyages.

Then Sindbad the Sailor had Sindbad the Porter dine with him and gave him a hundred pieces of gold, saying to him, "You have cheered us today." The porter thanked him, took his present, and went on his way, meditating and marveling at the events that befall mankind. He spent that night at home, and as soon as it was morning, he went to the house of Sindbad the Sailor, who welcomed him, spoke courteously to him, and asked him to sit. When the rest of his companions arrived, he set food and drink before them, and when they were cheerful and merry, he said to them:

The Second Voyage of Sindbad

FRIENDS, AS I TOLD you yesterday, I lived a most enjoyable life of unalloyed pleasure until it occurred to me one day to travel abroad, and I felt a longing for trading, seeing other countries and islands, and making profit. Having made my resolve, I took out a large sum of money and bought goods and travel gear, packed them up, and went down to the shore. There I found a fine new ship, with sails of good cloth, numerous crewmen, and abundant equipment. I loaded my bales on it, as did a group of other merchants, and we sailed on the same day. We sailed under fair weather and journeyed from sea to sea and from island to island, and wherever we landed, we met merchants, high officials, and sellers and buyers, and we sold, bought, and bartered.

We continued in this fashion until fate brought us to a beautiful island abounding with trees, ripe fruits, fragrant flowers, singing birds, and clear streams, but there was not a single inhabitant nor a breathing soul around. The captain anchored the ship at the island, and the merchants and other passengers landed there, to divert themselves with the sight of the trees and birds and to glorify the One Omnipotent God and wonder at the power of the Almighty King. I landed with the rest and sat down by a spring of pure water among the trees. I had with me some food, and I sat there eating what the Almighty God had allotted me. The breeze was cool, and the place was pleasant; so I dozed off and rested there until the sweetness of the breeze and fragrance of the flowers lulled me into a deep sleep.

When I awoke, I did not find a single soul around, neither man nor demon. The ship had sailed with all the passengers and left me behind, none of the merchants or the crew taking any notice of me. I searched right and left, but found no one but myself. I felt extremely unhappy and outraged, and my spleen was about to burst from the severity of my anxiety, grief, and fatigue, for I was all alone with nothing of worldly goods and without food or drink. I felt desolate and despaired of life, saying to myself, "Not every time the jar is saved in time. If I escaped safely the first time, by finding someone who took me with him from the shore of that island to the inhabited part, this time I am very far from the prospect of finding someone who will deliver me out of here." Then I began to weep and wail for myself until I was completely overcome by grief, blaming myself for what I had done and for having embarked on the hardships of travel, after I had been reposing peacefully in my own house and in my own country, happily enjoying good food and good drink and good clothes, without need for money or goods. I regretted leaving Baghdad on this sea journey, especially after the hardships I had endured on the first and after my narrow escape from destruction, saying, "We are God's and to God we return." I felt like a madman.

At last, I arose and began to walk on the island, turning right and left, for I was unable to sit still in any one place. Then I climbed a tall tree and looked to the right and left but saw nothing but sky and water and trees and birds and islands and sands. Then I looked closely and saw a large, white object. I climbed down and walked in its direction until I reached it and found it to be a huge white dome of great height and circumference. I drew closer and walked around it but found that it had no door, and because of its extreme smoothness, I had neither the power nor the nimbleness to climb it. I marked the spot where I stood and went around the dome to measure its circumference and found it to be a good fifty paces. I stood, thinking of a way to get inside, as the day was about to end and the sun was about to set. Suddenly, the sun disappeared, and it grew dark. I therefore thought that a cloud had come over the sun, but since it was summer, I wondered at that. I raised my head to look at the object and saw that it was a great bird, with a huge body and outspread wings, flying in the air and veiling the sun from the island. My wonder increased, and I recalled a story I heard from tourists and travelers that there is on certain islands an enormous bird, called the Rukh, which feeds its young on elephants, and I became certain that the dome I saw was one of the Rukh's eggs and wondered at the works of God the Almighty.

While I was in this state, the bird alighted on the egg and brooded over it with its wing and, stretching its legs behind on the ground, went to sleep. Glory be to Him who never sleeps! I unwound my turban, twisted it with a rope and, girding my waist with it, tied it fast to the bird's feet, saying to myself, "Perhaps, this bird will carry me to a land where there are cities and people. That will be better than staying on this island." I spent that night without sleep, fearing that the bird might fly with me while I was unaware. When dawn broke and it was light, the bird rose from its egg, uttered a loud cry, and flew with me up into the sky. It soared higher and higher until I thought that it had reached the pinnacle of heaven. Then it began to descend gradually until it alighted with me on the ground, resting on a high place. As soon as I reached the ground, I hastened to unbind myself, and, loosening my turban from its feet, while shaking with fear, although it was unaware and took no notice of me, I walked away. Then it picked up something with its talons from the ground and flew high into the sky. When I looked at it carefully, I saw that it was an enormous serpent, which the bird had taken and flown with toward the sea. And I wondered at that.

Then I walked about the place and found myself on a crest overlooking a large, wide, and deep valley at the foot of a huge and lofty mountain that was so high no one could see the top nor climb to it, so I blamed myself for what I had done, saying, "I wish that I had stayed on the island, which is better than this desolate place, for there I might at least have eaten of its various fruits and drunk from its streams, whereas this place has neither trees nor fruits nor streams. There is no power and no strength save in God the Almighty, the Magnificent. Every time I escape from a calamity, I fall into one that is greater and more perilous." Then I arose and, gathering my strength, walked in that valley and saw that its ground was composed of diamonds, with which they perforate minerals and jewels, as well as porcelain and onyx, which is such a hard and dense stone that neither stone nor steel has any effect on it and which nobody can cut or break except with the leadstone. Moreover, the valley was full of serpents and snakes, each as big as a palm tree, indeed so huge that it could swallow an elephant. These serpents came out at night and hid themselves during the day, fearing that the Rukh or eagles might carry them away and cut them in pieces, for a reason of which I was unaware. I stood there, regretting what I had done and saying to myself, "By God, I have hastened my own destruction."

As the day was waning, I walked in that valley and began looking for a place to spend the night, being afraid of the serpents, forgetting my food and drink and subsistence, and thinking only of saving my life. Soon I saw a cave nearby. It had a narrow entrance, and when I went in I saw a big stone lying by that entrance. I pushed the stone and closed the entrance from the inside, saying to myself, "I am safe here now, and as soon as it is day, I will go out and see what fate will bring." But when I took a look inside, I saw a huge snake brooding over its eggs. My hair stood on end, and I raised my head, committing myself to fate and divine decree. I spent the entire night without sleep, and as soon as it was dawn, I removed the stone with which I had closed the entrance of the cave and went out, like a drunken man, feeling dizzy from excessive hunger, sleeplessness, and fear.

I walked in the valley in this condition, when suddenly a big slaughtered sheep fell before me, but when I saw no one else around, I was amazed, and I recalled a story I used to hear a long time ago from some merchants, tourists, and travelers that the mountains of the diamonds are so perilous that no one can gain access to them, but that the merchants who deal in diamonds employ a device to get them. They take a sheep, slaughter it, skin it, cut up the meat, and throw it from the top of the mountain into the valley. When the meat falls, still fresh, the diamonds stick to it. Then they leave it there till midday, when the eagles and vultures swoop down on it, pick it up with their talons, and fly with it to the top of the mountain. The merchants then rush, shouting at them, and scare them away from the meat. Then the merchants come to the meat, take the diamonds sticking to it, and carry them back to their country. No one can obtain diamonds except by this method.

When I saw that slaughtered sheep and recalled that story, I approached the carcass and began to pick a great number of diamonds and to put them into my pockets and the folds of my clothes, and I continued to fill my pockets, my clothes, my belt, and my turban. While I was thus engaged, another carcass suddenly fell before me. I bound myself to it with my turban and, lying on my back, placed it on my chest and held on to it. Thus it was raised above the ground. Suddenly, an eagle swooped down on it, caught it with his talons, and flew up into the air with it and with me clinging to it. The eagle continued to soar until it reached the top of the mountain and, alighting there, was about to tear off a piece of meat, when suddenly a loud cry and the sound of clattering with a piece of wood came from behind the eagle, who took fright and flew away.

I unbound myself from the carcass, with my clothes stained with its blood, and stood by its side. Suddenly, the merchant, who had shouted at the eagle, approached the carcass and saw me standing there, but he did not utter a word, for he was frightened of me. Then he came closer to the carcass, and when he turned it over and found nothing on it, he uttered a loud cry and said, "What a disappointment! There is no power and no strength, save in God the Almighty, the Magnificent. May God save us from Satan the accursed," and he kept expressing regret, wringing his hands and saying, "What a pity! How did this happen?" I went to him, and he said to me, "Who are you, and what brings you to this place?" I said to him, "Don't be afraid, for I am a human being, and one of the best men. I was a merchant, and I have a strange and extraordinary tale to tell, and the reason for my coming to this valley and this mountain is marvelous to relate. Don't worry, for you will receive from me what will please you. I have with me a great deal of diamonds, each one better than what you would have gotten, and I will give you a portion that will satisfy

you. Don't fear and don't worry." When he heard this, he thanked me
and invoked a blessing on me, and we began to converse.

When the other merchants, each of whom had thrown down a
slaughtered sheep, heard me conversing with their companion, they
came to meet me. They saluted me, congratulated me on my safety,
and took me with them. I told them my whole story, relating to them
what I had suffered on this voyage and the cause of my coming to
this valley. Then I gave the merchant, to whose slaughtered sheep I
had attached myself, a large portion of diamonds, and that made
him happy, and he thanked me and invoked a blessing on me, and
the merchants said to me, "By God, you have been granted a new
life, for no one has come to this place before and escaped from it,
but God be praised for your safety." They spent the night in a pleasant and safe place, and I spent the night with them, extremely happy
for my safe escape from the Valley of Serpents and my arrival in an
inhabited place.

When it was morning, we arose and journeyed along the ridge of
the high mountain, seeing many snakes in the valley below, and we
continued walking until we came to a large and pleasant island with
a grove of camphor trees, each of which might provide a hundred
men with shade. When someone wishes to obtain some camphor, he
makes a perforation in the upper part of the tree with a piercing rod
and catches what descends from it. The liquid camphor, which is
the juice of that tree, flows and later hardens, like gum. Afterwards,
the tree dries and becomes firewood. We also saw in that island,
besides cattle, a kind of beast called the rhinoceros, which pastures
as cows and buffaloes do in our country, and feeds on the leaves of
trees, but the body of that beast is bigger than that of a camel. It is a
huge beast, with a single horn in the middle of its head, thick and
twenty feet long and resembling the figure of a man. Travelers and
tourists on land and in the mountains report that this beast called
the rhinoceros carries a huge elephant on its horn and grazes with it
in the island and on the shores, without feeling its weight, and when
the elephant dies on the horn, its fat melts under the heat of the sun
and flows on the head of the rhinoceros and, entering his eyes,
blinds it. Then it lies down by the shore, and the Rukh picks it up
with its talons and carries it together with the elephant to feed to its
young. I also saw in that island a great number of a certain kind of
buffalo, the like of which is not seen among us.

The merchants exchanged goods and provisions with me and paid
me money for some of the diamonds I carried in my pockets from the
valley. They carried my goods for me, and I journeyed with them,
from town to town and from valley to valley, buying and selling and
viewing foreign countries and what God has created until we reached
Basra, where I stayed for a few days, then headed for Baghdad. When

I reached my quarter and entered my home, with a great quantity of diamonds and a considerable amount of goods and provisions, I met with my family and other relatives and gave alms and distributed presents to all my relatives and friends. Then I began to eat and drink well and wear handsome clothes, associating with friends and companions and forgetting all I had suffered, and I continued to lead a happy, merry, and carefree life of sport and merriment. And all who heard of my return came to me and inquired about my voyage and the countries I saw, and I told them, relating to them what I had seen and what I had suffered, and they were amazed at the extent of my hardships and congratulated me on my safety. That was the end of the second voyage. Tomorrow, the Almighty God willing, I will tell you the story of my third voyage.

WHEN SINDBAD the Sailor finished telling his story to Sindbad the Porter and the other guests, they all marveled at it. After they had supper, he gave Sindbad the Porter a hundred pieces of gold, which he took and, after thanking Sindbad the Sailor and invoking a blessing on him, went on his way, marveling at what Sindbad had suffered. The following day, as soon as it was light, the porter arose, and after performing his morning prayer, came to the house of Sindbad, as he had bidden him. The porter went in, wished him good morning, and Sindbad welcomed him and sat with him until the rest of his friends and companions arrived. After they had eaten and drunk and enjoyed themselves and felt relaxed and merry, Sindbad the Sailor began his story.

The Third Voyage of Sindbad

FRIENDS, THE STORY of my third voyage is more amazing than the two you have already heard, and God in His wisdom knows best what He keeps hidden. When I returned from my second voyage, I led a life of ease and happiness, rejoicing in my safety, having gained great wealth, for God had compensated me for everything I had lost, as I had related to you yesterday. I lived in Baghdad for some time, in prosperity and peace and happiness, until my soul began to long for travel and sightseeing and commerce and profit, and the soul is naturally prone to evil. Having made my resolve, I bought a great quantity of goods suited for a sea voyage, packed them up, and journeyed with them from Baghdad to Basra. Then I went to the seashore where I found a large ship in which there were many merchants and other passengers who seemed to be good people—men of rectitude, piety, and kindness. I embarked with them on that ship, and we sailed, relying on the blessing and aid and favor of the Almighty God, feeling happy in the expectation of a safe and prosperous voyage. We

sailed from sea to sea and from island to island and from city to city,
buying and selling and diverting ourselves with the sights and feeling exceedingly content and happy until one day we found ourselves
in the middle of a roaring, raging sea. The captain stood at the side
of the ship and examined the sea in all directions. Then he slapped
his face, furled the sails, cast the anchors, plucked his beard, tore
his clothes, and uttered a loud cry. When we asked him, "Captain,
what is the matter?" he said, "O fellows, may God preserve you. The
wind has prevailed against us and forced us into the middle of the
sea, and fate and our ill fortune have brought us to the Mountain of
the Apes. No one has ever come here and escaped safely." I was sure
that we were all going to perish, and no sooner had the captain finished his speech than the ship was surrounded by ape-like creatures
who came in great number, like locusts, and swarmed on the boat
and on the shore. We were afraid that if we killed, struck, or chased
away any of them, they would easily kill us because of their number,
for numbers prevail over courage. We also feared that they would
plunder our goods and provisions. They are the ugliest of beasts,
with a terrifying appearance, covered with hair like black felt. They
have black faces, yellow eyes, and small size, no more than four
spans. No one understands their language nor knows who they are,
for they shun the society of men. They climbed up the anchor cables
of the ship, on every side, and cut them with their teeth, and they
cut likewise all the ropes; so the ship swerved with the wind and
stopped on the shore, below the mountain. They seized all the merchants and the other passengers and, landing us on the island, took
the ship with everything in it and disappeared into an unknown
place, leaving us behind.

We stayed on the island, eating of its vegetables and fruits and
drinking of its streams until one day we saw a stately mansion, situated in the middle of the island. We walked in its direction, and
when we reached it, we found it to be a strong castle, with high walls
and a gate of ebony, with two leaves, both of which were open. We
entered and found inside a large courtyard, around which there
were many high doors, and at the upper end of which there was a
large, high bench, on which rested stoves and copper cooking pots
hanging above. Around the bench lay many scattered bones. But
we saw no one and were very much surprised. Then we sat down in
the courtyard for a while and soon fell asleep and slept from midmorning till sundown, when suddenly we felt the earth trembling
under us, heard a rumbling noise in the air, and saw descending on
us from the top of the castle a huge figure in the likeness of a man,
black in color and tall in stature, as if he were a huge palm-tree, with
eyes like torches; fangs like the tusks of a boar; a big mouth, like the
mouth of a whale; lips like the lips of a camel, hanging down on his

breast; ears like two barges, hanging down on his shoulders; and nails like the claws of a lion. When we saw him, we fainted, like men stricken dead with anxiety and terror.

When he descended, he sat on the bench for a while, then he got up and, coming to us, grabbed my hand from among my fellow merchants and, lifting me up in the air, turned me over, as I dangled from his hand like a little morsel, and felt my body as a butcher feels a sheep for the slaughter. But finding me feeble from grief, lean from the toil of the journey, and without much meat, he let me go and picked up one of my companions, turned him over, felt him, as he had done with me, and released him. He kept turning us over and feeling us, one after one, until he came to the captain of our ship, who was a fat, stout, and broad-shouldered man, a man of vigor and vitality. He was pleased by the captain, and he seized him, as a butcher seizes an animal he is about to slaughter, and, throwing him on the ground, set his foot on his neck and broke it. Then he fetched a long spit and thrust it through the captain's mouth until it came out from his posterior. Then he lit a big fire and set over it the spit on which the captain was spitted, turning it over the coal, until the flesh was roasted. Then he took the spit off the fire and, placing the body before him, separated the joints, as one separates the joints of a chicken, and proceeded to tear the flesh with his nails and eat it until he devoured all the flesh and gnawed the bones, and nothing was left of the captain except some bones, which he threw on one side. Then he sat on the bench for a while and fell asleep, snoring like a slaughtered sheep or cow, and slept till morning, when he got up and went on his way.

When we were sure that he was gone, we began to talk with one another, weeping for ourselves and saying, "We wish that we had drowned in the sea or been eaten by the apes, for that would have been better than being roasted on the coals. By God, this is a vile death, but what God wills comes to pass, and there is no power and no strength save in God the Almighty, the Magnificent. We will die miserably, and no one will know, for there is no escape from this place." We got up and walked in the island to look for a means of escape or a place to hide, feeling that death was lighter to bear than being roasted on the fire. But we failed to find a hiding place, and as the evening overtook us, we returned to the castle, driven by great fear.

No sooner had we sat down than the earth began to tremble under us, and that black creature approached us and began to turn us over and feel us, one after one, as he had done the first time, until he found one he liked, seized him, and did to him what he had done to the captain, on the first day. Then he roasted him and, after eating him, lay down on the bench and slept, snoring all night, like a slaughtered beast. In the morning, he got up and went on his way, leaving us, as usual.

We drew together and said to one another, "By God, if we throw ourselves into the sea and drown, it will be better than dying by fire, for this is a horrible death." One of us said, "Listen to me! Let us find a way to kill him and rid ourselves of this affliction and relieve all Muslims of his aggression and tyranny." I said to them, "Listen, friends! If we have to kill him, let us transport these planks of wood and some of the firewood and make for ourselves a raft and, after we find a way to kill him, embark on the raft and let the sea take us wherever God wishes. Then we will sit there until a ship passes by and picks us up. And if we fail to kill him, we can still embark on the raft and set out in the sea, even though we may drown, in order that we may escape from being slaughtered and roasted on the fire. If we escape, we escape, and if we drown, we die like martyrs." They all replied, "By God, this is a good plan," and we agreed to carry it out; so we carried the wood out of the castle, built a raft, tied it to the seashore and, after putting some food on it, returned to the castle.

When it was evening, the earth trembled under us, and in came the black creature, like a raging dog. He proceeded to turn us over and to feel us, one after one, until he picked one of us and did to him what he had done to his predecessors. Then he ate him and lay to sleep on the bench, snoring like thunder. We got up, took two of the iron spits of those set up there, and put them in the blazing fire until they became red-hot, like burning coals. Then, gripping the spits tightly, we went to the black creature, who was fast asleep, snoring, and, pushing the spits with all our united strength and determination, thrust them deep into his eyes. He uttered a great, terrifying cry. Then he got up resolutely from the bench and began to search for us, while we fled from him to the right and left, in unspeakable terror, sure of destruction and despairing of escape. But being blind, he was unable to see us, and he groped his way to the door, and went out, as his screams made the ground tremble under us and made us quake with terror. When he went out, we followed him, as he went searching for us. Then he returned with a female, even bigger than he and more hideous in appearance. When we saw him and saw that his female companion was more horrible than he, we were in utmost terror. When the female saw us, we hurried to the raft, untied it and, embarking on it, pushed it into the sea, while the two stood, throwing big rocks on us until most of us died, except for three, me and two companions.

The raft conveyed us to another island. There, we walked till the end of the day, and, when it was night, we went to sleep. We were barely asleep when we were aroused by an enormous serpent with a wide belly. It surrounded us and, approaching one of us, swallowed him to his shoulders, then swallowed the rest of him, and we heard his ribs crack inside its belly. Then it went on its way, leaving us in utter amazement and grief for our companion and fear for our lives, thinking to ourselves, "By God, this is amazing, for each death is more terrible than the preceding one. We rejoiced at our escape from the black creatures, but our joy did not last. There is no power and no strength, save in God. By God, we have escaped from the black creature and from drowning, but how shall we escape from this accursed monster?"

Then we walked in the island, eating of its fruits and drinking of its streams, and when it was evening, we found a huge, tall tree, climbed it, and went to sleep there, I myself being on the highest branch. As soon as it was dark, the serpent came and, looking right and left, headed for the tree on which we were, and climbed until it reached my companion. Then it swallowed him to his shoulders, coiled with him around the tree, as I heard his bones crack in its belly, then swallowed him whole, while I looked on. Then it slid down from the tree and went on its way.

I stayed on the tree for the rest of the night, and when it was daylight, I climbed down, like a man stricken dead with terror. I thought of throwing myself into the sea and delivering myself from the world. But I could not bring myself to do it, for life is dear. So I tied a wide piece of wood crosswise to my feet, tied two similar ones to my right side, to my left side, and to my chest, and tied another, very wide and long, crosswise to my head. Thus I was in the middle of these pieces of wood which surrounded me and, having fastened them tightly to my body, I threw myself on the ground and lay, with the wood enclosing me like a closet.

When it was dark, the serpent came, as usual, saw me, and headed for me, but it could not swallow me with the wood surrounding me. Then it began to circle around me, while I looked on, like a man stricken dead with terror. Then the serpent began to turn away from me and come back to me, and every time it tried to swallow me it was prevented by the wood that was tied to me on every side, and it continued in this fashion from sunset to sunrise. When it was light, it went its way, in the utmost vexation and rage. Then I moved my hands and untied myself from the pieces of wood, feeling almost dead from what I had suffered from that serpent.

I then walked in the island until I reached the shore and, happening to look toward the sea, saw a ship on the waves, in the distance. I took a big branch and began to make signs with it and call out to the passengers. When they saw me, they said to each other, "We must see what this is, for it may be a man." They came closer, and when they heard my cries for help, they came to me and took me with them in the ship. Then they inquired about my situation, and I related to them what had happened to me, from beginning to end, and what hardships I had suffered, and they marveled at that. Then they gave me some of their clothes to make myself decent and offered me some food and some cool sweet water. I ate and drank until I had enough, and I felt refreshed, relaxed, and very comfortable, and my vigor returned. God the Almighty had brought me to life after death, and I thanked Him and praised Him for his abundant blessings, after I had been certain of destruction, thinking that I was in a dream.

We sailed, with God's permission, with a fair wind, until we came to an island called the Salahita Island. The captain cast anchor there, and all the merchants and other passengers landed with their goods to sell and buy. Then the captain turned to me and said, "Listen to me! You are a poor stranger who has, as you told us, suffered many horrors, and I wish to benefit you with something that will help you to return to your country, so that you will pray for me." I replied, "Very well, you will have my prayers." He said, "There was a passenger with us whom we lost, and we don't know whether he is alive or dead, for he has left no trace. I would like to give you his goods, and you will take charge of them to sell them in this island, and we will pay you an amount commensurate with your work and trouble and take the rest with us back to Baghdad, find his family, and give it to them, together with the proceeds of the sale. Will you receive the goods and take them to the island to sell them, like the other merchants?" I replied, "Sir, I hear and obey, with gratitude and thanks," and I invoked a blessing on him and thanked him. He then ordered the porters and sailors to carry the goods to the island and deliver them to me. The ship's clerk said to him, "What are those bales that the porters and sailors are carrying out and in whose merchant's name shall I register them?" The captain replied, "Register them in the name of Sindbad the Sailor, who was with us on that island and who drowned, without leaving any trace. I wish this stranger to sell these goods, and I will give him an amount commensurate with his work and trouble and keep the rest of the money with us until we reach Baghdad and, if we find Sindbad, give it to him and, if we don't, give it to his family." The clerk replied, "This is a good and wise plan." When I heard the captain mention that the goods were in my name, I said to myself, "By God, I am Sindbad the Sailor who was lost on that island!"

Then I controlled myself and waited patiently until the merchants came back to the ship and assembled to chat and consult on the affairs of buying and selling. I approached the captain and said to him, "Sir, do you know anything about the man whose goods you gave me to sell?" The captain replied, "I know nothing about him, except that he was a man from Baghdad, called Sindbad the Sailor. We cast anchor at one of the islands, and he was lost, and we have not heard anything about him to this day." I uttered a great cry and said, "O captain, may God preserve you! I am Sindbad the Sailor. When you cast anchor at that island, and the merchants and the rest of the passengers landed, I landed with them. I took with me something to eat, and sat in a place, enjoying myself; then I dozed off and fell into a deep sleep." When the merchants and the other passengers heard my words, they gathered around me, some believing me, some disbelieving. Soon, one of the merchants, hearing me mention the valley of diamonds approached me and said to them, "Listen to what I have to say, fellows! When I related to you the most extraordinary events that I encountered in my travels and how the merchants threw the slaughtered sheep into the valley of diamonds, and I threw mine with theirs, as was my habit, and how I found a man attached to my slaughtered sheep, you did not believe me and thought that I was lying." They said, "Yes, you did tell us that story, and we did not believe you." The merchant said, "This is the very man who gave me the unmatched expensive diamonds, compensating me with more than I would have gotten from my slaughtered sheep, and who traveled with me as my companion until we reached Basra, where he bade us farewell and headed to his city, while we returned to ours. This is the very man who told us that his name was Sindbad the Sailor and related to us how the ship had left, while he was sitting in that island. This man has come to us, in order that you may believe my story. All those goods are his property, for he informed us of them when he first met us, and the truth of his words is evident." When the captain heard the merchant's words, he stood up and, coming up to me, stared at me for a while and asked me, "What is the mark on your bales?" I said, "The mark is such and such," and when I informed him of a matter that had occurred between us when I embarked in the ship, in Basra, he became convinced that I was indeed Sindbad the Sailor, and he embraced me, saluted me, and congratulated me on my safety, saying, "By God, sir, your story is extraordinary and wonderful. God be praised for reuniting you with us and returning your goods and property to you."

Afterwards, I disposed of my goods, according to the best of my skill, and made a great deal of profit, and I felt exceedingly happy and congratulated myself on my safety and the recovery of my property. We continued to sell and buy in the islands until we reached the Indus Valley, where we likewise sold and bought and enjoyed the sights. I saw in the sea there many wonders and strange things. Among the things I saw was a fish in the form of a cow and a creature in the form of an ass. I also saw a bird that comes out of a seashell, lays its eggs on the surface of the water, and hatches them there but never comes up from the sea to the land.

Then we continued our voyage, with God's permission, until, with the aid of a fair wind, we reached Basra, where I stayed for a short time and headed for Baghdad. I went to my house, where I greeted my family and my friends and companions, rejoicing in my safe return to my country and city and home and family. I gave alms and gifts and clothed the widows and the orphans. Then I gathered around me my friends and companions and began to enjoy myself with them, eating well and drinking well, and diverting and entertaining myself, and I forgot all that had happened to me and all the hardships and perils I had suffered. On that voyage, I gained what cannot be numbered or calculated. These then were the most extraordinary events of that voyage. Tomorrow, God willing, come to me, and I will tell you the story of the fourth voyage, which is more wonderful than those of the preceding voyages.

THEN SINDBAD the Sailor gave the porter a hundred pieces of gold, as usual, and ordered that the table be spread. After the table was spread, and the guests dined, still marveling at that story and its events, the porter took the money and went on his way, marveling at what he had heard. The porter spent the night in his house, and as soon as it was morning, he performed his morning prayer and headed to Sindbad the Sailor. He went in and saluted him, and Sindbad received him with gladness and cheer and sat with him until the rest of his companions arrived. When food was served, and they ate and drank and felt merry, Sindbad began his story, saying:

The Fourth Voyage of Sindbad

FRIENDS, WHEN I returned to Baghdad and to the society of my family and friends and companions, I lived in the utmost happiness, pleasure, and ease and forgot what I had experienced, because of my great profit and my immersion in sport and mirth in the society of friends and companions. Thus I lived a most delightful life until my wicked soul suggested to me to travel to foreign countries, and I felt a longing for meeting other races and for selling and gain. Having made my resolve, I purchased precious goods, suited for a sea voyage, and, having packed up more bales than usual, journeyed from Baghdad to Basra, where I loaded my bales in a ship and embarked with some of the chief merchants of the town.

We set out on our voyage and sailed, with the blessing of the Almighty God, in the sea, and the journey was pleasant, as we sailed, for many nights and days, from sea to sea and island to island until one day a contrary wind rose against us. So the captain cast the ship's anchors and brought it to a standstill, fearing that it would sink in midocean. While we were praying and imploring the Almighty God, a violent storm suddenly blew against us, tore the sails to pieces, and threw the people, with all their bales, provisions, and possessions, into the sea. I too was submerged like the rest. I kept myself afloat half the day, and when I was about to give up, the Almighty God provided me with one of the wooden planks of the ship, and I and some other merchants climbed on it, and we paddled with our feet, with the aid of the wind and the waves, for a day and a night. On the midmorning of the following day, a squall blew, and the waves rose, casting us on an island, almost dead from lack of sleep, exhaustion, hunger, thirst, and fear.

We walked along the shores of that island and found abundant vegetation, of which we ate a little to stay our hunger and to sustain ourselves. We spent the night on the shore, and when it was daylight, we arose and wandered in the island to the right and left until we saw a building in the distance. We walked toward that building and kept walking until we stood at its door. While we stood there, out came a group of naked men, who, without speaking to us, seized us and took us to their king. He ordered us to sit, and we sat. Then they brought us some strange food, the like of which we had never seen in our lives. My stomach revolted from it, and unlike my companions, I refrained from eating it, and my refraining was, by the favor of the Almighty God, the cause of my being alive till now. For when my companions ate of that food, they were dazed and began to eat like madmen, and their states changed. Then the people brought them coconut oil, and gave them to drink from it and anointed them with it. When they drank of that oil, their eyes rolled in their heads, and they proceeded to devour an unusual amount of food. When I saw them in that condition, I was puzzled and felt sorry for them, and I became extremely anxious and fearful for myself from these naked men. I looked at them carefully and realized that they were Magians and that the king of their city was a demon. Whenever someone came to their country, or they spotted him or chanced to meet him in the valley or on the roads, they brought him to their king, gave him of that food to eat and anointed him with that oil, so that his belly would expand and he would overeat, feeling stupefied, losing judgment, and becoming like an idiot. Then they gave him more and more of that food to eat and of that oil to drink, and when he became fat and stocky, they slaughtered him, roasted him, and gave him to their king to eat, while they themselves ate the flesh without roasting it or cooking it.

When I realized the situation, I was extremely anxious for myself and my companions, who, in their stupefaction, did not know what was being done to them. They were committed to a man who took them out every day and let them pasture on that island, like cattle.

In the meantime, I wasted away and became emaciated from hunger and fear, and my skin shriveled on my bones. When the Magians saw me in this condition, they left me alone and forgot me, not one of them taking any notice of me, until one day I found a way to slip out of the building and walked away. Then I saw a herdsman sitting on something elevated in the middle of the sea, and when I looked at him, I realized that he was the man to whom they had committed my companions to be taken out to pasture. With him there were many men like them. As soon as the man saw me, he knew that I was in possession of my reason and that I was not afflicted like my companions. He signed to me from afar, saying, "Turn back, and take the road on your right, and it will lead you into the king's highway." I turned back, as he had told me and, finding a road on my right, began to follow it, sometimes running from fear, sometimes walking slowly, in order to catch my breath, and I kept following the road until I disappeared from the sight of the man who had directed me to it, and we were no longer able to see each other.

By then, the sun had set, and it had become dark. I sat down to rest and tried to sleep, but I could not sleep that night because of my extreme fear, hunger, and fatigue. When the night was half spent, I rose and walked in the island until it was daylight, and the sun rose over the tops of the hills and over the plains. I was tired, hungry, and thirsty; so I ate of the herbs and the plants that were on that island until I had enough to allay my hunger. Then I walked the whole day and the next night, and whenever I felt hungry, I ate of the plants to stay my stomach, and I walked on like this for seven days and nights.

On the morning of the eighth day, I happened to cast a glance and saw a vague object in the distance. I walked toward it and kept walking until I reached it, after sunset. I stood scrutinizing it from a distance, still fearful because of what I had suffered the first and the second time, and found that it was a group of men gathering peppercorn. When I approached them, and they saw me, they hastened to me and, surrounding me on all sides, asked me, "Who are you, and from where do you come?" I said to them, "Fellows, I am a poor stranger," and I informed them of my case and how I had suffered hardships and horrors. When they heard my words, they said, "By God, this is extraordinary, but tell us how you escaped from these black men and how you slipped by them, when they are so numerous on this island, and they eat people?" So I related to them what had happened to me with them and how they had given my companions the food I refrained from eating. They congratulated me on my safety and marveled at my story.

They seated me among them until they finished their work. Then they brought me some good food, which I ate, being hungry, and rested for a while. Then they took me and embarked with me in a ship and went to their island and their homes. There, they presented me to their king, and I saluted him, and he welcomed me, treated me with respect, and asked me about my case. I related to him all that had happened to me, from the day I left Baghdad until I came to him, and he, as well as all those present in his assembly, marveled greatly at my story. Then he asked me to sit and gave orders to bring the food, and I ate until I had enough, washed my hands, and offered thanks to the Almighty God and praised him for His favor. Then I left the presence of the king and went sightseeing in his city and found it flourishing, populous, and prosperous, abounding with food, markets, and buyers and sellers. I rejoiced in my arrival in that city and felt at ease there, as I made friends with its people who, together with their king, favored me and honored me more than even the chief men of that city.

I saw that all the men, great and small, rode fine horses, but without saddles, and wondered at that, so I said to the king, "My lord, why don't you ride on a saddle, for it offers the rider comfort and greater control?" He asked, "What kind of thing is a saddle, for I have never seen nor used one in all my life." I said to him, "Will you permit me to make you a saddle to ride on and experience its quality?" He said, "Very well." I said, "Let them fetch me some wood," and he gave orders to bring me everything I required. Then I asked for a skilled carpenter and sat with him and showed him the construction of the saddle and how to make it. Then I took some wool, carded it, and made a felt pad out of it. Then I brought leather and, covering the saddle with it, polished it and attached the straps and the girth. Afterward, I brought a blacksmith and showed him how to make the stirrups, and he forged a great pair of stirrups which I filed and plated with tin and to which I attached fringes of silk. Then I brought one of the best of the king's horses, saddled him, attaching the stirrups to the saddle; bridled him; and led him to the king, who was pleased by the saddle and received it with approval and thanks. He seated himself on the saddle and was greatly pleased with it and gave me a large reward for it.

When his vizier saw that I had made the saddle, he asked me for one, and I made one like it. Moreover, all the leading men and high officials began to order saddles, and I kept making them and selling them, having taught the carpenter and blacksmith how to make saddles and stirrups. Thus I amassed a great deal of money, and was highly esteemed and greatly loved, and I continued to enjoy a high status with the king and his entourage, as well as the leading men of the city and the lords of the state.

One day, I sat with the king, in the utmost happiness and honor, when he said to me, "You are honored and loved among us, and you have become one of us, and we cannot part from you, nor can we bear your departure from our city. I wish you to obey me in a certain matter, without contradicting me." I said to him, "What does your majesty desire of me, for I cannot deny you, since I am indebted to you for your favors, benefits, and kindness, and, praise be to God, I have become one of your servants." He said, "I wish to marry you among us to a lovely, elegant, and charming woman, a woman of beauty and wealth, and you shall reside with us and live with me in my palace. Therefore, do not deny me or argue with me." When I heard the king's words, I remained silent, for I was too embarrassed to say anything. He said, "Son, why don't you answer me?" I replied, "My lord and king of the age, the command is yours." So he immediately summoned the judge and the witnesses and married me to a fine lady of high rank, noble birth, great lineage, surpassing beauty, and abundant wealth, possessing a great many buildings and dwellings. Then he gave me a great, beautiful house, standing alone, and gave me servants and attendants, and assigned me stipends and supplies. So I lived in the utmost ease, contentment, and happiness and forgot all the weariness, trouble, and hardship I had suffered. I said to myself, "If I ever go back to my country, I will take her with me. But whatever is predestined to happen will happen, and no one knows what will befall him," for I loved her and she loved me very much, and we lived in harmony, enjoying great prosperity and happiness.

One day, God the Almighty caused the wife of my neighbor, who was one of my companions, to die, and I went to see him to offer my condolences for the loss of his wife and found him in a sorry plight, anxious, weary, and distracted. I offered my condolences and began to comfort him, saying, "Don't mourn for your wife. God the Almighty will compensate you with a better wife and will grant you a long life, if it be His will." He wept bitterly, saying, "O my friend, how will God compensate me with a better wife, when I have only one day to live?" I said, "Friend, be rational and do not prophecy your own death, for you are well and in good health." He said, "By your life, brother, tomorrow you will lose me and never in your life will you see me again." I asked, "How so?" He said, "Today, they will bury my wife and bury me with her in the tomb, for it is the custom of our country, when the wife dies, to bury the husband alive with her, and when the husband dies, to bury the wife alive with him, in order that neither of them may enjoy life after the other." I said to him, "By God, this is a most vile custom, and no one should endure it."

While we were conversing, most of the people of the city came, offered their condolences for the death of my friend's wife and his own death, and began to prepare her, according to their custom. They brought a coffin and, placing the woman in it, carried her and took her husband with them, outside the city, until they reached a place in the side of a mountain by the sea. They advanced to a spot

328 The Arabian Nights

and lifted from it a large stone, revealing a stone-lined well. They threw the woman down into that well, which seemed to lead into a vast cavern beneath the mountain. Then they brought the husband and, tying a rope of palm fibers under his armpits, let him down the well, with a jug of sweet water and seven loaves of bread. When he was down, he undid the rope, and they drew it up, covered the mouth of the well with that large stone as it was before, and went on their way, leaving my friend with his wife in the cavern.

I said to myself, "By God, this death is worse than the first." Then I went to the king and said to him, "O my lord, why do you bury the living with the dead in your country?" He replied, "It is the custom of our country, when the husband dies, to bury his wife alive with him, and when the wife dies, to bury her husband alive with her, so that they may always be together, in life and in death. This custom we have received from our forefathers." I asked him, "O king of the age, will you do to a foreigner like me as you have done to that man, if his wife dies?" He replied, "Yes, we bury him and do to him as you have seen." When I heard his words, I was galled, dismayed, stricken with grief for myself, and dazed with fear that my wife might die before me and they bury me alive with her. Then I tried to divert my mind, by keeping busy, and to console myself, thinking, "Maybe I will die before her, for no one knows who will go first and who will follow."

But a short time later, my wife fell ill, and a few days later died. Most of the people of the city came to offer their condolences for her death to me and to her relatives. The king too came to offer his condolences, as was their custom. Then they brought a woman to wash her, and they washed her and arrayed her in her richest clothes and gold ornaments, necklaces, and jewels. Then they put her in the coffin and carried her to the side of the mountain and, removing the stone from the mouth of the well, they threw her in. Then all my friends and my wife's relatives turned to me to bid me the last farewell, while I was crying out among them, "I am a foreigner, and I cannot endure your custom." They did not pay any attention to my words, but, seizing me, they bound me by force and let me down the well into the large cavern beneath the mountain, with seven loaves of bread and a jug of sweet water, as was their custom. Then they said to me, "Untie yourself from the ropes," but I refused, and they threw the ropes down on me, covered the opening of the well, and departed.

I saw in that cavern many dead bodies that exhaled a putrid and loathsome smell, and I blamed myself for what I had done, saying to myself, "By God, I deserve everything that has happened to me." I could not distinguish night from day, and I sustained myself with very little food, not eating until I felt the pangs of hunger, nor drinking until I became extremely thirsty, fearing that my food and water would be exhausted. I said to myself, "There is no power and no strength, save in God the Almighty, the Magnificent. What possessed me to marry in this city? Every time I say to myself that I have escaped one calamity, I fall into a worse one. By God, this death is a vile death. I wish that I had drowned in the sea or died on the mountain; that would have been better than this horrible death." And I continued to blame myself. Then I threw myself down on the bones of the dead, begging, in the extremity of my despair, the Almighty God for a speedy death, but found it not, and I continued in this state until my stomach was lacerated by hunger, and my throat was inflamed with thirst. So I sat up and, groping for the bread, ate a little morsel and drank a mouthful of water. Then I stood up and began to explore that cavern. I found that it was wide and empty, except that its floor was covered with dead bodies and rotten bones from long ago. I made myself a place in the side of the cavern, far from the fresh bodies, and went to sleep there. Eventually my provisions dwindled until I had only a very little left. During each day, or more than a day, I had eaten only a morsel and drunk only a mouthful, fearing that the food and water would run out before my death.

I remained in this situation until one day, while I sat wondering what I would do when I ran out of food and water, the rock was suddenly removed from its place, and the light beamed on me. I said to myself, "I wonder what is happening," and saw people standing at the opening of the well who let down a dead man and a living woman, weeping and wailing for herself, and they let down with her food and water. I kept staring at the woman, without being seen by her, while they covered the mouth of the well with the stones and went on their way. Then I took the shinbone of a dead man and, going to the woman, struck her on the crown of the head, and she fell down unconscious. I struck her a second and a third time until she died. She had on her plenty of apparel, ornaments, necklaces, jewels, and precious metals, and I took all she had, together with the bread and water, and sat in the place I had made for myself in the side of the cavern where I used to sleep, and continued to eat only a little of that food, just enough to sustain me, for fear that it would be exhausted quickly and I would die of hunger and thirst.

I remained in the cavern for some time, and whenever they buried a dead person, I killed the living one who was buried with him and took his food and water to sustain myself until one day I woke up from my sleep and heard something rummaging in the side of the cavern. I said to myself, "What can it be?" Then I got up and, with a shinbone in my hand, I walked toward the noise and found out that it was a wild beast which, when it became aware of me, ran away and fled from me. I followed it to the far end of the cavern and saw a spot of light, like a star, now appearing, now disappearing. When I saw it, I walked toward it, and the closer I got to it, the larger and brighter it

became until I was certain that it was an opening in the cavern leading to the open air. I said to myself, "There must be an explanation
for this. Either it is a second opening, like the one from which they
let me down, or it is a fissure in the rock." I stood reflecting for a
while; then I advanced toward the light and found that it was a hole
in the side of the mountain which the wild beasts had made and
through which they entered the cavern and ate of the dead bodies
until they had their fill and went out as they came.

When I saw the hole, I felt relieved from my anxiety and worry,
certain of life, after having been on the verge of death, and as happy
as if I had been in a dream. Then I tried until I succeeded to climb
out of the hole, finding myself on the side of a great mountain overlooking the sea and acting as a barrier between the sea, on the one
side, and the island and the city, on the other, so that none could
come to that part from the city. I praised and thanked the Almighty
God, feeling extremely happy and regaining my courage. Then I
returned through the hole to the cavern and brought out all the food
and water I had saved. Then I changed my clothes, putting on some
of the clothes of the dead, and gathered a great many of all kinds of
necklaces of pearls and precious stones, ornaments of gold and silver set with gems, and other valuables I found on the corpses and,
using the clothes of the dead to pack the jewelry in bundles, carried
them out through the hole to the side of the mountain and stood on
the seashore.

Every day I went into the cavern and explored it, and whenever
they buried someone alive, I killed him, whether he was male or
female, took his food and water and, coming out of the cavern, sat
on the seashore to wait for deliverance by the Almighty God, by
means of a passing ship. For some time, I kept gathering all the jewelry I could find, tying it up in bundles in the clothes of the dead,
and carrying it out of the cavern.

One day, as I was sitting on the seashore, thinking about my situation, I saw a ship passing in the middle of a roaring, surging sea.
I took a white shirt that I had taken from one of the dead, tied it to
a stick, and ran along the seashore, making with it signals to the
people on the ship, until, happening to glance in my direction, they
saw me and turned toward me, and when they heard my cries, they
sent a boat with a group of men. When they came close to me,
they said, "Who are you, and why are you sitting in this place, and
how did you reach this mountain, for in all our lives we have never
known anyone who has reached it?" I said, "I am a merchant, who
had been shipwrecked, and I saved myself by getting on a wooden
plank, together with my belongings, and, with God's help and by my
own exertions, skill, and great toil, I landed at this place, with my
belongings." They took me with them in the boat, carrying all I had

taken from the cavern, bundled in the clothes and shrouds of the dead, embarked in the ship, and took me with all my belongings to the captain.

The captain said to me, "Fellow, how did you reach this great mountain, which bars the shore from the great city behind it, for I have been sailing in this sea and passing by this mountain all my life, but I have never seen anyone here, except the birds and the wild beasts?" I replied, "I was a merchant on a large ship that was wrecked, and I was thrown into the sea with all my merchandise, which consisted of the fabrics and clothes that you see. But I placed them on one of the wide wooden planks of the ship, and fate and fortune aided me, and I landed on the mountain, where I have been waiting for someone to pass by and take me with him." I did not tell them, however, about what had happened to me in the city or in the cavern, for fear that they might have with them on the ship someone from that city. Then I took out a good portion of my property and presented it to the captain, saying, "Sir, you are the cause of my rescue from this mountain. Take this gift in gratitude for what you have done." But he refused my gift, saying, "We take nothing from anyone, and when we see a shipwrecked man on the seashore or on an island, we take him with us, feed him and give him to drink, and if he is naked, clothe him, and, when we reach a safe harbor treat him with kindness and charity and give him a present, for the sake of the Almighty God." When I heard his words, I offered prayers, wishing him a long life.

We sailed from sea to sea and from island to island, while I anticipated my deliverance and rejoiced in my safety, but every time I recalled my stay with my dead wife in that cavern, I almost lost my mind. At last, with the help of the Almighty God, we arrived safely in Basra, where I stayed for a few days, then headed for Baghdad. There, I came to my quarter, entered my house, and met my relatives and friends, inquiring about their condition, and they rejoiced and congratulated me on my safe return. Then I stored all I had brought with me in my storerooms, gave alms and clothed the widows and the orphans, and bestowed gifts. I felt extremely joyful and happy and returned to my former habit of associating with friends and companions and indulging in sport and pleasure. These, then, are the most extraordinary events of my fourth voyage. Dine with me now, brother, and come back tomorrow, as usual, and I will tell you the story of what happened to me on the fifth voyage, for it is more extraordinary and more wonderful than the preceding one.

THEN SINDBAD the Sailor gave the porter a hundred pieces of gold and ordered that the table be spread, and after the guests dined, they went their way, in great amazement, for each story was more extraordinary than the preceding one. Sindbad the Porter went to his house, where he spent the night in the utmost joy, happiness, and wonder. As soon as it was daylight, he got up, performed his morning prayer, and walked until he came to Sindbad the Sailor. He walked in, wished him good morning, and Sindbad welcomed him and asked him to sit with him until the rest of his companions arrived. They ate and drank, enjoyed themselves, and felt merry, and when they turned to conversation, Sindbad the Sailor began his story saying:

The Fifth Voyage of Sindbad

FRIENDS, WHEN I returned from the fourth voyage, I indulged in sport, pleasure, and delight, rejoicing greatly in my gains, profits, and benefits, and forgot all I had experienced and suffered until I began to think again of traveling to see foreign countries and islands. Having made my resolve, I bought valuable merchandise suited to a sea voyage, packed up my bales, and journeyed from Baghdad to Basra. I walked along the shore and saw a large, tall, and goodly ship, newly fitted. It pleased me and I bought it. Then I hired a captain and crew, over whom I set some of my slaves and pages as superintendents, and loaded my bales on the ship. Then a group of merchants joined me, loaded their bales on the ship, and paid me the freight. We set out in all joy and cheerfulness, rejoicing in the prospect of a safe and prosperous voyage, and sailed from sea to sea and from island to island, landing to see the sights of the islands and towns and to sell and buy.

We continued in this fashion until one day we came to a large uninhabited island, waste and desolate, except for a vast white dome. The merchants landed to look at the dome, which was in reality a huge Rukh's egg, but, not knowing what it was, they struck it with stones, and when they broke it, much fluid ran out of it, and the young Rukh appeared inside. They drew it out of the shell, slaughtered it, and took from it a great deal of meat. While this was going on, I was on the ship, uninformed and unaware of it until one of the passengers came to me and said, "Sir, go and look at that egg, which we thought to be a dome." I went to look at the egg and arrived just when the merchants were striking it. I cried out to them, "Don't do this, for the Rukh will come, demolish our ship, and destroy us all." But they did not heed my words.

While they were thus engaged, the sun suddenly disappeared, and the day grew dark, as if a dark cloud was passing above us. We raised our heads to see what had veiled the sun and saw that it was the Rukh's wings that had blocked the sunlight and made the day dark, for when the Rukh came and saw its egg broken, it cried out at us, and its mate came, and they circled above the ship, shrieking with voices louder than thunder. I called out to the captain and the sailors, saying, "Push off the ship, and let us escape before we perish." The captain hurried and, as soon as the merchants embarked, unfastened the ship and sailed away from the island. When the Rukhs saw that we were on the open sea, they disappeared for a while.

We sailed, making speed, in the desire to leave their land behind and escape from them, but suddenly they caught up with us, each carrying in its talons a huge rock from a mountain. Then the male bird threw its rock on us, but the captain steered the ship aside, and the rock missed it by a little distance, and fell into the water with such force that we saw the bottom of the sea, and the ship went up and down, almost out of control. Then the female bird threw on us its rock, which was smaller than the first, but as it had been ordained, it fell on the stern of the ship, smashed it, sent the rudder flying in twenty pieces, and threw all the passengers into the sea.

I struggled for dear life to save myself until the Almighty God provided me with one of the wooden planks of the ship, to which I clung and, getting on it, began to paddle with my feet, while the wind and the waves helped me forward. The ship had sunk near an island in the middle of the sea, and fate cast me, according to God's will, on that island, where I landed, like a dead man, on my last breath from extreme hardship and fatigue and hunger and thirst. I threw myself on the seashore and lay for a while until I began to recover myself and feel better. Then I walked in the island and found that it was like one of the gardens of Paradise. Its trees were laden with fruits, its streams flowing, and its birds singing the glory of the Omnipotent, Everlasting One. There was an abundance of trees, fruits, and all kinds of flowers. So I ate of the fruits until I satisfied my hunger and drank of the streams until I quenched my thirst, and I thanked the Almighty God and praised Him.

I sat in the island until it was evening, and night approached, without seeing anyone or hearing any voice. I was still feeling almost dead from fatigue and fear; so I lay down and slept till the morning. Then I got up and walked among the trees until I came to a spring of running water, beside which sat a comely old man clad with a waistcloth made of tree leaves. I said to myself, "Perhaps the old man has landed on the island, being one of those who have been shipwrecked." I drew near him and saluted him, and he returned my salutation with a sign but remained silent. I said to him, "Old man, why are you sitting here?" He moved his head mournfully and motioned with his hand, meaning to say, "Carry me on your shoulders, and take me to the other side of the stream." I said to myself, "I will do this old man a favor and transport him to the other side of the stream, for God may reward me for it." I went to him, carried him on my shoulders, and took him to the place to which he had pointed. I said to him, "Get down at your ease," but he did not get off my shoulders. Instead, he wrapped his legs around my neck, and when I saw that their hide was

as black and rough as that of a buffalo, I was frightened and tried to
throw him off. But he pressed his legs around my neck and choked
my throat until I blacked out and fell unconscious to the ground, like
a dead man. He raised his legs and beat me on the back and shoulders, causing me intense pain. I got up, feeling tired from the burden,
and he kept riding on my shoulders and motioning me with his hand
to take him among the trees to the best of the fruits, and whenever
I disobeyed him, he gave me, with his feet, blows more painful than
the blows of the whip. He continued to direct me with his hand to
any place he wished to go, and I continued to take him to it until we
made our way among the trees to the middle of the island. Whenever
I loitered or went leisurely, he beat me, for he held me like a captive.
He never got off my shoulders, day or night, urinating and defecating
on me, and whenever he wished to sleep, he would wrap his legs
around my neck and sleep a little, then arise and beat me, and I
would get up quickly, unable to disobey him because of the severity of
the pain I suffered from him. I continued with him in this condition,
suffering from extreme exhaustion and blaming myself for having
taken pity on him and carried him on my shoulders. I said to myself,
"I have done this person a good deed, and it has turned evil to myself.
By God, I will never do good to anyone, as long as I live," and I began
to beg, at every turn and every step, the Almighty God for death,
because of the severity of my fatigue and distress.

I continued in this situation for some time until one day I came
with him to a place in the island where there was an abundance of
gourds, many of which were dry. I selected one that was large and
dry, cut it at the neck and cleansed it. Then I went with it to a
grapevine and filled it with the juice of the grapes. Then I plugged
the gourd, placed it in the sun, and left it there several days until the
juice turned into wine, from which I began to drink every day in
order to find some relief from the exhausting burden of that obsti-
nate devil, for I felt invigorated whenever I was intoxicated.

One day he saw me drinking and signed to me with his hand,
meaning to say, "What is this?" I said to him, "This is an excellent
drink that invigorates and delights." Then I ran with him and danced
among the trees, clapping my hands and singing and enjoying
myself, in the exhilaration of intoxication. When he saw me in
that state, he motioned to me to give him the gourd, in order that
he might drink from it. Being afraid of him, I gave it to him, and he
drank all that was in it and threw it to the ground. Then he became
enraptured and began to shake on my shoulders, and as he became
extremely intoxicated and sank into torpor, all his limbs and muscles
relaxed, and he began to sway back and forth on my shoulders.
When I realized that he was drunk and that he was unconscious, I
held his feet and loosened them from my neck and, stooping with

him, I sat down and threw him to the ground, hardly believing that I had delivered myself from him. But, fearing that he might recover from his drunkenness and harm me, I took a huge stone from among the trees, came to him, struck him on the head as he lay asleep, mingling his flesh with his blood, and killed him. May God have no mercy on him!

Then I walked in the island, feeling relieved, until I came back to the spot on the seashore where I had been before. I remained there for some time, eating of the fruits of the island and drinking of its water and waiting for a ship to pass by, until one day, as I sat thinking about what had happened to me and reflecting on my situation, saying to myself, "I wonder whether God will preserve me and I will return to my country and be reunited with my relatives and friends," a ship suddenly approached from the middle of the roaring, raging sea and continued until it set anchor at the island, and its passengers landed. I walked toward them, and when they saw me, they all quickly hurried to me and gathered around me, inquiring about my situation and the reason for my coming to that island. I told them about my situation and what had happened to me, and they were amazed and said, "The man who rode on your shoulders is called the Old Man of the Sea, and no one was ever beneath his limbs and escaped safely, except yourself. God be praised for your safety." Then they brought me some food, and I ate until I had enough, and they gave me some clothes, which I wore to make myself decent. Then they took me with them in the ship, and we journeyed many days and nights until fate drove us to a city of tall buildings, all of which overlooked the sea. This city is called the City of the Apes, and when night comes, the inhabitants come out of the gates overlooking the sea and, embarking in boats and ships, spend the night there, for fear that the apes may descend on them from the mountains.

I landed, and while I was enjoying the sights of the city, the ship sailed, without my knowledge. I regretted having disembarked in that city, remembering my companions and what had happened to us with the apes the first and the second time, and I sat down, weeping and mourning. Then one of the inhabitants came to me and said, "Sir, you seem to be a stranger in this place." I replied, "Yes, I am a poor stranger. I was in a ship that anchored here, and I landed to see the sights of the city, and when I went back, I could not find the ship." He said, "Come with us and get into the boat, for if you spend the night here, the apes will destroy you." I said, "I hear and obey," and I got up immediately and embarked with them in the boat, and they pushed it off from the shore until we were a mile away. We spent the night in the boat, and when it was morning, they returned to the city, landed, and each of them went to his business. Such has been their habit every night, and whoever remains behind in the city

at night, the apes come and destroy him. During the day, the apes go
outside the city and eat of the fruits in the orchards and sleep in the
mountains until the evening, at which time they return to the city.

This city is located in the farthest parts of the land of the blacks.
One of the strangest things I experienced in the inhabitants' treatment of me was as follows. One of those with whom I spent the night
in the boat said to me, "Sir, you are a stranger here. Do you have any
craft you can work at?" I replied, "No, by God, my friend, I have no
trade and no handicraft, for I was a merchant, a man of property and
wealth, and I owned a ship laden with abundant goods, but it was
wrecked in the sea, and everything in it sank. I escaped from drowning only by the grace of God, for He provided me with a plank of
wood on which I floated and saved myself." When he heard my
words, he got up and brought me a cotton bag and said, "Take this
bag, fill it with pebbles from the shore, and go with a group of the
inhabitants, whom I will help you join and to whom I will commend
you, and do as they do, and perhaps you will gain what will help you
to return to your country."

Then he took me with him until we came outside the city, where I
picked small pebbles until the bag was filled. Soon a group of men
emerged from the city, and he put me in their charge and commended me to them, saying, "This man is a stranger. Take him with
you and teach him how to pick, so that he may gain his living and
God may reward you." They said, "We hear and obey," and they welcomed me and took me with them, and proceeded, each carrying a
cotton bag like mine, filled with pebbles. We walked until we came
to a spacious valley, full of trees so tall that no one could climb
them. The valley was also full of apes, which, when they saw us, fled
and climbed up into the trees. The men began to pelt the apes with
the pebbles from the bags, and the apes began to pluck the fruits of
those trees and to throw them at the men, and as I looked at the
fruits the apes were throwing, I found that they were coconuts.

When I saw what the men were doing, I chose a huge tree full of
apes and, advancing to it, began to pelt them, while they plucked the
nuts and threw them at me. I began to collect the nuts as the men
did, and before my bag was empty of pebbles I had collected plenty
of nuts. When the men finished the work, they gathered together all
the nuts, and each of them carried as many as he could, and we
returned to the city, arriving before the end of the day. Then I went
to my friend, who had helped me join the group, and gave him all the
nuts I had gathered, thanking him for his kindness, but he said to
me, "Take the nuts, sell them, and use the money." Then he gave me
a key to a room in his house, saying, "Keep there whatever is left of
the nuts, and go out every day with the men, as you did today, and of
what you bring with you separate the bad and sell them, and use the

money, but keep the best in that room, so that you may gather enough to help you with your voyage." I said to him, "May the Almighty God reward you," and did as he told me, going out daily to gather pebbles, join the men, and do as they did, while they commended me to each other and guided me to the trees bearing the most nuts. I continued in this manner for some time, during which I gathered a great store of excellent coconuts and sold a great many, making a good deal of money, with which I bought whatever I saw and liked. So I thrived and felt happy in that city.

One day, as I was standing on the seashore, a ship arrived, cast anchor, and landed a group of merchants, who proceeded to sell and buy and exchange goods for coconuts and other commodities. I went to my friend and told him about the ship that had arrived and said that I would like to return to my country. He said, "It is for you to decide." So I thanked him for his kindness and bade him farewell. Then I went to the ship, met the captain, and, booking a passage, loaded my store of coconuts on the ship. We set out and continued to sail from sea to sea and from island to island, and at every island we landed, I sold and traded with coconuts until God compensated me with more than I had possessed before and lost.

Among other places we visited, we came to an island abounding in cinnamon and pepper. Some people told us that they had seen on every cluster of peppers a large leaf that shades it and protects it from the rain, and when the rain stops, the leaf flips over and assumes its place at its side. From that island I took with me a large quantity of pepper and cinnamon, in exchange for coconuts. Then we passed by the Island of the 'Usrat, from which comes the Comorin aloewood, and by another island, which is a five-day journey in length and from which comes the Chinese aloewood, which is superior to the Comorin. But the inhabitants of this island are inferior to those of the first, both in their religion and in their way of life, for they are given to lewdness and wine drinking and know no prayer nor the call to prayer. Then we came to the island of the pearl fishers, where I gave the divers some coconuts and asked them to dive, and try my luck for me. They dived in the bay and brought up a great number of large and valuable pearls, saying, "O master, by God, you are very lucky," and I took everything they brought up with me to the ship.

Then we sailed until we reached Basra, where I stayed for a few days, then headed for Baghdad. I came to my quarter, entered my house, and saluted my relatives and friends, and they congratulated me on my safety. Then I stored all the goods and gear I had brought with me, clothed the widows and the orphans, gave alms, and bestowed gifts on my relatives, friends, and all those dear to me. God had given me fourfold what I had lost, and because of my gains and the great profit I had made, I forgot what had happened to me and

the toil I had suffered, and resumed my association with my friends
and companions. These then are the most extraordinary events of
my fifth voyage. Let us have supper now, and tomorrow, come, and I
will tell you the story of my sixth voyage, for it is more wonderful
than this.

THEY SPREAD the table, and the guests dined, and when they finished Sindbad gave the porter a hundred pieces of gold, which he
took and went on his way, marveling at what he had heard. He spent
the night in his house, and as soon as it was morning, he got up, performed his morning prayer, and went to the house of Sindbad the
Sailor. He went in and wished him good morning and Sindbad the
Sailor asked him to sit and talked to him until the rest of his friends
arrived. They talked for a while, then the table was spread, and they
ate and drank and enjoyed themselves and felt merry. Then Sindbad
the Sailor began the story of the sixth voyage, saying:

The Sixth Voyage of Sindbad

DEAR FRIENDS, AFTER I returned from my fifth voyage, I forgot
what I had suffered, indulging in sport, play, and merriment and
leading a life of the utmost joy and happiness until one day a group
of merchants came by, showing signs of travel. Their sight reminded
me of the days of my return from my travel and my joy at seeing my
country again and reuniting with my relatives and friends and dear
ones. So I felt a longing for travel and trade, and I resolved to undertake another voyage. I bought valuable, rich merchandise suited to a
sea voyage, packed it up in bales, and traveled from Baghdad to
Basra. There, I found a large ship, full of prominent people and merchants with valuable goods, and I loaded my bales in the ship, and
we departed from Basra peacefully.

We sailed from place to place and from city to city, selling and buying, seeing the sights of the different countries and enjoying our
voyage and our good luck and profit. We continued in this way until
one day the captain suddenly cried out, screaming, threw down his
turban, slapped his face, plucked his beard, and fell down in the hold
of the ship, in extreme anguish and grief. All the merchants and other
passengers gathered around him and asked, "Captain, what is the
matter?" He said, "We have strayed from our course and entered a
sea of which we don't know the routes. If God does not provide us
with a means of escape from this sea, we will all perish. Pray to the
Almighty God to save us from this predicament." Then he climbed
the mast, in order to loosen the sails, but a strong wind blew against
the ship, driving it backward, and the rudder broke, near a high
mountain. The captain came down from the mast and said, "There is
no power and no strength save in God the Almighty, the Magnificent,

and no one can prevent that which has been decreed. By God, we have fallen into a great peril, from which there is no escape." The passengers wept for themselves and bade each other farewell, having given themselves up for lost. Soon the ship veered toward the mountain and smashed against it, so that its planks scattered, and all that was in it sank into the sea. The merchants fell into the sea, and some of them drowned, while others held onto the mountain and landed on it. I was among those who landed.

That mountain was on a large island whose shores were strewn with wrecked ships and an abundance of goods, gear, and wealth that dazzled the mind, cast there by the sea from the ships that had been destroyed and whose passengers had drowned. I climbed to the upper part of the island, began to explore, and saw a stream of sweet water that issued from one side of the mountain and entered from the other. Then all the other passengers climbed to the upper part and wandered in the island, like madmen, for their minds were confounded by the profusion of goods and wealth they saw strewn on the shores.

I saw in that stream a great many rubies and royal pearls and all kinds of jewels and precious stones, which covered the bed of the stream like gravel, so that all the channels, which ran through the fields, glittered from their profusion. I saw also in that island an abundance of the best Chinese as well as Comorin aloewood. Moreover, in that island there is a gushing spring of some sort of crude ambergris, which flows like wax under the intense heat of the sun, and flows in a stream down to the seashore, where the sea beasts come up, swallow it, and return with it into the sea. When it gets hot in their stomachs, they eject it from their mouths into the water, and it rises to the surface, where it congeals and changes its color. Then the waves throw it on the shore, and the travelers and merchants who know it take it and sell it. As for the crude ambergris that is not swallowed, it flows over the side of that spring and congeals on the ground. When the sun rises, it flows, and its scent fills the whole valley with a musk-like fragrance, and when the sun sets, it congeals again. But that place where the ambergris is found, no one can reach, for the mountains surround the whole island, and no one can climb them.

We continued to wander in that island, marveling at the riches that the Almighty God had created there, but feeling perplexed in our predicament and sorely afraid. We had collected on the shore of the island a small amount of food, which we used sparingly, eating only every day or two, worried that the food would run out and we would die of starvation and fear. Whenever one of us died, we washed him, wrapped him in a shroud from the clothes cast on the shore by the sea, and buried him until most of us had died, except for a few who were weakened by a stomach ailment contracted from the sea. It was not long before all my friends and companions died, one by one.

I was left all alone in the island, with very little food. I wept for
myself, thinking, "I wish that I had died before my companions, for
they would have at least washed me and buried me. There is no
power and no strength save in God the Almighty, the Magnificent." A
little while later, I arose and dug for myself a deep hole on the shore,
saying to myself, "When I grow weak and feel that I am about to die,
I will lie in this grave and die in it, and the wind will blow the sand
on me and cover me, and I will have my burial." I blamed myself for
my lack of sense in leaving my country and city and traveling to foreign countries, after all I had suffered during the first, the second,
the third, the fourth, and the fifth voyages, each marked by greater
perils and horrors than the preceding one, each time hardly believing in my narrow escape. And I repented and renounced the sea and
all travel in the sea, especially since I had no need of money, of
which I had enough and, indeed, so much more that I could not
spend or exhaust even half of it for the rest of my life.

After a while, however, I reflected and said to myself, "By God, the
stream must have a beginning and an end, and it must lead to an
inhabited part. The best plan will be to make a little raft, big enough
to sit in, take it down, launch it on the stream, and drift with the
current. If I find a way out, I will escape safely, the Almighty God
permitting, and if I don't, it is better to die in the stream than in this
place," and I sighed for myself.

Then I got up and proceeded to gather pieces of Comorin and
Chinese aloewood from the island and tied them together on the
shore with the ropes of wrecked ships. Then I took from the ships
planks of even size and fixed them firmly on the wood. In this way, I
made me a raft, which was a little narrower in width than the width
of the stream. Then I attached a piece of wood on each side, to serve
as oars, and launched it on the stream. Then I took some of the
jewels, precious stones, and pearls that were as large as gravel and
some of the best crude, pure ambergris, as well as other goods,
together with whatever was left of the food, loaded everything on the
raft, and did what the poet said:

> If you suffer injustice, save yourself
> And leave the house behind to mourn its builder.
> Your country you'll replace by another,
> But for yourself, you'll find no other self.
> Nor be too fretful at the blows of fate,
> For every misfortune begins and ends,
> And he who in a certain place his death impends,
> Will in no other place suffer that fate.
> Nor for your mission trust another man,
> For none is as loyal as you yourself.

I drifted with the stream, wondering what would happen to me, until I came to the place where the stream entered beneath the mountain and took the raft with it. I found myself in intense darkness, and the raft bore me with the current through a narrow tunnel beneath the mountain, and the sides of the raft began to rub against the sides of the tunnel, and my head began to rub against the roof. I was unable to go back, and I blamed myself for what I had done to myself and said, "If this tunnel becomes any narrower, the raft will not pass through, and since it cannot go back, I will inevitably perish miserably here." I prostrated myself on the raft, because of the narrowness of the channel, and continued to drift, not knowing night from day, because of the darkness beneath the mountain, and feeling concerned for myself and terrified that I might perish. In this condition, I continued my course along the stream, which sometimes widened and sometimes narrowed, until the intensity of the darkness and distress wearied me, and I fell asleep as I lay prostrate on the raft, which drifted, while I slept in utter oblivion.

When I awoke and opened my eyes, I found myself in the light, in the open air, and found the raft moored to an island, in the middle of a group of Indians and blacks. As soon as they saw me rise, they approached me and spoke to me in their language, but I did not understand what they said and kept thinking that I was still asleep and that this was a dream occasioned by my grief and distress. When they spoke to me, and I did not reply, not knowing their language, one of them came to me and said in Arabic, "Peace be on you, friend! Who are you, from where do you come, and what is the reason for your coming here? We are the owners of these lands and fields, which we came to irrigate, and we found you asleep on the raft. So we held it and moored it here, waiting for you to rise at your leisure. Tell us what is the reason for your coming here?" I said, "For God's sake, sir, bring me some food, for I am hungry. After that ask me what you wish." He hastened and brought me food, and I ate my fill until I felt satisfied and relaxed, and my spirit revived. I praised the Almighty God and rejoiced in my escape from that stream and in my finding them. Then I told them my story from beginning to end and how I had suffered from the narrowness of that stream.

They talked among themselves, saying, "We must take him with us and present him to our king, so that he may tell him his story." Then they took me, together with the raft and all that was on it of goods, jewels, precious stones, and gold ornaments, presented me to their king, and acquainted him with what had happened. He saluted me, welcomed me, and inquired about my condition and what I had experienced. I told him my story from beginning to end, at which he marveled exceedingly and congratulated me on my safety. Then I fetched from the raft a large quantity of jewels, precious stones, ambergris, and aloewood and presented them to the king, who accepted them, treated me very courteously, and gave me a lodging in his palace, where I stayed permanently. I associated with the best and most prominent people, who treated me with great respect. The visitors to that island came to me and questioned me about the affairs of my country, and I told them, and I, in turn, questioned them and was informed about the affairs in their own countries. One day the king himself questioned me about the conditions in my country and the way the caliph governs in Baghdad, and I told him about the caliph's just rule. The king marveled at that and said, "By God, the caliph's methods are wise and his ways praiseworthy, and you have made me love him. Therefore, I would like to prepare a present and send it with you to him." I said, "I hear and obey, my lord. I will convey the present to him and inform him that you are his sincere friend."

I continued to live with the king in great honor, consideration, and contentment for some time until one day, sitting in the king's palace, I heard that a group of people from the city had prepared for themselves a ship, with the intention of sailing to the environs of Basra. I said to myself, "I cannot do better than to travel with these people." I arose at once and, kissing the king's hand, informed him of my wish to travel with that group in the ship they had prepared, for I longed for my country and my family. The king said, "The decision is yours, yet if you wish to stay with us, we will be very glad, for we have enjoyed your company." I said, "By God, my lord, you have overwhelmed me with your kindness and your favors, but I long for my country and my family and friends." When he heard my reply, he summoned the merchants who had prepared the ship, commended me to them, paid my fare, and bestowed on me a great many gifts. He also entrusted me with a magnificent gift for the Caliph Harun al-Rashid in Baghdad. Then I bade the king, as well as my frequent companions, farewell and embarked with the merchants in the ship.

We sailed with a fair wind, committing ourselves to the care of the Almighty and Glorious God, and continued to travel from sea to sea and from island to island until, with the permission of the Almighty God, we reached Basra safely. I disembarked and spent a few days there to equip myself and pack up my goods. Then I headed for Baghdad, the Abode of Peace, and went to the Caliph Harun al-Rashid and conveyed the king's gift to him. Then I came to my quarter, entered my house, and stored my goods and gear. Soon my relatives and friends came to see me, and I bestowed gifts on all, and gave alms.

A little while later, the caliph summoned me and asked me the reason for the gift and from where it came. I said, "By God, O Commander of the Faithful, I do not know the name of the city from which this gift came, nor do I know the way to it. When the ship I was in was wrecked, I landed on an island, where I made me a raft and launched it on a stream in the middle of that island." Then I related to him what had happened to me on my journey and how I had escaped from the stream and reached that city safely. I also related to him what had happened to me in that city and explained the reason for the gift. The caliph marveled exceedingly, and he ordered the historians to record my story and deposit it in his library, so that whoever reads it might be edified by it, and he treated me very generously.

I resumed my former way of life in Baghdad and forgot all that I had experienced and suffered, living a life of sport, play, and pleasure. This, then, friends, is the story of my sixth voyage. Tomorrow, God the Almighty willing, I will tell you the story of my seventh voyage, for it is stranger and more wonderful than all the others.

SINDBAD ORDERED THAT the table be spread, and the guests dined with him. Then Sindbad the Sailor gave Sindbad the Porter a hundred pieces of gold, and the porter took the money and went on his way, as did the rest of the company, all marveling exceedingly at that story. Sindbad the Porter spent the night at his house, and as soon as he performed his morning prayer, he went to the house of Sindbad the Sailor. Then the rest of the group began to arrive, and when they were all assembled, Sindbad the Sailor began to tell them the story of his seventh voyage, saying,

The Seventh Voyage of Sindbad

FELLOWS, AFTER I returned from my sixth voyage, I resumed my former way of life and continued to lead a life of contentment and happiness, indulging day and night in play, diversion, and pleasure, having secured great gains and profits, until I began to long again to sail the seas, associate with fellow merchants, see foreign countries, and hear new things. I made my resolve and, packing up a quantity of precious goods suited to a sea voyage, carried them from Baghdad to Basra, where I found a ship ready to set sail, with a group of prominent merchants. I embarked with them, and we became friends, as we sailed with a fair wind in peace and good health until we passed by a city called the City of China, and while we were in the utmost joy and happiness, talking among ourselves about travel and commerce, a violent head wind blew suddenly, and a heavy rain began to fall on us until we and our bales were drenched. So we covered the bales with felt and canvas, fearing that the goods would be spoiled by the rain, and began to pray and implore God the Almighty to deliver us from the peril we were in. Then the captain, girding his waist and tucking up his clothes, climbed up the mast and began to look to the right and left. Then he looked at the people in the ship and began to slap his face and pluck his beard. We asked him, "Captain, what is the matter?" And he said, "Implore the Almighty God for deliverance from the peril we are in, and weep for yourselves and bid each other farewell, for the wind has prevailed against us and driven us into the farthest of the seas of the world." He then descended from the mast, opened a chest, and took out of it a cotton bag. Then he untied the bag, took out of it some dust, like ashes, wetted it with water, and, waiting a little, smelled it. Then he took out of the chest a small book and began to read in it. Then he said to us, "Passengers, in this book there is an amazing statement that whoever comes to this place will never leave it safely and will surely perish, for this region is called the Province of the Kings, and in it is the tomb of our Lord Solomon, the son of David (peace be on him), and there are huge, horrible-looking whales, and whenever a ship enters this region, one of them rises from the sea and swallows it with everything in it."

When we heard the captain's explanation, we were dumbfounded, and hardly had he finished his words when the ship suddenly began to rise out of the water and drop again, and we heard a great cry, like a peel of thunder, at which we were struck almost dead with terror, sure of our destruction. Suddenly we saw a whale heading for the boat, like a towering mountain, and we were terrified and wept bitterly for ourselves and prepared for death. We kept looking at that whale, marveling at its terrible shape, when suddenly another whale, the most huge and most terrible we had ever seen, approached us, and while we bade each other farewell and wept for ourselves, a third whale, even greater than the other two, approached, and we were stupefied and driven mad with terror. Then the three whales began to circle the ship, and the third whale lunged at the ship to swallow it, when suddenly a violent gust of wind blew, and the ship rose and fell on a massive reef, breaking in pieces, and all the merchants and the other passengers and the bales sank in the sea.

I took off all my clothes, except for a shirt, and swam until I caught a plank of wood from the ship and hung on to it. Then I got on it and held on to it, while the wind and the waves toyed with me on the surface of the water, carrying me up and down. I was in the worst of plights, with fear and distress and hunger and thirst. I blamed myself for what I had done and for incurring more hardships, after a life of ease, and said to myself, "O Sindbad the Sailor, you don't learn, for every time you suffer hardships and weariness, yet you don't repent and renounce travel in the sea, and when you renounce, you lie to yourself. I deserve my plight, which had been decreed by God the Almighty to cure me of my greed, which is the root of all my suffering, for I have abundant wealth." I returned to my reason and said to myself, "In this voyage, I repent to the Almighty God with a sincere repentance, and I will never again embark on travel, nor mention it, nor even think of it, for the rest of my life." I continued to implore the Almighty God and to weep, recalling my former days of play and pleasure and cheer and contentment and happiness.

I continued in this condition for a whole day and a second, at the end of which I came to a large island abounding in trees and streams. I landed and ate of the fruits of those trees and drank of the waters of those streams until I felt refreshed and regained my strength and recovered my spirit. Then I walked in the island and found on the other side a great river of sweet water, running with a strong current, and I remembered the raft I had made last time and said to myself, "I must make me a raft like that one; perhaps I will get out of here. If I get out safely, I will have my wish and vow to the Almighty God to foreswear travel, and if I perish, I will find rest from toil and misery."

Then I gathered many pieces of wood from the trees, which were of the finest sandalwood, the like of which does not exist anywhere else, although I did not know it at the time. Then I found a way to twist grasses and twigs into a kind of rope, with which I bound the raft, saying to myself, "If I escape safely, it will be by the grace of God." Then I got on the raft and proceeded along the river, leaving that part of the island behind. I lay on the raft for three days. I did not eat, but I drank from the water of the river, to quench my thirst, until I was giddy like a young bird from extreme weariness, hunger, and fear.

At the end of this time, the raft brought me to a high mountain, beneath which ran the river. When I saw this, I was frightened, recalling what I had suffered from the narrowness of that other stream during my preceding voyage. I tried to stop the raft and get off on the side of the mountain, but the current overpowered me and drew the raft, with me on it, beneath the mountain. I was sure that I would perish and said, "There is no power and no strength save in God the Almighty, the Magnificent," but after a short distance, the raft emerged in a wide space, a great valley, through which the river roared with a noise like thunder and ran with a swiftness like that of the wind. I held on to the raft, for fear of falling, while the waves tossed it to the right and left in the middle of the river. The raft continued to descend with the current, along the valley, while I was unable to stop or steer it toward the bank, until it brought me to a large, well-built, and populous city. When the people saw me on the raft, descending in the middle of the river with the current, they cast a net and ropes on the raft and drew it ashore.

I fell among them like a dead man, from extreme hunger, lack of sleep, and fear. Soon there approached me from among the people a venerable old man, who welcomed me and threw over me an abundance of handsome clothes, which I put on to make myself decent. Then he took me to the bath and brought me refreshing cordials and sweet perfumes. After the bath, he took me to his house, and his family received me joyfully. Then he seated me in a pleasant place and prepared sumptuous food for me, and I ate my fill and thanked the Almighty God for my safety. Then his pages brought me hot water, with which I washed my hands, and his maids brought me silk towels, with which I dried them and wiped my mouth. Then he prepared for me a private apartment in a part of his house and charged his pages and maids to wait on me and fulfill my needs, and they served me attentively. I stayed in the guest apartment for three days, enjoying delicious food and drink and sweet scents, until my fear subsided, my energy returned, and I felt at ease.

On the fourth day, the old man came to me and said, "Son, we have enjoyed your company, and God be praised for your safety. Would you like now to go down with me to the bank of the river and sell your goods in the market? Perhaps with the money you get, you will buy something with which to traffic." I remained silent for a while, thinking to myself, "What goods do I have, and what does he mean?" He added, "Son, don't worry and don't think too much about it. Let us go to the market, and if we find anyone who will offer a price that will content you, I will receive the money for you, and if we don't, I will keep them for you in my storerooms until the days of buying and selling arrive." I thought about it and said to myself, "Let me do what he asks and see what these goods are." Then I said to him, "Uncle, I hear and obey. I cannot contradict you in anything, for what you do has God's blessing." So I went with him to the market and found out that he had taken the raft apart and delivered the sandalwood, of which it was made, to the broker who was announcing it for sale. The merchants came and opened the bidding, and they increased their offers until the bidding stopped at one thousand dinars. Then the old man turned to me and said, "Listen, son, this is the price of your goods at the present time. Would you like to sell them at this price, or would you like to wait and let me keep them for you in my storerooms to sell them for a higher price at the right time?" I replied, "Sir, I leave it to you; do as you wish." He said, "Son, will you sell me this wood for a hundred dinars above what the merchants have offered?" I said, "Yes, it is done." Then he ordered his servants to carry the wood to his storerooms, and we returned to his house, where we sat, and he counted the money in payment for the wood and, fetching bags, put the money in them, locked them up with an iron lock, and gave me the key.

Some days later, the old man said to me, "Son, I would like to propose something to you, and I hope that you will comply." I said, "What is it?" He replied, "Son, I am a very old man, and I am without a son, but I do have a daughter who is young and charming and endowed with great wealth and beauty. I would like to marry her to you, so that you may live with her here in our country. Then I will give you all I have, for I have become an old man, and you will take my place." I remained silent, and he added, "Son, accept my proposal, for I wish you good. If you obey me, I will marry my daughter to you, and you will be as my son and will possess all I have. If you wish to travel to your country and engage in trade, no one will prevent you. This is your property, at your disposal, to do with it what you wish and choose." I said to him, "By God, uncle, you have become as a father to me. I have suffered many horrors that have rendered me bewildered and lacking in judgment. It is for you to decide as you wish." Then he ordered his pages to bring the judge and witnesses, and when they came, he married me to his daughter, celebrating with a great entertainment and a great feast. When I went in to my wife, I found her extremely beautiful, with a graceful figure and a lovely gait, clad in rich apparel and covered with gold ornaments, necklaces, jewels, and precious stones, worth thousands of thousands of dinars and beyond the means of anyone. When I saw her, she pleased me, and we loved one another. I lived with her for some time, leading an extremely happy and joyful life. Soon her father died and was admitted to the mercy of God. We prepared him and buried him, and I took possession of all his property, and his servants became my servants to serve me at my bidding. Then the merchants appointed me to his office, for he was their chief, and that meant that none of them purchased anything without his knowledge and permission.

When I mingled with the people of the city, I noticed that they were transformed at the beginning of each month, in that they grew wings with which they flew to the upper region of the sky, and no one remained in the city except women and children. I said to myself, "When the first day of the month comes, I will ask some of them to carry me with them to where they go." When the day came, and their colors and shapes changed, I went to one of them and said, "For God's sake, carry me with you, so that I may divert myself and then return." He said, "This is not possible," but I pressed him until he granted me the favor. So I went with them, without telling any of my family or servants or friends, and he took me on his back and flew with me up into the air and kept flying upward until we were so high that I heard the angels glorifying God in the vault of heaven. I marveled at that and exclaimed, "Glory be to God, and His is the praise."

Hardly had I finished my prayer when a fire came out of heaven and almost consumed us. They flew down and, dropping me on a high mountain, departed, feeling very angry with me, and left me alone. I blamed myself for what I had done and said to myself, "There is no power and no strength, save in God the Almighty, the Magnificent. Every time I escape from a calamity, I fall into a worse one."

I sat on the mountain, not knowing where to go, when suddenly two young men passed by. They were like twin moons, each holding a walking staff of red gold. I approached them and saluted them, and they returned my salutation. Then I asked them, "For God's sake, tell me who and what you are." They replied, "We are servants of the Almighty God," and, giving me a walking staff of gold, like the ones they had with them, went on their way and left me. I walked along the ridge of the mountain, leaning on the staff and wondering about the two young men, when suddenly a serpent emerged from beneath the mountain, with a man in its mouth, whom it had swallowed to his navel, while he was screaming and crying out, "Whoever delivers me, God will deliver him from every difficulty." I went close to the serpent and struck it on its head with the gold staff, and it threw the man from its mouth. Then he approached me and said, "Since you have saved me from this serpent, I will never leave you, and you have become my companion on this mountain."

Soon a group of people approached us, and when I looked, I saw among them the man who had carried me on his shoulders and flew up with me. I approached him and, speaking courteously to him, offered my apologies and said, "Friend, this is not the way friends treat friends." He replied, "It was you who almost destroyed us by glorifying God on my back." I said, "Excuse me, for I had no knowledge of this, and I will never utter another word again." Finally, he consented to take me with him, on condition that I would refrain from mentioning the name of God or glorifying Him on his back. Then he carried me and flew up with me, as he had done before, until he brought me to my house.

My wife met me, greeted me, and, congratulating me on my safety, said, "Beware of going out again or associating with those people, for they are brothers of the devils and do not worship God." I asked her, "But how did your father then get along with them?" She replied, "My father was not one of them, nor did he as they did. Now that he is dead, I think that you should sell all our possessions, buy goods with the money, and go back to your country and family, and I will go with you, for I have no reason to stay in this city, since both my father and mother are dead." So I sold my father-in-law's property, little by little, and waited to find someone who would go to Baghdad, so that I might go with him.

Soon, a group of men in the city decided to travel and, failing to find a ship, bought wood and built for themselves a large one. I booked passage with them, paying them the fare in full, and embarked with my wife and all we could carry of our property, leaving our land and buildings behind. We set out and sailed with a fair wind from sea to sea and from island to island until we reached Basra, where, without tarrying, I booked passage on a boat and, loading our belongings, headed for Baghdad. Then I came to my quarter, entered my house, and met my family and friends and loved ones, and stored in my storerooms all the goods I had brought with me. My family had given up hope of my return, for when they calculated the time of my absence during the seventh voyage, they found that it was twenty-seven years. When I related to them all my experiences, they marveled exceedingly and congratulated me on my safety.

Then I vowed to the Almighty God never to travel again by land or sea, after the seventh voyage, which was the one to end all voyages. I also refrained from indulging my appetites and thanked the Almighty and Glorious God and praised Him and glorified Him for having brought me back to my native country and to my family. Consider, O Sindbad the Porter, what I had gone through.

SINDBAD THE PORTER said to Sindbad the Sailor, "For God's sake, pardon me the wrong I did you," and they continued to enjoy their fellowship and friendship, in all cheer and joy, until there came to them death, the destroyer of delights, sunderer of companies, wrecker of palaces, and builder of tombs.

CONTEXTS

Early Witnesses

ANONYMOUS

A Ninth-Century Fragment of the
Thousand Nights†

(1) In the name of Allah the Merciful, the Compassionate.
(2)   N I G H T
(3) And when it was the following night
(4) said Dīnāzād, "O my Delectable One, if you are
(5) not asleep, relate to me the tale
(6) which you promised me and quote striking examples of the
(7) excellencies and shortcomings, the cunning and stupidity
(8) the generosity and avarice, and the courage and cowardice
(9) that are in man, instinctive or acquired
(10) or pertain to his distinctive characteristics or to courtly manners,
     Syrian
(11) or Bedouin.
(12) [And Shīrāzād related to her a ta]le of elegant beauty
(13) [of So-and-So the ? and] his [f]ame (or [c]raft)
(14) [sh]e becomes more worthy than they who are (or do) not
(15) [or] else more crafty (or malicious) than they.
(16) [(traces only at the end of the line)]

AL-MASʿŪDĪ

Meadows of Gold (Murūj al-Dhahab)

Many of those well acquainted with their *akhbār* (pseudo-historical tales of ʿAbīd [ʿUbaid] ibn Sharyah and others of the court of Muʿāwīyah) state that these *akhbār* are apographal, embellished, and fabricated, strung together by those who drew nigh to the kings by relating them and who duped their contemporaries with memorising and reciting them (as authentic. They state, furthermore), that they are of the same type as the books which have been transmitted

---

† This and the following selection are from "New Light on the Early History of the *Arabian Nights*" by Nabia Abbott, from *Journal of Near Eastern Studies*, Vol. 8, No. 3 (July 1949), pp. 133, 150–51. Reprinted by permission of the University of Chicago Press Journals.

to us and translated for us from the Persian [Pahlavi], Indian and Greek—books composed in like manner as the above mentioned—such as the book of *Hazār Afsāna*, or translated from the Persian to the Arabic of a *Thousand Khurāfāt*, (fantastic tales) for khurāfa in Persian is called *afsāna*. The people call this book *A Thousand Nights [and a Night]*. It is the story of the king and the wazir and his daughter and her nurse [or maid, or sister, or the wazir and his two daughters] named Shīrāzād [Shīrazād] and Dīnāzād [Dīnārazād] and such as the *Book of Farza [Jaliʿad] and Shīmās* and what is in it of the stories of the kings of India and their wazirs. And such as the *Book of Sindbād* and other books of this nature.

IBN ISḤĀQ AL-NADĪM

The Fihrist[†]

Section One

Thus saith Muḥammad ibn Isḥāq [al-*Nadīm*]: The first people to collect stories, devoting books to them and safeguarding them in libraries, some of them being written as though animals were speaking, were the early Persians. Then the Ashkānian kings, the third dynasty of Persian monarchs, took notice of this [literature]. The Sāsānian kings in their time adding to it and extending it. The Arabs translated it into the Arabic language and then, when masters of literary style and eloquence became interested, they refined and elaborated it, composing what was similar to it in content.

The first book to be written with this content was the book *Hazār Afsān*, which means "a thousand stories." The basis for this [name] was that one of their kings used to marry a woman, spend a night with her, and kill her the next day. Then he married a concubine of royal blood who had intelligence and wit. She was called Shahrāzād, and when she came to him she would begin a story, but leave off at the end of the night, which induced the king to spare her, asking her to finish it the night following. This happened to her for a thousand nights, during which time he [the king] had intercourse with her, until because of him she was granted a son, whom she showed to him, informing him of the trick played upon him. Then, appreciating her intelligence, he was well disposed towards her and kept her alive. The king had a head of the household named Dīnār Zād who was in league with her in this matter. It is said that this book was

† From Vol. 2 of *Fihrist Al Nadīm*, vol. 1 and 2, edited and translated by Bayard Dodge. © 1970 by Columbia University Press. Reprinted with the permission of the publisher.

composed for *Humā'ī*, the daughter of *Bahrām*, there being also additional information about it.

Thus saith Muḥammad ibn Isḥāq [al-*Nadīm*]: The truth is, if Allāh so wills, that the first person to enjoy evening stories was *Alexander*, who had a group [of companions] to make him laugh and tell him stories which he did not seek [only] for amusement but [also he sought] to safeguard and preserve [them]. Thus also the kings who came after him made use of the book *Hazār Afsān*, which although it was spread over a thousand nights contained less than two hundred tales, because one story might be told during a number of nights. I have seen it in complete form a number of times and it is truly a coarse book, without warmth in the telling.

Thus saith Muḥammad ibn Isḥāq [al-*Nadīm*]: Abū ʿAbd Allāh Muḥammad ibn ʿAbdūs al-*Jahshiyārī*, author of *The Book of Viziers*, began the compiling of a book in which he was to select a thousand tales from the stories of the Arabs, Persians, Greeks, and others. Each section (story) was separate, not connected with any other. He summoned to his presence the storytellers, from whom he obtained the best things about which they knew and which they did well. He also selected whatever pleased him from the books composed of stories and fables. As he was of a superior type, there were collected for him four hundred and eighty nights, each night being a complete story, comprising more or less than fifty pages. Death overtook him before he fulfilled his plan for completing a thousand stories. I saw a number of the sections of this book written in the handwriting of Abū al-*Ṭayyib* [ibn Idrīs], the brother of al-*Shāfiʿī*.

Before that time there was a group of people who composed stories and fables in the speech of humans, birds, and beasts. Among them there were ʿAbd Allāh ibn al-*Muqaffaʿ*; *Sahl* ibn Hārūn; *ʿAlī* ibn Dāʾūd, the secretary of *Zubaydah*; and others besides them. I have dealt thoroughly with these [authors] and what they composed in the appropriate places in this book.

There is the book *Kalīlah wa-Dimnah* about which they have disagreed. It is said to be the work of the Indians (Hindus), information about that being in the first part of the book. It is also said to be the work of the Ashkānian kings to which the Indians made false claims, or of the Persians and falsely claimed by the Indians. One group has said that the man who composed parts of it was *Buzurjmihr*, the wise man, but it is Allāh who knows about that.

There was the book *Sindbādh al-Ḥakīm*, which is in two transcriptions, one long and one short. They disagreed about it, too, just as they disagreed about *Kalīlah wa-Dimnah*. What is most probable and the closest to the truth is that the Indians composed it.

* * *

Modern Echoes

EDGAR ALLAN POE

The Thousand-and-Second Tale of Scheherazade[†]

Truth is stranger than fiction. —Old Saying.[1]

Having had occasion, lately, in the course of some Oriental investiga-
tions, to consult the *Tellmenow Isitsöornot,* a work which (like the Zohar
of Simeon Jochaides) is scarcely known at all,[2] even in Europe, and
which has never been quoted, to my knowledge, by any American—if
we except, perhaps, the author of the "Curiosities of American Literature;"[3]—having had occasion, I say, to turn over some pages of the
first-mentioned very remarkable work, I was not a little astonished
to discover that the literary world has hitherto been strangely in
error respecting the fate of the vizier's daughter, Scheherazade, as
that fate is depicted in the "Arabian Nights;" and that the *dénoue-
ment* there given, if not altogether inaccurate, as far as it goes, is at
least to blame in not having gone very much farther.

For full information on this interesting topic, I must refer the
inquisitive reader to the "Isitsöornot" itself; but, in the mean time, I
shall be pardoned for giving a summary of what I there discovered.

It will be remembered, that, in the usual version of the tales, a certain monarch, having good cause to be jealous of his queen, not only
puts her to death, but makes a vow, by his beard and the prophet, to
espouse each night the most beautiful maiden in his dominions, and
the next morning to deliver her up to the executioner.

[†] From *Collected Works of Edgar Allan Poe: Vol. III; Tales and Sketches 1843–1849,* edited
by Thomas Ollive Mabbott, with the assistance of Eleanor D. Kewer and Maureen
C. Mabbott, pp. 1151–74, Cambridge, Mass.: The Belknap Press of Harvard University
Press. Copyright © 1978 by the President and Fellows of Harvard College. Reprinted by
permission of the publisher.

1. Motto: Compare Byron's *Don Juan,* XIV, c1, 1, and see *Politian,* V, 40; "How to Write a Blackwood Article"; "A Tale of the Ragged Mountains," and "Von Kempelen and His Discovery."

2. Unlike the *Tellmenow Isitsō ornot,* the *Zohar* is a real work, mentioned as Poe describes it
in the first edition of Irving's classic, *A History of New York by Dietrich Knickerbocker*
(1809), Book IV, chapter 4, paragraph 12. Known since the last part of the thirteenth
century, the *Zohar* is a collection of esoteric material long ascribed to a second-century
rabbi, Simeon ben Jochai (Jochiades); it is one source of the Kabbala.

3. The "Curiosities" referred to was supplied by Griswold for an American edition of Isaac
D'Israeli's *Curiosities of Literature* (1844) and is also mentioned in "The Angel of the
Odd" at n. 3 and in *Doings of Gotham,* Letter VI.

Having fulfilled this vow for many years to the letter, and with a religious punctuality and method that conferred great credit upon him as a man of devout feelings and excellent sense, he was interrupted one afternoon (no doubt at his prayers) by a visit from his grand vizier, to whose daughter, it appears, there had occurred an idea.

Her name was Scheherazade, and her idea was, that she would either redeem the land from the depopulating tax upon its beauty, or perish, after the approved fashion of all heroines, in the attempt.

Accordingly, and although we do not find to be leap-year, (which makes the sacrifice more meritorious,) she deputes her father, the grand vizier, to make an offer to the king of her hand. This hand the king eagerly accepts—(he had intended to take it at all events, and had put off the matter from day to day, only through fear of the vizier,)—but, in accepting it now, he gives all parties very distinctly to understand, that, grand vizier or no grand vizier, he has not the slightest design of giving up one iota of his vow or of his privileges. When, therefore, the fair Scheherazade insisted upon marrying the king, and did actually marry him despite her father's excellent advice not to do anything of the kind—when she would and did marry him, I say, will I nill I, it was with her beautiful black eyes as thoroughly open as the nature of the case would allow.

It seems, however, that this politic damsel (who had been reading Machiavelli, beyond doubt,) had a very ingenious little plot in her mind.[4] On the night of the wedding, she contrived, upon I forget what specious pretence, to have her sister occupy a couch sufficiently near that of the royal pair to admit of easy conversation from bed to bed; and, a little before cock-crowing, she took care to awaken the good monarch, her husband, (who bore her none the worse will because he intended to wring her neck on the morrow,)—she managed to awaken him, I say, (although, on account of a capital conscience and an easy digestion, he slept well,) by the profound interest of a story (about a rat and a black cat, I think,) which she was narrating (all in an undertone, of course,) to her sister. When the day broke, it so happened that this history was not altogether finished, and that Scheherazade, in the nature of things, could not finish it just then, since it was high time for her to get up and be bowstrung—a thing very little more pleasant than hanging, only a trifle more genteel!

The king's curiosity, however, prevailing, I am sorry to say, even over his sound religious principles, induced him for this once to postpone

---

4. Compare Butler's couplet in *Hudibras*, I, i, 741–742: "There is a Machiavelian plot,/Tho' ev'ry nare olfact it not"—used as the motto to "The Folio Club."

the fulfilment of his vow until next morning, for the purpose and with the hope of hearing that night how it fared in the end with the black cat (a black cat, I think it was)[5] and the rat.

The night having arrived, however, the lady Scheherazade not only put the finishing stroke to the black cat and the rat, (the rat was blue,) but before she well knew what she was about, found herself deep in the intricacies of a narration, having reference (if I am not altogether mistaken) to a pink horse (with green wings) that went, in a violent manner, by clockwork, and was wound up with an indigo key. With this history the king was even more profoundly interested than with the other—and, as the day broke before its conclusion, (notwithstanding all the queen's endeavors to get through with it in time for the bowstringing,) there was again no resource but to postpone that ceremony as before, for twenty-four hours. The next night there happened a similar accident with a similar result; and then the next—and then again the next; so that, in the end, the good monarch, having been unavoidably deprived of all opportunity to keep his vow during a period of no less than one thousand and one nights, either forgets it altogether by the expiration of this time, or gets himself absolved of it in the regular way, or, (what is more probable) breaks it outright, as well as the head of his father confessor. At all events, Scheherazade, who, being lineally descended from Eve, fell heir, perhaps, to the whole seven baskets of talk, which the latter lady, we all know, picked up from under the trees in the garden of Eden;[6] Scheherazade, I say, finally triumphed, and the tariff upon beauty was repealed.

Now, this conclusion (which is that of the story as we have it upon record) is, no doubt, excessively proper and pleasant—but, alas! like a great many pleasant things, is more pleasant than true; and I am indebted altogether to the "Isitsöornot" for the means of correcting the error. *"Le mieux,"* says a French proverb, *"est l'ennemi du bien,"*[7] and, in mentioning that Scheherazade had inherited the seven baskets of talk, I should have added, that she put them out at compound interest until they amounted to seventy-seven.

"My dear sister," said she, on the thousand-and-second night, (I quote the language of the "Isitöornot" at this point, *verbatim*,) "my

---

5. For other special mention of black cats, see "Instinct vs Reason," "The Black Cat," and "Desultory Notes on Cats."
6. Says the *New-York Mirror*, May 30, 1835, in an article captioned "The Ladies": "The Rabbins ought to be ashamed of themselves for their scandalous libel, in saying that ten baskets of chatter were let down from heaven, and that the women appropriated nine of them." The story is given in other forms in other periodicals of the time.
7. "The better is the enemy of the good" is from one of the *Contes Moreaux* of Voltaire, written in 1772 (Beuchot edition, 1828), XVI, 407, "Dans ses écrits un sage Italien/Dit que le mieux est l'ennemi du bien." Adolph Bowski, in the New York *Times Book Review*, August 21, 1921, says that "Il meglio e l'inimico del bene" is an old Italian proverb.

dear sister," said she, "now that all this little difficulty about the bowstring has blown over, and that this odious tax is so happily repealed, I feel that I have been guilty of great indiscretion in withholding from you and the king (who, I am sorry to say, snores—a thing no gentleman would do,) the full conclusion of the history of Sinbad the sailor. This person went through numerous other and more interesting adventures than those which I related; but the truth is, I felt sleepy on the particular night of their narration, and so was seduced into cutting them short—a grievous piece of misconduct, for which I only trust that Allah will forgive me. But even yet it is not too late to remedy my great neglect—and as soon as I have given the king a pinch or two in order to wake him up so far that he may stop making that horrible noise, I will forthwith entertain you (and him if he pleases) with the sequel of this very remarkable story."

Hereupon the sister of Scheherazade, as I have it from the "Isitsöornot," expressed no very particular intensity of gratification; but the king having been sufficiently pinched, at length ceased snoring, and finally said "Hum!" and then "Hoo!" when the queen understanding these words (which are no doubt Arabic) to signify that he was all attention, and would do his best not to snore any more—the queen, I say, having arranged these matters to her satisfaction, reentered thus, at once, into the history of Sinbad the sailor:

"'At length, in my old age,' (these are the words of Sinbad himself, as retailed by Scheherazade,)—'at length, in my old age, and after enjoying many years of tranquillity at home, I became once more possessed with a desire of visiting foreign countries; and one day, without acquainting any of my family with my design, I packed up some bundles of such merchandise as was most precious and least bulky, and, engaging a porter to carry them, went with him down to the sea-shore, to await the arrival of any chance vessel that might convey me out of the kingdom into some region which I had not as yet explored.

"'Having deposited the packages upon the sands, we sat down beneath some trees, and looked out into the ocean in the hope of perceiving a ship, but during several hours we saw none whatever. At length I fancied that I could hear a singular buzzing or humming sound—and the porter, after listening awhile, declared that he also could distinguish it. Presently it grew louder, and then still louder, so that we could have no doubt that the object which caused it was approaching us. At length, on the edge of the horizon, we discovered a black speck, which rapidly increased in size until we made it out to be a vast monster, swimming with a great part of its body above the surface of the sea. It came towards us with inconceivable swiftness, throwing up huge waves of foam around its breast, and illuminating all that part of the sea through which it passed, with a long line of fire that extended far off into the distance.[8]

"'As the thing drew near we saw it very distinctly. Its length was equal to that of three of the loftiest trees that grow, and it was as wide as the great hall of audience in your palace, O most sublime and munificent of the caliphs. Its body, which was unlike that of ordinary fishes, was as solid as a rock, and of a jetty blackness throughout all that portion of it which floated above the water, with the exception of a narrow blood-red streak that completely begirdled it. The belly, which floated beneath the surface, and of which we could get only a glimpse now and then as the monster rose and fell with the billows, was entirely covered with metallic scales, of a color like that of the moon in misty weather. The back was flat and nearly white, and from it there extended upwards of six spines, about half the length of the whole body.

"'This horrible creature had no mouth that we could perceive; but, as if to make up for this deficiency, it was provided with at least four score of eyes, that protruded from their sockets like those of the green dragon-fly, and were arranged all around the body in two rows, one above the other, and parallel to the blood-red streak, which seemed to answer the purpose of an eyebrow. Two or three of these dreadful eyes were much larger than the others, and had the appearance of solid gold.

"'Although this beast approached us, as I have before said, with the greatest rapidity, it must have been moved altogether by necromancy—for it had neither fins like a fish nor web-feet like a duck, nor wings like the sea-shell which is blown along in the manner of a vessel;[9] nor yet did it writhe itself forward as do the eels. Its head and its tail were shaped precisely alike, only, not far from the latter, were two small holes that served for nostrils, and through which the monster puffed out its thick breath with prodigious violence, and with a shrieking, disagreeable noise.

"'Our terror at beholding this hideous thing was very great; but it was even surpassed by our astonishment, when, upon getting a nearer look, we perceived upon the creature's back a vast number of animals about the size and shape of men, and altogether much resembling them, except that they wore no garments (as men do,) being supplied (by nature, no doubt,) with an ugly, uncomfortable covering, a good deal like cloth, but fitting so tight to the skin, as to

---

8. The monster described is a battleship propelled by steam and manned by sailors. The first steamship of the United States Navy to be driven by a screw propeller, the *Princeton*, was new in 1844. Despite subsequent worthy service, it is chiefly remembered as the scene of a gun explosion on February 28, 1844 that killed two cabinet officers.
9. For another reference to the sea animal called the argonaut or paper nautilus, see "Parody on Drake" and note (Mabbott, I, 301–302).

render the poor wretches laughably awkward, and put them apparently to severe pain. On the very tips of their heads were certain square-looking boxes, which, at first sight, I thought might have been intended to answer as turbans, but I soon discovered that they were excessively heavy and solid, and I therefore concluded they were contrivances designed, by their great weight, to keep the heads of the animals steady and safe upon their shoulders. Around the necks of the creatures were fastened black collars, (badges of servitude, no doubt,) such as we keep on our dogs, only much wider and infinitely stiffer—so that it was quite impossible for these poor victims to move their heads in any direction without moving the body at the same time; and thus they were doomed to perpetual contemplation of their noses—a view puggish and snubby in a wonderful if not positively in an awful degree.

"'When the monster had nearly reached the shore where we stood, it suddenly pushed out one of its eyes to a great extent, and emitted from it a terrible flash of fire, accompanied by a dense cloud of smoke, and a noise that I can compare to nothing but thunder. As the smoke cleared away, we saw one of the odd man-animals standing near the head of the large beast with a trumpet in his hand, through which (putting it to his mouth) he presently addressed us in loud, harsh, and disagreeable accents, that, perhaps, we should have mistaken for language, had they not come altogether through the nose.

"'Being thus evidently spoken to, I was at a loss how to reply, as I could in no manner understand what was said; and in this difficulty I turned to the porter, who was near swooning through affright, and demanded of him his opinion as to what species of monster it was, what it wanted, and what kind of creatures those were that so swarmed upon its back. To this the porter replied, as well as he could for trepidation, that he had once before heard of this sea-beast; that it was a cruel demon, with bowels of sulphur and blood of fire, created by evil genii as the means of inflicting misery upon mankind; that the things upon its back were vermin, such as sometimes infest cats and dogs, only a little larger and more savage; and that these vermin had their uses, however evil—for, through the torture they caused the beast by their nibblings and stingings, it was goaded into that degree of wrath which was requisite to make it roar and commit ill, and so fulfil the vengeful and malicious designs of the wicked genii.

"'This account determined me to take to my heels, and, without once even looking behind me, I ran at full speed up into the hills, while the porter ran equally fast, although nearly in an opposite direction, so that, by these means, he finally made his escape with my bundles, of which I have no doubt he took excellent care—although this is a point I cannot determine, as I do not remember that I ever beheld him again.

"'For myself, I was so hotly pursued by a swarm of the men-vermin (who had come to the shore in boats) that I was very soon overtaken, bound hand and foot, and conveyed to the beast, which immediately swam out again into the middle of the sea.

"'I now bitterly repented my folly in quitting a comfortable home to peril my life in such adventures as this; but regret being useless, I made the best of my condition, and exerted myself to secure the good-will of the man-animal that owned the trumpet, and who appeared to exercise authority over its fellows. I succeeded so well in this endeavor that, in a few days, the creature bestowed upon me various tokens of its favor, and, in the end, even went to the trouble of teaching me the rudiments of what it was vain enough to denominate its language; so that, at length, I was enabled to converse with it readily, and came to make it comprehend the ardent desire I had of seeing the world.

"'*Washish squashish squeak, Sinbad, hey-diddle diddle, grunt unt grumble, hiss, fiss, whiss,*' said he to me, one day after dinner—but I beg a thousand pardons, I had forgotten that your majesty is not conversant with the dialect of the Cock-neighs,[1] (so the man-animals were called; I presume because their language formed the connecting link between that of the horse and that of the rooster.) With your permission, I will translate. '*Washish squashish,*' and so forth:—that is to say, 'I am happy to find, my dear Sinbad, that you are really a very excellent fellow; we are now about doing a thing which is called circumnavigating the globe; and since you are so desirous of seeing the world, I will strain a point and give you a free passage upon the back of the beast.'"

When the Lady Scheherazade had proceeded thus far, relates the "Isitsöornot," the king turned over from his left side to his right, and said—

"It is, in fact, *very* surprising, my dear queen, that you omitted, hitherto, these latter adventures of Sinbad. Do you know I think them exceedingly entertaining and strange?"

The king having thus expressed himself, we are told, the fair Scheherazade resumed her history in the following words:—

"Sinbad went on in this manner, with his narrative—'I thanked the man-animal for its kindness, and soon found myself very much at home on the beast, which swam at a prodigious rate through the ocean; although the surface of the latter is, in that part of the world, by no means flat, but round like a pomegranate, so that we went—so to say—either up hill or down hill all the time.'"

"That, I think, was very singular," interrupted the king.

"Nevertheless, it is quite true," replied Scheherazade.

---

1. Cockneys. The quotation, obviously, is meaningless gibberish.

"I have my doubts," rejoined the king; "but, pray, be so good as to go on with the story."

"I will," said the queen. "'The beast,' continued Sinbad, 'swam, as I have related, up hill and down hill, until, at length, we arrived at an island, many hundreds of miles in circumference, but which, nevertheless, had been built in the middle of the sea by a colony of little things like caterpillars.'"*²

"Hum!" said the king.

"'Leaving this island,' said Sinbad—(for Scheherazade, it must be understood, took no notice of her husband's ill-mannered ejaculation)—'leaving this island, we came to another where the forests were of solid stone, and so hard that they shivered to pieces the finest-tempered axes with which we endeavored to cut them down.'"†³

"Hum!" said the king, again; but Scheherazade, paying him no attention, continued in the language of Sinbad.

"'Passing beyond this last island, we reached a country where there was a cave that ran to the distance of thirty or forty miles within the bowels of the earth, and that contained a greater number of far more spacious and more magnificent palaces than are to be found in all Damascus and Bagdad. From the roofs of these palaces there hung myriads of gems, like diamonds, but larger than men; and in among the streets of towers and pyramids and temples, there flowed immense rivers as black as ebony, and swarming with fish that had no eyes.'"‡⁴

"Hum!" said the king.

"'We then swam into a region of the sea where we found a lofty mountain, down whose sides there streamed torrents of melted metal,

* The coralites.
2. A corallite is a fossil coral. Poe spoke of "the coral worm" in "Instinct vs Reason," and of "the corralliferi" in "Julius Rodman."
† "One of the most remarkable natural curiosities in Texas is a petrified forest, near the head of Pasigono river. It consists of several hundred trees, in an erect position, all turned to stone. Some trees, now growing, are partly petrified. This is a startling fact for natural philosophers, and must cause them to modify the existing theory of petrifaction."—*Kennedy*.
3. This wonder is from the *Weekly Reveille* cited in the introduction. The first paragraph of Poe's footnote follows verbatim—ascription and all—the headnote to the article on "Prairie and Mountain Life." The source is Chapter V of William Kennedy's *Texas* (London, 1841), I, 120, or p. 69 in the New York 1844 reprint.
    The second paragraph of the long footnote was added in Griswold's edition, but came from the same article in the *Reveille:* "That the forest exists there, at the head of the Chayenne river, in the vicinity of the Black Hills, is as certain as that there are no stone trees around St. Louis, and very few wooden ones on the Platte." The spelling today is Cheyenne.
    The third paragraph, also added in Griswold's edition, came from the *Asiatic Journal*, 3 ser. III, 359, August, 1844—a short article headed "Petrified Forest near Cairo."
‡ The Mammoth Cave of Kentucky.
4. The Mammoth Cave, known before 1800, was the subject of at least three books possibly known to Poe, which were published respectively by Nahum Ward in 1816, Edmund F. Lee in 1835, and Alexander Bullett in 1844.

some of which were twelve miles wide and sixty miles long;§[5] while from an abyss on the summit, issued so vast a quantity of ashes that the sun was entirely blotted out from the heavens,[6] and it became darker than the darkest midnight; so that when we were even at the distance of a hundred and fifty miles from the mountain, it was impossible to see the whitest object, however close we held it to our eyes.'"*

"Hum!" said the king.

"'After quitting this coast, the beast continued his voyage until we met with a land in which the nature of things seemed reversed—for we here saw a great lake, at the bottom of which, more than a hundred feet beneath the surface of the water, there flourished in full leaf a forest of tall and luxuriant trees.'"†

"Hoo!" said the king.

"'Some hundred miles farther on brought us to a climate where the atmosphere was so dense as to sustain iron or steel, just as our own does feathers.'"‡[7]

"Fiddle de dee," said the king.

"'Proceeding still in the same direction, we presently arrived at the most magnificent region in the whole world. Through it there meandered a glorious river for several thousands of miles. This river was of unspeakable depth, and of a transparency richer than that of amber. It was from three to six miles in width; and its banks, which arose on either side to twelve hundred feet in perpendicular height, were crowned with ever-blossoming trees, and perpetual sweet-scented flowers, that made the whole territory one gorgeous garden; but the name of this luxuriant land was the kingdom of Horror, and to enter it was inevitable death.'"§[8]

---

§   In Iceland, 1783.

5. The lava flow of 1783 from the Laki fissure in Iceland is recognized as the greatest in recorded history. The note on Iceland and the subsequent notes on Hekla (in Iceland) and other volcanic explosions, and on the earthquake at Caracas in Venezuela, are from Hugh Murray's *Encyclopaedia of Geography* (1836), I, 215, 217, and 221.

6. Compare "To M. L. Shew," lines 3–4, "The blotting utterly from out high heaven/The sacred sun."

*   "During the eruption of Hecla in 1766, clouds of this kind produced such a degree of darkness that, at Glaumba, which is more than fifty leagues from the mountain, people could only find their way by groping. During the eruption of Vesuvius, in 1794, at Caserta, four leagues distant, people could only walk by the light of torches. On the first of May, 1812, a cloud of volcanic ashes and sand, coming from a volcano in the island of St. Vincent covered the whole of Barbadoes, spreading over it so intense a darkness that, at mid-day, in the open air, one could not perceive the trees or other objects near him, or even a white handkerchief placed at the distance of six inches from the eye."—*Murray*, p. 215, *Phil. edit.*

†   "In the year 1790, in the Caraccas, during an earthquake, a portion of the granite soil sank and left a lake eight hundred yards in diameter, and from eighty to a hundred feet deep. It was a part of the forest of Aripao which sank, and the trees remained green for several months under the water."—*Murray*, p. 221.

‡   The hardest steel ever manufactured may, under the action of a blowpipe, be reduced to an impalpable powder, which will float readily in the atmospheric air.

7. This item was added in Griswold's edition. Poe's source for powdered steel is undiscovered.

§   The region of the Niger. See *Simmond's "Colonial Magazine."*

8. Poe's source is a series of four articles by Richard Mouat in *Simmond's Colonial Magazine*, June–September 1844 (II, 138, 311, 416, and III, 115), called "A Narrative of the Niger Expedition."

"Humph!" said the king.

"'We left this kingdom in great haste, and, after some days, came to another, where we were astonished to perceive myriads of monstrous animals with horns resembling scythes upon their heads. These hideous beasts dig for themselves vast caverns in the soil, of a funnel shape, and line the sides of them with rocks, so disposed one upon the other that they fall instantly, when trodden upon by other animals, thus precipitating them into the monsters' dens, where their blood is immediately sucked, and their carcasses afterwards hurled contemptuously out to an immense distance from the caverns of death.'"[*9]

"Pooh!" said the king.

"'Continuing our progress, we perceived a district abounding with vegetables that grew not upon any soil, but in the air.[†1] There were others that sprang from the substance of other vegetables;[‡2] others that derived their sustenance from the bodies of living animals;[§3] and then, again, there were others that glowed all over with intense fire;[*]

---

[*] The *Myrmeleon*—lion-ant. The term "monster" is equally applicable to small abnormal things and to great, while such epithets as "vast" are merely comparative. The cavern of the myrmeleon is *vast* in comparison with the hole of the common red ant. A grain of silex is, also, a "rock."

9. See Thomas Wyatt's *Synopsis of Natural History*, p. 135. The lion-ant is also mentioned in Poe's "Instinct vs Reason," and in "Julius Rodman," Chapter III.

[†] The *Epidendron, Flos Aeris* of the family of the *Orchideœ*, grows with merely the surface of its roots attached to a tree or other object, from which it derives no nutriment—subsisting altogether upon air.

1. See Patrick Keith's *System of Physiological Botany* (1816), II, 429, with credit to "Willdenow, *Princ. Bot.*, 263." The *Epidendron* is also mentioned in "How to Write a Blackwood Article," and in "Eleonora." A specimen, which had an odor like vanilla, was exhibited at a meeting of the Horticultural Society described in an article reprinted in the Philadelphia *Public Ledger*, July 22, 1839, from the *Baltimore Patriot*. See Cornelia Varner, in the *Journal of English and Germanic Philology*, January 1933, p. 78.

[‡] The *Parasites*, such as the wonderful *Rafflesia Arnoldi*.

2. The *Rafflesia Arnoldi* is a giant parasitic plant, a blossom without stalk or leaves, measuring three feet across—the largest flower known. It was discovered in Sumatra in 1818.

[§] *Schouw* advocates a class of plants that grow upon living animals—the *Plantœ Epizoœ*. Of this class are the *Fuci* and *Algœ*.

Mr. J. B. Williams, of Salem, Mass., presented the "National Institute," with an insect from New Zealand, with the following description:—"'The Hotte,' a decided caterpillar, or worm, is found growing at the foot of the *Rata* tree, with a plant growing out of its head. This most peculiar and most extraordinary insect travels up both the *Rata* and *Perriri* trees, and entering into the top, eats its way, perforating the trunk of the tree until it reaches the root, it then comes out of the root, and dies, or remains dormant, and the plant propagates out of its head; the body remains perfect and entire, of a harder substance than when alive. From this insect the natives make a coloring for tattooing."

3. Joachim Frederik Schouw (1789–1852) was a Danish botanist, some of whose writings were translated into English.

The National Institute, founded in 1840 at Washington, D.C., was a forerunner and urgent proponent of the Smithsonian Institution. Many of the communications it received were published in newspapers in Washington and elsewhere. John B. Williams of Salem was for a time United States consul at Auckland, New Zealand. His gift, in 1844, of the "Hotté, a remarkable insect or worm," further described in words followed almost verbatim in Poe's note, is recorded in the third *Bulletin* of the Institute (1845), page 369. Notes concerning a second gift from Williams appear in the fourth *Bulletin* (1846), pages 483, 493, 506–507.

[*] In mines and natural caves we find a species of cryptogamous *fungus* that emits an intense phosphorescence.

others that moved from place to place at pleasure;[†4] and what is still more wonderful, we discovered flowers that lived and breathed and moved their limbs at will, and had, moreover, the detestable passion of mankind for enslaving other creatures, and confining them in horrid and solitary prisons until the fulfillment of appointed tasks.'"[‡5]

"Pshaw!" said the king.

"'Quitting this land, we soon arrived at another in which the bees and the birds are mathematicians of such genius and erudition, that they give daily instructions in the science of geometry to the wise men of the empire. The king of the place having offered a reward for the solution of two very difficult problems, they were solved upon the spot—the one by the bees, and the other by the birds; but the king keeping their solutions a secret, it was only after the most profound researches and labor, and the writing of an infinity of big books, during a long series of years, that the men-mathematicians at length arrived at the identical solutions which had been given upon the spot by the bees and by the birds.'"[§6]

---

† The orchis, scabius and vallisneria.

4. This group was added in Griswold's edition. The orchis, or orchid, needs no comment. The scabius, or scabious, is any one of more than 70 species of the teasel family, supposedly remedial for scabies, or mange; some kinds are the Mourning Bride, the Horseweed, and the Daisy Fleabane. The "Valisnerian lotus" is mentioned in "Al Aaraaf," I, 74; the correct spelling is Vallisneria.

‡ "The corolla of this flower, (*Aristolochia Clematitis*,) which is tubular, but terminating upwards in a ligulate limb, is inflated into a globular figure at the base. The tubular part is internally beset with stiff hairs, pointing downwards. The globular part contains the pistil, which consists merely of a germen and stigma, together with the surrounding stamens. But the stamens, being shorter than even the germen, cannot discharge the pollen so as to throw it upon the stigma, as the flower stands always upright till after impregnation. And hence, without some additional and peculiar aid, the pollen must necessarily fall down to the bottom of the flower. Now, the aid that nature has furnished in this case, is that of the *Tipula Pennicornis*, a small insect, which, entering the tube of the corolla in quest of honey, descends to the bottom, and rummages about till it becomes quite covered with pollen; but, not being able to force its way out again, owing to the downward position of the hairs, which converge to a point like the wires of a mouse-trap, and being somewhat impatient of its confinement, it brushes backwards and forwards, trying every corner, till, after repeatedly traversing the stigma, it covers it with pollen sufficient for its impregnation, in consequence of which the flower soon begins to droop, and the hairs to shrink to the side of the tube, effecting an easy passage for the escape of the insect." —Rev. P. Keith—"*System of Physiological Botany*."

5. In the footnote, Poe quotes from Keith, vol. II, p. 354.

§ The bees—ever since bees were—have been constructing their cells with just such sides, in just such number, and at just such inclinations, as it has been demonstrated (in a problem involving the profoundest mathematical principles) are the very sides, in the very number, and at the very angles, which will afford the creatures the most room that is compatible with the greatest stability of structure.

During the latter part of the last century, the question arose among mathematicians— "to determine the best form that can be given to the sails of a windmill, according to their varying distances from the revolving vanes, and likewise from the centres of revolution." This is an excessively complex problem; for it is, in other words, to find the best possible position at an infinity of varied distances, and at an infinity of points on the arm. There were a thousand futile attempts to answer the query on the part of the most illustrious mathematicians; and when, at length, an undeniable solution was discovered, men found that the wings of a bird had given it with absolute precision, ever since the first bird had traversed the air.

6. Compare "Instinct vs Reason" on the perfect construction of the bees' honeycomb.

"Oh my!" said the king.

"'We had scarcely lost sight of this empire when we found our-selves close upon another, from whose shores there flew over our heads a flock of fowls a mile in breadth, and two hundred and forty miles long; so that, although they flew a mile during every minute, it required no less than four hours for the whole flock to pass over us—in which there were several millions of millions of fowls.'"[*][7]

"Oh fy!" said the king.

"'No sooner had we got rid of these birds, which occasioned us great annoyance, than we were terrified by the appearance of a fowl of another kind, and infinitely larger than even the rocs which I met in my former voyages; for it was bigger than the biggest of the domes upon your seraglio, oh, most Munificent of Caliphs. This terrible fowl had no head that we could perceive, but was fashioned entirely of belly, which was of a prodigious fatness and roundness, of a soft looking substance, smooth, shining and striped with various colors. In its talons, the mon-ster was bearing away to his eyrie in the heavens, a house from which it had knocked off the roof, and in the interior of which we distinctly saw human beings, who, beyond doubt, were in a state of frightful despair at the horrible fate which awaited them. We shouted with all our might, in the hope of frightening the bird into letting go of its prey; but it merely gave a snort or puff, as if of rage, and then let fall upon our heads a heavy sack which proved to be filled with sand!'"[8]

"Stuff!" said the king.

"'It was just after this adventure that we encountered a continent of immense extent and of prodigious solidity, but which, neverthe-less, was supported entirely upon the back of a sky-blue cow that had no fewer than four hundred horns.'"[†][9]

"*That*, now, I believe," said the king, "because I have read some-thing of the kind before, in a book."

"'We passed immediately beneath this continent, (swimming in between the legs of the cow,) and, after some hours, found ourselves in a wonderful country indeed, which, I was informed by the man-animal, was his own native land, inhabited by things of his own

---

[*]   He observed a flock of pigeons passing betwixt Frankfort and the Indiana territory, one mile at least in breadth; it took up four hours in passing; which, at the rate of one mile per minute, gives a length of 240 miles; and, supposing three pigeons to each square yard, gives 2,230,272,000 pigeons—"*Travels in Canada and the United States,*" *by Lieut. F. Hall.*

7.   Tremendous flights of passenger pigeons darkening the sky were a familiar spectacle in the Middle West through much of the nineteenth century. The last survivor of the species died in the Cincinnati Zoo in 1914.

8.   The monster is a balloon with car, which discharges ballast.

[†]   "The earth is upheld by a cow of a blue color, having horns four hundred in number." —*Sale's Koran.*

9.   See also "Lionizing" for a "Grand Turk's" discussion of these legends. Poe's exact source is uncertain; it is not in the Koran itself.

species. This elevated the man-animal very much in my esteem; and in fact, I now began to feel ashamed of the contemptuous familiarity with which I had treated him; for I found that the man-animals in general were a nation of the most powerful magicians, who lived with worms in their brains,[‡1] which, no doubt, served to stimulate them by their painful writhings and wrigglings to the most miraculous efforts of imagination.'"

"Nonsense!" said the king.

"'Among the magicians, were domesticated several animals of very singular kinds; for example, there was a huge horse whose bones were iron and whose blood was boiling water. In place of corn, he had black stones for his usual food; and yet, in spite of so hard a diet, he was so strong and swift that he would drag a load more weighty than the grandest temple in this city, at a rate surpassing that of the flight of most birds.'"[§2]

"Twattle!" said the king.

"'I saw, also, among these people a hen without feathers, but bigger than a camel; instead of flesh and bone she had iron and brick; her blood, like that of the horse, (to whom, in fact, she was nearly related,) was boiling water; and like him she ate nothing but wood or black stones. This hen brought forth very frequently, a hundred chickens in the day; and, after birth, they took up their residence for several weeks within the stomach of their mother.'"[*3]

---

‡ "The *Entozoa*, or intestinal worms, have repeatedly been observed in the muscles, and in the cerebral substance of men."—*See Wyatt's Physiology*, p. 143.

1. The reference should be to Wyatt's *Synopsis of Natural History*, p. 143. Poe refers to the *Entozoa* in an article in *Alexander's Weekly Messenger*, April 15, 1840, and in a review of Charles Lamb in the *Broadway Journal*, September 13, 1845. The scientist first observing the phenomenon was a Philadelphian, Professor John Morgan (1735–1789), who published "Of a Living Snake in a Living Horse's Eye" in the *Transactions of the American Philosophical Society* (1787). Compare "the animalculae which infest the brain" in "The Island of the Fay."

§ On the great Western Railway, between London and Exeter, a speed of 71 miles per hour has been attained. A train weighing 90 tons was whirled from Puddington to Didcot (53 miles,) in 51 minutes.

2. See the introductory note on the speed of trains.

* The *Eccaleobion*.

3. The *Eccaleobion* (a word formed from Greek, meaning "that which brings forth life") was being demonstrated in New York in the summer of 1844. It had been shown in London some five years earlier. Cornelia Varner printed a notice from the Philadelphia *Public Ledger* of May 23, 1839, which says: "A London paper states that a curious exhibition, under the name of 'Eccaleobion,' is about to be opened in Pall-Mall"; it may have been brought to America the same year. The *Monthly Review* (London), for November 1839, reviews and quotes from *The Eccaleobion. A Treatise on Artificial Incubation. By William Bucknell. Published for the Author*—a pamphlet describing "an exhibition that has been established in London and is in practical operation—viz. the hatching of chickens by artificial heat . . . on a scale that might produce a hundred birds every day." The *New-York Tribune* for May 23, 1844 (p. 3, col. 7) carried an advertisement under the heading "ECCALEOBION.—HATCHING EGGS BY STEAM," saying: "The proprietor of this wonderful invention . . . is happy to announce the re-opening of the Exhibition at No. 285 Broadway, opposite Washington Hall, from 9 a.m. until sunset daily," with some further words of praise. A brief statement of hours and prices—"Tickets 25 cts. Children 12½ cts."—was repeated almost daily for months. On June 10, the *Tribune* carried a paragraph (p. 2, col. 7):

"Fal lal!" said the king.

"'One of this nation of mighty conjurors created a man out of brass and wood, and leather, and endowed him with such ingenuity that he would have beaten at chess, all the race of mankind with the exception of the great Caliph, Haroun Alraschid.[†4] Another of these magi constructed (of like material) a creature that put to shame even the genius of him who made it; for so great were its reasoning powers that, in a second, it performed calculations of so vast an extent that they would have required the united labor of fifty thousand fleshly men for a year.[‡5] But a still more wonderful conjuror fashioned for himself a mighty thing that was neither man nor beast, but which had brains of lead, intermixed with a black matter like pitch, and fingers that it employed with such incredible speed and dexterity that it would have had no trouble in writing out twenty thousand copies of the Koran in an hour; and this with so exquisite a precision, that in all the copies there should not be found one to vary from another by the breadth of the finest hair. This thing was of prodigious strength, so that it erected or overthrew the mightiest empires at a breath; but its powers were exercised equally for evil and for good.'"[6]

> The greatest curiosity that ever was in the United States is the wonderful Eccaleobion, 285 Broadway, displaying the laws established by the creator for the production of life. The idea of producing life by machinery is certainly worthy of attention. The curious and reflecting mind may have food for his thoughts. And no person can go from the Eccaleobion dissatisfied What would our forefathers have thought had they been told that for 25¢ they could see *chickens hatched by steam?* Their first thought would be, "We'll go and see it."
>
> N. P. Willis was impressed, and wrote some paragraphs in which he commented:
>
> The chirruping of chickens saluted our ears as we opened the door, and we observed that a corner of the room was picketed off, where a dozen or two of these *pseudo*-orphans (who had lost their mother by not having been suffered to have one), were pecking at gravel and evidently doing well . . . It began to look very much as if mothers were a superfluity.

See his *Complete Prose Works* (1846), p. 676.

†   Maelzel's Automaton Chess-player.

4. The footnote was added in Griswold's edition. See Poe's essay on "Maelzel's Chess-Player" (*SLM,* April 1836), and a book on the subject by the Poe scholar, Henry Ridgely Evans, 1939. The machine's ability to defeat the redoubtable Haroun Alraschid is perhaps suggested by a story—repeated by Evans, p. 28—that Maelzel's hidden player, William Schlumberger, took a hint *not* to checkmate the venerable Charles Carroll of Carrollton.

‡   Babbage's Calculating Machine.

5. Charles Babbage, professor of mathematics at Cambridge, wanted a machine to help him prepare tables of logarithms, and traveled about Europe studying mechanical processes. Discouraged by withdrawal of government aid, he had not finished his labors after eighteen years; but a machine to add, subtract, divide, and multiply was perfected, according to an article, "Difference Machines," in the *Edinburgh Review,* July 1834. Poe, in his essay on "Maelzel's Chess-Player" refers to Babbage on the basis of statements he ascribes to Brewster's *Letters on Natural Magic.*

6. The "thing" is, of course, the printing press, which was rapidly developed during the eighteen-thirties and forties through innovation after innovation by the Hoe Company of New York. Poe hailed "The Mirror Steam-Press" soon after its installation in the summer of 1844. See his *Complete Works* (1846), p. 725: "Now (thanks to Mr. Hoe), we have a steam-press, which *puts up three fingers for a sheet of white paper, pulls it down into its bosom, gives it a squeeze that makes an impression, and then lays it into the palm of an iron hand which deposites it evenly on a heap—at the rate of two thousand an hour!*"

"Ridiculous!" said the king.

"'Among this nation of necromancers there was also one who had in his veins the blood of the salamanders; for he made no scruple of sitting down to smoke his chibouc in a red-hot oven until his dinner was thoroughly roasted upon its floor.[§7] Another had the faculty of converting the common metals into gold, without even looking at them during the process.[*8] Another had such a delicacy of touch that he made a wire so fine as to be invisible.[†9] Another had such quickness of perception that he counted all the separate motions of an elastic body, while it was springing backwards and forwards at the rate of nine hundred millions of times in a second.'"[‡1]

"Absurd!" said the king.

"'Another of these magicians, by means of a fluid that nobody ever yet saw, could make the corpses of his friends brandish their arms, kick out their legs, fight, or even get up and dance at his will.[§2] Another had cultivated his voice to so great an extent that he could have made himself heard from one end of the earth to the other.[*3] Another had so long an arm that he could sit down in Damascus and indite a letter at Bagdad—or indeed at any distance whatsoever.[†4] Another commanded the lightning to come down to him out of the heavens, and it came at his call; and served

§   *Chabert*, and, since him, a hundred others.
7. Poe from here on takes many notes from Dionysius Lardner's *Course of Lectures*. The account of John Xavier Chabert is from page 25. In London, Chabert sat in an oven, but had protection between himself and the floor upon which he broiled a beefsteak.
*   The Electrotype.
8. "Electrotype" is defined by the *Century Dictionary* as "a copy in metal (precipitated by galvanic action, usually in the form of a thin sheet) of any engraved or molded surface." Lardner (p. 36) touched on the process of electrotyping, then comparatively new. To Poe it seems to have suggested alchemy.
†   *Wollaston* made a platinum for the field of views in a telescope, a wire one eighteen-thousandth part of an inch in thickness. It could be seen only by means of the microscope.
9. William Hyde Wollaston (1766–1828), English scientist who made many important contributions to chemistry, physics, and optics, discovered the means of making platinum available for industrial use. Lardner, p. 35, gave as Wollaston's estimate the figure Poe mentions. Poe referred to "Wollaston's wires" in "Marginalia," number 129 (*Godey's*, August 1845, p. 50).
‡   Newton demonstrated that the retina beneath the influence of the violet ray of the spectrum, vibrated 900,000,000 of times in a second.
1. Lardner (pp. 40–41) discussed vibrations of the retina, but Poe's figure is not mentioned there and may have been Poe's own calculation from other data.
§   The Voltaic pile.
2. Lardner, pp. 11–12, discussed the Voltaic Pile, invented by and named for Count Alessandro Volta (1745–1827), which by chemical action between two dissimilar metals produced electricity like that produced by the Galvanic battery. See the effects of the Galvanic battery as described in "Loss of Breath," "Premature Burial," and "Some Words with a Mummy."
*   The Electro Telegraph transmits intelligence instantaneously—at least so far as regards any distance upon the earth.
3. The practicality of Morse's telegraph was strikingly demonstrated by Morse's message transmitted from Washington to Baltimore on May 24, 1844.
†   The Electro Telegraph Printing Apparatus.
4. This item was added in the *Broadway Journal* text. Lardner, pp. 18–19, said that Morse had demonstrated an experimental instrument in 1837. He had 153 miles of wire when *Brother Jonathan* published an article on his experiments, October 28, 1843. He had indeed thought of a printing telegraph before he planned transmitting an audible signal.

him for a plaything when it came.[5] Another took two loud sounds and out of them made a silence. Another constructed a deep darkness out of two brilliant lights.[‡6] Another made ice in a red-hot furnace.[§7] Another directed the sun to paint his portrait, and the sun did.[*8] Another took this luminary with the moon and the planets, and having first weighed them with scrupulous accuracy, probed into their depths and found out the solidity of the substance of which they are made. But the whole nation is, indeed, of so surprising a necromantic ability, that not even their infants, nor their commonest cats and dogs have any difficulty in seeing objects that do not exist at all, or that for twenty millions of years before the birth of the nation itself, had been blotted out from the face of creation.'"[†9]

"Preposterous!" said the king.

"'The wives and daughters of these incomparably great and wise magi,'" continued Scheherazade, without being in any manner disturbed by these frequent and most ungentlemanly interruptions on the part of her husband—"'the wives and daughters of these eminent

5. Franklin's kite?
‡ Common experiments in Natural Philosophy. If two red rays from two luminous points be admitted into a dark chamber so as to fall on a white surface, and differ in their length by 0.0000258 of an inch, their intensity is doubled. So also if the difference in length be any whole-number multiple of that fraction. A multiple by 2¼, 3¼, &c., gives an intensity equal to one ray only; but a miltiple by 2½, 3½, &c., gives the result of total darkness. In violet rays similar effects arise when the difference in length is 0.0000157 of an inch; and with all other rays the results are the same—the difference varying with a uniform increase from the violet to the red.
    Analogous experiments in respect to sound produce analogous results.
6. Two examples of waves canceling each other—a phenomenon described by Lardner on p. 40. The explanatory paragraph was added to the footnote in Griswold's edition.
§ Place a platina crucible over a spirit lamp, and keep it a red heat; pour in some sulphuric acid, which, though the most volatile of bodies at a common temperature, will be found to become completely fixed in a hot crucible, and not a drop evaporates—being surrounded by an atmosphere of its own, it does not, in fact, touch the sides. A few drops of water are now introduced, when the acid immediately coming in contact with the heated sides of the crucible, flies off in sulphurous acid vapor, and so rapid is its progress, that the caloric of the water passes off with it, which falls a lump of ice to the bottom; and by taking advantage of the moment before it is allowed to re-melt, it may be turned out a lump of ice from a red-hot vessel.
7. This item—added in the *Broadway Journal*—is taken practically verbatim from an article headed "Production of Ice in a Red Hot Crucible" in the *Weekly Reveille*, November 18, 1844, credited to a "Mining Journal."
* The Daguerreotype.
8. The daguerreotype, invented by L. J. M. Daguerre of Paris, was first published in 1839. Poe was already much interested in daguerreotypes when he wrote about them in *Alexander's Weekly Messenger* of January 15 and May 6, 1840.
† Although light travels 167,000 miles in a second, the distance of 161 Cygni, (the only star whose distance is ascertained,) is so inconceivably great, that its rays would require more than ten years to reach the earth. For stars beyond this, 20—or even 1000 years—would be a moderate estimate. Thus, if they had been annihilated 20, or 1000 years ago, we might still see them to-day, by the light which *started* from their surfaces, 20 or 1000 years in the past time. That many which we see daily are really extinct, is not impossible—not even improbable.
9. Poe's very significant changes in text and footnotes revealed by the variants suggest the tremendous advances being made in the science of astronomy. He had clearly made use of Lardner's information in the first version of his tale, but in the final version, which may have been prepared in 1848 or 1849, he incorporated much more detailed, more accurate, and more awesomely impressive information, some of which he used also in *Eureka,* which he was writing in 1847.

conjurors are every thing that is accomplished and refined; and would be every thing that is interesting and beautiful, but for an unhappy fatality that besets them, and from which not even the miraculous powers of their husbands and fathers has, hitherto, been adequate to save. Some fatalities come in certain shapes, and some in others—but this of which I speak, has come in the shape of a crotchet.'"

"A what?" said the king.

"'A crotchet,'" said Scheherazade. "'One of the evil genii who are perpetually upon the watch to inflict ill, has put it into the heads of these accomplished ladies that the thing which we describe as personal beauty, consists altogether in the protuberance of the region which lies not very far below the small of the back. Perfection of loveliness, they say, is in the direct ratio of the extent of this hump. Having been long possessed of this idea, and bolsters being cheap in that country, the days have long gone by since it was possible to distinguish a woman from a dromedary –'"[1]

"Stop!" said the king—"I can't stand that, and I won't. You have already given me a dreadful headache with your lies. The day, too, I perceive, is beginning to break. How long have we been married?— my conscience is getting to be troublesome again. And then that dromedary touch—do you take me for a fool? Upon the whole, you might as well get up and be throttled."

These words, as I learn from the Isitsöornot, both grieved and astonished Scheherazade; but, as she knew the king to be a man of scrupulous integrity, and quite unlikely to forfeit his word, she submitted to her fate with a good grace. She derived, however, great consolation, (during the tightening of the bowstring,) from the reflection that much of the history remained still untold, and that the petulance of her brute of a husband had reaped for him a most righteous reward,[2] in depriving him of many inconceivable adventures.

MARCEL PROUST

From Remembrance of Things Past[†]

The idea of death took up permanent residence within me in the way that love sometimes does. Not that I loved death, I abhorred it. But after a preliminary stage in which, no doubt, I thought about it from

---

1. For other comments on the absurdity of bustles, see "The Spectacles" and "Mellonta Tauta."
2. Compare "A righteous man's reward," St. Matthew 10:41.
† From *Remembrance of Things Past*, Vol. 3, by Marcel Proust, translated by C. K. Scott-Moncrieff and Terence Kilmartin and A. Mayor, translation copyright © 1981 by Random House, Inc., and Chatto & Windus. Reprinted by permission of Random House, Inc., and The Random House Group Ltd.

time to time as one does about a woman with whom one is not yet in love, its image adhered now to the most profound layer of my mind, so completely that I could not give my attention to anything without that thing first traversing the idea of death, and even if no object occupied my attention and I remained in a state of complete repose, the idea of death still kept me company as faithfully as the idea of my self. And, on that day on which I had become a half-dead man, I do not think that it was the accidents characterising this condition—my inability to walk downstairs, to remember a name, to get up from a chair—that had, even by an unconscious train of thought, given rise to this idea of death, this conviction that I was already almost dead, it seems to me rather that the idea had come simultaneously with the symptoms, that inevitably the mind, great mirror that it is, reflected a new reality. Yet still I did not see how from my present ailments one could pass, without warning of what was to come, to total death. Then, however, I thought of other people, of the countless people who die every day without the gap between their illness and their death seeming to us extraordinary. I thought also that it was only because I saw them from within—rather than because I saw them in the deceptive colours of hope—that certain of my ailments, taken singly, did not seem to me to be fatal although I believed that I would soon die, just as those who are most convinced that their hour has come are, nevertheless, easily persuaded that if they are unable to pronounce certain words, this is nothing so serious as aphasia or a stroke, but a symptom merely of a local fatigue of the tongue, or a nervous condition analogous to a stutter, or the lassitude which follows indigestion.

No doubt my books too, like my fleshly being, would in the end one day die. But death is a thing that we must resign ourselves to. We accept the thought that in ten years we ourselves, in a hundred years our books, will have ceased to exist. Eternal duration is promised no more to men's works than to men.

In my awareness of the approach of death I resembled a dying soldier, and like him too, before I died, I had something to write. But my task was longer than his, my words had to reach more than a single person. My task was long. By day, the most I could hope for was to try to sleep. If I worked, it would be only at night. But I should need many nights, a hundred perhaps, or even a thousand. And I should live in the anxiety of not knowing whether the master of my destiny might not prove less indulgent than the Sultan Shahriyar, whether in the morning, when I broke off my story, he would consent to a further reprieve and permit me to resume my narrative the following evening. Not that I had the slightest pretension to be writing a new version, in any way, of the *Thousand and One Nights*, or of that other book written by night, Saint-Simon's *Memoirs*, or of any of those books which I had loved with a child's simplicity and to

which I had been as superstitiously attached as later to my loves, so
that I could not imagine without horror any work which should be
unlike them. But—as Elstir had found with Chardin—you can make
a new version of what you love only by first renouncing it. So my
book, though it might be as long as the *Thousand and One Nights*,
would be entirely different. True, when you are in love with some
particular book, you would like yourself to write something that
closely resembles it, but this love of the moment must be sacrificed,
you must think not of your own taste but of a truth which far from
asking you what your preferences are forbids you to pay attention to
them. And only if you faithfully follow this truth will you sometimes
find that you have stumbled again upon what you renounced, find
that, by forgetting these works themselves, you have written the
Thousand and One Nights or the *Memoirs* of Saint-Simon of another
age. But for me was there still time? Was it not too late?

And I had to ask myself not only: "Is there still time?" but also: "Am
I well enough?" Ill health, which by compelling me, like a severe direc-
tor of conscience, to die to the world, had rendered me good service
("for unless the grain of wheat dies after it has been sown, it will abide
alone; but if it dies, it will bring forth much fruit"), and which, after
idleness had preserved me from the dangers of facility, was perhaps
going to protect me from idleness, that same ill health had consumed
my strength and as I had first noticed long ago, particularly when I
had ceased to love Albertine, the strength of my memory. But was not
the re-creation by the memory of impressions which had then to be
deepened, illumined, transformed into equivalents of understanding,
was not this process one of the conditions, almost the very essence of
the work of art as I had just now in the library conceived it? Ah! if
only I now possessed the strength which had still been intact on that
evening brought back to my mind by the sight of *François le Champi*!
Was not that the evening when my mother had abdicated her authority, the evening from which dated, together with the slow death of my
grandmother, the decline of my health and my will? All these things
had been decided in that moment when, no longer able to bear the
prospect of waiting till morning to place my lips upon my mother's
face, I had made up my mind, jumped out of bed and gone in my
night-shirt to post myself at the window through which the moonlight entered my room until I should hear the sounds of M. Swann's
departure. My parents had gone with him to the door, I had heard the
garden gate open, give a peal of its bell, and close. . . .

While I was asking myself these questions, it occurred to me suddenly that, if I still had the strength to accomplish my work, this
afternoon—like certain days long ago at Combray which had influenced me—which in its brief compass had given me both the idea of
my work and the fear of being unable to bring it to fruition, would

certainly impress upon it that form of which as a child I had had a presentiment in the church at Combray but which ordinarily throughout our lives, is invisible to us: the form of Time.

* * *

TĀHĀ HUSAYN

From The Dreams of Scheherazade[†]

On the thousand and ninth night, Shahrayar woke with a start, but that which had disturbed him was no longer to be heard. He groped around his couch in the dark expecting his hands to encounter something strange, but there was nothing to be found. He sat up, trying to pierce the gloom with his eyes, and stared about him. He pricked up his ears, attentively listening to the silence which invaded his room, and yet neither could his eyes fathom the dark nor could his ears catch a sound. Unable to discover the cause of his unrest he was now convinced that a spirit had visited him during his sleep and had woken him with violence. Such aimless spirits are often to be encountered, wandering in the black of night, whispering in a secret language to the souls of sleepers and sometimes to the sleepless too. This language is not always comprehended but the weird and ghostly words have an unexpected and often diverse effect on peoples' lives, trailing good in their wake, and occasionally evil.

Nevertheless, Shahrayar was soon able to compose his spirit, and a brief smile flashed across his lips as lightning streaks across the sky. Yet he sensed, surging within him, a feeling which though not harsh was at the same time sharp and insistent. He felt an emotion which contained a slight sadness, a slight despair and a nostalgia for an age which had passed and would never return. Then, serenity restored once more, he laid himself down. Closing his eyes and resting his hands upon his chest he prayed hard for the balm of sleep.

Sleep, it seemed, was but waiting for this prayer, for no sooner had the call come than the merciful spirit stretched out its arms and embraced the grief-stricken being with a movement of gentle and tender pity. It was not long before the king slipped into oblivion, sinking into the depths of a calm and sweet slumber.

After sleeping for some time, short or long, he could not tell, the king once again woke with a start, frightened. Once again he tried to pierce

[†] From *The Dreams of Scheherazade*, translated by Magdi Wahba (Cairo: General Egyptian Book Organization, 1974).

the darkness with his eyes and listened hard with his ears; once again he groped around him. But as he could neither see nor hear anything unfamiliar, he decided that the strangeness must lie within himself.

He rose wearily from his couch and began to walk aimlessly about the room. On reaching a window, he opened it and let the rays of the moon into the chamber. As the moonlight poured through the window like a torrent that would brook no resistance, every corner was bathed in light. Yet the king, gazing round the room could see nothing odd or unpleasant.

Breathing in the midnight air, he leaned out of the window and tried to look into the surrounding darkness. All that was visible was a few trees pointing upwards to the night sky. Splashed with light by moonbeams, they appeared to be sheathed in pure silver. Their branches reached outwards, undulating softly in the breeze as though lulling to sleep the birds which had alighted on them at sunset. The birds had truly found peace and rest in the subdued yet rhythmical movement of the branches, for they slept serenely, undisturbed except for an occasional dream passing through their small heads. Dreams which caused them to utter brief yet sweet-sounding calls while their wings quivered fitfully in a gentle tremor.

For a long time Shahrayar stood gazing out of the window trying to catch other sounds in the vast oppressive silence of the space around him. Solace came, however, in resting his eyes upon the soft light of the moon and in listening to the sweet strains which reached his ears from time to time.

When his spirits were calm again and serenity pervaded his soul, he drew back from the window with heavy steps. But instead of going to his couch, he threw himself onto a divan, determined to wait for dawn. Sleep, his own bed, and the evil spirit which had spent the night tormenting him, were all equally distasteful.

And yet, hardly was he at ease on his divan than his mind began to wander once more. No sooner had he settled down than he was locked as if in a pitying and tender embrace by the arms of sleep entwined about his neck. And the king drifted off into a deep and refreshing slumber for an uncertain length of time, lulled by sleep lurking behind his bed.

Then he woke up in a fright for the third time. Once more he tried to pierce the darkness with his eyes and listened intently, but to no avail. He clapped his hands and the door was flung open by the guards who rushed into the room carrying lanterns.

"Did you notice anything strange?", asked the king.

"No, Your Majesty, nothing," answered the captain of the guard.

The king murmured in a tired voice:

"How curious! I have not been able to sleep all night."

Rising, he walked wearily out of his room, with guards in front and behind him. Silently, unaware of his surroundings, he went straight to the wing of the palace which contained the queen's apartments. The guards took their leave of him as he entered the queen's bedroom alone, paying no attention to her attendants, who were unable to hide their surprise on seeing the king at this late hour of the night. But they said nothing, for it did not become them to speak, although some signs of amazement must have appeared on their faces, as they darted surreptitious glances at the king.

The king closed the door gently behind him, and tiptoed to the queen's bedside. He gazed at her for a long time, as she lay fast asleep. He listened to the rhythmical sound of her breathing, but the queen herself was blissfully unaware of the presence of this man who, snake-like, had quietly glided into her room, not heeding the customs of the palace.

Drawing back slightly, the king found an armchair and sat down quietly, careful not to rouse the queen from her slumbers. When he had settled himself comfortably he bowed his head as if absorbed in contemplation. But he did not wait long, for the voice of Scheherazade reached his ears soon afterwards throwing him into a disarray of spirit, causing him almost to take leave of his senses. Then suddenly, remembering something, he regained his composure and stared into space as he listened to the gentle and innocent murmurings which reached him from Scheherazade, his beloved queen. Her voice reminded him of the babbling of a brook near which he used to sit as the sun was setting in the west. He would listen to its sweet singing and play idly with the pebbles on the banks. His spirit was intoxicated by the perfumes which were wafted from the bank by rose, narcissus and jasmine, all seeming to conspire for his pleasure.

* * *

CRITICISM

HUGO VON HOFMANNSTHAL

A Thousand and One Nights[†]

We had this book in our hands when we were boys; and when we were twenty, and believed ourselves to be far from childhood, we took it in our hands again, and again it took hold of us—how strongly did it hold us again! In the youth of our heart, in the loneliness of our soul we found ourselves in a very big city that was threatening and seductive and full of secrets, like Baghdad and Basra. The seductions and threats were curiously intermixed; overcome by an uncanny feeling, our heart was still full of yearning; we dreaded inner loneliness, we dreaded being lost and yet a sense of courage and desire pulled us forward, pulled us along a labyrinthine path, always between faces, between possibilities, riches, somber, half-concealed expressions, half-open doors, pandering and evil looks, into the enormous bazaar that surrounded us. How similar we were to these princes, who have strayed far from their native land, to these merchant sons, whose father has died and who abandon themselves to the temptations of life—how we believed ourselves to be like them. Like a magical board, on whose surface inlaid gemstones, glowing like eyes, create fantastical and uncanny figures, so the book burned in our hands; as the living signs of these destinies flowed into one another intertwined, so an abyss of forms and intuitions, of yearning and lust opened itself inside us. Now that we are men, this book advances toward us for the third time, and only now are we truly to possess it.

What we saw before our eyes in the past were adaptations and retellings; and who can adapt a poetic whole without destroying its most idiosyncratic beauty, its most profound power? The actual adventure is of course indestructible and, retold again and again, retains its power; yet here are not only adventures and events, here is a poetic world—and what would it be like for us if we only knew Homer from the retellings of his adventures? Here is a poem, composed of course by more than one person; it is, however, as though emanating from a single soul; it is a whole, a world through and through. And what a world! Next to it, Homer might in some instances seem bland and un-naive. Here there is variety and profundity, ardor of the imagination and penetrating wisdom of the

† From *Gesammelte Werke in Einzelausgaben: Prosa II*, edited by Herbert Steiner (Frankfurt a.M.: S. Fischer, 1951), pp. 311–20. Translated from the German by Kathryn Stergiopoulos.

world; here is an endless sequence of events, dreams, wise speeches, pranks, indecencies, mysteries; here, the boldest spirituality and the most complete sensuality are woven into one. All our senses, from the highest to the lowest, cannot but be stirred; everything that is in us comes alive here and is called to enjoyment.

There are stories upon stories, extending to the monstrous, to the absurd; there are adventures and pranks, extending into the grotesque, into the vulgar; there are conversations braided out of riddles and parables, out of allegories, becoming almost tiresome; yet in the atmosphere of this whole, the monstrous is not monstrous, the obscene is not vulgar, the general is not tiresome, and the whole is nothing but wondrous: a complete, incomparable, sublime sensuality holds the whole together.

In reality, we knew nothing when, out of this book, we knew only its events; they might have seemed to us gruesome and ghostly, but it was only because they had been torn out of their atmosphere of life. In this book there is no place for horror: the most prodigious life pervades it through and through. The most prodigious sensuality is here key. Sensuality is in this poem what light is in the paintings of Rembrandt, what color is on the panels of Titian. Were it confined somewhere and were it to break through its confines at several points, then this sensuality could offend; since it flows through this whole, through this world unconfined, it is a revelation.

We move from the highest world to the lowest, from the caliph to the barber, from the wretched fisherman to the princely merchant, and it is *one* humanity that surrounds us, that lifts and carries us in a gentle, wide wave; we are amid spirits, amid magicians, amid demons and yet we feel ourselves at home again. A never-failing concreteness paints for us the halls, exquisitely paved with flagstones, paints for us the fountains, paints for us the old bandit-mother, her head swarming with vermin; it arranges the table, decorates it with beautiful bowls and jars, lets us smell all foods, fatty, spicy, and sweet, lets us smell the drinks made of pomegranate seeds and peeled almonds, prepared rich with sugar and fragrant spices, and cooled in the snow; it depicts for us with the same relish the hump of the hunchback and the hideousness of mean old men with slobbering mouths and squinting eyes; it lets the donkey driver, but also the donkey, the enchanted dog and the bronze statue of a dead king all talk, each full of wisdom, full of truth; it paints with the same equanimity, no, with the same enormous pleasure the pack of a worn-out donkey, the pomp of an emir, and from gesture to gesture, unendingly, the erotic pantomime of lovers, whom, after a thousand adventures, an illuminated, fragrant room finally brings together.

Who would want to try to rip apart a fabric so completely full of wonders such as this one? And yet we feel tempted to trace the artifice, which is undoubtedly applied in a thousand places, so that such an enormous mass of material concerning external reality may not oppress us with its weight, or even become unbearable in the long run. And then the reverse occurs: the longer we read, the more easily we abandon ourselves to this world, we lose ourselves in the medium of the most incomprehensible, most naive poetry and possess ourselves all the more: just as one swimming in beautiful waters loses his heaviness but becomes all the more aware of feeling his body as enjoyable and magical. This leads us to the innermost nature of Oriental poetry, indeed to the secret weaving of language; for this mystery, which in the greatest, densest appearance of life, releases us from every feeling of oppression, from all baseness, is the deepest element of Eastern language and Eastern poetry both: in them everything is a trope, everything a branch of age-old roots, everything thinkable in more than one way, everything in suspension. The first root is sensual, primitive, concise, forceful; in quiet transitions it is left behind for new related, almost no longer related meanings; even in the most remote meaning, however, something of the word's age-old sound still rings out, and, as in a cloudy mirror, the image of that first sensation still casts a shadow. Here we see language and poetry—at this level they are one—making the most unconscious and most unrestrained use of this, their essence. In the limitless concreteness of depiction the material seems to impose itself on us with the greatest force; yet what comes so close to us that it could offend us if only it were limited to the nearest word-sense dissolves in a magical mist because of the polysemy of the expression, such that we intuit behind the nearest sense another one, of which it is a transposition. We do not lose sight, therefore, of the real, first sense; yet where it is vulgar, it shakes off its vulgar mystery and often leaves us with a gripping feeling, suspended between what it sensualizes and something higher behind it that takes us up to the magnificent, up to the sublime at lightning speed.

I mean this very simply and would like to be understood. Yet when I speak about a trope, a transposed meaning, the reader's mind will follow its habitual path and not venture there, where I want it to be. The reader will think of a transcendental sense, a hidden, higher meaning where I want to reveal a far less artificial and far more beautiful phenomenon that permeates the whole fabric of these poetic compositions: this language—and it is the responsibility of an excellent translation to allow us to feel through it and throughout it the nakedness of the original language like the body of a female dancer through her robes—this language is not polished into abstract concepts; its movement-words, its object-words are primal words, formed in order to depict sensually and naively, lightheartedly, and powerfully a majestic, patriarchal life and nomadic comings and goings, nothing but sensual, forceful, pure settings, free of every vulgarity. Here we are far away from such a primeval state of the world, and Baghdad and Basra are not the dwelling places of patriarchs. The distance, however, is still not so great that an unspoiled language bristling with impressions would not be able to tie this modern setting to that age-old one in a thousand ways. Just to express a lascivious gesture, an audacious reach for the bowl, a greedy guzzling and gobbling down of delicious foods, a brutal beating, an almost animal emotion of fear or lust, this language has at its disposal nothing but those primal words and phrases, to which something magnificent always clings, something awe-inspiring and naive, something of hallowed nature, majestic settings, eternal purity. No ornamentation is intended, no suggestion of something higher, no allegory—no other allegory at least than one which would help paint the sensual even more sensually, the living even more vividly. The mouth does not open wide in order to summon a higher world; it is merely like a breathing through the pores, but we are breathing through the pores of this naively poetic language the air of an age-old, holy world, in which angels and demons float through and forest and desert-animals are venerated like patriarchs and kings. In this way the vulgarity, the unseemly particularity, even the swearword become, not infrequently, like a window, through which we believe to be peeking into a mysteriously illuminated world of intuitions, indeed, into even higher mysteries.

As we see boundless sensuality illuminate itself from within with its own light, so this whole is at the same time interwoven with a poetic spirituality, in which we advance from first awareness to complete understanding with the most vivid delight. An intuition, a presence of God that is indescribable lies in all of these sensual things. The canopy of the radiant sun or the holy, starry sky are always outstretched over this confusion of the human, animal, and demonic, and like a gentle, pure, and great wind, the eternal, simple, holy sentiments—hospitality, piety, faithfulness—blow through the whole. In the story of Ali Shar and the loyal Zumurrud, to pick out one of a thousand pages, there is a moment that I would not trade for any other glorious passage in our most venerated books. And it is almost nothing. The lover wants to free his beloved, who has been stolen from him by a wicked old Christian. He has scouted out the house, he is under the window around midnight, a signal is agreed upon, he only has to give it—yet he must wait for a little while longer. Then a leaden sleep descends upon him, as untimely as it is irresistible—as though fate had breathed on him, paralyzingly, from the darkness. "Sitting in the darkness of the wall, under the window," it is said, "he fell asleep. Praise and Bless Him, whom slumber never befalls."

I do not know which aspect of Homer or Dante I would place next to these lines, to let arise in this way, out of nothing, in the midst of a wild adventure, the feeling of God just like the moon, when it rises over the edge of the sky and peeks into the life of mankind. Yet what could be said about the wise speeches of birds and of other animals, about the profound answers of lovely young women, about the adages and truths that go to the heart, which dying fathers and old, wise kings whisper into the ears of young people, and finally what could be said about the inexhaustible dialogues, with which lovers distance from and raise above themselves their bliss and the burden of their rapture, all but giving it back to existence. And as they raise their bliss above themselves by articulating it in the words of the poets, in the words of holy books, so the boy raises his shyness above himself, the beggar his poverty, and the thirsty one his thirst. By being in every mouth like the air that everyone shares, the pious, lucid words of the poets take away the baseness from all things; above thousands of interwoven destinies is suspended their eternal element pure and free, expressed in eternally beautiful, imperishable words. These adventurers, whose entire core is a voracious striving, a tumultuous suffering, and an absolute enjoyment, seem to be there only for the sake of the magnificent poems suspended above them—but what would these poems be, what would they be to us if they did not arise out of a living world?

This living world is incomparable and suffused with unending exhilaration, an inextinguishable, passionate, childlike exhilaration that intricately weaves everything, brings everything together: the caliph with the poor fisherman, the demon with the huckstress, the most beautiful of the beautiful with the hunchbacked beggar, body with body and soul with soul. What were we looking at when we found this book to be a labyrinth and full of uncanniness? It is inexpressibly joyous. It flutters with unending exhilaration even around the evil deed, the evil occurrence. The lover wants to free his beloved; he is under the windows around midnight; she, in the dark, awaits his signal, then a leaden sleep descends upon him. A giant Kurd, the most ferocious, most despicable of the forty thieves, slips into the street, sees the one sleeping, listens for the one waiting. He claps his hands at random, the beautiful Zumurrud lets herself down onto his shoulders, and he gallops ahead, carrying the beautiful, light burden as if it were nothing. She wonders at his strength. "Is this Ali Shar?" she asks herself, "who trots ahead there beneath me, more untiring than a young horse? Can this be my beloved, who wrote to me he was emaciated and weak, close to death out of sorrow and desire for me?" And he is galloping ahead, and she is becoming more anxious, and since he does not answer her, she reaches her hand onto his face: "since it was the face of the hideous Kurd, rough and prickly, it felt to the touch like the snout of a pig, which in its gluttony has gobbled up a live hen, and the tail feathers are sticking out from its throat." It is unseemly to tear out the detail in this way—yet this setting, this deliberation, this meditation on the beautiful while she is dashing ahead through the night on the shoulders of the vile thief, this moment of discovery and this incredible simile, which immediately thrusts us out into the light of day, into the farmstead, and which one never forgets—I do not know where anything similar could be found, except now and then in the most exhilarating, most naïve, most audacious passages in the comedies of the enchanting Lope de Vega. What were we thinking when we found this book to be uncanny? It is a maze, but a maze of pleasure. It is a book that could turn a prison into an agreeable abode. It is what Stendhal said about it. It is the book that one ought to be able to completely forget time and time again in order to read it with renewed pleasure again and again.

JOSEF HOROVITZ

The Origins of *The Arabian Nights*†

THE influence which the Arabs (that is, learned men who wrote in Arabic, whether Arabians, Persians or whatever their origin) exercised on the science of mediæval Europe has been often described; it is less generally known that a very great part also of the stories, with which the West amused itself in the Middle Ages, became known to it through Arabic channels. In science the instructors of the Arabs were above all the Greeks, whose inheritance they (the Arabs) then handed on to the West enriched by many valuable renderings of their own. Of the tales passed on to the Western world many had their home in India and had reached the Arabs themselves by way of Persia. The Indian pattern for princes, "Kalîla and Dimna," known in many Western lands also as "The Fables of Bidpai;" the book of the Wiles of Women, much read in Europe under the name of "The Seven Wise Masters;" the legend of Barlaom and Josaphat, a remodelling of the history of Buddha—these and other writings, which are all still preserved for us in Arabic, go back, some to altogether lost, some to existing, some to reconstructable, Indian originals. The collection of Oriental tales most famous in Europe

---

† From *Islamic Culture* 1 (1927): 36–57. Translated from the German typescript.

today—that of The Thousand and One Nights—was unknown to Europe in the Middle Ages, though, as we shall presently see, at least the contents of the introduction had penetrated by oral transmission to Italy in the thirteenth Christian century at latest. From the sixteenth century onward European philosophy and science become emancipated from the Arab influence; but in the sphere of amusing narrative the East celebrates a new triumph, even after the rebirth of European genius. The tales of the Thousand and One Nights, first made known by Galland's French translation at the beginning of the eighteenth century, spread to every part of Europe and called forth many imitations; their popularity in the modern West is not less than was that of the Seven Wise Masters or the Fables of Bidpai in the Middle Ages.

Jean Antoine Galland (b. 1646) had by travel learnt to know the East and had spent a long while in Constantinople, Asia Minor, Syria and Palestine. Though there already the story-tellers had fascinated him, he became acquainted with the Arabic tales of the Thousand and One Nights first through a manuscript which was sent to him to Paris from Syria, after his return. His translation appeared under the title: "Les Mille et Une Nuits, contes Arabes traduits en Francois par M. Galland," at first in twelve volumes, at Paris and Lyon from 1704 to 1717. The extraordinary success which the translation had is largely due to Galland, for he strove to adapt the performance to the taste of his European readers and often rewrote rather than translated; had he confined himself strictly to the Arabic text his work would not have found the same applause in Europe of that day. The Arabic original text, however, remained still for a long while inaccessible. In 1814, a hundred years after the appearance of Galland's translation, a learned Arabist in Calcutta first applied himself to its publication; his translation, published "Under the patronage of the College of Fort William," did not, however, go beyond the first two volumes. In the following decades, on the other hand, several complete editions of the Arabic text came out: in 1835, the Egyptian edition which proceeded from the State Press at Bulâq newly established by the creator of Modern Egypt, Mehemed Ali; in 1839–42, again in Calcutta, the edition edited by Sir W. H. Macnaghten, an Anglo-Indian official; and from 1825–45 the edition begun by Professor Habicht of Breslau and completed later by H. L. Fleischer, which frankly contains many things which belong not at all to the Thousand and One Nights. These texts, however much they differ in particulars, all agree in this: that they are altogether innocent of certain stories like Aladdin and Ali Baba which have become especially popular in Europe. Already the question from what source Galland had taken those stories must have led to curiosity concerning those particular Arabic manuscripts which he had used for his translation;

but it was not till 1887 that the librarian of the Paris National Library, H. Zotenberg, undertook a close examination of the Galland Bequest, when it was found to include three volumes of a manuscript of the Thousand and One Nights dating from the fifteenth century, agreeing with a somewhat latter MS. preserved in the Vatican. Both, however, present not the full text, but only the first 281 Nights. The Galland MS. is the oldest of all hitherto known. According to a recent newspaper report, indeed, a much older MS. is said to have cropped up in Leningrad, but this report is, as Professor Kratschkovsky has very kindly communicated to me in reply to my enquiry, totally without foundation; there are only two, long familiar, MSS. in Leningrad belonging to the nineteenth century. The American Arabist, D. B. MacDonald, who some years ago published a story according to the Galland MS., is planning the publication of the whole of Galland's text and will soon, it is hoped, be able to carry out this plan. The same man of letters has busied himself with the elucidation of the relative position of the different textual variations to one another and thus has lighted upon many disregarded or unknown MSS. of the work. As catalogues of the important Eastern collections of MSS., especially private collections, are either nonexistent or inaccessible, it would be a kindness if readers of this article who are in a position to furnish information regarding such manuscripts would decide to publish it. The date of a MS. is not by any means the only detail of importance; a recent MS. may prove to be the transcription of a hitherto unknown or noteworthy original, and accurate data as to the tales included in the MS. and the order in which they follow one another, would be most welcome.

The Galland MS. does not represent, perhaps, the form which the Thousand and One Nights had assumed in the fifteenth century, but only the form which was at that time popular in Egypt. For, as the language of Galland's text in itself shows, the tales had at that time long slipped out of the hands of writers who cared for correctness of language and fallen into those of the popular story-tellers; and it is self-evident that for these the essential point was not the accurate restoration of the traditional text. Similarly a manuscript going back to the 15th century has been preserved for us, in which we see such a story-teller at his work. It is the Tübinger MS. of the story of Sul and Shumul, which was published in text and translation by Chr. Seybold in 1902. That this tale is an ingredient of the Thousand and One Nights is indicated in the Tübinger MS. by the fact that it is divided into Nights, that it is narrated by Shahrazād, and that the narrator at the outset of each night is requested by her sister to continue her story. To be sure, that is not the case throughout the course of the tale, but many quite different formulas of introduction occur, such as: "The reporter further relates" or the address "My Masters" directed from the story-teller to his audience. There can be no doubt but that the Syrian author—for such, by his familiarity with the geography of Syria, he proclaims himself to be—wished to let the story appear as a part of the Thousand and One Nights and attempted, though without success, to incorporate a story, certainly not quite unknown, but never reckoned as belonging to the Thousand and One Nights, in that collection. We shall come to know of more than one example of works originally outside the collection finding their way into it, and the attempt which the writer of Sul and Shumul made in vain succeeded in such cases. In the collection, in the form in which it was current in Egypt in the fifteenth century, are found already, as the Galland MS. indicates, besides the frame-story, the story of the Merchant and the Geni, the Fisherman and the Geni, the Porter and the Three Ladies of Baghdad, the Three Apples, the Hunchback, Nûr-ud-dîn and Qamr-uz-Zamân with the stories included in them. A Tübinger MS. of the 16th century, forming part of the second volume of the collected work, shows us that in the interval the great knight-errantry romance of Umar un-Numan had already found a way into the collection; and the various MSS. of the Thousand and One Nights are differentiated among other things by their inclusion or omission of that voluminous romance and by the position which they assign to it in the series. That the frame-story at least goes back to a period considerably more remote than the Galland MS. is established by this fact alone: that it was already known in Italy in the fourteenth Christian century. Already Wilhelm von Schlegel had observed that the story of Astolfo and Giocondo narrated in Canto 28 of Ariosto's *Orlando Furioso* must have some bond of kinship with the frame-story of the Thousand and One Nights, although the two differ in not quite unessential particulars. Since then Pio Raina has directed attention to a "novella" of Giovanni Sercambi (1347–1424) which in many features stands nearer to the frame-narrative than does the Canto of Ariosto, while in others it is more akin to the latter. Sercambi, as later Ariosto, transfers the scene of the story to Italy, and the heroes in both cases are Italians. The local colour shows no longer any trace of the Oriental, and one gets the impression that the tale must already have been known in Italy a long while before, probably through travellers who had learnt to know it in the East. If already these Italian parallels allow us to conclude that the frame-narrative must have been widely known in the East in the thirteenth century, positive indications permit us to date back some centuries further not only the frame-tale itself but also the collection to which it forms the introduction. Both Al-Maqrizi and Al-Maqqari have preserved for us a statement of Ibn

Sa'îd, who died in 673 or 685 A.H., which he derived from the Târîkh of "Qurtubi"—a name which is here probably a mistake for that of Al-Qurti, who composed a History of Egypt between 555 and 567 A.H. This Qurti had in his work compared the love adventures of the Fatemite Khalîfa Al-Amir bi Ahkâm Illâh (495–524 A.H.) with the tales of the Thousand and One Nights. Under this title the collection was well known in Egypt at least as early as about the middle of the sixth Islamic century. Numerous stories of our Thousand and One Nights are concerned with Egypt and its capital, though it is not an Egyptian Sultan whose name is most often mentioned, but Harûn ar-Rashîd, a Khalîfa of Baghdâd. That of itself brings us near to accept that the collection must have been current in the East of the Khalîfa's empire for a longer time at least; and in fact we find the earliest information as to its origin and contents in the works of two Baghdâdî authors of the fourth Islamic century. Al-Mas'ûdi in his Murûj-adh-dhahab, completed in 336 and revised in 346 A.H., compares certain tales to "the books translated for us from the Persian, Indian and Greek, as for example the book Hazâr Afsânah which, translated from Persian into Arabic, means the Thousand Adventures (Khurâfa). And"—he goes on to say—"people name it Thousand (in some MSS. Thousand and One) Nights. Such is the story of the King and his Wazir whose daughter and her nurse" (some MSS. have "her slave" and others "his two daughters") who are named Shahrazâd and Dînazâd; or the book Kal'âd and Shimâs with the stories therein contained of the King of India and the Wazîr, likewise the book Sindbâd and others of this sort."

Thus we see that, in the fourth Islamic century, there existed in Baghdad a work translated from the Persian, of which the title was Alf Khurâfa but which was known as Alf Laila, and in which the *dramatis personæ* were the same as in our Thousand and One Nights. Moreover, both the other stories mentioned by Al-Mas'-ûdi, that of Shimâs and that of Sindbâd (by which the book of the Wiles of Women is here meant, not that of the Seafarer), which in our texts are brought within the frame of the Thousand and One Nights, had then already been translated into Arabic, but stood outside the Thousand Nights. It further appears from the Fihrist of Ibn Abi Ya'qûb an-Nadîm compiled in 377 A.H. that not only—with the exception of the King's brother—the *dramatis personæ* were the same as in the frame-story of our Thousand and One Nights, but they played the same parts. "The first people who composed adventures," so he reports, "who made separate books of them and incorporated them in libraries, were the old Persians. The Ashghani (Arsaki) Kings were addicted to them with especial zeal. In the times of (their successors) the Sassanid dynasty, new material was added and it (this literature) extended and the Arabs translated the tales into their language. Men of eloquence and grammatical knowledge then took them up, began to polish them, embellished them and fashioned them to taste. The first book of the kind to be thus treated was the book Hazâr Afsânah, which means Thousand Adventures, the occasion of which was the following:

"One of their Kings had the custom, when he married a woman and had spent the night with her, to kill her in the morning. Now he one day married a King's daughter who possessed intelligence and wit and was called Shahrazâd, and who when she came to him began to entertain him with adventures. Withal she proceeded with her tale in such a way towards the end of the night that the King was induced to spare her and to beg her on the following night to finish her story, until a thousand nights were thus passed. During this time he lived with her until she had a child by him, the which she showed him, and therewith informed him of the stratagem she had employed against him. He, however, recognised her wit, inclined to her and spared her life. The King had a housekeeper, Dînazâd by name, who supported her therein. It is said that this book was composed for Humaï, the daughter of Bahman; other statements have, however, been made concerning it. Muhammad ibn Ishâq (the author of the Fihrist) says thereof—but whether it be true; God knoweth—that the first who passed the nights with stories was Alexander and that he had people to make him laugh and recount adventures to him; this he did not for pleasure, but in order to be wakeful and on the alert. And for that purpose the Kings used the book Hazâr Afsân, which contained a thousand nights and less than two hundred stories (Samar), for generally a story stretches over several nights. I have several times seen the book complete: it is a thin, limp (lit. cold) book."

Here, indeed, Shahrazâd is called a King's daughter, whereas already Al Mas'ûdi, like our own versions, describes her as daughter of the Wazîr, and Dinazâd, who by Al-Mas'ûdi is introduced as the nurse and according to the Fihrist was the housekeeper of the King, appears in our versions as the sister of Shahrazâd. In spite of such divergences, however, and although the brother of the King is missing both in the Fihrist and Mas'ûdi, it is clear that the introduction to the Thousand Nights of the fourth Islamic century is essentially the same as that of our Thousand and One Nights. The change of the title from 1,000 nights to 1,001 nights, as which Al Qurti knew it, is explained by the preference, to be observed also in other matters, of Orientals for uneven numbers, especially those which overstep a round number by one, or fall short of it by one. Thus the Islamic rosary consists of 99 beads, not a hundred; thus according to the Parsis 9,999 Spirits, not 10,000 guard the righteous. Authentic precedents for the number 1,001 seem to be first forthcoming at a time when Turkish influence had already made itself supreme everywhere in the East; and perhaps

E. Littmann is right in ascribing the adoption of 1,001 for a large number to the Turkish alliteration "bin bir" (1,001).

An Arabica "Book of the 1,001 Slaves" and also a "Book of the 1,001 Handmaids" is known to us from the seventh Islamic century, and in the same century Nâsir-ud-dîn Tûsi uses 1,001 to indicate a large quantity. From the Fihrist we learn of a further book of the "Thousand Nights," quite different from the Hazâr Afsân, which Muhammad Al-Jahshiyârî, who died in 881 A.H. (942 A.D.), had compiled. "He gathered out of books and from the mouths of the night story-tellers (Musâmirûn) 1,000 tales and adventures of Arabian, Persian, Greek and other origin, of which each stood alone without connection with the others and of which each represented a night. He had elaborated 480 nights, each of which took up about 50 pages when death prevented him from continuing the work." Manifestly Al-Jahshiyârî was not dependent on the already mentioned 1,000 Adventures which, according to Mas'ûdi, people called the 1,000 Nights; he had made his own selection of stories from oral and written sources and cannot have taken over the frame-story of the Thousand Adventures unaltered, if he took it at all. For that would have meant that each story was carried on to the following night, or was brought into connection with the one before it, whereas the Fihrist expressly states that the opposite was the case. Thus much, however, it seems that we must conclude from his words: that Al-Jahshiyârî without the model of the 1,000 Adventures never would have come to name his collection "The Thousand Nights." That model must therefore have been extant at any rate in the year 300 A.H., though whether the Persian original or already an Arabic translation lay before him, who can say. There is nothing improbable in the latter supposition, for translations of Persian works into Arabic had been undertaken much earlier. Instances date already from the time of Hishâm bin Abdul Malik (v. Mas'ûdi Tanbih 106) and several from the time of Mansûr (136–158 A.H.). A poet named Rasti, who is said to have lived in the time of Mahmûd of Ghazni, is also mentioned in connection with the Persian Hazâr Afsânah; it is not clear, however, if it is meant that he translated the Hazâr Afsânah into Persian verse as Rudagi did the Kalîla wa Dimna. Anyhow, as little of this poetical lucubration has reached us as of the prose text of the Hazâr Afsânah. This was not the only Persian story-book that was known in Baghdâd in the fourth Islamic century; the author of the Fihrist mentions a whole series of other similar tales and collections of tales with their names.

It is established from the statements of Mas'ûdi and the Fihrist that our Thousand and One Nights goes back by the roundabout way through the "Thousand Nights" of Baghdâd to the Persian Hazâr Afsânah. Of the age of this Persian work, however, we know nothing certain. According to the Fihrist, indeed, "as people say" it was written for Humaï the daughter of Bahman, but what Persian legend tell us of that lady does not put us in the position to establish her historical identity. This Humaï, also named Chihrazâd, is indeed identified by some Arabic chroniclers with the Esther of the Bible and is said to have afterwards become the wife of Ahashverosh (Xerxes); but this identification depends not on contemporary tradition, but is merely the result of a combination of certain biblical data with similar data of Persian origin. After the learned men who were concerned with the Persian national tradition had learnt from the Book of Esther that there had once been a Persian queen of Jewish origin they made the attempt to identify her among the names of Persian queens and so hit on Humaï Chihrazâd. The renowned Dutch Orientalist, M. J. de Goeje, has gone even a step further: since Humaï is identical with Esther and at the same time also bore the name of Chihrazâd, therefore she should be identified with the Shahrazâd of the Hazâr Afsânah. He also thinks that he can recognise in the biblical Book of Esther the frame-tale of the Thousand and One Nights, which therefore must go back to the second or third pre-Christian Century, the conjectural period of origin of the biblical book. But the analogies which de Goeje finds are altogether insignificant, quite apart from the fact that the Hazâr Afsânah were said to be compiled *for* not *from* Humaï. She therefore has nothing to do with Shahrazâd, the teller of stories. Certainly, both in the Thousand and One Nights and in the Book of Esther the part of deliverer from sore peril falls to a woman, but the methods which lead up to safety are quite different: Esther's achievement with those means was to unmask the persecutor of her people, but Shahrazâd knew how to postpone, by means of story-telling, longer and ever longer the decision of her fate, and so in the end converted the tyrant to clemency. Esther delivers her people: Shahrazâd at least does directly save others of her sex, but the life of Esther herself is not threatened while Shahrazâd fights above all for her own life. Though the stories thus run quite differently from one another, still it cannot be denied that they have particular features in common, which is explained simply by the fact that both stories are acted on the same stage, the court of the Persian King.

We had already spoken of the fact that Indian stories and collections of stories had been translated into Persian, or more accurately into Pahlavi, such as Kalîla wa Dimna and presumably also the Book of Women's Wiles. These works, which in the second Islamic century were further translated into Arabic, have retained traces of their Indian origin in the names of the characters as well as in peculiar features. The Hazâr Afsânah, on the contrary, by such names a Shariyâr,

Shahrazâd, Dînâzâd at first sight give the impression of being Persian of the soil. All three are genuine Persian names and only that of Shâhzamân is a hybrid formation, not found in older times, from Persian Shâh and Arabic zamân. But precisely this name and its bearer are unknown to the oldest form of the frame-story, as Al-Mas'udi and the Fihrist have preserved it for us. However, the retention of such Persian names in the Arabic version can only demonstrate with certainty that the story, as is otherwise established, flowed to the Arabs from a Persian channel, not that the Persian version was the original. Moreover, when we remember that even Ariosto and, before him, Sercambi gave the heroes of their story Italian names, we shall be cautioned, and shall deduce from the Persian names nothing more than that the frame-story, whatever its origin, had become at home in Persia in the third or fourth Islamic century. We have no positive data for the theory, but general considerations as well as the existence of Indian parallels closely analogous in all essentials point to it, that the Persian Hazâr Afsânah went back to an Indian original.

Examples of several stories being held together by a frame-narrative are to be found already in Ancient Egypt; but the way in which the tales of the Thousand and One Nights are fitted into the frame is specifically Indian, and just that particular feature is noticeable elsewhere in Indian literature: that stories are strung together with the object of warding off or rendering impossible a dreaded event. Just so, in the Indian Sukasaptati, does the wise Papagai bind to the house the woman who in her husband's absence wished to visit her lover by concluding every day the fragment of a story with the words: "The rest I shall tell you to-morrow if you stay at home." But we can go much further. In one of the canonical books of the Jains the following story is quoted: A King, who had the custom of telling the women of his palace one after another to come to spend the night with him, once married a maiden of low origin whose wit and beauty had enchanted him. When it came to the turn of the maiden to go to the King, she took with her her maid-servant, whom she had ordered to ask for a story at the time when the King should come to rest and so to propound her request that the King should hear it. When, then, the maid begs for a story, her mistress replies that she must wait until the King has gone to sleep. The King pretends to be asleep and the Queen begins to propound a kind of riddle which the servant does not understand, and the explanation of which the mistress defers till the following evening. The King, eager to hear the answer, lets the damsel come again to him on the following evening, and she was able for six months so continuously to bind him by her stories that he neglected all his other women for love of her. So here again a clever woman succeeded in inducing the King to listen to her night after night, though, to be sure, her life was in no way threatened as in the

Thousand and One Nights. As an allusion to this story, as E. Leumann has shown, is found already in the versified abridgment of the same Sutra, its diffusion in at least the fifth or sixth century after Christ is ascertained. If thus for the last part of the Frame-story—the only one which Al-Mas'ûdi and the Fihrist transmit to us—Indian origin is very probable, it is no less so for the two parts which precede it in our texts. The first part of the frame is made up of the story of the husband brought to despair by his wife's faithlessness, who recovers cheerfulness and health when he sees that others of his kind have fared no better. This motive is known already to the Buddhistic Tripi-taki, which in 251 was translated into Chinese. The second part of the frame relates the story of the woman kept imprisoned by the Geni, who yet found means to deceive him with another man, and is already to be found in a Buddhistic Jataka. Only the point, first attested by Al-Mas'ûdi and the Fihrist, that the Queen was to have been killed, seems not to be referable to older Indian literature. Of this point we can only say that the Persian Hazâr Afsânah already knew it; not that it is of Persian or of Indian origin. An Indian book that can be regarded as the original of the Hazâr Afsânah, is not known; the parallels collated by E. Cosquin by way of proof, with the fact that Persia of old had to thank the Indians for so many stories, makes it at least probable, however, that the Hazâr Afsânah also were translated from the Indian or wrought upon an Indian model.

If we compare the table of contents given in the Fihrist with the frame-story of our own text we find, as already observed, that it is taken only from the third part. Whether the Hazâr Afsânah said noth-ing at all as to the reason which led to the King's cruelty towards women, or whether the author of the Fihrist and Al-Mas'ûdi omitted it for the sake of brevity, we cannot decide. Ariosto and Sercambi, on the other hand, know not the part of the frame-story which alone the Arabic writers reproduce, but only the first and second part of the frame-story of our text.

The table of contents of the Fihrist, however, is not sufficiently detailed to enable us to judge in what manner the individual stories were linked together inside the frame. A. Gelber has sought to answer the question, clear to him but never put by any of his predecessors, whether the queenly narrator was only—as in our texts—thinking of delay, or whether she was not really, by the choice and arrangement of her stories, endeavouring to change the mind of her hearer. After the pattern of other Indian collections, one might suppose that alternating stories, which spoke now for and now against the cor-ruptness of women would have been retailed; or such as impress upon the mind the necessity of careful deliberation and the danger of precipitate action. Gelber, however, has not given himself the trouble to reconstruct such an older selection and arrangement approximately from existing vestiges and parallels, and so his book brings us no nearer to a solution of this question; if it is still solvable, which, in face of the alterations which the original Thousand Nights have undergone since then, from the beginning until now, is not exactly probable. In spite of such alterations we might expect to come upon stories of Indian origin, even outside the frame-story, in our texts if an Indian work were really at the bottom of it. In fact many of the plots are also to be found in Indian stories, which does not, however, in itself prove that the stories must have been derived from India, since the same plots are to be found also outside India; only where the plots are linked together in exactly the same way as in an Indian story, can a borrowing be held as proved. Peculiar touches have, however, been preserved which become easily intelligible when the Indian manners and customs presupposed by them are taken into consideration. For example, when the condemned physician takes vengeance on the King by poisoning the pages of the book which he bequeathes to him, the case is, as J. Gildemeister has already pointed out, not extraordinary in India, where books are written on palm-leaves and are rubbed with a poisonous fluid as a protection against ants. On the other hand, the presumably original Indian names of the heroes of the frame-story (and perhaps of other stories too) were already, in the version of the Hazâr Afsânah, changed into Persian. For a Persian touching up an original Indian work it was of first importance to replace the Indian names, outlandish-sounding to his readers, by names familiar to them; although another procedure was possible and had been employed in the case of Kalîla wa Dimna, for example. In our text, however, not only have the Indian names almost completely disappeared, but, outside the frame-story, the probable Persian names of the Hazâr Afsânah have also mostly been replaced by Arabic; only a few like Shâpûr or Ardshîr may still descend from the Hazâr Afsânah. While the latter may have been a version or translation of an Indian original, and perhaps contained only tales of Indian origin, it is none the less established by the statements of the Fihrist, as we have already seen, that, at the time when the Hazâr Afsânah were translated into Arabic, Persian stories had long been available to the Arabs; as we know from Al-Jahshiyârî that he gathered such in his Thousand Nights, so they may well have found their way into the older Alf Lailah. All this is mere conjecture, therefore; for even of the Arabic translation of the Hazâr Afsânah we know only the frame-story, and the oldest text of the Thousand and One Nights preserved to us, as above indicated, dates only from the ninth Islamic century. Besides Indian and Persian stories, Al-Jahshiyârî gathered similar stories of Greek origin, and has likewise preserved for us in the Fihrist the names of a whole series of narratives of Greek origin translated into

Arabic in the fourth Islamic century. Even in the Thousand and One Nights we find, if not whole stories, at any rate episodes of which the Greek origin is probable. The reader need only recall the passage in Sindbâd's third voyage where the captain is eaten by the giant, the latter, however, has his eye put out by the other prisoners. Here the agreement with the legend of Polyphemus is so close that we may well derive the Arabic story from the Greek; probably it reached the Arabs through a prose version of the contents of Homer's epic, such as the Byzantines loved.

But the Arabic light literature of the fourth Islamic century was not by any means derived only from such loans from Indians, Persians and Greeks. Already in the heathen times the deeds of tribal heroes and the life and vicissitudes of the desert, and of the Arabian princely courts, had formed the subject of "Night Stories" (samar). Islam added to this a new element. The Quran itself is full of stories about the former Prophets, the predecessors of Muhammad. The characters of the Bible history both Old and New Testament, and also Alexander (dhu'l-Qarnain), the Seven Sleepers of Ephesus (Ashâb al-Kahf), the tribes of 'Ad and Thamûd are brought repeatedly before the eyes of the Arabs, for the encouragement of the Prophet and his followers and as a warning to opponents. The new urban culture, which blossomed forth in the most important centres of the newly-founded Arab world-empire, created new themes for the activity of the story-tellers; we hear of some such who, in the markets, satisfied the requirements of the masses, and of others who beguiled the time for the ruler and his court what time the winecup circled. Al-Mas'ûdi tells us how a public story-teller, "a man who speaks in the street and proffers to the people tales and anecdotes and drolleries" was brought before the Khalîfa Al-Mu'tadid (279–89 A.H.) and had to repeat his stories. Many titles, too, of purely Arabic tales, which were common in Baghdâd in the fourth Islamic century are enumerated for us by the author of the Fihrist. He devotes a special section to the various Arabian lovers of both heathen and Islamic times whose histories had been treated in literary form. From this group he distinguishes another, "of lovers whose names occur in the night-stories" (asma ul-'ushshâq alladhîna tadkhulû ahâdîth-uhum fî's-samar), which, in contradistinction to the others, formed the subject of oral delivery and of which several were set in the time of the Ummayyads.

Besides such sentimental or realistic love-tales, the wonderful and supernatural had its lovers, for we hear at the same time, in the Fihrist, of stories treating of the love of men for jinn and of jinn for men, while others are dedicated to the wonders of the sea. The heroes of all these love stories, as well as of the stories of the wonders of the sea, bear true Arabic names and the author of the Fihrist observes in conclusion that this sort of entertaining literature enjoyed special

popularity under the Abbasids and above all in the time of the Khalîfah Al Muqtadir (295–320 A.H.) He adds: "The copyists have composed (writings of this sort) and have lied (in doing so)" and he goes on
to name two writers who notoriously ascribed their own compilations
to other authors. So far as names of Arab rulers appear in these titles
they belong exclusively to the Ummayad period; the Prince who, in
the Thousand and One Nights has become the Khalîfah, Hârûn, is
not once named in them, and the authors of the works mentioned in
the Fihrist had, notoriously, scruples against introducing a member of
the ruling house in their stories. Yet it is certain that the name of
Hârûn had by then acquired great popularity, not so much owing to
his personal qualities as to the fact that not long after the end of his
reign peace and security vanished from Bâghdâd, and his time
appeared to survivors, amid the disorders which burst upon them, as a
lost paradise. It may be stated for certain that stories which were told
at first of other rulers were later on transferred to the time of Hârûn;
to name one example, the public story-teller who was summoned to
the palace, as above mentioned on the authority of Al-Mas'ûdi, is
shown in a tale of the Thousand and One Nights, no longer at the
court of Al-Mu'tadid, but at that of Hârûn, and is introduced there by
Masrûr. Hârûn has not, however, been able altogether to drive out the
memory of earlier rulers from our texts. There are still in the Thousand and One Nights stories which are set in the time of 'Abdulmalik
or Hishâm, not to speak of those which take place under the rule of
later Khalifahs of the dynasty of the Abbasids and other Sultâns. It has
even been supposed that the night-wanderings which Hârûn undertook along with his Wazîr and his executioner in order to learn to
know the secrets of his capital were transferred to him afterwards; at
any rate some story-writers relate similar adventures of the Khalîfah
An-Nâsir (575–622 A.H.). Hârûn figures often in the love-stories
which take place in citizen circles of Baghdâd quite extraneously, as a
deus ex machina to unite the lovers or relieve them from their former
woes. But besides these stories in which he must be content with the
role of the typical Khalîfah, there are anecdotes in which, more in
accord with historical accuracy, he comes on in conversation with his
court poets and singers—anecdotes such as are regarded as authentic
in historical and historico-literary works. Popular fantasy imagined an
offset to the brilliant ruler, who governed all the kingdoms of the
earth, in the form of his legendary son, As-Sabti, who, like St. Alexius,
left the palace of his royal father to earn his bread as a day-labourer—an
Islamic saintly legend which the ascetic's flight from the world glorifies.
We may suppose that a part of the stories grouped around Hârûn
had their origin in Baghdâd somewhere between the fourth and
fifth Islamic centuries, and that they there found their way into the
collection.

We have already seen that the Thousand and One Nights was well known in Egypt in the sixth Islamic century, and all our texts also present stories of undoubtedly Egyptian origin. These stories, then added, depict by preference the life of the merchants and artisans, are well told, and in many of them the wonderful plays a very modest part. In particular, a number of tales of roguery belong to this stratum, in which the dishonesty and corruption of the police appear in the light of criticism. This kind of story—as Th. Nollinger has pointed out, who was the first to characterise the Egyptian stratum—has been familiar in Egypt from of old; already Herodotus offers us an example of it in the legend of Rampsinitos. On the other hand these tales bear much resemblance to the "genero picaresco" of the Spaniard; and that stories of this kind were told in Spain as early as the Islamic period we learn from a passage in Al-Maqqari, in which a distinguishing feature of one of these Egyptian tales of the Thousand and One Nights is transferred to Seville of the fifth Islamic century; the thief already fastened to the cross—in the Thousand and One Nights it is a woman thief—manages to beguile a passing Bedawi, who sets him free, whereupon he binds his liberator to the cross and slips off with that liberator's property. Many stories of the Egyptian group seem to have been enlarged afterwards by the inclusion of plots of wonder and of witchcraft. One peculiarity, as J. Oestrup has brought out, distinguishes the demons who figure in these Egyptian legends in contrast to those of the Indo-Persian group: whereas in the latter the superhuman beings take an intimate interest in the fate of the heroes, in the late Egyptian group they are altogether dependent on the possessor of the ring or other talisman which governs them without there being any question of their own feelings. V. Chauvin, in his work "La récension Egyptienne des mille et une nuits" has attempted to prove that these later Egyptian insertions—whole stories as well as mere postscripts to those earlier existing—are the work of a Jew who had gone over to Islam; only thus can be explained the fact that conversions to Islam are so frequent in these stories, and that they are strongly flavoured with Jewish ideas. But stories of conversion of a similar kind are to be found already in much earlier times in authors of pure Islamic origin, and the originally Jewish ideas in question had by then been long the common property of Islamic popular belief and were not at all restricted to the Jewish converts.

The three principal categories—the Indo-Persian from Hazâr Afsânah, the Bâghdâd stories from the spheres of the city and the court, and the Egyptian tales of roguery and witchcraft stories do not at all account for the whole contents of our text. These and similar writings owe their inclusion first to the endeavour to fill out the frame and complete the number, not at the outset meant to be taken literally, of

1,001, but also to the changing taste of the readers or hearers who ever demanded something new. The introduction and the stories which were there at the beginning have been least affected by this effort; for the rest, however, the public story-tellers, for whom the collection served as a text-book, had, as already stated, no special interest to respect the original text as it had been handed down to them. As a text-book of such a story-teller the Tübinger MS. of the story of Sul and Shumûl declares itself by the occasional occurrence in it of the address "My Masters," directed to the audience. While eminent persons suffered them to come to their houses for the entertainment of their guests, the simple folk crowded in courtyards and even in the public squares around these story-tellers and later on followed them into the coffee-houses to which, from their coming into vogue in the ninth Islamic century, they transferred their activity. We have evidences of the way in which these story-tellers delivered the Thousand and One Nights only at a later time, through European travellers of the eighteenth century. The most intimate is the description which the English physician Patrick Russell, who from 1750–71 practised at Aleppo and to whom we are indebted for a "Natural History of Aleppo," furnishes us in that work. He describes to us how the narrator paces up and down the room, standing still only when the scene described calls for an emphatic pause. He then goes on to say: "He is commonly heard with great attention and not unfrequently in the midst of some interesting adventure, when the expectation of his audience is raised to the highest pitch, he breaks off abruptly and makes his escape from the room, leaving both his heroine and his audience in the utmost embarrassment." Russell then describes how those who sit near the door try to prevent him, and demand that he shall end the tale before he leaves the place; how he, however, always contrives to escape, and how the audience must reserve their curiosity for the following evening. This trick of the story-tellers has its traces in our texts in the fact that a "Night" often breaks off in the middle of the story; the story-teller, who derived a modest revenue in some places from the sale of sugar which he furnished for the coffee, in others only from the voluntary contributions of the audience, must have been as concerned as the keeper of the coffee-house to secure his audience also for the next evening. Not long after Russell, the Thousand and One Nights seems to have disappeared from the repertory of the public story-tellers, for E. W. Lane, who lived in Cairo from 1825 to 1828 and has also in his "Manners and Customs of the modern Egyptians" made detailed mention of the activity of the public story-tellers, declares that the stories of the Thousand and One Nights, which only a few years before had been recited, were now no more to be heard, and manuscript copies of the work were so rare that the hard-worked story-tellers could not afford them. Soon after Lane, printed editions of the text of the collection made it generally accessible, and the public story-tellers, whose audience consisted essentially of the illiterate had no longer any difficulty in procuring a copy; but, nevertheless, the Thousand and One Nights still remained excluded from their programme. Yâ'qûb Artin Pasha reports that it is a common superstition in Cairo that he who reads the Thousand and One Nights right through must die in the same year. A story-teller, questioned by me in Cairo in 1906, knew nothing of that, but explained that the language of the text was not correct enough for him, whereupon, on a close investigation of his argument, it transpired that he had never read the Thousand and One Nights. Another peculiarity of the story-tellers must be signalised, which is also to be observed in our text: they like to transpose the scenes which they depict to the immediate neighbourhood, well known to their hearers, so that they can turn now and again to one or other of them with such words as: "Thou, Hasan, knowest the house full well. Thou passest by it every morning of thy life." Our editions all depend on manuscripts of Egyptian origin, and so show intimate acquaintance with the topography of Cairo and its neighbourhood.

Let us now throw a glance on the books, once independent, which in the course of time became absorbed in the collection. There is first of all the story of Sindbâd or the Seven Wise Masters, the Indian original of which has not yet indeed been discovered, but which in design and spirit betrays its land of birth; some have even wished to derive the name Sindbâd from the Indian Siddāhpati, a theory with which the long "A" of the Arabic form is not, however, to be harmonised. Its theme is that, so often treated in India, of the wiles and infidelity of woman, of which the stories inserted in the frame-tale furnish proof. The work had been done into Arabic verse by the poet Abân al-Lâhiqi who died in 200 A.H.; the Arabic prose version which served as groundwork must therefor have appeared in the second Islamic century. In the frame-narrative this book shows some kinship with another collection which, as we have seen, is mentioned as early as in the third Islamic century under the name of Kal'âd wa Shimâs: the individual stories, however which the frame encloses are quite different from those in the Sindbâd book. The Shimâs book is avowedly of Indian origin, but seems to have reached the Arabs by way of some Christian recension. We possess other such recensions, though in the versions received into the Thousand and One Nights the specifically Christian passages are discarded.

The voyages of Sindbâd, also, formed originally an independent work. In the fourth Islamic century there existed a number of such travel-romances, and even in the Thousand and One Nights this literature of Mirabilia is represented by other stories besides that of Sindbâd, as, for instance, by the history of Saif ul-Mulûk. In such tales we have before us the Arabic adaptation of older travel-legends known to East and West, to which, however, all sorts of information, true and false, has been added, just as the Arab merchants and sea-farers brought it home from their voyages to countries of the East. Reports of several such voyages have been preserved to us, and one of them goes back to a merchant who in 237 A.H. travelled all through China. From this and from a similar work, the Ajâibul Hind of Captain Buzurg ibn Shahriyâr, much has been incorporated in the voyages of Sindbâd. M. J. de Goeje has shown that the "Navigatio" of St. Brandan is very strongly influenced by the voyages of Sindbâd and other Oriental writings and Asin y Palacios has recently carried his proofs still further. The author of the "Navigatio," or his author-ity, seems to have been in the East about the year 1000 A.D., and to have heard these stories there.

There are also two great chivalry-romances in the Thousand and One Nights, that of 'Umar un-Numan, which the Tübinger MS. of the ninth Islamic century recognises already as belonging to the Thousand and One Nights, and that of 'Ajîb and Gharîb. While the former reflects the shock of the encounter of Islam with the Frank-ish chivalry—a period which has left behind its echo also in other stories of the collection—in 'Ajîb and Gharîb survives in some sort the remembrance of the struggles between Arabs and Persians in pre-Islamic and early Islamic times; there crops out in it a spirit of fanaticism which was altogether foreign to those early times and was first roused by the inroads of the Crusaders.

In the once similarly independent book of the learned slave, Tawaddud, we have before us a story less noteworthy for its content than for its literary after-effects. In the slave-market Tawaddud, who had herself advised her husband to free himself from want by selling her, fell to an officer of the palace and was offered to the Khalîfa for purchase. The Khalîfa, however, to make sure whether she really possessed all the excellences ascribed to her, subjected her to a searching examination, in which she not only answered all ques-tions, but on her side also put questions to her examiners, which they were unable to answer. Therefor the Khalîfa bade her ask a favour for herself and, in accordance with her request, united her to her former lord. Possibly we have to see a prototype of this story in a work, quoted in the Fihrist and translated from the Greek, of which the title runs: *Kitab al-failsuf alladhi buliya bi'l-Jariati Qitar Waha-dith al falasifah fi amriha*. To the narrator of Tawaddud the fate of his characters is of secondary consideration, the essential part for him is the questions and answers which cover the most diverse fields of knowledge—theology, astronomy, medicine and philosophy. Works of a similar nature were multifarious and common in the Middle Ages, not only among the Arabs but also among the Persians, in the

Christian East and in the West. In the Islamic world the most renowned example of this literature is the Questions of Adbullah ibn Salam, which, besides the Arabic, has been adapted into Persian, Turkish, Urdu and Malay, and which, through a Latin translation, became known in Christian Europe as early as the thirteenth century. All these Question-books are in arrangement and even in contents akin to one another, but the relations in which the story of Tawaddud stands to a Spanish folk-book the *Historia de la doncella Teodor* which continued to be widely read till the end of the nineteenth century is much closer. Not only is the frame-story in both exactly consonant, but even the name of the heroine is the same in either case, for Teodor is derived from the Arabic Tûdur, as the name actually runs in one Arabic MS. through alteration of the terminal "d" into "r." Many of the questions, also, in the Spanish version are in agreement with the Arabic text and it is noteworthy that the oldest Spanish text preserved to us contains nothing specifically Christian; the Christian elements introduced into the later Spanish versions are taken from a similar folk-book, the Dialogue of the Emperor Hadrian with the Child Epitus. In the Arabic text, only one of the examiners is mentioned by name, the renowned Ibrâhîm an-Nazzâm (d. 231 A.H.), who also lives again in the Spanish under the nearly corresponding name of *Abrahem el trobador,* the surname Nazzâm, which Ibrâhîm bore on account of his handicraft—*Kana yanzimu 'l-hirz*—is here wrongly taken in the sense of versifier, a meaning which Nazzâm can also bear. The Arabic book probably originated at a time when the memory of those philosophers of the second Islamic century was still alive, whereas the oldest Spanish versions known to us date from the fourteenth century at latest, possibly from the thirteenth century. The Spanish text first appeared in print in 1520, an edition followed by numerous others in unbroken succession till 1890, while a Portuguese edition is catalogued as late as the year 1906.

The *Hasaniya* of Abul Futuwwa, which in Sir John Malcolm's time was much read in Persia, represents a Shî'a adaptation of the above.

Another story of the Thousand and One Nights which equally is still preserved as an independent book in Arabic, Persian and Turkish, the Story of Saif ul-Mulûk, attracts attention on account of its introduction. In this it is reported that a King Muhammad ibn Sabā'ik caused search to be made for the finest story and finally received that of Saif ul-Mulûk through a merchant Hasan in Damascus. Now there is no King of this name, though Mahmûd ibn Sabuktegin is famed throughout the whole East of the Islamic world and the Persian version of the story names him in place of that Muhammad. It is there told how Mahmûd heard from his court poet, Unsuri a story which greatly pleased him. The Wazîr of Mahmûd, the same Ahmad ibn Hasan Maimandi who still survives in numerous anecdotes, being tormented by envy, thereupon set to work to move heaven and earth in order to discover an even finer story, till at last he secured that of Saif ul-Mulûk. This introduction of the Persian version clearly preserves the original, and in the Arabic setting the famous Wazîr has been made into the merchant Hasan. The story itself is of no particular consequence, nor had it its original home in Persia, but presents itself in essentials as an adaptation of Sindbâd's voyages.

In like manner the group of marvellous travels appertain to the story of Bulûqyâ; for it is not a question here of journeys into lands inhabited by foreign folk, but of journeys for religious motives into realms which are otherwise inaccessible to mortals. Bulûqyâ is the name of a King of Bani Israîl in Egypt who in searching through the treasure-chamber of his father finds a book in which the appearance of the Prophet Muhammad is foretold. Bulûqyâ then sets out in search of him, reaches Jerusalem and there hears from 'Affân that whoever can get hold of the signet-ring of Solomon will become by its possession lord of genii and of men; the ring, however, is still on the finger of Solomon, whose body rests in a place beyond the Seven Seas. In order to pass over the seas a herb is needed with which the feet must be rubbed, and which is said to be in the possession of the King of the Serpents. 'Affân persuades Bulûqyâ to take him with him, saying that, once in possession of the ring, their every wish will be fulfilled and they will be then able to live until the appearance of Muhammad. They come at last to Solomon's corpse, but as 'Affân is trying to pull off the ring he is burnt to ashes, while Bulûqyâ's life is saved, thanks to the intervention of the angel Gabriel, from whom he learns that it will be a good while before the Prophet appears. Thereupon he continues his journeys and reaches the realm of the believing genii, Jabal Qâf, the Confluence of the Two Seas, and finally the Earthly Paradise; whence Al-Khidhr in a second whisks him back to his own home. In this story we have before us, in the form of travel description, a whole compendium of Islamic cosmology and eschatology. Even Hell, which he did not himself visit, was described to Bulûqyâ by the King of the believing genii. The story stands near to the Heaven and Hell journeys such as are common among Jews and Christians, Parsis and Muslims and reach their highest point in Dante's Divina Comedia. How strongly Dante was influenced by Islamic eschatology M. Asin y Palacios has lately sought to prove in his book *La escatologia Musulman en la Divina Comedia* published in 1919. The name of Bulûqyâ has its ultimate origin in the biblical Book of Kings and is miswritten from that of Hilqiyâhû, the High Priest who in the reign of Josiah finds the Book of the law which had been left to oblivion just as Bulûqyâ finds the Taurât in his father's treasure-chamber. In an extant version apart from the Thousand and One Nights Bulûqyâ is expressly said to be the son of Ushiyâ, *i.e.*, Josiah. As Hilqiyâhû has become Bulûqyâ, so Shâfân, who according to the biblical account also took part in the finding of the Book of the Law has become 'Affân. Already at the beginning of the fourth Islamic century Hamza al-Isfahâni names the story of Bulûqyâ, together with that of King 'Og, as an example of Jewish tales. King 'Og is in fact much mentioned in the Jewish legends, but Hilqiyâhû (Bulûqyâ) hardly at all; none the less is Hamza right to characterise his story as Jewish, because apart from the disfigured Hebrew names of the characters, the eschatological lore depends in many respects on Jewish ideas, and the wanderings of Bulûqyâ show much resemblance to the Jewish tales of Rabbi Joshua ben Levi and the Midrash Konen. The oldest extant version of the Bulûqyâ-story is to be found in Thalabi's Qisas ul-Anbiyā and is there reported in the name of Al Jauzaqi (d. 388 A.H.) who traces it back to Abd us-Salâm, the Jewish convert of the Prophet, to whom it is nowhere ascribed in older sources; at latest, however, it must have originated between 250 and 300 A.H.

Finally, there is yet another tale to be mentioned, which is not to be found in the ordinary editions of the Thousand and One Nights, but in certain MSS. of Christian origin—Christian Arabs have also of yore acquired merit for the maintenance of the Thousand and One Nights—the tale of the wise Haiqâr. Haiqâr, the Wazîr of Sanherib, King of Babel, adopts his nephew in childhood, but afterwards turns him out of the house because he will not take to heart his instruction. To avenge himself, the nephew forges a letter of Haiqâr to the Kings of Egypt and Persia which he plays into the hands of Sanherib, while at the same time he arranges for his uncle to receive an equally false letter of Sanherib. In his pretended letter Haiqâr promises the two Kings to betray the empire of his lord on their arrival at the Eagle's Plain, while Sanherib in his letter to Haiqâr orders the latter to make a sham attack on himself in order to offer a war bait to the two rulers. When Sanherib read Haiqâr's letter and by the subsequent conduct of the latter thought himself confirmed in the opinion that he was betrayed by him, he determines to have him put to death. Haqâr's wife, however, induces the executioner to kill another in his place, while Haiqâr remains hidden. On the news of the fall of the wise Wazîr the neighbouring Kings grow overbearing and demand of Sanherib the solution of apparently insoluble problems unless he wishes to be deprived of his Kingdom. In the country's hour of need the executioner resolves to confess the truth to the King. Whereupon Haiqâr is restored to favour, solves all the problems and in the end once again attempts, by a series of wise admonitions, to lead his nephew Nadan back into the right way. This story was known in the Middle Ages to all the Christian peoples of the East and also to the Slavs and Byzantines, and traces of it are to be found in the Talmud as early as the fourth century. But some five hundred years earlier, the Book of Tobit in the Apocrypha of the Old Testament, which knows the wise Akiakaros and his nephew Nadan, plays upon it, and finally the excavations at Elephantine in Egypt have brought to light a papyrus which preserves for us fragments of the tale in Aramaic script of the fifth pre-Christian century. Some have wished to ascribe a Jewish origin to the story because it was common among the Jews at such an early period, but already the names of the chief characters are all Assyrian, not only Haiqâr and Nadan but also that of the executioner Abu Sumaik, who is called in the papyrus version, in good Assyrian, Nabûsumiskun; the scene is the court of the Assyrian King and everything favours the theory that we have here a popular tale which had its origin somewhere about the seventh pre-Christian century in the Assyrian capital, Niniveh, or at least was located there.

Besides such whole books or independent tales, several collections of smaller pieces inter-related by their contents have been taken into the Thousand and One Nights. Animal fables, legends—these latter mostly of Jewish ancestry—anecdotes about verses and their origin, controversy-stories (like that in which the various complexions strive for supremacy) stories of stupid answers and other fooleries. Most of these pieces are also to be found elsewhere in Arabic literature, especially in books of *Adab,* and are taken from them, so plainly that even the names of the authorities to which they go back originally are preserved in the text.

All printed editions of the Arabic text agree, as already observed, in this: that they none of them contain some of the stories most beloved in Europe since the time of Galland, such as that of Aladdin and the Wonderful Lamp and that of Ali Baba and the Forty Thieves. That Aladdin does actually form an ingredient of certain variants of the Thousand and One Nights, however, is proved by the discoveries of Zotenberg, who found Arabic texts of this story in Paris. The case of Ali Baba is somewhat different: After all attempts for a decade to discover an Arabic text of this tale had been in vain, D. B. MacDonald observed that one had been lying in the Bodleian at Oxford since 1860 and was even correctly indicated in the MS. catalogue of the collection. This text, written about 1800, which was made known by Macdonald in 1910, has, however, nothing to show that it belongs to the Thousand and One Nights. The Oxford text, indeed, is not very different from that used by Galland, though it does not accord with it in all particulars, and the hitherto undiscovered Arabic text of Galland might quite well, despite the Oxford version, figure as part of the Thousand and One Nights like that of Aladdin.

The tales of the Thousand and One Nights are narrated in prose, and that is the proper form of narrative. True, the insertions of rhymed prose or verse are extraordinarily frequent, but both very seldom serve to carry on the story; their function being above all the description of men and things and the expression of emotions. Rhymed prose (*saj'*) was customary among the Arabs of old in the pronouncements of seers and judges. It then almost disappeared— except for its use in the Koran—from Arabic literature. From the middle of the third Islamic century it first appears again, more frequent, till by the beginning of the fourth century it has made good its entry into solemn and official speech and finally into the style of private correspondence. In the Thousand and One Nights, too, it is repeatedly employed for letters and dialogues.

Whilst rhymed prose does not occur in the older Arabic narrative literature, it has at all times known poetical insertions. Already in the accounts of the Ayâm ul-'Arab they are usual; the biography of the Prophet (Sîrah) does not disdain them, no more does the historical literature of the first century of Islam. But there the same thing is to be noted as in the Thousand and One Nights: the inlaid verses are not a continuation but an interruption of the narrative. The hero himself expresses his emotions in verses which indeed frequently contain allusions to the events in which he is taking part, but furnish no account of them. He sings the fame of his ancestry; participators in the events praise him in eulogy, lament for the fallen in elegy—that is especially the task of women—or insult the enemy. It is true that Arabic literature, from the third Islamic century, knows stories brought into the form of verse; Abân al-Lâhiqī, for example, (who died in 200 A.H.) wrought narrative works of Indian and Persian origin into poetic shape. In the Thousand and One Nights, however, we extremely seldom find narrative verse properly so called. There the verses which are put in the mouths of the personages give expression to their feelings, or to the judgment of the author, and often are brought in to transport the readers to general considerations from the tension of the moment; letters and inscriptions, too, are often composed in verse-form. Again, it is very seldom that the name of the poet is mentioned; often, however, the verse is stated to be a quotation by such formulas as "as the poet saith," or "as it has been said," and often quotations of this sort are strung together, verses of different poets on the same theme being cited one after another. Even where verses are not expressly acknowledged as quotations they are generally recognisable as such. Cases in which the verse has been a part of the story from the first are not very frequent, the great majority even of those verses which are introduced with a simple "Then he began to speak" are not composed by the narrator but are borrowings made by him from other poets. I have devoted some attention to this question and from about 1,280 various verses or verse-groups in Macnaghten's edition some 350 poets can be pointed out with certainty to whom, on the evidence of their own Diwans or various works of Adab, they belong. It is noticeable also that the poets of heathen or early Islamic times are only seldom quoted, while on the other hand the poets of later times up to the eighth Islamic century are quoted frequently. It would be interesting to ascertain how far the oldest texts, especially the Galland MSS., contain the same verses as our own editions. The fixing of the origin of the verse is of importance as well for the history of the origin of particular tales as for the rectification of the text, for very many of them appear to be disfigured in our editions.

The old book of the Thousand Nights is not preserved to us and, except Al-Mas'ûdi, the author of the Fihrist, and Al Qurti, no Arabic man of letters has anywhere mentioned it. After it ceased to serve for the entertainment of the cultivated, it no longer appertained to the literature of which learned men took note. What the public story-tellers offered to their ignorant audiences appeared to them unworthy of attention. It was the aim of the story-tellers to entertain their hearers, not to hand on a book in the form in which it had come down to them. It is therefore not easy for us to circumscribe the scope and contents of the Thousand and One Nights, for the contents have not always in different countries and times been exactly the same; and nothing else is left for us but to reckon as included in it everything which in any of the texts which have come to us is produced as belonging to the Thousand and One Nights. What is no better attested than, for example, Sul and Shumûl, we have a right to exclude, for the narrator who wished to insinuate it into the collection only half carried out his attempt. Where, however, such attempts have succeeded, we must recognise the accomplished fact. We are not dealing with a work handed down in a fixed form, but with a collection which is constantly being supplemented. The Thousand and One Nights had become the basin into which all the numerous streams of Arabic Story discharge their flow; or, to express it otherwise, a microcosmos in which all the various *genres* of the Arabic story-teller's art appear. There remains the important problem of classifying the individual stories under these various *genres*, and to compare the stories inside the Arabian Nights which belong to one and the same category one with another, as also with representatives of the same *genre* outside the collection. V. Chauvin, in his *Bibliographie des ouvrages arabes* has provided data for the solving of this problem.

The fables, parables, legends, traditions, fairy-tales, jokes, novels and learned stories do not always occur in independent shape, but appear sometimes bound to others by ever fresh entanglements, from which they must first be extricated ere we can compare them, as

original literary entities, with others of their kind. In the case of anecdotes, especially, there is a foundation of definite historical events,
which often have undergone only trifling alterations; while in the traditional stories such events have left but a faint echo. Certain traits
which recur in all literatures are appropriated in the Thousand and
One Nights to specified personages of the Arabo-Islamic sphere of
culture, and are by preference transferred to places which lie within
the horizon of that sphere. Finally, the stories and legends abound in
themes which recur not only in the literatures of the most widely different peoples of the East and West, but also in the popular traditional lore of every part of the earth, even among illiterate peoples.

The Thousand and One Nights is a mirror of the Arabic-Islamic
world of the first six centuries; it resembles a kaleidoscope in which
the plots of the popular story-teller's art of all peoples and times pass
before us in their motley variety.

JORGE LUIS BORGES

The Translators of *The Thousand and One Nights*[†]

1. Captain Burton

At Trieste, in 1872, in a palace with damp statues and deficient
hygienic facilities, a gentleman on whose face an African scar told
its tale—Captain Richard Francis Burton, the English consul—
embarked on a famous translation of the *Quitab alif laila ua laila,*
which the *roumis* know by the title *The Thousand and One Nights.*
One of the secret aims of his work was the annihilation of another
gentleman (also weatherbeaten, and with a dark and Moorish beard)
who was compiling a vast dictionary in England and who died long
before he was annihilated by Burton. That gentleman was Edward
Lane, the Orientalist, author of a highly scrupulous version of *The
Thousand and One Nights* that had supplanted a version by Galland.
Lane translated against Galland, Burton against Lane; to understand Burton we must understand this hostile dynasty.

I shall begin with the founder. As is known, Jean Antoine Galland
was a French Arabist who came back from Istanbul with a diligent
collection of coins, a monograph on the spread of coffee, a copy of

[†] Translated by Esther Allen from *Selected Non-Fictions* by Jorge Luis Borges, edited by
Eliot Weinberger, copyright © 1999 by Maria Kodama; translation copyright © 1999 by
Penguin Putnam, Inc. Used by permission of Viking Penguin, a division of Penguin
Group (USA), Inc., Penguin Group (Canada), a Division of Pearson Canada, Inc., and
Penguin Group Ltd. (UK).

the *Nights* in Arabic, and a supplementary Maronite whose memory was no less inspired than Scheherazade's. To this obscure consultant—whose name I do not wish to forget: it was Hanna, they say—we owe certain fundamental tales unknown to the original: the stories of Aladdin; the Forty Thieves; Prince Ahmad and the Fairy Peri-Banu; Abu al-Hassan, the Sleeper and the Waker; the night adventure of Caliph Harun al-Rashid; the two sisters who envied their younger sister. The mere mention of these names amply demonstrates that Galland established the canon, incorporating stories that time would render indispensable and that the translators to come—his enemies—would not dare omit.

Another fact is also undeniable. The most famous and eloquent encomiums of *The Thousand and One Nights*—by Coleridge, Thomas De Quincey, Stendhal, Tennyson, Edgar Allan Poe, Newman—are from readers of Galland's translation. Two hundred years and ten better translations have passed, but the man in Europe or the Americas who thinks of *The Thousand and One Nights* thinks, invariably, of this first translation. The Spanish adjective *milyunanochesco* [thousand-and-one-nights-esque]—*milyunanochero* is too Argentine, *milyunanocturno* overly variant—has nothing to do with the erudite obscenities of Burton or Mardrus, and everything to do with Antoine Galland's bijoux and sorceries.

Word for word, Galland's version is the most poorly written of them all, the least faithful, and the weakest, but it was the most widely read. Those who grew intimate with it experienced happiness and astonishment. Its Orientalism, which seems frugal to us now, was bedazzling to men who took snuff and composed tragedies in five acts. Twelve exquisite volumes appeared from 1707 to 1717, twelve volumes that were innumerably read and that passed into various languages, including Hindi and Arabic. We, their mere anachronistic readers of the twentieth century, perceive only the cloying flavor of the eighteenth century in them and not the evaporated aroma of the Orient which two hundred years ago was their novelty and their glory. No one is to blame for this disjunction, Galland least of all. At times, shifts in the language work against him. In the preface to a German translation of *The Thousand and One Nights*, Dr. Weil recorded that the merchants of the inexcusable Galland equip themselves with a "valise full of dates" each time the tale obliges them to cross the desert. It could be argued that in 1710 the mention of dates alone sufficed to erase the image of a valise, but that is unnecessary: *valise*, then, was a subspecies of saddlebag.

There have been other attacks. In a befuddled panegyric that survives in his 1921 *Morceaux choisis*, André Gide vituperates the licenses of Antoine Galland, all the better to erase (with a candor

that entirely surpasses his reputation) the notion of the literalness of
Mardrus, who is as *fin de siècle* as Galland is eighteenth-century, and
much more unfaithful.

Galland's discretions are urbane, inspired by decorum, not moral-
ity. I copy down a few lines from the third page of his *Nights*: *"Il alla
droit a l'appartement de cette princesse, qui, ne s'attendant pas à le
revoir, avait reçu dans son lit un des derniers officiers de sa maison"*
[He went directly to the chamber of that princess, who, not expecting to see him again, had received in her bed one of the lowliest servants of his household]. Burton concretizes this nebulous *officier*:
"a black cook of loathsome aspect and foul with kitchen grease and
grime." Each, in his way, distorts: the original is less ceremonious
than Galland and less greasy than Burton. (Effects of decorum: in
Galland's measured prose, *"recevoir dans son lit"* has a brutal ring.)

Ninety years after Antoine Galland's death, an alternate translator
of the *Nights* is born: Edward Lane. His biographers never fail to
repeat that he is the son of Dr. Theophilus Lane, a Hereford
prebendary. This generative datum (and the terrible Form of holy
cow that it evokes) may be all we need. The Arabized Lane lived five
studious years in Cairo, "almost exclusively among Muslims, speaking and listening to their language, conforming to their customs
with the greatest care, and received by all of them as an equal." Yet
neither the high Egyptian nights nor the black and opulent coffee
with cardamom seed nor the frequent literary discussions with the
Doctors of the Law nor the venerable muslin turban nor the meals
eaten with his fingers made him forget his British reticence, the delicate central solitude of the masters of the earth. Consequently, his
exceedingly erudite version of the *Nights* is (or seems to be) a mere
encyclopedia of evasion. The original is not professionally obscene;
Galland corrects occasional indelicacies because he believes them
to be in bad taste. Lane seeks them out and persecutes them like an
inquisitor. His probity makes no pact with silence: he prefers an
alarmed chorus of notes in a cramped supplementary volume, which
murmur things like: *I shall overlook an episode of the most reprehen-
sible sort; I suppress a repugnant explanation; Here, a line far too
coarse for translation; I must of necessity suppress the other anecdote;
Hereafter, a series of omissions; Here, the story of the slave Bujait,
wholly inappropriate for translation*. Mutilation does not exclude
death: some tales are rejected in their entirety "because they cannot
be purified without destruction." This responsible and total repudia-
tion does not strike me as illogical: what I condemn is the Puritan
subterfuge. Lane is a virtuoso of the subterfuge, an undoubted precursor of the still more bizarre reticences of Hollywood. My notes
furnish me with a pair of examples. In night 391, a fisherman offers

a fish to the king of kings, who wishes to know if it is male or female and is told it is a hermaphrodite. Lane succeeds in taming this inadmissible colloquy by translating that the king asks what species the fish in question belongs to, and the astute fisherman replies that it is of a mixed species. The tale of night 217 speaks of a king with two wives, who lay one night with the first and the following night with the second, and so they all were happy. Lane accounts for the good fortune of this monarch by saying that he treated his wives "with impartiality." . . . One reason for this was that he destined his work for "the parlor table," a center for placid reading and chaste conversation.

The most oblique and fleeting reference to carnal matters is enough to make Lane forget his honor in a profusion of convolutions and occultations. There is no other fault in him. When free of the peculiar contact of this temptation, Lane is of an admirable veracity. He has no objective, which is a positive advantage. He does not seek to bring out the barbaric color of the *Nights* like Captain Burton, or to forget it and attenuate it like Galland, who domesticated his Arabs so they would not be irreparably out of place in Paris. Lane is at great pains to be an authentic descendant of Hagar. Galland was completely ignorant of all literal precision; Lane justifies his interpretation of each problematic word. Galland invoked an invisible manuscript and a dead Maronite: Lane furnishes editions and page numbers. Galland did not bother about notes: Lane accumulates a chaos of clarifications which, in organized form, make up a separate volume. To be different: this is the rule the precursor imposes. Lane will follow the rule: he needs only to abstain from abridging the original.

The beautiful Newman-Arnold exchange (1861–62)—more memorable than its two interlocutors—extensively argued the two general ways of translating. Newman championed the literal mode, the retention of all verbal singularities: Arnold the severe elimination of details that distract or detain. The latter procedure may provide the charms of uniformity and seriousness; the former, continuous small surprises. Both are less important than the translator and his literary habits. To translate the spirit is so enormous and phantasmal an intent that it may well be innocuous; to translate the letter, a requirement so extravagant that there is no risk of its ever being attempted. More serious than these infinite aspirations is the retention or suppression of certain particularities; more serious than these preferences and oversights is the movement of the syntax. Lane's syntax is delightful, as befits the refined parlor table. His vocabulary is often excessively festooned with Latin words, unaided by any artifice of brevity. He is careless; on the opening page of his translation he places the adjective *romantic* in the bearded mouth of a twelfth-century

Muslim, which is a kind of futurism. At times this lack of sensitivity serves him well, for it allows him to include very commonplace words in a noble paragraph, with involuntary good results. The most rewarding example of such a cooperation of heterogenous words must be: "And in this palace is the last information respecting lords collected in the dust." The following invocation may be another: "By the Living One who does not die or have to die, in the name of He to whom glory and permanence belong." In Burton—the occasional precursor of the always fantastical Mardrus—I would be suspicious of so satisfyingly Oriental a formula; in Lane, such passages are so scarce that I must suppose them to be involuntary, in other words, genuine.

The scandalous decorum of the versions by Galland and Lane has given rise to a whole genre of witticisms that are traditionally repeated. I myself have not failed to respect this tradition. It is common knowledge that the two translators did not fulfill their obligation to the unfortunate man who witnessed the Night of Power, to the imprecations of a thirteenth-century garbage collector cheated by a dervish, and to the customs of Sodom. It is common knowledge that they disinfected the Nights.

Their detractors argue that this process destroys or wounds the good-hearted naiveté of the original. They are in error; *The Book of the Thousand Nights and a Night* is not (morally) ingenuous; it is an adaptation of ancient stories to the lowbrow or ribald tastes of the Cairo middle classes. Except in the exemplary tales of the *Sindibad-namah*, the indecencies of *The Thousand and One Nights* have nothing to do with the freedom of the paradisiacal state. They are speculations on the part of the editor: their aim is a round of guffaws, their heroes are never more than porters, beggars, or eunuchs. The ancient love stories of the repertory, those which relate cases from the desert or the cities of Arabia, are not obscene, and neither is any production of pre-Islamic literature. They are impassioned and sad, and one of their favorite themes is death for love, the death that an opinion rendered by the *ulamas* declared no less holy than that of a martyr who bears witness to the faith. . . . If we approve of this argument, we may see the timidities of Galland and Lane as the restoration of a primal text.

I know of another defense, a better one. An evasion of the original's erotic opportunities is not an unpardonable sin in the sight of the Lord when the primary aim is to emphasize the atmosphere of magic. To offer mankind a new *Decameron* is a commercial enterprise like so many others; to offer an "Ancient Mariner," now, or a *"Bateau ivre,"* is a thing that warrants entry into a higher celestial sphere. Littmann observes that *The Thousand and One Nights* is, above all, a repertory of marvels. The universal imposition of this assumption on every

Western mind is Galland's work; let there be no doubt on that score. Less fortunate than we, the Arabs claim to think little of the original; they are already well acquainted with the men, mores, talismans, deserts, and demons that the tales reveal to us.

In a passage somewhere in his work, Rafael Cansinos Asséns swears he can salute the stars in fourteen classical and modern languages. Burton dreamed in seventeen languages and claimed to have mastered thirty-five: Semitic, Dravidian, Indo-European, Ethiopic . . . This vast wealth does not complete his definition: it is merely a trait that tallies with the others, all equally excessive. No one was less vulnerable to the frequent gibes in *Hudibras* against learned men who are capable of saying absolutely nothing in several languages. Burton was a man who had a considerable amount to say, and the seventy-two volumes of his complete works say it still. I will note a few titles at random: *Goa and the Blue Mountains* (1851); *A Complete System of Bayonet Exercise* (1853); *Personal Narrative of a Pilgrimage to El-Medinah and Meccah* (1855); *The Lake Regions of Central Equatorial Africa* (1860); *The City of the Saints* (1861); *The Highlands of the Brazil* (1869); *On an Hermaphrodite from the Cape de Verde Islands* (1866); *Letters from the Battlefields of Paraguay* (1870); *Ultima Thule* (1875); *To the Gold Coast for Gold* (1883); *The Book of the Sword* (first volume, 1884); *The Perfumed Garden of Cheikh Nefzaoui*—a posthumous work consigned to the flames by Lady Burton, along with the *Priapeia, or the Sporting Epigrams of Divers Poets on Priapus*. The writer can be deduced from this catalogue: the English captain with his passion for geography and for the innumerable ways of being a man that are known to mankind. I will not defame his memory by comparing him to Morand, that sedentary, bilingual gentleman who infinitely ascends and descends in the elevators of identical international hotels, and who pays homage to the sight of a trunk. . . . Burton, disguised as an Afghani, made the pilgrimage to the holy cities of Arabia; his voice begged the Lord to deny his bones and skin, his dolorous flesh and blood, to the Flames of Wrath and Justice; his mouth, dried out by the *samun*, left a kiss on the aerolith that is worshiped in the Kaaba. The adventure is famous: the slightest rumor that an uncircumcised man, a *nasráni*, was profaning the sanctuary would have meant certain death. Before that, in the guise of a dervish, he practiced medicine in Cairo— alternating it with prestidigitation and magic so as to gain the trust of the sick. In 1858, he commanded an expedition to the secret sources of the Nile, a mission that led him to discover Lake Tanganyika. During that undertaking he was attacked by a high fever; in 1855, the Somalis thrust a javelin through his jaws (Burton was coming from Harar, a city in the interior of Abyssinia that was forbidden to Europeans). Nine years later, he essayed the terrible hospitality of the ceremonious cannibals of Dahomey; on his return there was no scarcity of rumors (possibly spread and certainly encouraged by Burton himself) that, like Shakespeare's omnivorous proconsul,[1] he had "eaten strange flesh." The Jews, democracy, the British Foreign Office, and Christianity were his preferred objects of loathing; Lord Byron and Islam, his venerations. Of the writer's solitary trade he made something valiant and plural: he plunged into his work at dawn, in a vast chamber multiplied by eleven tables, with the materials for a book on each one—and, on a few, a bright spray of jasmine in a vase of water. He inspired illustrious friendships and loves: among the former I will name only that of Swinburne, who dedicated the second series of *Poems and Ballads* to him—"in recognition of a friendship which I must always count among the highest honours of my life"—and who mourned his death in many stanzas. A man of words and deeds, Burton could well take up the boast of al-Mutanabbi's *Diwan:*

> The horse, the desert, the night know me
> Guest and sword, paper and pen.

It will be observed that, from his amateur cannibal to his dreaming polyglot, I have not rejected those of Richard Burton's personae that, without diminishment of fervor, we could call legendary. My reason is clear: the Burton of the Burton legend is the translator of the *Nights.* I have sometimes suspected that the radical distinction between poetry and prose lies in the very different expectations of readers: poetry presupposes an intensity that is not tolerated in prose. Something similar happens with Burton's work: it has a preordained prestige with which no other Arabist has ever been able to compete. The attractions of the forbidden are rightfully his. There was a single edition, limited to one thousand copies for the thousand subscribers of the Burton Club, with a legally binding commitment never to reprint. (The Leonard C. Smithers re-edition "omits given

---

1. I allude to Mark Anthony, invoked by Caesar's apostrophe: "On the Alps/It is reported, thou didst eat strange flesh/which some did die to look on . . . " In these lines, I think I glimpse some inverted reflection of the zoological myth of the basilisk, a serpent whose gaze is fatal. Pliny (*Natural History* VIII, par. 33) tells us nothing of the posthumous aptitudes of this ophidian, but the conjunction of the two ideas of seeing (*mirar*) and dying (*morir*)—"*vedi Napoli e poi mori*" [see Naples and die]—must have influenced Shakespeare.

The gaze of the basilisk was poisonous; the Divinity, however, can kill with pure splendor—or pure radiation of *manna*. The direct sight of God is intolerable. Moses covers his face on Mount Horeb, "for he was afraid to look on God"; Hakim, the prophet of Khorasan, used a four-fold veil of white silk in order not to blind men's eyes. Cf. also Isaiah 6:5, and 1 Kings 19:13.

passages in dreadful taste, whose elimination will be mourned by no one"; Bennett Cerf's representative selection—which purports to be unabridged—proceeds from this purified text.) I will venture a hyperbole: to peruse *The Thousand and One Nights* in Sir Richard's translation is no less incredible than to read it in "a plain and literal translation with explantory notes" by Sinbad the Sailor.

The problems Burton resolved are innumerable, but a convenient fiction can reduce them to three: to justify and expand his reputation as an Arabist; to differ from Lane as ostensibly as possible; and to interest nineteenth-century British gentlemen in the written version of thirteenth-century oral Muslim tales. The first of these aims was perhaps incompatible with the third; the second led him into a serious lapse, which I must now disclose. Hundreds of couplets and songs occur in the *Nights*; Lane (incapable of falsehood except with respect to the flesh) translated them precisely into a comfortable prose. Burton was a poet: in 1880 he had privately published *The Kasidah of Haji Abdu*, an evolutionist rhapsody that Lady Burton always deemed far superior to FitzGerald's *Rubáiyát*. His rival's "prosaic" solution did not fail to arouse Burton's indignation, and he opted for a rendering into English verse—a procedure that was unfortunate from the start, since it contradicted his own rule of total literalness. His ear was as greatly offended against as his sense of logic, for it is not impossible that this quatrain is among the best he came up with:

> A night whose stars refused to run their course,
> A night of those which never seem outworn:
> Like Resurrection-day, of longsome length
> To him that watched and waited for the morn.[2]

And it is entirely possible that this one is not the worst:

> A sun on wand in knoll of sand she showed,
> Clad in her cramoisy-hued chemisette:
> Of her lips honey-dew she gave me drink,
> And with her rosy cheeks quencht fire she set.

I have alluded to the fundamental difference between the original audience of the tales and Burton's club of subscribers. The former were roguish, prone to exaggeration, illiterate, infinitely suspicious of

---

2. Also memorable is this variation on the themes of Abulmeca de Ronda and Jorge Manrique: "Where is the wight who peopled in the past/Hind-land and Sind; and there the tyrant played?"

the present, and credulous of remote marvels; the latter were the respectable men of the West End, well equipped for disdain and erudition but not for belly laughs or terror. The first audience appreciated the fact that the whale died when it heard the man's cry; the second, that there had ever been men who lent credence to any fatal capacity of such a cry. The text's marvels—undoubtedly adequate in Kordofan or Bûlâq, where they were offered up as true—ran the risk of seeming rather threadbare in England. (No one requires that the truth be plausible or instantly ingenious: few readers of the *Life and Correspondence of Karl Marx* will indignantly demand the symmetry of Toulet's *Contrerimes* or the severe precision of an acrostic.) To keep his subscribers with him, Burton abounded in explanatory notes on "the manners and customs of Muslim men," a territory previously occupied by Lane. Clothing, everyday customs, religious practices, architecture, references to history or to the Koran, games, arts, mythology—all had already been elucidated in the inconvenient precursor's three volumes. Predictably, what was missing was the erotic. Burton (whose first stylistic effort was a highly personal account of the brothels of Bengal) was rampantly capable of filling this gap. Among the delinquent delectations over which he lingered, a good example is a certain random note in the seventh volume, which the index wittily entitles "*capotes mélancoliques*" [melancholy French letters]. The *Edinburgh Review* accused him of writing for the sewer; the *Encyclopedia Britannica* declared that an unabridged translation was unacceptable and that Edward Lane's version "remained unsurpassed for any truly serious use." Let us not wax too indignant over this obscure theory of the scientific and documentary superiority of expurgation: Burton was courting these animosities. Furthermore, the slightly varying variations of physical love did not entirely consume the attention of his commentary, which is encyclopedic and seditious and of an interest that increases in inverse proportion to its necessity. Thus volume 6 (which I have before me) includes some three hundred notes, among which are the following: a condemnation of jails and a defense of corporal punishment and fines; some examples of the Islamic respect for bread; a legend about the hairiness of Queen Belkis' legs; an enumeration of the four colors that are emblematic of death; a theory and practice of Oriental ingratitude; the information that angels prefer a piebald mount, while Djinns favor horses with a bright bay coat; a synopsis of the mythology surrounding the secret Night of Power or Night of Nights; a denunciation of the superficiality of Andrew Lang; a diatribe against rule by democracy; a census of the names of Mohammed, on Earth, in the Fire, and in the Garden; a mention of the Amalekite people, of long years and large stature; a note on the private parts of the Muslim, which for the man extend from the navel to his knees, and for the woman from the top of the head to the tips of her toes; a consideration of the *asa'o* [roasted beef] of the Argentine gaucho; a warning about the discomforts of "equitation" when the steed is human; an allusion to a grandiose plan for cross-breeding baboons with women and thus deriving a sub-race of good proletarians. At fifty, a man has accumulated affections, ironies, obscenities, and copious anecdotes; Burton unburdened himself of them in his notes.

The basic problem remains: how to entertain nineteenth-century gentlemen with the pulp fictions of the thirteenth century? The stylistic poverty of the *Nights* is well known. Burton speaks somewhere of the "dry and business-like tone" of the Arab prosifiers, in contrast to the rhetorical luxuriance of the Persians. Littmann, the ninth translator, accuses himself of having interpolated words such as *asked, begged, answered,* in five thousand pages that know of no other formula than an invariable *said.* Burton lovingly abounds in this type of substitution. His vocabulary is as unparalleled as his notes. Archaic words coexist with slang, the lingo of prisoners or sailors with technical terms. He does not shy away from the glorious hybridization of English: neither Morris' Scandinavian repertory nor Johnson's Latin has his blessing, but rather the contact and reverberation of the two. Neologisms and foreignisms are in plentiful supply: *castrato, inconséquence, hauteur, in gloria, bagnio, langue fourree, pundonor, vendetta, Wazir.* Each of these is indubitably the *mot fuste,* but their interspersion amounts to a kind of skewing of the original. A good skewing, since such verbal—and syntactical—pranks beguile the occasionally exhausting course of the *Nights.* Burton administers them carefully: first he translates gravely, "Sulayman, Son of David (on the twain be peace!)"; then—once this majesty is familiar to us—he reduces it to "Solomon Davidson." A king who, for the other translators, is "King of Samarcand in Persia," is, for Burton, "King of Samarcand in Barbarian-land"; a merchant who, for the others, is "ill-tempered," is "a man of wrath." That is not all: Burton rewrites in its entirety—with the addition of circumstantial details and physiological traits—the initial and final story. He thus, in 1885, inaugurates a procedure whose perfection (or whose *reductio ad absurdum*) we will now consider in Mardrus. An Englishman is always more timeless than a Frenchman: Burton's heterogenous style is less antiquated than Mardrus', which is noticeably dated.

2. *Doctor Mardrus*

Mardrus' destiny is a paradoxical one. To him has been ascribed the *moral* virtue of being the most truthful translator of *The Thousand*

and One Nights, a book of admirable lascivity, whose purchasers were previously hoodwinked by Galland's good manners and Lane's Puritan qualms. His prodigious literalness, thoroughly demonstrated by the inarguable subtitle, "Literal and complete translation of the Arabic text," is revered, along with the inspired idea of writing *The Book of the Thousand Nights and One Night*. The history of this title is instructive; we should review it before proceeding with our investigation of Mardrus.

Masudi's *Meadows of Gold and Mines of Precious Stones* describes an anthology titled *Hazar afsana*, Persian words whose true meaning is "a thousand adventures," but which people renamed "a thousand nights." Another tenth-century document, the *Fihrist*, narrates the opening tale of the series; the king's heartbroken oath that every night he will wed a virgin whom he will have beheaded at dawn, and the resolution of Scheherazade, who diverts him with marvelous stories until a thousand nights have revolved over the two of them and she shows him his son. This invention—far superior to the future and analogous devices of Chaucer's pious cavalcade or Giovanni Boccaccio's epidemic—is said to be posterior to the title, and was devised in the aim of justifying it. . . . Be that as it may, the early figure of 1000 quickly increased to 1001. How did this additional and now indispensable night emerge, this prototype of Pico della Mirandola's *Book of All Things and Also Many Others*, so derided by Quevedo and later Voltaire? Littmann suggests a contamination of the Turkish phrase *"bin bir,"* literally "a thousand and one," but commonly used to mean "many." In early 1840, Lane advanced a more beautiful reason: the magical dread of even numbers. The title's adventures certainly did not end there. Antoine Galland, in 1704, eliminated the original's repetition and translated *The Thousand and One Nights*, a name now familiar in all the nations of Europe except England, which prefers *The Arabian Nights*. In 1839, the editor of the Calcutta edition, W. H. Macnaghten, had the singular scruple of translating *Quitab alif laila ua laila* as *Book of the Thousand Nights and One Night*. This renovation through spelling did not go unremarked. John Payne, in 1882, began publishing his *Book of the Thousand Nights and One Night*; Captain Burton, in 1885, his *Book of the Thousand Nights and a Night*; J. C. Mardrus, in 1899, his *Livre des mille nuits et une nuit*.

I turn to the passage that made me definitively doubt this last translator's veracity. It belongs to the doctrinal story of the City of Brass, which in all other versions extends from the end of night 566 through part of night 578, but which Dr. Mardrus has transposed (for what cause, his Guardian Angel alone knows) to nights 338–346. I shall not insist on this point; we must not waste our consternation on this inconceivable reform of an ideal calendar. Scheherazade-Mardrus relates:

> The water ran through four channels worked in the chamber's floor with charming meanderings, and each channel had a bed of a special color; the first channel had a bed of pink porphyry; the second of topaz, the third of emerald, and the fourth of turquoise; so that the water was tinted the color of the bed, and bathed by the attenuated light filtered in through the silks above, it projected onto the surrounding objects and the marble walls all the sweetness of a seascape.

As an attempt at visual prose in the manner of *The Portrait of Dorian Gray*, I accept (and even salute) this description; as a "literal and complete" version of a passage composed in the thirteenth century, I repeat that it alarms me unendingly. The reasons are multiple. A Scheherazade without Mardrus describes by enumerating parts, not by mutual reaction; does not attest to circumstantial details like that of water that takes on the color of its bed; does not define the quality of light filtered by silk; and does not allude to the Salon des Aquarellistes in the final image. Another small flaw: "charming meanderings" is not Arabic, it is very distinctly French. I do not know if the foregoing reasons are sufficient; they were not enough for me, and I had the indolent pleasure of comparing the three German versions by Weil, Henning, and Littmann, and the two English versions by Lane and Sir Richard Burton. In them I confirmed that the original of Mardrus' ten lines was this: "The four drains ran into a fountain, which was of marble in various colors."

Mardrus' interpolations are not uniform. At times they are brazenly anachronistic—as if suddenly Marchand's withdrawal were being discussed. For example:

> They were overlooking a dream city. . . . As far as the gaze fixed on horizons drowned by the night could reach, the vale of bronze was terraced with the cupolas of palaces, the balconies of houses, and serene gardens; canals illuminated by the moon ran in a thousand clear circuits in the shadow of the peaks, while away in the distance, a sea of metal contained the sky's reflected fires in its cold bosom.

Or this passage, whose Gallicism is no less public:

> A magnificent carpet of glorious colors and dexterous wool opened its odorless flowers in a meadow without sap, and lived all the artificial life of its verdant groves full of birds and animals, surprised in their exact natural beauty and their precise lines.

(Here the Arabic editions state: "To the sides were carpets, with a variety of birds and beasts embroidered in red gold and white silver, but with eyes of pearls and rubies. Whoever saw them could not cease to wonder at them.")

Mardrus cannot cease to wonder at the poverty of the "Oriental color" of *The Thousand and One Nights*. With a stamina worthy of Cecil B. de Mille, he heaps on the viziers, the kisses, the palm trees, and the moons. He happens to read, in night 570:

> They arrived at a column of black stone, in which a man was buried up to his armpits. He had two enormous wings and four arms; two of which were like the arms of the sons of Adam, and two like a lion's forepaws, with iron claws. The hair on his head was like a horse's tail, and his eyes were like embers, and he had in his forehead a third eye which was like the eye of a lynx.

He translates luxuriantly:

> One evening the caravan came to a column of black stone, to which was chained a strange being, only half of whose body could be seen, for the other half was buried in the ground. The bust that emerged from the earth seemed to be some monstrous spawn riveted there by the force of the infernal powers. It was black and as large as the trunk of an old, rotting palm tree, stripped of its fronds. It had two enormous black wings and four hands, of which two were like the clawed paws of a lion. A tuft of coarse bristles like a wild ass's tail whipped wildly over its frightful skull. Beneath its orbital arches flamed two red pupils, while its double-horned forehead was pierced by a single eye, which opened, immobile and fixed, shooting out green sparks like the gaze of a tiger or a panther.

Somewhat later he writes:

> The bronze of the walls, the fiery gemstones of the cupolas, the ivory terraces, the canals and all the sea, as well as the shadows projected towards the West, merged harmoniously beneath the nocturnal breeze and the magical moon.

"Magical," for a man of the thirteenth century, must have been a very precise classification, and not the gallant doctor's mere urbane adjective. . . . I suspect that the Arabic language is incapable of a "literal and complete" version of Mardrus' paragraph, and neither is Latin or the Spanish of Miguel de Cervantes.

The Book of the Thousand and One Nights abounds in two procedures: one (purely formal), rhymed prose; the other, moral predications. The first, retained by Burton and by Littmann, coincides with the narrator's moments of animation: people of comely aspect, palaces, gardens, magical operations, mentions of the Divinity, sunsets, battles, dawns, the beginnings and endings of tales. Mardrus, perhaps mercifully, omits it. The second requires two faculties: that of majestically combining abstract words and that of offering up stock comments without embarrassment. Mardrus lacks both. From the line memorably translated by Lane as "And in this palace is the last information respecting lords collected in the dust," the good Doctor barely extracts: "They passed on, all of them! They had barely the time to repose in the shadow of my towers." The angel's confession—"I am imprisoned by Power, confined by Splendor, and punished for as long as the Eternal commands it, to whom Force and Glory belong"—is, for Mardrus' reader, "I am chained here by the Invisible Force until the extinction of the centuries."

Nor does sorcery have in Mardrus a co-conspirator of good will. He is incapable of mentioning the supernatural without smirking. He feigns to translate, for example:

> One day when Caliph Abdelmelik, hearing tell of certain vessels of antique copper whose contents were a strange black smoke-cloud of diabolical form, marveled greatly and seemed to place in doubt the reality of facts so commonly known, the traveller Talib ben-Sahl had to intervene.

In this paragraph (like the others I have cited, it belongs to the Story of the City of Brass, which, in Mardrus, is made of imposing Bronze), the deliberate candor of "so commonly known" and the rather implausible doubts of Caliph Abdelmelik are two personal contributions by the translator.

Mardrus continually strives to complete the work neglected by those languid, anonymous Arabs. He adds Art Nouveau passages, fine obscenities, brief comical interludes, circumstantial details, symmetries, vast quantities of visual Orientalism. An example among so many: in night 573, the Emir Musa bin Nusayr orders his blacksmiths and carpenters to construct a strong ladder of wood and iron. Mardrus (in his night 344) reforms this dull episode, adding that the men of the camp went in search of dry branches, peeled them with knives and scimitars, and bound them together with turbans, belts, camel ropes, leather cinches, and tack, until they had built a tall ladder that they propped against the wall, supporting it with stones on both sides. . . . In general, it can be said that Mardrus does not translate the book's words but its scenes: a freedom denied to translators, but tolerated in illustrators, who are allowed to add these kinds of details. . . . I do not know if these smiling diversions are what infuse the work with such a happy air, the air of a far-fetched personal yarn rather than of a laborious hefting of dictionaries. But to me the

Mardrus "translation" is the most readable of them all—after, Burton's incomparable version, which is not truthful either. (In Burton, the falsification is of another order. It resides in the gigantic employ of a gaudy English, crammed with archaic and barbaric words.)

I would greatly deplore it (not for Mardrus, for myself) if any constabulary intent were read into the foregoing scrutiny. Mardrus is the only Arabist whose glory was promoted by men of letters, with such unbridled success that even the Arabists still know who he is. André Gide was among the first to praise him, in August 1889; I do not think Cancela and Capdevila will be the last. My aim is not to demolish this admiration but to substantiate it. To celebrate Mardrus' fidelity is to leave out the soul of Mardrus, to ignore Mardrus entirely. It is his infidelity, his happy and creative infidelity, that must matter to us.

3. *Enno Littmann*

Fatherland to a famous Arabic edition of *The Thousand and One Nights*, Germany can take (vain) glory in four versions: by the "librarian though Israelite" Gustav Weil—the adversative is from the Catalan pages of a certain encyclopedia—; by Max Henning, translator of the Koran; by the man of letters Félix Paul Greve; and by Enno Littmann, decipherer of the Ethiopic inscriptions in the fortress of Axum. The first of these versions, in four volumes (1839–42), is the most pleasurable, as its author—exiled from Africa and Asia by dysentery—strives to maintain or substitute for the Oriental style. His interpolations earn my deepest respect. He has some intruders at a gathering say, "We do not wish to be like the morning, which disperses all revelries." Of a generous king, he assures us, "The fire that burns for his guests brings to mind the Inferno and the dew of his benign hand is like the Deluge"; of another he tells us that his hands "were liberal as the sea." These fine apocrypha are not unworthy of Burton or Mardrus, and the translator assigned them to the parts in verse, where this graceful animation can be an *ersatz* or replacement for the original rhymes. Where the prose is concerned, I see that he translated it as is, with certain justified omissions, equidistant from hypocrisy and immodesty. Burton praised his work—"as faithful as a translation of a popular nature can be." Not in vain was Dr. Weil Jewish, "though librarian"; in his language I think I perceive something of the flavor of Scripture.

The second version (1895–97) dispenses with the enchantments of accuracy, but also with those of style. I am speaking of the one provided by Henning, a Leipzig Arabist, to Philippe Reclam's *Universalbibliothek*. This is an expurgated version, though the publisher claims otherwise. The style is dogged and flat. Its most indisputable virtue must be its length. The editions of Bûlâq and Breslau are represented, along with the Zotenberg manuscripts and Burton's *Supplemental Nights*. Henning, translator of Sir Richard, is, word for word, superior to Henning, translator of Arabic, which is merely a confirmation of Sir Richard's primacy over the Arabs. In the book's preface and conclusion, praises of Burton abound—almost deprived of their authority by the information that Burton wielded "the language of Chaucer, equivalent to medieval Arabic." A mention of Chaucer as *one* of the sources of Burton's vocabulary would have been more reasonable. (Another is Sir Thomas Urquhart's Rabelais.)

The third version, Greve's, derives from Burton's English and repeats it, excluding only the encyclopedic notes. Insel-Verlag published it before the war.

The fourth (1923–28) comes to supplant the previous one and, like it, runs to six volumes. It is signed by Enno Littmann, decipherer of the monuments of Axum, cataloguer of the 283 Ethiopic manuscripts found in Jerusalem, contributor to the *Zeitschrift für Assyriologie*. Though it does not engage in Burton's indulgent loitering, Littmann's translation is entirely frank. The most ineffable obscenities do not give him pause; he renders them into his placid German, only rarely into Latin. He omits not a single word, not even those that register—1000 times—the passage from one night to the next. He neglects or refuses all local color: express instructions from the publisher were necessary to make him retain the name of Allah and not substitute it with God. Like Burton and John Payne, he translates Arabic verse into Western verse. He notes ingenuously that if the ritual announcement "So-and-so pronounced these verses" were followed by a paragraph of German prose, his readers would be disconcerted. He provides whatever notes are necessary for a basic understanding of the text: twenty or so per volume, all of them laconic. He is always lucid, readable, mediocre. He follows (he tells us) the very breath of the Arabic. If the *Encyclopedia Britannica* contains no errors, his translation is the best of all those in circulation. I hear that the Arabists agree; it matters not at all that a mere man of letters—and he of the merely Argentine Republic—prefers to dissent.

My reason is this: the versions by Burton and Mardrus, and even by Galland, can only be conceived of *in the wake of a literature*. Whatever their blemishes or merits, these characteristic works presuppose a rich (prior) process. In some way, the almost inexhaustible process of English is adumbrated in Burton—John Donne's hard obscenity, the gigantic vocabularies of Shakespeare and Cyril Tourneur, Swinburne's affinity for the archaic, the crass erudition of the authors of 17th-century chapbooks, the energy and imprecision, the love of tempests and magic. In Mardrus' laughing paragraphs, *Salammbô* and La Fontaine, the *Mannequin d'osier* and the *ballets russes* all coexist. In Littmann, who like Washington cannot tell a lie, there is nothing but the probity of Germany. This is so little, so very little. The commerce between Germany and the *Nights* should have produced something more.

Whether in philosophy or in the novel, Germany possesses a literature of the fantastic—rather, it possesses *only* a literature of the fantastic. There are marvels in the *Nights* that I would like to see rethought in German. As I formulate this desire, I think of the repertory's deliberate wonders—the all-powerful slaves of a lamp or a ring; Queen Lab, who transforms Muslims into birds; the copper boatman with talismans and formulae on his chest—and of those more general ones that proceed from its collective nature, from the need to complete one thousand and one episodes. Once they had run out of magic, the copyists had to fall back on historical or pious notices whose inclusion seems to attest to the good faith of the rest. The ruby that ascends into the sky and the earliest description of Sumatra, details of the court of the Abbasids and silver angels whose food is the justification of the Lord, all dwell together in a single volume. It is, finally, a poetic mixture; and I would say the same of certain repetitions. Is it not portentous that on night 602 King Schahriah hears his own story from the queen's lips? Like the general framework, a given tale often contains within itself other tales of equal length: stages within the stage as in the tragedy of *Hamlet*, raised to the power of a dream. A clear and difficult line from Tennyson seems to define them:

Laborious orient ivory, sphere in sphere.

To further heighten the astonishment, these adventitious Hydra's heads can be more concrete than the body: Schahriah, the fantastical king "of the Islands of China and Hindustan," receives news of Tarik ibn Ziyad, governor of Tangiers and victor in the battle of Guadalete. . . . The threshold is confused with the mirror, the mask lies beneath the face, no one knows any longer which is the true man and which are his idols. And none of it matters; the disorder is as acceptable and trivial as the inventions of a daydream.

Chance has played at symmetries, contrasts, digressions. What might a man—a Kafka—do if he organized and intensified this play, remade it in line with the Germanic distortion, the *unheimlichkeit* of Germany?

References

Among the volumes consulted, I must enumerate:
Les Mille et une Nuits, contes arabes traduits par Galland. Paris, s.d.

The Thousand and One Nights, commonly called The Arabian Nights' Entertainments. A new translation from the Arabic by E.W. Lane. London, 1839.
The Book of the Thousand Nights and a Night. A plain and literal translation by Richard F. Burton. London (?) n.d. Vols. VI, VII, VIII.
The Arabian Nights. A complete [sic] *and unabridged selection from the famous literal translation of R. F. Burton.* New York, 1932.
Le Livre des mille nuits et une nuit. Traduction littérale et complète du texte arabe par le Dr. J. C. Mardrus. Paris, 1906.
Tausend und eine Nacht. Aus dem Arabischen übertragen von Max Henning. Leipzig, 1897.
Die Erzählungen aus den Tausendundein Nächten. Nach dem arabischen Urtext der Calcuttaer Ausgabe vom Jahre 1839 übertragen von Enno Littmann. Leipzig, 1928.

FRANCESCO GABRIELI

The *Thousand and One Nights* in European Culture[†]

During the last years of the Sun King, lovely Shahrazad, together with Red Riding Hood and Perrault's Cat in Boots, made her entry into Europe. As is well known, she owed her introduction to Antoine Galland (1646–1715), the learned and brilliant French Orientalist who had spent many years in Constantinople and the Levant, observing that world with the same attentive interest as Pietro Della Valla, yet greater preparation. It was upon Galland's return to his homeland that, with the publication of his first free version of *The Thousand and One Nights*, the West came to be submitted to the reign of the Eastern tale and fable. Galland's attitude toward the many written and oral materials of which he made use reveals the typical literary taste of the *grand siècle*. No Romantic abandonment before the letter; classical harmony of line and sobriety of color; elimination and attenuation of anything that could *brave l'honnête* in the Arabic original, and which would later excite the taste of other palates, accustomed to strong drugs. But despite all this, Galland showed a substantial fidelity as an interpreter and also an instinctual felicity in his choice and presentation of the material, which allowed him immediately to grasp hold of the pearls in the collection: Qamar al-Zaman and Aladdin, Ali Baba and the Forty Thieves, the Flying Horse, Shams ad-Din and Nur ad-Din, the cycle of the Hunchback of Baghdad, Sindbad the Sailor. . . . This Orient was exotic enough to provoke the interest of the nascent Enlightenment, and it was orderly and pure enough not to scandalize a precious literary priest or a forbidding Cato. Precisely what, a few decades later, would be held against Galland—the fact that "he clothed his Sultans in the

†   From *Storia e civiltà musulmana* (Naples: R. Ricciardi, 1947), pp. 99–107. Translated from the Italian by Daniel Heller-Roazen.

French style," that he adapted the work to the artistic and moral scruples of time—was a not insignificant element in the clamorous success of his version. The French and European eighteenth century went into ecstasy over just such a domesticated *turquerie*.

Throughout the eighteenth century, the reprints of Galland's *The Thousand and One Nights* became ever more numerous, and in their wake came a whole swarm of imitations, continuations, and remakes of Oriental tales under the sign of Shahrazad. A few years before Galland's death, François Pétis de la Croix began to publish a collection of Arabic, Persian, and Turkish tales that had been freely manipulated and edited, giving his anthology the obviously competing title *A Thousand and One Days*. At the end of the century, Chavis and Cazotte together published a collection in Geneva, *Cabinet des fées*, titled *Sultan Shahrayar's Evenings* (*Les veillées du sultan Chahriyar*): a partial continuation of Galland's work, which, having been interrupted by the translator's death, contained only some three hundred and fifty of the thousand and one nights. It was the age of the Revolution and the Terror, and the graceful images of Oriental sprites and fairies floated for a brief while, soothing exasperated fears and passions. Perhaps Shahrazad had been by the side of André Chenier's *jeune captive* in the St. Lazare prison? Of course, in those same years, Shahrazad had also emigrated from France. In her composite but still gracious Arabo-Turkish-French garb, she had joyfully greeted curious and thoughtful minds across Europe: Wieland and Herder in Germany, Carlo Gozzi in Venice. . . . In 1722, Venice already witnessed the first Italian retranslation of Galland's French *A Thousand and One Nights*, which was no doubt known to the author of *Turandot* and *The Love of the Three Oranges*. The fabulous and somewhat fictitious Orient that the Arabist of the Collège de France had revealed to European culture could be perfectly framed by the marble, water, light, color, and masks of a dying Venice.

The intellectualistic curiosity with which the eighteenth century looked toward the Orient was, with Romanticism, to become a fantastic and sentimental passion. As erudition raised itself to the level of philology and Sylvestre De Sacy, the founder of modern Arabic scholarship, began to study the originals of *The Thousand and One Nights*, distinguishing between its various strata and reconstructing its composition and history, interest for the great book grew, spreading throughout Europe. In Germany, Egypt, and India, the three editions of the text that remain fundamental to this day began to appear in print (revealing, what is more, a highly composite and fluctuating tradition of narrative material, which had been hidden under a single title). This was the beginning of the age in which there were to be direct translations from the Arabic, in addition to the persistent retranslations of Galland. Lane in England and Hammer Purgstall and Weil in Germany presented to their compatriots new, larger, and more faithful English and German editions of *The Thousand and One Nights*, which were to be the source of ecstasy for the Romantic generation as well as those that followed it through to the end of the nineteenth century. The more or less mannered Muslim Orient, with its repertory of minarets and pavilions, odalisques and dervishes, scimitars and turbans, Bedouins and Sultans, had already made its triumphant entry in Romantic poetry, lending its attire to the studied wisdom of the old Goethe no less than to the exuberant, coloristic imagination of Byron and the young Hugo. But one can easily picture the interest and fervor with which the epoch of Brentano, the Grimm brothers, and Fauriel found in the disclosure of the best-known and studied *Thousand and One Nights* a treasure of Oriental storytelling and, moreover, authentic folklore. The influence that the collection exerted on the cultural and artistic training of many of the great writers of the nineteenth century can be perceived in echoes in their works and their autobiographical confessions, from Stendhal to Flaubert, from Dickens to Tennyson, from Ohlenschläger to Tolstoy. But *The Thousand and One Nights'* most direct and profound influence is undoubted on the work of a less illustrious, though still noble artistic figure, the German Wilhelm Hauff (1802–1827), familiar to us Italians through Maria Pezzè Pascolato's magisterial versions and adaptations. The young Swabian poet had lived his few days in the most fervent Romantic worship of the bewitching Orient, which he discovered in the pages of *A Thousand and One Nights*. He identified so deeply with that world as to become himself a kind of Shahrazad, telling German youth exquisite Oriental tales, which are often founded on echoes, characters, and milieus of authentic Arabic narrative patrimony. What impressions do Hauff's tales leave on those who know, as directly as is possible, their distant models? On the artistic side, one must judge in favor of the imitator, who knew how to build and develop his plots with a mastery that is not inferior—and that, indeed, is often superior—to the crude Oriental bards of whom he presents himself as the epigone (think of Stork Caliph, the Ship of the Dead, the Adventures of Said, the Little Muk, and like pleasures of our adolescence). Hauff shows a formal refinement, a capacity for characterization, a sense of measure that is altogether Western and only rarely achieved by the Arabic originals. On the other hand, if we pass from an essential aesthetic judgment to a cultural judgment, considering the fidelity with which Hauff renders the Arabo-Muslim world and ethos, we can hardly fail to note that the stylization of this Romantic Orient remains rather mannered. As far as the immediate spontaneity of representation is concerned, Hauff's tales certainly cannot compete with the suggestive realism of *The Thousand and One Nights*, at least where the *Nights* are realistic, which is not always the case, as we shall see. Hauff's work, in short, has all the merits and defects of a *Nachdichtung*, a free recreation on given motifs. It is unable as well as unwilling to usurp in fidelity and authenticity the place of the originals, from which it draws its motifs.

Toward the end of the nineteenth century and the beginning of the twentieth, the fortunes of *The Thousand and One Nights* appeared in a new light, reflecting and accompanying, once again, the evolution of European taste and thought. Enlightened curiosity and Romantic passion had been both directed less toward the form than toward the content of the work, its exotic world of characters, customs, and the milieu they all revealed. Now there followed a more formal, literary interest, which tended to consider *The Thousand and One Nights* as a work of art, discovering in it at once the voice and the spirit of the Orient in exemplary form. These were the years of European Symbolism and the Decadent Movement, in which Fitzgerald's Omar Khayyàm enchanted the Anglo-Saxon world, the Goncourt brothers discovered the art of the Far East, and a new, delicate love of the Orient unfolded in the refined circles of intellectuals in England and France. In England and France, two new complete versions of *The Thousand and One Nights*, both of high literary aspirations, simultaneously belied and fed the new attitude. Richard Burton, the tireless English traveler, pilgrim to Mecca, and rover of all seven seas, driven by the demon of exploratory curiosity, published in 1885 in Benares (that is, in reality in London) a sumptuous translation of *The Thousand and One Nights* that was later to obscure, in its fame, the preceding English versions by Lane and Payne, becoming a classic of exotic literature. Not long later, between 1899 and 1904, the Levantine physician and man of letters, J. C. Mardrus gave to France the first complete version of *The Thousand and One Nights*, which drove out the old and incomplete Galland from the place it had till then occupied. Despite their great diversity, Burton's and Mardrus's versions share certain common characteristics, mirroring what I would define as the "decadent" phase of the European interest for the famous collection. Each underlines its own character of completeness and literalness with respect to the originals, whose form and spirit each aims to render equally well; each translates the many lines of poetry inserted into the prose of the text, which Galland had omitted altogether and which Lane had often abbreviated on the grounds that the lines were generally of no importance to the action and seemed insipid or bizarre to European taste. Finally, both Burton and Mardrus show an ambitious care for language and style, which leads—especially as far as Mardrus is concerned—to a true, harmonious work of art (in Burton, the non-English Orientalist at times has an easier task turning to the Arabic text!).

But how faithful are these renditions to the authentic spirit of the original? Lawrence of Arabia, a competent judge, did not hesitate to prefer Lane's simplicity and lack of ornament to Burton's convolutions. Every Arabist who reads Mardrus, while admiring the splendid French form of his literary language, asks himself from time to time if old Galland, with his self-assured and traditional storytelling, was not after all closer to the spirit of the original than the supremely refined nineteenth-century exegete. In other words, Burton and Mardrus lend their *Thousand and One Nights* a high literary tone, subtle stylistic finishing, and a solemn and moving poetic breath that is almost always lacking in the original. While the two versions both exaggerate the rough elements in this Oriental work for different—though perhaps humanly identical—reasons, the reader's ultimate impression is one of a refined and exquisite world of unlimited and fantastic wealth, profound and mysterious wisdom, and insuperable harmony. At least this is how Mardrus's version was greeted by dilettantish enthusiasts of Oriental things (see, for example, Julia's book, *Les Mille et une nuits et l'enchanteur Mardrus*). In this sense, it is worth noting the influence that Mardrus's translation exerted on French artistic movements at the beginning of the twentieth century, when Mardrus's Shahrazad reigned supreme in Baskt's ballet, Rabaud's operas, and Dulac's illustrations. This unhistorical depiction of the Orient as an arcane source of pleasure, beauty, and death was later to fall into decline and, losing the brilliance of its artistic expression, to wind up cheaply evoked in the "Oriental" films dear to the suburbs.

At this point, the reader will perhaps wonder which of the various interpretations of *The Thousand and One Nights* that we have mentioned may be considered the least distant from the original, and which, more exactly, the nonspecialist should use to obtain a faithful general impression of this classic of world literature. To the second question, we may answer immediately that, for those who read German, the best complete version that has so far been made is the recent edition by Enno Littmann (Leipzig, 1921–28). Littmann is an Orientalist who has known how to temper literary dignity with a scrupulous respect for the letter and the spirit of the original. In Italian, readers must still content themselves with more or less openly avowed second-hand versions, first of Galland's and later of Mardrus's French editions, which vary from adaptations for children to the complacently illustrated books featured in newspaper kiosks. Today, however, work has begun on a new translation, which will see the light of day as soon as contemporary contingencies have ended; it is direct and complete, the work of a group of Arabists that hopes to offer to the largest Italian public a serious basis for forming a judgment about the famous book.

Since the author of these lines is a member of this group, it is not inopportune now to announce some directions for such a judgment, which will also positively take account of the exposition of the fate of *The Thousand and One Nights* that has been offered.

Far from being that rare and exquisite work of art that decadent readers of the fin de siècle, projecting their own extenuated refinement, saw in it, *The Thousand and One Nights* is a book of the common people in the good and less than good senses of that expression. This is the reason why the sheikhs of Al-Azhar, pedantic champions of learned Arabic literature, despite it; this is also why the European Romantics, who rightly saw in it a *Wunderhorn*, a magic horn of Oriental fable and folklore, extolled it. Excepting the occasional rhetorical flourish in rhymed prose, certain affections, and learned seventeenth-century additions in inserted lines of poetry, the form of *The Thousand and One Nights* is simple, rough, and unkempt, in great contrast to the beautiful style that characterizes so much of the prose of Arabic literature. The content of the collection is a true narrative ocean, into which elements of the most varied provenance have flowed. The most ancient is that of Indian storytelling, to which one may trace the scheme and frame of the work, the tale of Shahrazad (whose name, however, is Iranian, not Indian); the first tales that follow; and the tale and apologia of Sindbad the Wise. Next, there is the Persian element, whose traces may be found in the details of names and demonology. Then there is the Arabic element, which is of varying age. Then there is the Jewish element, and so on and so forth. It should be understood that the Arabic narrative furnishes the major nucleus. Occasionally, it contains echoes of the oldest genuine phase, dating from pre-Islamic and early Islamic times. Generally, however, it reflects the Egyptian Arabism of the fifteenth and sixteenth centuries, under the Mamluks and the Turks (some scholars have argued that the definitive period of compilation can be dated as late as the eighteenth century, but the principal manuscript used by Galland dates from before 1500).

The comparatist may find precedents and parallels to this immense material in the literature of tales and fables from the East and the West. The literary elaboration in *The Thousand and One Nights* is not uniform. It runs from the true small masterpiece to the vapid banality of the storyteller and the narrative hack, along a scale in which scholars have had trouble distinguishing any single authorial personalities. Despite such diversity of materials and artistic treatment, a uniform Muslim patina covers *The Thousand and One Nights*, lending the collection, in a certain sense, a unitary aspect. The world that *The Thousand and One Nights* portrays results from the juxtaposition and sometimes fusion of two elements: the supernatural, involving the superstitious and the thaumaturgical; and the realistic, involving human cunning and canniness. Genies and demons, benign sprites and malign bogeys persecute and assist human beings, leading them toward happiness or ruin, surrounding them with blinding treasures or pushing them toward extreme desperation. But human diligence also asserts itself, untangling the often complicated threads of the adventure. Merchants and reckless youths, disgraceful lovers and simpletons, sponger thieves and adventurers, disciplined and mystical wanderers, princesses of the harem and merry people of the street—they all make up the teeming crowd of these pages. In the cracks of the stylization of the fantastic and the marvelous, one can almost always detect the authentic common life of the medieval Orient, that of Cairo in the time of the Ayyubid and Mamluk dynasties, which can to this day be glimpsed in the poorer neighborhoods of the Egyptian capital, and whose customs and ways of life, still almost identical to those depicted in *The Thousand and One Nights*, were described, a century ago, in a magisterial book by Lane. In short, *The Thousand and One Nights* mainly mirror the life of the people and, therefore, the life of the higher classes as seen through the avid and curious eyes of the people (it suffices, from this perspective, to think of the famous tale of Aladdin, which is not included in the vulgate edition of the collection but which is related to it). The *Nights* preserve the fatalism, the superficial and superstitious piety of the people's mentality. Somehow this finds a way of coexisting with sporadic bouts of obscenity in crude and irritating forms, which have been at times sweetened or refined by translators, as we have indicated, and which have so contributed to the exaggerated fame of the collection as a classic of Arabo-Muslim pornography.

The reader who seeks in *The Thousand and One Nights* not folkloric material but artistic enjoyment, therefore, should not expect from these some 1,200 pages a perpetual marvel and uninterrupted pleasure. Once accustomed to the novelty of the milieu and the dress, he will find large gray zones, repetitions and doubles, puerile common superstitions, and monotonous nursery rhymes for children awake at night or ne'er-do-well habitués of Cairene cafés. He will find an absence of the control of art, which is lethal for four fifths of Oriental art and which is here aggravated by the sometimes mechanical and fortuitous path that has led to the definitive collection. Often this will cause the European reader sorely to miss his Grimm and Andersen, the *Novellino* and Boccaccio. But while not everything is gold, not everything is rubbish, and here and there jewels glimmer in tales that, in entirety or in parts, are in every way the equals of the most famous short stories of the West. Everyone remembers them, and at the start of these pages we have recalled them; some of them, which most deserve their fame, have been reworked and adapted in the fairy-tale traditions of every country. But I would like to draw the attention of a future reader of a complete edition to many of the minor or brief stories, which are often inserted, in whole groups, within longer tales.

Here one can glimpse the sparkle of a wit and the splendor of a figurative and dramatic power that is worthy of the most genuine Arabic tradition, and which is not adulterated (as is so often the case) by the opaque mediocrity of an age of decadence. I would also draw the reader's attention to the realistic stories set in a plain Cairene milieu (for example, the two about Dalila and Ali Zaibaq), which have nothing to fear from comparisons with the richest Spanish picaresque narratives. It is certainly tiring to pick "gold from the dung of Ennius" (*de stercore Ennii*), especially if Ennius is here the anonymous, ungraspable, uncongenial bard of the Orient, who sometimes molds a work of art and sometimes contaminates and ruins with his uncouth hands an ancient narrative material, whose origins are lost in distant centuries and far-off regions in the Asiatic cradle of civilization. But where the selection is rich and varied, who would not rather choose for himself, according to his own genius and taste, and not rely on an anthologist? Like every great book of humanity, in whose margins generations after generations seem to have left the traces of their feelings, passions, and dreams, *The Thousand and One Nights* deserves to be known once and for all in its entirety, before being distilled into finer drinks for distraction and solace along our harsh journey.

MIA IRENE GERHARDT

From The Art of Story-Telling[†]

* * *

Frame-stories

A frame-story[1] may be defined as a narrative whole composed of two distinct but connected parts: a story, or stories, told by a character or several characters in another story of lesser dimensions and subordinate interest, which thus encloses the former as a frame encloses a picture. The '1001 Nights' presents three basic types of the pattern, determined by the function of the framed story in relation to the plot of the framework: we may call them the entertaining frame, the time-gaining frame and the ransom frame. They will be discussed here in this order, which corresponds to an increasing importance of the issue involved in the telling of the framed story.

[†]   From *The Art of Story-Telling: A Literal Study of the Thousand and One Nights* (Leiden: Brill, 1963).

1.   The following pages were published, in French translation and somewhat less developed, in Mia I. Gerhardt, "*La Technique du récit à cadre dans less* 1001 *Nuits*," *Arabica* 8 (1961), pp. 137–157.

ENTERTAINING FRAME

The simplest type is the entertaining frame; it merely presents a character (or several in turn) telling a story for the pleasure of one or more
listeners. It mostly dispenses with elaborate stage-setting, except in
those Harûn stories that begin by making the disguised caliph assist at
some intriguing scene. The interest concentrates on the framed story,
which is told for its own sake and serves merely to provide entertainment, or occasionally, to satisfy curiosity. Harûn er-Rashîd needs
stories to allay his restlessness and prepare him for sleep; and other
caliphs too, thought not endowed with the distinctive feature of
insomnia, often ask one of their familiars to relate a memorable experience, by way of pastime. Even the mamluk sultan Baibars, the story
says, *had a liking for all that is told among the folk, and all that men
choose to believe; and he always wanted to assist in person and to listen
when there was talk about such things* (IV, 776); so he had the captains
of his watch assembled to hear about the strange events they met with
in the course of their careers. (If this is authentic, it might be a case of
"life imitating art": Baibars modelling himself upon the caliphs as presented in fiction.) Normally, the entertainer is of a humbler condition
than the listener who is being entertained; there are no examples, in
the '1001 Nights', of a caliph telling a story himself. Only in SINDBAD
THE SAILOR, the customary roles are reversed, and the distinguished,
wealthy man's entertaining—in every sense of the word—the poor
man gives added point to the frame.

In this type, structural interference between the frame and the
related story is comparatively rare. Most often, the listening caliph
simply dismisses the teller with a few words of comment, and a
reward. Occasionally, he orders that the persons about whom he has
just heard be brought before him, to make their acquaintance and
bestow benefits upon them: thus, el-Mamûn wants to see the six
well-spoken slave-girls (46), and the generous merchant (103).
However, already here there is sometimes a striving to connect
frame and story more closely, making each of them dependent on
the other for its point. The stories of the Ladies of Baghdad account
for their strange behaviour, as described in the framework; in NOC-
TURNAL ADVENTURES, too, the autobiographical stories of the three
protagonists explain the puzzling things that were first related about
them. A less spectacular, but extremely skilful connexion is made
in ABU EL-HASAN FROM KHORASÂN, where a veritable little mystery
is set up in the frame, to be solved in the story. The caliph's amazement and displeasure at noticing valuable property marked with the
name of his grandfather el-Mutawakkil in the house of an unknown
businessman, are dispelled when he is told how this came about
through his grandfather's magnanimity. Still, the only case where

the entertaining frame is an integral part of the whole, not only completely motivated, but functional in bringing out the story's intention, is, again, SINDBAD THE SAILOR.

To this first, simple type belongs also the very elaborate and historically interesting frame of SAIF EL-MULÛK, which even has a title of its own, STORY OF KING MOHAMMED IBN SABAÏK AND THE MERCHANT HASAN. It shows how high a value was set, at the time, upon a good story, and it certainly has some foundation in fact, for all the romantic embellishment of the circumstances. The figure of the dignified sheik, who gives permission to copy the SAIF EL-MULÛK story, but strictly specifies the kinds of public worthy or unworthy of hearing it, may in a certain measure correspond to the reality of a good story-telling period.[2] It also seems authentic that the story is copied from a book, and carefully checked, whereas the king, every time he wants to hear it again, has it read out aloud to him.—Artistically, however, this unique frame is a misfit, because, as Lane already remarked,[3] the story it serves to frame does not live up to it. After having been made to expect something incomparable, the reader is disappointed by an unoriginal and mediocre piece, remarkable chiefly for its length.

The entertaining frame, which prepares the telling of the story and surrounds it with a definite atmosphere, certainly adds to the appeal of the whole; from a technical point of view, though, it most often remains relatively ingenuous. The frame-story offers other, less obvious possibilities.

TIME-GAINING FRAME

The time-gaining frame, a more complicated type than the one just discussed, serves notably to string together large collections of stories, whose function within the frame is to help put off an execution or another calamitous event. This pattern, apparently of Indian origin,[4] is not indigenous in the '1001 Nights'; it is found only in a few stories that were adapted from the Persian. Nevertheless it occupies

---

2. Josef Horovitz, "Saif al-Mulûk," *Mitteilungen des Seminars für Orientalische Sprachen zu Berlin* 6:2 (1903), pp. 52–56.

3. E. W. Lane, *The Thousand and One Nights, Commonly Called, in England, The Arabian Nights' Entertainment*, 3 vols. (London: E. Stanely Poole, 1877), p. III: 343; he therefore put the framing story in a note.

4. There seems little doubt that the time-gaining frame, like other framing and inserting devices, is an Indian invention. It is displayed to advantage in the *Parrot Book*, which we possess i.a. in a 14th-century Persian adaptation; the original Sanskrit text, "Seventy tales of a Parrot", of which a mention occurs in the 12th century, but which may have been considerably older, is lost. See, however, also for the Shehrezâd story, B. E. Perry, "The Origin of the Book of Sindbad," *Fabula* 3 (1960), 1–94, on the SEVEN VIZIRS.

a place of unique importance, as it furnished the framework for the collection itself: Shehrezâd temporizes by making one story follow another, until at last she has gained her victory.

The Shehrezâd story, though made up from bits and pieces[5] and having an indefinable air of foreignness and oddity about it, is all that a framing story should be. The story-teller who patched it together is a little long in coming to the point, but he struggles valiantly along with a firm purpose in mind.[6] First, the misconduct of the two queens shows that women can be very depraved, then the demon episode illustrates their appalling boldness and resourcefulness in depravity, and finally, in striking contrast to this black picture of womanhood, Shehrezâd appears on the scene, self-sacrificing, chaste, learned; she, too, is bold and resourceful, but she uses her gifts nobly, not viciously. She is going to play for time, to save herself and many other girls fated to die, just by telling stories. It is no wonder that this plot had a world-wide success: it works up a quite unexpectedly charming and simple suspense situation, to which the story-book itself will finally furnish the denouement.

Notwithstanding this excellent start, though, as a framed collection the '1001 Nights' has no firm structure: the working-out falls short of the idea. As soon as the telling of the stories begins, the framework seems gradually to fade away. King Shehriyâr rarely comments on what he has heard:[7] only in the little series of fables in the first part of the book, a compiler put in some grateful remarks and requests: "*O Shehrezâd, you have given me still more wise warnings and lessons by what you have told. Do you also know any stories about the animals of the field?*" (II, 248).[8] The last of such remarks occurs, as an afterthought, at the end of 22; from then on, there is no more comment between the stories,[9] which follow each other without transition or with a simple "Furthermore it is told . . . ". The failure to keep the framework functioning throughout the collection is illustrated by the fact that its conclusion varies in the different texts,

---

5. On this point, see notably Emmanuel Cosquin, "*Le Prologue-cadre des Mille et une Nuits,*" in *Études folkloriques: Recherches sur les migrations des contes populaires et leur point de départ* (Paris: Champion, 1922), pp. 265–347. There is much to be said for the view, held by several scholars, that the version found in the *1001 Nights* is rather firmer and more coherent.

6. As Karl Dryoff, "*Zur Entstehung und Geschichte des arabischen Buches Tausend und eine Nacht,*" in Felix Paul Greve, *Die Erzählungen aus den Tausend und ein Nächten*, 12 vols. (Leipzig: Insel Verlag, 1907–1908), pp. XII:229–307, so well puts it: ". . . kein bedeutender Künstler; er benützt unbedenklich fremde Lappen und stückt ohne besonderen eigenen Aufwand ein neues Gebilde daraus zusammen; aber wir müssen doch anerkennen, dass er mit Energie auf sein Ziel lossteuert."

7. Except in the "translation" of Mardrus, who made up little comic dialogues between the king and Shehrezâd.

8. After no. 12; also before 9 and after 11, 14, 16, 17 and 19.

9. In one single instance, Shehrezâd is made to point out the moral of a tale she has just told, THE JUST KING ANUSHARWÂN.

and sometimes is lacking altogether.—All this must partly be put down to the plot itself, which, involving only one reciter and one listener (two if we count Dinazâd in), is not solid enough, as it were, to carry the weight of so many stories. A very large framed collection is more convincingly presented when the roles are distributed among a little company, every member of it telling a story in his turn while the others listen. A larger cast also favours the exchange of comment, which lends variety and depth to the whole; and above all, it offers an opportunity for creating a relation between the personality and circumstances of each character, and the stories he tells.[1]

Such a relation between the framed stories and the frame is lacking in the '1001 Nights'. To be sure, it would have been difficult to keep up in so vast a collection, and necessarily would have limited its scope. Yet, especially in the beginning it is somewhat surprising when Shehrezâd's stories seem so ill-adapted to the dangerous situation she had put herself in. The first one, THE MERCHANT AND THE DEMON, already presents two wicked wives, and in the second one, THE FISHERMAN AND THE DEMON, the last part seems a particularly tactless choice under the circumstances: the queen's morbid infatuation with the negro slave can scarcely have been a pleasant topic to king Shehriyâr. In the fourth one, THE THREE APPLES, the plot turns again upon a negro slave supposed to have won his mistress's favours, although the suspicion turns out to be unfounded. All in all, in the first few stories, if we try to connect them with the frame, Shehrezâd appears to be rubbing in the king's conjugal misfortune, rather than helping him to get over it; unless we interpret her choice as destined to show the king that he is not the only one to suffer, but nothing bears out this interpretation.[2]

The obvious explanation is that the compilers did not consider the point; they did not strive to interrelate stories and frame, nor to keep alive the interest in the framing story itself. Consequently, just as they did, we gradually forget Shehrezâd and her plight, and concentrate all our attention upon the stories she tells. There remains only the rhythmical division into Nights, with its standing transition formulas, to remind us in passing of the clever woman who is still playing for time.

---

1. Baccaccio and Chaucer, and in some measure also Marguerite de Navarre, made expert use of the possibilities of this pattern. The Persian poet Nizami (12th century), in *The seven Princesses*, connects the seven narrations with each other and with the framework by a subtle use of symbols and moral implications; the result is enchanting, but from a story-telling point of view almost over-refined.
2. An attempt to trace the developing of a long moral lesson throughout the whole of the '1001 Nights' has been made by Adolf Gelber, *Tausend und eine Nacht: Der Sinn der Erzählungen der Scheherezade* (Vienna/Leipzig: Moritz Perles, 1917); but his constructions are the opposite of convincing. The same applies to Marie Lahy-Hollebecque, *Le Féminisme de Schéhérazade: La Révélation des Mille et une nuits* (Paris: Radot, 1927), who bases his demonstration on Mardrus.

Apart from the Shehrezâd story, the time-gaining frame is something of a rarity in the '1001 Nights'. A doubtful case is THE SERPENT QUEEN, where it does not become quite clear whether the long framed story with its oversized insertion[3] is told for its own sake, or to put off the young hero's return to the upper world, which will cause the Serpent Queen's death. At first she refuses to let him go, and keeps him occupied with the story of Bulûkiya; later, when he has obtained permission to return, he voluntarily stays on for a while to hear the story of Janshâh. I confess that I should need more data on the framework of THE SERPENT QUEEN[4]—which looks like a batch of old material in a mediocre Egyptian version—to grasp its implications.

The framed collection of THE SEVEN VIZIRS[5] on the contrary, an adaptation from the Persian that was incorporated in the '1001 Nights' by later compilers, is carefully arranged in an elegant time-gaining frame. The telling of the stories is doubly functional here, as it serves a double purpose: to persuade, as well as to gain time. A king's favourite has treacherously accused the prince, his son, of trying to seduce her, and the king proposes to put his son to death. His vizirs are trying to save the prince, not only by the delaying action of the stories, but also by making them furnish arguments against the deed: they try to exemplify the dangers of rashness and the malice of women, while the spiteful favourite retaliates by telling about unreliable vizirs and the wickedness of men. The advantages of the pattern are evident: a captivating interrelation of framework and stories, and, in the series of stories itself, a debate effect that makes for variety and surprise. The result might have been a structural masterpiece, if only the stories were to the purpose; but, oddly enough, most of them are not.[6] The first vizir, already, opens the

---

3. The JANSHÂH story, forcibly inserted in BULÛKIYA, is doubtless a random addition; the narrator did not even trouble to put it in the first person.

4. There is some information on the framed stories, especially BULÛKIYA; * * * on the framework, I have found none at all.

5. Studies about the BOOK OF SINDBAD in its numerous versions—Persian, Arabic, Syriac, Hebrew, Greek, Latin, Romance languages—are countless; I include only a few specimens in my Bibliography. The version that came to be incorporated, apparently at a late date, in the '1001 Nights', derives from an Arabic prose version which was adapted from the Persian, probably in the 8th century, and gave rise to many imitations, among which seems to count JALI'ÂD AND WIRD KHÂN. It has long been unanimously supposed that the Persian version, in its turn, was adapted from an Indian original, of which, however, no trace has ever been found. Perry 1960, clearly dissatisfied with the old "India theory" as a whole, defends fresh views: Persian origin, possibly a 2nd-century Greek prototype, JALI'ÂD AND WIRD KHÂN the model (also Persian) rather than an imitation.

6. Theodor Nöldeke, "Sindban oder die sieben weisen Meister," Zeitschrift der deutschen Morgenländischen Gesellschaft 33 (1879), 522–523, aptly established that originally, the vizirs' stories formed two parallel series, the first one devoted to the theme of rashness and the second one to that of women's malice. This arrangement, which can never have been very efficacious, to judge by what is still left of it, has got broken up and obfuscated in the '1001 Nights'-version, especially towards the end.

series with a tale in which a woman, tactfully defending her virtue, has the *beau rôle*. The first tale of the second vizir is, at best, a warning against stinginess, and in that of the fourth vizir, the husband is really more immoral than the wife (139a, e, k). The favourite, in her turn, misses the mark with her fourth story (139m), about a man who invents an unusual stratagem to conquer his beloved, but without meaning or doing any harm at all. And so on: even the gem of the series as it stands in the '1001 Nights', the memorable WOMAN WITH FIVE SUITORS, is too ambiguous to make the point required by the framing story. Told by the sixth vizir, it certainly sets forth an uncommonly fine example of the malice of women, but it is the men who are dissolute and abuse their power; the woman merely takes advantage of their illicit pursuits to further her own, relatively legitimate aim—freeing her lover from prison—and shames them quite deservedly. All these inconsistencies detract from the effect of the pattern; they may, however, be due not to carelessness on the part of the original creator, but to the transformations which the story underwent in the course of transmission.

Thus, the '1001 Nights' offers no examples of a particularly skilful use of the time-gaining frame. And yet, the two are inseparable in every reader's memory. Beyond all technical cavilling, the compelling plot of the Shehrezâd story remains one of the most remarkable artistic achievements of the book.

Ransom Frame

Lastly, there is the ransom frame, which must be examined here with particular care, as it is represented in the '1001 Nights' by some very interesting pieces, more or less connected with and dependent upon each other, as I hope to show. In this type, the telling of stories has a paramount function: it serves to redeem a human life. The frame is set up to show how somebody came to be threatened with imminent execution; the story or stories told, either by the condemned man himself or by people intervening in his favour, may, if found good enough, redeem him. A very important issue depends, therefore, on their quality, and on the taste of the listener who holds the decision in his hands.

The very first story of the '1001 Nights' in all known recensions, THE MERCHANT AND THE DEMON, shows the pattern in its simplest form. A merchant travelling in the desert is menaced by a demon; three sheiks save his life by telling a story each. Now it has often been remarked upon, and every reader can see for himself, that Shehrezâd is given a surprisingly insignificant piece for a beginning. Indeed, its shortcomings are only too apparent. The arrival of the three sheiks with their animals at the right time and place is in no way motivated; the demon, after each story, willingly renounces a third of the merchant's blood, so that there is no uncertainty as to the final success; and worst of all, the three narrations rather monotonously develop the same motif, the transformation of human beings into animals. Almost any story in the collection might have made a better opening than this one.

Macdonald[7] has attempted to offer, for this anomaly, a historical explanation, which seems very plausible; it is connected with an anecdote apropos of the Arabic word *khurâfa*, meaning "a (pleasant) fictitious story". A 13th-century author states, giving the chain of witnesses, that Mohammed once told Aïsha a story about a man named Khurâfa, who was captured by three demons, and redeemed by three passers-by who each told an amazing incident (one of these involving a transformation). Our THE MERCHANT AND THE DEMON is so like the Khurâfa story as to appear just another, somewhat more elaborate version of it. Macdonald therefore surmises that it is a left-over, taken along with the Shehrezâd frame, of an older form of the '1001 Nights', composed throughout of simple, relatively short, and purely Arabic stories such as this one.

If the Khurâfa story really goes back to Mohammed's time, the ransom frame would be quite an old pattern indeed. If, on the other hand, it was made up later, as an attempt to provide the word *khurâfa* with an etymology,[8] it may have been modelled upon THE MERCHANT AND THE DEMON, though on internal criteria this latter seems the younger one. Yet even in that case, the place of honour assigned to THE MERCHANT AND THE DEMON is still well explained by its being assuredly one of the oldest stories in the book, "of a pro-nounced desert and Arabic type,"[9] as Macdonald says.

From a literary point of view, the question is how we are to understand the peculiar ransom frame here displayed, and what assured the lasting success of this pattern. Its two essential features seem to be: the value of good stories, rated so high that they balance the scales against a human life; and the fact that the bargain is made—in this oldest form, represented also by the Khurâfa story—not with another human being, but with a demon, of the species called Jinni (plural Jinn).

The lively appreciation of a good story may perhaps be explained, to a certain extent, by the conditions of life in pre-Islamic and early Islamic times. In a society where entertainments were few and read-ing not within everybody's reach, the resources of human inter-course were of great importance: they not only provided diversion, but ranked among man's principal means of asserting himself as a

---

7. Duncan Black Macdonald, "The Earlier History of the Arabian Nights," *The Journal of the Royal Asiatic Society* (1924), pp. 372–379.
8. This is quite possible, and all the more probable as there is still another, similar anecdote extant to explain the word: Dyroff 1908, pp. 253–254.
9. Macdonald 1924, p. 376.

civilized being. Stories, as much as poetry, could be perpetuated by oral tradition, and there is ample proof that they were. Later, when a more refined urban culture prevailed over desert life, the particular form of pastime offered by story-telling found its professionals; this development affirms its lasting popularity, of which the '1001 Nights' in all its aspects offers such interesting proof.

Stranger, at first sight, seems the role of the demons. In the Khurâfa story, they take the man prisoner for no reason at all, and then deliberate among themselves what they shall do: kill him, enslave him, or let him off. THE MERCHANT AND THE DEMON gives a motivation: the merchant has accidently killed the Jinni's son, and the father has a right to revenge. But in both cases, the stories told by the human intercessors apparently afford such gratification to the Jinn that they willingly consent to let their captive go free. As the '1001 Nights'-story has it: *when the third sheik had told his story, even more wonderful than the first two, the demon was all amazement; he wriggled with pleasure, and exclaimed: "Lo, I acquit you of the rest of the merchant's debt, and I grant his freedom unto you all."* (I, 48).

There is an odd naïveté, at the same time endearing and puzzling, in this gratitude of an other-world being for stories from this world. But no doubt it seems stranger to us than it did to the Arabs, who lived on a footing of relative familiarity with Jinn and regarded them as different, certainly, from humans, but not basically or incommensurably so.[1] (They are not immortal, and may be killed by men; most of them accepted Islam.) The implication of the stories under discussion seems to be, if we put it in modern terms, that Jinn are subject to boredom and want entertainment, just as humans do. Their wanton capturing of Khurâfa and then not quite knowing what to do with him is well in keeping with this interpretation. And we might even remember, in this context, the Koran's telling how the Jinn try to ascend to the lowest spheres of heaven because they want to overhear the angels, who chase them away by hurling meteors at them.[2] Fundamentally, the ransom frame as presented here affirms human superiority: Jinn may be stronger than men and often redoubtable, but men's words charm them, men's lives are more interesting than theirs.

Let us now turn to a general survey of the beginning of the '1001 Nights'. In the chief mss. of the Oriental family as well as in ZER, the first five pieces are the following:

(1) THE MERCHANT AND THE DEMON.
(2) THE FISHERMAN AND THE DEMON, + THE PETRIFIED PRINCE.
(3) THE THREE LADIES.

1. On Jinn, see especially the fine article of Duncan Black Macdonald, "From the Arabian Nights to Spirit," *The Moslem World* 9 (1919), 336–348.
2. *Koran*, Sura 72; transl. Arthur J. Arberry, *The Koran Interpreted*, 2 vols. (London: Allen & Unwin 1955), II:305–307.

(4) THE THREE APPLES + NÛR ED-DÎN AND SHEMS ED-DÎN.

(5) THE HUNCHBACK.

Of these five stories, four display the ransom frame in one form or another; and, curiously enough, thereafter it is not found any more in the whole of the '1001 Nights.'[3] Oestrup did remark that the first stories of the collection are characterized by an "Einschachtelungs-methode,"[4] which, however, he did not analyse in detail, nor try to explain. To find out the possible reasons for this recurrence of the same pattern in just one place of the book, we must closely examine the first five stories, and compare them from a structural point of view.

After (1) THE MERCHANT AND THE DEMON, already discussed, follows (2) THE FISHERMAN AND THE DEMON, which treats the same theme: when the fisherman has unintentionally liberated the menacing demon (a Mârid this time) who is resolved to kill him, he says to himself: "*This is a demon, and I am a human being, Allah has given me intelligence; so by my astuteness and intelligence I will undo him, even as he meant to undo me in his treacherous wickedness.*" (I, 54). And he defeats the demon by his superior human wit. This piece is the only one of the five that is not a frame-story; its first part employs the kindred insertion technique, its sequel, THE PETRIFIED PRINCE, is half-appended, half-inserted in a somewhat puzzling manner,[5] probably due either to an unskilful narrator or to damage in transmission. In the next story, the Baghdadian (3) THE THREE LADIES, the ransom device crops up in an unsatisfactory form, as we shall presently see. To (4) THE THREE APPLES, a short and well-constructed Harûn story of the Baghdad period, was joined later the much longer, Egyptian, NÛR ED-DÎN AND SHEMS ED-DÎN, in such a way that the latter functions as a ransom for the culprit of the former. And lastly, there is THE HUNCHBACK, a ransom-frame story throughout, and a highly complicated one, displaying no less than eleven stories within its frame. —In the last three pieces, the old frame-pattern is, as it were, secularized: instead of a Jinni, it is a caliph or a king, or a wealthy lady, who threatens people's lives and listens to the ransom stories.[6] It will be necessary now to discuss these last three pieces one by one, with special reference to the way in which the ransom frame is employed in each of them, in order to establish their relation to the opening story and to each other.

---

3. The ransom device is merely hinted at in introducing one of the little inserted stories in OMAR IBN EN-NU'MÂN.
4. Johannes Oestrup, *Studien über 1001 Nacht*, trans. O. Rescher (Stuttgart: W. Heppeler, 1925), p. 48. The same remark already in Dyroff 1908, pp. 263–264, with some, mostly excellent, comment.
5. Notably, the intriguing motif of the fishes who recite verse in the frying-pan when an apparition comes out of the wall, remains, in what follows, completely blind.
6. In the Indian Vetālā stories (written down by Somadeva in the 11th century) the pattern appears reversed: the demon tells *casus*-stories, and the king has to furnish answers to save his life, although by speaking he frustrates his enterprise.

TZVETAN TODOROV

Narrative-Men[†]

"What is character but the determination of incident? What is incident but the illustration of character? What is either a picture or a novel that is *not* of character? What else do we seek in it and find in it?"

These questions occur in a famous essay by Henry James, *The Art of Fiction* (1884). Two general ideas emerge from them; the first concerns the unbreakable link between the different elements of narrative: action and character. There is no character except in action, no action independent of character. But surreptitiously, a second idea appears in the last lines: if the two are indissolubly linked, one is more important than the other nonetheless—character, that is, characterization, that is, psychology. Every narrative is "an illustration of character."

We rarely have occasion to observe so pure a case of egocentricity presenting itself as universality. Though James's theoretical ideal may have been a narrative in which everything is subservient to the psychology of the characters, it is difficult to ignore a whole tendency in literature, in which the actions are not there to "illustrate" character but in which, on the contrary, the characters are subservient to the action; where, moreover, the word "character" signifies something altogether different from psychological coherence or the description of idiosyncrasy. This tendency, of which the *Odyssey,* the *Decameron,* the *Arabian Nights,* and *The Saragossa Manuscript* are among the most famous examples, can be considered as a limit-case of literary *a-psychologism.*

Let us try to observe this situation more closely, taking the last two works as our examples.

We are usually satisfied, in speaking of such works as the *Arabian Nights,* with saying that they lack internal analysis of the characters, that there is no description of psychological states. But this way of describing a-psychologism is tautological. To characterize this phenomenon more accurately, we should start from a certain image of narrative movement when narrative obeys a causal structure. We might then represent each moment of the narrative in the form of a simple proposition, which enters into a relation of consecution (noted by +) or a relation of consequence (noted by →) with the propositions preceding and following it.

The first opposition between the narrative James extols and that of the *Arabian Nights* can be illustrated as follows: if there is a proposition "X sees Y," the important thing for James is X; for Scheherazade, Y.

[†] From *The Poetics of Prose* by Tzvetan Todorov, pp. 66–79. English translation © 1977 by Cornell University. Originally published in French as *La Poetique de la Prose.* Copyright © 1971 by Editions du Seuil. Reprinted by permission of Georges Borchardt, Inc., for Editions du Seuil.

Psychological narrative regards each action as a means of access to the personality in question, as an expression if not a symptom. Action is not considered in itself, it is *transitive* with regard to its subject. A-psychological narrative, on the contrary, is characterized by intransitive actions: action is important in itself and not as an indication of this or that character trait. The *Arabian Nights* derive, we might say, from a *predicative* literature: the emphasis will always fall on the predicate and not on the subject of the proposition. The best-known example of this effacement of the grammatical subject is the story of Sinbad the Sailor. Even Odysseus emerges more clearly characterized from his adventures than Sinbad. We know that Odysseus is cunning, prudent, and so forth. Nothing of the kind can be said about Sinbad, whose narrative (though told in the first person) is impersonal; we should note it not as "X sees Y" but as "Y is seen." Only the coldest travel narrative can compete with Sinbad's tales in impersonality— though we have Sterne's *Sentimental Journey* to remind us that not all travel narratives are cold.

The suppression of psychology occurs here within the narrative proposition; it continues even more successfully in the field of relations among propositions. A certain character trait provokes an action; but there are two different ways of doing this. We might speak of an *immediate* causality as opposed to a *mediated* causality. The first would be of the type "X is brave → X challenges the monster." In the second, the appearance of the first proposition would have no immediate consequence, but in the course of the narrative X would appear as someone who acted bravely. This is a diffused, discontinuous causality, which is expressed not by a single action but by secondary aspects of a series of actions, often remote from one another.

But the *Arabian Nights* does not acknowledge this second causality. No sooner are we told that the sultana's sisters are jealous than they substitute a dog, a cat, and a piece of wood for her children. Kassim is greedy; therefore he goes looking for money. All character traits are immediately causal; as soon as they appear, they provoke an action. Moreover the distance between the psychological trait and the action it provokes is minimal; rather than an opposition between quality and action, we are concerned with an opposition between two aspects of the action, durative and punctual or iterative and noniterative. Sinbad likes to travel (character trait) → Sinbad takes a trip (action): the distance between the two tends toward a total reduction.

Another way of observing the reduction of this distance is to inquire if the same attributive proposition can have, in the course of the narrative, several different consequences. In a nineteenth-century novel, the proposition "X is jealous of Y" can lead to "X withdraws from society," "X commits suicide," "X courts Y," "X hurts Y." In the *Arabian Nights,* there is only one possibility: "X is jealous of Y→X hurts Y." The stability of the relationship between the two propositions deprives the first of any autonomy, of any intransitive meaning. The implication tends to become an identity. If the consequences are more numerous, the first proposition will have a greater value of its own.

Here we touch on a curious property of psychological causality. A character trait is not simply the cause of an action, nor simply its effect: it is both at once, just as action is. X kills his wife because he is cruel; but he is cruel because he kills his wife. Causal analysis of narrative does not refer back to a first and immutable origin, which would be the meaning and law of subsequent images. In other words, in its pure state, we must be able to grasp this causality outside of linear time. The cause is not a primordial *before*, it is only one element of the "cause-and-effect" couple, in which neither is thereby superior to the other.

Hence it would be more accurate to say that psychological causality duplicates the causality of events (of actions) rather than that it takes its place. Actions provoke one another, and as a by-product a psychological cause-and-effect coupling appears, but on a different level. Here we can raise the question of psychological coherence; such psychological by-products may or may not form a system. The *Arabian Nights* again affords us an extreme example, in the tale of Ali Baba. The wife of Kassim, Ali Baba's brother, is anxious about her husband's disappearance. "She wept all night long." The next day, Ali Baba brings home the pieces of his brother's body and says, by way of consolation: "Sister-in-law, your suffering is all the greater because you had so little reason to expect it. Though the harm is past remedy, if something is yet capable of consoling you, I offer to unite what little God has granted me to whatever you possess, by marrying you." The sister-in-law's reaction: "She did not refuse the match, but rather regarded it as a reasonable cause of consolation. Drying her tears, which she had begun to shed in abundance, stifling the shrill cries customary to women who have lost their husbands, she gave Ali Baba sufficient evidence that she would accept his offer." In this fashion Kassim's wife moves from despair to joy. Similar examples are countless.

Obviously, by contesting the existence of a psychological coherence in such a case we enter the realm of common sense. There is doubtless another psychology in which these two consecutive actions form a unity. But the *Arabian Nights* belong to the realm of common sense (of folklore), and the abundance of examples suffices to convince us that we are not concerned here with another psychology, nor even with an antipsychology, but with an a-psychology.

Character is not always, as James claims, the determination of incident, nor does every narrative consist of "the illustration of character." Then what is character? The *Arabian Nights* gives us a very clear answer, which is repeated and confirmed by *The Saragossa Manuscript*: a character is a potential story that is the story of his life. Every new character signifies a new plot. We are in the realm of narrative-men.

This phenomenon profoundly affects the structure of narrative.

Digression and Embedding

The appearance of a new character invariably involves the interruption of the preceding story, so that a new story, the one which explains the "now I am here" of the new character, may be told to us. A second story is enclosed within the first; this device is called *embedding*.

This is obviously not the only excuse for embedding. The *Arabian Nights* already affords us a number of others: for example, in "The Fisherman and the Genie," the embedded stories serve as arguments. The fisherman justifies his pitilessness toward the genie by the story of Duban; within the latter story, the king defends his position by the story of the jealous man and the parrot; the vizier defends his by the story of the prince and the ghoul. If the characters remain the same in the embedded story and in the embedding one, this kind of motivation becomes pointless. In the "Story of the Two Jealous Sisters," the narrative of the kidnapping of the sultan's children from the palace and of their recognition by the sultan encloses the narrative of the acquisition of the magic objects; temporal succession is the only motivation. But the presence of narrative-men is certainly the most striking form of embedding.

The formal structure of embedding coincides (nor is such a coincidence an accident) with that of a syntactic form, a particular case of subordination, which in fact modern linguistics calls *embedding*. To reveal this structure, let us take a German example, since German syntax permits much more spectacular examples of embedding than English or French:

Derjenige, der den Mann, der den Pfahl, der auf der Brücke, der auf dem Weg, der nach Worms führt, liegt, steht, umgeworfen hat, anzeigt, bekommt eine Belohnung.

(Whoever identifies the one who upset the post which was placed on the bridge which is on the road which goes to Worms will get a reward.)

In the German sentence, the appearance of a noun immediately provokes a subordinate clause which, so to speak, tells its story; but since this second clause also contains a noun, it requires in its turn a subordinate clause, and so on, until an arbitrary interruption, at which point each of the interrupted clauses is completed one after the other. The narrative of embedding has precisely the same structure, the role of the noun being played by the character: each new character involves a new story.

The *Arabian Nights* contain examples of embedding quite as dizzying. The record seems to be held by the narrative which offers us the story of the bloody chest. Here

    Scheherazade tells that
        Jaafer tells that
           the tailor tells that
                the barber tells that
                    his brother (and he has six brothers) tells that . . .

The last story is a story to the fifth degree; but it is true that the two first degrees are entirely forgotten and no longer have any role to play. Which is not the case in one of the stories of *The Saragossa Manuscript*, where

    Alfonso tells that
        Avadoro tells that
           Don Lope tells that
              Busqueros tells that
              Frasquetta tells that . . .

and where all the degrees, except for the first, are closely linked and incomprehensible if isolated from one another.

Even if the embedded story is not directly linked to the embedding story (by identity of characters), characters can pass from one story to the other. Thus the barber intervenes in the tailor's story (he saves the hunchback's life). As for Frasquetta, she crosses all the intermediary degrees to appear in Avadoro's story (she is the mistress of the Knight of Toledo); so does Busqueros. Such shifts from one degree to the next have a comic effect in *The Saragossa Manuscript*.

Embedding reaches its apogee with the process of self-embedding, that is, when the embedding story happens to be, at some fifth or sixth degree, embedded by itself. This "laying bare of the device" is present in the *Arabian Nights*, as Borges has pointed out: "No [interpolation] is more disturbing than that of the six hundred and second night, most magical of all. On this night, the king hears from the queen's mouth her own story. He hears the initial story, which includes all the others, which—monstrously—includes itself. . . . If the queen continues, the king will sit still and listen forever to the truncated version of the *Arabian Nights*, henceforth infinite and circular. . . ." Nothing will ever again escape the narrative world, spreading over the whole of experience.

The importance of embedding is indicated by the dimensions of the embedded stories. Can we even call them digressions when they are longer than the story from which they digress? Can we regard as an addition or as a gratuitous embedding all the tales of the *Arabian Nights* because they are embedded in Scheherazade's tale? The same is true of *The Saragossa Manuscript:* whereas the basic story seemed to be Alfonso's, actually it is the loquacious Avadoro's tales which spread over more than three-quarters of the book.

But what is the internal significance of embedding, why are all these means assembled to give it so much emphasis? The structure of narrative provides the answer: embedding is an articulation of the most essential property of all narrative. For the embedding narrative is the *narrative of a narrative*. By telling the story of another narrative, the first narrative achieves its fundamental theme and at the same time is reflected in this image of itself. The embedded narrative is the image of that great abstract narrative of which all the others are merely infinitesimal parts as well as the image of the embedding narrative which directly precedes it. To be the narrative of a narrative is the fate of all narrative which realizes itself through embedding.

The *Arabian Nights* reveal and symbolize this property of narrative with a particular clarity. It is often said that folklore is characterized by the repetition of the same story; and indeed it is not rare, in one of the *Nights*, for the same adventure to be related twice if not more often. But this repetition has a specific function which is unknown: it serves not only to reiterate the same adventure but also to introduce the narrative which a character makes of it. Most of the time it is this narrative which counts for the subsequent development of the plot. It is not the adventures Queen Badur survives which win her King Armanos' pardon, but the narrative of them she recounts. If Turmente cannot further his plot, it is because he is not permitted to tell his story to the caliph. Prince Firuz wins the heart of the Princess of Bengal not by having his adventure but by telling it to her. The act of narrating is never, in the *Arabian Nights*, a transparent act; on the contrary, it is the mainspring of the action.

Loquacity and Curiosity—Life and Death

The speech-act receives, in the *Arabian Nights*, an interpretation which leaves no further doubt as to its importance. If all the characters incessantly tell stories, it is because this action has received a supreme consecration: narrating equals living. The most obvious example is that of Scheherazade herself, who lives exclusively to the degree that she can continue to tell stories; but this situation is ceaselessly repeated within the tale. The dervish has incurred a genie's wrath, but by telling him the story of the envious man, he wins pardon. The slave has committed a crime; to save his life, his master, as the caliph tells him, has but one recourse: "If you tell me a story more amazing than this one, I shall pardon your slave. If not,

I shall have him put to death." Four persons are accused of the murder of a hunchback; one of them, the inspector of kitchens, tells the king: "O fortunate King, will you give us the gift of life if I tell you the adventure which befell me yesterday, before I met the hunchback who was put into my room by stealth? It is surely more amazing than this man's story." "If it is as you say," replies the king, "I shall grant all four of you your lives."

Narrative equals life; absence of narrative, death. If Scheherazade finds no more tales to tell, she will be beheaded. This is what happens to the physician Duban when he is threatened by death: he asks the king permission to tell the story of the crocodile; permission is not granted, and Duban perishes. But he is revenged by the same means, and the image of this vengeance is one of the finest in all the *Arabian Nights*: he offers the pitiless king a book to read while the decapitation is taking place. The executioner does his work; Duban's severed head speaks:

> O king, you may look through the book."
> The king opened the book. He found its pages stuck together. Putting his finger in his mouth, he wet it with saliva and turned the first page. Then he turned the second, and those that followed. He continued in this fashion, for the pages parted only with difficulty, until he came to the seventh leaf. He looked at the page and saw nothing written there.
> "Physician," he said, "I see nothing written on this leaf."
> "Keep turning the pages," replied the head.
> He opened more leaves, and still found nothing. Scarcely a moment had elapsed, when the drug entered his body; the book was impregnated with poison. Then he took a step, staggered, and fell to the ground.

The blank page is poisoned. The book which tells no story kills. The absence of narrative signifies death.

Consider, after such a tragic illustration, this pleasanter version of the power of nonnarrative. A dervish tells every passerby how to gain possession of a certain talking bird, but all have failed and been turned into black stones. Princess Parizade is the first to capture the bird, and she releases the other less fortunate candidates. "All sought to find the dervish as they passed by, to thank him for his welcome and his counsel, which they had found sincere if not salutary; but he had died and none could discover whether it had been of old age or because he was no longer necessary to teach the way to the conquest of the three things over which Princess Parizade had just triumphed." The man is merely a narrative; once the narrative is no longer necessary, he can die. It is the narrator who kills him, for he no longer has a function.

Finally, the imperfect narrative also equals, in such circumstances, death. Hence the inspector of kitchens who claimed that
his story was better than the hunchback's ends it by addressing the
king: "Such is the amazing tale I wanted to tell you yesterday and
which I recount today in all its details. Is it not more astounding
than the hunchback's adventure?" "No, it is not, and your boast
bears no relation to the truth," answered the King of China, "I must
have all four of you hanged."

Absence of narrative is not the only counterpart of narrative-as-
life; to want to hear a narrative is also to run mortal risks. If loquacity
saves from death, curiosity leads to it. This law underlies the plot of
one of the richest tales, "The Porter and the Ladies." Three young
ladies of Baghdad receive several unknown men in their house; they
stipulate only one condition in return for the pleasures they promise
to bestow: "about anything you are going to see, ask no explanation."
But what the men see is so strange that they ask the three ladies to
tell their story. No sooner has this desire been expressed than the
ladies call in their slaves: "Each slave chose his man, rushed upon
him, and cast him to the ground, striking him with the flat of his
sword." The men must be killed because their request for a narrative,
their curiosity, is liable to the death penalty. How do they escape?
Thanks to the curiosity of their executioners. For one of the ladies
says: "I shall give each of them permission to continue on his way, on
condition that he tell his story, recounting the series of adventures
which led to his visiting us here. If they refuse, you will cut off their
heads." The listener's curiosity, when it does not mean his own death,
restores life to the condemned men, who in return can escape only
on condition that they tell a story. Finally, a third reversal: the caliph,
who was present in disguise among the guests of the three ladies,
invites them the next day to his palace; he forgives them everything,
but on one condition: they must tell. . . . The characters of this book
are obsessed by stories; the cry of the *Arabian Nights* is not "Your
money or your life!" but "Your story or your life!"

This curiosity is the source of both countless narratives and incessant dangers. The dervish can live happily in the company of the ten
young men, all blind in the right eye, on one condition: "ask no indiscreet question about our infirmity or our condition." But the question
is asked, and peace is at an end. To discover the answer, the dervish
ventures into a magnificent palace; there he lives like a king, surrounded by forty lovely ladies. One day they depart, telling him, if he
would remain in such happiness, not to enter a certain room. They
warn him: "We fear you will not be able to protect yourself against that
indiscreet curiosity which will be the cause of your downfall." Naturally,
faced with the choice between happiness and curiosity, the dervish

chooses curiosity. Just as Sinbad, for all his misfortunes, sets out again after each voyage: he wants life to tell him stories, one narrative after the other.

The palpable result of such curiosity is the *Arabian Nights*. If its characters had preferred happiness, the book would not exist.

Narrative: Supplier and Supplied

For the characters to be able to live, they must narrate. Thus the first narrative subdivides and multiplies into a thousand and one nights of narratives. Now let us attempt to take the opposite point of view, no longer that of the embedding narrative but that of the embedded narrative, and inquire: why does the embedded narrative need to be included within another narrative? How can we account for the fact that it is not self-sufficient but requires an extension, a context in which it becomes simply a part of another narrative?

If we consider the narrative in this way, not as enclosing other narratives but as being enclosed by them, a curious property is revealed. Each narrative seems to have something excessive, a supplement which remains outside the closed form produced by the development of the plot. At the same time, and for this very reason, this something-more, proper to the narrative, is also something-less. The supplement is also a lack; in order to supply this lack created by the supplement, another narrative is necessary. Hence the narrative of the ungrateful king who puts Duban to death after the latter has saved his life has something more than this narrative itself; besides, it is for this reason, with a view to this supplement, that the fisherman tells the story, a supplement which can be summed up in a formula: never pity the ungrateful. The supplement must be integrated into another story; hence it becomes the simple argument which the fisherman employs when he becomes involved in an adventure similar to Duban's, with the genie. But the story of the fisherman and the genie also has a supplement which requires another story; and there is no reason for this process to stop anywhere. The attempt to supply is therefore vain—there will always be a supplement awaiting a narrative-to-come.

This supplement takes several forms in the *Arabian Nights*. One of the most familiar is that of the argument, as in the preceding example; the narrative becomes a means of convincing the interlocutor. Further, at higher levels of embedding, the supplement is transformed into a simple verbal formula, a sentence or proverb meant to be used by the characters as much as by the readers. Finally a wider integration of the reader is also possible (though it is not characteristic of the *Arabian Nights*). Behavior provoked by reading is also a supplement, and a law is established: The more this supplement is consumed within the narrative, the less reaction this narrative provokes on the part of its reader. We may weep when reading *Manon Lescaut*, but not when reading the *Arabian Nights*.

Here is an example of a one-sentence proverb or moral. Two friends argue about the origin of wealth: Is it enough to have some money to begin with? There follows a story illustrating one of the positions being defended, then comes a story which illustrates the other; and at the end, a conclusion is reached: "Money is not always a sure means of amassing more and becoming rich."

As in the case of psychological cause and effect, we must here conceive of this logical relation outside of linear time. The narrative precedes or follows the maxim, or both at once. Similarly, in the *Decameron*, certain novellas are created to illustrate a metaphor (for example, "scraping the bottom of the barrel") and at the same time they create that metaphor. It is pointless to ask today whether the metaphor engendered the narrative, or the narrative engendered the metaphor. Borges has even suggested an inverted explanation of the existence of the entire *Arabian Nights*: "This invention [the stories Scheherazade tells] . . . is apparently posterior to the title and was imagined in order to justify it." The question of origins need not be raised; we are beyond the origin and unable to conceive of it. The supplied narrative is no more original than the supplying narrative, nor vice versa. Each narrative refers us to another, in a series of reflections which can end only by becoming perpetual—for example, by self-embedding.

Such is the incessant proliferation of narratives in this marvelous story-machine, the *Arabian Nights*. Every narrative must make its own narration explicit; but to do so a new narrative must appear in which this narration is no more than a part of the story. Hence the narrating story always becomes a narrated story as well, in which the new story is reflected and finds its own image. Furthermore, every narrative must create new ones—within itself, in order that its characters can go on living, and outside itself, so that the supplement it inevitably produces may be consumed there. The many translators of the *Arabian Nights* all seem to have yielded to the power of this narrative machine. None has been content with a simple translation merely faithful to the original; each translator has added and suppressed stories (which is also a way of creating new narratives, narrative always being a selection); a secondary speech-act, translation represents in itself a new tale which no longer awaits its narrator. Borges has told a part of this tale in his "Translators of the *Arabian Nights*."

There are, then, so many reasons for narrative never to stop that we cannot help wondering: What happened before the first narrative? And what will happen after the last? The *Arabian Nights* have not failed to provide an answer, ironic though it may be, for those

who want to know the "before" and the "after." The first story,
Scheherazade's, begins with these words, meaningful on every level
(but one should not open the book to look for them—it should be
possible to guess what they are, so appropriate are they to their
place): "It is told . . . " No need to search out the origin of narrative
in time—it is time which originates in narrative. And if before the first
narrative there is an "it *has been* told," after the last there will be an "it
will be told." For the story to stop, we must be told that the marveling
caliph orders it to be inscribed in letters of gold in the annals of the
realm; or again that "this story . . . spread and was told everywhere
down to the last detail."

ANDRAS HAMORI

A Comic Romance from *The Thousand and One Nights: The Tale of Two Viziers*[†]

I. Patterned tales

In the general introduction to the Thousand and One Nights text
published by Macnaghten (Calcutta 1839) the redactor[1] assures us
that the book is not proposed for the idling away of vacant hours.
"The stories of the ancients are a lesson to those who live after them,
so that a man may ponder the instructive things that befell others . . .
and take warning. Praise to Him who made the tales of the ancients
into a lesson to those who live after them"![2] What lesson or lessons,
he does not say.

[†] From *Arabica* 30.1 (1983): 38–56. Reprinted by permission of Koninklijke BRILL NV.
1. "Redactor" is a term of convenience. The composition of the book (the collection of coin-
    cidence stories at the beginning, or the pairing of certain stories, such as '*Aziz and 'Aziza*
    and *Dunyā and Taj al-Mulūk,* or the two tales discussed in this essay) suggests arrange-
    ment for effect. How many hands' work this is, we cannot know.
       I use the Macnaghten text (4 vols., Calcutta and London 1839–42). The differences
    between it and the first Būlāq edition (1835) are at times substantial. For example, in the
    Tale of Two Viziers the Sultan of Basra is angered at Badr ad-Dīn because Badr ad-Dīn, in
    mourning for his father, fails to present himself at court (p. 160). In the Būlāq text (pp.
    58–59) the cause of the Sultan's displeasure is not nearly so clear. In the Calcutta text the
    reunion of hero and heroine is followed by a few pages, in which Badr ad-Dīn treats the
    Sultan of Egypt to a pedantic display of erudition. The Būlāq text ends more naturally
    with the happy ending of the lovers' story. One could study these texts, fruitfully, from a
    comparative or historical viewpoint, but this essay deals with one version alone. A beauti-
    ful new book on the *Thousand and One Nights*. André MIQUEL's *Sept contest de Mille el
    Une Nuits* (Paris 1981) only became available to me after this essay had been completed.
    The approaches are different and the overlap is slight, but many observations in Miquel's
    chapter on our tale will also enrich reflection along the lines followed in this essay. (E.g.,
    on the rhythms of the marvelous and the ordinary, and the setting of the father-son rela-
    tion in the latter).
2. *Macnaghten* I. 1.

Counsels of practical conduct—hold your tongue, beware of the
envious, don't underestimate women—would be easy to extract.
Some of the tales have a cautionary air.[3] But if asked what the paramount lesson was, the lesson in the singular, the redactor would, I
think, have agreed with the caliph in the story of Ghānim ibn Ayyūb:
"The caliph ordered that all that had happened should be recorded . . .
so that those living after him might read of these events, stand amazed
before the manifold workings of God's decrees and entrust their
affairs to the Creator of night and day."[4]

Such is the obvious moral of the patterned tales—*The Porter and
the Three Ladies, The Two Viziers,* etc.—in which certain motifs
form, by variation and echo, bold schemes of symmetries and contrasts. In these tales piety sanctions wonder at coincidence, and
approves delight in the mere intricacy of design. As the pattern rises
into view the devout audience glimpses the hand of God.

But the design and the pious reading of it do not account for the
whole effect. Plot and pattern, all the colorful and marvellous events
that form them, involve, as folk-tales often do, great moral or phe-
nomenological themes: power, justice, compulsion, lust and love.
The pattern does not cannibalize these themes. On the contrary,
since the pattern employs variations on a motif it is apt to throw into
relief various facets of the theme cast up by that motif. The great
tales of the Thousand and One Nights blend detached tranquility
with the sharp tang of experience.

In the following pages I will try to show (in sections 2 and 3) how
in the *Tale of Two Viziers* pattern and plot lead the audience through
various views of certain themes, and (in section 4) how certain narrative techniques enhance the story's intricacy and verve. A synopsis
of the tale is attached at the end of this essay.

Before turning to the tale I shall offer a few observations on the
genesis of such patterns, and on the way in which the pattern may
thrust certain themes on the narrative. I hope to show that no
antecedent authorial scheme need account for the play of pattern,
plot, and theme, because the dialectic play of these elements is the
result of basic combinatory possibilities governing the composition
(or aggregation) of the text. Trusting the rules of this play as a guide
to significant details of configuration will, at the very least, give
reflection a shape. Perhaps it will also prove an avenue of escape
from the circularity of interpretation.

---

3. E.g. the story of 'Azîz and 'Azîza, which reflects the kind of moral speculation we find, in
    learned form, in ibn Qayyim al-Jawzīya's *Rawḍot al-muḥibbin* and similar books. Cf. my
    essay, "Notes on two love stories from the Thousand and One Nights." *Studia Islamica*
    1976 (fasc. 43) pp. 65–80.
4. *Macnaghten* 1, 350. " . . . ḥattā yaqra'ahu lladhī ya'ii min ba'dihi fayata'ajjaba min
    taṣarrufāti l-aqdār, wa-yufawwiḍa l-anira ilā khāliqi l-layli wan-nahār."

People are paradigm makers. For intellectual and esthetic reasons, we like to sort objects into classes and explore the relations among kinds of order. For a transparent example, here is a diagram drawn by the Anglo-Saxon monk Byrhtferth, a man "stretching out to grasp the outline of the universal coherence of man and nature":

Season of the year:	spring	summer	autumn	winter
Age of man:	childhood	adolescence	manhood	old age
Element:	air	fire	earth	water
Effects:	moist & hot	hot & dry	dry & cold	cold & moist
Temperament:	sanguine	choleric	melancholic	phlegmatic

"He could not elaborate this system; he could draw no conclusions from it; but it pleased him and it went on pleasing his monastic successors until the early years of the twelfth century."[5]

Such orders and variations also rule the patterned tale. A similar table can be drawn up, for example, to diagram the dangers that precede the first meeting between our hero and heroine. The neatness of distribution may tempt one to exaggerate the importance of such a chart:

Actor:	Hero	Heroine
Menaced by:	Royal patron	Royal suitor
Cause of breach:	preoccupation with mourning	preoccupation with a planned engagement
Danger:	loss of status and threat to life	loss of status and threat to life

It may seem at first glance that the first table contains well defined sets whose membership is finite, the second only selections from ill-defined sets whose members, being arbitrary variations on some element, cannot be fully enumerated. But in fact there is no hard and fast line.

In the first table the seasons form a set well defined by time-honored convention, but the ages of man, we suspect, are fitted to the occasion. If no congruence were sought, their division might be fixed in some other, equally plausible way. Conversely, in the second table there are sets to which a little tampering with definitions can give an air of completeness: hero vs. heroine; loyalty to the dead adoptive

5. R. W. SOUTHERN, *Medieval Humanism and Other Studies* (Harper Torchbook ed., New York 1970) 165. For an Islamic example of similar tabulation of universal harmonies, cf. al-Kirmānī's chart of the correspondances among the emanations of being, the heavenly spheres, the Ismā'īlī hierarchy (*nāṭiq, asās, imām, ḥāb,* etc.) and the degrees of gnosis, in *Rāḥat al-'aql,* ed. Muḥammad Kāmil Ḥusayn and Muḥammad Muṣṭafā Ḥilmi (Cairo, 1953) 138.

parent vs. loyalty to the not-yet-seen fiancé. Folktales like sharp edges. Because neatly divided domains are clearest to the imagination, and most readily thought of and remembered, in folktales the variation of elements tends towards completeness of classification.[6] This is the other side of Byrhferth's coin, where the esthetic, the sheer pleasure in the contemplation of harmonious permutations, disguises itself as a kind of science.

Both diagrams might be regarded as tests of hypotheses. Byrhferth's table tests and proves, to its author's satisfaction, that the world is harmonious. Our table of the dangers in the *Tale of Two Viziers* could be read as a sample collected in support of an inductive generalization about the behaviour of powerful people with morbidly thin skins. This would be a perverse interpretation, but it brings us to an important distinction.

If someone were to propose this last as the one and only reading of our story, we would cry imposture. The formal likeness to the first table is not in question but, we would argue, the second table offers no more than program notes to the tale (or part of it, to be exact) and the tale makes no hypotheses. Rather, in the part in question, it displays varied aspects of a generalization (about the fickleness of the powerful) which is a ready motif in the story-teller's lexicon of plotting elements. It happens here to be the material used for paradigmatic variation. It is not discovered through logical operations. One is tempted to continue: not does the particular motif (the fickleness of the powerful) need have any primacy over the form (the paradigmatic variation of an arbitrary motif) except the primacy of marble over a marble statue.[7]

It is certainly true of the tale that "art, with its 'craving for the concrete' tends to break into discrete parts even what seems general and homogeneous."[8] But the extreme statement of the primacy of form needs to be somewhat modified.

In the patterned tale a "pattern" (there may be several) is founded on the permutation of motifs that fall into some definable category. It is true that this could be a category of anything at all, except that categories of love, or betrayal, or crime and punishment are more interesting than categories of cabbages. The sculpture is made of marble rather than sugar-candy.

---

6. Cf. V. Propp. *Morphology of the Folktale* (trans. L. Scott, revised by L. Wagner, Austin and London 1968) 53–4, on the distribution of helpers.
7. The motif *need not* have primacy over the form, but that is not to say it cannot. A storyteller may certainly plan themes, moral, or even an allegorical interpretation in advance. I am speaking here of the limiting case of storytelling by the aggregation of narrative elements, where the dialectic process leading to a subtle moral meditation is set in train by the mere decision to use a certain form.
8. V. Shklovski, *O teorii prozy* (Moscow 1929) 33 (German trans. *Theorie der Prosa* Frankfurt 1966, p. 38). The phrase "craving for the concrete" is credited to Carlyle. I do not know the English original.

The mustering of variants leads the story-teller to focus on what they are variants of. "What was but the confused part of a great confusion gains, when like is joined to like, its particular quality; it is then that it becomes itself."[9] The theme thus brought into focus by the pattern may affect the plot by pushing the tale towards a counter-theme, modification or denial of the first theme. In the *Tale of Two Viziers* the pattern of dangers stresses the underlying motif "selfish love." This leads to the counter-theme "unselfish love" (and so of course to a set of which the earlier set "examples of selfish love" and the countertheme are both members). This is a formally plausible process. But not only formally: once the pattern has cast up a moral theme, the questioning countertheme will begin to press.[1] The rules that generate narrative become rules of meditation.

In story-telling the dialectic of form and theme is inextricably bound to the workings of two other elementary (and contradictory) principles: retardation and economy.[2] In the *Tale of Two Vizers* retardation—teasing the audience by putting off the consummation of the story—uses the common two-tier scheme.[3] The lovers are brought together from afar, then separated, then again brought together from afar. It is this scheme that affords opportunity for an important element of design: the hero's twofold passage from a metonymy of death—cemetery and death sentence—to the marriage bed. Of economy of plotting, an example is furnished by the dangers to Badr ad-Dīn and Sitt al-Ḥusn. As we have seen, a single underlying motif brings these about: in each case injured pride shifts a powerful man's affection to ill-will. It is obvious that such economy is favorable to patterning built on symmetries. Thus the economy of formulaic motivation brings an esthetic bonus, and a thematic one as well by thrusting into the foreground the theme that underlies the variations.

2. The Theme of Time in Pattern and Plot

Both the first and the last among the chief motifs in the *Tale of Two Viziers* are familiar. The first hinges on a daydream of a chain of events. (E.g., the milkmaid imagines bartering her way to wealth). The links of this chain stretch far into the future; a distant link jars the dreamer into a reaction that immediately and ludicrously disposes of the daydream. (The milkmaid envisions how, rich and married, she will deal with troublesome children; in her imaginative ardor she kicks the milkpail and there is an end to her wealth). In the last motif, a person

---

9. A. Jolles, *Einfache Formen* (3rd ed., Tubingen 1965) 21.
1. E.g., the themes of retribution and justice in the *Porter and the Three Ladies*.
2. V. Shklovski, *O teorii prozy* 32–60 (*Theorie der Prosa* 37–61).
3. Cf. Propp. *Morphology* 92–96, on the ways in which stories are combined.

is tricked into inability to distinguish between illusion and reality
(E.g., in the introduction to the *Taming of the Shrew*).

These motifs are tied in our tale to two unusual experiences of
time. As the first motif is developed (and the daydream is, amazingly,
fulfilled) time shows itself uncommonly accommodating in the
simultaneous occurrence of events that seem to belong together
(the brothers' marriages, the conception and birth of their children).
In the second, as Badr ad-Dīn asks "Did I wake or sleep?", identity of
scene drugs consciousness into the illusion that time has been
recaptured: indeed, that the lost time was never lost at all. The first
of these experiences has a curiosity and the second a poignancy, but
they truly come into their own, we shall see, as pattern and plot
mount them in a larger gallery of experiences.

The illusion that restitution can be found and the past recaptured
is prepared and deepened by the shift in the pattern of events from
simultaneity to repetition. After the marriages and births comes a
last coincidence: the royal wrath threatening both hero and heroine.
The next coincidence is, as it were, longitudinal: Badr ad-Dīn is
taken from the cemetery to Sitt al-Ḥusn's bedroom; near the end of
the tale he will be taken, under sentence of death and in a closed box
(a portable grave?), to her bedroom.

The network of coincidences, both lateral and longitudinal, *and the
subtle shift from the former to the latter,* suggest that all coincidence is
of the same order and that the loss of time can be as fully remedied as
separation in space. This is how the patterning of coincidences lures
the *reader* to share Badr ad-Dīn's illusion when it appears to him, in
his wife's bedroom, that the ten years never passed.

In yet another way the pattern of the tale hints at recurrence. As
we have seen, each love scene is preceded by a metonymy of the
hero's death. The first of these is grim enough. The second is comic:
the sentence of death and the ominous box in which he is kept by
day are a joke for everybody except the hero. (This ascent from the
grim to the comic is an expansion of the path of emotion within
the single archetypal move from the brush with death to love). We
(the audience; not neccessarily the characters) are made to sense
cycles—the comically oriented cycle, spring after winter.

These illusions of recapture and recurrence, stressed by the pattern, are dashed against the irreversibility of time, stressed by the
plot. The story makes no statements about time. It contrasts illusions about it with facts.

In an Indian version, our story might be a parable of *māyā*, and
the passage of time would then be no more real than the brothers'
original reverie. If it appeared in the form of a Hellenistic novel,
chances are that the lovers would not seem a day older on the last

page than when they first looked at one another. But in the *Tale of Two Viziers* the characters suffer the wear and tear of time.

The reality of the past is brought home to Badr ad-Dīn when he touches a finger to the scar on his forehead. The motif of the scar is the kind of gift the Muse bestows on good story tellers: it does several jobs for one telling. The bloodied head is emblematic of the last retardatory scene; the scar is functional as a mark of the past carried on Badr ad-Dīn's person; but it is also just what it is, the scar of the past.

Nor are the other characters spared. As they project their simultaneous marriages and all the rest, the two brothers envision symmetries in the lives of each generation. The series of symmetrical events is completed, in unforeseen fashion, but then the symmetry breaks down. Shams ad-Dīn lives, but both Nūr ad-Dīn, Badr ad-Dīn's father, and the pastry cook, Badr ad-Dīn's adoptive father, die. Why did the narrator have to kill off the pastry cook rather than reward him at the end of the tale? The pastry cook dies so that at the happy ending no father substitute should disturb the asymmetry.[4]

This devaluation of symmetry also affects the recognitions that bring the story to its end. Badr ad-Dīn's son has to eat the pastry and praise it to his grandmother before Badr ad-Dīn himself is recognized. The succession of generations—reminder of mortality—has replaced on the story's stage the brash confident reveries of the contemporaries.

3. *Love*

Two twists of fate are of the greatest importance for plot and pattern alike: the dangers to Sitt al-Ḥusn (who is threatened with a loathsome and degrading marriage which she would rather die than endure) and to Badr ad-Dīn Ḥasan (whose life is threatened by the king of Basra). Both dangers are motivated by royal caprice of a particular kind: affection turned by injured self-love to hatred.

The like motivation of the simultaneous dangers throws the pattern into relief. But the two kings' evil changes of heart also enter a network of themes we have not yet discussed: the themes of selfish and unselfish love.

The plot is set in motion, and the first separation is caused, by self-love: the brothers' quarrel comes from blind insistence on the requisites of a pompous self-esteem. Conversely, the movement towards recognition and reparation will owe its beginning to Badr al-Dīn's sound love for his son: *fa-hājat fīhi l-maḥabbatu l-ilāhiya*, "divine love stirred in his heart."[5] When the child mistakes the

4. In the Būlāq text (p. 66) there is no mention of the cook's death.
5. *Macnaghten* I, 181.

stranger's love for lust, rock and bloodied head turn the listener, mind and heart, to the contrast between the good and flawed loves.

How does this contrast affect the love of the hero and heroine? A comparison with the Greek romances is again helpful. The adventures (though not their sequence) are similar: meeting, separation, great perils, sexual dangers to the heroine, loss of social status for the hero. The metonymies of death in our tale recall the motif of apparent death in the Greek romance.[6] But there is an enormous difference: the Greek romances are most of them stories of chaste lovers who after many trials manage to marry. In our tale hero and heroine spend their wedding night together and then do not see each other for a decade. In the *Two Viziers* there is no doubt that sensuous gratification is a very nice thing, but it is not by itself enough for a satisfactory conclusion to the story.

It cannot be said of course that during the years of separation a change comes over Badr ad-Dīn's character. In the patterned tale the actors are ruled by events and Badr ad-Dīn does not in any significant sense have "character." Yet we cannot help but feel that something morally important has happened to him. It is this. As the tale exhibits and contrasts different aspects of the theme of time, so too it exhibits and contrasts different aspects of the theme of love. There is love tainted with self love (and consequently injustice), there is raw, beautiful sensuous love, and there is the selfless "divine love." Badr ad-Dīn's story can end only after he has experienced, as pastry cook in Damascus, the divorce from his first manner of existence (a metamorphosis usual in this genre of narrative), and after he has felt selfless love.

What do the themes of time and love have to do with each other? It seems conceivable that pattern and plot, by the dialectic process I sketched above, thrust upon the story-teller (or chain of story tellers) the various facets of these themes quite independently of one another. There might be two intertwined mazes then whose crossings mean nothing.

But to read the story in this infelicitous way—to choke off all reflection that these crossings invite—would be perverse. The crossings are too much in evidence to be dismissed. There are the rock and the scar: the sign that refutes the illusion about time results from a confusion between the divine love and the tainted love. The divine love itself needs the sequence of generations, before it can appear.

There is also a sturdily comic moment that brings the perplexity about time right into the lovers' embrace. In the first love scene the audience is teased by a comic delay. Badr ad-Dīn undresses in an

---

6. For a discussion of the Greek romances, with many observations of great profit to the readers of the 1001 Nights, see M. BAKHTIN, *Esthétique et théorie du roman* (Paris, 1978, trans. of *Voprosy literatury i éstetiki*, Moscow 1975) 239–260.

unseemly neat fashion (this scene, another gift of the Muse to the narrator and gift of fate in the story, will be discussed in the next section) and the lady must make the first move: "She drew him to her, and Badr ad-Dīn drew her to him and embraced her . . . ."[7] At the end of the tale the teasing delay recurs, a minor repetition among major ones. The delay is now caused by Badr ad-Dīn's puzzlement over the real or illusory nature of the past. He thinks this, he thinks that, until at last "she hugged him to her breast, and he hugged her to his breast, then he thought a bit and said . . . ."[8] The technical aspects of this repetition are certainly of the common stock: the comic retardation of a love-scene, the motif of the forward lady, the formulaic syntax. But no matter how automatically technique generates this crossing of the themes of time and love, the crossing is there and affects our mood and thought.

These crossings are not to be mistaken for clues to an encoded message. There is no cunningly hidden statement of some "if/then" form. Certainly, the crossings stress that the story belongs to the large family of myths and archetypes of the comic ascent from loss, terror, and death to love. It belongs to the family of literary works in which recognition is the source of joy rather than disaster.[9]

There is no encoded statement: the crossings between the themes of love and time are felicitous and significant simply because they exist. Reflection on love is inextricable from reflection on time, because a human being exists in time differently from a stock or stone. The selfless love is between two people as they move through their continually shortening time. The selfish love is for an object that only coincidentally, and quite inconveniently, happens to be mortal. The story's structure conjures up the structure of a mood of thought.

Badr al-Din's puzzlement is not about time alone. He suffers an equally bothersome unraveling of identity.

Similar *māyā* stories (e.g., the tale in which the king puts his head in a pail of water and, before lifting it out, lives through many changes of fortune) are therapeutic in intent: they teach the unreality of the phenomenal self.

No such teaching seems intended here, but certainly the self is questioned. Given the apparent continuity of the scenes in the bedroom, Badr ad-Dīn the pastry cook of Damascus should prove a figure dreamt by Badr ad-Dīn the married husband, but no such thing happens. Certainty eludes Badr ad-Dīn. His comic vacillation is, in this respect, the surface to a profound unease. If memory cannot discriminate between reality and illusion, the self (both in its linear

7. *Macnaghten* I, 171.
8. *Macnaghten* I, 193.
9. N. FRYE treats many aspects of this literary type in *Anatomy of Criticism* (Princeton 1957) 163–86.

time and in its remembered, configurational time) must crumble. Violence has been done to our hero's self (in addition to the violence to his social identity, a stock-in-trade of romance)—he may therefore learn to extend to others the privilege of constituting themselves as selves. In other words, he may learn to love.

4. Strip-Tease

We have seen the many roles of the rock that bloodies Badr ad-Dīn's head. I want to discuss another such detail in which several threads of narrative come together. When the genies take the sleeping Badr ad-Dīn from his beautiful cousin's arms, his clothes are left in her bedroom. These clothes and the documents wrapped in them permit the girl's father to learn his vanished son-in-law's identity. Near the end of the story, the clothes are still there, and greatly contribute to Badr ad-Dīn's confusion, which gives conclusive proof of who he is.

Badr ad-Dīn's undressing is described in such detail that, like Badr ad-Dīn, the listener will find himself on intimately familiar ground when the clothes are seen again. Detailed description often prepares recognition. Here, for example, is the description of the mule on which the vizier sets forth after the break with his brother. This wonderfully equipped mule will draw the attention of the vizier of Basra to Nūr ad-Dīn:[1]

> He ordered some of his servants to saddle for him the Nubian she-mule with its padded saddle. It was a dapple-gray mule, its back loftly as a dome. Its saddle was gilt, its stirrups were from India, its caparison would have done Chosroes honor. It was like a bride adorned and displayed before her wedding night. He ordered the servant to place a silk rug on it and then a prayer-rug, and this prayer-rug overhung the saddlebags.

The contrast between this passage and the one immediately following could not be greater. The vizier orders his retinue to let him ride out alone—and then he is no longer a speaking character but a figure traveling across vast distances. Nouns dominated the last paragraph; now, as the language shifts to rapid narration, they yield to verbs:[2]

1. *Macnaghten* I, 151. *"Amara ba'da ghilmānihi an yashudda lahu baghlata n-nawbati bi-sarjihā l-mudarrabi wa-hiya baghlatun zarzūriya, 'āliyatu z̧qzahri ka-annahā qubbatun mabnīya, sarjuhā dhahabun wa-rikābātuhā hindiya, 'alayhā 'abā'atun kasrawīya, wa-hiya ka'annahā a'rūsatun majlīya. Wa-amarahu an yaj'ala 'alayhā bisāṭan ḥarirun wa-ja'ala l-khurja min taḥti s-sajjāda."*

2. *Loc. cit.* *"Wa-asra'a wa-rakiba l-baghlata wa-akhadha ma'ahu shay'an qulilan mina z-zādi wa-kharaja min miṣra wa-staqbala l-barra fa-mā jā'a 'alayhi z̧-zuhru ḥattā dakhala 'alā mad-inati Bilbaysa fa-nazala 'an baghlatihi wa-starāḥa wa-rayyaḥa l-baghlata wa-akhadha shay'an mina z-zādi fa-akaluhu wa-akhadha min Bilbaysa mā ya'kuluhu wa-mā ya'lifuhu 'alā baghlatihi wa-staqbala l-barra fa-mā jā'a 'alayhi l-laylu ḥattā dakhala baladan yuqālu lahu s-Sa'diya . . ."* (Later at yet another stop *"istarāḥa wa-rayyaḥa,"* etc.).

I transliterated these two passages inconsistently, using pausal forms in the former to stress the rhythm.

He mounted the mule hurriedly, took some provisions and rode out of Cairo making for the open country. Shortly after noon he entered the city of Bilbays. He got off his mule, rested and rested the mule, and took some of his provisions and ate. He took from Bilbays something for himself to eat and something to feed his mule, and made for the open country. Shortly after nightfall he entered a place called as-Sa'diya, and he spent the night there . . .

This paragraph is an altogether different affair. Besides providing linguistic variety, the syntax, with its stripped down sequence of verbs and their repetitions, seems a backdrop to the action: ceaseless, rapid, but monotonous.

Let us now return to Badr ad-Dīn's wedding. After the genies bring him to Cairo where Sitt al-Ḥusn is about to be married to the hunchback groom, events move quickly. The poor hunchback is brusquely removed; the young woman, still thinking she must marry him, makes ready to struggle and die if she must; Badr ad-Dīn reassures her, pretending that she was meant for him all along.

She is very glad indeed, and in another minute she is naked:[3]

She smiled, and was glad, and laughed sweetly, and said: "By God, this is balm to my heart. Embrace me then: hold me." She had no other clothes on now, and she lifted her dress to her neck . . .

What does Badr al-Dīn do?[4]

When Badr al-Dīn saw this, desire stirred in him and he arose and loosened his clothes. The gold purse which he had received from the Jew, and in which the thousand dinars were, he wrapped in his trousers and put under the end of the mattress. Then he took off his turban and hung it on the chair. Then he only had his fine shirt on, and the shirt was embroidered with gold—and then Sitt al-Ḥusn stepped to him and drew him to her and Badr al-Dīn drew her to him and embraced her . . .

3. Macnaghten 1, 171. "Tabassamat wa-fariḥat wa-ḍaḥikat ḍaḥakan laṭifan wa-qālat: 'Wallāhi laqad atfa'ta nāri, fa-billāhī khudhnī ilā 'indika wa-ḍummani ilā ḥiḍnik. Wa-kāna min ghayri libāsin wa-kashafat thawbahā ilā raqabatiha . . . ." My loose translation of min ghayri libāsin is a coward's hedging his bets. Dozy argues (Dictionnaire détaillé des noms des vêtements chez les arabes, Amsterdam 1845, pp. 395–96) from parallel passages in the Habicht-Fleischer text that libās means sarāwil, "trousers," both here and where Badr ad-Dīn is found in Damascus bi-lā libās, Macnaghten 1, 1972).

4. Loc. cit. "Fa-lammā naẓara Badr ad-Dīn dhālika taḥarrakat fihi sh-shahwatu fa-qāma wa-ḥalla libāsahu, thumma l-kīsu dh-dhahabu lladhī kāna akhadhahu mina l-yahūdīyi lladhī kāna fihi alfu dīnārin . . . laffahu fi sirwālihi wa-ḥaṭṭahu taḥta dhayli ṭ-ṭarrāḥati, wa-qala'a shāshahu wa-'allaqahā 'alā l-kursiyi wa-baqiya bil-qamīṣi r-rafi'i wa-kāna l-qamīṣu ṭarrazan bidh-dhahabi fa-'inda dhālika qāmat ilayhi Sitt al-Ḥusn wajadhabathu ilayhā wa-jadhabahā Badr ad-Dīn . . . ."

Even on a first reading we may guess from the density of the description that these clothes will have a role to play, but as in a thriller we suspend our knowledge that the heroine will get off the rails in time, here too we bracket our guess and innocently watch the narrative strip-tease. The absurd double relative clause is functional because it fixes the purse in our minds, but for now it is quite redundant—we already know the origin and contents of the purse—and comic teasing is its only work. A naked girl is waiting and we have to find our way out of a double relative clause first! The long undressing seems a comic obverse of the tenser retardatory scene in which the tiring-women (*mawāshiṭ*) displayed the bride in a number of splendid garments in preparation for her marriage to the repulsive stable-boy.[5]

If we are annoyed at Badr ad-Dīn's fussy precision, we can only laugh in exasperation when the narrator shoves Badr ad-Dīn aside (as the grammatical subject shifts in *haqiya . . . wa-kāna . . .*) and sets about, with a delicious meta-fussbudgetry, to describe Badr ad-Dīn's shirt. "At this Sitt al-Ḥusn stepped to him" and a good thing too, we say, she is interrupting these excessively circumspect fellows, lover and narrator both.

Comic retardation, the creation of linguistic texture, labeling certain objects for eventual recognition—these are all part of the work done by this scene, but most important of all is the repetition of the scene near the end of the tale.

Having awakened, to his astonishment, in Sitt al-Ḥusn's bedroom. Badr ad-Dīn is once again preoccupied with something—this time it is the wake-or-dream puzzle—and once again Sitt al-Ḥusn "drew him to her breast . . ." etc. Here the narrative accomplishes several things.

First, this is the satisfying culmination of the pattern. Repetition (of the room, with the old clothes where they were ten years ago, but also of his delaying and her embrace) brings to its happy conclusion the story in which repetition, in the form of various coincidences, played such an important role.

Second, it is a healing repetition. The first love scene was followed by separation and suffering. This is a time for reintegration; that is why the narrative puts such emphasis, after the reunion, on Badr ad-Dīn's interview with the king and his appointment as vizier.[6] The healing power shows in a small comic detail. Sitt al-Husn is first to speak, calling from her bed to Badr al-Dīn:[7] "Won't you come in, my lord? You've been a long time in the privy." This is repetition too, for when she woke

---

5. *Macnaghten* I, 166–69.
6. The interview is emphasized in the Macnaghten, but not in the Būlāq text (cf. note 1, p. 453).
7. *Macnaghten* I, 192.

alone after the wedding night, ten years ago, she really thought that that was where Badr ad-Dīn had gone. Now as old wounds heal, the old error is recalled in mock error. (This repetition is a gift of narrative economy. The privy is an obvious place for getting characters offstage. The repulsive stable-boy, for example, removes himself from the lady's chamber when he goes to the privy and walks straight into the afreet's clutches. A practiced story-teller will have a sharp sense of the effects that the ordering of such conventions can offer.

Third, the irony in this scene—the heroine's knowledge of how the means of his perplexity were contrived—creates a form of delicious collusion between Sitt al-Ḥusn and the audience. On the other hand, Badr ad-Dīn is the hero whose fortunes were followed in detail. Which character speaks with the voice of the audience? The knowing character's loving irony, the puzzled character's tangle of illusion and reality—these are both our voices, the two coexistent voices, to be exact, in which we say "I."

5. Stories as Ransom

After Badr ad-Dīn is found by his uncle, the mock threat to his life is ostensibly precipitated by a mistake of the most trivial kind. His expostulations, that too little pepper in a dish cannot be a capital offense, are natural enough. In his case of course it is reintegration that masquerades as injustice: he goes through a carnevalesque taming of injustice. He is a lucky fellow. For others disaster may indeed follow from trivial causes.

The *Tale of Two Viziers* is nested in the story of the murdered lady whose body, hacked into pieces, is found in a chest fished out of the Tigris.[8] It is discovered that Ja'far al-Barmakī's slave Rayḥān was, by mere filching and fibbing, indirectly responsible for the innocent woman's death, and the *Tale of Two Viziers* is told by Ja'far in the hope that Rayḥān's life will be spared if the caliph finds the web of fated events in the tale even more astounding than the coincidences that brought about the murder.

There are certain similarities between the *Murdered Lady* and the *Two Viziers*. In each of the tales the hero's child plays an unwitting role in bringing about "recognition." The children's actions seem two sides of a coin: in the *Two Viziers* the child eats the pastry; in the *Murdered Lady* the child loses the apples. There is a difference though: in the *Two Viziers* the recognition is sound and the tale is a comedy; in the *Murdered Lady* the recognition is false and the end is disaster.

Rayḥān's ransom, the *Tale of Two Viziers* in which coincidence forms a comic pattern, is a kind of ransom for the tale of the murdered

8. *Macnughten* I, 141–48.

lady itself. In the *Murdered Lady*, lack of intelligent government of one's affairs and impulsive reliance on coincidence lead to the spilling of innocent blood. God who weaves coincidence into his designs seems to have let go of the shuttle.[9]

This is a form of paradigmatic variation at the level of the ordering of the stories. Irreconcilable aspects of a topic are mustered and set side by side. This happens in a number of cases in the Thousand and One Nights. I have tried to show elsewhere the pairing of *'Aziz and 'Aziza* and the story in which it is nested, *Dunyā and Tāj al-Mulūk*.[1] A clear and astonishing example is the story of Qamar az-Zamān. Its first half, a story of young lovers, is linked to its second half, a kind of Phaedra story, by many precise echoes of theme and motif.

The whole story of the two viziers is informed by shifting contrasts and masquerades. The young man who is a vizier's son and destined to be a vizier puts in ten years as a pastry cook: folly (*'adam al-tadbīr*) proves to be a flourish in the pattern of divine decree; at one moment the groom is a hunchback stableboy and in the next a dashing young man (*she* is certainly muddled by it all: "Who is my husband then," she asks, "he you, or both"?[2]). The child and the slave in charge of

---

9. There is an evident antinomy here. How is one to reconcile the need for intelligent government of one's affairs (*tadbīr*) with the divine determination of events and men's learning to "entrust their affairs to the Creator of night and day"?
    The two notions coexist. In the *Two Viziers*. Shams ad-Dīn says (*Macnaghten* I, 154): "But for my folly and lack of foresight this would not have happened" (*mā hasala dhālika illā min qillati 'aqlī wa-'adami tadbīrī*). Two lines down, the same events happened "by the will of God" (*bi-irādati ilāhi*). There is no irony in this. Pious predestinarian and mere determinist both know that in the practice of daily life a human being cannot in good faith disown or renounce his acts of will.
    The Sunni theologians tried various tricks for reconciling divine determination and human mental acts. To the non-theologian these seem subtleties on the high-wire. But piety can simply accept the relativity of the matter. An-Nawawī's celebrated collection of forty traditions begins with "Acts are judged according to intentions" and follows this up, two traditions later, with a firmly predestinarian view of human acts. The Basran ascetic Muslim ibn Yasār (d. 718 or 720) put it like this: "Act . . . like someone who knows that only his own acts can still save him, and trust (*tawakkal*) in God like someone who knows that only that will strike him which was meant for him." (Cited in J. VAN ESS, *Zwischen Hadīt und Theologie*, Berlin 1975, pp. 152–53. I owe the reference, and the English wording, to Eric L. ORMSBY. *An Islamic Version of Theodicy: The Dispute over al-Ghazīlī's "Best of All Possible Worlds,"* unpublished Princeton University Press, forthcoming).
    There is an amusing discussion of *tabīr* and the *maqādīr* in al-Jāhiz's essay *Al-Ma'āsh wal-ma'ād*, in *Rasā'il al-Jāhiz*, ed. 'Abd as-Salām Muhammud Hārūn, (2 vols, Cairo 1964) 1, 121–22. According to al-Jāhiz, people of knowledge hold in higher esteem a thoughtful and wary man, even if he is brought down by fate, than a heedless man, even if he succeeds. In any case, it is unusual that the heedless prospers and the wary is brought down, and one should go by the usual order of things, *innumā l-ashyā'u bi-'awāmmihā*.
    The tales accept this relativity and highlight now *tadhīr*, now passive acceptance.
    The paradoxical nature of the matter is brought out in the tale of the physician Dūbān. Brought before the king he has cured and who now fears his skill, Dūbān, having no premonition that he is about to be killed, recites
    > *lā yanfa'u l-tadbīru 'abdan 'ājizan*
    > *fa-trukhu laslam fī na'īnun dā'imi*
    and similar verses. (*Macnaghten* 1, 34). This is certainly ironic; the physician lives in a fool's paradise. But more than ironic, it is scandalous; for what could he have managed better?
1. Cf. the article cited in no. 3, p. 454.
2. *Macnaghten* I, 171.

him weep for pity while they stuff themselves with pastries. These are elements of the mode M. Bakhtin called "carnevalesque" in his discussion of the Menippean satire and similar genres.[3] In the *Tale of Two Viziers* the carnival ends happily. But the larger carnival of the two stories set side by side is no longer informed by the comic ascent. There is only pure juxtaposition—a carnival in which both possibilities are equally valid.

This dissecting vision of the "manifold workings of God's decrees" is not softened by milky optimism. One tale in it calls to another; a pattern is seen, but no more than that.

Rayḥān's life is saved, at any rate. Ransom stories do succeed— one hardly expects the narrator to acknowledge the futility of his art. The ransom stories have an obvious narrative use: they produce interesting nestings. But formal benefits to the narrator are perhaps not all. Why can lives be bought for stories?

The marvellous may be regarded quite simply as equivalent value, the story as a kind of blood money. A merchant tosses away a datestone and it kills a genie's son. Three tales of the marvellous make up the price of the merchant's life.

More interestingly, storytelling binds narrator and listener. It is like a circulation of gifts. There is an illuminating example in the Sanskrit *Ocean of Story*: one person must tell a certain tale to another, who must then pass it on to another in order to lift the various curses that had been on all three.[4]

But there is one more thing. When genie, caliph and king turn into listeners as the story begins, they turn into *us*. When the competent reader of a patterned tale sees the caliph listen to the tale, the caliph becomes a competent reader, with his glimpse of the play of individual plans, passions, and necessity.

> The strong man has ever first in his thoughts that all things follow from the necessity of divine nature[5] so that whatsoever he deems to be hurtful and evil and whatsoever, accordingly, seems to him impious, horrible, unjust, and base, assumes that appearance owing to his own disordered, fragmentary, and confused view of the universe. Wherefore he strives before all things to conceive things as they really are, and to remove the hindrances to true knowledge, such as are hatred, anger, envy,

---

3. Pp. 125–36 in the German translation of his *Problemy poètiki Dostoevskogo* (*Probleme der Poetik Dostoevskijs*. Munich 1971).

4. *The Ocean of Story*, by Somadeva, trans. C. H. TAWNEY with notes by N. M. PENZER (10 vol., London 1924–28). 1, 10.

5. "The necessity of divine nature." A philosopher would agree: so would Ibn al-'Arabi and his heirs. Others, of the *ahl al-sunna*, would be horrorstruck.

   For the simple believer Spinoza's phrase could be changed into "the divine will" or "divine wisdom," but the striving for serene satisfaction with that will—*iṭmi 'nān* and *riḍā*—would be the same.

derision, pride, and similar emotions, which I have mentioned above. Thus he endeavors as we said before as far as in him lies to do good, and to go on his way rejoicing. . . .[6]

Whence it appears, how potent is the wise man and how much he surpasses the ignorant man, who is driven only by his lusts. For the ignorant man is not only distracted in various ways by external causes without ever gaining the true acquiescence of his spirit, but moreover lives, as it were unwitting of himself, and of God and of things. . . .[7]

For the simple believer Spinoza's phrase could be changed into «the divine will» or «divine wisdom», but the striving for serene satisfaction with that will—*irmi'nān and* ridā—would be the same.

The listener within the tale resembles the "competent reader" also in this that he is neither a "strong man" nor one of those who still live "unwitting of themselves." He sees the characters all at sea in their lives, buffeted by passion and reason and yet carried where necessity will have them. He sees more than the characters see, but is barely awakened from the unwitting life. He now has a little hoard of detachment and a little hoard of charity. That being so, the merchant will live, Sheherezade will keep her head on her shoulders.[8]

Synopsis

Shams ad-Dīn and Nūr ad-Dīn are brothers who jointly hold the office of vizier in Egypt. One day they imagine how pleasant it would be if they married at the same time, had children at the same time, and these—son and daughter—married each other. The question of bride-wealth comes up and causes a quarrel. Hurt in his pride, Nūr ad-Dīn leaves Cairo. His travels take him to Basra where he is adopted by the vizier, whose daughter he marries. It so happens that Shams ad-Dīn does get married at the same time, and the hoped for

---

6. SPINOZA, *Ethics* (trans. R. H. M. ELWES, Dover Books ed., New York 1951) note to Part IV. Proposition lxxiii.
7. *Ethics*, note to Part V, Proposition xlii.
8. In the longer of the two quotes above, "as far as in him lies" is the innocent looking phrase admitting the checks from the abominations of nature and history. We might choose to see certain oddities in our tale (e.g., Shams ad-Dīn's failure look for Badr ad-Dīn sooner, or the vizier of Basra's remark that Nūr ad-Dīn should travel no further because *inna l-hilā kharāh,* "the land is a wreck" *Macnaghten* I, 152) as signals that anodyne serenities are easily subverted. But there is really no need for hints; the tale of the murdered lady is, even as it completes the pattern, our book's "as far as in him lies." To be sure, we do wonder at Shams ad-Dīn's lackadaisical behavior, much as the rabbis wondered why Joseph, during all the good years in Egypt, neglected to let his father know that he was alive and well. It is fair to say though that in both tales there are points where we are told just enough to keep the story going and are trusted not to heckle the narrator about the rest. Where the plot could be easily extended to account for an unmotivated event (worry about the king's anger; worry about injuries to honor, etc., in Shams ad-Dīn's case) the critic can live without hypotheses.

son (to N.) and daughter (to S.) are born. The old vizier of Basra retires and Nūr ad-Dīn takes his office. When his son Ḥasan Badr ad-Dīn is fifteen years old Nūr ad-Dīn dies. On his deathbed he dictates to Badr ad-Dīn a summary of what has happened to him.

After his father's death Badr ad-Dīn mourns so deeply that for two months he does not present himself at court. The Sultan of Basra, infuriated by this, appoints someone else as vizier; Nūr ad-Dīn's property is confiscated and Badr ad-Dīn's life is in danger. He flees, wanders blindly and ends up at his father's tomb. Here he meets a Jewish merchant who owes his father money and gives him a purse of gold. He goes to sleep in the cemetery.

In the meantime in Egypt Shams ad-Dīn's daughter Sitt al-Ḥusn is also in trouble. The king of Egypt wishes to marry the girl, but her father refuses—she is meant for his brother's son. The king orders her married to a repulsive hunchback stableboy. At one point she exclaims that she will die rather than submit to this groom; later we learn that her father would have killed her if she had submitted.

Genies impressed with the beauty of the hero and heroine transport the sleeping Badr ad-Dīn to Cairo and when he awakes arrange for the stableboy to spend the night upended in a privy and for B. to spend the night in Sitt al-Ḥusn's bed. When B. falls asleep they mean to take him back to the cemetery in Basra, but the genie carrying him is shot down by an angel and the young man ends up deposited in Damascus.

Upon hearing his story everybody thinks him crazy, but he is protected and then adopted by a pastry cook. He works in the cook's shop, which he later inherits.

In Cairo, the disappearance of B. is inexplicable, but after some confusion the identity of the mysterious night-guest is learned from the documents wrapped in his clothes which the genies had left there. A son is born to Sitt al-Ḥusn. Ten years later, after the boys at school make fun of the child, 'Ajīb, because he has no known father. Shams ad-Dīn finally decides to travel east and make inquiries concerning Badr ad-Dīn.

When the search party of Shams ad-Dīn, Sitt al-Ḥusn and 'Ajīb stop for a few days in Damascus, 'Ajīb enters Badr ad-Dīn's shop. Badr al-Dīn is drawn to the boy: indeed, his affection for him is such that he follows him and his servant after they leave the shop. 'Ajīb mistakes the nature of B.'s affection and throws a stone at him that bloodies his head and knocks him out cold.

The family go on to Basra where they find no information but do meet Nūr ad-Dīn's widow who agrees to go with them to Egypt.

On the return trip, when another stop is made in Damascus, 'Ajīb and his servant go back to the shop, where they are treated to a confection of pomegranate seeds. When the boy returns to his family, his grandmother offers him a similar dessert which the boy, already full, finds inferior. The grandmother orders her servant to bring her some of the confection from the cook's shop, and recognizes that the sample can only have been made by her son Badr ad-Dīn.

In order to make sure that the cook is Badr ad-Dīn, and indeed the man who was with Sitt al-Ḥusn on her wedding night, Shams ad-Dīn orders his servants to wreck Badr ad-Dīn's shop and tie him up. B. is carried back to Cairo in a box from which he is let out only by night. He is told that he will be crucified for having put too little pepper in the pomegranate seeds.

Badr ad-Dīn is asleep when he is carried into Sitt al-Ḥusn's chamber. It is exactly as he left it: turban on the chair, purse under the mattress, etc. He cannot tell whether he has really spent ten years as a cook in Damascus or dreamt it, and remains bewildered even after he touches a finger to the scar left by 'Ajīb's rock. In the morning the vizier Shams ad-Dīn enters and explains all. Badr ad-Dīn is presented to the king of Egypt, and shows such *'ilm* and *adab* that he is made one of the king's close companions (*nadīm*). All live happily for the rest of their lives.

HEINZ GROTZFELD

Neglected Conclusions of the *Arabian Nights*: Gleanings in Forgotten and Overlooked Recensions[†]

Certainly no other work of Arabic literature has become so universally known in the West as the *Stories of Thousand and One Nights*, more commonly called *The Arabian Nights' Entertainments* or simply *The Arabian Nights*. Since their first appearance in Europe (Galland's French translation 1704 sqq.; English and German translations of Galland only a few years later), the *Nights* met with lively interest from a large public. In the latter part of the 18th century, this interest generated something like a run on manuscripts of the *Nights*, especially in the English world, as is documented by the relatively large number of Arabic MSS of the *Nights* that were purchased by British residents or travellers in the East and are now to be found in British libraries. Even the I Calcutta edition of the Nights of 1814 and 1818 as well as the II Calcutta edition of 1839–1842 are due to British

[†] From "Neglected Conclusions of the *Arabian Nights*: Gleanings in Forgotten and Overlooked Recensions," *Journal of Arabic Literature* 16 (1985): 73–87. Reprinted by permission of Koninklijke BRILL NV.

activities, since they are both based on MSS brought from Syria or Egypt to India by Englishmen.[1] On the continent, too, one library or another contains MSS of the *Nights,* most of them, however, purchased after 1800 and representing the same recension as the Bulaq edition; a considerable number of older MSS of the *Nights* are to be found only in the Bibliothèque Nationale de Paris.

The interest in MSS of the *Nights,* which is to be observed in the 18th century, diminished at the beginning of the 19th century. Arabists, anyway, did not make the most of the MSS treasured in European libraries. They were satisfied with picking out stories which had not been translated at that time and, in their own translations or expansions of Galland, simply added them to the repertoire of *Nights* stories already existing. There are two exceptions. One is Joseph von Hammer, whose French translation, made in Constantinople from 1804 to 1806 on the basis of a complete Egyptian MS and sent to Silvestre de Sacy for publication, came out only in 1823, not in its original form, but in a stylistically rather unsatisfactory German version for which his publisher Cotta was responsible. The important information given by Hammer in his introduction about the *Nights,* the complete list of the stories, their order and segmentation into nights, as well as his view of the history of the work, had been published earlier in the *Fundgruben* and the *Journal Asiatique.* The other exception is Maximilian Habicht, "who, through close intercourse with Orientals during his long residence in Paris, had come to embrace entirely the irresponsible Oriental attitude towards MSS and editing" (Macdonald 1909, p. 687) and made out of fragments of the *Nights* and other material a compilation of his own, which he published in the years 1825–1839 (vols. I–VIII of the Breslau edition; the remaining four vols. were published after Habicht's death by H. L. Fleischer, 1842–1843).

The Bulaq edition of 1835, which was widely circulated both in the Arab world and in Europe, and the II Calcutta edition, which is of the same recension, superseded almost completely all other texts and formed the general notion of the *Arabian Nights.* For more than half a century it was neither questioned nor contested that the text of the Bulaq and II Calcutta editions was the true and authentic

---

1. Cf. Macdonald, D. B., *A preliminary classification of some MSS of the Arabian Nights.* In: *A Volume of Oriental Studies, presented to E. G. Browne*; ed. by T. W. Arnold and R. A. Nicholson, Cambridge 1922, pp. 313 and 305. The "Egyptian MS brought to India by the late Major Turner Macan", from which II Calcutta was printed, is lost. I rather doubt if this MS was a *complete* ZER-copy. Bulaq and II Calcutta differ chiefly in the first quarter, Calcutta presenting in its prose passages an unrevised "middle Arabic" like any other MS of ZER. In the three remaining quarters, the text of Bulaq and II Calcutta is almost identical, Calcutta presenting here the same "polished" Arabic as Bulaq, which is somewhat strange. But this can easily be explained by the—heretical—assumption that these parts of II Calcutta were printed directly or indirectly from the *printed* Bulaq text.

text. This opinion did not change even when in 1887 H. Zotenberg in his *Notice sur quelques manuscrits des Mille et Une Nuits et la traduction de Galland* showed that the text of the Bulaq and II Calcutta editions represented only one recension of the work[2] and that other recensions of the *Nights* were attested by manuscript evidence much older than any evidence for ZER.[3] It is not that the results of Zotenberg's research were disregarded. But a process not uncommon in the history of texts made it possible to preserve the generally accepted notion of the *Nights* more or less unaffected by them: ZER was given, by tacit convention, the status of a *canonical* text, whereas other recensions were degraded to the rank of *apocrypha*. Still another group of texts was classified as *pseudepigrapha,* e.g. the Breslau edition, which was revealed by Macdonald to be a compilation made by its editor Habicht.[4] Even texts which since Galland had been considered to be integral parts of the *Nights,* e.g. Aladdin or Ali Baba, became classified as spurious.[5] Disregarding "apocryphal" or "pseudepigraphical" material may frequently be of little or no consequence. But focusing the view on ZER rather blocked philological research concerning the text. It is one of the purposes of this paper to show that a careful study of "apocryphal" materials can throw new light on the history of the *Nights.*

The original conclusion of the *Nights* seems to be lost. Galland never had a text for the conclusion he gave to his *Mille et Une Nuits,* and he was considered—wrongly, see n. 3 on p. 478—to have invented this end himself. Thus it was not before the early 19th century, when copies of ZER came into the hands of Europeans, that an Arabic text of the end of the *Nights* became known in Europe. Hammer boasted of being the first European to have discovered the unexpected conclusion of the *Nights* (for his *unexpected* conclusion, see below). The conclusion of the *Nights* as it stands in the Bulaq and II Calcutta editions is no doubt a very simple piece of literature.[6] Nevertheless, it reflects the conclusion outlined in the latter half of the 10th century in the following famous passage of the *Fihrist:*

2. Zotenberg called this recension "la rédaction moderne d'Égypte", Macdonald introduced the abbreviation ZER—Zotenberg's Egyptian Recension.
3. All known manuscript evidences for ZER were transcribed shortly before or after 1800; in all probability, the compilation of ZER itself had been carried out only a few years earlier. Mardrus's affirmation that he owned the very MS "de la fin du XVIIᵉ siècle" from which the Bulaq edition was printed (cf. Chauvin IV, p. 109) is a lie.
4. Macdonald, D. B., *Maximilian Habicht and his reconsion of the Thousand and One Nights,* JRAS 1909, p. 685–704.
5. It was out of reverence for their first translator that Mia Gerhardt, *The Art of Story-Telling,* Leiden 1963, p. 15, did not call them so, but euphemistically spoke of "Galland's orphan stories".
6. Burton expanded it with passages taken from the Breslau edition. Lane translated the end as he had found it in his Bulaq copy.

" . . . until she had passed a thousand nights, while he at the
same time was having intercourse with her as his wife, until she
was given a child by him, which she showed to him, informing
him of the stratagem she had used with him. Then he admired
her undertaking and inclined to her and preserved her alive.
And the king had a qahramāna who was called Dīnārzād, and
she assisted her in that."[7]

The central idea of the conclusion in ZER, thus, is obviously the
same as that of a *Nights*-recension which circulated in Bagdad 800
years earlier, though more obscured than at that time.

We do not know what the conclusion was in the Indian archetype
nor in *Hazār Afsānah*, the Persian recension. Reflexes of the frame
story in the popular literatures of India and its neighbouring countries compel us to assume that in the original form of the frame
story, Shahrazād continues to tell her stories, in the well-known
manner, thus postponing her execution from one day to the other,
until she has given birth to a child[8] and therefore feels safe enough
to reveal her stratagem to the king, whereupon the king preserves
her alive and definitely makes her his queen. The new title the work
was given in the Arabic world, *alf layla*,[9] in which the number was
taken literally, suggests that Shahrazād has to survive a fixed number
of nights by the telling of stories, not the period until she has
reached the status of mother, which then safeguards her against execution. The connection between Shahrazād's reaching this status
and her ending the story-telling became obscured. That seems to be
the case already in the conclusion summarized in the *Fihrist*. The
wording of the *Fihrist*, however, does not exclude, even if it does not
suggest, that Shahrazād needed exactly 1000 nights to become a
mother. Compared with that conclusion, ZER presents a slight but
not unimportant change: during the 1001 nights, Shahrazād has
borne the king three children. It is difficult to decide whether
Shahrazād now has three children because naive tradition could not
imagine the king and Shahrazād enjoying the delight of communion
1001 nights successively without the number of children Shahrazād
is plausibly to have in that time, and therefore amended the number,
or whether she has them because three children were thought to

---

7. Ibn an-Nadîm, *Kitāb al-Fihrist, maqāla* 8, *fann* 1; I quote the translation of Macdonald,
   D. B., *The earlier history of the Arabian Nights*, JRAS 1924, pp. 353–397; p. 365.
8. Or until she was pregnant, as in the frame-story of the *Hundred and One Nights*, which
   corresponds much better to our feeling of plausibility. It is quite unreasonable of ZER to
   demand the audience or the reader to believe that Shahrazād managed to hide her three
   pregnancies from the king.
9. The oldest documentary evidence for the actual title *alf layla wa-layla* is from the 12th
   century and comes from the Cairo Geniza; see S. D. Goitein in JAOS 78, 1958, pp.
   301–302.

touch the king's heart more effectively than only one child. The latter does not seem to be wholly incompatible with ZER, since here changed numbers occur in two other places in the frame-story as well. In the well-known orgy observed by Shāhzamān, the queen enters the garden together with twenty slave girls and twenty male slaves; in G (see n. 3, p. 481) and other earlier texts, the queen is escorted only by twenty slave girls, ten of whom, however, are disguised male slaves, which becomes clear to Shāhzamān only some time later, when they strip off their clothes. In ZER, the trophies of the young woman held captive in the chest are five hundred and seventy seal-rings; in G and most of the other texts, the number is ninety-eight. The change in both instances is no doubt due to a defective or somewhat illegible text.[1] Nevertheless, it shows the predilection of the redactor of ZER, or more likely of one of his predecessors, for strengthening essential elements of the narration by quantitative arguments.

By linking the end of Shahrazād's story-telling with the thousand and first night, the internal logic of the conclusion is lost: when Shahrazād on the 1001th night requests the king to grant her a wish, namely to exempt her from slaughter for the sake of her three children whom she presents to him, her step has not been prepared in the narrative. Nor has any reason been given—except through the title—that she should do so this very night, since the period of story-telling has nowhere previously been limited, unlike the period of seven days in the *Book of the Seven Sages*, where the span to be bridged by telling stories is set in advance by the horoscope of the hero. One or other among the copyists or compilers of *Nights*-recensions also realized this lack. Hammer owned (and translated) a ZER-MS containing a revised ZER-version. Its conclusion says that on the 1001th night, after the story of Ma'rūf the Cobbler, king Shahriyār was bored by Shahrazād's story-telling and ordered her to be excuted the following morning, whereupon Shahrazād sent for her three children and asked for mercy, which was granted her, in the same way as in the other ZER-versions. This surprising turn, which could have been borrowed from a parody of the frame-story, fully explains why Shahrazād must proceed to act as well as why she finishes telling stories to the king.[2]

---

1. The number 570 is obviously a *tashīf* of 98, the *rasm* of a carelessly written ṭamāniya wa-tis 'īn being very close to that of *ḫamsimi'a wa-sab'īn*; it is to be found already in the Paris MS 3612, which is prior to the compilation of ZER. The twenty male slaves have been added in order to make plausible a text in which the passage relating the disguise had been dropped, obviously by a copyist who was unable to guess how the story could have run.

2. Burton missed the point of this modification or interpolation. Though he knew that this reading was to be found in some MSS, he accused Trébutien, the French translator of Hammer-Zinserling, that he "cannot deny himself the pleasure of a French touch" (X, p. 54, n. 2).

Even the author of the poor conclusion which ends the recension contained in the so-called Ṣabbāgh-MS[3] conceived such a double motivation, though one which perfectly fits the poorness of the composition: Shahrazād has related to the king all she knew (*hāḏā mā 'indī min tawārīḫ as-sālifīn wan-nās al-awwalān*), "and when king Shahriyār had heard all the tales of Shahrazād, and since God had blessed him by her (sc. with children) during the time he had been occupied by listening to her tales, he said to himself: 'By God, this wife is intelligent, erudite, reasonable, experienced, so I must not slay her, specially since God has blessed me by her with two children.' And he continued that night admiring her wisdom, and his love for her increased in his heart. In the following morning, he rose and went to the cabinet, bestowed a robe of honour and all kinds of favour upon her father the wazīr, and lived together with her in happiness and delight until the angel of Death came to them and made them dwell in the grave" (MS arabe 4679, fol. 401b). In these artless, simple or poor conclusions[4] we meet the same deterioration that is often to be observed in stories transmitted by long oral tradition: the elements as such of the stories are still preserved, but the original connection between them has become distorted or totally lost. So it is reasonable to assume that the conclusions of ZER and the Sabbāgh-MS reproduce what was known about the end of the *Nights* from oral tradition in a more or less skilful arrangement by the respective compiler.

There exists, however, an elaborate skilful conclusion, entirely different from that of ZER. It is attested by some manuscript sources considerably older than ZER, and one printed one, namely Habicht's edition. But since this edition, following Macdonald's article in *JRAS* 1909, was discredited in its entirety, though parts of it reproduce "authentic" *Nights*-material, particularly fragments of *Nights*-recensions prior to ZER, its conclusion was no longer paid any attention.

So far, I know of four sources for this conclusion:

H: Habicht's edition or compilation of the *Nights*; the end of his compilation, nights 885–end, is based upon the transcript made by Ibn an-Najjār (Habicht's Tunisian friend) of a fragment of a *Nights*-recension transcribed in 1123/1711 (see Macdonald 1909, p. 696).

---

3. Paris, Bibliothèque Nationale, MS arabe 4678–4679, formerly marked "Supplément arabe 2522–2523", transcribed at the beginning of the 19th century in Paris by Michel Ṣabbāg from an unknown MS which had been transcribed in 1115/1703 in Bagdad, according to its colophon copied literally by Ṣabbāg; cf. Zotenberg p. 202.
4. Burton says that the Wortley Montague MS in the Bodleian Library "has no especial conclusion relating the marriage of the two brother kings with the two sisters" (XV, p. 351). Does this mean that the MS has a poor conclusion, like that in ZER, or no conclusion at all?

K: MS Edebiyât 38 in Kayseri, Raşid Efendi kütüphane; this MS is
described by H. Ritter in *Oriens* 2, 1949, pp. 287–289; on the
basis of its script Ritter gives the 16th or the 17th century as the
date of its transcription ("frühestens 10.jh.H."). The text is
divided into nights, but the nights are not numbered, the space
for the numbers, which probably were to have been rubricated,
not having been filled.

B: MS We.662 in Berlin, Stiftung Preussischer Kulturbesitz-
Staatsbibliothek (formerly Royal Library), Nr. 9104 in Ahlwardt's
catalogue; the transcription of the part concerning us is from
1173/1759. The night-formulae and the numbering have been
crossed out (see below p. 484).

P: MS arabe 3619 in Paris, Bibliothèque Nationale; the MS. was
formerly marked "Supplément arabe 1721 II" (so in Zotenberg
1887, p. 214); "d'origine égyptienne écrit au XVIIᵉ siècle ou au
commencement du XVIIIᵉ siècle".

The conclusion of these sources differs from the conclusion
attested by the *Fihrist* and narrated in ZER, in that Shahrazâd does
not implore the king's mercy by referring to her status as mother of
his child or children, but "converts" the king by telling stories which
make him reflect on his own situation so that he begins to doubt
whether it was right to execute his wives after the bridal night. No
sooner is Shahrazâd sure that her stories have taken effect than she
begins to tell the prologue/frame-story of the *Nights* themselves,
somewhat condensed and slightly alienated in that the characters
have no names, but are labelled "the king", "the wazīr", "the wazīr's
daughter" and "her sister", and the scene is simply "a town":[5]

It has reached me, o auspicious King, that someone said: People pretend that a man once declared to his mates: I will set
forth to you a means of security against annoy. A friend of mine
once related to me and said: We attained to security against
annoy, and the origin of it was other than this; that is, it was the
following: I over-travelled whilome lands and climes and towns
and visited the cities of high renown . . . Towards the last of my
life, I entered a city,[6] wherein was a king of the Chosroës and
the Tobbas and the Caesars. Now that city had been peopled

5. This is certainly what was originally intended. The beginning of H and B is still in accord
with this intention. In the sequel, names have slipped into the narration: the younger
brother lives in Samarcand, the elder in Şīn. In K, the alleged friend who relates the story
came to "a town in Şīn".
6. Burton has added here "of the cities of China" and explained in note 6 that this "is taken
from the sequence of the prologue where the elder brother's kingdom is placed in China".
He missed the point that in this tale, which he qualifies as "a rechauffé of the Introduction" (note 4), persons and places must remain nameless. *Fīâḫir al-ʿumr* (H = the text
translated by Burton; B) is no doubt a corruption of *fī āḫir al-ʿumrān* (K); the best reading
is to be found in P: *daḫaltu madīna fī āḫir al-ʿumrān* 'I came to a town at the end of the
civilized world' (fol. 163b).

with its inhabitants by means of justice and equity; but its then king was a tyrant dire who despoiled lives and souls at his desire; in fine, there was no warming oneself at his fire, for that indeed he oppressed the believing band and wasted the land. Now he had a younger brother, who was king in Samarcand of the Persians, and the two kings sojourned a while of time, each in his own city and stead, till they yearned unto each other and the elder king despatched his Wazir to fetch his younger brother . . .

(Burton XII, pp. 192–193; I shall skip the rest of the story, which ends as follows)

. . . on the fifth night she told him anecdotes of Kings and Wazirs and Notables. Brief, she ceased not to entertain him many days and nights, while the king still said to himself, 'Whenas I shall have heard the end of the tale, I will do her die,' and the people redoubled their marvel and admiration. Also the folk of the circuits and cities heard of this thing, to wit, that the king had turned from his custom and from that which he had imposed upon himself and had renounced his heresy, wherefor they rejoiced and the lieges returned to the capital and took up their abode therein, after they had departed thence; and they were in constant prayer to Allah Almighty that He would stablish the king in his present stead. And this <said shahrazad> is the end of that which my friend[7] related to me." Quoth Shahriyar, "O Shahrazad, finish for us the tale thy friend told thee, inasmuch as it resembleth the story of a King whom I knew; but fain would I hear that which betided the people of this city and what they said of the affair of the king, so I may return from the case wherein I was."[8] Shahrazad replies that, "when the folk heard how the king had put away from him his malpractice and returned from his unrighteous wont, they rejoiced in this with joy exceeding and offered up prayers for him. Then they talked one with other of the cause of the slaughter of the maidens <and they told this story and it became obvious for them, that only women had caused all that>[9] and the wise said, 'Women are not all alike, nor are the fingers of the hand alike.' " (Burton XII, p. 197).

7. This short-cut *isnād* is in contradiction with the longer *isnād* in the introductory passage, but it is no doubt that of the older version.
8. The words *hādihi l-ḥikāya tušbih li-ḥikāyal malik anā aʿrif-hu* are certainly an integral part of this revelation scene; so is the king's request to hear about the reaction of the subjects *urīd an asmaʿ mā ǧarā li-ahl hādihi l-madīna wa-mā qālū min amr al-malik*. But the subsequent final clause *li-arǧiʿ ʿam-mā kuntu fīhi* is not quite logical. An emendation *lammā raǧaʿ ʿam-mā kān fīhi* 'when he returned from the case wherein he was', which, regarding the *rasm*, seems to suggest itself, would make the text reasonable.
9. This passage has been dropped from H, but the following statement of the wise presupposes at least *sabab hādā an-nisā*; the addition is from B, fol. 114b; nearly the same text is to be found in K, fol. 124b.

The king comes to himself and awakens from his drunkenness; he acknowledges that the story was his own and that he has deserved God's wrath and punishment, and he thanks God for having sent him Shahrazād to guide him back on the right way. Shahrazād, then, lectures on the interrelation between ruler and army, between ruler and subjects, on the indispensability of a good wazīr (which is all somewhat inappropriate in this context), argues by reference to sūra 33:35 that there are also chaste women,[1] and by relating the Story of the Concubine and the Caliph (Burton XII, pp. 199–201; Chauvin's Nr. 178) and the Story of the Concubine of al-Maamun[2] (Burton XII, pp. 202–206; Chauvin's Nr. 179) she demonstrates for Shahriyār that his case is not as unique as he thought, because "that which hath befallen thee, verily, it hath befallen many kings before thee . . . all they were more majestical of puissance than thou, mightier of kingship and had troops more manifold" (Burton XII, p. 199). The king is now fully convinced that he was wrong and that Shahrazād has no equal. He arranges his marriage with her, and marries Dīnāzād to his brother Shāhzamān, who in Samarcand behaved the same way as he had done until Shahrazād entered the scene. Dīnāzād, however, stipulates that the two kings and the two sisters should live together for ever. So the wazīr is sent to Samarcand as their governor. The king orders the stories told by Shahrazād to be recorded by the annalists; they fill thirty volumes. There is no mention in these texts of a child, much less three children, as an argument for granting mercy to Shahrazād.[3]

The texts of the four sources mentioned above are essentially identical, the variants in number and nature being within the usual confines. But though derived from one and the same version, they constitute the end of two different recensions of the Nights. In H, this conclusion follows the "Tale of the King and his Son and his

---

1. Women qualified as muslimāt, mu'mināt, qānitāt, ṣādiqāt . . . ḥāfiẓāt (sc. furūğahunna) must exist in reality, as they are mentioned in this āya.

2. The name of the Caliph in this story is al-Ma'mūn al-Ḥākim bi-amrillāh. The ism of the historical caliph al-Ḥākim (who reigned from 996 to 1021) was al-Manṣūr. The scene of the story is Cairo.

3. The spread of this conclusion in the 17th century is attested indirectly by Galland. He had tried in vain to get a complete copy of the Nights, nor had he ever had at his disposal an Arabic text of an end-fragment. The ending of his translation therefore has been suspected, until quite recently, to be of Galland's own invention. But from oral information he knew at least the basic concept of this conclusion: as early as August 1702, two years before he published the first volume of his translation, he outlined in a letter "le dessein de ce grand ouvrage: (. . .) De nuit en nuit la nouvelle sultane le mesne [Schahriar] jusques à mille et une et l'oblige, en la laissant vivre, de se défaire de la prévention où il étoit généralement contre toutes les femmes". The words in italics are to be found in the conclusion of Galland's translation, in which Shahrazād does not present children, but is granted mercy because the king's "esprit étoit adouci" and the king is convinced of Shahrazād's chastity. (The quotation from Galland's letter in M. Abdel-Halim, Galland, sa vie et son œuvre, Paris 1964, pp. 286–287).

Wife and the seven Wazirs" (i.e. the Arabic version of the *Book of Sindibād* or *Book of the Seven Sages*); the transition from this tale to the conclusion is seamless and logical:

> King Shahriban (i.e. Shahriyār's name in the Breslau edition) marvelled at this history and said, 'By Allah, verily, injustice slayeth its folk!'[4] And he was edified[5] by that, wherewith Shahrazad bespoke him, and sought help of Allah the Most High. Then he said to her, 'Tell me another of thy tales, O Shahrazad; supply me with a pleasant story and this shall be the completion of the story-telling.' Shahrazad replied, 'With love and gladness! It has reached me, O auspicious King, that a man once declared . . . ' (Burton XII, p. 192; see above p. 477).

In the three other texts, this conclusion is interwoven with the "Tale of Baibars and the Sixteen Captains of Police"[6] as follows: the 16th Captain tells to King Baibars the prologue-story as if related to himself by a friend. The stories told in the Breslau edition by the 14th, 15th, 16th Captain (*n, o, p* in Burton's translation) in this recension of the Baibars-cycle are told by the 13th, 14th and 15th respectively (this shift is already prepared in the first half of the cycle: the 5th Captain relates two stories, his "own" and that of the 6th Captain). The stories of the Clever Thief and of the Old Sharper (Burton's *na* and *nb*) remain in their place in the order of tales between *n* and *o*. The 15th Captain thus tells, in the first person singular, the story of the traveller who was threatened by a robber sitting on his breast with a knife drawn in his hand, but is delivered by a crocodile which came

> 'forth of the river and snatching him up from off my breast plunged into the water, with him still hending knife in hand, even within the jaws of the beast which was in the river. And I praised God for having escaped from the one who wanted to slay me.' The king[7] marvelled and said: 'Injustice harms[8] its folk.' Then he was alarmed[9] in his heart and said: 'By God, I was in foolishness before these exhortations, and the coming of this maiden is nothing but (a sign of God's) mercy.' Then he said:

---

4. Text: *al-baġyu yaqtulu ahlahū*. This looks like a proverb, a variant of the one recorded by al-Maydānī, *Maǧmaʿ al-amṯāl*, Cairo 1953, nr. 555 = Freytag, Proverbia Maidanii, cap. II, nr. 129: *albaġyu āḫiru muddati l-qawmi, yaʿnī anna ẓ-ẓulma iḏā mtadda madāhu, āḏana bi-nqirāḍi muddatihim.*

5. Text: *ittaʿaẓa*; but see the parallel texts, n. 9 below.

6. Translated by Burton from the Breslau edition, XII, pp. 2–44.

7. In K, the king is nameless; P: *al-malik aẓ-Ẓāhir*; in B, his name is Šahribāz.

8. B: *yaḍurru*; P: *yuhliku*; K: *yusriʿu* (= ?).

9. B: *irtāʿa fī nafsihī*; K: *irtadaʿa*, obviously a *taṣḥīf* instead of *irtāʿa*. This passage is not in P, nor is the following dialogue between the king and Shahrazād.

'I conjure thee, O Shahrazad, supply me with another one of
these pleasant tales and exhortations, and this shall be the completion of the Story of King az-Zāhir and the sixteen Captains.'
And she said: 'Well, then came forward another Captain, and
he was the sixteenth of the Captains, and said: 'I will set forth to
you a means of security against annoy. One of my friends once
related to me . . . ' (B, fol. 113a; I have borrowed from Burton
XII, p. 44 and 192 the translations of the corresponding parts in
the Breslau edition—H).

The text of the story told by the 16th Captain (see p. 479) is somewhat fuller in B than in H, which is, for its part, close to the text of
K. B and K coincide, however, in minor details both internal (e.g.
even the first wives of the two brother-kings are sisters) and external
(e.g. the 16th Captain's story has night-divisions at the same places),
so there is no doubt that B and K derive from the same version, the
fuller text of B being due to a more recent polishing. In P, a considerable portion of the text is missing here: the "Tale of the two Kings"
which is told by the Captain, breaks off after the words characteriz-
ing the elder kind (' . . . and wasted the land'); then follows immediately the "Tale of the Concubine of the Caliph" (fol. 163b, lines
5–6). The lacuna is superficially dissimulated by the interpolation
of *fa-taʿaǧǧab al-malik aẓ-Ẓāhir min hāḏihi l-umūr, fa-lā taʿaǧǧab
ayyuhā l-malik Šahriyār* at the end of the second Concubine-tale
(fol. 170a). Even the division into nights continues; the numbering,
however, runs thus: fol. 163a: 908; fol. 165b: 909; fol. 168a: 1000 (!).
Shahrazād finishes telling her stories in that night.
    Incorporating the prologue-story into the Baibars-cycle involved a
threefold oblique narration, which necessitated some adjustments
in the text to be transcribed. The redactor mastered this task well,
but eventually, certainly because of failing attention, made a mistake, which then was copied by over-scrupulous scribes. In K, as in
B (P: lacuna), the Baibars-cycle ends as follows (somewhat less
abruptly than in the Breslau edition, vol. 11, p. 399):

    ' . . . and this is the end of what my friend related to me, O King
    az-Zāhir.' Those who were attending and King az-Zāhir mar-
    velled, then they dispersed. And this is <said shahrazad> what
    reached me from their invitation. Then King Shahriyar said:
    'This is indeed marvellous, but O Shahrazad, this story which
    the Captain related *to me (ahkā lī)*, resembles the story of a king
    whom I know . . . '

He then asks what the reaction of the subjects was, "so I may return
from the case wherein I was." (K, fol. 122b). Shahrazād replies by
using nearly the same words as in H (see above p. 477), though on the

basis of the premises of this composition she cannot have any further information. In the text of B, the inappropriate *to me* has been eliminated. The story then continues and ends in the same way as in H.

The literary ambition and the skill of this composition—at least of parts of it—are clearly discernible in spite of the somewhat degenerated versions in which it is accessible to us. Redactional mistakes as the aforementioned one indicate that this conclusion was not originally composed for these versions, but is a "recycled" fragment.[1] Since the recensions into which this conclusion has been inserted were in all probability compiled as early as the 16th century,[2] the recensions to which this conclusion originally belonged must be considerably older.

Such an early date of origin is suggested by some characteristic details in which the Story of the Two Kings and the Wazīr's Daughter, i.e. the prologue-story, agrees with the prologue in Galland's MS, the earliest extant MS of the *Nights*.[3] As in G, the story immediately begins with two kings who are brothers (ZER begins with a king who divides his kingdom and assigns it to either of his two sons); the younger brother returns to his castle, as in G, to take leave of his wife (in ZER he returns because he forgot *ḥāǧa* 'something' or *ḥaraza* 'a pearl') and, as in G, he perceives in the garden the wife of his brother together with ten white slave girls and ten male negro slaves (in ZER the number is twenty for each group). The lover of the younger brother's wife is "a man" (*raǧul*, K and B) or "a strange man" (*raǧul aǧnabī*, H), which fits in better with the "man from the kitchen-boys" (*raǧl min ṣubyān al-maṭbaḥ*) in G than with the "negro slave" in ZER. Last not least, the epithets *ǧabbār—lā yuṣṭalā lahū bin-nār* ("a tyrant dire—there was no warming oneself at his fire", see above p. 477) which characterize the elder brother occur even in G among the epithets of Shahriyār (they are not found in ZER nor in any other MS which is independent of the G-group).[4] This congruence does not necessarily imply that this conclusion ever constituted the end of that recension of which G is an initial fragment, since the prologue in

---

1. In most cases fragments of older recensions were inserted into the new compilation without extensive revision. So quite often it is not difficult to detect such *spolia* by inconsistent distribution of the roles (speaker, hearer etc.), stylistic peculiarities and the like. The ZER-text however, specially the printed one, has undergone a careful revision.
2. The corruptions found in the text of K, the oldest of the four MSS and carefully calligraphed, show that already that text had been transmitted within a long written tradition.
3. Paris, Bibliothèque Nationale, arabe 3609-3611 (formerly marked "ancien fonds 1508, 1507, 1506"). This MS, commonly designated as G, was transcribed after 1425, the year in which the *ašrafī*-dinar (mentioned in 3610, fol. 43b) was introduced, and before 943/1535, the earliest date of a reader's expression of thanks at the end of 3610.
4. *lā yuṣṭalā lahū bin-nār* is among the epithets of 'Umar ibn an-Nu'mān at the beginning of the 'Umar-Romance.

G, too, is most probably a literary spolium;[5] it implies, however, that a prologue like that of G and a conclusion like that of H and K, B, P once formed the beginning and the end of a recension of the *Nights* considerably earlier than G.

Though the conclusion incontestably bears an Islamic stamp and at first sight hardly has anything in common with the conclusion summarized by Ibn an-Nadīm, we have to ask ourselves, considering the great age of the composition, whether it is a totally new creation achieved without any knowledge of other conclusions of the *Nights*—or at least without any regard to them—, or whether the author of this composition has perhaps also inserted, besides comparatively young elements such as the two concubine tales,[6] fragments of older recensions. I think we have good reasons to assume that this composition includes an element which was part not only of a very old recension of the *Nights,* but also, most probably, of the Indian archetype. Ibn an-Nadīm's words concerning the end of the *Nights,* "until she was given a child by him, which she showed to him, informing him of the stratagem she had used with him", imply, no doubt, the device by which in this composition the king is informed of the matter. For, how did Shahrazād instruct the king? It is hardly conceivable that the structural element par excellence of the (older parts of the) *Nights,* namely telling a story for the most varied purposes (to obtain ransom, to gain time, to entertain, to instruct), should not be employed here: for Shahrazād nothing is better suited to reveal her stratagem to the king than to relate to him the story in its alienated form in which Shahriyār recognizes himself and his own fate as in a mirror. I have no doubt that in the recension of the *Nights* which the author of the *Fihrist* had before his eyes the conclusion was introduced by this revelation story, but I consider it also very likely that this was the case already in the Indian archetype of the *Nights.*

Since the king is converted from his hatred for women to an indulgent attitude towards them, and does not simply show mercy, as he does in the *Fihrist*/ZER-conclusion, there is no need for Shahrazād to produce a child, or three children respectively, as an argument to obtain pardon. Children would even mar the picture of

---

5. It does not come up to the same stylistic and narrative level as the tales inserted into the frame, which are, by the way, far better in the version of G than in ZER. Shahrazād's first tale however, that of the Merchant and the Jinnī, is as poor as in the printed texts, which proves that even it was part of the initial fragment left from preceding recensions.
6. The tale of the Concubine of al-Ḥākim can have taken its actual shape only after the eccentric person of the historical al-Ḥākim had been transfigured by time, so that he could become a nucleus of popular story or romance. The Zuwayla-Gate mentioned in all the texts was built in 1092; as a *terminus ante quem non,* such an early date is rather insignificant.—Also six of the seven poems describing the bride's seven dresses in the Tale of Nūr al-Dīn and his Son (Burton I, pp. 217–219) are used (again?) here for the same purpose.

the sumptuous wedding by which this composition is closed. Therefore I assume that the author of this conclusion dropped the children-
motif on purpose.

A third version of the end is found in the recension represented by
the so-called MS Reinhardt.[7] After the tale of Hārūn ar-Rashīd and
Abū Ḥasan, The Merchant of Oman, which is the last tale of this
recension (nights 946–952 in ZER), Shahrazād immediately begins
the Tale of the Two Kings and the Wazīr's Daughters, without any
preparatory transition except for the usual *wa-ḥukiya*, "one relates".
The first part of this tale repeats almost verbatim, without any
abridgement, the prologue of this recension,[8] the two kings and
their father, for instance, being given their names. Only the latter
part of the tale is more condensed (the two daughters of the wazīr
remain nameless here):

> (Shahrazād is still talking:) '. . . and she occupied him with
> tales and stories until she got pregnant and gave birth to a boy,
> got pregnant once again with a girl, and for a third time got
> pregnant with a boy. They bought white and black slave girls
> and populated the palace anew, as it had been before, the king
> not being aware of any of this.' The king turned his face to her
> (i.e. he pricked his ears) and asked: 'Where are *my* children?'—
> She replied: 'They are here.' Then he said: 'So that is the way to
> let me know! By God, if you had not acted in this manner and
> caught me with your stories, you would not have remained alive
> until now. Well done!' Shahrazād replied: 'A woman is worth
> only as much as her intelligence and her faith. Women are very
> different from one another.' And she ordered (*amarat*) her sister
> Dunyazad to bring the children. . . . (4281, fol. 477b—478a)

The king rejoices at his children and tells Shahrazād that he loves
her still more. Complying with her request, he brings back servants
and domestics to the palace;[9] he writes a letter to his brother relating to him this happy ending; the brother sends his congratulations
and gifts for all of them, "and King Shah Baz and the wazir's daughter abode in all solace of life and its delight until there came the

---

7. Strasbourg, Bibliothèque Nationale et Universitaire, MS 4278–4281. Date of transcription 1247/1831–2. As for the date of the compilation, see n. 1 on p. 484. Table of contents
in Chauvin, *Bibliographie* IV, pp. 210–212.
8. The prologue has been considerably remodelled in its details: the seats of the two kings
have been exchanged; the younger brother is deceived by his chief concubine, the elder
by his wife; the number of slave girls and male slaves who accompany the queen into the
garden has been raised to eighty; Shahrazād is the younger of the two daughters of the
wazīr.
9. The untrue slaves had all been executed, so the palace, at least the *haramlik*, had been
totally depopulated.

Destroyer of delights and the Sunderer of societies" (the translation of this frequent end-clausula is borrowed from Burton).

I have evidence that the Reinhardt MS is the original copy of this recension or compilation;[1] so the date of transcription, 1247/1832, is at the same time that of the compilation. In view of this recent date one is not inclined to assume that the end of this recension is a proof of another ancient conclusion of the *Nights*. Nevertheless, it cannot be contested that this conclusion comes closest to that summarized by Ibn an-Nadīm: There are children involved;[2] Shahrazād reveals her stratagem to the king; the king admires her intelligence, he inclines towards her and preserves her alive. Shahrazād's sister has, in this conclusion, the same function as Shahrazād's accomplice in the *Fihrist*-version: she is only a nurse (thus, there is no need to marry her to the king's brother); there is no trace of a "conversion" or "listening to reason". These congruences are not accidental; there must be a connection between the end of the recension known to Ibn an-Nadīm and the conclusion of the Reinhardt MS. It is not likely that the compiler of this recension knew a version of the conclusions discussed above. It is true that he did not hesitate to recast stories radically, as is shown by the prologue, but if he had rewritten the end, there should be some traces left from the former text. As to Shahrazād's device of informing the king of her stratagem, namely relating his own story to him, there is no model for it in the finale of ZER (which was certainly known to the compiler), nor does it follow immediately from what the *Fihrist* (which the compiler can hardly have known) says about the end. On the other hand, it is obvious that the stories are gathered from very shifting traditions; even such tales as occur under the same title in ZER are not all taken from ZER-fragments; the tale of Tawaddud, for instance, is from a tradition which can be traced back to the 16th century,[3] quite independently of ZER. Thus, we cannot but deduce that the compiler of the Reinhardt MS knew a model stemming from a separate tradition, and we must for the present accept the curious fact that the latest

1. The text has been divided into nights by relatively long formulae with separate spaces left for the numbers of the nights. The night-formulae always fill half a page; the nights themselves measure two and a half pages, the formulae not included. The scribe has evidently inserted the night-formula rather automatically, on every third or fourth page, into the text he was copying. But he has made a mistake, for there is one too many: after the formula used for the 1001st night, there is yet another, which was crossed out later. If the MS was a transcription from a compilation already lying before the copyist's eyes, the lines that were crossed out and the free space for the night-number would not have been copied.
2. The composition does not say how many children Shahrazād herself is supposed to have. The number of the heroine's children in Shahrazād's revelation-story is no doubt borrowed from ZER.
3. The version of Tawaddud is very different from that in ZER, but close to freely circulating versions of the story, e.g. that of MS We.702 in Berlin (Ahlwardt Nr. 9179), transcribed in 1055/1645.

recension of the *Nights* obviously presents the very conclusion which is closest to its original form.[4]

Since ZER was regarded as canonical not only in Europe but also in the Arabic World, other recensions were less appreciated even there. The *Nights*-fragment B, then, less than a hundred years after its transcription was considered to be trash and was rehashed; by means of a rather superficial revision it was turned into a "new" work: *Kitāb samarīyāt wa-qisas ʿibarīyāt*. The redactor's work, however, consisted chiefly in crossing out the Night-formulae and numbers and in adding a few excerpts from other books as well as a new title page (cf. Ahlwardt Nr. 9103 and 9104). We should not let ourselves be deluded by this procedure, any more than that unknown Arabic reader of the "new" work who wrote the following beneath its new title: *hāda kitāb min sīrat alf layla ilā intihāʾ as-sīra* ("this is a part of the Story of the Thousand Nights right to the end of the story").

JEROME W. CLINTON

Madness and Cure in the *1001 Nights*[†]

Introduction[1]

The stories of the *Thousand and One Nights* appear on first encounter to appeal principally through their exotic, fantastic and sensational features. And, indeed, they are filled with kings and caliphs and all the panoply of court life, with enormous and terrifying jinns, with magicians both good and evil, and of both sexes, and with adventures that are by turns horrible, wonderful, bloody and sublime. Yet the collection opens with the instruction that we are to read these tales, not to be amused or distracted, but to be admonished and restrained.

"The lives of former generations are a lesson to posterity. A man may review the remarkable events that have befallen others, and so be admonished. He may consider the history of people of preceding ages, and so be restrained. Praised be He who has ordained that the

---

4. "A quite modern MS may carry a more complete tradition than one centuries older" (Macdonald 1922, p. 321).

† From *Studia Islamica* 61 (1985): 107–25. Reprinted by permission.

1. I presented an earlier version of this paper at the MESA meetings in Philadelphia in November 1982. At various stages in the revision of it into its present form I have benefited from the comments of Andras Hamori, Nahoma Clinton, and Betsy S. Halpern whom I would like both to thank here and to absolve of responsibility for any deficiencies that remain.

history of former generations be a lesson to those which follow. Thus are the tales of the Thousand and One Nights".[2]

That is, we are invited to see events and characters in them that are so like us that reading about them will illumine our understanding of ourselves and of others like us.

The very first tale in the collection, and the one that both introduces the others and sets their narration in motion, seems to deny that promise. The elements of the fantastic, exotic and sensational are so strong within it that it is difficult to see beyond them. Yet at bottom, the tale of Shahriyar and Shahrizad is about male wounding and how it can destroy the bond between men and women.[3] The theme is one that is both general and ordinary. It is also a story about justice, and about madness and its cure. If on first encounter it excites our interest by its strangeness, it is its profound familiarity that engrosses us at last.

The Madness of Shahriyar

The world to which the tale of Shahriyar and Shahrizad first introduces us is one of apparent tranquility and order. Shahriyar has ruled in justice for twenty years. His brother, Shahzaman, is so secure upon his throne that he feels free to leave his kingdom in his vazir's charge while he goes off on a prolonged visit to his brother. The infidelity of Shahzaman's wife makes an ugly ripple in this serene surface, but that of Shahriyar's wife shatters it with destructive force. After Shahriyar witnesses her debauch, he first abandons his throne altogether, then, after his encounter with the jinn and the kidnapped bride, he returns to his throne, but transformed into a monster of injustice.

Shahriyar, in a word, has gone mad. That is, for a monarch who is loved and admired throughout his kingdom first to abandon his throne without a moment's warning or reflection, and then to make war on his subjects in this calculated but violent way are acts of madness. The task which the clever and heroic Shahrizad sets herself is to cure him of this madness, both "to rescue the daughters of Muslims from death," and to restore that peace and order which initially reigned in the state. The means by which she attempts this cure is the series of tales that fills up their nights for the next three years or so. Since the cure works, she has arguably understood the king's affliction correctly. But as she does not present her diagnosis

---

2. *Alf Laila wa Laila,* Bulaq edition of A. H. 1252, offset in Baghdad by Qasim Muhammad al-Rajab, p. 2.
3. The tale is here presented in a context that unites Islamic Iran with its pre-Islamic past. E. Cosquin has found a Sanskrit analogue for its principal theme, the betrayal of the monarch by his queen in the palace garden, that he considers its original. *Le prologue-cadre des 1001 Nuits. Etudes folkloriques,* pp. 265–347. Paris, 1922.

anywhere in explicit terms, we are obliged to infer it from the symptoms, just as she did. A formidable task, but not an impossible one, particularly since we have, as she did not, the considerable advantage of being able to witness the event that traumatizes Shahriyar as he is experiencing it.

That infidelity, and particularly the manner of it, tells us a good deal. Shahriyar's wife has chosen not only to cuckold him, an act of tremendous hostility by itself, but also to do so with a man who is as opposite and inferior to him as Islamic court society can provide, a black slave. She has made her act of infidelity a kind of rite of the harem by involving forty of her male and female slaves. Moreover, it is a rite that she apparently celebrates every time the king leaves the palace. And although it is carried out in the apparent seclusion of the harem, with so many privy to the secret, it can hardly have been a secret at all, except from Shahriyar. When Shahriyar confronts both the fact and the manner of his wife's betrayal of him, he has to confront as well the realization that what has only now become known to him has long been common knowledge in the court.

The physical context of this traumatic event gives added symbolic weight to it. As Shahriyar looks down on his wife and her attendants, he is observing her in what was for him the most secret and secure point in his kingdom. The garden is at the heart of the castle and protected by its walls, and the walls of the castle are protected both by his own twenty years of just rule and by those of his father as well. The garden is not simply a quiet and beautiful place within the palace, it is a symbol and metaphor both for Shahriyar's psyche and self, and for the quality of his performance as ruler of his kingdom.[4] Shahriyar's wife has invaded, violated and betrayed him in the very center of his personal and public being. The blow is too much for him to endure, and as the author says, "his wits flew off." He physically flees as well, abandoning throne and state, and deferring vengeance, to find if anyone in all the world has suffered as he and Shahzaman have.

Let us leave him there and return for a moment to the traumatic scene that put him to flight. The adultery of Shahzaman's wife foreshadows that of Shahriyar's. Since events rarely come singly in such

---

4. The palace garden, which was often given a celestial name, provided a paradisial setting for a monarch who was perceived as the brother of the sun and moon, and the shah often held court there during major festivals of the year. (cf. J. W. Clinton, *The Divan of Manuchihri Damghani*, Minneapolis 1972, chapters 1, 5 and 6) An ideal monarch was one who made the whole of his kingdom just such a paradisial garden. In the *Shahnamah* the justice of Daridun is described thus : "By his goodness he protected everyone from evil, as padishahs ought to do. He adorned the world like paradise, planting cypresses and rose bushes instead of (ordinary) plants." (Abul-Qasim Firdausi, *Shahnamah*. ed. Ye. E. Bertels, Moscow 1960, volume 1, page 81.) It also symbolized both his state as well as that of the kingdom. When Faridun receives back the body of his son, Iraj, who has been murdered by his two brothers, he manifests his grief by weeping, tearing his hair, and laying the palace garden waste. (volume 1. p. 106)

tales, when we learn that Shahzaman's wife has betrayed him, we know, or can reasonably assume, that we will shortly encounter the infidelity of his elder brother's wife. Yet, psychologically, the first betrayal cannot altogether prepare us for the second. The adultery of Shahzaman's wife, however surprising and unpleasant, is private and has the air of a more routine act of infidelity. The only hint of symbolic defiance is in her choice of a black slave as her lover. What Shahriyar must confront is on a much vaster scale and is much more heavily freighted than what his brother has endured.

Our first introduction to Shahriyar has also not prepared us to see him humiliated in quite this way. On the contrary, Shahriyar has been described to us as a just ruler, and the presumptions is that a ruler who is just and equitable whith his subjects will be so with his family and friends as well. Nor should we interpret his justice as rigid and authoritarian. The Perso-Islamic ideal of justice is one that rests as much on the exercise of wisdom and mercy as on the strict enforcement of the law. That Shahriyar conformed to this ideal may be inferred from the statement that his subjects loved him. The adultery of Shahriyar's wife is a puzzling response to such justice, or, rather, its ferocious and defiant character is. It obliges us to look at the question of justice, his justice, again. Unless we can find something in the story to show that Shahriyar, at least, mistreated his wife, her actions will appear as inexplicable or as arising from some inborn predisposition to malice.

This latter assumption is, in fact, the one that informs most interpretations of the tale.[5] The argument runs that the wives of Shahriyar, Shahzaman and the captive of the jinn are innately wicked women who treat their respective mates with unjustified and excessive cruelty. Based on this sample of womankind, Shahriyar's policy of bride murder is certainly extreme, but not altogether wrong-headed. The problem is that his sample is skewed, and what Shahrizad does through her tales and her own example is to expand his sample to include a number of virtuous women.

This reading is supported in the text principally by the expectations set up by the infidelity of Shahzaman's wife. Since she is arguably "in the wrong", by implication Shahriyar's wife is as well. The norms of the society in which the story takes place, and of the audience that heard it, which assumed that women were morally inferior to men, and were animated almost exclusively by their

---

5. I have in mind those of Mia I. Gerhardt (*The Art of Storytelling*. E. J. Brill, Leiden 1963. p. 398), and of the earlier translators such as Lane and Burton, in particular. See, for example. Lane's note 27 on p. 38 of volume one of the three volume edition of his work (London, 1859). M. Mahdi sees the wives as rebellious, though not actually depraved. "Remarks on the 1001 Nights." *Interpretation*, volume 2/2–3 (winter) 1973, pp. 157–168.

passions, have had much to do with sustaining this view, as well.[6] It would be a much easier interpretation to sustain if Shahriyar moved directly from the discovery of his wife's treachery to her execution, and the institution of the draconian policy by which he hopes to prevent another such shattering confrontation. For the interlude with the jinn and his captive bride provide us with compelling evidence that Shahriyar's wife is not a monster, but a woman with a compelling and legitimate grievance.

The jinn is a gigantic, powerful being before whom Shahriyar, though monarch of a great realm, is as humble as his wife's lover, the black slave Mas'ood, is before him. Yet Shahriyar sees the jinn as essentially like him and his brother in his vulnerability to female treachery. And since this kind of humiliation is proportionate to one's greatness, he feels indeed that the jinn has suffered a worse indignity than he and his brother have.

By identifying himself with the jinn, Shahriyar invites us to see in this incident a dramatization of how he himself perceives what has happened to him. How telling it is then to realize that he sees the jinn as the aggrieved party in this drama. In doing this, he overlooks, or gives no value, to the great injustice that the woman has endured. The jinn stole her away from her husband on her wedding night and has since kept her locked up at the bottom of the sea, releasing her temporarily only when it suits him to do so. Surely, she is the one who has suffered injustice. And if she has, like Shahriyar's wife, taken her vengeance on the jinn in a way that is most damaging to his sense of himself, she has done so because that is virtually the only means left open to her of expressing her very justified anger against him. She cannot physically oppose the jinn. He is too strong. She cannot flee him. He would find her wherever she went. She cannot plead with him. Had he any regard for her wishes, he would not have kidnapped her in the first place. And were she somehow to escape, the bridegroom and her family would not welcome her back after so long and problematic an absence.[7]

If Shahriyar sees the jinn as playing his role in this drama, then the bride is playing his wife's. Like her, she is a woman coveted as a precious object and stored away like one to be enjoyed as he wills. Her humanity is ignored or denied. The jinn's theft of the bride thus becomes a metaphor for a young woman's sense of betrayal when

6. As one of the poems in the text puts it, "Never trust in women, nor rely upon their vows, /Since all their likes and dislikes and but the itch between their thighs." (*Alf Laila, op. cit.,* p. 4)

7. Judith Grossman draws attention to the injustice of the jinn's treatment of the bride, but does not pursue its implications for the treatment of the royal wives of the two brothers. ("Infidelity and Fiction: The Discovery of Women's Subjectivity in the *Arabian Nights.*" *The Georgia Review,* XXXIV, 1 (Spring 1980), pp. 113–126).

the romantic connection she had hoped would begin with her wedding is never formed. And she awakes to find herself bound inescapably to a man whose principal interest in her is a desire to protect his exclusive sexual access to her. She had hoped to marry a man and finds herself instead the prisoner of a monster whose vastly greater power is vulnerable in only one place.

Perhaps we should explain Shahriyar's lapse in justice here as a temporary aberration. After all, he has endured a great deal and is not in his right mind. He has been obliged by the threat of a painful death to cuckold the jinn after just having endured the experience of being himself cuckolded. The woman who has compelled him to this humiliating and frightening act, has also just taken his signet ring, a symbol both of wholeness and of identity, and strung it like a bead on a necklace along with hundreds of others. Symbolically, he has been transformed from monarch of a vast realm to a mere cypher. Yet such moments of stress only release what has been in the unconscious all along. The jinn and the bride rise to view from the depths of the sea, but they come out of Shahriyar's psyche as much as they come out of the sea. For Shahriyar the injustice does not lie in kidnapping a bride or in keeping her locked away against her will, but only in that bride's violation of her captor's exclusive sexual control of her.

The exercise of justice requires the recognition and acceptance of the humanity of those subjected to judgement. Commerce with those who are more or less than human requires different protocols. Shahriyar's sphere of humanity includes only males. He sees the jinn as human, although he is not, but cannot see the bride as human, althought she is. Her power, like that of all women, seems superhuman to him, and more than he can defend himself from by ordinary means. He does not see that he is largely to blame for the fact that their power is directed against him. The jinn has created an enemy for himself by his injustice. In his madness, Shahriyar cannot accept that, nor the responsibility for his wife's infidelity that such acceptance would imply. Instead, he interprets what has occurred as final and unarguable proof that all women are evil and bent on the betrayal of men, and that all men are like him, vulnerable to their power. The vision that might have cured him only feeds his psychosis. He returns to the palace, takes vengeance on his wife and her servants, and institutes his war on women, putting boxes around them from which no amount of determination and cunning will allow them to escape.

Why should his wife's infidelity, however flagrant, shatter Shahriyar so completely ? The trauma he has endured is surely enough to explain a serious and disabling neurosis, but not the murderous and violent psychosis into which he falls. Shahzaman's deep depression was cured because he saw that his older, more powerful brother had suffered an even worse humiliation than he had. Shahriyar's encounter with the jinn parallels the experience of his younger brother in exactly these terms, yet he is, if anything, made worse by it. There is an apparent alleviation of his symptoms in that he is able to return to the palace and resume his responsibilities as king. But as we see, this is really a deeper madness masquerading as cure. Why?

Shahriyar's madness bespeaks not simply an inability to treat women as his equals, but a deep-seated fear of and rage against them. By whatever psychoanalytic theory we prefer, we can reasonably assume that the source of this fear and rage is a childhood trauma that involved his mother and which included the essential elements of the later trauma that so disordered his wits. That is, his mother, like his wife used her intimate bond with him to betray him cruelly at the very center of his being. It is impossible to know much more than this.

When we look to the beginning of the story to discover what the relation of Shahriyar to his mother was like, the only evidence we find is negative. There is the old king and his two sons, but no mention of the queen, nor even of daughters, for that matter. There is no evidence of any feminine presence at the court at all. Moreover, this complete absence of the feminine at their father's court is true for the courts of the two sons, as well. The wives of Shahriyar and Shahzaman play no active role in the life of either court. Shahzaman's wife neither makes the journey to visit Shahriyar with her husband, nor is there to bid him farewell. Shahriyar's wife neither welcomes Shahzaman on his arrival, nor takes responsibility for his entertainment. Yet in other stories of the collection, wives and daughters play just such active roles in the court. Indeed, neither wife is allowed to identify herself except by the negative act of her adultery. The failure to give them their own identities both reduces their status within the story, and indicates a general denigration of women on the part of Shahriyar and Shahzaman. If royal wives are treated thus, what can the lot of other women be?

In short, the evidence of the story, though meagre and negative, suggests that Shahriyar and Shahzaman are men who have grown up entirely in a context that gives women no importance. As a consequence, neither has been able to form a positive bond either with women or with those feminine qualities in themselves which are called the anima in Jungian psychology.[8] While this need not affect a

---

8. Jung distinguishes his use of the term from its more general meaning of "spirit" in his essay, "Concerning the Archetypes, with Special Reference to the Anima Concept." (*Collected Works* translated by R. F. C. Hull, volume 9, part 1, second edition, Princeton University Press 1968). The fullest treatment of the mother archetype, which includes an extended treatment of the anima, as well, is that of Erich Neuman, *The Great Mother : An Analysis of an Archetype.* translated by R. Manheim (Princeton University Press 1963). In this context, chapters three, "The Two Characters of the Feminine", and eleven, "Negative Elementary Character", are of most interest.

man's performance in an essentially masculine society, particularly during the years of his early manhood, when his principal need is to establish himself in a man's world, it can have a devastating effect on his psyche when he reaches middle age. As Jung puts it in the essay referred to above:

> "After the middle of life, however, permanent loss of the anima means a diminution of vitality, of flexibility and of human kindness. The result, as a rule, is premature rigidity, crustiness, stereotypy, fanatical one-sidedness, obstinacy, pedantry, . . . "[9]

When one adds to this, as I think one should for the case of Shahriyar but not Shahzaman, both a childhood trauma like that I have suggested and the burden of ruling a vast kingdom, the result is a personality of great fragility and instability. Such a personality would also be unusually vulnerable to attack from the feminine.

Shahriyar's traumatic confrontation with his wife's infidelity would have been difficult for him to endure with a healthy ego. As it is, it drives him into a dramatic flight from reality. The captive bride compounds this trauma by making him live through it again, and then takes from him symbolically what she and Shahriyar's wife have already deprived him of, his identity and sense of wholeness. When he returns to the court he initiates a compulsive, psychotic behavior that is particularly suited to the wound he has suffered. He both attempts to form that positive bond with the feminine that he lacks by marrying a new bride each night, but then he destroys her before she can use that bond of intimacy to wound him further.

There is an ambiguity in Shahriyar's continuing to seek at least sexual connection with women. On the one hand it provides him with the opportunity of exercising his control over them, and, not incidentally, of punishing the courtiers who knew of his humiliation. Their daughters are the first murdered. On the other, it indicates that he still desires, somehow, to form a bond with the feminine.

The Cure

Enter Shahrizad. She is both the first woman in the story to have a name, and with it an individual personality, and the first to exercise a deciding measure of control over her own life. No explanation is offered for her uncharacteristic independence. Since there is no mention of either her mother or of any brothers, perhaps we are to assume that the vazir has raised his daughter exclusively himself, and raised her somewhat as a son, that is, as a person of value and

---

9. *Ibid*, page 71, paragraph 147.

importance. Whatever the reason, she has acquired what was a rare accomplishment in a woman, a solid knowledge of poetry and of history, particularly of the kings of other nations and times. We know that such historical works were characteristically composed in the form of stories and incidents from the lives of individual rulers, accompanied by comments on their virtues and failings. That is, Shahrizad is a learned student of royal, male behavior, and has a rich store of tales at her disposal. By implication, it is upon the basis of this knowledge that she has discovered a remedy for the Shah's madness and a solution for the dilemma it poses for the court and populace.

It is worth noting here, that the cure for his madness comes not from the diligent, loyal vazir as one would expect, but from his daughter. The logic of this is that since the wounding to the king's psyche that is the cause of his psychosis comes from the feminine side, the cure for it must come from there as well.

Stories, however, must provide their own narrative logic. Shahrizad's aptitude for the task and her superiority to her father as a physician for this particular ill in the body politic is made plain in their brief discourse and the two tales that are imbedded in it. The vazir has returned home after scouring the community for another maid to sacrifice to the king (feeling angry, oppressed and fearful). Yet it is hard to feel much sympathy for him. He is, to begin with, the instrument of the Shah's cruel policy. Moreover, he has not succeeded either in opposing that policy or in dissuading him from it during the preceding three years. As a result the kingdom is on the verge of dissolution. Finally, if he was Shahriyar's vazir before the trauma that engendered this policy, he has also failed to protect the king from that trauma by warning him of the queen's infidelity before it had become common knowledge. He is not, in short, a very skilfull, effective or virtuous vazir. All that one can say in his favor is that he has used his position to protect his own daughters.

When she learns of his dilemma, Shahrizad, whom we know to be a learned and thoughtful young woman, makes a remarkable suggestion. She will marry the king and either be a sacrifice for Muslim women, or the cause of their deliverance. Shahrizad is not offering simply to buy her father a little time with her life. She hopes to rescue all the women of the kingdom by her action. She has a plan. Her father does not ask her about that, but tries to dissuade her from risking her life. When she is adamant in her resolve, he tells her two stories intended to exemplify the unhappy consequences of her decision. Despite having allowed and encouraged the development of her abilities it appears that he doesn't really believe in them. Not only has he failed to discover a cure himself, he is unable even to ally himself with the one who has found a cure. Shahrizad must look for help to the only other woman in the family, her younger sister, Dinazad.

JEROME W. CLINTON

In the first of the vazir's stories, a farmer uses his secret knowledge of the speech of animals to punish the ass who has encouraged the ox to feign illness in order to escape the heavy labor of plowing. At the conclusion of this story the ox, having been told by the ass that if he continues to avoid labor in this way he will wind up at the butcher's shop, frisks about to show the farmer how eager for the yoke he now is. When the farmer laughs at this, his wife asks why. And when he won't tell her—for to do so would be to forfeit his life—she effects the transition to the second story by insisting that he do so.

In the second story, the farmer is on the point of yielding to his wife's foolish insistence that he reveal his secret, even if it kills him, when his secret knowledge allows him to learn from the cock how to deal with such a headstrong wife. He beats her out of her murderous whim, and peace is restored.

These are amusing but undistinguished stories. What strikes one most on reading them is how poorly they fit the occasion. It is hard to find the vazir or Shahrizad or Shahriyar in them, and harder still to see how the moral of either, or both, applies to Shahrizad's decision to marry Shahriyar. The ass is punished for not minding his own business, but very lightly. He must plow in the ox's place for two days. The ox takes poor advice, but is rewarded with two day's rest and learns as well the valuable lesson that there are worse fates than hard labor. In the second story the wife is punished for her selfishness, for being willing to sacrifice her husband's life only to learn the secret of what makes him laugh. The only moral that the vazir draws from this story, or from both the stories, is that he should perhaps beat Shahrizad for her disobedience as the farmer did his wife. But this is based on the most superficial of comparisons. Although both are disobedient, Shahrizad's motive is the opposite of the farmer's wife's. She would disobey her father in order to save his life and those of all young women in the kingdom. Moreover, she would do so at the risk of her own.

Whatever their virtues as tales, in this context they function principally to demonstrate what we have already suspected, that the vazir is inept and will be unable to cure the king and save the realm on his own. The tales are worse than irrelevant, they undermine the very point he wishes to make. In the first, the farmer's special knowledge—magic—allows him to manipulate his animals for their own good, as Shahrizad would use her special knowledge to manipulate or instruct the king for his. In the second, the farmer learns that his magic can cause him harm unless he has the wisdom to understand human nature as well. Shahrizad must be both clever and wise if she is to succeed.

Both the tales teach one to consider the motives of those who offer advice very carefully, and to distrust those who, like the vazir, act out of self interest. There is another message in these tales, and one that bears on Shahriyar's mode of curing the king. It is that a dull, irrelevant tale convinces no one.

Quite naturally, Shahrizad is unmoved by these tales and repeats the very phrase with which she met her father's first attempt to dissuade her, "There is no escape from this (course)." She understands what is at stake and what is required, as her father does not. He is no more able to stop her than he is able to stop the king.

Shahrizad has both grasped why the king has gone mad and seen the significance of his continuing to seek a bond with women. Were he completely lacking in compassion she would have no hope of initiating her plan. She has wagered everything on his agreeing to her request for permission to say farewell to her sister. The solution Shahrizad has chosen assumes that there is a sane and reasonable Shahriyar trying to get out of the mad and murderous one. It is also a very feminine one. Not armed rebellion, not assasination, not elimination or defeat of the king by any means. She has chosen rather to educate him in the variety and complexity of human personality, both male and, in particular, female. In doing this she will help him develop the positive anima he lacks, to provide him with that part of his education that he missed because the feminine presence was missing or negative in his childhood. And she will do this by means of a talking cure—although it is one that conforms to the expectations of Baghdad, not Vienna. That is, the doctor does the talking, not the patient, and tells tales that address the patient's concerns.[1]

Shahrizad's first sequence of tales both makes the ends of her method implicit, and adumbrates the message she principally wishes to convey. The frame of the sequence is provided by the story of the merchant who accidentally kills the son of a jinn. The jinn plans to kill the merchant in retaliation, but is persuaded to delay his execution for a year so that the merchant can settle his affairs at home. When the merchant, true to his word, returns at the end of the year to meet his fate, he encounters three travellers who on hearing his story are moved to pity and offer to barter their own strange adventures for his life. The jinn accepts their proposal. The tale to this point has two clear messages, or, one moral and one message. The moral is that a harsh, retributive justice that takes no account of individual guilt is monstrous. While the merchant is, however accidentally, responsible for the death of the jinn's child, the jinn's exaction of his life for his son's seems excessive to three chance passers

---

1. Confirmation that this mode of therapy is effective may be found in Bruno Bettelheim's *The Uses Of Enchantment: The Meaning And Importance of Fairy Tales.* (A. Knopf, New York 1976). Bettelheim is here concerned with children, but the therapeutic mode he examines seems relevant to the situation of a Shahriyar as well.

by—all of whom are men of experience, and possibly learned as well. How much crueler would they find Shahriyar's decision to punish the women of his kingdom as he has. He is murdering innocent young women for no greater crime than being female.

The message is as important as the moral, and is symmetrical with the earlier message that a dull, irrelevant tale has no value. It is that a good tale is a fair exchange for at least a portion of the price on one's head. When the king agrees to delay Shahrizad's death one night in order to hear the end of the tale, he implicitly accepts the same bargain that the jinn has. If the stories are good enough, he will release his victim, Shahrizad and, by extension, all the young women of his kingdom. At the same time he is making clear whether consciously or not, that he is willing to listen to tales that touch on the sensitive issue of his madness.

At least one commentator finds Shahrizad's choice of these tales tactless and painful to the king.[2] Bettelheim has shown, however, that children troubled by a particularly painful problem, such as the death of a parent, prefer stories that deal directly with the problem, especially when they suggest that there is a means of resolving it successfully. And this, as we shall see, is precisely what Shahrizad's tales do. We should also keep in mind that Shahrizad has begun by accepting the king's psychosis and putting herself physically in his power. It is unlikely that he would perceive her as a threat when he has already dispatched so many young women like her in the preceding three years.

Having first addressed the question of the absolute injustice of Shahriyar's war on women, Shahrizad turns in the three stories to that of the innate character of women and its relation to their power. The narration of each of the travellers presents a different portion of her lesson. In the first, the bad wife is a witch who enchants the concubine and son of her husband out of malice and jealousy, and then tries to wreak vengeance on him by tricking him into having them slaughtered. Could a woman be more evil ? Yet it is another woman, the daughter of the sheikh's herdsman, who helps him to defeat his wife's evil scheme and rescue his son by putting her white magic at his disposal.

Women clearly come in at least two kinds, good and evil. Both kinds have that great power that Shahriyar fears—here given the form of witchcraft, as it so often is both in and out of folktales. Yet how they use that power depends on their own innate character. We and Shahriyar are surely meant to see Shahrizad as like the herdsman's daughter in this tale since she and her father stand to Shahriyar very much as the daughter and her father stand to the merchant. Certainly we are meant to assume that she, like that daughter, is a virtuous woman. And even if her abilities seem at times magical to

2. Gerhardt, *Storytelling*, p. 399.

Shahriyar, he need not fear them for she intends to use them only for his benefit, to undo the evil his wife has done him. Indeed, the message here, and it is one that is repeated in the tales that follow, is that given reasonable security and protection women are quite happy to be guided by men in the exercise of their powers. There is no quarrel here with the Islamic belief that women ought to be subordinated to men, only an insistence that with that subordination come respect and protection.

In the second story, two evil brothers conspire to murder their good and prosperous brother. He is saved by a female jinn to whom he has given protection and shown kindness when she, in human form, asked it of him. The brothers are punished by being changed into dogs for ten years, but their brother forgives them their crimes against him. The good merchant is not only a master of worldly matters, witness his repeated assistance to his feckless brothers, but capable of kindness and a deep loving bond with a woman. He does not exclude his wife from his life, but gives her so central a place in it that he neglects his brothers and they grow murderously jealous. The reward of the second sheikh's granting his wife the kindness and love she has asked for is his own salvation. When she reveals that great and unsuspected power of hers, she uses it to save him from certain death and to transport him swiftly and safely home. The good merchant's wicked brothers also remind us, and Shahriyar, that it is not only women who are capable of great evil.

There is another message here as well. The good brother would forgive his evil siblings completely despite the grossness of their crime. The jinniyya wishes to punish them with death, which indeed they deserve by the standards of strict justice, even though they are her husband's brothers. They err in opposite directions. A more reasonable punishments is the one that the two wicked brothers receive at last. Having behaved metaphorically like dogs to their brother, they are made to suffer for ten years as actual dogs. This is a punishment more merciful than death, yet commensurate with their crime.

The story of the third sheikh comes to the nub of Shahriyar's psychosis, obliging him to relive vicariously the trauma that engendered it. The third sheikh does not simply discover his wife in bed with a black slave, like Shahriyar, he witnesses her relishing the experience. Then, before he can gather his wits to act, she turns him into a dog.

In turning the sheikh literally into a dog, the wife has here accomplished in real, if fantastic, fact, what the wives of Shahzaman and Shahriyar have done psychologically—turned them into what are in Islamic terms the vilest of creatures. Here again the device of giving flesh to metaphor has been used, and to surpisingly similar ends. The brothers have been made into dogs in order to force upon them the realization that they have committed a grave crime in attempting to murder their brother. Surely, they ought to have realized this without any such extraordinary admonition, but as their brother said, "Satan made their actions seem good to them." When the third sheikh is obliged to suffer the same punishment, it suggests that he, too, has committed some grave crime of which he is himself not aware. However much he is made to suffer, the sheikh is not an altogether innocent victim. Or put another way, his wife is not wholly unjustified in her betrayal of him. And since the situation of the third sheikh so closely parallels that of Shahriyar, it is hard not to see here a subtle suggestion on Shahrizad's part that Shahriyar consider the measure of his responsibility for his own wife's infidelity.

The close parallels between the king and the sheikh continue with further telling implications for Shahriyar. The sheikh turned dog then runs into a butcher's shop, and there begins to devour bones indiscriminately. The butcher's shop is an apt metaphor for Shahriyar's kingdom as it has become during the preceding three years, as the dog's indiscriminate consumption of bones is a metaphor for Shahriyar's "devouring" of his kingdom's young women. In the shop, again, it is not the butcher but his daughter who releases the victim from his spell. But she goes a step further than the herdsman's daughter, and teaches him how to punish his wife not by killing her but by working on her a transformation like that she has inflicted on him. Since she was eager to bear an inappropriate burden, a man not her husband, her husband now turns her into a beast of burden who must bear whoever wishes to ride her, but at no pleasure to herself. Again, vengeance is acceptable, but it should fit the crime. The third sheikh is a man of healthy ego, and he finds the appropriate punishment at once, but he is able to accomplish it only with the aid of the butcher's daughter. The vazir's daughter will guide Shahriyar back to that mastery of justice that he formerly enjoyed.

The third tale is only a fraction as long as the other two. Yet the jinn is delighted with it and accepts it as equal in value to the other two. He is right to do so for the tale is a treasure. It recapitulates the themes of the first two, presents an analysis of Shahriyar's affliction and foreshadows the successful resolution of the therapy. The conclusion of this sequence does the latter as well. Once Shahrizad has returned Shahriyar to his normal self by means of her tales, he, like the jinn, will release all those whom he now holds under threat of death—the young women of his kingdom.

Framing the Thousand and One Nights

The interpretation of the tale of Shahriyar and Shahrizad that I have given has, I think, important implications for understanding how the tale functions as a frame tale for the *Thousand and One Nights*.

Some commentators have characterized the tale as an inferior example of the framing tale. There is but a single narrator which is monotonous in itself. Moreover, it lacks the surface links between narrator and tale or tales that are to be found in Chaucer and Bocaccio.[3] One need not look so far afield. They are well-framed sequences of tales included in the *Nights* themselves that have those very features which the tale of Shahriyar and Shahrizad lacks. In the Barber of Baghdad, for instance, or even the sequence we have just looked at, there is a lively, many-sided interplay between the narrators and the tales they tell. Once Shahrizad has been launched on her narration, the personalities of the frame tale essentially vanish from view for some three years, reappearing only to provide the happy ending that concludes at least some manuscripts.

While I have no wish to quarrel with these criticisms, I would like to suggest that they may be off the point. As I see it the problem is not with the tale but with the criteria used to judge it. The linkages between the tale of Shahriyar and Shahrizad and those which follow are not narrative and superficial, but thematic and psychological. The themes articulated here recur thoughout the *Nights* in ways that have not yet been explored in any detail. For example, in the next sequence of tales, although most of the tales that compose it display nothing like the close thematic relation to the tale of Shahriyar and Shahrizad that those just analyzed do, the last tale returns us to their world once more. Here, again, we have the familiar triangle of a faithless queen, her black slave lover and a king who has been cruelly damaged by her. There is also a kingdom that has been put at risk, albeit in a way very different from that of Shahriyar. The protagonist, a king from outside the enchanted realm, slays the slave, tricks the evil queen into releasing her husband and the people of his realm from her spell, and restores order and tranquility to the realm. In short, this tale provides another teaching for Shahriyar that continues the lessons of the earlier stories, and seems to be intended to remind the audience of the special context in which these tales are being told.

The exploration of these questions is the subject for another study. My only intention in raising them here is to point out that the psychological realities of the tales in the *Thousand and One Nights* form an essential dimension both of their appeal and of the narrative unity into which they have been formed.

---

3. Gerhardt, for example, quotes with approval the comment of Dryoff that the tale is an energetic but botched effort. She also dismisses earlier attempts to articulate a coherent or unifying theme in the collection as unpersuasive (*The Art of Storytelling, op. cit.*, pp. 398–99). Ferial J. Ghazoul has recently shown the limitations of this view from a structuralist perspective in her illuminating study, *The Arabian Nights: A Structural Analysis* (Cairo Associated Institution for the Study and Presentation of Arab Values, Cairo 1980).

ABDELFATTAH KILITO

The Eye and the Needle[†]

Idris (=Enoch) was the first to write with a stylus, the first to work
with a needle and to wear sewn clothes, the first to take an interest
in astronomy and arithmetic.
—Tha'labi, *Qisas al-anbiya'*

Stories are a school of wisdom, but it takes time—quite some time—
to acquire it. It is only after having told all her stories that Shahrazad
turns toward the king to indicate the course that he should take: "You
were surprised at what was inflicted upon you by women; and yet,
before you, the kings of Persia were subject to troubles and misfortunes far graver than yours. . . . There is, in that, sufficient warning for
the man gifted with sense and an admonishment for the prudent
man." The stories were many mirrors in which the king contemplated
his own story. Thanks to them, he succeeded in overcoming his solitude. Far from being unique, his case fits within the context of a series
of analogous cases; through identifying with fictional characters, he
acquired a new vision of things and abandoned his resentment.

But there is another patient who needs the stories: the reader of the
Nights. From the first lines, the compiler of the collection addresses
the reader in terms that recall those of Shahrazad: "The conduct of
the Ancients must serve as lesson for their descendants. One ought to
consider what happened to them to educate oneself. One ought to
become acquainted with the story of ancient peoples to know, in this
way, how to distinguish good from evil. Glory to He who recalls their
example, so that it may be pondered by their descendants. This is the
case of the tales titled *The Thousand and One Nights*."

The text uses the word *'ibra*, which means warning, admonishment,
example. The *'ibra* is the effect the story produces, the path it opens to
reflection. It is interesting to remark that *'ibra* is close to the verb
'abara, which means to pass, to cross a bridge, to get over a river, a
ford. As a rule, everyone who listens to a story feels concerned; he
then "crosses" the distance that separates himself from the narrator,
who often tells his own story. At the start, therefore, the narrator and
the listener are on two banks of a river; their meeting is marked by
incomprehension, even hostility, and then a reconciliation, a junction,
gradually comes to pass. The listener crosses the bridge built by the
story, finding himself on the same bank as the narrator.

[†] From *L'Œil et l'aiguille: Essais sur "les Mille et une nuits"* (Paris: La Découverte, 1992),
pp. 104–11. Translated from the French by Zachary E. Woolfe. Reprinted by permission
of Editions La Découverte.

Who is a good reader of the *Nights*? Definitely not the one who would see there only the extraordinary stories, the ones that distract and astonish. The good reader is the one who satisfies two conditions. In the first place, he must practice *'ibra*, that is, reflect, when he learns what has happened to others, on what could have happened to him. The stories are thus paradigms that orient choices and clarify action. This is what is asserted by the compiler, who sees in the use of reflection, in instruction by examples, an act of piety, a submission to the will of God, who enjoins us to ponder narratives related to our predecessors so that we may admit our limits and not fall into excess.

In the second place, the reader is implicitly invited to write the stories, or to recopy them, if possible in golden letters, as do so many of the characters of the *Nights*. Thus set, they will be constantly available, bringing him pleasure and knowledge. On what material should one write them? Entrusted to a book, they run the risk of becoming external, foreign; the ideal would then be to write them on one's own body, and even—horrible prospect—on the corner of one's eye.

In the *Nights*, in fact, one finds a sentence which is often repeated, and which leaves one perplexed. It would even be frightening, if we ever took it into our heads to follow it literally (but how could one do otherwise, given that it refers precisely to the letter, to the graphic sign?). It is a sentence concerning the eye in its relationship to writing, to sewing, a sentence that, bringing the organ of vision dangerously close to the needle, threatens the one who reads it with sudden blindness.

It appears for the first time in the "Story of the Merchant and the Genie," which begins Shahrazad's narrative cycle. In the course of a voyage, a merchant stops under a tree, eats some dates and throws the pits aside. Hardly has he stopped than a genie appears and wants to kill him. The reason is that a pit hit the genie's son in the chest and he died! The merchant, however, obtains a reprieve of one year, at the end of which he returns to the spot where he saw the genie. There he meets an old man to whom he tells his story. The old man listens with astonishment, then says: "By God, I admire your respect for the given word, and I find your story extraordinary. If one could write it with a needle on the inner corner of the eye, it would spur reflection in those who know to reflect."

Shaken by what he has just heard, the old man thinks, therefore, that the story ought to be written on the eye, on his and on everyone's. He is so overwhelmed that he seeks to incorporate the story into his own being, to make it his, to insert it in his vision, to see through it. *It regards him*. [*Ça le regarde.*] The story exceeds its frame and, threatening the hearer, summons him to do something. He will never separate himself from it; he will carry it with him, on him. Sewn on the inner corner of his eye, it will form a second eye, an eye in the eye. The ear will be taken over by the eye. The old man fears that he may forget the story, or at least forget why it was told; his duty is to protect it, to preserve it by inscribing it on the most fragile part of his body, the most precious, the most cherished.

The story of the merchant is the only story in the *Nights* in which the sentence concerning the eye is uttered by the listener. In the other stories, it is the character-narrators who use it at the moment when they begin telling the story of their misfortunes. It is used in this way in the story of the young king whose lower half is paralyzed following his wife's curses, in the story of the three Calanders, in that of Qamar and Buddur, and in that of the young man of Oman. The narrators do not tell a story that is foreign to them or that they know only by hearsay; it is a question of their own story, a story that they have experienced and in which they are implicated: ". . . Something happened to me that was so astonishing, so strange that if one wrote it by needle on the corner of the eye, it would give matter for reflection to those who want to reflect." At the moment when they begin to speak, they find themselves in a very painful position; their physical integrity is compromised, or their life may even be in danger. The expression that they utter marks a solemn and poignant story. It would hardly suit a humorous story, like that of the barber of Baghdad and his brothers. Each of them experienced an adventure from which he did not emerge unscathed, yet the comic aspect of the situations leaves no place for compassion and commiseration; in telling the story of his brothers, the barber seeks to make his listeners laugh, not to touch them with pity. The eye and the needle are effective in tragic stories alone.

To my knowledge, the blinding expression can be found only in the *Nights*. I encountered it again, but in another form, in the *Kitab al-hayawan* by al-Jahiz ("the man with the bulging cornea"!): "Knowledge gives to you according to what you give to it; if I could lodge it in the deepest part of my heart or preserve it on the inner corner of my eye, I would do so." Only the needle is missing. But it is implicitly present, for with what other point could one sew knowledge to the bottom of the heart and on the corner of the eye?

On the inner corner of the eye, next to the nose, on this minuscule space, a story ought to be sewn. With what thread? The reference to sewing is justified not only by the needle but also by the verb *kataba*, which means both to write and to sew. To write is to sew.

Let us try to *see* what the expression means. First of all, let us notice that, insofar as it acts as a means of opening, a mark of beginning, the sentence has a phatic function. It aims to arouse interest, to solicit attention. Moreover, it comments on and praises in advance the story that it highlights and which appears as having a special force, an inestimable value: it is fitting to receive such a story not distractedly but in an attitude of respect, meditation, even fear.

It is true that the expression introduces only some tales, but it could announce many others, all those that describe a painful or sad experience. It could even serve as the epigraph to the book of the *Nights*, which, we have seen, presents the conduct of the Ancients as a subject of meditation for their descendants. The reader is invited, in other words, to transcribe the book on the corner of his eye.

Better, perhaps, to close one's eyes, to look away from the sharp point of the needle. This is what Galland did: doubtless frightened by the unbearable prospect it revealed, he decided not to see it, and so he excluded it from his translation. In erasing it, he concealed the most disquieting enigma of the *Nights*. To be sure, he did not eliminate the expression entirely. He even cites it in the story that he titled "The Three Apples," but so softened that at first one hardly recognizes it: ". . . if one could put in writing all that happened between this lady and me, it would be a story that could be useful to mankind." In "translating" it, which is to say, in rewriting it, Galland took away its mystery, its dark zone; he transformed it into a sentence that is banal, seemly, *invisible*. Yet the eye and the needle were to torment him: in the "Story of the Merchant and the Genie," he indicates that the date's pit hit not the chest, but the eye of the genie's son. A rather mysterious alchemy transformed the needle destined for the reader into the pit that gouges out the eye of a little genie before killing him.

The phrase is indeed frightening. To puncture one's eyes after having heard a story is an act that only Oedipus committed. It is true that it was his own story, told by Tiresias, the blind soothsayer. None of the heroes of the *Nights* inscribed his own story on his eye, except perhaps the three Calanders, each blinded in one eye after dramatic circumstances. They tell how they lost the left eye (the right eye according to Mahdi's edition), and the first two begin their narrative by mentioning the famous expression; blind in one eye, they cite precisely the sentence that punctures the eye. Their story is engraved by the needle of destiny on their destroyed pupil. Indelible, it accompanies them wherever they go; the lost eye encapsulates it, displays it, represents it to the eyes of all. Such a mark alters the gaze and displays the world in a new, unusual light. The three one-eyed men have a different perception of things, and their undeclared intention is to lead their listeners to share their way of seeing, that is, to lead them to puncture their own left eyes. I tell you my story and you give me your eye, the eye that I no longer have.

But no one will make this sacrifice. One ought to write the story on the corner of one's eye, but no one will do it. Underlying the expression is the bitter observation that the receiver is negligent, distracted, ungrateful, and that the story will not give him cause for reflection. For he does not know how to reflect; he does not perceive his reflection in the mirror that is held before him; he does not grasp the injunction, the plea—articulated or mute—contained within the story, within every story: do not forget me, for I speak of you.

The story will not, then, be written by the needle on the inner corner of the eye. It will be written by a stylus on the pages of a book. But this moment when the story is noted, recorded, and past, and beyond which there is nothing more to tell, this final moment is, in reality, initial, inaugural. Indeed, the story is written before being told, before the hero lives his adventures, even before he is born. It is written in an original book, source of all that is produced in the world, and from which all books arise. Everything is already marked and engraved in this book, which is invisible, unreadable, but whose text is *realized*, manifesting itself by events and by stories. And all that is written is only a reproduction of this archetypal book, drafted at the dawn of time.

Every character in the *Nights* carries, inscribed on his body, an extract of this primordial book, the text of which determines his destiny and controls the least of his movements. He is not, however, able to read it—not that he is a bad reader, but the eye is incapable of seeing what is written on the forehead. Indeed, it is on this topmost part of the face that the signs of destiny are inscribed. And now it is time to quote another expression from the *Nights*: "What an unhappy destiny I have had, since my birth, engraved on my brow, forever decreed in the world of divine mystery!" Or again: " . . . No cunning outwits destiny, and one cannot know how to flee what is written on one's brow." Having come from the book where everything is set out in advance, the character ultimately succeeds in reaching another book, the one in which his story will be recorded, and which will be a reflection of the first. Writing thus renders itself essential, anterior and posterior, inceptive and conclusive.

DAVID PINAULT

Story-Telling Techniques in *The Arabian Nights*[†]

* * *

B. *Oral performance and literary language in* The Arabian Nights

"Abū 'Abd Allāh Muhammad ibn 'Abdūs al-Jahshiyārī," we are informed in al-Nadīm's *Fihrist*, "author of *The Book of Viziers*, began the compiling of a book in which he was to select a thousand tales from the stories of the Arabs, Persians, Greeks, and others. Each section . . . was separate, not connected with any other. He summoned

[†]　From *Story-Telling Techniques in the Arabian Nights* (Leiden: Brill, 1992). Reprinted by permission of Koninklijke BRILL NV.

to his presence the storytellers, from whom he obtained the best things about which they knew and which they did well. He also selected whatever pleased him from the books composed of stories and fables . . . There were collected for him four hundred and eighty nights, each night being a complete story . . . Death overtook him before he fulfilled his plan for completing a thousand stories (p. 355)."[1]

This reference to al-Jahshiyārī (an 'Abbasid government official and secretary of the tenth century AD) offers us a glimpse of how medieval Arabic story-anthologies were created. This particular composer drew on both written sources and the oral performances of professional storytellers. The two influences—literary and oral—should be borne in mind when evaluating a collection such as the *Alf laylah*.

Richard Hole, an English scholar who in 1797 published a series of lectures entitled *Remarks on the Arabian Nights' Entertainments*, recorded travelers' comments on the *Alf laylah*:

> Colonel Capper, in his observations on the passage to India through Egypt and across the great Desert, says, that "before any person decides on the merit of these books, he should be eye-witness of the effect they produce on those who best understand them. I have more than once seen the Arabians on the Desert sitting round a fire, listening to these stories with such attention and pleasure as totally to forget the fatigue and hardship with which an instant before they were entirely overcome."[2]

This observation reminds us that the tales comprising the *Alf laylah* were originally oral evening-entertainments and were meant to be recited and listened to. The performance-dimension of the *Nights* is reflected in the very manuscripts used to record various versions of the tales. For storytellers who could afford them, texts incorporating some or all of the *Alf laylah* adventures served as reference material and sources of narrative inspiration. In his study on "The Earlier History of the Arabian Nights" MacDonald makes reference to the story-manuscripts comprising the library of a professional reciter in Damascus.[3] Lane remarks on public recitations from the *Nights* in Cairo during the early nineteenth century; but he also notes that the cost of a complete *Alf laylah* manuscript was too high for most reciters. According to Lane the '*Anātirah* (or storytellers who recited the adventures of the Arab hero 'Antar) frequently read aloud from written texts of the tale as part of their public performance.[4]

1. Page numbers in parentheses are to the text herein.
2. Richard Hole, *Remarks on the Arabian Nights' Entertainments* (London: Cadell & Davies, 1797; reprint: New York: Garland Publishing, 1970), p. 7.
3. Duncan Black Macdonald, "The Earlier History of the Arabian Nights," *The Journal of the Royal Asiatic Society* (1924), p. 370.
4. Edward William Lane, *Manners and Customs of the Modern Egyptians* (London: J.M. Dent & Sons, Everyman's Library edition, 1954), pp. 419–420.

Peter Molan has drawn attention to phrases such as *qālā al-rāwī* ("the storyteller said") and *qāla sāḥib al-ḥadīth* ("the master of the tale said") which recur throughout many manuscript texts of the *Nights*. Such phrases are in Molan's description "anomalous" or extrinsic to the dialogue and narrative context within which they occur. He argues that instances of anomalous *qāla* are linked to the oral provenience of stories recorded in *Alf laylah* manuscripts.[5] As I analyze individual Arabic manuscripts in later chapters of this study I will present some of those points at which anomalous *qāla* recurs in each text. By way of summary I note the following. Phrases such as *qāla sāḥib al-ḥadīth* tend to appear at transition points in the given text: anomalous *qāla* often occurs between the conclusion of a poem and the resumption of the prose narrative; or it may come at the end of a minor story told by a character within a larger narrative, thus indicating a return to the major narrative frame. The copyists who inserted *qāla al-rāwī* or *qāla sāḥib al-ḥadīth* in their texts sometimes penned such phrases in disproportionately large letters or in an ink which varied from that of the surrounding text. Thus we can hypothesize that anomalous *qāla* served as a visual guide and marker alerting any reciter who glanced at the page of an imminent change in narrative voice.[6]

The *Alf laylah* text occasionally discloses other allusions to its oral performance background, as in this passage from the tale of *Maryam the Christian*:

As for that young maiden's departure from her father's city, there is a curious story and wondrous matter behind that, which we will utter in proper order, so that the hearer might delight therein and grow cheerful therefrom.

(wa-qad kāna li-khurūj tilka al-jāriyah min madīnat abīhā ḥadīth gharīb wa-amr 'ajīb nasūquhu 'alā al-tartīb ḥattā yaṭraba al-sāmi' wayaṭīb)[7]

---

5. Peter D. Molan, "The *Arabian Nights*: the Oral Connection," *Edebiyât* n.s. vol. II, nos. 1 & 2 (1988), p. 195.

6. For examples of MSS in which *qālā al-rāwī* and other instances of anomalous *qāla* are penned in disproportionately large lettering see Paris 3651, fol. 40b et seq. (*The City of Brass*) and Paris 3663, fol. 85a et seq. (*The False Caliph*). See also the Leiden edition of the *Alf laylah*, vol. 2, plates 55–56 (Christ Church Arabic MS 207) and plates 71–72 (Paris 3612). In Paris 3668, fol. 53b et seq. (*The City of Brass*), red ink is used for phrases such as *qāla al-rāwī* and for other words which indicate changes of speaker in dialogue portions of the text, in contrast to the black ink used for the bulk of the narrative.

7. B vol. 2 (Night 878), p. 431. See also the beginning of the *Nights* in the Leiden edition (vol. 1, p. 56): *wa-yatsḍammanuhu* [sic] *ayḍan siyar jalīlah yata'allamu sāmi'uhā al-firāsah* ("It also contains many splendid accounts; the person who hears them may learn discernment"). The latter phrase is retained in the incipit of many texts of the Syrian family. Note also Scheherazade's statement as she begins the recitation of *Nūr al-Dīn and the Lady Shams al-Nahār* (Leiden, vol. 1, p. 379): *wa-hawa ḥadīt[h] Abū* [sic] *al-Ḥasan . . . wa-mā jarā lahu ma'a jāriyal al-khalīfah Shams al-Nahār yaṭraba al-sāmi' wa-huwa bahjat ḥusn al-lawāli'* ("This is the tale of Abū al-Ḥasan . . . and what happened to him with the caliph's servant-girl Shams al-Nahār. The person who hears it will delight therein, if he is lucky enough [to hear it]").

The phrasing of this sentence (" . . . which we will utter . . . so that the hearer might delight therein . . . ") implies the presence of a reciter and an audience of listeners rather than a relationship of writer and reader. Those familiar with medieval Arabic literature will recognize in the text above the use of *saj'*, the prose-rhyme often favored for public recitation. Taken together the phrasing and rhyme-form recall the oral performance environment within which the *Nights* evolved.

Yet the published Arabic editions of the *Alf laylah* are far from being straightforward unaltered transcriptions of oral vernacular performances. The B and MN texts are the products of learned editors of the eighteenth and nineteenth centuries who rewrote much of the material in their source-manuscripts in accordance with the principles of *fuṣḥā* or classical literary Arabic. They normalized the spelling of individual words, substituted elevated diction for colloquial expressions, formalized dialogue so as to remove traces of influence from the vernacular, and altered the grammatical structure of sentences to align them with the rules of *fuṣḥā*. Even the fourteenth-century G manuscript, which is much more colloquial than B or MN in its language, is influenced by classical literary models. Extravagant and sometimes incorrect use is made of literary grammatical constructions as ornaments with which to embellish the text. In this the G manuscript only follows the practice of the Ayyubid and Mamluk periods, eras characterized by literary works in which the author strained for rhetorical effects by the elaborate use of classical *fuṣḥā* constructions. As Mahdi remarks, the wording of G comprises a "third language," neither purely colloquial nor exclusively literary, in which both *fuṣḥā* and colloquial are employed in the presentation of each tale. Thus the *Alf laylah*, as revealed through the very diverse texts in which it is recorded, cannot be described only as a collection of transcribed oral folktales: for it survives as the crafted composition of authors who used various forms of written literary Arabic to capture an oral narrative tradition. In evaluating the stories of the *Nights* it will be wise to acknowledge the interaction implicit therein of the text's oral performance background and the transforming process of written composition.[8]

Throughout the present study I use the term 'redactor' in discussing the authorship of individual *Alf laylah* tales. As Andras Hamori remarks:

> 'Redactor' is a term of convenience. The composition of the book [i.e., the *Alf-laylah*] . . . suggests arrangement for effect. How many hands' work this is, we cannot know.[9]

8. Muhsin Mahdi, ed. *The Thousand and One Nights (Alf layla wa-layla) from the Earliest Known Sources*, 2 vols. (Leiden: E. J. Brill, 1984). See also Johann Fück, *ʿArabīya: Recherches sur l'histoire de la langue et du style arabe* (Paris: Librairie Marcel Didier, 1955), pp. 177–191.
9. Andras Hamori, "A Comic Romance from the Thousand and One Nights: the Tale of Two Viziers," *Arabice* 30:1 (1983), p. 38, n. 1.

Each redactor will doubtless have benefitted from the creativity of oral reciters who transmitted and embellished the given tale before it was committed to writing. He also will have been influenced by the textual revisions introduced by preceding generations of scribes. The term redactor indicates that person who stands at the end of this chain of oral and textual transmission, that person responsible for the shape in which the story reaches us in its final written form in a given manuscript or printed text.

C. A Description of Selected Storytelling Techniques from the Nights

In this section I describe narrative devices used by redactors in numerous stories found in the *Alf laylah*. The terms will recur in later chapters of the present study as I examine individual tales.

I. REPETITIVE DESIGNATION

Under this heading I group repeated references to some character or object which appears insignificant when first mentioned but which reappears later to intrude suddenly on the narrative. At the moment of the initial designation the given object seems unimportant and the reference casual and incidental. Later in the story, however, the object is brought forward once more and proves to play a significant role.

A good example of this technique can be found in one of the early episodes in the frame-story of King Shāhrayār and Scheherazade as presented in the Leiden edition of the G manuscript.[1] Shāhrayār's brother Shāhzamān arrives for a visit, and the G redactor offers a detailed description of the guest-quarters where Shāhzamān is housed: a palace overlooking an enclosed garden and facing a second house containing the women's quarters. Furthermore, it is carefully explained that his chambers have windows overlooking the garden. Finally, we are told that the nobleman repeatedly sighs and laments, "No one has ever had happen to him what happened to me!," a reference to the adulterous betrayal by his wife which opened the story. These references seem incidental enough at first, but in fact the redactor has made mention of all these details—the women's quarters, the garden, the guest-chamber windows which happen to overlook the garden, Shāhzamān's lament—by way of foreshadowing and preparation for the next development in the plot. One day King Shāhrayār departs to go hunting, and Shāhzamān, the redactor tells us, chances to look out his window at the garden which is visible below. Suddenly he sees his brother's wife, followed by an entourage of men

1. Mahdi, op. cit., p. 773, n.3.

and women, emerge from the harem opposite and enter the garden. From his window-perch he sees them all join lustily in sexual congress. Shāhzamān then realizes that his repeated lament is untrue, for his brother too has had happen to him what happened to Shāhzamān.

Another instance of repetitive designation emerges in the Leiden version of *The Merchant and the Genie*.[2] The tale opens with a description of the protagonist putting loaves of bread and dates in his saddlebag as provisions for a journey he is about to undertake. Trivial enough data this seems at first, a description of the food a man takes on a business trip. But to the contrary: in the next scene the merchant pauses in his journey for lunch and eats his dates, flinging away the date-stones at random. Shortly thereafter a wrathful genie appears, which informs the man that his life is now forfeit: the date-stones he flung away so thoughtlessly at lunch struck and killed the genie's invisible son; in turn the genie must now kill him. The hapless merchant pleads for mercy, a plea which will ultimately trigger the stories-told-for-ransom which comprise the bulk of this narrative-cycle.

Thus in the two examples cited above the initial reference establishes an object (e.g., a garden-window or a saddlebag full of dates) in the background of a scene and readies it for its appearance at the proper moment. Repetitive designation creates thereby an effect of apparently casual foreshadowing and allows the audience the pleasure of recognition at that later moment when the object reappears and proves significant.

II. LEITWORTSTIL

In his work *The Art of Biblical Literature* Robert Alter explains that the term *Leitwortstil* ("leading-word style") was coined by Martin Buber and Franz Rosenzweig and applied to the field of Biblical textual studies. Alter states that the term designates the "purposeful repetition of words" in a given literary piece. The individual *Leitwort* or "leading word" usually expresses a motif or theme important to the given story; the repetition of this *Leitwort* ensures that the theme will gradually force itself on the reader's attention.[3]

In the preface to his German Bible translation Buber discusses the triliteral root system in Hebrew and the opportunities it offers for verbal repetition. He labels this technique of repetition as a *Leitwortstil* and defines the term as follows:

> A *Leitwort* is a word or a word-root that recurs significantly in a text, in a continuum of texts, or in a configuration of texts: by

2. Ibid.
3. Robert Alter, *The Art of Biblical Narrative* (New York: Basic Books, 1981), p. 92.

following these repetitions, one is able to decipher or grasp a meaning of the text . . . The repetition, as we have said, need not be merely of the word itself but also of the word-root; in fact, the very difference of words can often intensify the dynamic action of the repetition. I call it "dynamic" because between combinations of sounds related to one another in this manner a kind of movement takes place: if one imagines the entire text deployed before him one can sense waves moving back and forth between the words.[4]

What is true for Hebrew triliteral roots and the Bible holds good, I believe, for Arabic and the *Arabic Nights*. *Leitwortstil* can be discerned at work in the MN version of *The Magian City*, a minor narrative enframed within *The Tale of the First Lady* (which in turn belongs to the story-cycle known as *The Porter and the Three Ladies of Baghdad*).[5]

Three sisters leave Baghdad to undertake a business trip by sea. Their ship goes off course, and for several days the vessel drifts without direction. Neither captain nor crew has any idea where they are; but after a number of days an unknown shore is sighted. The lookout cries, "Good news! . . . I see what looks like a city"; and the ship is brought to harbor. The captain goes ashore to investigate:

> He was gone for some time; then he came to us and said, "Come, go up to the city and marvel at what God has done to His creatures, and seek refuge from His wrath! (*wa-ista 'idhū min sukhṭihi*). And so we went up to the city.

> Then when I came to the gate I saw people with staves in their hands at the gate of the city. So I drew near to them, and behold!: they had been metamorphosed and had become stone (*wa-idhā hum maskhūṭīn wa-qad ṣārū aḥjāran*). Then we entered the city and found everyone in it metamorphosed into black stone (*maskhūṭan aḥjāran sūdan*). And in it [i.e., in the city] there were neither houses with inhabitants nor people to tend the hearths. We marveled at that and then traversed the markets.[6]

A note by Edward Lane from his translation of the *Nights* suggests the significance of the verbal root *s-kh-ṭ* which occurs three times in the above passage:

4. Quoted and translated by Alter, op. cit., p. 93.
5. The MN version of *The Magian City* is found in vol. 1, pp. 123–128. B (vol. 1, pp. 44-46) and Leiden (vol. 1, pp. 203–207) lack MN's pattern of *Leitwörter*. The three versions are compared in D. Pinault, "Stylistic Features in Selected Tales from *The Thousand and One Nights*" (Ph.D. diss., University of Pennsylvania, 1986), pp. 172–194.
6. MN vol. 1, p. 123.

The term "maskhooṭ," employed to signify "a human being converted by the wrath of God into stone," is commonly applied in
Egypt to an ancient statue. Hence the Arabs have become
familiar with the idea of cities whose inhabitants are petrified,
such as that described in "The Story of the First of the Three
Ladies of Baghdad."[7]

In his *Arabic-English Lexicon* Lane also notes that the primary
sense of the passive participle *maskhūṭ* is "transformed, or metamorphosed . . . in consequence of having incurred the wrath of God." In
addition, Lane records the gerund *sukhṭ*, which he defines as "dislike, displeasure, disapprobation, or discontent."[8]

The term *maskhūṭ* may of course be understood in a very general
sense simply to mean "transformed" or "metamorphosed." Burton's
commentary on this tale notes that *maskhūṭ* is "mostly applied to
change of shape as man enchanted to monkey, and in vulgar par-
lance applied to a statue (of stone, etc.)"; elsewhere in his edition of
the *Nights* he offers the gloss "transformed (mostly in something
hideous), a statue."[9] But the connotations enumerated by Lane are
brought forward in the MN edition by the captain's exclamation at
the beginning of the Magian City episode: *ta 'ajjabū min ṣan' Allāh fī
khalqiki wa-ista'īdhū min sukhṭihi* ("Marvel at what God has done to
His creatures, and seek refuge from His wrath!"). The redactor uses
this sentence to achieve a resonance of meanings between *sukhṭ*
("divine wrath") and *maskhūṭ* ("metamorphosed"), words derived
from the same verbal root, *s-kh-ṭ*. The presence of the noun *sukhṭ*
gives *maskhūṭ* a religious connotation; and the implication that
arises from this juxtaposition of words is that the city's inhabitants
were transformed specifically as a punishment for having aroused
God's anger.

Of interest to our discussion is a remark by 'Abd al-Qāhir al-Jurjānī
(d. AD 1078) on the subject of context and meaning in his work *Dalā'il
al-i'jāz* ("Demonstrations of Qur'anic Inimitability"):

It becomes clear then, with a clarity that leaves no place for
doubt, that verbal expressions are not remarkable for their excellence insofar as they are mere abstracted utterances, nor insofar
as they are isolated words. Rather the worth or lack of worth of a
given expression depends on the harmony established between

---

7. Edward William Lane, *The Arabian Nights' Entertainments* (New York: Tudor Publishing
   Co., 1927), p. 1209, n. 1.
8. Edward William Lane, *An Arabic-English Lexicon* (Beirut: Librairie du Liban, 1968), vol. 4,
   p. 1325.
9. Richard Burton, *Book of the Thousand Nights and a Night* (London: Burton Club for Private Subscribers, "Bagdad Edition," n.d.), vol. 1, p. 165, n. 1, and vol. 10, p. 362.

the meaning of a given expression and the meaning [of the word or phrase] which follows that expression.[1]

As G. J. H. van Gelder notes in his analysis of al-Jurjānī's work: "The qualities do not depend on the single words but on the 'wonderful harmony' (*ittisāq 'ajīb*) in the passage."[2] Al-Jurjānī's insight can be applied to the 'harmony of meanings' found in a story such as *The Magian City*. By placing the phrase *ista'idhū min sukhṭihi* immediately before the sentences describing the lost city and its metamorphosed populace, the MN redactor reminds the reader of the root-meaning of *maskhūṭ*, with its original denotation of God's wrath against the impious. The words *sukhṭ* and *maskhūṭ* will recur throughout this narrative-frame as related *Leitwörter* highlighting the tale's moralistic concerns.

The story continues with a description of how passengers and crew disembark and then wander the lifeless city. The protagonist ventures on her own into a palace where she discovers the preserved corpses of a king and queen, each of which has been transformed into black stone (and each described with the term *maskhūṭ*). Finally she encounters a young man who alone has survived the fate of all the other inhabitants. He tells her the story of this city, explaining that all its people were Magians and devoted to the worship of fire. He himself, however, was secretly Muslim. Year after year divine warnings visited the city to the effect that the infidel inhabitants must abandon their fire-worship and turn to the true God; to no avail. And so, the young man explains:

> They never ceased with their adherence to the way they were, until there descended upon them hatred and divine wrath (*al-maqt wa-al sukhṭ*) from heaven, one morning at dawn. And so they were transformed into black stone (*fa-sukhiṭū ahjāran sūdan*), and their riding beasts and cattle as well.[3]

The Magian City frame ends when the protagonist rejoins her companions and conveys to them the story she has just heard:

> I reported to them what I had seen, and I told them the tale of the young man and the reason for the metamorphosis of this city (*wa-sabab sukhṭ hādhihi al-madīnah*) and what had happened to them; and they marveled at that.[4]

1. Abd al-Qāhir al-Jurjānī, *Dalā'il al-i'jīz*, ed. Muhammad 'Abd al-Mun'im Khafājī (Cairo: Maktabat al-Qāhirah, 1969), p. 90.
2. G. J. H. van Gelder, *Beyond the Line: Classical Arabic Literary Critics on the Coherence and Unity of the Poem* (Leiden: E.J. Brill, 1982), p. 131.
3. MN vol. 1, p. 127.
4. MN vol. 1, p. 128.

Thus in this story the condition of the city's inhabitants (*maskhūt*, *sukhiṭū*) is explained as a consequence of divine wrath (*al-sukhṭ*), with the two states described in terms of the single root *s-kh-ṭ*. Not only does this motif-word accent relationships among events within *The Magian City*; it also demarcates this enframed minor narrative at both beginning and end and distinguishes the tale from the surrounding major narrative.

In other *Alf laylah* stories one notes the operation of what may be termed (as an extension of Buber's model) *Leitsätze* ("leading-sentences"): entire clauses or sentences which are repeated at salient points throughout a narrative and encapsulate its theme. In chapter 2 we will see how the *Leitsatz* "Spare me and God will spare you" is used to link minor narratives to the overarching tale of *The Fisherman and the Genie*. The sentence "This is a warning to whoso would be warned" is a familiar moralistic utterance encountered frequently throughout the *Nights*; in *The City of Brass*, however (as will be shown in chapter 4), the redactor repeatedly introduces variants of this conventional admonition (all built around the *Leitwörter* '*ibrah*—"warning"—and *i'tabara*—"to take warning") so as to draw attention to the thematic concerns which unite the various episodes in the tale.

III. Thematic Patterning and Formal Patterning

In those stories from the *Alf laylah* (as with works of fiction in general) which are especially well crafted, the structure is disposed so as to draw the audience's attention to certain narrative elements over others. Recurrent vocabulary, repeated gestures, accumulations of descriptive phrases around selected objects: such patterns guide the audience in picking out particular actions as important in the flow of narrative. And once the audience has had its attention drawn to the patterns which give shape to a story, it experiences the pleasure of recognition: so *this* is the revelation toward which the storyteller is guiding us; *this* must be the object which constitutes the story's focus. The reader attempting to discern such patterns in a story, however, should beware of examining too narrowly any one given incident from the tale, for an individual dialogue or isolated event, taken alone, may not have enough context to let the observer establish its significance for the story at hand. The observer's emphasis, rather, should be on the particular event as it exists in relation to the rest of the narrative and the way in which the events and other narrative elements in a story join to form a structural pattern.

In my study of individual tales I have noted two kinds of structural patterning, thematic and formal. By thematic patterning I mean the distribution of recurrent concepts and moralistic motifs among the various incidents and frames of a story. In a skilfully crafted tale, thematic patterning may be arranged so as to emphasize the unifying argument or salient idea which disparate events and disparate narrative frames have in common.

Thematic patterning binds the tales contained within *The Fisherman and the Genie*. The argument of this narrative-cycle may be baldly stated as: violence against one's benefactors or intimate companions, whether triggered by mistrust, envy, or jealous rage, leads inevitably to regret and repentance. This concept is illustrated both in the major narrative of the *Fisherman* and in its enframed minor narratives such as *Yunan and Duban* and *The Jealous Husband and the Parrot* (I discuss these tales in chapter 2). Of course all these stories are also linked thematically to the outermost narrative frame, where Scheherazade is quite literally trying to talk her way out of violent death at the hands of a husband who himself is dominated by mistrust and jealous rage.

Another example of thematic patterning can be found in *The City of Brass* (analyzed below in chapter 4), a story which at first glance may appear to have little structural unity. The primary action, in which a party of travellers crosses the North African desert in search of ancient brass bottles, is continually interrupted by subsidiary narratives: the tale recorded on inscriptions in the lost palace of Kūsh ibn Shaddād; the imprisoned *'ifrīt*'s account of Solomon's war with the jinn; and the encounter with Queen Tadmur and the automata which guard her corpse. But each of these minor narratives introduces a character who confesses that he once proudly enjoyed worldly prosperity: subsequently, we learn, the given character has been brought low by God and forced to acknowledge Him as greater than all worldly pomp. These minor tales ultimately reinforce the theme of the major narrative: riches and pomp tempt one away from God; asceticism is the way to salvation. Thus a clearly discernible thematic pattern of pride—punishment from God—submission to the Divine Will unifies the otherwise divergent stories which are gathered into this tale.

By formal patterning I mean the organization of the events, actions and gestures which constitute a narrative and give shape to a story; when done well, formal patterning allows the audience the pleasure of discerning and anticipating the structure of the plot as it unfolds. An example can be found in *The Tale of the Three Shaykhs*, where three old men come upon a merchant in the desert about to be slain by a demon which has a claim of blood-vengeance against him (we have encountered the earlier part of this tale already, in my analysis of incidents from *The Merchant and the Genie*). First the redactor takes care to note that each shaykh has with him some object of interest: the first, a chained gazelle; the second, a pair of black hunting dogs; the third, a mule. Then the first shaykh approaches the genie and pleads with it for the merchant's life: if you grant me one-third of the blood-claim due you from this man, he states, I will recite for you a wondrous tale concerning this chained gazelle. The demon accepts, and the audience can already recognize the symmetries of the formal patterning at work in this story-cycle: each of the three shaykhs in turn will advance to tell a wondrous tale concerning his animal and claim one-third of the blood-punishment. And such in fact is what happens: the merchant is saved by the recitation of the three tales.[5]

A more elaborate instance of formal patterning is at work in a story-cycle entitled *The Tale of the Hunchback*.[6] Four characters, a Christian broker, a steward, a Jewish doctor, and a tailor, are summoned before a sultan and each must tell a satisfyingly amazing anecdote in order to have his life spared. This story-as-ransom motif obviously connects the entire cycle with the Scheherazade frame, where the heroine also recites tales to avert death. But there is more. Each of the four characters in *The Hunchback* tells a story in which he describes an encounter with a young man who has been mysteriously maimed or crippled. In each encounter the narrator asks the young man how he suffered his hurt, and the latter's explanation constitutes the tale offered to the sultan as ransom. The last of the four reciters, the tailor, tells how at a marriage-feast he met a young man who had been lamed. The youth recounts the misfortunes whereby he came to be crippled; and it turns out that the person responsible for this injury, an insufferably garrulous barber, is seated at the same table as the tailor. No sooner does the youth conclude his tale than the barber insists on offering the tailor and his friends a succession of stories, first one about himself, then a good

---

5. Such at least is the structure of this story-cycle as found in B (vol. 1, pp. 7–10) and MN (vol. 1, pp. 12–20); but it is of interest to note that, from the point of view of formal patterning, G (as found in the Leiden ed., vol. 1, pp. 78–86) is markedly deficient. As in the two Egyptian texts, in G the first of three shaykhs advances to claim one-third of the blood-punishment, and the audience is prepared for a pattern of three stories. The first two shaykhs bring forward their beasts and recite wondrous tales concerning them, as in B and MN. But when it comes the third shaykh's turn, he is not described in G's version as having with him any animal; hence he quite literally has no tale worth speaking of. And G in fact at this juncture (Leiden, p. 86) contains no more than the bald statement:

> The third shaykh told the genie a tale more wondrous and stranger than the other two tales. Then the genie marvelled greatly and shook with pleasure and said, "I grant you one-third of the blood-claim."

Thus in G we are told only that the shaykh recited his story, but we are not permitted to hear the story itself, in contrast to the pattern followed with the full recitals given by the first two shaykhs. The audience is denied hearing the third tale which it had been led to expect by the narrative's structure. The passage quoted above shows that G acknowledges the structure dictated by the formal patterning of the three shaykhs and the blood-punishment divided into thirds; but G disposes of this structure at the end in very perfunctory fashion.

6. The story is found in Leiden, vol. 1, pp. 280–379; B vol. 1, pp. 73–106; and MN vol. 1, pp. 199–278.

half-dozen anecdotes about his six unfortunate brothers. The tales narrated by the barber are not demanded as any kind of ransom by the tailor, in contrast to the four tales required by the sultan in the overarching *Hunchback* cycle. Nor do the barber's stories seem controlled by a common thematic concern or moral argument. All six brothers suffer harm, but some deserve punishment for their foolishness or lust, while others (especially the third and fourth brothers) are clearly innocent victims of malicious sharpsters. But common to the vignettes in this series is that each tells how one of the brothers was blinded, castrated or somehow deprived of lips and ears.[7] This structural pattern of mutilation links the six tales formally to one another and in turn unites the *Barber* cycle as a whole with *The Hunchback*, where each of the four enframed tales also displays a formal patterning of mutilation/crippling. Thus the stories contained in *The Barber's Six Brothers* constitute an example of a narrative cycle where the unity lacking at the thematic level is compensated for by a consistent formal patterning.

IV. DRAMATIC VISUALIZATION

I define dramatic visualization as the representing of an object or character with an abundance of descriptive detail, or the mimetic rendering of gestures and dialogue in such a way as to make the given scene 'visual' or imaginatively present to an audience. I contrast 'dramatic visualization' with 'summary presentation,' where an author informs his audience of an object or event in abbreviated fashion without dramatizing the scene or encouraging the audience to form a visual picture of it. In *The Rhetoric of Fiction* Wayne Booth analyzes the modern novel by making analogous distinctions between what he calls "showing" and "telling": when an author "shows" his audience something he renders it dramatically so as to give the "intensity of realistic illusion"; when he "tells" his audience about a thing he is using his authorial powers to summarize an event or render judgment on a character's behavior, without, however, using descriptive detail to make the given event or character imaginatively present.[8]

---

7. Some of these mutilations are central to the given story, others incidental. One significant variant among the three editions occurs in the account of *The Barber's Fifth Brother*. The Egyptian texts (MN, vol. 1, p. 271 and B, vol. 1, p. 103) conclude this story by having thieves fall upon the barber's fifth brother and cut off his ears, an incident not found in the Leiden version. This act is not essential to the story proper of the fifth brother, but it does link the tale to its larger frame by bringing forward the motif of maiming/mutilation which characterizes all the stories of the *Hunchback* cycle. As such the Egyptian versions of *The Barber's Fifth Brother* offer a more consistent example than does the Syrian text of the use of formal patterning as a means of achieving structural unity for a series of otherwise unrelated tales.

8. Wayne Booth, *The Rhetoric of Fiction* (Chicago: University of Chicago Press, 1961), pp. 3–9, 40.

To understand how these techniques function let us compare the wording of analogous scenes in two different *Alf laylah* stories. Both portray exemplary punishment in the form of amputation which is to be inflicted on the protagonist. The first scene is from *The Lover Who Pretended to be a Thief*. Khālid, governor of Basrah, is confronted with the men of a family who have caught a handsome young man breaking into their home. They accuse the boy of theft, and the prisoner confesses freely. To Khālid the youth seems too well-spoken and of too noble a bearing to be a thief; yet given the boy's insistence on his own guilt, the governor has no choice but to order the legally mandated punishment. Suspecting nevertheless that the prisoner is for some reason concealing the truth, Khālid counsels him privately to "state that which may ward off from you the punishment of amputation" the next morning when he is to be interrogated one last time by the judge before the sentence is executed (not till the end of the story do we learn that the youth is a lover who had entered the home for a tryst with the daughter of the house, and that he has allowed himself to be labeled a thief so as to protect her honor). The punishment-scene reads as follows:

> When morning dawned the people assembled to see the youth's hand cut off; and there was not a single person in Basrah, neither man nor woman, who failed to be present so as to see the punishment of this young man. Khālid came riding up, and with him were prominent dignitaries and others from among the people of Basrah. Then he summoned the judges and called for the young man to be brought. And so he approached, stumbling in his chains; and not one of the people saw him without weeping for him. And the voices of the women rose up in lamentation.
>
> The judge thereupon ordered the women to be silenced; and then he said to him, "These persons contend that you entered their home and stole their possessions. Perhaps you stole less than the amount which makes this a crime legally necessitating such punishment?"
>
> "On the contrary," he replied. "I stole precisely an amount which necessitates such punishment."
>
> He said, "Perhaps you were co-owner with these persons in some of those possessions."
>
> "On the contrary," he replied. "Those things belong entirely to them. I have no legal claim to those things."
>
> At this point Khālid grew angry. He himself stood up, went over to him and struck him in the face with his whip, quoting aloud this verse:
>
> Man wishes to be given his desire
> But God refuses all save what *He* desires.

Thereupon he called for the butcher so that the latter might cut off his hand. And so he came, and he took out the knife. Then he stretched out the boy's hand and placed upon it the knife.

But suddenly there rushed forward a young woman from the midst of the women, clad in soiled and tattered clothes. She screamed and threw herself upon him. She drew back her veil, to reveal a face like the moon for beauty. And there rose up from the people a great outcry.[9]

The beloved has appeared: she will sacrifice her reputation and their love-secret so as to save the boy from punishment.

We will return to the lovers in a moment, but let us look first at our second amputation-scene, this one from *The Reward of Charity*. A capricious king has ordered that henceforth no one in his realm is to offer alms or bestow charity under any circumstances; all those caught violating this command will have their hands chopped off. In what follows a starving beggar approaches a woman who proves to be the protagonist:

The beggar said to the woman, "Give me something in the way of charity!"

She replied, "How can I give you alms when the king is cutting off the hand of everyone who gives alms?"

He said, "I beg you in God's name, give me something in the way of alms!"

So when he asked her in God's name she felt pity for him and gave him two loaves of bread as an act of charity.

Thereafter report of this reached the king and he ordered that she be brought to him. Then when she appeared he cut off her hands and she returned to her home.[1]

Brief, brutal, and to the point.

But the two passages, juxtaposed as they are here, trigger a question: why is dramatic visualization employed in the amputation-scene from *The Lover,* while the redactor contents himself with the technique of summary presentation in an analogous episode from *The Reward of Charity*? The answer I believe is related to the fact that the punishment-scene in *The Lover* is the climax of the entire story. Throughout the *Alf laylah* dramatic visualization is reserved especially for scenes which form the heart of a given narrative. Such is the case here. What *follows* the girl's appearance in the public square is narrated succinctly: the boy's punishment is averted, the couple's love is made known, and Khālid prevails on the girl's father to allow them to

9. B vol. 1 (Night 298), p. 471.
1. B vol. 1 (Night 348), p. 527.

marry. But the redactor lingers over the spectacle of punishment: the wailing crowds, the pathetic glimpse of the youth stumbling in his chains, the extended dialogue between judge and prisoner, and the sketch of the frustrated Khālid giving up all attempt to save the boy and lashing out with his whip. The effect of all this visualized detail is to slow the pace of narration; and we are not permitted any resolution till the last possible moment, when the heroine is introduced just as the butcher is about to apply his knife. Thus the technique of dramatic visualization enables the storyteller to heighten the tension in a scene and increase his audience's experience of pleasurable suspense.

By way of contrast the amputation in *The Reward of Charity* is not the narrative focus of the story at all. The punishment is presented in summary fashion because it is only a prelude to the true climax: the scene where the woman's generous impulse is vindicated. Mutilated as she is and subsequently expelled to the desert with her infant son clinging to her, she wanders until she comes upon a stream:

> She knelt down to drink, because of the extreme thirst which had overtaken her from her walking and her fatigue and her sorrow. But when she bent over, the boy fell into the water. She sat weeping greatly for her child.
>
> And while she was crying, behold!: two men passed by; and they said to her, "What is making you weep?"
>
> She answered them, "I had a boy who was holding me about the neck, and he fell into the water."
>
> They said to her, "Would you like us to bring him forth for you?"
>
> She replied, "Yes," and so they called on God most high. Thereupon the child came forth to her unharmed; nothing ill had befallen him.
>
> Then they said to her, "Would you like God to restore your hands to you as they had been?"
>
> She replied, "Yes," and so they called on God—all praise and glory to Him!—and her hands were restored to her, more beautiful than they ever had been before.
>
> Then they said to her, "Do you know who we are?"
>
> She replied, "Only God knows!"
>
> They said, "We are your two loaves of bread, which you bestowed in charity on the beggar."[2]

The redactor has reserved dramatic visualization for the scene which most merits it, that episode illustrating the moralistic theme which drives the whole narrative.

* * *

2. Ibid., p. 527.

The Arabian Nights:
A Chronology

c. 850	Oldest surviving fragment of *A Thousand Nights*.
900s	Three Arabic authors—al-Masʿūdī, Ibn al-Nadīm, and al-Jahshīyārī—mention *A Thousand and One Nights,* reporting that it constitutes a translation of a Persian collection titled *A Thousand Stories*.
c. 1150	A document contained in the Cairo Synagogue Geniza testifies to the existence of a book titled *A Thousand and One Nights*.
1300s	Period of composition of the earliest surviving Arabic edition of *The Thousand and One Nights*, a Syrian manuscript later edited by Antoine Galland and Muhsin Mahdi. This version contains two hundred and eighty-one nights, during which thirty-five stories are told.
1704–1717	Antoine Galland's French edition of *The Thousand and One Nights*, consisting of a partial translation of the fourteenth-century Syrian manuscript and tales told to him orally.
1706	Publication of the first English language translation of Galland's *Nights*. Translations from the French into other European languages soon follow: German (1712), Italian (1722), Dutch (1732), Danish (1745), Russian (1763), Flemish (1794), and Yiddish (1794).
1800s	Translation of Galland's into Turkish, Persian, and various languages of India, Asia, and Africa as well as into European languages.
1814–18	First modern Arabic edition of *The Thousand and One Nights*, printed in Calcutta ("Calcutta I"). It is based on a manuscript dating from 1770 but also includes other tales (among which thirty-six stories involving Sindbad).

1825–43	Bilingual Arabic-German edition published in Breslau ("Breslau" or "Habicht"). Containing approximately one hundred and thirty tales, it is based on several Arabic editions of varying age and provenance.
1835	Second modern Arabic edition of the *Nights*, printed in Bulaq, Egypt. Containing one thousand and one nights, this text will be used for later editions of the work that aspire to completeness.
1838–41	E. W. Lane's translation, *The Arabian Nights' Entertainment*, based on the Bulaq, Calcutta I, and Breslau editions.
1839–42	Second edition of the Arabic text printed in Calcutta ("Calcutta II"), edited by Macnaghten. It contains one thousand and one nights and, like the Bulaq edition, will be often used in translations of a total text.
1882–84	John Payne's translation, *The Book of the Thousand Nights and a Night*, based on the Calcutta II and Breslau editions.
1885–88	Richard Burton's translation, *The Book of Thousand Nights and a Night*, based on the Bulaq, Calcutta II, and Breslau editions.
1899–1906	J. C. Mardrus's French translation of the Bulaq edition, supplemented by Calcutta II and Breslau, as well as other unnamed sources.
1921–28	Enno Littmann's German translation of Calcutta II, with references to the Bulaq and Breslau editions.
1949	Francesco Gabrieli's Italian edition of the *Nights*, based principally on the Bulaq text, as well as Calcutta II.
1984	Muhsin Mahdi publishes a partial critical edition *Thousand and One Nights* in Arabic, based on the fourteenth-century Syrian manuscript.
1990	Husain Haddawy's translation into English of Mahdi's edition of the fourteenth-century Syrian manuscript, *The Arabian Nights*.
1995	Hussayn Haddawy's translation of selected tales from the *Nights* not included in the fourteenth-century Syrian manuscript, *The Arabian Nights II*.
2005	Jamel Eddine Bensheikh and André Miquel's French edition of the *Nights*, based on the Bulaq and Calcutta II editions.

Selected Bibliography

• Indicates items included or excerpted in this Norton Critical Edition.

• Abbott, Nadia. "A Ninth Century Fragment of the Thousand Nights." *Journal of Near East Studies* 8 (1949): 129–64.

Bencheikh, Jamel Eddine. *Les Mille et une nuits ou la parole prisonnière*. Paris, Gallimard, 1988.

• Borges, Jorge Luis. "The Thousand and One Nights." In *Seven Nights*. Trans. Eliot Weinberger. New York: New Directions, 1984, 42–57.

Campell, Kay Hardy et al., eds. *The 1001 Nights: Critical Essays and Annotated Bibliography*. Cambridge, Mass.: Dar Mahjar, 1985.

Caracciolo, Peter L., ed. *The Arabian Nights in English Literature*. London, Macmillan, 1988.

De Sacy, Silvestre. *"Mémoires sur l'orgine du recueil de contes intitulés les Mille et une nuits."* *Mémoire de l'Académie des inscriptions et belles-lettres* 10 (1833): 30–64.

Elisseéff, Nikita. *Thèmes et motifs des Mille et une nuits, Essai de Classification*. Beirut, Institut français de Damas, 1949.

• Gabrieli, Francesco. "Le mille e una notte nella cultura europea." *Storia e civiltà mussulmana*. Napoli: R. Ricciardi, 1947, 99–107.

• Gerhardt, Mia I. *The Art of Story-Telling: A Literary Study of the Thousand and One Nights*. Leiden: E. J. Brill, 1963.

Ghazoul, Ferial J. *Nocturnal Poetics: The Arabian Nights in Comparative Context*. Cairo: American University in Cairo Press, 1996.

Goitein, Shelomo Dov. "The Oldest Documentary Evidence for the Title Alf Laila wa-Laila." *Journal of the American Oriental Society* 78 (1959): 301–02.

Hammer-Purgstall, Freiherr Joseph von. "Sur l'origine des Mille et une Nuits." *Journal Asiatique*, 1st ser., 10 (1827): 253–56.

• Hamori, Andras. "A Comic Romance from *The Thousand and One Nights: The Tale of the Two Viziers*." *Arabica* 30.1 (1983): 38–56.

———. "Notes on Two Love Stories from *The Thousand and One Nights*." *Studia Islamica* 43 (1976): 65–80.

———. *On the Art of Medieval Arabic Literature*. Princeton: Princeton UP, 1974.

• Horovitz, Joseph. "The Origins of the *Arabian Nights*." *Islamic Culture* 1 (1927): 36–57.

Irwin, Robert. *The Arabian Nights: A Companion*. London: Penguin Books, 1994.

Kilito, Abdelfattah. *Al-Hikāya wa-al-ta'wīl: Dirāsāt fī'al-sard al-'arabī*. Casablanca: Toubkal, 1988.

———. *The Author and His Doubles: Essays on Classical Arabic Culture*. Trans. Michael Cooperson, with a Foreword by Roger Allen. Syracuse, N.Y.: Syracuse University Press, 2001.

• ———. *L'Œil et l'aiguille: Essais sur "les Mille et une nuits."* Paris: La Découverte, 1992.

Knipp, C. "The *Arabian Nights* in England." *Journal of Arabic Literature* 5 (1964): 44–74.

SELECTED BIBLIOGRAPHY523

MacDonald, Duncan Black "The Earlier History of the Arabian Nights." *Journal of the Royal Asiatic Society* (1924): 353–97.

Mahdi, Muhsin. *The Thousand and One Nights*. Leiden: Brill, 1995.

Marzolph, Ulrich, ed. *The Arabian Nights Reader*. Detroit: Wayne State Press, 2006.

Marzolph, Ulrich, and Richard van Leeuwen, eds. *The Arabian Nights Encyclopedia*. 2 vols. Santa Barbara, CA: ABC-Clio, 2004.

Molan, Peter D. "The *Arabian Nights*: The Oral Connection." *Edebiyât* N.S. II, 1–2 (1988): 191–204.

Ouyang, Wen-chin, and Geert Jan van Gelder, eds. *New Perspectives on Arabian Nights: Ideological Variations and Narrative Horizons*. London: Routledge, 2005.

Perry, B. E. "The Origin of the Book of Sinbad." *Fabula* 3 (1959): 1–94.

• Pinault, David. *Story-Telling Techniques in the Arabian Nights*. Leiden: Brill, 1992.

Propp, Vladimir. *The Morphology of the Folk-Tale*. 2nd ed. Trans. Lawrence Scott with an introduction by Svatava Pirkova-Jakobson. Austin: University of Texas Press, 1968.

Schlegel, August Wilhelm von. "Lettre à M. le Baron de Sacy." *Journal Asiatique* 3rd ser. 1 (1836): 575–80.

• Todorov, Tzvetan. *The Poetics of Prose*. Trans. Richard Howard, with a new foreword by Jonathan Culler. Ithaca, N.Y.: Cornell University Press, 1977.

Wood, Michael. "The Last Night of All." *PMLA* 122.5 (2007): 1394–402.

BIBLIOGRAPHY